תהלים

THE PSALMS

THE SONCINO BOOKS OF THE BIBLE

(Complete in fourteen volumes)

SONCINO BOOKS OF THE BIBLE
EDITOR: REV. DR. A. COHEN, M.A., Ph.D., D.H.L.

The Psalms

HEBREW TEXT & ENGLISH TRANSLATION
WITH AN INTRODUCTION
AND COMMENTARY

by
THE REV. DR. A. COHEN, M.A., Ph.D., D.H.L.

Revised by
RABBI E. ORATZ, M.A., Ph.D.

Assisted by
RAV SHALOM SHAHAR

*Declare His glory among the
nations,
His marvellous works among all
the peoples*

PSALM XCVI. 3

THE SONCINO PRESS, LTD.
London・Jerusalem・New York

© COPYRIGHT 1992
THE SONCINO PRESS, LTD.

FIRST EDITION 1945
(TWELVE IMPRESSIONS)
REVISED SECOND EDITION 1992

PUBLISHER'S NOTE
*Thanks are due to the
Jewish Publication Society of America
for permission to use their very beautiful
English text of the Scriptures.*

All rights reserved including the right to
reproduce this book or parts thereof in
any form.

Library of Congress Cataloging-in-Publication Data

Bible. O.T. Psalms. English. Jewish Publication Society. 1992.
  The Psalms : Hebrew text & English translation, with an
introduction and commentary / by A. Cohen ; revised by E. Oratz
assisted by Shalom Shahar. -- Rev. 2nd ed.
    p. cm. -- (The Soncino books of the Bible)
Biblical verses in English and Hebrew.
Includes bibliographical references and index.
ISBN 1–871055–65–2 : $13.95
(Formerly ISBN 0–900689–32–3)
ISBN 0–871055–70–9 (14 volume set)
  1. Bible. O.T. Psalms--Commentaries. I. Cohen, A. (Abraham),
1887– . II. Oratz, Ephraim. III. Title. IV. Series.
BS1424.C59 1992
223' .2077--dc20

91-36934
CIP
rev

PRINTED IN THE UNITED STATES OF AMERICA

PUBLISHER'S PREFACE
TO THE REVISED SECOND EDITION

JUST over forty-six years ago, THE PSALMS, the first in a series of the SONCINO BOOKS OF THE BIBLE, saw the light of the day, to be followed in the next six years by the remaining thirteen books. Whereas the earlier edition drew from various non-Jewish, as well as Jewish sources, the publishers now feel that there is a need to acquaint the reader with the pure Jewish view of these holy books, and this revised edition therefore is based entirely on the traditional classic Jewish commentaries and source material. Significant new material from these commentaries and sources has been incorporated in this revised edition.

We are indebted to the Judaica Press for allowing us to use material from the Judaica Books of the Hagiographa—The Holy Writings.

A special note of thanks to Rabbi Zvi Lampel for his extensive aid in the editing of this volume.

לְהַנְצָחַת זֵכֶר

אָבִינוּ

הָרַב ר' מָרְדְכַי יַעֲקֹב בְּר' שְׂרַגָא פַייוֶועל

"מָה אָהַבְתִּי תוֹרָתֶךָ
כָּל הַיוֹם הִיא שִׂיחָתִי"
לָמַד וְלִמֵד, עָשָׂה וְקִיֵם
אֶת כָּל דִבְרֵי תַלְמוּד תוֹרָתֶךָ
בְּאַהֲבָה

Given as a Living Memorial
to

Rabbi Max Jacob Mintz

**for whom Torah was a Tree of Life
He lived it daily with love
He guarded it zealously
He brought passion and brillance
in its teachings to our family
and to the larger Jewish
community.**

**The legacy of our Father will continue
to enrich our lives and the lives of
the generations who will come after us.**

May His Memory Be Blessed

Naomi and Louis Feder
and Family

וְאֵת זֵכֶר

אִמֵּנוּ

הָרַבָּנִית מַלְכָּה בַּת ר׳ נָחוּם הַכֹּהֵן

Malcha Mintz

"תְּנוּ לָהּ מִפְּרִי יָדֶיהָ
וִיהַלְלוּהָ בַשְּׁעָרִים מַעֲשֶׂיהָ"

**The center of our family in her younger years,
Its Matriarch in her later years.
Her mantle was dignity
and grace.
In her right hand was practical wisdom
In her left hand, perennial youth.
"She will taste from the fruit of her labors
and her deeds will proclaim her praise."**

**The legacy of our Mother will continue
to enrich our lives and the lives of
the generations who will come after us.**

May Her Memory Be Blessed

Naomi and Louis Feder
and Family

CONTENTS

ix

PREFACE TO THE FIRST EDITION

My one purpose has been to assist the reader to a deeper appreciation of this precious jewel in the spiritual treasury of Israel.

Among the Books of the Hebrew Scriptures, the Psalter has always made the most direct appeal to the human heart. If this work succeeds in re-awaking in some men and women today the fervent love which past generations felt for these sublime religious poems, the labour involved will have been well expended.

In my comments I have endeavoured throughout to exercise an independent judgment in deciding among a variety of translations and explanations. The Targum, Talmud, Midrash and the classical Jewish Commentaries have been consulted and freely drawn upon.

The translation is that issued by the Jewish Publication Society of America which is generally most faithful to the original and reflects Jewish tradition. It is, however, not accepted as final; and when there is disagreement with its rendering, an alternative is proposed which is deemed preferable. All Biblical references accord with chapter and verse of the Hebrew text, reproduced in the American-Jewish translation.

I have to acknowledge my indebtedness to Mr. J. Davidson, Director of the Soncino Press, for his constant attention to the many technical matters involved in the preparation and publication of the volume.

A. COHEN

[Editor's note—This Preface has been revised for the Second Edition.]

INTRODUCTION

In Rabbinical literature the designation of the Book of Psalms is *Sefer Tehillim* (sometimes contracted to *Tillim*), 'the Book of Praises,' and this name has passed into traditional usage among Jews, although only one Psalm has the word *tehillah*, 'praise,' in its superscription (cxlv), although it does appear twenty eight times in various grammatical forms throughout the book. When referring to Psalms included in the Jewish liturgy, the Talmudical authorities mention them as 'verses of praise,' employing the Aramaic term *zimra*, which is cognate with the Hebrew *mizmor* found in the heading of fifty-seven Psalms, translated in the LXX by *psalmos*. Both in Hebrew and in Greek the root-meaning is to play instrumental music, and then to sing to musical accompaniment.

That, in effect, explains the origin of most of the compositions in this Biblical Book. The singing of hymns by a choir of Levites and by the assembly of worshippers, with an accompaniment of string and wind instruments, was a feature of the religious service in the Temple. 2 Chronicles vii: 6 describes the Levites as standing *with instruments of music of the Lord, which David the king had made, to give thanks unto the Lord, for His mercy endureth for ever, with the praises of David by their hand.* In ibid. xxix: 30, Hezekiah the king and the officers tell the Levites *to sing praises unto the Lord with the words of David ....* In the building of the Temple described in the Book of Ezra (iii. 10) we find *the Levites, sons of Asaf, with the cymbals to praise God by* (the words of) *David, king of Israel.* Many of the Psalms present clear evidence of this liturgical use, and were associated with the days of the week or festival occasions by a tradition which is independently attested both by the LXX and the Talmud. It does not follow that all the Psalms were so employed; indeed some of them would scarcely have been

suitable for the purpose. But regarded as a whole, the Book may be fairly described as the hymnal of the Temple.

In the Masoretic text the Psalter heads the third division of the Hebrew Bible, the so-called Hagiographa or 'holy writings.' In the Talmud (B.B. 14b) the order is given as 'Ruth, Psalms,' etc. According to another arrangement, formerly in vogue among the Sephardic Jews, Chronicles preceded Psalms.

In the enumeration of the Masoretic text there are 150 Psalms. The Palestinian Talmud, however, has an allusion to 147, the number being obtained by combining i and ii, ix and x, cxiv and cxv. The Midrash on Psalms remarks that 'Moses gave Israel the Five Books of the Torah, and, correspondingly, David gave them the five Books of the Psalms.' Such a division is apparent from the doxology which occurs at the end of xli, lxxii, lxxxix and cvi, while the closing Psalm is in its entirety the culminating doxology.

In subject-matter the Psalms may be classified under three main heads:

(i) *Praise.* Most common of all is the extolment of God for His goodness and mercy to Israel and all His creatures, His vindication of the righteous when persecuted by the wicked, His Kingship over all mankind, and His might as the Creator and Ruler of the universe. Allied themes are praise of the Torah which contains His revealed will; of Zion, chosen by Him as His dwelling-place on earth; and of David and his dynasty appointed by Him to sit upon the throne of Israel.

(ii) *Elegy.* The minor key is struck in numerous Psalms which tell of the sufferings of individuals and of Israel as a people. In accordance with the accepted doctrine that personal and national calamity is the sequel of sin, earnest confession of guilt and the plea for pardon appear conspicuously in this group. The note of supplication for relief and ease is also heard.

(iii) *Ethics.* Several Psalms of a didactic,

or instructive, character are likewise included. They deal with the right way of living, denounce prevalent vices which bring unhappiness to people as a whole or endanger the existence of individuals, and they proclaim the joy which ensues from loyalty to God's will.

The Psalms are more than beautiful literary compositions; they are essentially human documents. They reflect life in its varied aspects as it was experienced by members of the Israelite community. In particular, the hardships of existence are faithfully mirrored: the struggles of the godly to remain faithful to their ideals in the face of oppression; the disturbing doubts created in their hearts by the triumph of evil-doers; the stern fight of the sinner for the victory of his better self; the conquest of despair by resolute faith in the righteousness of God.

Such experiences are not limited to one people or one age; they are recurrent and world-wide. Hence the unfading appeal of the Psalms. They echo the thought and the feeling, the aspiration and the yearning, of countless men and women in every era. In their matchless phrases the human soul has found, for tens of centuries, an outlet in its own struggle from the depths to reach the heights. They describe good fortune of a different nature; the kind whose primary goal is to encourage man not to be disturbed by any wrongdoing he might observe in his daily living. They accentuate the positive in living and foster the desire to follow God's teachings. To all seekers of God they remain a grateful aid in their quest.

AUTHORSHIP

In the Midrashic passage quoted above the statement occurred: 'David gave Israel the five Books of the Psalms.' Traditional language speaks of 'the Psalms of David.' But the headings ascribe one psalm to Moses, two to King Solomon, twelve to Asaph, one to Heman, and one to Ethan. Many have no

superscription, and the Talmud makes it clear that and thus came to be the popular impression that the whole of the Psalter is ascribed to him. 'David wrote the Book of Psalms, including in it the works of the elders, namely, Adam, Malchizedek, Abraham, Moses, Heman, Jeduthun, Asaf, and the three sons of Korah' (B.B. 14b). It was, accordingly, asserted that the Psalter was partly a collection of composite authorship, though compiled by David.

The fact that the book as it exists was completed in the reign of David was accepted by the great Jewish commentators of the Middle Ages—Rashi, Ibn Ezra and Kimchi. Several Psalms, though connected by them with the Babylonian captivity, were admittedly products of prophetic spirit.

An examination of the contents of the Book leads unmistakably to the conclusion that it is made up of distinctive groups apart from individual Psalms. The 'Songs of Ascents' (cxx-cxxxiv) are, for example, a distinctive group; so are the Korahite Psalms (xlii-xlix, lxxxiv-lxxxviii), the Asaph Psalms (lxxiii-lxxxiii) and the Hallel Psalms (cxi-cxviii).

Of the 150 Psalms, seventy-three have the superscription *leDavid*. Most of these portray circumstances which harmonize with his adventurous career. Some commentators explain that *leDavid* does not always mean 'written by David,' but at times 'concerning David' or 'in style of David.' Others maintain that these Psalms were indeed composed by David. In fact, R. Meir stated: All the praises which are stated in the Book of Psalms, David uttered all of them (Pes. 117a).

Song-writing was an ancient art in Israel, of which the most striking illustrations preserved in the Scriptures are the Song of the Red Sea (Exod. xv) and the Song of Deborah (Judges v). It is recorded that David was renowned as a harpist (1 Sam. xvi. 18), and he also possessed skill as a poet. His pathetic lament over the death of Saul and Jonathan (2 Sam. i. 19ff.) and later over Abner (2 Sam. iii.

33f.) are specimens of his poetical composition. The song authored by him in 2 Sam. xxii. appears again in Ps. xviii. In his 'last words' (2 Sam. xxiii. 1) he is described as 'the sweet singer of Israel.' David said of himself, *The spirit of the LORD spoke by me, and His word was upon my tongue*, which indicates some form of authorship. In 1 Sam. xvi. 18 we read a description of David who, in his youth, was 'skillful in playing' and was called in before Saul to play on his harp (op. cit. 23).

RELIGIOUS AND ETHICAL DOCTRINE

In the Psalter, the leading ideas and the main currents of thought are easily discerned because they constantly recur and stand forth boldly. They may be briefly defined as follows:

GOD. The awareness of God was most intimate and all-pervading with the Psalmists. They had the consciousness that man and peoples are at all times in His presence and subject to His scrutiny. Under the strain of adverse circumstances the writers may have temporarily experienced His having 'hidden His face' from them, but they were saved from despair by their invincible trust in Him; never did they succumb to the fiction that He was unmindful or indifferent of what was happening.

God is at once transcendent and immanent. His throne is in the remote heavens and the earth is His 'footstool.' Surrounded by the angelic hosts, He bears sway over all the inhabitants of the world. Nevertheless, He dwells with the lowly of spirit, is the Protector of the weary, and near to all who call upon Him in truth. He provides for the needs of His creatures, even the beasts and birds. The universe and all it contains are sustained, guided and controlled by His spirit which brought order out of chaos and secures the continuance of order.

Allusions to His might as 'Creator of heaven and earth' are frequent; but far more numerous are the places where His attributes of love, mercy, holiness and justice are extolled. The ethical essence of His nature is the aspect of Him which colours the whole of the Psalter, not as an abstract doctrine but as the inspiration of man's living.

MAN. The paradox of the human being is often in the minds of the writers. Set beside the vastness of the universe and the boundless majesty of God, man is an infinitesimal creature and wholly without significance. Yet he is the crown of the Divine creative work, endowed with the godly spirit, and appointed to rule in the terrestrial sphere. His supreme purpose in life is to use his powers and opportunities so that they glorify the name of his Maker. Man's duty to praise God, not only in words but far more so in his daily activities, is a dominant keynote in the Psalms. By these means his truest happiness is promoted, and the earth yields to him the abundant blessings which the Creator intended, and he gains immortality in the afterlife. Man's concern is to earn these rewards with his life upon earth; above all, to utilize it as the occasion for praising God.

SIN. Man is presented with the choice of good and evil. The good is that which is in harmony with God's will and has His approval. Evil is rebellion against the Divine Sovereignty. The wrong which an individual does to his fellow, or a strong nation to a weak neighbour, is a defiance of the expressed command of God and cannot be overlooked by Him. Confronted with the spectacle of evil victorious over righteousness, the Psalmists were perplexed and voiced a protest; but they certainly never wavered that retribution would overtake the evil-doer and right be vindicated. The primary function of an earthly king is to administer justice within his realm, protect the weak from exploitation, and ensure security to his subjects. Precisely so is it with God, the King of the earth. It is in this sense that the frequent reference to the destruction of the wicked is to be correctly understood. The motive was not

malicious joy over the penalties which would be inflicted upon malefactors but relief in the demonstration that faith in God had been proved justified.

REVELATION. Such a consciousness of right and wrong was rooted in the conviction that God had made His will known at Sinai. His Torah revealed the reality of sin and taught the principles of right conduct. By loyalty to His precepts individual life and national life are elevated to a higher plane, peace and prosperity ensue. Through the Torah man is able to learn how he can come to 'dwell with God.' Most purposeful are the first two Psalms which are introductory to the Psalter and summarize its main thesis. Two ways of life are open to a person and a people: the way of the Torah leading to well-being, or alternatively, the way of rejection of the Torah ending in ruin. The Torah is the beacon-light which offers the mariners upon the sea of life warning and true direction.

ISRAEL AND ZION. The citadel of national and spiritual life, the people of Israel and Zion are set in the centre of the cosmos. The historic consciousness was vividly alive in the Psalmists. Especially in the times of vicissitude, the only way to sustain the courage and refresh the hope of the people was to turn their minds back to the past in order to draw renewed hope for the future. Though God is discovered in the works of creation, His presence can be constantly witnessed in the facts of history. Israel's history, it is emphasized, is an essential source of Israel's religion; its lessons must be remembered to assure the national future. Not for self-glorification do the Psalmists bring this truth home to their people. The doctrine of 'the chosen of God' never has the purpose of exciting a sense of superiority, but rather of inducing a sense of responsibility to a cause which aims at the true advancement of all mankind. God selected Zion as the centre upon earth from which should spread a universal Kingdom with all peoples subject to the Divine rule. All may enroll in His service, and none who wish to submit to His Sovereignty are excluded. The note of universalism rings out clear in many of the Psalms. From this point of view lxxxvii is perhaps the most remarkable in the Psalter.

The Messianic hope is similarly not restricted to Israel's aggrandisement. The nation's vindication is but a prelude to a more comprehensive design. A whole series of Psalms herald the advent of God as the Judge of the world, Whose rule of equity will become the cause of universal rejoicing. The ultimate aspiration is that all humanity will acknowledge the Divine Kingship; and the supreme, as well as final, call is *Let every thing that hath breath praise the* LORD.

HEBREW POETRY

In classical, Arabic, and western literature, the difference between poetry and prose is that the former is contained within a framework of metre—a regular succession of long and short syllables—and (sometimes) rhyme. In Biblical Hebrew, rhyme is hardly ever found and metre, in the defined sense, is unknown. Nevertheless an obvious distinction does exist between sections of the Scriptures which may be classified respectively as prose and poetry. The construction of a Psalm is clearly unlike that of a chapter of a historical Book, and for an appreciation of the language and style of the Psalter the differences must be appreciated.

The Psalms were not read, but chanted or sung in more elaborate form. The singing was often in the antiphonal method, i.e. two parties sharing the recital: one party chanting a line to which the other responded. Such a procedure inevitably gave rise to 'parallelism' which is the most notable feature of Hebrew poetry. Parallelism may take various forms, the most common being:

(i) *Synonymous*, the thought reproduced in different words, e.g.:

(a) *LORD, who shall sojourn in Thy Tabernacle?*

(b) *Who shall dwell upon Thy holy mountain?* (xv. 1).

(ii) *Anthithetic*, the thought reinforced by

the method of contrast, e.g.:

(a) *For the L*ORD *regardeth the way of the righteous;*

(b) *But the way of the wicked shall perish* (i. 6).

(iii) *Synthetic*, the thought continuing from line to line to build up a cumulative effect, e.g.:

Happy is the man that

(a) *hath not walked in the counsel of the wicked,*

(b) *nor stood in the way of sinners,*

(c) *nor sat in the seat of the scornful* (i. 1).

This use of parallelism is an important aid to the understanding of the text. A word in one line may elucidate an obscure word in another, and the clue may at times extend to the entire clause.

Usually the verse is made up of two equal halves, but may consist of three divisions and occasionally more. The verses are normally grouped into strophes of equal length. The introductory Psalm, for example, consists of six verses, the first and second three each comprising a strophe. In Ps. ii verses 1-3, 4-6, 7-9 and 10-12 are strophes of three verses. Unequal length is also frequent, as in Ps. iv where the first and third strophes have three verses, but the second only two.

A few Psalms are constructed on the plan of an alphabetic acrostic. They are xxv, xxxiv, xxxvii, cxi, cxii, cxix (eight-fold) and cxlv. Traces of this construction are also distinguishable in ix and x.

ROLE OF THE PSALM

Rabbi Yudan stated in the name of Rabbi Yehudah: 'Everything that David stated in his Psalms was said pertaining to himself, pertaining to all of Israel, and pertaining to all times' (Midrash Shocher Tov on Psalm xviii).

The construction of the Psalms, their style and content make them suitable for use as prayer by all people, at all times, for all occasions: in sorrow as in happiness and joy; as an expression of thanks and as the language for beseeching; by individuals and by multitudes. Many verses from the Psalms and many Psalms in their entirety have become incorporated in the standard Prayer Book for weekdays, Sabbath and Holy days.

The Book of Psalms has accompanied the Jewish people through all periods. In it they found solace during times of darkness and followed its radiant light of spiritual direction. Its verses gave the people strength to with- stand edicts and onslaughts; courage and hope to look to a brighter tomorrow. The Jewish people never despaired, even during the most dreadful epochs of their history, as they drew their faith in the future from the inspiring and reassuring verses of the Psalms. Malbim, in his commentary on Psalms, points out that every person can find his own experience in it—in every prayer, in every supplication; in every Psalm of thanks or salvation, affliction or respite, voiced by the individual or the public—through the march of time and into the storms that buffet the traveller on the roaring sea with its thunderous waves.

The Book of Psalms clarifies the possibilities for each human being, as well as for all of mankind, that under all circumstances, contentment and tranquility are attainable.

Rabbi Samson Raphael Hirsch, in the introduction to his commentary on Psalms, states: 'For, far beyond the confines of the Jewish people, even today, the Psalms still serve to lift up to God the emotions of all those who seek Him, to bring them enlightenment, consolation and strength, and to inspire them to show self-sacrificing devotion in their conduct on earth.'

[Editor's note—This Introduction has been revised for the Second Edition.]

תהלים

THE PSALMS

THE BOOK OF PSALMS

BOOK I
(PSALMS I–XLI)

1   # PSALM I   א

1 HAPPY is the man that hath not
   walked in the counsel of the
   wicked,
Nor stood in the way of sinners,
Nor sat in the seat of the scornful.

2 But his delight is in the law of the
   LORD ;
And in His law doth he meditate
   day and night.

אַשְׁרֵי הָאִישׁ אֲשֶׁר ׀ לֹא הָלַךְ
בַּעֲצַת רְשָׁעִים
וּבְדֶרֶךְ חַטָּאִים לֹא עָמָד
וּבְמוֹשַׁב לֵצִים לֹא יָשָׁב:
כִּי אִם־בְּתוֹרַת יְהֹוָה חֶפְצוֹ 2
וּבְתוֹרָתוֹ יֶהְגֶּה יוֹמָם וָלָיְלָה:

THE TWO WAYS

THE first and second Psalms constitute an introduction to the Psalter, announcing a theme
which is one of the main motifs that run through this Book of the Bible. Man falls into two
categories: the godly—those devoted to God—and the ungodly. The contrast between these
in their behaviour and fate is a subject upon which the Psalms frequently dwell. Thus, the
Talmud (Ber. 9b) declares: '*Happy is the man* (i. 1) and *Why are the nations in an uproar etc.?*
(ii. 1) form one Psalm.' In confirmation of this view a Rabbi pointed out: 'Every Psalm which
was dear to David he opened with *happy* and concluded with *happy*. He opened with *happy*,
as it is written *Happy is the man*, and concluded with *happy*, as it is written *Happy are all they
that take refuge in Him* (ii. 12).'

1-3   THE WAY OF THE GODLY

1. *happy is the man.* lit. 'the happiness of the
man.' The phrase is frequent in the Bible, and
it signifies the spiritual joy and tranquility of
heart which result from trust in God (Cf. Malbim
and Daath Sofrim). Rashi and Metsudath David
render 'the praises of the man are that etc.'

hath not walked. To avoid the possibility of
contamination, the godly man avoids association with evildoers (cf. Metsudath David).

walked, stood, sat: The verbs describe successive steps in a career of evil: (*a*) accepting the
principles of deliberate sinners; (*b*) flirting with
those who adopt a frivolous, light-hearted attitude; (*c*) being in constant companionship with
those who ridicule the Torah and scorn their
religion (Malbim, Hirsch).

wicked. Common term for the ungodly, the

opposite being *tsaddik*, 'the righteous.' They
wilfully and persistently violate the commands
of God (Malbim).

sinners. These men 'miss' (such is the root
meaning) the true way of living, either from
ignorance or lack of moral strength (Malbim).

seat of the scornful. Or, 'company of scoffers.'
The worst type of all: scorners of piety who
deliberately choose evil and delight in corrupting others (see Metsudath Zion).

2. *but his delight.* The characteristic of the
godly man is negative in his refusal to associate
with the wicked, but also positive in the concentration of his mind upon understanding the
law (the revealed will) of God. Conformity to
His law, it should be noted, is not an irksome
burden, but a *delight* (Metsudath David).

doth he meditate. Fulfilling the exhortation
addressed to Joshua (Joshua i. 8).

3 And he shall be like a tree planted
    by streams of water,
  That bringeth forth its fruit in its
    season,
  And whose leaf doth not wither;
  And in whatsoever he doeth he
    shall prosper.

4 Not so the wicked;
  But they are like the chaff which
    the wind driveth away.

5 Therefore the wicked shall not
    stand in the judgment,
  Nor sinners in the congregation of
    the righteous.

6 For the LORD regardeth the way of
    the righteous;
  But the way of the wicked shall
    perish.

וְהָיָה כְּעֵץ שָׁתוּל עַל־פַּלְנֵי מָיִם 3
אֲשֶׁר פִּרְיוֹ ׀ יִתֵּן בְּעִתּוֹ
וְעָלֵהוּ לֹא־יִבּוֹל
וְכֹל אֲשֶׁר־יַעֲשֶׂה יַצְלִיחַ:
לֹא־כֵן הָרְשָׁעִים 4
כִּי אִם־כַּמֹּץ אֲשֶׁר־תִּדְּפֶנּוּ רוּחַ:
עַל־כֵּן ׀ לֹא־יָקֻמוּ רְשָׁעִים בַּמִּשְׁפָּט 5
וְחַטָּאִים בַּעֲדַת צַדִּיקִים:
כִּי־יוֹדֵעַ יְהֹוָה דֶּרֶךְ צַדִּיקִים 6
וְדֶרֶךְ רְשָׁעִים תֹּאבֵד:

3. *like a tree*. The imagery is also found in Jer. xvii. 5-8. Like the tree which draws its vitalizing moisture from a constant source, so the godly man derives strength of purpose from the unfailing Spirit of God (cf. Hirsch). Fortified in this manner, he may be buffeted by the troubles which overtake him, but he comes through them with unshaken resolve, like a firmly rooted tree which 'even if all the winds in the world come and blow upon it, it cannot be stirred from its place' (Aboth iii. 22).

he shall prosper. He ultimately succeeds in his undertakings because obstacles fail to turn him from his purpose (Hirsch). His trust in God enables him to draw upon hidden reserves of power with which he overrides the storm and safely reaches his goal.

4-6 THE WAY OF THE UNGODLY

4. *like the chaff*. In contrast to the tree which no wind can uproot. In the Holy Land, wheat was threshed on hilltops which were swept by the wind. The corn remained and the chaff was carried away. Similarly, although the un-godly may triumph temporarily, they lack stability and do not endure (Metsudath David).

5. *therefore*. Because the wicked have sinned in this world (Kimchi).

in the judgment. God is the Judge of the universe and the wicked receive condemnation at His hands.

nor sinners in the congregation of the righteous. God makes a distinction between the two classes in the fate which befalls them. The righteous will enjoy their share in the world to come, while the sinners will perish entirely (Kimchi).

6. *regardeth*. He concerns Himself with *the way of the righteous* so that it prospers (Kimchi).

way of the wicked shall perish. Without the support of God, their lives are doomed and they have no hope of attaining their goal (Hirsch). The psalm is a fundamental teaching in the approach to success in life. In order to merit reward from God, one must associate with the righteous and avoid consorting with the wicked.

1 Why are the nations in an uproar?
And why do the peoples mutter
in vain?

2 The kings of the earth stand up,
And the rulers take counsel
together,
Against the Lord, and against His
anointed:

3 'Let us break their bands asunder,
And cast away their cords from us.'

A PLOT AGAINST GOD'S ANOINTED

COMMENTATORS differ as to whether the subject of this Psalm is the King Messiah or King David. Rashi's comment is: 'Our Rabbis expound it as relating to King Messiah; but according to its plain meaning it is proper to interpret it in connection with David, in light of the statement: *And when the Philistines heard that David was anointed king over Israel, all the Philistines went up to seek David* (2 Sam. v. 17).' The succession to the throne of Israel became the occasion of a political crisis which threatened the country with war. The Psalm demonstrates how that which is true of the life of the individual, applies equally to nations as a whole. They, too, will perish if instead of placing their power in the service of God's moral law, they abuse their might by contradicting that law (Hirsch).

1–3 KINGS PLAN AN ATTACK

1. *why.* The question is twofold. It is addressed to the nations and expresses wonder at their futile attempts to gather against God and his anointed, and according to the Midrash (Shocher Tov) it is also a question addressed to God: Why are the wicked not punished for their misdeeds? (Daath Sofrim).

in an uproar. The same word as in lv. 15, *In the house of God we walked with the throng.* It conveys the idea of a noisy assembly (cf. Meiri).

mutter in vain. Better, 'meditate a vain thing' (Rashi). The plan they had gathered to consider, viz. the overthrow of the newly crowned king, is 'an empty scheme' (Kimchi).

2. *the kings of the earth. Eretz* means 'earth' or 'land.' Here the reference is to the kings of the Philistines and of the surrounding nations,

(Kimchi) and the phrase stands in opposition to *My king* (verse 6).

against the Lord. An attack upon Israel's king would be a revolt against God Who had willed his kingship (Kimchi).

His anointed. The ceremony of dedication to a divinely ordained office included the pouring of oil upon the head. It was done at the consecration of a priest (Exod. xxviii. 41), a king (1 Sam. x. 1), and occasionally a prophet (1 Kings xix. 16). David called Saul *the Lord's anointed* (1 Sam. xxiv. 6). Although the text could be translated *His Messiah*, it may apply as well to an ordinary king.

3. *let us break their bands asunder.* The consensus to appoint David as king (Redak). Or, they fear becoming vassals of Israel under the Messiah (Metsudath David). The *bands* and *cords* refer to the limitations and duties imposed on people and nations by God's moral

4 He that sitteth in heaven laugheth,
The Lord hath them in derision.

5 Then will He speak unto them in
His wrath,
And affright them in His sore
displeasure:

6 'Truly it is I that have established
My king
Upon Zion, My holy mountain.'

7 I will tell of the decree:
The Lord said unto me: 'Thou
art My son,
This day have I begotten thee.

8 Ask of Me, and I will give the
nations for thine inheritance,
And the ends of the earth for thy
possession.

9 Thou shalt break them with a rod
of iron;
Thou shalt dash them in pieces
like a potter's vessel.'

יוֹשֵׁב בַּשָּׁמַיִם יִשְׂחָק 4
אֲדֹנָי יִלְעַג־לָמוֹ:

אָז יְדַבֵּר אֵלֵימוֹ בְאַפּוֹ 5
וּבַחֲרוֹנוֹ יְבַהֲלֵמוֹ:

וַאֲנִי נָסַכְתִּי מַלְכִּי 6
עַל־צִיּוֹן הַר־קָדְשִׁי:

אֲסַפְּרָה אֶל־חֹק 7
יְהֹוָה אָמַר אֵלַי בְּנִי אַתָּה
אֲנִי הַיּוֹם יְלִדְתִּיךָ:

שְׁאַל מִמֶּנִּי וְאֶתְּנָה גוֹיִם נַחֲלָתֶךָ 8
וַאֲחֻזָּתְךָ אַפְסֵי־אָרֶץ:

תְּרֹעֵם בְּשֵׁבֶט בַּרְזֶל 9
כִּכְלִי יוֹצֵר תְּנַפְּצֵם:

---

law. These were in contradiction to their interests and, therefore, their goal was to break them asunder (Hirsch).

4-6   GOD DERIDES THE PLOT

4. As in the Book of Job, the reader is transported to the heavenly regions to witness the working out of God's designs.

He that sitteth in heaven. Better, 'He Who is enthroned in heaven' (as in cxxiii. 1), the King of kings.

laugheth. A bold anthropomorphism which makes the scene vivid (cf. xxxvii. 13, lix. 9).

5. *then.* At the moment when He decides to intervene and frustrate their plans (cf. Kimchi).

6. *truly it is I.* The pronoun is stressed in the Hebrew to mark a contrast. *I* have willed the king to reign, so how dare *you* conspire to overthrow him! (Metsudath David).

My king. A king chosen by Me.

Zion. A poetical name for Jerusalem, for which

My holy mountain is another epithet (cf. *the city of our God, His holy mountain,* xlviii. 2).

7-9   THE KING SPEAKS

7. *I will tell of the decree.* The king claims that he is no usurper of the crown, nor has he assumed the kingship to gratify his personal ambition. He holds his office by Divine decree.

thou art My son. See lxxxix. 28 where God declares of David: *I will also appoint him firstborn, the highest of the kings of the earth.*

this day have I begotten thee. To be understood in a figurative sense. On the day of his enthronement, the king was *begotten* of God as His servant to guide the destinies of His people. When the throne was promised to Solomon, God gave the assurance: *I will be to him for a father, and he shall be to Me for a son* (2 Sam vii. 14) (Rashi).

8. *ask of Me.* The language of the verse is poetical hyperbole. So close is the relationship

10 Now therefore, O ye kings, be
    wise;
  Be admonished, ye judges of the
    earth.

11 Serve the Lord with fear,
  And rejoice with trembling.

12 Do homage in purity, lest He be
    angry, and ye perish in the way,
  When suddenly His wrath is
    kindled.
  Happy are all they that take
    refuge in Him.

10 וְעַתָּה מְלָכִים הַשְׂכִּילוּ

הִוָּסְרוּ שֹׁפְטֵי אָרֶץ:

11 עִבְדוּ אֶת־יְהֹוָה בְּיִרְאָה

וְגִילוּ בִּרְעָדָה:

12 נַשְּׁקוּ־בַר פֶּן־יֶאֱנַף ׀ וְתֹאבְדוּ דֶרֶךְ

כִּי־יִבְעַר כִּמְעַט אַפּוֹ

אַשְׁרֵי כָּל־חוֹסֵי בוֹ:

between God and His anointed that any request
would be granted, even dominion over the
whole earth (Metsudath David). Not that any
such ambitious thought is in the king's mind;
but it indicates the hopelessness of any attempt
to dethrone him (cf. Daath Sofrim).

9. If the plotters venture to proceed with their
scheme, their fate will be utter destruction, like
the shattering of an earthenware vessel
(Kimchi).

rod of iron. i.e. a sword (Rashi).

a potter's vessel. Easily broken and then beyond repair (Jer. xix. 11).

10-12 EXHORTATION TO THE SCHEMERS

10. Two ways confront the schemers. One
is to rebel against God's decree, which will
bring upon them severe retribution; the other
is to submit to His will with happiness as its
sequel. They are exhorted to adopt the second
alternative.

judges. Rulers whose function was to administer justice.

11. *serve the Lord with fear.* Humbly yield to
His decree respecting the kingship, fearing the
consequences of His anger (cf. Kimchi).

rejoice with trembling. Instead of seeking my
downfall, rejoice in His choice of a king, standing in awe of His infinite Majesty.

12. *do homage in purity. Do homage* is lit.
'kiss' (cf. 1 Sam. x. 1), for to kiss the hand of
one's master is a symbolic act of homage. The
word for *purity* occurs in the phrase *pure in heart*
(lxxiii. 1) (Kimchi). The psalm entreats them
to gird themselves in purity as opposed to
violence and wrongdoing if the wrath of God is
to be averted (Hirsch). Rashi renders 'yearn for
absolute purity of the heart,' i.e., accept His
kingdom without reservation.

ye perish in the way. A reminiscence of *the way
of the wicked shall perish* (i. 6) (Rashi).

happy are all they. The Psalm ends on the same
note as that struck at the beginning of Ps. i.
Rashi, as in i. 1, renders *ashrei* as a noun. According to this rendition the verse states that
the delight of the one who trusts in God will
become manifest to all.

3

1 A Psalm of David, when he fled from Absalom his son.

2 LORD, how many are mine adversaries become!
Many are they that rise up against me.

3 Many there are that say of my soul:
'There is no salvation for him in God.'   Selah

4 But Thou, O LORD, art a shield about me;
My glory, and the lifter up of my head.

מִזְמוֹר לְדָוִד בְּבָרְחוֹ
מִפְּנֵי ׀ אַבְשָׁלוֹם בְּנוֹ:
2 יְהוָה מָה־רַבּוּ צָרָי
רַבִּים קָמִים עָלָי:
3 רַבִּים אֹמְרִים לְנַפְשִׁי
אֵין יְשׁוּעָתָה לּוֹ בֵאלֹהִים סֶלָה:
4 וְאַתָּה יְהוָה מָגֵן בַּעֲדִי
כְּבוֹדִי וּמֵרִים רֹאשִׁי:

A PRAYER IN DISTRESS

THE Psalm speaks for itself. It is a sublime expression of trust in God's help when beset by relentless enemies. A close connection with Ps. iv. is discernible, and the latter is to be understood as its sequel. The first of the two Psalms is accordingly a cry of one's heart called forth by the present danger, culminating in the realization that God has not forsaken him. He brings courage to all those who find themselves in a similar state of peril or misery (Hirsch). The second Psalm is a song of relief uttered when the peril seemed less imminent. The circumstance is specified in the superscription.

1. *when he fled from Absalom.* See 2 Sam. xv-xvii.

2-3 HIS DANGEROUS PLIGHT

2. *how many are mine adversaries become.* A messenger brought David the information: *The hearts of the men of Israel are after Absalom* (2 Sam. xv. 13); as is clear from that narrative, the rebel son, as Kimchi delineates, had a considerable following.

3. *my soul.* Hebrew idiom for 'me,' occurring so frequently in the Psalter.

there is no salvation for him in God. His situation appeared so desperate, that it was generally believed that he had lost his share in the world to come and that nothing could help him. He was not expected to regain the throne (Kimchi). *Selah.* Occurs 71 times in the Psalms. A term meant for the musicians who accompanied the recital of the Psalms in the Temple, probably an indication that a change in tune was to be introduced at this point (Ibn Ezra, Kimchi).

4-5 GOD IS HIS SURE TO HELP

4. *a shield about me.* As God had assured Abraham: *I am thy shield* (Gen. xv. 1). Thus protected, he is confident of escape from his peril.

my glory. God is the bestower of his regal dignity, no human being can deprive him of it (Metsudath).

the lifter up of my head. When David fled, *he had his head covered, and went barefoot* (2 Sam. xv. 30). He was bowed under his humiliation, but God would enable him to hold his head high again (Metsudath David).

5 With my voice I call unto the
   LORD,
   And He answereth me out of His
   holy mountain.   Selah

6 I lay me down, and I sleep;
   I awake, for the LORD sustaineth
   me.

7 I am not afraid of ten thousands of
   people,
   That have set themselves against
   me round about.

8 Arise, O LORD; save me, O my
   God;
   For Thou hast smitten all mine
   enemies upon the cheek,
   Thou hast broken the teeth of the
   wicked.

9 Salvation belongeth unto the LORD;
   Thy blessing be upon Thy people.
                           Selah

קוֹלִי אֶל־יְהֹוָה אֶקְרָא 5
וַיַּעֲנֵנִי מֵהַר קָדְשׁוֹ סֶלָה:
אֲנִי שָׁכַבְתִּי וָאִישָׁנָה 6
הֱקִיצוֹתִי כִּי יְהֹוָה יִסְמְכֵנִי:
לֹא־אִירָא מֵרִבְבוֹת עָם 7
אֲשֶׁר סָבִיב שָׁתוּ עָלָי:
קוּמָה יְהֹוָה ׀ הוֹשִׁיעֵנִי אֱלֹהַי 8
כִּי־הִכִּיתָ אֶת־כָּל־אֹיְבַי לֶחִי
שִׁנֵּי רְשָׁעִים שִׁבַּרְתָּ:
לַיהֹוָה הַיְשׁוּעָה 9
עַל־עַמְּךָ בִרְכָתֶךָ סֶּלָה:

5. *I call … He answereth.* Whenever I cry, He responds. The recollection of His saving power in days past drives away the feeling of despair (cf. Kimchi).

out of His holy mountain. Mt. Zion (see ii. 6) where the holy ark was situated. Kimchi suggests Mt. Moriah which, although not yet sanctified, was known to be the future site for the sanctuary. From his position on the Mount of Olives, David had a clear view of the Temple Mount.

6-7 HIS FEELING OF CONFIDENCE

6. *I sleep.* The knowledge that he had God as a shield made it possible for him to sleep at night, when the danger of sudden attack was greatest (Kimchi).

for the LORD sustaineth me. His first thought on waking is his indebtedness to the mercy of God for coming safely through the night. It fortifies him to face what the new day may bring (cf. Rashi).

7. *I am not afraid of ten thousands of people.* Conscious that he has God as his Helper, the numerical strength of his enemies does not dismay him (Metsudath David).

8-9 PRAYER FOR DELIVERANCE

8. *arise, O LORD.* A recollection of Israel's watchword when confronted with danger (Num. x. 35: see also lxviii. 2).

Thou hast smitten. Either the memory of what God had done on his behalf in the past is an assurance that it will happen again; or we have here the Hebrew idiom known as 'the prophetic perfect' whereby an event still to take place is described as having actually happened. If the latter, the sense is: I am certain a time will come when Thou wilt have smitten (Kimchi).

broken the teeth of the wicked. Deprived them of their power to harm (cf. lviii. 7).

9. *salvation belongeth unto the LORD.* With Him alone rests the issue of the crisis through which he was passing (Metsudath David). Granted His redemptive might, he would triumph over his foes.

Thy blessing be upon Thy people. Although his subjects, unmindful of their allegiance, had sided with the usurper, he has no bitter feelings towards them and invokes upon them God's blessing (Metsudath David).

4

ד

1 For the Leader; with string-music.
A Psalm of David.

2 Answer me when I call, O God of
my righteousness,
Thou who didst set me free when
I was in distress;
Be gracious unto me, and hear my
prayer.

3 O ye sons of men, how long shall
my glory be put to shame,
In that ye love vanity, and seek
after falsehood? Selah

4 But know that the LORD hath set
apart the godly man as His own;

לַמְנַצֵּחַ בִּנְגִינוֹת מִזְמוֹר לְדָוִד׃

2 בְּקָרְאִי עֲנֵנִי ׀ אֱלֹהֵי צִדְקִי
בַּצָּר הִרְחַבְתָּ לִּי
חָנֵּנִי וּשְׁמַע תְּפִלָּתִי׃

3 בְּנֵי־אִישׁ עַד־מֶה כְבוֹדִי לִכְלִמָּה
תֶּאֱהָבוּן רִיק תְּבַקְשׁוּ כָזָב סֶלָה׃

4 וּדְעוּ כִּי־הִפְלָה יְהוָה חָסִיד לוֹ

A PRAYER IN RELIEF

THE same spirit pervades this Psalm as the former, and the two should be read together. The writer now feels that his reliance upon God in his time of trouble has been justified and a sense of tranquillity possesses him.

1. *the Leader.* The word is found in 2 Chron. ii. 1 to describe the overseer of the men who were building the Temple. In the Psalm headings it refers to the director of music. He receives his instruction regarding the accompaniment of the Psalm in the words that follow (Kimchi).

with string-music. Better, 'with musical instruments.' This refers to a particular group of instruments. Other instruments were included in the composition of the Temple orchestra (Ibn Ezra).

2–4 APPEAL TO GOD AND HIS ENEMIES

2. *God of my righteousness.* The Hebrew word for 'innocent' is the same as 'righteous' (*tsaddik*). So here the phrase is best translated 'God of my vindication.' He prays to Him to prove him in the right (Metsudath David).

Thou Who didst set me free when I was in distress. lit. 'in narrowness Thou hast broadened (a space) for me' (Metsudath David). He had been hemmed in by relentless pursuers, and God had made it possible for him to move more freely.

be gracious unto me. As in the recent past, so also in days to come (Rashi).

3. *ye sons of men.* Hebrew *ish,* not the more usual *adam.* He addresses himself to the leaders among the rebels, not to the rank and file (Kimchi) who had been misled.

my glory. My personal dignity as king, which has been humiliated by the uprising.

ye love vanity. Same Hebrew word as *in vain* (ii. 1); the vain scheme to crown Absalom to which they had applied themselves (Kimchi).

seek after falsehood. Kazab here means that which will fail and bring disappointment, as in *a spring of water, whose waters fail not* (Isaiah lviii. 11). Their aim to make Absalom king will be nullified by God (Kimchi).

4. *but know.* Rather, 'and know.' He gives the conclusive reason why they should abandon their plan, viz. his kingship was determined by God (cf. Metsudath David).

the godly man. Hebrew *chasid,* a frequent word in the Psalms, refers to a person who demonstrates his love of God by dealing so favourably

The LORD will hear when I call
unto Him.

5 Tremble, and sin not;
Commune with your own heart
upon your bed, and be still.
Selah

6 Offer the sacrifices of righteousness,
And put your trust in the LORD.

7 Many there are that say: 'Oh that
we could see some good!'
LORD, lift Thou up the light of
Thy countenance upon us.

8 Thou hast put gladness in my heart,
More than when their corn and
their wine increase.

9 In peace will I both lay me down
and sleep;
For Thou, LORD, makest me dwell
alone in safety.

יְהֹוָה יִשְׁמַע בְּקָרְאִי אֵלָיו׃
5 רִגְזוּ וְאַל־תֶּחֱטָאוּ אִמְרוּ בִלְבַבְכֶם
עַל־מִשְׁכַּבְכֶם וְדֹמּוּ סֶלָה׃
6 זִבְחוּ זִבְחֵי־צֶדֶק
וּבִטְחוּ אֶל־יְהֹוָה׃
7 רַבִּים אֹמְרִים מִי־יַרְאֵנוּ טוֹב
נְסָה־עָלֵינוּ אוֹר פָּנֶיךָ יְהֹוָה׃
8 נָתַתָּה שִׂמְחָה בְלִבִּי
מֵעֵת דְּגָנָם וְתִירוֹשָׁם רָבּוּ׃
9 בְּשָׁלוֹם יַחְדָּו אֶשְׁכְּבָה וְאִישָׁן
כִּי־אַתָּה יְהֹוָה לְבָדָד
לָבֶטַח תּוֹשִׁיבֵנִי׃

with his fellow man as to treat kindly even those who have harmed him. It is towards such a person that God manifests his love and favour. David, a prime example of a *chasid*, as seen in his dealings with Saul (1 Sam. xxiv. 18), is confident that his petition will not go unanswered (cf. Kimchi).

5-6 WHAT HIS ENEMIES SHOULD DO

5. *tremble.* Be afraid of God, if not of me (Kimchi).

sin not. The rebellion was a denial of God's will with regard to his right to the throne, and consequently an act of sinfulness.

commune with your own heart. In the quietness of the night let your conscience speak and convince you of the error of your ways (Kimchi, Metsudath David).

and be still. Put an end to your rebellious activities against me (Kimchi).

6. *sacrifices of righteousness.* Offerings brought with a pure motive and penitent heart (li. 19) as opposed to *an offering of abomination* (Isa. i. 13) (cf. Kimchi).

7-9 HIS CONFIDENCE IN GOD

7. *Oh that we could see some good!* R.V. more

lit. *'who will shew us any good?'* The condition of the people was hard at that time and many were discontented. In their longing for an improvement, they were ready to turn to any leader who made them promises; and so they had rallied around Absalom (Rashi, Kimchi).

LORD, lift Thou up the light of Thy countenance. A quotation from the priestly benediction (Num. vi. 26). David hopes for better things for the people by praying that He will show them the right path to take (Daath Sofrim).

8. *Thou hast put gladness in my heart.* He has experienced a God-sent joy which he contrasts with the rejoicing that men make over an abundant harvest. His is infinitely superior (Metsudath David).

9. *in peace will I ... sleep. Both* is lit. 'together.' His mind now freed from anxiety, lying down and sleep become united, and he is not kept awake by fear of impending danger (Metsudath David).

dwell ... in safety. Cf. Deut. xxxiii. 28. Even without human allies he is able to enjoy safety (Rashi). Kimchi favours the rendering 'For Thou, LORD, alone makest me dwell'; to Him alone he is indebted for his safety.

5

1 For the Leader; upon the Nehiloth. A Psalm of David.

2 Give ear to my words, O LORD,
Consider my meditation.

3 Hearken unto the voice of my cry,
my King, and my God;
For unto Thee do I pray.

4 O LORD, in the morning shalt Thou
hear my voice;
In the morning will I order my
prayer unto Thee, and will look
forward.

5 For Thou art not a God that hath
pleasure in wickedness;
Evil shall not sojourn with Thee.

ה

לַמְנַצֵּחַ אֶל־הַנְּחִילוֹת מִזְמוֹר לְדָוִד:

2 אֲמָרַי הַאֲזִינָה וְיהוָה
בִּינָה הֲגִיגִי:

3 הַקְשִׁיבָה לְקוֹל שַׁוְעִי מַלְכִּי וֵאלֹהָי
כִּי־אֵלֶיךָ אֶתְפַּלָּל:

4 יהוָה בֹּקֶר תִּשְׁמַע קוֹלִי
בֹּקֶר אֶעֱרָךְ־לְךָ וַאֲצַפֶּה:

5 כִּי לֹא אֵל־חָפֵץ רֶשַׁע אָתָּה
לֹא יְגֻרְךָ רָע:

A PRAYER FOR ASSISTANCE

THE tone of this Psalm is like that of the preceding and the circumstance are somewhat similar. The speaker is exposed to danger from treacherous foes (Meiri). He offers a prayer in which he expresses his conviction that God Who hates evil will not allow wrongdoers to triumph. In addition, he asks God to help him lead a righteous life and that he not be led astray by the wicked (verses 9-10).

1. *Nehiloth.* lit. 'a swarm of bees.' The name was applied to a string instrument which produced a droning sound similar to that of bees (Meiri).

2-4 INTRODUCTORY INVOCATION

2. *meditation.* Unspoken prayer in the recesses of the heart (cf. xix. 15) (Meiri). David reinforces his plea by asking God to understand the thoughts of his heart when he no longer has the strength to utter his prayer by mouth (Rashi).

3. *my King.* As a subject appeals to his monarch to right his cause, so I, a king, turn to the King of kings to justify me (cf. Kimchi).

my God. Elohim, the Deity in His role of Judge.

4. *in the morning.* The appropriate time to offer prayer, before the secular duties of the

day commence (see lix. 17, lxxxviii. 14) (Kimchi).

will I order my prayer. Others render 'will I prepare myself before Thee' (cf. Meiri, Metsudath David). Malbim suggests 'I value Thee as I do the morning.' Just as the dawn signifies the end of darkness, so shall You come as a saviour to end my days of sorrow.

will look forward. As I wait for dawn to break, so shall I wait for Your salvation (Malbim).

5-7 GOD IS AGAINST WORKERS OF EVIL

5. *hath pleasure in.* God is not partial to wickedness.

sojourn with Thee. The qualifications of those who may *sojourn* with God are enumerated in Ps. xv. Malbim prefers 'shall not intimidate You.'

6 The boasters shall not stand in Thy
   sight;
   Thou hatest all workers of iniquity.

7 Thou destroyest them that speak
   falsehood;
   The Lord abhorreth the man of
   blood and of deceit.

8 But as for me, in the abundance of
   Thy lovingkindness will I come
   into Thy house;
   I will bow down toward Thy holy
   temple in the fear of Thee.

9 O Lord, lead me in Thy righteousness because of them that
   lie in wait for me;
   Make Thy way straight before
   my face.

‎6 לֹא־יִתְיַצְּבוּ הוֹלְלִים לְנֶגֶד עֵינֶיךָ
‎שָׂנֵאתָ כָּל־פֹּעֲלֵי אָוֶן:
‎7 תְּאַבֵּד דֹּבְרֵי כָזָב
‎אִישׁ־דָּמִים וּמִרְמָה יְתָעֵב ׀ יְהֹוָה:
‎8 וַאֲנִי בְּרֹב חַסְדְּךָ אָבוֹא בֵיתֶךָ
‎אֶשְׁתַּחֲוֶה אֶל־הֵיכַל־קָדְשְׁךָ בְּיִרְאָתֶךָ:
‎9 יְהֹוָה ׀ נְחֵנִי בְצִדְקָתֶךָ לְמַעַן שׁוֹרְרָי
‎הוֹשַׁר לְפָנַי דַּרְכֶּךָ:

6. *boasters.* A graphic account of their conduct is given in lxxiii. 8f.

shall not stand in Thy sight. Parallel to preceding *an evil man shall not sojourn with Thee*;
God does not tolerate their presence.

7. *abhorreth.* God's essence naturally repels
deception and violence (Malbim).

    8   HIS RIGHT TO ENTER THE SANCTUARY

8. *but as for me.* The Hebrew, common in the
Psalter, marks a strong antithesis. Unlike the
wicked who do not have any rightful place in
God's house, the psalmist does, for the reasons
he states (Kimchi).

the abundance of Thy lovingkindness. God will
be gracious to him and, accordingly, he will
come to offer thanks in the sanctuary
(Metsudath David).

I will bow down. lit. 'prostrate myself' with
face to the ground, the posture of humble
supplication.

Thy holy temple. Both 'Thy house' and 'Thy
holy temple' refer to the holy of holies in the
sanctuary where the ark was kept. Those wishing to bow down to God would face in that

direction (Kimchi). Daath Sofrim points out
that at the time of the writing of this Psalm, the
sanctuary in Jerusalem had not yet been built.
The ark was situated in Shiloh and later in Nob
and Gibeon. Those unable to reach these places
would face towards them whilst at prayer.

in fear of Thee. Better, 'in reverence of Thee,'
yirah being expressive of reverential awe in
connection with God. This is an additional
reason why he contrasts himself with those
who have no place in the Sanctuary; his heart
is filled with humility and submission towards
God (cf. Malbim). This verse has been appropriately selected for recital upon entering a
synagogue (*P.B.*, p. 2).

    9-11   HIS PRAYER FOR VINDICATION

9. *lead me in thy righteousness.* This is my
request to You, that You keep me steadfast in
the right path (Kimchi).

because of them that lie in wait for me. Opposed by unscrupulous men, he might be
tempted to resort to their ways. His request is
accordingly for proper instruction and to be
strengthened in his righteous ways (Malbim).

make Thy way straight. Appreciating the

10 For there is no sincerity in their
    mouth;
    Their inward part is a yawning
    gulf,
    Their throat is an open sepulchre;
    They make smooth their tongue.

11 Hold them guilty, O God,
    Let them fall by their own
    counsels;
    Cast them down in the multitude
    of their transgressions;
    For they have rebelled against
    Thee.

12 So shall all those that take refuge
    in Thee rejoice,
    They shall ever shout for joy,
    And Thou shalt shelter them;
    Let them also that love Thy name
    exult in Thee.

13 For Thou dost bless the righteous;
    O LORD, Thou dost encompass
    him with favour as with a
    shield.

10 כִּי אֵין בְּפִיהוּ נְכוֹנָה קִרְבָּם הַוּוֹת
קֶבֶר־פָּתוּחַ גְּרֹנָם לְשׁוֹנָם יַחֲלִיקוּן:
11 הַאֲשִׁימֵם ׀ אֱלֹהִים יִפְּלוּ
מִמֹּעֲצוֹתֵיהֶם
בְּרֹב פִּשְׁעֵיהֶם הַדִּיחֵמוֹ
כִּי־מָרוּ בָךְ:
12 וְיִשְׂמְחוּ כָל־חוֹסֵי בָךְ לְעוֹלָם יְרַנֵּנוּ
וְתָסֵךְ עָלֵימוֹ וְיַעְלְצוּ בְךָ
אֹהֲבֵי שְׁמֶךָ:
13 כִּי־אַתָּה תְּבָרֵךְ צַדִּיק יְהוָה
כַּצִּנָּה רָצוֹן תַּעְטְרֶנּוּ:

---

difficulty in keeping to God's way in his time of danger, he begs that it be made *straight* for him, i.e. level, with its obstacles removed (cf. Isa. xl. 4) (cf. Malbim).

10. *no sincerity in their mouth.* They *speak peace with their neighbours, but evil is in their heart* (xxviii. 3).

inward part. When they devise their schemes they are treacherous (Rashi). They are continually conspiring and are consequently devoid of sincerity (Hirsch).

their throat is an open sepulchre. The words they utter lure the unwary to the doom prepared for them (Hirsch).

11. *hold them guilty.* If they are condemned by God, their plots must fail and punishment overtake them!

let them fall by their own counsels. Let their wickedness be the cause of their own undoing.

They will fall into the pit that they have dug for the innocent (cf. Malbim).

cast them down. From their position of influence, so that they cannot work mischief.

they have rebelled against Thee. Plotting against the king, God's anointed, is rebellion against Him (Kimchi).

12-13 THE JOY OF THE RIGHTEOUS

12. With the overthrow of the wicked, those who look to God will rejoice and find shelter from misery and oppression (Hirsch).

that love Thy name. Who pay allegiance to God and are faithful to His will (Hirsch).

13. *shield.* Not the same word as in iii. 4. It is a shield of the largest size, which covers the whole body. God is a complete protection to the righteous (cf. Rashi; see also Rashi Psalm xci. 4).

PSALM VI

6

ו

1 For the Leader; with string-music;
on the Sheminith. A Psalm of
David

2 O Lᴏʀᴅ, rebuke me not in Thine
anger,
Neither chasten me in Thy wrath.

3 Be gracious unto me, O Lᴏʀᴅ, for
I languish away;
Heal me, O Lᴏʀᴅ, for my bones
are affrighted.

4 My soul also is sore affrighted;
And Thou, O Lᴏʀᴅ, how long?

5 Return, O Lᴏʀᴅ, deliver my soul;
Save me for Thy mercy's sake.

לַמְנַצֵּחַ בִּנְגִינוֹת עַל־הַשְּׁמִינִית
מִזְמוֹר לְדָוִד׃
2 יְהוָה אַל־בְּאַפְּךָ תוֹכִיחֵנִי
וְאַל־בַּחֲמָתְךָ תְיַסְּרֵנִי׃
3 חָנֵּנִי יְהוָה כִּי אֻמְלַל אָנִי
רְפָאֵנִי יְהוָה כִּי נִבְהֲלוּ עֲצָמָי׃
4 וְנַפְשִׁי נִבְהֲלָה מְאֹד
וְאַתְּ יְהוָה עַד־מָתָי׃
5 שׁוּבָה יְהוָה חַלְּצָה נַפְשִׁי
הוֹשִׁיעֵנִי לְמַעַן חַסְדֶּךָ׃

ואתה ק׳ v. 4.

A PRAYER IN SICKNESS

A sᴜꜰꜰᴇʀᴇʀ, his body agonized and his mind troubled by ill-wishers who taunt him as being forsaken by God, David sees himself on the verge of death. He sends a fervent prayer up to heaven for relief, with the knowledge that it is futile to expect help from man. God alone can save him. He is confident that God would hear his supplication and grant him renewed strength (verses 9, 10). The Psalm is included in the daily Jewish liturgy (P.B., p. 62f.) among the penitential prayers.

1. *on the Sheminith.* An eight-stringed harp (Rashi). The Talmud (Arachin 13b) renders 'on the eighth string,' explaining that the standard harp had seven strings while the one mentioned in this Psalm refers to the harp that is to be used in the messianic era.

2-4 Cʀʏ ᴏꜰ Sᴜꜰꜰᴇʀɪɴɢ

2. *rebuke me not in Thine anger.* Calamity and illness are divinely appointed means of punishment for sin. Stricken by a painful malady, David sees in his condition evidence of God's displeasure. He humbly admits that he had deserved 'rebuke,' but appeals that it should be in mercy and not in anger (cf. Jer. x. 24) (Meiri).

3. *I languish away.* lit., I am devastated and weak (Rashi).

heal me. The sickness being a visitation from

God, He alone can cure it.

my bones are affrighted. His bodily frame is torn with agony (cf. Kimchi).

4. *my soul also.* His mind is agitated by what has happened to him. Apart from the severity of the illness which may prove fatal (Kimchi), he is deeply disturbed at the thought of having incurred God's wrath (Daath Sofrim).

how long? A poignant exclamation rather than a question: how long will the Divine displeasure last! (Daath Sofrim).

5-8 Pʟᴇᴀ ꜰᴏʀ Dᴇʟɪᴠᴇʀᴀɴᴄᴇ

5. *return.* i.e. from Thine anger (Rashi). See Exod xxxii. 12. Possibly *return ... deliver* means 'deliver again,' as in the past so too now (cf. Hirsch).

deliver my soul. From sickness (Rashi).

6 For in death there is no remem-
brance of Thee;
In the nether-world who will give
Thee thanks?

7 I am weary with my groaning;
Every night make I my bed to
swim;
I melt away my couch with my
tears.

8 Mine eye is dimmed because of
vexation;
It waxeth old because of all mine
adversaries.

9 Depart from me, all ye workers
of iniquity;
For the LORD hath heard the
voice of my weeping.

10 The LORD hath heard my supplication;
The LORD receiveth my prayer.

11 All mine enemies shall be
ashamed and sore affrighted;
They shall turn back, they shall
be ashamed suddenly.

כִּי אֵין בַּמָּוֶת זִכְרֶךָ 6
בִּשְׁאוֹל מִי יוֹדֶה־לָּךְ:
יָגַעְתִּי ׀ בְּאַנְחָתִי 7
אַשְׂחֶה בְכָל־לַיְלָה מִטָּתִי
בְּדִמְעָתִי עַרְשִׂי אַמְסֶה:
עָשְׁשָׁה מִכַּעַס עֵינִי 8
עָתְקָה בְּכָל־צוֹרְרָי:
סוּרוּ מִמֶּנִּי כָּל־פֹּעֲלֵי אָוֶן 9
כִּי־שָׁמַע יְהוָה קוֹל בִּכְיִי:
שָׁמַע יְהוָה תְּחִנָּתִי 10
יְהוָה תְּפִלָּתִי יִקָּח:
יֵבֹשׁוּ ׀ וְיִבָּהֲלוּ מְאֹד כָּל־אֹיְבָי 11
יָשֻׁבוּ יֵבֹשׁוּ רָגַע:

for Thy mercy's sake. He appeals to the attribute of mercy which God had revealed as one of His essential characteristics (Exod. xxxiv. 6)

6. *in death there is no remembrance of Thee*. (See xxx. 10, lxxxviii. 11, cxv. 17; Isa. xxxviii. 18). Only during man's lifetime has he the opportunity to win God's approval by fulfilment of His commands.

the nether-world. Hebrew *Sheol*, often rendered as the grave and, in effect, having the same meaning as *in death* mentioned earlier in the verse (Daath Sofrim). It is an existence connected with silence (cxv. 17), darkness (cxliii. 3), and oblivion (lxxxviii. 13). In Psalm xxx. 4 it describes Gehinom (Kimchi) and the thought of being consigned there always arouses a feeling of horror and dismay; but the righteous are upheld by the knowledge that their stay will not be eternal. God will not leave them in *Sheol*, but will eventually bring them up to enjoy His Presence (xxx. 4).

give Thee thanks. In gratitude of His love.

7. *I am weary*. Worn out.

make ... to swim. Finding sleep impossible, he spends the night weeping over his sufferings.

I melt away. This follows Kimchi's rendering. Rashi has 'I soak.'

8. *mine eye ... because of vexation*. His vision has become unclear (Rashi). Cf. *mine eye wasteth away with vexation* (xxxi. 10). The vexation is caused by the gloating of his enemies over the suffering he has endured (Kimchi).

it waxeth old. His sight fails as in a man of advanced age (Meiri).

9-11 HIS PRAYER ANSWERED

9. *the LORD hath heard*. A marked transition occurs here. The words ring with joyful relief and the note of complaint ends. The verb can be understood as the prophetic perfect (Kimchi).

11. *shall be ashamed*. When they witness my recovery (Kimchi).

sore affrighted. Lest God's anger be directed against them and they have to endure the pains he had suffered (Malbim).

they shall turn back. In dismay at the frustration of their hopes. They shall repent and make peace with me (Kimchi).

PSALM VII

7

ז

1 Shiggaion of David, which he sang
unto the LORD, concerning
Cush a Benjamite.

2 O LORD my God, in Thee have I
taken refuge;
Save me from all them that pursue
me, and deliver me;

3 Lest he tear my soul like a lion,
Rending it in pieces, while there is
none to deliver.

4 O LORD my God, if I have done
this;
If there be iniquity in my hands;

5 If I have requited him that did
evil unto me,
Or spoiled mine adversary unto
emptiness;

שִׁגָּיוֹן לְדָוִד אֲשֶׁר־שָׁר לַיהוָה
עַל־דִּבְרֵי־כוּשׁ בֶּן־יְמִינִי׃

2 יְהוָה אֱלֹהַי בְּךָ חָסִיתִי
הוֹשִׁיעֵנִי מִכָּל־רֹדְפַי וְהַצִּילֵנִי׃

3 פֶּן־יִטְרֹף כְּאַרְיֵה נַפְשִׁי
פֹּרֵק וְאֵין מַצִּיל׃

4 יְהוָה אֱלֹהַי אִם־עָשִׂיתִי זֹאת
אִם־יֶשׁ־עָוֶל בְּכַפָּי׃

5 אִם־גָּמַלְתִּי שׁוֹלְמִי רָע
וָאֲחַלְּצָה צוֹרְרִי רֵיקָם׃

APPEAL TO THE HEAVENLY JUDGE

ANOTHER prayer for protection while under attack by ruthless foes. The title states that David composed the Psalm as a piece *concerning Cush a Benjamite*. The Bible makes no other mention of this name; but in the Talmud (M.K. 16b) Cush is identified with Saul, and the language of the Psalm fits quite well to the circumstances of the episode with that king in David's life. He laments that he had not accorded Saul the honour due him by not grieving sufficiently over his death.

1. *Shiggaion.* Various explanations have been offered. Rashi prefers 'a mistaken choice.' Menachem (quoted by Rashi) maintains that the reference is to a type of musical instrument, while the Talmud (M.K. 16b) has 'in error' (see introduction).

2-3 HIS DANGER

2. *in Thee have I taken refuge.* Not in human aid does he trust to escape from his peril, but in God (cf. Kimchi). This is one of the basic thoughts in the Psalter.

from all them that pursue me. The plural suggests that although Saul was his archenemy, by the king's command, many were hunting him down (cf. Kimchi).

3. *lest he tear.* The singular points to Saul as the instigator of the attempt on his life (Kimchi).

my soul. i.e. 'me' or 'my life.'

like a lion. King Saul, like the king of the beasts, is mighty and prevailing (Kimchi). According to the Midrash Shocher Tov, Doeg and Ahitofel are the ones compared to lions as they were ready to destroy David by mutilating his good name.

4-6 PROTESTATION OF INNOCENCE

4. *if I have done this.* viz. the act mentioned in the next verse (Rashi). He had been accused of disloyalty.

5. *if I have requited him that did evil unto me.* Better, 'if I have rewarded evil unto him that was at peace with me' (so Ibn Ezra, Kimchi). The implication is, "I deny having been disloyal to Saul before his onslaught upon me. Though mistreated by him, I fought his battles and never allowed him to come to any harm."

or spoiled mine adversary unto emptiness.

6 Let the enemy pursue my soul,
 and overtake it,
And tread my life down to the
 earth;
Yea, let him lay my glory in the
 dust.   Selah

7 Arise, O Lord, in Thine anger,
Lift up Thyself in indignation
 against mine adversaries;
Yea, awake for me at the judgment
 which Thou hast commanded.

8 And let the congregation of the
 peoples compass Thee about,
And over them return Thou on
 high.

9 O Lord, who ministerest judgment to the peoples,
Judge me, O Lord,
According to my righteousness,
 and according to mine integrity that is in me.

10 Oh that a full measure of evil
 might come upon the wicked,
And that Thou wouldest establish the righteous;
For the righteous God trieth the
 hearts and reins.

11 My shield is with God,
Who saveth the upright in heart.

Better "(I, who have spared my adversary by letting him go free)," the clause being parenthetical. What greater proof could there be that David had no evil designs against Saul than the occasions when he had spared the king's life? (See 1 Sam. xxiv., xxvi) (Kimchi).

6. *my glory.* If he is guilty of the charge, he not only asks that death should overtake him, but that his personal honour be overwhelmed with shame.

7-11 PRAYER FOR GOD'S INTERVENTION

7. *in Thine anger.* God being just, He is indignant at the injustice which has been done to the innocent (Metsudath David). Let Him display His wrath and justify me.

lift up Thyself, etc. Hirsch renders this as 'lift up Thyself against the excesses of my oppressors; yea, awaken for me the judgment which

Thou hast decreed.' The words echo the bold challenge of Abraham: *Shall not the Judge of all the earth do justly?* (Gen. xviii. 25).

8. *let the congregation ... about.* David refers to God as judge over all the nations. He asks that they should come to recognize Him and submit to His judgment (Hirsch).

over them return Thou on high. To take Your seat upon the heavenly throne as sovereign ruler and execute justice (cf. Hirsch).

9. Returning to the immediate present, David, acknowledging that God will judge the nations, petitions God to judge him favourably as he is innocent (Hirsch).

10. *Oh that a full measure of evil might come upon the wicked.* Better, 'Oh let the wickedness of the wicked come to an end.' *Wicked* indicates the guilty party in the suit; may his evil plan be brought to an end.

16

12 God is a righteous judge,
   Yea, a God that hath indignation
     every day:

13 If a man turn not, He will whet
    His sword,
   He hath bent His bow, and made
    it ready;

14 He hath also prepared for him the
    weapons of death,
   Yea, His arrows which He made
    sharp.

15 Behold, he travaileth with iniquity;
   Yea, he conceiveth mischief, and
    bringeth forth falsehood.

16 He hath digged a pit, and
    hollowed it,
   And is fallen into the ditch which
    he made.

17 His mischief shall return upon
    his own head,
   And his violence shall come down
    upon his own pate.

18 I will give thanks unto the LORD
    according to His righteousness;
   And will sing praise to the name
    of the LORD Most High.

אֱלֹהִים שׁוֹפֵט צַדִּיק 12
וְאֵל זֹעֵם בְּכָל־יוֹם׃

אִם־לֹא יָשׁוּב חַרְבּוֹ יִלְטוֹשׁ 13
קַשְׁתּוֹ דָרַךְ וַיְכוֹנְנֶהָ׃

וְלוֹ הֵכִין כְּלֵי־מָוֶת 14
חִצָּיו לְדֹלְקִים יִפְעָל׃

הִנֵּה יְחַבֶּל־אָוֶן 15
וְהָרָה עָמָל וְיָלַד שָׁקֶר׃

בּוֹר כָּרָה וַיַּחְפְּרֵהוּ 16
וַיִּפֹּל בְּשַׁחַת יִפְעָל׃

יָשׁוּב עֲמָלוֹ בְרֹאשׁוֹ 17
וְעַל קָדְקֳדוֹ חֲמָסוֹ יֵרֵד׃

אוֹדֶה יְהוָה כְּצִדְקוֹ 18
וַאֲזַמְּרָה שֵׁם־יְהוָה עֶלְיוֹן׃

---

hearts and reins. In the Bible, 'heart' is the seat of the more lofty emotions, while *reins* (kidneys) are the center of physical urges and desires (see Hirsch on Leviticus 3:4). Combined, they determine a man's character and actions (see xxvi, 2; Jer. xi. 20, xvii. 10, xx. 12).

11. *my shield is with God.* More lit. 'upon God.' His defence is dependence upon God as the Protector of the just (Kimchi).

12-17 FATE OF THE WICKED

12. *every day.* God constantly shows His displeasure to the wicked (Hirsch). Alternatively, the subject of the second half of the verse is the evil man, and the verse reads 'God judges the righteous (according to his righteousness), and also judges the evil man who angers Him every day 'he who is constantly sinning against Him' (Kimchi).

13. *turn not.* Does not repent of his evil (Rashi).

whet His sword. For the imagery, see Deut. xxxii. 41f. The wicked are God's enemies against whom He comes arrayed like a warrior (Rashi).

14. *His arrows.* See xviii. 15, where *arrows* has 'lightnings' as its parallel.

which He made sharp. Better, 'He maketh arrows for them that pursue (me).'

15. *he travaileth.* The subject is the unrighteous man. The hatching of evil designs is described in a metaphorical language connected with childbirth (Rashi).

17. *his mischief.* The harm he intended for others recoils upon himself.

18 GRATITUDE TO HIS VINDICATOR

LORD Most High. Who is above all His creations and is supreme ruler, doing as He wishes (Kimchi).

PSALM VIII

8

1 For the Leader; upon the Gittith.
  A Psalm of David.

2 O LORD, our Lord,
  How glorious is Thy name in all
    the earth!
  Whose majesty is rehearsed above
    the heavens.

3 Out of the mouth of babes and
    sucklings hast Thou founded
    strength,
  Because of Thine adversaries;
  That Thou mightest still the
    enemy and the avenger.

ח

לַמְנַצֵּחַ עַל־הַגִּתִּית מִזְמוֹר לְדָוִד׃

2 יְהוָה אֲדֹנֵינוּ

מָה־אַדִּיר שִׁמְךָ בְּכָל־הָאָרֶץ

אֲשֶׁר תְּנָה הוֹדְךָ עַל־הַשָּׁמָיִם׃

3 מִפִּי עוֹלְלִים וְיֹנְקִים יִסַּדְתָּ עֹז

לְמַעַן צוֹרְרֶיךָ

לְהַשְׁבִּית אוֹיֵב וּמִתְנַקֵּם׃

THE PARADOX OF MAN

A NEW note is struck. Instead of supplication in a time of danger, we have a profound reflection upon man's status in the universe as testimony to the infinite greatness of God. The Psalmist meditates upon the grandeur of His creation and the place which the human being occupies therein. On the one hand, man is so insignificant in comparison with the vastness of God's works that it is surprising that the Creator deigns to give him a thought. On the other hand, he is the human lord of the earth and endowed with powers which make him little less than divine. Both perceptions are true and there is no contradiction. The dignified position which man as a creature of God holds in the world is only proof of the incomparable majesty of His Maker.

1. *upon the Gittith.* Several explanations are possible. The Targum connects the term with the city name Gath, suggesting a musical instrument or melody which had a Philistine origin. The Midrash sees a connection with Hebrew *gath*, 'a winepress,' hence a tune associated with vintage songs. Ibn Ezra suggests that this composition was performed by Oved Edom, the Gittite, who was a Levite.

2-3 GOD'S MAJESTY

2. *Our LORD.* David exclaims God's name in contemplation of the Creator Whose mighty works are manifest in all corners of the universe (Kimchi). The God of Israel is no tribal or national deity, but the LORD of the whole universe. David speaks in the name of the people; hence *our* instead of 'my.'

Thy name. 'Name,' when applied to God, means more than the designation by which He is known. It denotes His nature as revealed in His acts (cf. Malbim).

rehearsed above the heavens. His glory belongs in the heavens. Yet, God, in His humility, has transferred His presence to earth so that we may behold His majestic power (Rashi). Kimchi explains this part of the verse in the past tense saying that the reason that God's name is glorious in all the earth is because He invested the heavens with the power to exert control over the earth and all that is within it.

3. *mouth of babes and sucklings.* God's miraculous power is evident from the moment a babe is born. The mother is ready to wean and her child is immediately able to suckle. We owe thanks to our Creator from our first day on this earth (Kimchi). Hirsch approaches this verse differently. He points out that every child born means another pure soul on earth. Thus even if the name of God was omitted from all scientific literature, it would never be erased from the Divine writings handed down anew to every generation. It is from the mouths of the babes of all future generations that God's name is established for ever.

18

4 When I behold Thy heavens, the
    work of Thy fingers,
  The moon and the stars, which
    Thou hast established;

5 What is man, that Thou art mind-
    ful of him?
  And the son of man, that Thou
    thinkest of him?

6 Yet Thou hast made him but little
    lower than the angels,
  And hast crowned him with glory
    and honour.

7 Thou hast made him to have
    dominion over the works of Thy
    hands;
  Thou hast put all things under his
    feet:

8 Sheep and oxen, all of them,
  Yea, and the beasts of the field;

9 The fowl of the air, and the fish of
    the sea;
  Whatsoever passeth through the
    paths of the seas.

10 O LORD, our Lord,
   How glorious is Thy name in all
     the earth!

כִּי־אֶרְאֶה שָׁמֶיךָ מַעֲשֵׂה אֶצְבְּעֹתֶיךָ 4

יָרֵחַ וְכוֹכָבִים אֲשֶׁר כּוֹנָנְתָּה:

מָה־אֱנוֹשׁ כִּי־תִזְכְּרֶנּוּ 5

וּבֶן־אָדָם כִּי תִפְקְדֶנּוּ:

וַתְּחַסְּרֵהוּ מְּעַט מֵאֱלֹהִים 6

וְכָבוֹד וְהָדָר תְּעַטְּרֵהוּ:

תַּמְשִׁילֵהוּ בְּמַעֲשֵׂי יָדֶיךָ 7

כֹּל שַׁתָּה תַחַת־רַגְלָיו:

צֹנֶה וַאֲלָפִים כֻּלָּם 8

וְגַם בַּהֲמוֹת שָׂדָי:

צִפּוֹר שָׁמַיִם וּדְגֵי הַיָּם 9

עֹבֵר אָרְחוֹת יַמִּים:

יְהוָה אֲדֹנֵינוּ 10

מָה־אַדִּיר שִׁמְךָ בְּכָל־הָאָרֶץ:

---

the enemy and the avenger. Those who attempt to deny the divinity of God. By taking note of the miracles to be seen in nature and in the creation of the human being, they will come to acknowledge the existence of the creator (Malbim). According to Rashi the reference is to the enemies of Israel who refuse to recognize them as God's nation.

4-5 MAN'S PHYSICAL INSIGNIFICANCE

4. *the moon and the stars.* The Psalm is the product of the author's thoughts induced at night, while he was gazing at the sky illumined by the moon and studded with stars. That is why there is no mention of the sun (Kimchi).

5. *man.* Hebrew *enosh,* i.e. a frail, mortal being (Malbim).

son of man. Hebrew *adam,* derived from *adamah* 'earth.' *Son of man* is the equivalent of 'earth-born.'

thinkest. lit. 'visitest.' The verb is used of God's providential care of the human being (cf. Gen. xxi. 1; Exod. iii. 16).

6-9 MAN'S SPIRITUAL PRE-EMINENCE

6. *little lower than the angels.* lit., 'less than God.' As compared with animals, the human being is on a far higher plane, owing to the Divine element which is in him. For all that, he is less that the angels (Metsudath David). The Talmud (R.H. 21b), quoting this verse, cites Moses as an example of one who was raised almost to the heights of Divine understanding.

glory and honour. Attributes ascribed to God as the supreme King of the universe (xxix. 1, civ. 1 cxlv. 5). He has bestowed them upon a man as the king of the terrestrial sphere.

7. *dominion.* This and the following verse are based on Gen. i. 28.

10 OPENING REFRAIN REPEATED

After enumerating the kindnesses which God has bestowed on mankind, David feels the need to reiterate that man is minute and insignificant when compared with the works of creation as a whole. Hence the repetition of the first verse (Kimchi).

PSALM IX

9   ט

1 For the Leader; upon Muth-
  labben.
  A Psalm of David.

2 I will give thanks unto the Lord
  with my whole heart;
  I will tell of all Thy marvellous
  works.

3 I will be glad and exult in Thee;
  I will sing praise to Thy name, O
  Most High:

4 When mine enemies are turned
  back,
  They stumble and perish at Thy
  presence;

5 For Thou hast maintained my
  right and my cause;
  Thou sattest upon the throne as
  the righteous Judge.

לַמְנַצֵּחַ עַל־מוּת לַבֵּן מִזְמוֹר לְדָוִד׃

2 אוֹדֶה יְהוָה בְּכָל־לִבִּי
אֲסַפְּרָה כָּל־נִפְלְאוֹתֶיךָ׃

3 אֶשְׂמְחָה וְאֶעֶלְצָה בָךְ
אֲזַמְּרָה שִׁמְךָ עֶלְיוֹן׃

4 בְּשׁוּב־אוֹיְבַי אָחוֹר
יִכָּשְׁלוּ וְיֹאבְדוּ מִפָּנֶיךָ׃

5 כִּי־עָשִׂיתָ מִשְׁפָּטִי וְדִינִי
יָשַׁבְתָּ לְכִסֵּא שׁוֹפֵט צֶדֶק׃

SONG OF THANKSGIVING

This is David's song of thanksgiving for victory over his enemies, although the danger has by no means passed. There are several ideas suggested as to which events David had in mind while composing this Psalm. Rashi maintains that the Psalm alludes to the future downfall of the empire of Edom and the final redemption. Kimchi is of the opinion that it refers to the defeat of Goliath, while Alshich proposes that David composed the Psalm as a result of the death of the first son borne to him by Bath-Sheba. In the Psalm David acknowledges that everything done by God is for good. A trace of an alphabetical acrostic is discernible in the verses of this Psalm and of the following one, although several letters are omitted.

1. *Muth-labben.* lit. 'death to the son.' Rashi and Kimchi explains that David composed this pæan on the death of a neighbouring ruler, named Labben, who had oppressed Israel— though there is no record of him in the Bible history. Rashi, quoting Menachem, also offers another suggestion, that the word 'labben' is derived from the Hebrew 'binah,' understanding. It is a direction given for the leader of the orchestra to study the score thoroughly, with understanding. (See also introductory paragraph above).

2-3   PRAISE TO GOD AFTER VICTORY

2. *with my whole heart.* Not with the lips only; the feeling of gratitude is deep-rooted (cf. Malbim).

marvellous works. Divine intervention which brought about Goliath's downfall (Kimchi), or, according to Rashi, the final redemption.

3. *Most High.* Sovereign over all kingdoms on earth (cf. vii. 18).

4-5   GOD THE VINDICATOR

4. *are turned back.* They fled in terror (Kimchi).

stumble. So that they are unable to retreat in safety but are destroyed.

5. *Thou hast maintained my right.* He does not attribute his triumph to his prowess as a warrior. He acknowledges that victory over Goliath was the result of a miracle (Kimchi).

the throne. Of judgment, as in verse 8 (Malbim).

20

6 Thou hast rebuked the nations,
Thou hast destroyed the wicked,
Thou hast blotted out their name
for ever and ever.

7 O thou enemy, the waste places
are come to an end for ever;
And the cities which thou didst
uproot,
Their very memorial is perished.

8 But the LORD is enthroned for
ever;
He hath established His throne for
judgment.

9 And He will judge the world in
righteousness,
He will minister judgment to the
peoples with equity.

10 The LORD also will be a high
tower for the oppressed,
A high tower in times of trouble;

11 And they that know Thy name
will put their trust in Thee;
For Thou, LORD, hast not forsaken them that seek Thee.

6 גָּעַרְתָּ גוֹיִם אִבַּדְתָּ רָשָׁע
שְׁמָם מָחִיתָ לְעוֹלָם וָעֶד:

7 הָאוֹיֵב ׀ תַּמּוּ חֳרָבוֹת לָנֶצַח
וְעָרִים נָתַשְׁתָּ אָבַד זִכְרָם הֵמָּה:

8 וַיהוָה לְעוֹלָם יֵשֵׁב
כּוֹנֵן לַמִּשְׁפָּט כִּסְאוֹ:

9 וְהוּא יִשְׁפֹּט־תֵּבֵל בְּצֶדֶק
יָדִין לְאֻמִּים בְּמֵישָׁרִים:

10 וִיהִי יְהוָה מִשְׂגָּב לַדָּךְ
מִשְׂגָּב לְעִתּוֹת בַּצָּרָה:

11 וְיִבְטְחוּ בְךָ יוֹדְעֵי שְׁמֶךָ
כִּי לֹא־עָזַבְתָּ דֹרְשֶׁיךָ יְהוָה:

6-7 COMPLETE DESTRUCTION OF HIS
ENEMIES

6. *wicked.* A term for the neighbouring
peoples (Esau according to Rashi, Goliath according to Kimchi, Labben according to Ibn
Ezra), who were ungodly in their conduct.

blotted out their names. No remembrance of
them remains, so thoroughly have they been
eliminated.

7. *O thou enemy.* An alternative translation
is: 'As for the enemy, they are ended as desolations forever; and (their) cities Thou hast
uprooted; the very memorial of them (i.e. the
enemy) is perished' (Kimchi). Most forceful is
the contrast drawn between the wicked nations
whose memory is blotted out and the eternity
of the Judge Who decreed their fate.

8-9 GOD THE JUDGE OF ALL

8. *the LORD is enthroned for ever.* From this

instance of retribution the Psalmist derives
the lesson that all the people of the earth are
under the jurisdiction of the eternal Judge.
They have to give account of their actions
before Him, and He pronounces judgement
equitably. The universality of this concept of
God should be noted.

10-11 GOD THE PROTECTOR

10. *higher tower.* As a fortress gives protection to those within its walls, so is God a
stronghold in which the righteous are safe from
destruction (Kimchi).

11. *they that know Thy name.* i.e. know how
to worship and obey Thee. For the converse, cf.
*Now the sons of Eli were base men; they knew
not the LORD* (1 Sam. ii. 12).

them that seek Thee. For help and counsel
(Hirsch).

12 Sing praises to the Lord, who
      dwelleth in Zion;
   Declare among the peoples His
      doings.

13 For He that avengeth blood hath
      remembered them;
   He hath not forgotten the cry of
      the humble.

14 Be gracious unto me, O Lord,
   Behold mine affliction at the
      hands of them that hate me;
   Thou that liftest me up from the
      gates of death;

15 That I may tell of all Thy praise
      in the gates of the daughter of
      Zion,
   That I may rejoice in Thy salva-
      tion.

16 The nations are sunk down in the
      pit that they made;
   In the net which they hid is their
      own foot taken.

זַמְּרוּ לַיהוָה יֹשֵׁב צִיּוֹן 12
הַגִּידוּ בָעַמִּים עֲלִילוֹתָיו:
כִּי־דֹרֵשׁ דָּמִים אוֹתָם זָכָר 13
לֹא־שָׁכַח צַעֲקַת עֲנִיִּים:
חָנְנֵנִי יְהוָה רְאֵה עָנְיִי מִשֹּׂנְאָי 14
מְרוֹמְמִי מִשַּׁעֲרֵי־מָוֶת:
לְמַעַן אֲסַפְּרָה כָּל־תְּהִלָּתֶיךָ 15
בְּשַׁעֲרֵי בַת־צִיּוֹן אָגִילָה בִּישׁוּעָתֶךָ:
טָבְעוּ גוֹיִם בְּשַׁחַת עָשׂוּ 16
בְּרֶשֶׁת־זוּ טָמָנוּ נִלְכְּדָה רַגְלָם:

____

v. 13. עניים ק׳

12-13 GOD THE AVENGER

12. *who dwelleth in Zion.* Whose Presence is
manifested in Jerusalem where the Sanctuary
was to be located (Kimchi).

declare among the peoples. Cf. xcvi. 3, cv. 1.
The salvation He wrought for Israel should be
made known to all nations, so that they might
come to declare the greatness of God whose
Sanctuary in Zion will one day benefit all of
mankind (Hirsch).

13. *He that avengeth blood.* According to
His assurance: *At the hand of man, even at the
hand of every man's brother, will I require
the life of man* (Gen. ix. 5). Bloodshed is a
most heinous offence in the sight of God. As
He told Cain: *The voice of thy brother's blood
crieth unto Me from the ground* (Gen. iv. 10);
and He follows and remembers all occurrences of Jewish blood that has ever been
spilt in order to avenge that blood at the time
that He deems fit (Metsudath David).

the humble. This follows the *kerë*, while the
kethib has *aniyim*—poor, who are usually
humble because of their poverty (Kimchi).

14-15 PRAYER OF THE HUMBLE

14. Sudden changes from praise to prayer are
frequent in the Psalter and we may have one
here. The following two verses may be understood as the 'cry of the humble.'

gates of death. Again in cvii. 18. Death is
associated with the gates of Sheol (Isa. xxxviii.
10) which leads to the grave (Malbim).

15. *gates.* The entrance to a city where people
congregated, and so the best place in which to
secure publicity (cf. Kimchi).

daughter of Zion. Jerusalem being the mother-
city (lxxxvii. 5), *daughter of Zion* represents its
inhabitants, the people of Israel.

16-17 RETRIBUTION OVERTAKES AGGRESSORS

16. The same thought as in vii. 16.

17 The LORD hath made Himself
   known, He hath executed
   judgment,
   The wicked is snared in the work
   of his own hands. Higgaion.
                   Selah

18 The wicked shall return to the
   nether-world,
   Even all the nations that forget
   God.

19 For the needy shall not alway be
   forgotten,
   Nor the expectation of the poor
   perish for ever.

20 Arise, O LORD, let not man prevail;
   Let the nations be judged in Thy
   sight.

21 Set terror over them, O LORD;
   Let the nations know they are but
   men.   Selah

נוֹדַע ׀ יְהֹוָה מִשְׁפָּט עָשָׂה 17
בְּפֹעַל כַּפָּיו נוֹקֵשׁ רָשָׁע הִגָּיוֹן סֶלָה:
יָשׁוּבוּ רְשָׁעִים לִשְׁאוֹלָה 18
כָּל־גּוֹיִם שְׁכֵחֵי אֱלֹהִים:
כִּי לֹא לָנֶצַח יִשָּׁכַח אֶבְיוֹן 19
תִּקְוַת עֲנָוִים תֹּאבַד לָעַד:
קוּמָה יְהֹוָה אַל־יָעֹז אֱנוֹשׁ 20
יִשָּׁפְטוּ גוֹיִם עַל־פָּנֶיךָ:
שִׁיתָה יְהֹוָה ׀ מוֹרָה לָהֶם יֵדְעוּ גוֹיִם 21
אֱנוֹשׁ הֵמָּה סֶלָה:

____

ע נ י י ם ק׳ v. 19.

---

17. *hath made Himself known.* By means of
the judgment carried out upon the enemies of
Israel, His Omnipotence has become revealed
to all (Rashi).

Higgaion. An expression to underline the truth
of the matter. It is connected to the verb
'haggah'—meditate. David is suggesting to
the wicked that they contemplate what has just
been said and believe it as absolute truth
(Malbim).

18-19   FATE OF THE WICKED

18. *return to the nether-world.* i.e. *Sheol.* The
phrase means nothing more than that they will
perish. For the verb, cf. *unto dust shall they
return.* (Gen. iii. 19).

forget God. Deliberately ignore His precepts
and rebel against His rule.

19. *needy ... poor.* The first word is used to
describe one who is utterly destitute, owning
absolutely nothing. As this is rare, the singular

is used. The latter word is the general term used
for those lacking material wealth. This is more
common and, therefore, the plural form is
given (Daath Sofrim). The verse describes the
people of Israel who are oppressed by the
nations (Rashi).

expectation. The hope that looks to God for aid.

20-21   CLOSING PRAYER

20. *arise.* Assert Thy majestic power against
the pretensions of men who, mighty in their
own esteem, are but weak mortals (*enosh*), and
insignificant in the eyes of God (Hirsch).

21. *set terror over them.* Display some awe-
inspiring demonstration of Thy might, to break
down their arrogance and induce a spirit of
humbleness in them.

men. Once more the Hebrew is *enosh.* Behind
the façade of vaunting national power is nothing but the fragility of mortal man (cf. Rashi,
Kimchi, Malbim).

10

1 Why standest Thou afar off,
O Lord?
Why hidest Thou Thyself in
times of trouble?

2 Through the pride of the wicked
the poor is hotly pursued,
They are taken in the devices that
they have imagined.

3 For the wicked boasteth of his
heart's desire,
And the covetous vaunteth himself,
though he contemn the Lord.

4 The wicked, in the pride of his
countenance [,saith]: 'He will
not require';
All his thoughts are: 'There is no
God.'

לָמָה יְהוָה תַּעֲמֹד בְּרָחוֹק
תַּעְלִים לְעִתּוֹת בַּצָּרָה:

2 בְּגַאֲוַת רָשָׁע יִדְלַק עָנִי
יִתָּפְשׂוּ ׀ בִּמְזִמּוֹת זוּ חָשָׁבוּ:

3 כִּי־הִלֵּל רָשָׁע עַל־תַּאֲוַת נַפְשׁוֹ
וּבֹצֵעַ בֵּרֵךְ נִאֵץ ׀ יְהוָה:

4 רָשָׁע כְּגֹבַהּ אַפּוֹ בַּל־יִדְרֹשׁ
אֵין אֱלֹהִים כָּל־מְזִמּוֹתָיו:

PRAYER OF THE OPPRESSED

A SIMILAR theme to that of Psalm IX. This Psalm, however is concerned with innocent suffering caused by godless persons within the body of Israel who are oppressing their weaker brethren (Hirsch). Rashi, in Talmud (Meg. 17b), is of the opinion that Psalms IX and X are considered one Psalm, hence the absence of an introductory verse to Psalm X.

1-2 APPEAL TO GOD FOR HELP

1. *afar off.* As though heedless of what is happening (Malbim).

times of trouble. When the innocent are wretched through the unlawful activities of the wicked (cf. Hirsch verse 2).

2. *pride.* Haughtiness which makes them indifferent to the disapproval of God and man alike.

they are taken. This translation follows Rashi: the innocent are taken in by the devices which the wicked have planned. R.V. *'let them be taken'* agrees with Kimchi and Meiri, who see the words as a prayer and petition that the wicked shall be ensnared in the traps that they laid for the defenceless.

3-11 DESCRIPTION OF THE WICKED

3. *boasteth of his heart's desire.* Since God has stood afar off as if heedless of what is happening, the wicked man pursues his aim openly and even boasts of it (Rashi).

vaunteth himself. Hebrew 'blesseth.' According to Kimchi the subject is the wicked man. He blesses the brazen and those who follow in his path, while condemning the Lord. Alternatively, "Those who laud the ways of the wicked are considered as if they have blasphemed the Lord." Rashi explains it as the brazen one applauding his actions and saying, "though I condemn the Lord, I succeed in my ways."

4. *He will not require.* He takes no account of man's deeds, so they can be performed with impunity (Rashi).

there is no God. Not that He is nonexistent, but He is not the Judge of men. Atheism, in the sense of denial of God's reality, never occurs in the Bible; the non-believers are they who scorn the belief that He cares how men act (cf. xiv. 1).

5 His ways prosper at all times;
  Thy judgments are far above out
      of his sight;
  As for all his adversaries, he
      puffeth at them.

6 He saith in his heart: 'I shall not
      be moved,
  I who to all generations shall not
      be in adversity.'

7 His mouth is full of cursing and
      deceit and oppression;
  Under his tongue is mischief and
      iniquity.

8 He sitteth in the lurking-places of
      the villages;
  In secret places doth he slay the
      innocent;
  His eyes are on the watch for the
      helpless.

9 He lieth in wait in a secret place
      as a lion in his lair,
  He lieth in wait to catch the poor;
  He doth catch the poor, when he
      draweth him up in his net.

10 He croucheth, he boweth down,
   And the helpless fall into his
       mighty claws.

11 He hath said in his heart: 'God
       hath forgotten;
   He hideth His face; He will never
       see.'

5 יַחִילוּ דְרָכָו ׀ בְּכָל־עֵת
מָרוֹם מִשְׁפָּטֶיךָ מִנֶּגְדּוֹ
כָּל־צֽוֹרְרָיו יָפִיחַ בָּהֶם׃

6 אָמַר בְּלִבּוֹ בַּל־אֶמּוֹט
לְדֹר וָדֹר אֲשֶׁר לֹא־בְרָע׃

7 אָלָה ׀ פִּיהוּ מָלֵא וּמִרְמוֹת וָתֹךְ
תַּחַת לְשׁוֹנוֹ עָמָל וָאָוֶן׃

8 יֵשֵׁב ׀ בְּמַאְרַב חֲצֵרִים
בַּמִּסְתָּרִים יַהֲרֹג נָקִי
עֵינָיו לְחֵלְכָה יִצְפֹּנוּ׃

9 יֶאֱרֹב בַּמִּסְתָּר ׀ כְּאַרְיֵה בְסֻכֹּה
יֶאֱרֹב לַחֲטוֹף עָנִי
יַחְטֹף עָנִי בְּמָשְׁכוֹ בְרִשְׁתּוֹ׃

10 וְדֹכֶה יָשֹׁחַ
וְנָפַל בַּעֲצוּמָיו חֶלְכָּאִים׃

11 אָמַר בְּלִבּוֹ שָׁכַח אֵל
הִסְתִּיר פָּנָיו בַּל־רָאָה לָנֶצַח׃

v. 5. דרכיו ק׳ v. 10. ידכה ק׳ v. 10. הל כאים ק׳

5. *his ways prosper at all times.* Because he triumphs in his evil design, he imagines to himself that it will always be so and no punishment will be exacted of him.

Thy judgments ... sight. The righteous speak of God's 'judgments' in that He punishes wrongdoing. The retort of the wicked man is that God is too far away from the human scene to observe and judge; therefore he does not allow the thought of such judgment to deter him (Hirsch).

adversaries. In his self-confidence he despises all who oppose him.

6. *to all generations.* He is so presumptuous that even the possibility of his death does not occur to him. Generations will pass away, but he will continue to prosper (Kimchi). Another explanation is: he lives on in his descendants and they too, he is sure, will have the same good fortune as himself (Malbim).

7. *under his tongue.* In readiness to be produced in speech as smooth words behind which lurk evil intentions (cf. Malbim).

8. *villages.* Unwalled settlements (Lev. xxv. 31) which are open to attack (Kimchi).

11. *he ... in his heart.* David emphasizes in this verse that nobody who believed that God paid attention to His creatures' actions could act in this manner; and so he ends his description of the wicked with the same psychological analysis as at the beginning. It also makes a fitting transition to the concluding portion of the Psalm in which he calls upon God to expose the falsity of that mental attitude.

12-16 APPEAL TO GOD

forget not the humble. A retort to the statement, *God hath forgotten* (Kimchi).

12 Arise, O Lord; O God, lift up
  Thy hand;
  Forget not the humble.
13 Wherefore doth the wicked contemn God,
  And say in his heart: 'Thou wilt
  not require'?
14 Thou hast seen; for Thou be-
  holdest trouble and vexation,
  to requite them with Thy
  hand;
  Unto Thee the helpless com-
  mitteth himself;
  Thou hast been the helper of the
  fatherless.
15 Break Thou the arm of the
  wicked;
  And as for the evil man, search
  out his wickedness, till none
  be found.
16 The Lord is King for ever and
  ever;
  The nations are perished out of
  His land.
17 Lord, Thou hast heard the desire
  of the humble:
  Thou wilt direct their heart, Thou
  wilt cause Thine ear to attend;
18 To right the fatherless and the
  oppressed,
  That man who is of the earth may
  be terrible no more.

קוּמָה יְהוָה אֵל נְשָׂא יָדֶךָ 12
אַל־תִּשְׁכַּח עֲנָוִים:
עַל־מֶה נִאֵץ רָשָׁע אֱלֹהִים 13
אָמַר בְּלִבּוֹ לֹא תִדְרֹשׁ:
רָאִתָה כִּי־אַתָּה עָמָל וָכַעַס תַּבִּיט לָתֵת בְּיָדֶךָ 14
עָלֶיךָ יַעֲזֹב חֵלֶכָה
יָתוֹם אַתָּה הָיִיתָ עוֹזֵר:
שְׁבֹר זְרוֹעַ רָשָׁע 15
וָרָע תִּדְרוֹשׁ־רִשְׁעוֹ בַל־תִּמְצָא:
יְהוָה מֶלֶךְ עוֹלָם וָעֶד 16
אָבְדוּ גוֹיִם מֵאַרְצוֹ:
תַּאֲוַת עֲנָוִים שָׁמַעְתָּ יְהוָה 17
תָּכִין לִבָּם תַּקְשִׁיב אָזְנֶךָ:
לִשְׁפֹּט יָתוֹם וָדָךְ בַּל־יוֹסִיף עוֹד 18
לַעֲרֹץ אֱנוֹשׁ מִן־הָאָרֶץ:

עֲנִיִּים ק׳ v. 12.

13. *wherefore.* David is jealous of God's
honour, and pleads that He should not permit
such contemptuous conduct to remain
unchallenged.

14. *Thou hast seen.* The conviction is expressed that God has not closed His eyes to
what has been happening (Kimchi).

fatherless. The widow and orphan are symbolic of the helpless who may be easily de-
frauded.

15. *arm.* The strength which has been used
so mercilessly.

till none be found. Many commentaries render
it more grammatically: 'till Thou find none.'
Let justice be exacted so that You no longer
find any wickedness, for they shall have returned to fear Thee.

16. *the Lord is King.* After having meted out
punishment to the wicked, God will be universally acclaimed as the Almighty, and no one
will ever dare to defy Him (Kimchi).

the nations ... out of His land. Hirsch calls attention to earth being referred to as His land—
and comments that after the earth shall have
become His land—after He will be acknowledged everywhere—the nations as menacing,
lawless powers, will disappear from the earth.

17-18 FAITH JUSTIFIED

17. *the desire of the humble.* As voiced in
their prayers to be freed from their oppressors
(Metsudath David).

Thou wilt direct their heart. So that they have
pure intentions while at prayer (Kimchi), or, so
that they may ask for the right things at the
appropriate time (Hirsch).

18. *man.* Hebrew *enosh* as in ix. 20f.

who is ... earth. Who originated from the earth's
dust and has his last resting-place there.

may be terrible no more. No longer inspire terror
in the hearts of the weak (Rashi).

יא

לַמְנַצֵּחַ לְדָוִד
בַּיהוָה ׀ חָסִיתִי אֵיךְ תֹּאמְרוּ לְנַפְשִׁי
נוּדוּ הַרְכֶם צִפּוֹר׃
2 כִּי הִנֵּה הָרְשָׁעִים יִדְרְכוּן קֶשֶׁת
כּוֹנְנוּ חִצָּם עַל־יֶתֶר
לִירוֹת בְּמוֹ־אֹפֶל לְיִשְׁרֵי־לֵב׃
3 כִּי הַשָּׁתוֹת יֵהָרֵסוּן
צַדִּיק מַה־פָּעָל׃

1 For the Leader. [A Psalm] of David.
In the Lord have I taken refuge;
How say ye to my soul:
'Flee thou! to your mountain, ye birds'?

2 For, lo, the wicked bend the bow,
They have made ready their arrow upon the string,
That they may shoot in darkness at the upright in heart.

3 When the foundations are destroyed,
What hath the righteous wrought?

נודי ק׳ v. 1.

SONG OF STEADFASTNESS

THE setting of this Psalm is similar to that of V and VII. It is a time of danger for the Psalmist and his life is threatened. Friends advise him to seek safety in flight, but he stands his ground because he has confidence in Divine protection. The Psalm seems to fit in best with what is told in 1 Sam. xviiif., and supplements the historical narrative. When Saul's obsession against David became apparent, it is natural to suppose that David received advice to flee. He remained, however, at the king's court until, after the second attempt upon his life failed, his wife persuaded him to go. His feelings in that crisis are here described.

1-3 FRIENDS ADVISE FLIGHT

1. *in the Lord have I taken refuge.* I have complete faith in God and find solace in the fact that everything that I go through is divinely ordained (Malbim).

to my soul. To me. The question is addressed to his enemies (Kimchi).

flee thou. According to the *kerë* the verb is fem. sing., apparently in agreement with *soul*. The *kethib* is plural, addressed to David and his close associates who shared his peril. The plural is retained in the suffix of *your mountain*, which makes it preferable to regard *ye birds* (in Hebrew collective sing.) as the subject of the verb. *Your mountain* refers to the mountainous area in which David was hiding from Saul. It can be understood thus: 'Go back to hide in your mountain. You are but as a bird that flies from place to place and finds no rest'

(Rashi). Hirsch renders, 'How can you say to me "Flee; my rock (i.e. faith) is only a bird." In other words, "How can you tell me to abandon the faith I cherish?"

2. In this and the next verses we have the words by which the friends counseled him (Hirsch).

shoot in darkness. Shoot from a dark place where they lurk (Malbim).

the upright in heart. The intended victims are innocent men.

3. *when the foundations are destroyed.* Society, like a building, rests upon foundations, and should these be undermined, there is likelihood of a collapse. The pillars of society are law and justice, which had been flouted by the men whose duty it was to uphold them—a reference to the murdered priests of Nob (1 Sam. xxii) (Rashi).

4 The LORD is in His holy temple,
The LORD, His throne is in heaven;
His eyes behold, His eyelids try,
the children of men.

5 The LORD trieth the righteous;
But the wicked and him that loveth
violence His soul hateth.

6 Upon the wicked He will cause to
rain coals;
Fire and brimstone and burning
wind shall be the portion of their
cup.

7 For the LORD is righteous, He
loveth righteousness;
The upright shall behold His
face.

4 יְהֹוָה ׀ בְּהֵיכַל קָדְשׁוֹ
יְהֹוָה בַּשָּׁמַיִם כִּסְאוֹ
עֵינָיו יֶחֱזוּ עַפְעַפָּיו יִבְחֲנוּ בְּנֵי אָדָם:

5 יְהֹוָה צַדִּיק יִבְחָן
וְרָשָׁע וְאֹהֵב חָמָס שָׂנְאָה נַפְשׁוֹ:

6 יַמְטֵר עַל־רְשָׁעִים פַּחִים
אֵשׁ וְגָפְרִית וְרוּחַ זִלְעָפוֹת
מְנָת כּוֹסָם:

7 כִּי־צַדִּיק יְהֹוָה צְדָקוֹת אָהֵב
יָשָׁר יֶחֱזוּ פָנֵימוֹ:

what hath the righteous wrought? If evil has triumphed and law and order has been flouted, of what value has the righteous man been to this world? (Hirsch). Others make God the subject of the verse and render it thus: "What has the LORD done about protecting the righteous and punishing the wicked? Is He not in control of the world?" (Malbim).

4-7 HIS CONFIDENCE IN GOD

4. *the* LORD *is in His holy temple.* That is the Psalmist's reply to his advisers. There is a God in heaven and He maintains the right. *Temple* stands for *heaven*, as in xviii. 7, xxix. 9.

His throne. Of Judgment (see ix. 5).

His eyelids try. A forceful image borrowed from human action. When a person closely scrutinizes an object, he contracts his eyelids. God, although enthroned in heaven, thoroughly examines the deeds of His creatures on earth (cf. Hirsch). The remoteness of the Divine dwelling-place in heaven was never held to be incompatible with God's detailed knowledge of what happens in the world. He is sometimes said 'to come down' and look upon the actions of men (see on xviii. 10).

5. *trieth the righteous.* God tests all men, even the righteous, by afflicting them (Rashi, Kimchi) and by allowing the wicked to prosper (Hirsch).

His soul hateth. So again in Isa. i. 14. The nature of God finds evil loathsome wherever it occurs.

6. *coals.* Of fire, as happened to Sodom and Gomorrah (Gen. xix. 24; cf. xviii. 9).

fire, etc. God uses the forces of nature as His instruments for destroying the wicked.

the portion of their cup. Their fate.

7. *the* LORD *is righteous.* Because righteousness is part of the Divine Essence, the righteousness of man must win His approval.

behold His face. The godly are, so to speak, admitted into His Presence and enjoy His radiance (cf. Metsudath David), whereas evil-doers are banished into darkness. As sin erects a barrier between man and God, goodness is an attractive force, drawing the human being into closer contact with his Maker.

12

1 For the Leader; on the Sheminith.
  A Psalm of David.

2 Help, LORD; for the godly man
    ceaseth;
  For the faithful fail from among
    the children of men.

3 They speak falsehood every one
    with his neighbour;
  With flattering lip, and with a
    double heart, do they speak.

4 May the LORD cut off all flattering
    lips,
  The tongue that speaketh proud
    things!

5 Who have said: 'Our tongue will
    we make mighty;
  Our lips are with us: who is lord
    over us?'

יב

לַמְנַצֵּחַ עַל־הַשְּׁמִינִית מִזְמוֹר לְדָוִד׃
2 הוֹשִׁיעָה יְהֹוָה כִּי־גָמַר חָסִיד
  כִּי־פַסּוּ אֱמוּנִים מִבְּנֵי אָדָם׃
3 שָׁוְא יְדַבְּרוּ אִישׁ אֶת־רֵעֵהוּ
  שְׂפַת חֲלָקוֹת בְּלֵב וָלֵב יְדַבֵּרוּ׃
4 יַכְרֵת יְהֹוָה כָּל־שִׂפְתֵי חֲלָקוֹת
  לָשׁוֹן מְדַבֶּרֶת גְּדֹלוֹת׃
5 אֲשֶׁר אָמְרוּ לִלְשֹׁנֵנוּ נַגְבִּיר
  שְׂפָתֵינוּ אִתָּנוּ מִי אָדוֹן לָנוּ׃

A PRAYER ANSWERED

A PSALM in which the state of affairs in human society is depicted as seemingly hopeless, the cause of the trouble being the evil tongue which spews forth lies, hatred, flattery and deception. The Psalm ends on a confident note that God will answer the prayer of the oppressed and human values will be restored. Rashi, in 2 Chron. xxii. 10, is of the opinion that this Psalm was composed in reference to the atrocities committed by Ataliah (2 Kings xi). David, with his spirit of holiness, foresaw that during the eight generations of his dynasty Ataliah would annihilate all the members of the royal family, except for the infant Josiah. In this Psalm David prays that all his progeny not be destroyed, and Josiah, who later became king, was indeed saved.

1. *Sheminith.* See on vi. 1.

2-5 THE PRAYER

2. *help.* More lit. 'save.' The answer comes in verse 6: *I will set him in safety.*

the godly man. Hebrew *chasid* (see on iv. 4). When the virtues are scorned and evil abounds, uprightness and concern for others become rare values, having all but vanished from society (Hirsch).

ceaseth. Disappears (Hirsch).

for the faithful fail. They grow fewer in number and, unless help comes from God, will disappear.

3. *they speak falsehood every one with his neighbour.* Falseness has become universal, and no society can endure when this vice is widely practiced (cf. Hirsch).

flattering lip. lit. 'lips of smooth things.' Instead of truth, whatever is agreeable and flattering to the hearer is spoken although not sincerely meant.

with a double heart. lit. 'with a heart and a heart.' They think one thing but express the opposite (Rashi).

4. *speaketh proud things.* Their 'big words' (so the Hebrew) are specified in the next verse.

5. *our tongue will we make mighty.* They forge their tongue into a powerful weapon to secure their ends, and are armed with lies and deceit (Metsudath David).

6 'For the oppression of the poor,
   for the sighing of the needy,
Now will I arise,' saith the LORD;
'I will set him in safety at whom
   they puff.'

7 The words of the LORD are pure
   words,
As silver tried in a crucible on the
   earth, refined seven times.

8 Thou wilt keep them, O LORD;
Thou wilt preserve us from this
   generation for ever.

9 The wicked walk on every side,
When vileness is exalted among
   the sons of men.

6 מִשֹּׁד עֲנִיִּים מֵאַנְקַת אֶבְיוֹנִים
עַתָּה אָקוּם יֹאמַר יְהוָה
אָשִׁית בְּיֵשַׁע יָפִיחַ לוֹ:
7 אִמְרוֹת יְהוָה אֲמָרוֹת טְהֹרוֹת
כֶּסֶף צָרוּף בַּעֲלִיל לָאָרֶץ
מְזֻקָּק שִׁבְעָתָיִם:
8 אַתָּה־יְהוָה תִּשְׁמְרֵם
תִּצְּרֶנּוּ ׀ מִן־הַדּוֹר זוּ לְעוֹלָם:
9 סָבִיב רְשָׁעִים יִתְהַלָּכוּן
כְּרֻם זֻלּוּת לִבְנֵי אָדָם:

our lips are with us. As forces at our command to make us strong (Metsudath David).

who is lord over us? Who can read our thoughts or suspect that what we speak is not the truth (Metsudath David).

6   GOD'S ANSWER

6. *for.* On account of.

sighing. Or 'groaning.' The same word is used regarding a prisoner (lxxix. 11, cii. 21).

now will I arise. To intervene on behalf of the sufferers (Rashi). In His wisdom God allows the oppressors to have the upper hand for a while although it means hardship for innocent victims; but He decides when the moment is opportune to assert His will (cf. Exod. ii. 24f.; Isa. xxxiii. 10).

at whom they puff. Better rendered as 'from those who trap them' (Kimchi). Rashi and Ibn Ezra maintain that the term denotes 'talking' as is found in the verse in Habakuk (ii. 3). Malbim and Hirsch explain that the verb 'puach' gives the impression of gentle whispering, and they render 'He whispers to him,' viz. the victim.

7-9   CONFIDENCE IN THE ANSWER

7. *pure words.* Unlike the deceitful words of men, the utterance of God is trustworthy (Hirsch).

as silver. Human speech may contain both truth and falsity, but God's word is like precious silver which has been repeatedly refined in the crucible and freed from every trace of dross (Hirsch).

crucible on the earth. Hebrew 'to the earth.' The purified metal is poured from the crucible into the mould in ground (cf. 1 Kings vii. 46) (Malbim).

seven times. The number seven is a symbol of thoroughness (cf. Kimchi).

8. *keep them.* Guard those who are attacked by these lying men (Rashi).

Thou wilt preserve us. Better 'him': each one of them, with personal care (Kimchi).

this generation. This class of unscrupulous persons (Kimchi).

9. *walk on every side,* etc. Wicked men are to be found everywhere when they who are set in authority are of vile character (Kimchi). The rulers are *sons of men* (*adam*, not *ish*, see on iv. 3, viii. 5), common men. Corruption spreads and affects those who wish to lead righteous lives (Daath Sofrim). In spite of this David is confident that God will protect the virtuous who are victimized (Metsudath David).

1 For the Leader. A Psalm of
David.

2 How long, O LORD, wilt Thou
forget me for ever?
How long wilt Thou hide Thy face
from me?

3 How long shall I take counsel in
my soul,
Having sorrow in my heart by
day?
How long shall mine enemy be
exalted over me?

4 Behold Thou, and answer me, O
LORD my God;

לַמְנַצֵּחַ מִזְמוֹר לְדָוִד׃

עַד־אָנָה יְהֹוָה תִּשְׁכָּחֵנִי נֶצַח 2
עַד־אָנָה ׀ תַּסְתִּיר אֶת־פָּנֶיךָ מִמֶּנִּי׃

עַד־אָנָה ׀ אָשִׁית עֵצוֹת בְּנַפְשִׁי 3
יָגוֹן בִּלְבָבִי יוֹמָם
עַד־אָנָה ׀ יָרוּם אֹיְבִי עָלָי׃

הַבִּיטָה עֲנֵנִי יְהֹוָה אֱלֹהָי 4

FROM DESPAIR TO HOPE

Mine enemy is again the subject, and both Rashi and Kimchi take the speaker to be Israel suffering
oppression from her neighbours. It can also be seen as an introduction to Psalm XIV. Feeling that
it has been abandoned, Israel is afraid that its faith might falter and it prays for the ability to
overcome its difficulties (Hirsch). The Psalm ends with an expression of sincere hope that their
faith in God will be justified and that God will respond to their pleas mercifully.

2-5 CRY OF DESPAIR

2. *how long ... for ever?* The conflicting
thoughts in his mind are vividly brought out by
four questions which force themselves upon
his attention: Will God forget me forever?
How long have I yet to wait for relief? How
long can I last in such circumstances? How
long will I suffer oppression under my enemy?

hide Thy face. Seemingly careless of my plight.

3. *take counsel in my soul.* Without Divine
help I must continue to devise my own plans on
how to escape from my predicament (Kimchi).

sorrow. The crushing weight of anxiety.

by day. Even while going about his regular

daily business, he cannot take his mind off his
troubles (Kimchi).

exalted. Hebrew 'high,' corresponding to the
English idiom 'have the upper hand.'

4. The antidote to the sensation of hopelessness is prayer.

behold Thou. In contrast to *how long wilt Thou
hide Thy face from me?* Look upon my
troubled life (Kimchi).

lighten mine eyes. Revive my spirit, restore my
courage. The eye reveals the inward disposition. Age, grief or trouble darkens it; but when
Jonathan recovered from the faintness of hunger after eating some honey, *his eyes bright-
ened* (1 Sam. xiv. 27).

Lighten mine eyes, lest I sleep the
   sleep of death;

5 Lest mine enemy say: 'I have
   prevailed against him';
Lest mine adversaries rejoice when
   I am moved.

6 But as for me, in Thy mercy do I
   trust;
My heart shall rejoice in Thy
   salvation.
I will sing unto the LORD,
Because He hath dealt bountifully
   with me.

הָאִ֥ירָה עֵינַי֮ פֶּן־אִישַׁ֪ן הַמָּ֥וֶת׃

5 פֶּן־יֹאמַ֣ר אֹיְבִ֣י יְכָלְתִּ֑יו
צָרַ֥י יָ֝גִ֗ילוּ כִּ֣י אֶמּֽוֹט׃

6 וַאֲנִ֤י ׀ בְּחַסְדְּךָ֣ בָטַחְתִּי֮
יָ֤גֵ֥ל לִבִּ֗י בִּישֽׁוּעָ֫תֶ֥ךָ
אָשִׁ֥ירָה לַיהֹוָ֑ה כִּ֖י גָמַ֣ל עָלָֽי׃

the sleep of death. The image of death as *sleep*
is frequently used in Job (cf. iii. 13, vii. 21, xiv.
12) and Jer. l. 27. The analogy finds expression
in two Talmudical sayings, 'Sleep is a sixtieth
part of death,' and 'The incomplete experience
of death is sleep.'

6   HOPE REVIVED

The offering of prayer restored David's trust in
God's aid, and faith gained the victory over
despondency.

my heart shall rejoice. Better, 'let my heart
rejoice.' Create the occasion when I shall have
reason to rejoice in Thy saving power.

I will sing. Render: 'let me sing'; give me cause
to sing because Thy favour to me has been
displayed. Nowhere in the whole realm of
literature is the doctrine of hope so pronounced
as in the Hebrew Scriptures, and especially the
Psalms. It is one of the secrets of the Bible's
imperishable appeal to the human heart. Trouble
seems to be an inseparable feature of man's
existence; inequalities and injustices are an
integral part of his lot. Nothing, however,
prevents an utter sinking of the heart and consequent breakdown of endurance as the hope
which springs from faith in God. Of this invincible trust the present Psalm is a most eloquent
expression.

1 For the Leader. [A Psalm] of
  David.
  The fool hath said in his heart:
  'There is no God';
  They have dealt corruptly, they
  have done abominably;
  There is none that doeth good.

2 The LORD looked forth from
  heaven upon the children of
  men,
  To see if there were any man of
  understanding, that did seek
  after God.

3 They are all corrupt, they are
  together become impure;
  There is none that doeth good,
  no, not one.

A CORRUPT WORLD

Two lines of interpretation have been applied to this Psalm. Rashi and Kimchi understand it as a description of the hard lot of Israel under the tribulations of Nebuchadnezzar and is written in the form of prophecy. Hirsch sees it as depicting the fate of the righteous elements in a generation of moral decadence. Psalm xiv is repeated in liii with a few variants.

1-3 WIDESPREAD CORRUPTION

1. *fool.* Hebrew *nabal* connotes moral, not intellectual, deficiency (Hirsch). In Isa. xxxii. 5f., where his conduct is described, the word is translated *vile person*, and that is its meaning here. He is a person lacking in sense of honour and decency, deliberately preferring evil to good.

said in his heart. 'Heart' is the seat of thought. The *nabal* had come to this definite conclusion, which he made the ruling principle of his life.

there is no God. Who observes human conduct and distinguishes between the virtuous and the vicious (see x. 4, lxxiii. 11) (Kimchi).

they have dealt corruptly. Unrestrained by belief in God as the world's Judge, mankind in general had grown utterly dissolute.

2. *the LORD looked forth from heaven.* Emphatically denying, therefore, the theory of the *nabal.* Even from His far-off abode in heaven, God scrutinizes the ways of men upon earth (Kimchi).

man of understanding. Who perceived the falsity of the statement *there is no God.*

seek after God. To act in a manner which would be in accord with His will.

3. *corrupt.* lit. 'turned aside,' from the path of righteousness.

become impure. This translation is too weak. The root (occurring again only in Job xv. 16) originally means 'to turn sour (of mind).' Render 'become tainted.'

4 'Shall not all the workers of
    iniquity know it,
  Who eat up My people as they eat
    bread,
  And call not upon the LORD?'

5 There are they in great fear;
  For God is with the righteous
    generation.

6 Ye would put to shame the counsel
    of the poor,
  But the LORD is his refuge.

7 Oh that the salvation of Israel were
    come out of Zion!
  When the LORD turneth the cap-
    tivity of His people,
  Let Jacob rejoice, let Israel be
    glad.

הֲלֹא יָדְעוּ כָּל־פֹּעֲלֵי אָוֶן 4
אֹכְלֵי עַמִּי אָכְלוּ לֶחֶם
יְהוָה לֹא קָרָאוּ:
שָׁם ׀ פָּחֲדוּ פָחַד 5
כִּי־אֱלֹהִים בְּדוֹר צַדִּיק:
עֲצַת־עָנִי תָבִישׁוּ 6
כִּי יְהוָה מַחְסֵהוּ:
מִי־יִתֵּן מִצִּיּוֹן יְשׁוּעַת יִשְׂרָאֵל 7
בְּשׁוּב יְהוָה שְׁבוּת עַמּוֹ
יָגֵל יַעֲקֹב יִשְׂמַח יִשְׂרָאֵל:

4-6 PUNISHMENT OF THE WICKED

4. In this verse God speaks.

shall not ... know it. Is it conceivable that they
are so lost to all understanding as to think God
will overlook such behaviour and not condemn
them? (Kimchi).

My people. "In the midst of such corruption
and perversion, there was one community in
human society which God called 'my people.'
The nation which had not forgotten Him, but
had placed their destiny entirely in His hands.
In the midst of atheism and world-wide lawlessness Israel, helpless and dispersed, has
kept alive the spark of recognition of the one
and only God, when everyone else had disre-
garded Him" (Hirsch).

as they eat bread. They devour my nation with
apparent ease, as if they were eating bread
(Kimchi).

call not upon the LORD. They have not acknowledged Him; for had they done so, they
would not have acted in so lawless a manner.

5. *there.* In whatever place God manifests
His judgment, dread overwhelms them.

God is with. To aid and protect.

the righteous generation. The class of persons
who may be designated *righteous;* the same use
of *generation* as in xii. 8.

6. *the counsel of the poor.* The reliance of the
afflicted upon the justice of God.

refuge. Which will be proved a sure stronghold.

7 CONCLUDING PRAYER

This verse is repeated in psalm liii. 7 with slight
variations.

Zion. The dwelling-place of the Divine Glory
from which He makes His Sovereignty known
in the world.

turneth the captivity. An idiom meaning 'restore the fortunes.' It does not necessarily
imply an actual state of exile, as is seen from
Hosea vi. 11 and Amos ix. 14, which are pre-
exilic.

1 A Psalm of David.
  LORD, who shall sojourn in Thy
    tabernacle?
  Who shall dwell upon Thy holy
    mountain?

2 He that walketh uprightly, and
    worketh righteousness,
  And speaketh truth in his heart;

3 That hath no slander upon his
    tongue,
  Nor doeth evil to his fellow,
  Nor taketh up a reproach against
    his neighbour;

GOD'S GUEST

THIS Psalm briefly outlines the requirements needed for those wishing to enter God's sanctuary, thereby becoming closer to Him both in this world and in the next. The Talmud (Makos 24a) remarks that the six hundred thirteen commandments of the Pentateuch are summarized in the eleven basic human characteristics mentioned in this Psalm, indicating that their moral purpose is here crystallized. These eleven principles all concern man's relationship with his fellow man, an area of conduct in which David's generation did not live up to the levels expected of them. As the Talmud Yerushalmi (Peah 1:1) comments: 'although they observed the commandments, they would fall in battle on account of their tale-bearing and slander.

1. *shall sojourn*, etc. The Hebrew *yagur* is used when a temporary dwelling is implied, while the word *yishkon* conveys the idea of a permanent abode while the term 'tabernacle' denotes our temporary lease on life on earth. 'Your holy mountain' is a reference to the heights to which man ascends at the end of his days, the sanctuary of God in heaven (Hirsch).

2. *walketh uprightly.* The same word occurs in God's exhortation to Abraham: *walk before Me and be thou whole-hearted* (Gen. xvii. 1)— perfect, without moral blemish.

righteousness. An all-embracing term for honest, straightforward dealing, the ethically right.

truth in his heart. Unlike those with *a double heart* (xii. 3). Inward sincerity is demanded.

3. *slander.* A vice strongly denounced in Jewish teaching. 'Whoever speaks slander is as though he denied the fundamental principle (the existence of God). The Holy One, blessed be He, says of him, "I and he cannot dwell together in the world"' (Talmud).

evil to his fellow. Wrongs him in a transaction (Tal. Mak. 24a).

taketh up a reproach. If attacked, he will refrain from retaliating. All the details mentioned in the verse illustrate the practical application of the Biblical rule, *Thou shalt love thy neighbour as thyself* (Lev. xix. 18).

4 In whose eyes a vile person is
    despised,
But he honoureth them that fear
    the LORD;
He that sweareth to his own hurt,
    and changeth not;

5 He that putteth not out his money
    on interest,
Nor taketh a bribe against the
    innocent.
He that doeth these things shall
    never be moved.

נִבְזֶה ׀ בְּעֵינָיו נִמְאָס 4
וְאֶת־יִרְאֵי יְהֹוָה יְכַבֵּד
נִשְׁבַּע לְהָרַע וְלֹא יָמֵר:
כַּסְפּוֹ ׀ לֹא־נָתַן בְּנֶשֶׁךְ 5
וְשֹׁחַד עַל־נָקִי לֹא־לָקָח
עֹשֵׂה אֵלֶּה לֹא יִמּוֹט לְעוֹלָם:

4. *a vile person is despised.* He judges a man by his true character and, if morally defective, does not allow other considerations to weigh in his estimate of him (Metsudath David). He reserves his respect for those who revere God. According to the Talmud (Mak. 24a), the Psalmist is alluding to Hezekiah, whose father Ahaz was an idolator. Upon the latter's death, his son did not honour him but showed that he despised his father's actions.

fear the LORD. Show reverence for Him by conformity to His will. Such *fear* is the beginning of knowledge and wisdom (cxi. 10; Prov. ix. 10), i.e. ethics, and to possess it is the distinguishing feature of men who lead a life of integrity. To *honour* them is consequently an indication of a good moral character, because like are attracted to like.

sweareth to his own hurt. Cf. Lev. v. 4. The sanctity of the plighted word, even when it proves difficult, is stressed in Jewish ethics. Though the inclination to quit is strong, the righteous man will stick to his resolve under all circumstances (Kimchi).

5. *money on interest.* Cf. Lev. xxv. 36f. and Deut. xxiii. 20f. on the latter reference.

bribe. The corruption of justice by bribery is severely condemned in the Bible (cf. Exod. xxiii. 8; Deut. xvi. 19, xxvii. 25). Nothing demarcates the concept of human society as depicted throughout the Scriptures, from the realities of the contemporary world, as does the unswerving insistence upon the corruptive power of a bribe. A healthy corporate body is only possible where the impartial rule of justice is complete and absolute; and the practice of bribery is a cancer which inevitably destroys its strength and stability.

that doeth these things. Rabbi Gamliel (Mak. 24a) commented: 'even if he practices only one of these things, he "shall never be moved."' Qualified to be a 'guest of God,' he benefits from His protection and successfully withstands the attacks of the wicked.

16

טז

מִכְתָּם לְדָוִד
שָׁמְרֵנִי אֵל כִּי־חָסִיתִי בָךְ:
2 אָמַרְתְּ לַיהוָה אֲדֹנָי אָתָּה
טוֹבָתִי בַּל־עָלֶיךָ:
3 לִקְדוֹשִׁים אֲשֶׁר־בָּאָרֶץ הֵמָּה
וְאַדִּירֵי כָּל־חֶפְצִי־בָם:
4 יִרְבּוּ עַצְּבוֹתָם אַחֵר מָהָרוּ

1 Michtam of David.
  Keep me, O God; for I have taken
  refuge in Thee.

2 I have said unto the LORD: 'Thou
  art my Lord;
  I have no good but in Thee';

3 As for the holy that are in the
  earth,
  They are the excellent in whom is
  all my delight.

4 Let the idols of them be multiplied
  that make suit unto another;

HAPPINESS THROUGH GOD

APART from the prayer in the opening words, the Psalm is a hymn of joy. Ineffable happiness has been David's lot because of his complete submission to God. It is pure speculation to assign the composition to any particular period in David's life.

1-2 HIS ACKNOWLEDGEMENT OF GOD

1. *Michtam.* The exact meaning of the term is not known. It may signify a musical arrangement (Rashi) or instrument (Kimchi). Ibn Ezra connects the word to 'fine,' denoting that the Psalm was an outstanding composition. Five more Psalms lxvi-lx, have the same heading, but no feature peculiar to the group can be discerned.

keep me, O God. A general prayer from a trusting soul, not a cry for help in a situation of danger.

2. *I have said.* lit. 'thou (fem.) hast said'; from the context we understand that the speaker is addressing his soul (Rashi).

my LORD. A noun, not the Divine Name: 'My Master,' to Whom I submit.

I have no good but in Thee. Better, 'Thou are not obligated to do good to me.'

3-4 HE ASSOCIATES ONLY WITH THE GODLY

3. *the holy.* Who have obeyed the exhortation: *Ye shall be holy, for I the LORD your God am holy* (Lev. xix. 2).

the excellent. Or, 'the nobles.' They are truly distinguished who are holy, not the men honoured because of their wealth or rank. In association with them he takes delight.

4. *let the idols,* etc. A preferable translation would be 'their sorrow shall be multiplied, (they) who exchange (the LORD) for another (god).' They will experience disappointments, whereas they who put their trust in the LORD will know no sorrow, as they believe everything to be a blessing from God. Cf. Proverbs x. 22. (See Hirsch).

Their drink-offerings of blood will
    I not offer,
Nor take their names upon my lips.

5 O Lord, the portion of mine
    inheritance and of my cup,
Thou maintainest my lot.

6 The lines are fallen unto me in
    pleasant places;
Yea, I have a goodly heritage.

7 I will bless the Lord, who hath
    given me counsel;
Yea, in the night seasons my reins
    instruct me.

8 I have set the Lord always before
    me;
Surely He is at my right hand, I
    shall not be moved.

בַּל־אַסִּיךְ נִסְכֵּיהֶם מִדָּם
וּבַל־אֶשָּׂא אֶת־שְׁמוֹתָם עַל־שְׂפָתָי:

5 יְהוָה מְנָת־חֶלְקִי וְכוֹסִי
אַתָּה תּוֹמִיךְ גּוֹרָלִי:

6 חֲבָלִים נָפְלוּ־לִי בַּנְּעִמִים
אַף־נַחֲלָת שָׁפְרָה עָלָי:

7 אֲבָרֵךְ אֶת־יְהוָה אֲשֶׁר יְעָצָנִי
אַף־לֵילוֹת יִסְּרוּנִי כִלְיוֹתָי:

8 שִׁוִּיתִי יְהוָה לְנֶגְדִּי תָמִיד
כִּי מִימִינִי בַּל־אֶמּוֹט:

drink-offerings of blood. Either to be understood lit. of blood-libations offered to idols
(Rashi), or, their drink offerings are even more
repugnant to me than bloodshed. It would be
spiritual suicide to render such homage to
powers other than God (Hirsch).

their names. The pagan deities which have
been preferred to the true God. Even to mention their names would soil his lips.

5-6   GOD IS HIS PORTION

5. *inheritance.* When the land of Israel was
allotted to the tribes, none of it was assigned to
the Levites, because God said *I am thy portion
and thine inheritance among the children of
Israel* (Num. xviii. 20). Similarly the Psalmist
urges that his inheritance is God, and he does
not long for a share of worldly goods (cf.
Hirsch).

cup. His thirst is that of the spirit which finds
its satisfaction in God (cf. xlii. 2).

Thou maintainest my lot. Kimchi remarks that
tomich is identical with *tomech,* the participle
of the verb; hence 'Thou hast guided me in the
choosing of my lot' (cf. Rashi). In a similar
vein Metsudath David renders 'Thou hast
helped me to realize that only in Thee can I
place my trust.'

6. *the lines.* The measuring-cords which mark
off the area falling to a lot, and then used on the
territory so allocated. His portion having been
assigned to him by God, it must be of the
choicest.

7-8   HIS RELATIONSHIP TO GOD

7. *I will bless the* Lord. Equals 'I will thank
Him.'

given me counsel. Granted me the understanding to choose Him as the Source of my welfare
(Kimchi).

the night seasons. In the stillness of the night
the voice of God seemed to speak to him and
direct his thoughts (Kimchi).

reins. See on vii. 10.

8. *I have set ... before me.* The annotator of
the *Shulchan Aruch* (the compendium of Jewish law), on the first paragraph, quotes these
words with the comment: 'This is a leading
principle in religion, and in the upward strivings
of the righteous who walk ever in the presence
of God.' To have the consciousness of being
always before Him must profoundly affect
man's conduct in every circumstance.

at my right hand. As my Guide and Helper.

I shall not be moved. Cf. xv. 5.

9 Therefore my heart is glad, and
 my glory rejoiceth;
 My flesh also dwelleth in safety;

10 For Thou wilt not abandon my
 soul to the nether-world;
 Neither wilt Thou suffer Thy
 godly one to see the pit.

11 Thou makest me to know the
 path of life;
 In Thy presence is fulness of joy,
 In Thy right hand bliss for
 evermore.

9 לָכֵן ׀ שָׂמַח לִבִּי וַיָּגֶל כְּבוֹדִי
אַף־בְּשָׂרִי יִשְׁכֹּן לָבֶטַח:
10 כִּי ׀ לֹא־תַעֲזֹב נַפְשִׁי לִשְׁאוֹל
לֹא־תִתֵּן חֲסִידְךָ לִרְאוֹת שָׁחַת:
11 תּוֹדִיעֵנִי אֹרַח חַיִּים
שֹׂבַע שְׂמָחוֹת אֶת־פָּנֶיךָ
נְעִמוֹת בִּימִינְךָ נֶצַח:

9-11 HIS HAPPINESS

9. *glory.* The soul which is the glory of the body (Kimchi; cf. the parallelism in *Let my soul not come into their council; unto their assembly let my glory not be united*, Gen. xlix. 6).

my flesh also dwelleth in safety. In addition to bliss of the spirit, his body enjoys security. The three terms, *heart, glory, flesh,* denote the constituent elements of the human being: mind, spirit and body (Malbim).

10. The last two verses carry an intimation of the immortality of the righteous, and are often quoted to convey that principle. Accordingly, the passage defines the first phrase in verse 9, as the latter half refers to the body during its life on earth (cf. Malbim).

Thou wilt not abandon my soul to the nether-world. Though my body returns to the earth, my soul will enjoy eternal spiritual bliss (Malbim).

to see the pit. i.e., to suffer early death; cf. *But Thou O God, will bring them down into the nethermost pit … they shall not live out half their days* (lv. 24) (Malbim).

11. *the path of life.* The way indicated by God to man in which he lives in the highest sense of that term: the way of righteousness (Kimchi). (Cf. *See, I have set before thee this day life and good, and death and evil*, Deut. xxx. 15).

in Thy presence is fulness of joy. lit. 'satisfaction of joys.' Worldly pleasures never completely satisfy as does the joy of the spirit derived from communion with God.

in Thy right hand. God has in His possession *delights that endure* which He dispenses to the righteous.

ג

תְּפִלָּה לְדָוִד

שִׁמְעָה יְהֹוָה ׀ צֶדֶק הַקְשִׁיבָה רִנָּתִי

הַאֲזִינָה תְפִלָּתִי בְּלֹא שִׂפְתֵי מִרְמָה:

מִלְּפָנֶיךָ מִשְׁפָּטִי יֵצֵא 2

עֵינֶיךָ תֶּחֱזֶינָה מֵישָׁרִים:

בָּחַנְתָּ לִבִּי ׀ פָּקַדְתָּ לַּיְלָה 3

צְרַפְתַּנִי בַל־תִּמְצָא

זַמֹּתִי בַּל־יַעֲבָר־פִּי:

לִפְעֻלּוֹת אָדָם בִּדְבַר שְׂפָתֶיךָ 4

אֲנִי שָׁמַרְתִּי אָרְחוֹת פָּרִיץ:

תָּמֹךְ אֲשׁוּרַי בְּמַעְגְּלוֹתֶיךָ 5

בַּל־נָמוֹטּוּ פְעָמָי:

17

1 A Prayer of David.
   Hear the right, O Lord, attend
      unto my cry;
   Give ear unto my prayer from lips
      without deceit.

2 Let my judgment come forth from
      Thy presence;
   Let Thine eyes behold equity.

3 Thou hast tried my heart, Thou
      hast visited it in the night;
   Thou hast tested me, and Thou
      findest not
   That I had a thought which should
      not pass my mouth.

4 As for the doings of men, by the
      word of Thy lips
   I have kept me from the ways of
      the violent.

5 My steps have held fast to Thy
      paths,
   My feet have not slipped.

A PRAYER

Two more Psalms are superscribed David's *prayer* (lxxxvi, cxlii). Despite some resemblances in the language of this and the preceding Psalm, the atmosphere is very different. In the latter there breathes a spirit of tranquillity and assurance; here agitation and anxiety prevail.

1-5 PLEA OF INNOCENCE

1. *hear the right*. Only because he knows that he has right on his side, he dares to supplicate God for aid.

cry. The Hebrew signifies a shrill and piercing sound wrung from the heart, expressive either of joy or suffering (Kimchi).

without deceit. He honestly believes that every word he utters in his prayer is truth.

2. *let my judgment come forth*. Others prefer to render 'Let my judgment be dismissed from before Thee,'—a plea to ignore his misdeeds (Kimchi, Metsudath David).

let thine eyes behold equity. As the all-wise Judge Who looks into men's hearts, look not upon my sins but discern where equity is to be found (Kimchi).

3. *in the night*. When the fine feelings of the heart are released (Kimchi). David presents the case that he has withstood many tests in the past (Daath Sofrim).

4. *by the word of Thy lips*. Obedient to God's will, he had not adopted the ways of lawlessness which his adversaries followed.

5. *Thy paths*. He kept steadfastly to the 'tracks' marked out for him by God, as distinct from *the ways of the violent*.

6 As for me, I call upon Thee, for
  Thou wilt answer me, O God;
  Incline Thine ear unto me, hear
  my speech.

7 Make passing great Thy mercies,
  O Thou that savest by Thy
  right hand
  From assailants them that take
  refuge in Thee.

8 Keep me as the apple of the eye,
  Hide me in the shadow of Thy
  wings,

9 From the wicked that oppress,
  My deadly enemies, that compass
  me about.

10 Their gross heart they have shut
   tight,
   With their mouth they speak
   proudly.

11 At our every step they have now
   encompassed us;
   They set their eyes to cast us
   down to the earth.

12 He is like a lion that is eager to
   tear in pieces,
   And like a young lion lurking in
   secret places.

6 אֲנִי קְרָאתִיךָ כִי־תַעֲנֵנִי אֵל
הַט־אָזְנְךָ לִי שְׁמַע אִמְרָתִי:

7 הַפְלֵה חֲסָדֶיךָ מוֹשִׁיעַ חוֹסִים
מִמִּתְקוֹמְמִים בִּימִינֶךָ:

8 שָׁמְרֵנִי כְּאִישׁוֹן בַּת־עָיִן
בְּצֵל כְּנָפֶיךָ תַּסְתִּירֵנִי:

9 מִפְּנֵי רְשָׁעִים זוּ שַׁדּוּנִי
אֹיְבַי בְּנֶפֶשׁ יַקִּיפוּ עָלָי:

10 חֶלְבָּמוֹ סָגְרוּ
פִּימוֹ דִּבְּרוּ בְגֵאוּת:

11 אַשֻּׁרֵנוּ עַתָּה סְבָבוּנִי
עֵינֵיהֶם יָשִׁיתוּ לִנְטוֹת בָּאָרֶץ:

12 דִּמְיֹנוֹ כְּאַרְיֵה יִכְסוֹף לִטְרוֹף
וְכִכְפִיר יֹשֵׁב בְּמִסְתָּרִים:

v. 11. סבבונו ק׳

6-9 HIS PETITION

6. *as for me.* Because I am conscious of my integrity, I pray for God's help in my trouble, confident that it will be granted.

7. *make passing great.* lit. 'make marvelous.' Intervene in a special way on my behalf.

Thy right hand. A symbol of overwhelming might (xx. 7, Exod. xv. 6).

8. *apple of the eye.* The pupil of the eye upon whose soundness sight depends, and therefore something to be protected with the utmost care (cf. Deut. xxxii. 10) (Rashi).

shadow of Thy wings. As a mother-bird guards her young. The phrase is common in the Psalter.

9. *my deadly enemies.* Hebrew 'my enemies at (the peril of my) soul'; enemies who demand my life (Kimchi).

10-12 HIS ENEMIES PORTRAYED

10. *gross heart.* Hebrew 'fat,' referring to their overindulgence which prevented them from beholding the acts of God and from fearing Him (Rashi). Alternatively, 'their fat has shut tight their mouth.' They spoke proudly of their material wealth and not of holy matters (Kimchi, Malbim).

speak proudly. They boast of their power.

11. *our every step.* Alluding to David and his men who were surrounded by enemies with escape seemingly impossible (Rashi).

they set their eyes. They keep a close watch for an opportunity to trap them (Kimchi).

12. *he is like a lion.* i.e., the enemy. It may refer to Saul who is compared to a lion in vii. 3 (Kimchi).

13 Arise, O Lord, confront him, cast
    him down;
    Deliver my soul from the wicked,
    by Thy sword;

14 From men, by Thy hand, O Lord,
    From men of the world, whose
    portion is in this life,
    And whose belly Thou fillest
    with Thy treasure;
    Who have children in plenty,
    And leave their abundance to
    their babes.

15 As for me, I shall behold Thy
    face in righteousness;
    I shall be satisfied, when I awake,
    with Thy likeness.

קוּמָה יְהֹוָה קַדְּמָה פָנָיו הַכְרִיעֵהוּ 13
פַּלְּטָה נַפְשִׁי מֵרָשָׁע חַרְבֶּךָ׃
מִמְתִים יָדְךָ ׀ יְהֹוָה מִמְתִים מֵחֶלֶד 14
חֶלְקָם בַּחַיִּים וּצְפוּנְךָ תְּמַלֵּא בִטְנָם
יִשְׂבְּעוּ בָנִים
וְהִנִּיחוּ יִתְרָם לְעוֹלְלֵיהֶם׃
אֲנִי בְּצֶדֶק אֶחֱזֶה פָנֶיךָ 15
אֶשְׂבְּעָה בְהָקִיץ תְּמוּנָתֶךָ׃

וצפונך ק׳ .v. 14

13-14 PRAYER FOR DELIVERANCE

13. *arise, O Lord.* See on iii. 8.

confront him. When he is about to spring upon me. Or, 'forestall him,' prevent him from springing.

cast him down. Better, 'make him crouch.' The verb is used in Gen. xlix. 9 and Num. xxiv. 9 of a lion on its haunches reduced to submission.

Thy sword. Cf. vii. 13.

14. *from men.* The 'wicked' from whom he prays to be saved. They are persons whose ideals are wholly material and their desires limited to earthly prosperity.

men of the world, whose portion is in this life. They aspire to nothing higher than the gratification of bodily enjoyment available in this world (Kimchi, Ibn Ezra).

Thy treasure. The good things of this world (Kimchi, Ibn Ezra).

children. Or, sons. Not only would they waste their own time in pursuing worldly pleasures, but that would also teach their children to do likewise (Kimchi).

leave their abundance. They enjoy prosperity throughout their lifetime and bequeath a rich inheritance to their grandchildren (Kimchi, Ibn Ezra).

15 HIS ASPIRATION

The thought of Ps. xvi is repeated. He does not envy the wealth of the ungodly, since his longing is for the joy of communion with God.

I shall behold. Or, 'may I behold' and 'may I be satisfied.' To *behold God's face* is to be in His Presence (xvi. 11).

when I awake, with Thy likeness. Like the end of xvi, the phrase refers to the awaking from the sleep of death (Rashi). Here again, however, the contrast is between a life devoted to self-interest and a life conscious of God. The clue to the meaning of *awake* is to be found in Num. xii. 6ff. Unlike other prophets to whom God revealed Himself in dreams, Moses had the experience of beholding *the likeness of the Lord.* That is the mystic privilege for which the Psalmist yearns, a *conscious* realization of the Divine Presence. With that he will be satisfied and exchange for it all the treasures of the earth.

18   יח

לַמְנַצֵּחַ לְעֶבֶד יְהוָה לְדָוִד אֲשֶׁר דִּבֶּר ׀ לַיהוָה אֶת־דִּבְרֵי
הַשִּׁירָה הַזֹּאת בְּיוֹם ׀ הִצִּיל־יְהוָה אוֹתוֹ מִכַּף כָּל־אֹיְבָיו
וּמִיַּד שָׁאוּל׃

2
3   יְהוָה ׀   וַיֹּאמַר אֶרְחָמְךָ יְהוָה חִזְקִי׃

אֵלִי צוּרִי אֶחֱסֶה־   סַלְעִי וּמְצוּדָתִי וּמְפַלְטִי

4   מְהֻלָּל   בּוֹ מָגִנִּי וְקֶרֶן־יִשְׁעִי מִשְׂגַּבִּי׃

5   אֲפָפוּנִי חֶבְלֵי־   אֶקְרָא יְהוָה וּמִן־אֹיְבַי אִוָּשֵׁעַ׃

6   חֶבְלֵי   מָוֶת וְנַחֲלֵי בְלִיַּעַל יְבַעֲתוּנִי׃

קִדְּמוּנִי מוֹקְשֵׁי   שְׁאוֹל סְבָבוּנִי

7   וְאֶל־   מָוֶת׃ בַּצַּר־לִי ׀ אֶקְרָא יְהוָה

יִשְׁמַע מֵהֵיכָלוֹ   אֱלֹהַי אֲשַׁוֵּעַ

8   וַתִּגְעַשׁ   קוֹלִי וְשַׁוְעָתִי לְפָנָיו ׀ תָּבוֹא בְאָזְנָיו׃

THE SONG OF DAVID

THE inflexible trust in God which David had displayed throughout his trials receives the testimony of its worth in this exultant hymn of thanksgiving. It has been embodied in his biography (2 Sam. xxii.), and a comparison discloses a number of verbal differences. Hirsch cites the explanation that the changes that appear in the Psalm were made by David himself when he later adapted the song as a national prayer. Rashi and others are of the opinion that the Psalm was first composed during David's old age, in reference to his earlier experiences, while Abarbanel maintains that David wrote the original version, in Samuel, during his younger years while still burdened by problems and surrounded by enemies. It is not so much a song of triumph as it is a prayer in times of distress.

1 For the Leader. [A Psalm] of David the servant of the Lord, who spoke unto the Lord the words of this song in the day that the Lord delivered him from the hand of all his enemies, and from the hand of Saul;

2 and he said:
I love thee, O Lord, my strength.

3 The Lord is my rock, and my fortress, and my deliverer;
My God, my rock, in Him I take refuge;
My shield, and my horn of salvation, my high tower.

4 Praised, I cry, is the Lord,
And I am saved from mine enemies.

5 The cords of Death compassed me,
And the floods of [1]Belial assailed me.

6 The cords of [1]Sheol surrounded me;
The snares of Death confronted me.

7 In my distress I called upon the Lord,
And cried unto my God;
Out of His temple He heard my voice,
And my cry came before Him into His ears.

8 Then the earth did shake and quake,

[1]*That is, the nether-world*

---

1. *the servant of the Lord.* The phrase was omitted in Samuel and inserted later by David who considered himself a servant of God (Hirsch).

2-4 INTRODUCTION

2. This entire verse does not occur in Samuel.

I love thee. An unusual verb is employed, denoting deep and fervent affection.

3. *rock.* Hebrew *sela*, a mountain crag. He applied the word to God, because he had once found refuge in such a crag when pursued by Saul (1 Sam. xxiii. 25) (Rashi).

fortress. Or, 'stronghold,' which had also provided him with protection (1 Sam. xxii. 4).

rock. Hebrew *tsur*, frequently used metaphorically of God as a support (nine times in Deut. xxxii.).

shield. Cf. v. 13.

my horn of salvation. 'Horn' as a symbol of irresistible strength is taken from the wild ox (Deut. xxxiii. 17).

high tower. Cf. ix. 10. Samuel adds: *My saviour, Thou savest me from violence.*

4. *praised, I cry, is the Lord.* This is in accordance with the Malbim's rendering. Al-

ternatively, 'with praises I cry out to the Lord, then will I be saved from mine enemies' (Rashi, Metsudath David).

5-7 HIS PERIL

5. *cords.* Samuel has 'waves'; the line occurs again in this form in cxvi. 3.

of Death. Cf. *there is but a step between me and death* (1 Sam. xx. 3).

Belial. lit. 'worthlessness.' *Men of Belial* is a Biblical phrase for persons of base character who resort to violence. The sense here is: floods of lawless aggression poured down upon me.

6. *cords … snares.* Used to trap hunted animals.

7. *His temple.* Heaven (Kimchi), as in xi. 4.

8-16 DIVINE INTERVENTION

8. God revealed Himself amidst upheavals of nature; literally, in Israel's past, and figuratively, in David's lifetime (Kimchi). (See Exod. xix. 16ff, Isa. vi. 4).

mountains. Samuel reads 'heavens'; but cf. Hab. iii. 6.

He was wroth. At the wickedness of men who persecuted the innocent.

וּמוֹסְדֵי הָרִים   וַתִּרְעַשׁ ׀ הָאָרֶץ
עָלָה   וַיִּתְגָּעֲשׁוּ כִּי־חָרָה לוֹ:   יִרְגָּזוּ 9
וְאֵשׁ מִפִּיו   עָשָׁן ׀ בְּאַפּוֹ
וַיֵּט   גֶּחָלִים בָּעֲרוּ מִמֶּנּוּ:   תֹּאכֵל 10
וַעֲרָפֶל תַּחַת   שָׁמַיִם וַיֵּרַד
וַיֵּדֶא   וַיִּרְכַּב עַל־כְּרוּב וַיָּעֹף   רַגְלָיו: 11
יָשֶׁת חֹשֶׁךְ ׀ סִתְרוֹ סְבִיבוֹתָיו   עַל־כַּנְפֵי־רוּחַ: 12
מְנֻגַּהּ   חֶשְׁכַת־מַיִם עָבֵי שְׁחָקִים: סֻכָּתוֹ 13
בָּרָד וְגַחֲלֵי־   נֶגְדּוֹ עָבָיו עָבְרוּ
וְעֶלְיוֹן   וַיַּרְעֵם בַּשָּׁמַיִם ׀ יְהוָה   אֵשׁ: 14
בָּרָד וְגַחֲלֵי־   יִתֵּן קֹלוֹ
וּבְרָקִים   וַיִּשְׁלַח חִצָּיו וַיְפִיצֵם   אֵשׁ: 15
וַיֵּרָאוּ ׀ אֲפִיקֵי   רֹב וַיְהֻמֵּם: 16
מִגַּעֲרָתְךָ   וַיִּגָּלוּ מוֹסְדוֹת תֵּבֵל   מָיִם
יִשְׁלַח מִמָּרוֹם   יְהוָה מִנִּשְׁמַת רוּחַ אַפֶּךָ: 17
יַצִּילֵנִי   יַמְשֵׁנִי מִמַּיִם רַבִּים: יִקָּחֵנִי 18
וּמִשֹּׂנְאַי כִּי־אָמְצוּ   מֵאֹיְבִי עָז

The foundations also of the mountains did tremble;
They were shaken, because He was wroth.

9 Smoke arose up in His nostrils,
And fire out of His mouth did devour;
Coals flamed forth from Him.

10 He bowed the heavens also, and came down;
And thick darkness was under His feet.

11 And He rode upon a cherub, and did fly;
Yea, He did swoop down upon the wings of the wind.

12 He made darkness His hiding-place, His pavilion round about Him;
Darkness of waters, thick clouds of the skies.

13 At the brightness before Him, there passed through His thick clouds
Hailstones and coals of fire.

14 The LORD also thundered in the heavens,
And the Most High gave forth His voice;
Hailstones and coals of fire.

15 And He sent out His arrows, and scattered them;
And He shot forth lightnings, and discomfited them.

16 And the channels of waters appeared,
And the foundations of the world were laid bare,
At Thy rebuke, O LORD,
At the blast of the breath of Thy nostrils.

17 He sent from on high, He took
   me;
   He drew me out of many waters.

18 He delivered me from mine
   enemy most strong,
   And from them that hated me,
   for they were too mighty for
   me.

9. The following verses vividly describe the manifestation of God's wrath by way of natural phenomena. The destruction that comes in its wake has a specific purpose in His Divine plan. The events alluded to are not necessarily from David's own life. The intention is to impress upon us the understanding that when catastrophic events shock humanity, the LORD is the prime cause and the occurrences take place under His guidance (Hirsch).

smoke. God's wrath, in its fierce heat, is said to *smoke* (lxxiv. 1) (Metsudath David).

fire. The consuming anger of God (xcvii. 3).

coals. Emblematic of His punishment (cxl. 11).

10. *came down.* To investigate and execute judgment (cf. Gen. xi. 5, xviii. 21) (Metsudath David).

thick darkness. In which He enshrouds Himself from human eyes (cf. xcvii. 2; 1 Kings viii. 12).

11. *cherub.* A winged heavenly creature. Cherubim guard the entrance to the Garden of Eden (Gen. iii. 24), replicas of them stand atop the lid of the ark of the covenant (Exod. xxv. 18f.), and God "rides" or "sits upon" them (2 Kings xix. 15). It is in this last aspect that the term is employed here. God descends to earth upon His throne of judgment.

swoop down. Hebrew *vayëdë*; in Samuel: *vayëra*, 'he was seen.' The word here better suits its context.

the wings of the wind. Upon which He is also said to *walk* (civ. 3).

12. *His hiding-place.* Omitted in Samuel.

darkness of waters. Samuel, *gathering of waters.* The reference is to black clouds which herald heavy rain (see Kimchi on Samuel).

13. *the brightness before Him.* Flashes of lightning. In Samuel the verse is abbreviated to: *at the brightness before Him coals of fire flamed forth.*

14. *His voice.* For thunder as the voice of God cf. xxix. 3.

Hailstones and ... fire, repeated from the end of the preceding verse, is lacking in Samuel.

15. *arrows.* Of lightning (cf. lxxvii. 18f.).

scattered them. The object is David's enemies (verse 4), against whom God had come forth in judgment (Rashi).

and He shot forth lightnings, Rab. 'He shot forth,' is more probably an adjective. Render: 'Yea, lightnings in abundance.'

16. *channels of waters.* Samuel, *of the sea.* The bed of the ocean was bared as the wind from God swept the waters aside.

foundations of the world. This refers to the oceans and the seas which are called the foundations of the earth. Cf. xxiv. 2 (Malbim).

Thy rebuke. The manifestation of God's reproof of the guilty.

blast ... of Thy nostrils. Cf. Exod. xv. 8.

17-21 · GOD'S DELIVERANCE OF HIM

17. *He sent from on high.* Better, 'He sent forth (His hand) from on high' (cf. cxliv. 7).

He took me. Rescued me.

He drew me out. The word again occurs only in Exod. ii. 10, concerning Moses' rescue, and means 'He relieved me of my troubles' (Kimchi on Samuel).

many waters. Often used as a symbol of a dangerous position (xxxii. 6, lxix. 2f.).

18. *mine enemy.* Saul or Goliath (Kimchi on Samuel).

them that hated me. Those who did battle with me (Metsudath David).

they were too mighty for me. I could not escape them without God's aid.

יְקַדְּמוּנִי בְיוֹם־אֵידִי   וַיְהִי־   מִמֶּנִּי: 19
וַיּוֹצִיאֵנִי לַמֶּרְחָב   יְהֹוָה־לְמִשְׁעָן לִי: 20
כִּי חָפֵץ כִּי   יִגְמְלֵנִי   יְחַלְּצֵנִי 21
כְּבֹר יָדַי יָשִׁיב   יְהֹוָה כְּצִדְקִי
כִּי־שָׁמַרְתִּי דַּרְכֵי יְהֹוָה   וְלֹא־   לִי: 22
כִּי כָל־מִשְׁפָּטָיו   רָשַׁעְתִּי מֵאֱלֹהָי: 23
וְחֻקֹּתָיו לֹא־אָסִיר מֶנִּי: וָאֱהִי   לְנֶגְדִּי 24
תָמִים עִמּוֹ וָאֶשְׁתַּמֵּר מֵעֲוֹנִי: וַיָּשֶׁב־יְהֹוָה לִי 25
כְּבֹר יָדַי לְנֶגֶד עֵינָיו: עִם־   כְצִדְקִי 26
עִם־גְּבַר תָּמִים   חָסִיד תִּתְחַסָּד
עִם־נָבָר תִּתְבָּרָר   וְעִם־   תִּתַּמָּם: 27
כִּי־אַתָּה עַם־עָנִי   עִקֵּשׁ תִּתְפַּתָּל: 28
וְעֵינַיִם רָמוֹת תַּשְׁפִּיל: כִּי־   תוֹשִׁיעַ 29
יְהֹוָה אֱלֹהַי יַגִּיהַּ   אַתָּה תָּאִיר נֵרִי
וּבֵאלֹהַי   כִּי־בְךָ אָרֻץ גְּדוּד   חָשְׁכִּי: 30

19 They confronted me in the day
    of my calamity;
   But the LORD was a stay unto me.

20 He brought me forth also into a
    large place;
   He delivered me, because He
    delighted in me.

21 The LORD rewarded me accord-
    ing to my righteousness;
   According to the cleanness of my
    hands hath He recompensed
    me.

22 For I have kept the ways of the
    LORD,
   And have not wickedly departed
    from my God.

23 For all His ordinances were be-
    fore me,
   And I put not away His statutes
    from me.

24 And I was single-hearted with
    Him,
   And I kept myself from mine
    iniquity.

25 Therefore hath the LORD recom-
    pensed me according to my
    righteousness,
   According to the cleanness of my
    hands in His eyes.

26 With the merciful Thou dost
    show Thyself merciful,
   With the upright man Thou dost
    show Thyself upright;

27 With the pure Thou dost show
    Thyself pure;
   And with the crooked Thou dost
    show Thyself subtle.

28 For Thou dost save the afflicted
    people;
   But the haughty eyes Thou dost
    humble.

29 For Thou dost light my lamp;
    The LORD my God doth lighten
      my darkness.

30 For by Thee I run upon a troop;
    And by my God do I scale a wall.

19. *calamity.* Or, 'distress,' the time when his plight was critical.

stay. The same word as *staff* in xxiii. 4, something to lean upon, a support.

20. *a large place.* Relief, opposite of 'straits' (see on iv. 2).

He delighted in me. He favoured me and desired to save me.

21. *rewarded me.* Or, 'dealt with me.'

righteousness. Guiltlessness in my relationship with Saul (Rashi).

cleanness of my hands. Unstained by wrong (cf. xxiv. 4, xxvi. 6).

recompensed. This verb and *rewarded* are in the imperfect mood in the Hebrew, and may be rendered 'deals with me' and 'doth He deal with me.'

22-25 HIS FAITHFULNESS TO GOD

The Psalmist has been speaking of his freedom from guilt regarding his behaviour with Saul; but the claim he now makes is of loyalty to God's precepts in general. He does not claim to be entirely innocent of any sin. Rather, he notes that if he had stumbled, he would have been quick to admit his mistake and atone for his wrongdoing (Daath Sofrim).

22. *wickedly departed from.* lit. 'acted wickedly from.'

23. *before me.* As a guide which I followed steadily and constantly.

I put not away. I did not set them aside in order to sin.

24. *single-hearted.* Same word as *uprightly* in xv. 2.

I kept myself from mine iniquity. i.e. I kept watch over myself so that I did not sin against Saul (Kimchi).

25. Repetition of verse 21 in a slightly different form.

26-28 GOD'S DEALINGS WITH MAN

26. *with the merciful.* God's attitude towards His creatures is determined by their conduct. If they are merciful with their fellows, God is merciful with them.

27. *crooked.* The perverse man who wilfully chooses evil rather than good.

Thou dost show Thyself subtle. Or, *shew Thyself froward.* With such a person one must also deal crookedly. God shows Himself to be an implacable opponent to those who persist in their evil ways, in that He does not let them go until they have been subdued (Hirsch).

28. *the afflicted people.* Those who suffer without cause at the hands of the merciless.

but the haughty eyes Thou doest humble. Samuel, *but Thine eyes are upon the haughty, that Thou mayest humble them. Haughty eyes* are an *abomination* to God (Prov. vi. 16). The vice of pride is frequently denounced in the Scriptures as evidence of a mentality which scorns all consideration for a neighbour's rights when these conflict with self-interest.

29-31 HIS EXPERIENCE OF GOD

29. *Thou dost light my lamp.* Samuel, *for Thou art my lamp, O LORD.* The burning lamp is taken to be a symbol of happiness and so the phrase means: Thou doest brighten my life (Hirsch).

30. *by Thee.* With Thine aid.

I run upon a troop. A reminiscence of his successful attack upon a *troop* of Amalekites (1 Sam. xxx. 8).

I scale a wall. Referring to the capture of the stronghold of Zion, over whose walls he figuratively leapt when the Jebusites boasted that it could not be taken (2 Sam. v. 6ff.) (Rashi).

הָאֵל תָּמִים ׀ דַּרְכּוֹ אִמְרַת־יְהוָה צְרוּפָה מָגֵן
31 אֶל־נֶגְדְּ שֹׁור:

הוּא לְכֹל ׀ הַחֹסִים בּוֹ: כִּי מִי אֱלוֹהַּ מִבַּלְעֲדֵי
32 יְהוָה

וּמִי־צוּר זוּלָתִי אֱלֹהֵינוּ: הָאֵל
33 הַמְאַזְּרֵנִי חָיִל וַיִּתֵּן תָּמִים דַּרְכִּי: וְעַל

מְשַׁוֶּה רַגְלַי כָּאַיָּלוֹת
34 בָּמֹתַי יַעֲמִידֵנִי: מְלַמֵּד יָדַי

לַמִּלְחָמָה וְנִחֲתָה קֶשֶׁת־נְחוּשָׁה זְרוֹעֹתָי: וַתִּתֶּן
35 לִי מָגֵן יִשְׁעֶךָ וִימִינְךָ תִסְעָדֵנִי וְעַנְוַתְךָ

36 תַּרְבֵּנִי: תַּרְחִיב צַעֲדִי תַחְתָּי וְלֹא
37 מָעֲדוּ קַרְסֻלָּי: אֶרְדּוֹף אוֹיְבַי

וָאַשִּׂיגֵם וְלֹא־אָשׁוּב עַד־כַּלּוֹתָם: אֲמָחָצֵם
38 וְלֹא־יֻכְלוּ קוּם יִפְּלוּ תַּחַת

39 רַגְלָי: וַתְּאַזְּרֵנִי חַיִל לַמִּלְחָמָה תַּכְרִיעַ
40 קָמַי תַּחְתָּי: וְאֹיְבַי נָתַתָּה לִי

---

31 As for God, His way is perfect;
The word of the LORD is tried;
He is a shield unto all them that
take refuge in Him.

32 For who is God, save the LORD?
And who is a Rock, except our
God?

33 The God that girdeth me with
strength,
And maketh my way straight;

34 Who maketh my feet like hinds',
And setteth me upon my high
places;

35 Who traineth my hands for war,
So that mine arms do bend a bow
of brass.

36 Thou hast also given me Thy
shield of salvation,
And Thy right hand hath holden
me up;
And Thy condescension hath
made me great.

37 Thou hast enlarged my steps
under me,
And my feet have not slipped.

38 I have pursued mine enemies,
and overtaken them;
Neither did I turn back till they
were consumed.

39 I have smitten them through, so
that they are not able to rise;
They are fallen under my feet.

40 For Thou hast girded me with
strength unto the battle;
Thou hast subdued under me
those that rose up against me.

41 Thou hast also made mine
enemies turn their backs unto
me,
And I did cut off them that hate
me.

31. *His way is perfect.* Defined by *His work is perfect, for all His ways are justice* (Deut. xxxii. 4). What He does is right.

word. Any promise He makes will assuredly be fulfilled, and His declaration stands the test of experience.

tried. Like metal *refined* of dross (see on xii. 7).

He is a shield … Him. The qualifying words *that take refuge in Him* necessarily narrow the number of those to whom God is a *shield* (Cf. Daath Sofrim). Even the laws of nature humble themselves before a person who takes refuge in Him (Malbim).

32-37 HIS INDEBTEDNESS TO GOD

32. *who is God, save the LORD?* The question does not imply a belief in the existence of other deities, but aims at stressing the reality of Israel's God, His ability to help and save, in contrast to the inertness of the objects worshipped by the heathen peoples.

Rock. Hebrew *tsur* (see verse 3).

33. *girdeth me with strength.* For battle, as explained in verse 40. David acknowledges that his might as a warrior, which had gained him a series of victories, was to be attributed to God's favour (Malbim).

maketh my way straight. lit. 'perfect,' removing every obstacle to success in my path. Also, as Ibn Ezra remarks, there is a connection of cause and effect between *God, His way is perfect* (verse 31) and God *maketh my way straight* (perfect). Since His deeds are just and proper, He guides His servants to act in like manner. As God helped him to triumph, so He directed the use to which to put his victory.

34. *like hinds.* Famed for swiftness and agility. God had endowed him with the power of rapid movement, a great asset in time of war, making a surprise attack possible (Metsudath David).

my high places. As hinds leap over the hills, so did God enable him to escape to high places when seeking refuge (Kimchi).

35. *who traineth my hands for war.* To resist adversaries. Again in cxliv. 1. No idea of the glorification of war is to be read into the verse. The Psalmist only exercises the prowess with which he has been divinely endowed for self-defence (cf. Malbim).

bend a bow of brass. Evidence of extraordinary strength. The weapon is mentioned again in Job xx. 24.

36. *Thy shield of salvation.* Thy protecting shield.

Thy … holden me up. Omitted in Samuel. God's 'right hand' is a symbol of military might (cf. Ex. xv. 6) and also of spiritual strength (cf. Deut. xxxiii. 2). It is possible that this verse alludes to the latter meaning after the Psalmist has previously referred to physical assistance from God in battle (Daath Sofrim).

Thy condescension hath made me great. lit. 'Thy humility.' A strange quality to ascribe to God, but it points to His readiness to descend from His supreme eminence to concern Himself with mundane affairs (cf. cxiii. 5f.) (cf. Daath Sofrim). He thus deigned to choose David, a shepherd, to become king of Israel.

37. *enlarged my steps.* I am no longer hemmed in, but free to move with firm steps.

my feet have not slipped. To have this happen in battle may be fatal, as it places one at a hopeless disadvantage when faced by an attacker.

38-46 HIS SUCCESSES DUE TO GOD

38. *I have pursued … overtaken.* Cf. Exod. xv. 9. Samuel has *destroyed* for 'overtaken.' The verbs in this and the next verses are in the imperfect and may be translated: 'I pursue … I smite … they fall … Thou subduest.'

39. *I have smitten.* Samuel prefixes *and I have consumed them.*

40. *those that rose up against me.* In iii. 2, the phrase means disloyal subjects who rebelled, but it also stands for enemies in general.

41. *turn their back.* In flight after defeat.

I did cut off. Or, 'I cut off.'

יְשַׁוְּעוּ ׀ וּמְשַׂנְאַי אַצְמִיתֵם׃ עֶרֶף 42
עַל־יְהֹוָה וְלֹא וְאֵין מוֹשִׁיעַ
כְּטִיט עָנֵם׃ וְאֶשְׁחָקֵם כְּעָפָר עַל־פְּנֵי־רוּחַ 43
תְּפַלְּטֵנִי מֵרִיבֵי חוּצוֹת אֲרִיקֵם׃ 44
עַם תְּשִׂימֵנִי לְרֹאשׁ גּוֹיִם עַם
לֹא־יָדַעְתִּי יַעַבְדוּנִי׃ לְשֵׁמַע אֹזֶן יִשָּׁמְעוּ 45
בְּנֵי בְּנֵי־נֵכָר יְכַחֲשׁוּ־לִי׃ לִי 46
חַי־יְהֹוָה וּבָרוּךְ נֵכָר יִבֹּלוּ וְיַחְרְגוּ מִמִּסְגְּרוֹתֵיהֶם׃ 47
הָאֵל צוּרִי וְיָרוּם אֱלוֹהֵי יִשְׁעִי׃ 48
וַיַּדְבֵּר עַמִּים הַנּוֹתֵן נְקָמוֹת לִי
מֵאִישׁ תַּחְתָּי׃ מְפַלְּטִי מֵאֹיְבָי אַף מִן־קָמַי תְּרוֹמְמֵנִי 49
עַל־כֵּן ׀ אוֹדְךָ בַגּוֹיִם חָמָס תַּצִּילֵנִי׃ 50
מְגַדִּל יְהֹוָה וּלְשִׁמְךָ אֲזַמֵּרָה׃ 51
וְעֹשֶׂה חֶסֶד ׀ יְשׁוּעוֹת מַלְכּוֹ
עַד־עוֹלָם׃ לְדָוִד וּלְזַרְעוֹ לִמְשִׁיחוֹ

42 They cried, but there was none
to save;
Even unto the LORD, but He
answered them not.

43 Then did I beat them small as the
dust before the wind;
I did cast them out as the mire of
the streets.

44 Thou hast delivered me from the
contentions of the people;
Thou hast made me the head of
the nations;
A people whom I have not known
serve me.

45 As soon as they hear of me, they
obey me;
The sons of the stranger dwindle
away before me.

46 The sons of the stranger fade
away,
And come trembling out of their
close places.

47 The LORD liveth, and blessed be
my Rock;
And exalted be the God of my
salvation;

48 Even the God that executeth
vengeance for me,
And subdueth peoples under me.

49 He delivereth me from mine
enemies;
Yea, Thou liftest me up above
them that rise up against me;
Thou deliverest me from the
violent man.

50 Therefore I will give thanks unto
Thee, O LORD, among the
nations,
And will sing praises unto Thy
name.

51 Great salvation giveth He to His
king;
And showeth mercy to His
anointed,
To David and to his seed, for
evermore.

42. *they cried.* Samuel, *they looked*, a slight variation in the Hebrew.

even unto the Lord. Although heathen peoples, they cried to Israel's God Whose might had been proved, but they received no response as their cry was not sincere (Kimchi).

43. *I beat them small.* Descriptive of the crushing defeat of the enemy. They were, so to speak, ground to dust and scattered (cf. 2 Kings xiii. 7). Samuel adds: *as the dust of the earth.*

cast them out … of the streets. The routed army was flung aside like refuse. For 'cast them out' (*arikem*) Samuel reads: *I did stamp them* (*adikkem*), adding *and did tread them down.*

44. *the contentions of the people.* Samuel, *my people*, showing that the reference is to the civil disturbance in the early period of David's reign when the house of Saul disputed his kingship (2 Sam. iii. 1) (Kimchi).

Thou hast made me the head of the nations. Samuel, *Thou hast kept me to be the head of the nations.* He was acknowledged the greatest king among the peoples of that part of the world (2 Sam. viii. 1ff.).

a people whom … serve me. Perhaps alluding to the Arameans (2 Sam. x. 19) (Kimchi).

45. In Samuel the two halves of the verse are transposed.

they obey me. Or, 'they offer me allegiance.' The account of David's prowess, when it reaches them, is sufficient to make them submit without a struggle.

sons of the stranger. Foreign peoples.

dwindle away before me. Better, 'come cringing to me.' lit., 'they lie to me.'

46. *fade away.* Like withering plants; they lose their vigour and display an eagerness to surrender.

close places. Fastnesses. For 'come trembling,' Samuel reads: *come haltingly.*

47-51 THANKS TO GOD

47. *the Lord liveth.* He is not like the inert idols worshipped by others. That is proven by David's remarkable career in which he traced the Hand of God.

blessed be my Rock. I am grateful to Him Who has been my Saviour.

exalted. In the esteem of man by the display of His might.

the God of my salvation. Samuel, *the God my Rock of salvation.*

48. *executeth vengeance.* In punishing the wicked. Alternatively, He gives me the power to execute vengeance upon my enemies on His behalf (Rashi, Kimchi).

subdueth. Samuel, *bringeth down.* The allusion may be to victories over neighbouring nations. Rashi renders, 'and He plagued the people and not me'; i.e., the nations were afflicted with diseases while I was spared.

49. *mine enemies.* At home and abroad.

violent men. Either men in general who resort to violence, or (Kimchi) an allusion to Saul.

50. *among the nations.* As the conqueror of foreign peoples, he will have the opportunity of letting them, as well as Israel, know how he is indebted to God for his triumphs.

51. *great salvation giveth He.* Hebrew *magdil*, in Samuel: *a tower of salvation is He* (*migdol*). Both variants occur in the Grace After Meals. One was assigned for weekdays, the other for the Sabbath and Holidays.

to His king. The king designated by God to occupy the throne of Israel.

mercy. Or, 'lovingkindness,' the visible expression of His selection of David as king.

His anointed. See on ii. 2.

to David … for evermore. David refers to himself by three titles: king, anointed, and shepherd, reflecting three stages in his life. He recognizes that through all of these stages God has been with him, and prays that He should likewise do kindness with his offspring for evermore (Abarbanel on Samuel).

19

יט

1 For the Leader.   A Psalm of
David.

2 The heavens declare the glory of
God,
And the firmament showeth His
handiwork;

3 Day unto day uttereth speech,
And night unto night revealeth
knowledge;

4 There is no speech, there are no
words,
Neither is their voice heard.

5 Their line is gone out through all
the earth,

לַמְנַצֵּחַ מִזְמוֹר לְדָוִד׃

2 הַשָּׁמַיִם מְסַפְּרִים כְּבוֹד־אֵל
וּמַעֲשֵׂה יָדָיו מַגִּיד הָרָקִיעַ׃

3 יוֹם לְיוֹם יַבִּיעַ אֹמֶר
וְלַיְלָה לְּלַיְלָה יְחַוֶּה־דָּעַת׃

4 אֵין־אֹמֶר וְאֵין דְּבָרִים
בְּלִי נִשְׁמָע קוֹלָם׃

5 בְּכָל־הָאָרֶץ ׀ יָצָא קַוָּם

THE WITNESSES TO GOD

THIS Psalm is divided into two sections. The first seven verses describe the manifestation of God in the universe. Anyone who thoughtfully contemplates nature, the heavens in particular, must come to the conclusion that the creation is the work of an omnipotent God. However, contemplating the laws of nature alone will not teach man how to act in the service of God or how to discover the truth of Divine Law. It is only the doctrine of Torah that can shape man's individual and communal life in accordance with God's will. From verse 8 the Psalmist shows us six ways in which Torah scholarship leads to a true comprehension of God and His universe as compared to scientific research. Man's goal should, therefore, be Torah. Only when this goal has been attained, will the fruits of his search be appreciated. The Torah will be found to be dearer than the most valuable goods on earth. New vistas of understanding will be open to him and his purpose in this world will be fully understood. The Psalm ends with a prayer that this concept and the manner in which it has been transmitted will find favour in the eyes of the LORD (Hirsch).

2-7   REVELATION OF GOD IN NATURE

2.   *heavens.* What can be seen in the sky by the naked eye is sufficient to proclaim a majestic Creator. The invention of astronomical instruments gives us infinitely greater cause for reverential wonder at the grandeur of God's handiwork.

the glory of God. His ineffable wisdom and power (Hirsch).

firmament. The term used in Gen. i. 6, the expanse of sky spread above the earth.

3.   *day unto day uttereth speech.* Each day 'pours out in a flow' (so lit.) to the next the tale of God's wondrous might in the rising and setting of the sun.

night unto night revealeth knowledge. Each night informs the next that there is an almighty Creator in the shining of the moon and stars.

4.   The message which is conveyed to man by the sight of the heavens comes to him without the employment of audible sound.

5.   *their line.* i.e. the measuring line used to determine the limits of a landed property. Here it extends to the whole world, and all its inhabitants receive the message (Hirsch).

in them. The heavens.

And their words to the end of the
world.
In them hath He set a tent for the
sun,
6 Which is as a bridegroom coming
out of his chamber,
And rejoiceth as a strong man to
run his course.
7 His going forth is from the end of
the heaven,
And his circuit unto the ends of it;
And there is nothing hid from the
heat thereof.
8 The law of the LORD is perfect,
restoring the soul;
The testimony of the LORD is sure,
making wise the simple.
9 The precepts of the LORD are
right, rejoicing the heart;
The commandment of the LORD
is pure, enlightening the eyes.
10 The fear of the LORD is clean,
enduring for ever;

וּבְקְצֵה תֵבֵל מִלֵּיהֶם
לַשֶּׁמֶשׁ שָׂם־אֹהֶל בָּהֶם׃
6 וְהוּא כְּחָתָן יֹצֵא מֵחֻפָּתוֹ
יָשִׂישׂ כְּגִבּוֹר לָרוּץ אֹרַח׃
7 מִקְצֵה הַשָּׁמַיִם מוֹצָאוֹ
וּתְקוּפָתוֹ עַל־קְצוֹתָם
וְאֵין נִסְתָּר מֵחַמָּתוֹ׃
8 תּוֹרַת יְהֹוָה תְּמִימָה מְשִׁיבַת נָפֶשׁ
עֵדוּת יְהֹוָה נֶאֱמָנָה מַחְכִּימַת פֶּתִי׃
9 פִּקּוּדֵי יְהֹוָה יְשָׁרִים מְשַׂמְּחֵי־לֵב
מִצְוַת יְהֹוָה בָּרָה מְאִירַת עֵינָיִם׃
10 יִרְאַת יְהֹוָה טְהוֹרָה עוֹמֶדֶת לָעַד

a tent for the sun. To many heathens the sun was an object of worship, since it was perceived that nature's vitality depended upon its warmth. In reality, it is one of God's creations, and the Psalmist images it as a resplendent being for whom the Creator provided an abode in the heavens.

6. *bridegroom.* Personification of splendour, virility and happiness (Isa. lxi. 10, lxii. 5).

strong man. Or, 'warrior.' Like a soldier eager for the fray, the sun rises at dawn to dispel the darkness of night (Cf. Kimchi).

7. The verse describes the impression of movement as it appears to the onlooker.

8-12 REVELATION OF GOD IN TORAH

8. *law.* Hebrew *Torah*, which properly means 'instruction, direction.'

restoring the soul. As God Himself does (xxiii. 3), it fortifies man's spirit. The phrase is used for satisfying hunger (Lam. i. 11, 19) and comforting one in distress (Lam. i. 16).

testimony. A regulation which attests the will of God.

sure. Reliable as guidance.

making wise the simple. The 'simple' man is often referred to in the Book of Proverbs as a person who is uncertain of himself. His heart is 'open' (so lit.) to influences both good and bad, and he therefore needs instruction and discipline (Daath Sofrim).

9. *precepts.* Particularized rules which are man's duty to obey.

rejoicing the heart. They bring inward happiness which flows from a clear conscience.

commandment. God's imperative; the general term for a law in the sphere of religious life.

pure ... eyes. Better, 'clear.' The adjective 'clear' is used of the sun (Cant. vi. 10). As the light of the sun is bright and limpid, so are the commandments flawless and eye-opening to man in his search for the right way of life.

10. *fear of the LORD.* The 'reverence' as expressed in the carrying out of His ordinances.

clean. Or 'pure.' He fears the LORD even when others are not watching, showing that his dedication to God is morally pure and non-dependent. (Cf. Kimchi).

The ordinances of the LORD are
  true, they are righteous altogether;

11 More to be desired are they than
  gold, yea, than much fine gold;
  Sweeter also than honey and the
  honeycomb.

12 Moreover by them is Thy servant
  warned;
  In keeping of them there is great
  reward.

13 Who can discern errors?
  Clear Thou me from hidden
  faults.

14 Keep back Thy servant also from
  presumptuous sins,
  That they may not have dominion
  over me; then shall I be
  faultless,
  And I shall be clear from great
  transgression.

15 Let the words of my mouth and
  the meditation of my heart be
  acceptable before Thee,
  O LORD, my Rock, and my Redeemer.

מִשְׁפְּטֵי־יְהֹוָה אֱמֶת צָדְקוּ יַחְדָּו:

11 הַנֶּחֱמָדִים מִזָּהָב וּמִפַּז רָב

וּמְתוּקִים מִדְּבַשׁ וְנֹפֶת צוּפִים:

12 גַּם־עַבְדְּךָ נִזְהָר בָּהֶם

בְּשָׁמְרָם עֵקֶב רָב:

13 שְׁגִיאוֹת מִי־יָבִין

מִנִּסְתָּרוֹת נַקֵּנִי:

14 גַּם מִזֵּדִים ׀ חֲשֹׂךְ עַבְדֶּךָ

אַל־יִמְשְׁלוּ־בִי

אָז אֵיתָם וְנִקֵּיתִי מִפֶּשַׁע רָב:

15 יִהְיוּ לְרָצוֹן ׀ אִמְרֵי־פִי וְהֶגְיוֹן

לִבִּי לְפָנֶיךָ יְהֹוָה צוּרִי וְגֹאֲלִי:

---

ordinances. Hebrew *mishpatim,* 'judgments'
for the regulation of man's intercourse with his
neighbour.

true. In conformity with principles of justice.

11.   *than gold.* Spiritual riches are superior to
material wealth as a means for obtaining true
happiness and lasting satisfaction.

sweeter also than honey. One may become
sated with the sweetness of honey, but not
with the joyful effects of faithfulness to God's
will (Kimchi).

honeycomb. lit. 'flowing of the combs,' the
purest form of honey (cf. Tal. Sot. 48b).

12.   *Thy servant.* The Psalmist.

warned. So that he does not fall into sin by
yielding to temptation (Hirsch).

great reward. Cf. Prov. xxii. 4. One is not a
loser by shunning evil methods of gaining
riches. God will prosper his way.

13-15   PRAYER FOR GOD'S HELP

13.   *who can discern errors?* However eager
he may be to remain loyal to God, he is liable
to make mistakes inadvertently. He therefore
prays for purification from *hidden faults,* those
undiscovered to himself (Kimchi, Hirsch).

14.   *presumptuous sins.* As distinct from *errors.* When the baser side of his nature prompts
him to do what he knows is wrong, he begs God
to restrain him (Metsudath David). The Hebrew elsewhere means 'presumptuous men,'
the arrogant and godless. If that is the intention
here, the prayer is for protection from their
oppression which may lead him to doubt God
(Ibn Ezra).

transgression. lit. 'rebellion' against the King
of kings.

15.   A beautiful concluding prayer for the
acceptance of the petitions he has just offered
with his lips and the thoughts in his heart of
which they were the verbal expression.

Rock. Upon Whom I rely when in danger,
physical or moral.

Redeemer. From the enslavement of evil men
or sin.

20

1 For the Leader. A Psalm of David.

2 The LORD answer thee in the day of trouble;
The name of the God of Jacob set thee up on high;

3 Send forth thy help from the sanctuary,
And support thee out of Zion;

4 Receive the memorial of all thy meal-offerings,
And accept the fat of thy burnt-sacrifice;   Selah

5 Grant thee according to thine own heart,
And fulfil all thy counsel.

ב

1 לַמְנַצֵּחַ מִזְמוֹר לְדָוִד׃

2 יַעַנְךָ יְהוָה בְּיוֹם צָרָה יְשַׂגֶּבְךָ שֵׁם ׀ אֱלֹהֵי יַעֲקֹב׃

3 יִשְׁלַח עֶזְרְךָ מִקֹּדֶשׁ וּמִצִּיּוֹן יִסְעָדֶךָּ׃

4 יִזְכֹּר כָּל־מִנְחֹתֶךָ וְעוֹלָתְךָ יְדַשְּׁנֶה סֶלָה׃

5 יִתֶּן־לְךָ כִלְבָבֶךָ וְכָל־עֲצָתְךָ יְמַלֵּא׃

PRAYER BEFORE A BATTLE

KIMCHI remarks that this is not a Psalm *by* David, but *on behalf of* him, and this view is accepted by many commentators. The occasion is the eve of a battle, and a prayer is offered for his victory. The ancient Syriac translation superscribes it as having been composed in connection with the war against the Ammonites. Verse 8 mentions *chariots and horses*, and these are specified in the account of the defeat of the Arameans who came to the assistance of this enemy (2 Sam. x. 18).

2-6 INTERCESSION FOR THE KING

2. *thee.* The king who led the army on the battlefield (Ibn Ezra), or who remained in Jerusalem bringing sacrifices to the Sanctuary and praying for their success (Rashi).

trouble. lit. 'narrowness,' i.e. crisis.

name. The character of God as revealed in His many saving acts in the past (cf. Prov. xviii. 10).

God of Jacob. That Patriarch is particularized because he had cause for erecting an altar to *God Who answered me in the day of my distress* (Gen. xxxv. 3) (Kimchi).

set thee up on high. Above the reach of his foes (Kimchi).

3. *help from the sanctuary … Zion.* See iii. 5. The army would be fighting on foreign soil, but not beyond God's help.

4. *receive the memorial of.* lit. 'remember,' a technical term in connection with the sacrifice (cf. Lev. ii. 2), when the object was to bring the offerer's cause to the mind, as it were, of God. The act of sacrificing before a battle was usual (see 1 Sam. vii. 9f., xiii. 9ff.) (Ibn Ezra).

accept the fat. Portion of the sacrificial animal always consumed on the altar (Lev. iii. 3ff.). 'Accept (the offering) as fat' (Rashi), or 'reduce it to ashes,' by fire from heaven (Ibn Ezra, Kimchi), i.e. receive it favourably (Rashi).

5. *according to thine own heart.* Not the heart's desires, but the heart's planning, as being the organ of thought (Cf. Targum).

counsel. Design for routing the enemy (Kimchi).

6 We will shout for joy in thy
    victory,
  And in the name of our God we
    will set up our standards;
  The LORD fulfil all thy petitions.

7 Now know I that the LORD saveth
    His anointed;
  He will answer him from His holy
    heaven
  With the mighty acts of His saving
    right hand.

8 Some trust in chariots, and some
    in horses;
  But we will make mention of the
    name of the LORD our God.

9 They are bowed down and fallen;
  But we are risen, and stand
    upright.

10 Save, LORD;
   Let the King answer us in the
     day that we call.

‬‎נְרַנְּנָה ׀ בִּישׁוּעָתֶךָ 6
‫וּבְשֵׁם־אֱלֹהֵינוּ נִדְגֹּל
‫יְמַלֵּא יְהוָה כָּל־מִשְׁאֲלוֹתֶיךָ׃
‫עַתָּה יָדַעְתִּי כִּי הוֹשִׁיעַ ׀ יְהוָה מְשִׁיחוֹ 7
‫יַעֲנֵהוּ מִשְּׁמֵי קָדְשׁוֹ
‫בִּגְבוּרוֹת יֵשַׁע יְמִינוֹ׃
‫אֵלֶּה בָרֶכֶב וְאֵלֶּה בַסּוּסִים 8
‫וַאֲנַחְנוּ ׀ בְּשֵׁם־יְהוָה אֱלֹהֵינוּ נַזְכִּיר׃
‫הֵמָּה כָּרְעוּ וְנָפָלוּ 9
‫וַאֲנַחְנוּ קַּמְנוּ וַנִּתְעוֹדָד׃
‫יְהוָה הוֹשִׁיעָה 10
‫הַמֶּלֶךְ יַעֲנֵנוּ בְיוֹם־קָרְאֵנוּ׃

---

6. *we will shout for joy.* Better, 'so that we may shout for joy,' and omit 'we will' in the next line. The prayer is continued in this verse.

set up our standards. Raise our flags in acknowledgment of the triumph which is ours through Divine aid (Metsudath David).

7-9   ASSURANCE OF VICTORY

7. *now know I.* The sacrifice having been offered, I am convinced.

saveth. Hebrew 'hath saved,' the prophetic perfect.

His anointed. See on ii. 2.

right hand. Cf. xvii. 7. The Hebrew is lit. 'with mighty acts of the salvation of His right hand.'

8. *some trust in chariots.* For instance, Pharaoh (Exod. xiv. 6).

we will make mention of the name of the LORD. Following the example of David in his contest with Goliath (1 Sam. xvii. 45). 'Other nations behold their god in chariots and horses, but we behold Him in His true nature as "The LORD"' (Hirsch).

9. *they are bowed down.* The enemy riders. Cf. Gen. xlix. 17 (Ibn Ezra).

10   CONCLUDING SUPPLICATION

save. Here the meaning is: 'give victory to.' The structure is not 'LORD, save the king; and may He answer us' (Ibn Ezra). When we call to God for help, we may expect Him to hear our cry and answer us because we have recognized Him as our king and have not placed our trust in a mortal monarch (Hirsch).

1 For the Leader. A Psalm of
David.

2 O Lord, in Thy strength the king
rejoiceth;
And in Thy salvation how greatly
doth he exult!

3 Thou hast given him his heart's
desire,
And the request of his lips Thou
hast not withholden.   Selah

4 For Thou meetest him with
choicest blessings;
Thou settest a crown of fine gold
on his head.

5 He asked life of Thee, Thou gavest
it him;
Even length of days for ever and
ever.

לַמְנַצֵּחַ מִזְמוֹר לְדָוִד׃

2 יְהוָה בְּעָזְּךָ יִשְׂמַח־מֶלֶךְ
וּבִישׁוּעָתְךָ מַה־יָּגֶל מְאֹד׃

3 תַּאֲוַת לִבּוֹ נָתַתָּה לּוֹ
וַאֲרֶשֶׁת שְׂפָתָיו בַּל־מָנַעְתָּ סֶּלָה׃

4 כִּי־תְקַדְּמֶנּוּ בִּרְכוֹת טוֹב
תָּשִׁית לְרֹאשׁוֹ עֲטֶרֶת פָּז׃

5 חַיִּים שָׁאַל מִמְּךָ נָתַתָּה לּוֹ
אֹרֶךְ יָמִים עוֹלָם וָעֶד׃

THANKSGIVING FOR VICTORY

The Targum, the ancient Aramaic translation of the Bible, interpreted this Psalm to be speaking of the Messianic king. Rashi adds that it may also refer to David and was composed as an answer to those who taunted him regarding Bath-Sheba. Hirsch understands it as a sequel to the preceding Psalm. The battle had been fought and won, and a hymn of thanksgiving was offered for the success of the campaign. Accordingly *le-David* again means 'on behalf of David.'

2-8   God's favour to the king

This section is the expression of the people's gratitude to God for the salvation He wrought in securing the triumph of the king or of the Messiah.

2. *in Thy strength*. Against which the chariots and horses of the enemy (xx. 8) were of no avail.

3. *his heart's desire*. The prayer of xx. 5 had been granted.

4. *Thou meetest him*. lit., thou precedest him. You sent the prophet Samuel to anoint him as king, though David never even thought in the direction of royalty.

a crown of fine gold. Only a metaphorical coronation is to be thought of. God confirmed the king's sovereignty by bestowing victory upon him. There may, however, be an allusion to 2 Sam. xii. 30: *And he took the crown of Malcam from off his head … and it was set on David's head* (Rashi). The verse continues: *and he brought forth the spoil of the city, exceeding much*, and this may define *choicest blessings* previously mentioned (Rashi).

5. *he asked life of Thee*. He prayed to God to prolong his years (Kimchi).

length of days for ever and ever. The addition of *for ever and ever* and the words that follow, suggest that the Messianic king is intended (Metsudath David); but the phrases can

6 His glory is great through Thy
   salvation;
   Honour and majesty dost Thou
   lay upon him.

7 For Thou makest him most
   blessed for ever;
   Thou makest him glad with joy in
   Thy presence.

8 For the king trusteth in the LORD,
   Yea, in the mercy of the Most
   High; he shall not be moved.

9 Thy hand shall be equal to all
   thine enemies;
   Thy right hand shall overtake
   those that hate thee.

10 Thou shalt make them as a fiery
   furnace in the time of thine
   anger;

גָּדוֹל כְּבוֹדוֹ בִּישׁוּעָתֶךָ 6
הוֹד וְהָדָר תְּשַׁוֶּה עָלָיו:
כִּי־תְשִׁיתֵהוּ בְרָכוֹת לָעַד 7
תְּחַדֵּהוּ בְשִׂמְחָה אֶת־פָּנֶיךָ:
כִּי־הַמֶּלֶךְ בֹּטֵחַ בַּיהוָה 8
וּבְחֶסֶד עֶלְיוֹן בַּל־יִמּוֹט:
תִּמְצָא יָדְךָ לְכָל־אֹיְבֶיךָ 9
יְמִינְךָ תִּמְצָא שֹׂנְאֶיךָ:
תְּשִׁיתֵמוֹ כְּתַנּוּר אֵשׁ לְעֵת פָּנֶיךָ 10

be naturally explained as referring to David.
For ever and ever may refer to the perpetuation
of his dynasty as promised by God through
Natan the Prophet (2 Sam. vii. 13) (Rashi). It
may also allude to the eternal length of days in
the World to Come (Kimchi).

6. *glory … honour … majesty.* His glory is
great only because of Thy salvation. He enjoys
honour and majesty only because Thou hast
conferred it upon him.

7. *most blessed.* lit. 'blessing,' the recipient
of God's blessing and a permanent example of
'one who is blessed' (Metsudath David). In
this sense Abraham was exhorted: *Be thou a
blessing* (Gen. xii. 2).

joy in Thy presence. Cf. xvi. 11.

8. *trusteth.* When confronted by enemies, he

makes 'mention of the name of the LORD (xx. 8),
and his trust received the rewards enumerated.

9-13 THE KING ADDRESSED

9. *thy hand.* By a sudden transition, common
in Hebrew, the subject is changed. In the first
part of the Psalm *thou* was God; in this section
it is the king (cf. Kimchi).

shall be equal to. lit. 'find,' which Kimchi
explains as 'suffice for.' According to others
(Ibn Ezra) it means 'reach unto' or 'overcome,' so that they cannot escape. Cf. 1 Sam
xxiii. 17.

10. *a fiery furnace.* Destroy them like fuel
in a furnace (for the image, cf. Mal. iii. 19).

in the time of Thine anger. Most commentaries render it as 'Thine anger' or lit. 'Thy
presence.'

The LORD shall swallow them up
   in His wrath,
And the fire shall devour them.

11 Their fruit shalt thou destroy
   from the earth,
And their seed from among the
   children of men.

12 For they intended evil against
   thee,
They imagined a device, wherewith they shall not prevail.

13 For thou shalt make them turn
   their back,
Thou shalt make ready with thy
   bowstrings against the face of
   them.

14 Be Thou exalted, O LORD, in
   Thy strength;
So will we sing and praise Thy
   power.

יְהוָה בְּאַפּוֹ יְבַלְּעֵם וְתֹאכְלֵם אֵשׁ׃

11 פִּרְיָמוֹ מֵאֶרֶץ תְּאַבֵּד
וְזַרְעָם מִבְּנֵי אָדָם׃

12 כִּי־נָטוּ עָלֶיךָ רָעָה
חָשְׁבוּ מְזִמָּה בַּל־יוּכָלוּ׃

13 כִּי תְּשִׁיתֵמוֹ שֶׁכֶם
בְּמֵיתָרֶיךָ תְּכוֹנֵן עַל־פְּנֵיהֶם׃

14 רוּמָה יְהוָה בְעֻזֶּךָ
נָשִׁירָה וּנְזַמְּרָה גְּבוּרָתֶךָ׃

swallow them up. That no trace of them remains upon the face of the earth.

11. *fruit*. Of their body, children (cf. cxxvii.
3, Lam. ii. 20). Since they were raised in the
spirit of wickedness and continue the evil ways
established by their fathers, they shall have no
future in this world (Hirsch).

and their seed. A prophetic allusion to the seed
of Esau (Amalek) which will be entirely oblit-
erated with the coming of the Messiah.

12. *they shall not prevail*. lit. 'they shall be
unable' to accomplish their design. The clause
may be understood as a prayer: 'They imagined a device; let us hope that it will fail'
(Daath Sofrim).

13. *make ready*. or 'aim' (cf. xi. 2). The idea
is to frighten them into submission by holding
the bow and arrow opposite their faces (Daath
Sofrim).

14 CONCLUDING PRAYER

Like the foregoing, the Psalm ends with a
supplication.

be Thou exalted. Exercise Thy kingly authority
over all the nations.

in Thy strength. It is due to God's strength,
rather than Israel's, that battles are won
(Kimchi).

Thy power. Which will give victory when aggression has to be resisted.

PSALM XXII

כב

1 For the Leader; upon Aijeleth
   ha-Shahar. A Psalm of David.

2 My God, my God, why hast Thou
   forsaken me,
   And art far from my help at the
   words of my cry?

3 O my God, I call by day, but
   Thou answerest not;
   And at night, and there is no sur-
   cease for me.

4 Yet Thou art holy,
   O Thou that art enthroned upon
   the praises of Israel.

לַמְנַצֵּחַ עַל־אַיֶּלֶת הַשַּׁחַר
מִזְמוֹר לְדָוִד׃
2 אֵלִי אֵלִי לָמָה עֲזַבְתָּנִי
רָחוֹק מִישׁוּעָתִי דִּבְרֵי שַׁאֲגָתִי׃
3 אֱלֹהַי אֶקְרָא יוֹמָם וְלֹא תַעֲנֶה
וְלַיְלָה וְלֹא־דוּמִיָּה לִי׃
4 וְאַתָּה קָדוֹשׁ
יוֹשֵׁב תְּהִלּוֹת יִשְׂרָאֵל׃

CRY FOR HELP

MOST commentators explain this Psalm as a prophetic reference to Haman's plot of annihilation, on the authority of the Talmud (Meg. 13a) which identifies *Aijeleth ha-Shahar* (in the heading) with Esther. The Talmud further explains that David knew that Mordecai was destined to be descended from Shimei ben Gera who had publicly cursed him (2 Sam. xvi. 5) and deserved the death sentence. David subsequently pardoned him with the thought in mind that a descendent of his would help save all of Israel. Kimchi and Hirsch see the Psalm as a general account of the suffering of the people of Israel. The 'shahar' alludes to the bright future that will emerge out of the darkness of exile. Others maintain that it is David's own personal story in which he laments his distress under Saul's persecution, or when confronted by the aggressive Philistine forces.

1. *upon Aijeleth ha-Shahar*. lit. 'the hind of the morning.' In all probability the name of a melodious instrument which accompanied the rendering of the Psalm.

2-9 HIS DESPAIR

2. *why hast Thou forsaken me?* A poignant cry of perplexity wrung from his lips in a moment of despair, when his prayer seemed to be unheeded. He feels that he has been abandoned by God, and his faith is sorely tried.

cry. The Hebrew word is commonly used of a lion's roar. When applied to the human being it signifies a shriek of agony.

3. *surcease*. Respite from his suffering.

4. *yet Thou art holy*. The victim is puzzled by his experience. How can his suffering be reconciled with the government of the world by a God Who is *holy* and, therefore, just? (Kimchi)

enthroned upon the praises of Israel. Often has Israel sent up to heaven thanksgiving for Divine salvation in times of distress, and their praises of God's mighty acts have become a throne of glory to Him. How, then, can He be indifferent to what is happening now! (Kimchi).

5 In Thee did our fathers trust;
   They trusted, and Thou didst
   deliver them.

6 Unto Thee they cried, and escaped;
   In Thee did they trust, and were
   not ashamed.

7 But I am a worm, and no man;
   A reproach of men, and despised
   of the people.

8 All they that see me laugh me to
   scorn;
   They shoot out the lip, they shake
   the head:

9 'Let him commit himself unto the
   Lord! let Him rescue him;
   Let Him deliver him, seeing He
   delighteth in him.'

10 For Thou art He that took me
   out of the womb;
   Thou madest me trust when I
   was upon my mother's breasts.

5 בְּךָ בָּטְחוּ אֲבֹתֵינוּ
בָּטְחוּ וַתְּפַלְּטֵמוֹ׃

6 אֵלֶיךָ זָעֲקוּ וְנִמְלָטוּ
בְּךָ בָטְחוּ וְלֹא־בוֹשׁוּ׃

7 וְאָנֹכִי תוֹלַעַת וְלֹא־אִישׁ
חֶרְפַּת אָדָם וּבְזוּי עָם׃

8 כָּל־רֹאַי יַלְעִגוּ לִי
יַפְטִירוּ בְשָׂפָה יָנִיעוּ רֹאשׁ׃

9 גֹּל אֶל־יְהוָה יְפַלְּטֵהוּ
יַצִּילֵהוּ כִּי חָפֵץ בּוֹ׃

10 כִּי־אַתָּה גֹחִי מִבָּטֶן
מַבְטִיחִי עַל־שְׁדֵי אִמִּי׃

5. *did our fathers trust.* Our fathers trusted in Thee when they were not in trouble, and when they were, Thou didst deliver them (Ibn Ezra).

6. *were not ashamed.* Not disappointed in their trust; it always proved reliable.

7. *worm.* Trodden under foot and treated with contempt. The language of this section is reminiscent of Isaiah's description of the suffering *Servant of the Lord*. The people of Israel is called *thou worm Jacob* (Isa. xli. 14).

and no man. I am not treated like a human being and have lost all sense of dignity. My name is used as an example of one who is to be despised (Metsudath David).

despised of the people. Cf. Isa. xlix. 7, liii. 3.

8. *they shoot out the lip.* lit. 'they separate with the lip'; they open their mouth wide to produce contemptuous words (cf. xxxv. 21).

they shake the head. An insulting gesture, as in xliv. 15, cix. 25.

9. This is the taunt directed at those who claim to be God's people (Hirsch).

let him commit himself. lit. 'roll (it).' Again in xxxvii. 5: *commit thy way unto the Lord*, but here the verb is used tauntingly.

10-22   HIS PLEA TO GOD

10. The mocking words of his persecutors have the effect of deepening his consciousness of what God had been to him since his birth.

for Thou are He. Better, 'Yeah, Thou art He.' His reply to the taunt is: Yes, I will commit myself to Him Who has taken care of me from the time I was born.

Thou madest me trust. Taught me to put my trust in Thee, i.e. my sense of reliance upon God was instilled in me from infancy.

11 Upon Thee I have been cast from
   my birth;
   Thou art my God from my
   mother's womb.

12 Be not far from me; for trouble is
   near;
   For there is none to help.

13 Many bulls have encompassed
   me;
   Strong bulls of Bashan have
   beset me round.

14 They open wide their mouth
   against me,
   As a ravening and a roaring lion.

15 I am poured out like water,
   And all my bones are out of joint;
   My heart is become like wax;
   It is melted in mine inmost parts.

16 My strength is dried up like a
   potsherd;
   And my tongue cleaveth to my
   throat;
   And Thou layest me in the dust
   of death.

17 For dogs have encompassed me;

עָלֶיךָ הָשְׁלַכְתִּי מֵרָחֶם 11
מִבֶּטֶן אִמִּי אֵלִי אָתָּה:
אַל־תִּרְחַק מִמֶּנִּי כִּי־צָרָה קְרוֹבָה 12
כִּי־אֵין עוֹזֵר:
סְבָבוּנִי פָּרִים רַבִּים 13
אַבִּירֵי בָשָׁן כִּתְּרוּנִי:
פָּצוּ עָלַי פִּיהֶם 14
אַרְיֵה טֹרֵף וְשֹׁאֵג:
כַּמַּיִם נִשְׁפַּכְתִּי 15
וְהִתְפָּרְדוּ כָּל־עַצְמוֹתָי
הָיָה לִבִּי כַּדּוֹנָג
נָמֵס בְּתוֹךְ מֵעָי:
יָבֵשׁ כַּחֶרֶשׂ כֹּחִי 16
וּלְשׁוֹנִי מֻדְבָּק מַלְקוֹחָי
וְלַעֲפַר־מָוֶת תִּשְׁפְּתֵנִי:
כִּי סְבָבוּנִי כְּלָבִים 17

11. *upon Thee I have been cast.* From the moment of my birth I have been dependent upon Thy protection for my existence.

12. *be not far from me.* As God had been near to him since his childhood and preserved him up to now, he prays that He will not be distant from him in his present danger (Kimchi).

13. *bulls.* He compares his enemies to powerful horned beasts which gore their victims.

have encompassed me. Throughout history, the powerful nations of the world have constantly shown hostility towards the Jewish people (Hirsch).

Bashan. District east of the Jordan, famed for its rich pasturage and cattle.

14. *open wide their mouth.* To spring upon him and rend him.

15. *poured out like water.* Cf. *the hearts of the people melted and became as water.* (Joshua vii. 5). Courage and strength deserted him, and he is left without power of resistance (Hirsch).

my bones are out of joint. My limbs are dislocated and cannot function in self-defence (Kimchi).

16. *throat.* lit. 'jaws.'

Thou layest me in the dust of death. Hirsch sees this as a question; 'Is it really your interest, then, to have me vanish from among the nations, and lay me down in the dust of death?'

17. *dogs.* These may be the mobs, the scum of the nations (Hirsch); the hostile enemies that surround Israel while in exile (Kimchi); or a specific reference to the sons of Haman (Medrash Shocher Tov).

A company of evil-doers have
inclosed me;
Like a lion, they are at my hands
and my feet.

18 I may count all my bones;
They look and gloat over me.

19 They part my garments among
them,
And for my vesture do they cast
lots.

20 But Thou, O LORD, be not far
off;
O Thou my strength, hasten to
help me.

21 Deliver my soul from the sword;
Mine only one from the power of
the dog.

22 Save me from the lion's mouth;
Yea, from the horns of the wild-
oxen do Thou answer me.

עֲדַת מְרֵעִים הִקִּיפוּנִי

כָּאֲרִי יָדַי וְרַגְלָי:

18 אֲסַפֵּר כָּל־עַצְמוֹתָי

הֵמָּה יַבִּיטוּ יִרְאוּ־בִי:

19 יְחַלְּקוּ בְגָדַי לָהֶם

וְעַל־לְבוּשִׁי יַפִּילוּ גוֹרָל:

20 וְאַתָּה יְהוָה אַל־תִּרְחָק

אֱיָלוּתִי לְעֶזְרָתִי חוּשָׁה:

21 הַצִּילָה מֵחֶרֶב נַפְשִׁי

מִיַּד־כֶּלֶב יְחִידָתִי:

22 הוֹשִׁיעֵנִי מִפִּי אַרְיֵה

וּמִקַּרְנֵי רֵמִים עֲנִיתָנִי:

like a lion, they are at my hands and my feet. The Hebrew is difficult, there being nothing to correspond with *they are at*. The Targum has 'biting like a lion my hands and my feet.' Malbim renders 'my hands and my feet are like those of a lion in that they are able to stand up to the enemy.' Kimchi connects 'like a lion' to the previous phrase: 'They encircle me as a lion encircles its prey, who in turn draws in its hands and feet in preparation, for the attack.' The captives in Babylon found themselves in a similar predicament as they were surrounded by the enemy on all sides.

18. *count all my bones.* Because the flesh of the body is wasted away (Kimchi, Metsudath).

they look and gloat over me. lit. 'as for them, they gaze, they stare at me.' They regard me with scorn and derision (Kimchi) maliciously delighting over my ill fortune (Rashi).

19. The language is imaginative, not factual. He pictures his enemies watching for his death so that they can strip his body and share his garments among them.

my vesture. The royal tunic which could not be divided without rendering it useless; therefore lots were cast to decide the possessor (Malbim).

20. *but Thou.* Emphatic in the Hebrew, to mark the contrast with his persecutors.

be not far off. Repeating the prayer of verse 12.

21. *sword.* Symbol of death by violence.

mine only one. My soul precious like 'an only child' (so lit.) (Kimchi).

dog. Cf. verse 17.

22. *wild-oxen.* Hebrew *reëm*, frequently mentioned as a figure of ferocity and destructive might. Other suggested renderings included 'bison,' 'unicorn,' and 'reindeer.'

do Thou answer me. Better, 'Thou hast answered me.' Just as God has answered him in the past and saved him from the horns of the ox, so should He rescue him now from the mouth of the lion and take him out of his exile (Kimchi).

23 I will declare Thy name unto my
    brethren;
  In the midst of the congregation
    will I praise Thee:
24 'Ye that fear the LORD, praise
    Him;
  All ye the seed of Jacob, glorify
    Him;
  And stand in awe of Him, all ye
    the seed of Israel.
25 For He hath not despised nor
    abhorred the lowliness of the
    poor;
  Neither hath He hid His face
    from him;
  But when he cried unto Him, He
    heard.'
26 From Thee cometh my praise in
    the great congregation;
  I will pay my vows before them
    that fear Him.
27 Let the humble eat and be
    satisfied;
  Let them praise the LORD that
    seek after Him;
  May your heart be quickened for
    ever!

אֲסַפְּרָה שִׁמְךָ לְאֶחָי 23
בְּתוֹךְ קָהָל אֲהַלְלֶךָּ:
יִרְאֵי יְהֹוָה ׀ הַלְלוּהוּ 24
כָּל־זֶרַע יַעֲקֹב כַּבְּדוּהוּ
וְגוּרוּ מִמֶּנּוּ כָּל־זֶרַע יִשְׂרָאֵל:
כִּי לֹא־בָזָה ׀ וְלֹא שִׁקַּץ עֱנוּת עָנִי 25
וְלֹא־הִסְתִּיר פָּנָיו מִמֶּנּוּ
וּבְשַׁוְּעוֹ אֵלָיו שָׁמֵעַ:
מֵאִתְּךָ תְהִלָּתִי בְּקָהָל רָב 26
נְדָרַי אֲשַׁלֵּם נֶגֶד יְרֵאָיו:
יֹאכְלוּ עֲנָוִים ׀ וְיִשְׂבָּעוּ 27
יְהַלְלוּ יְהֹוָה דֹּרְשָׁיו
יְחִי לְבַבְכֶם לָעַד:

23-32   GRATITUDE AND PRAISE

23. *Thy name.* Thy character as Saviour.

brethren. Those united to him by ties of race or faith (Cf. Kimchi).

congregation. Hebrew, 'assembly.' He will publish his experience as widely as possible.

24. This and verse 25 contain the wording of his proclamation of God's wondrous aid.

ye that fear the LORD. Addressed to a section of the community whose reverence of God distinguished them above the rest. So again cxv. 13, cxviii. 4.

25. *despised.* Heartless men who glory only in physical might and despise the weak (verse 7); not so God Who is considerate of their defenceless state.

poor. The helpless at the mercy of the strong.

hid His face. Cf. x. 11, xiii. 2.

26. *from Thee cometh my praise.* The salvation which has come to him from God is the cause of his public act of thanksgiving (Kimchi).

I will pay my vows. The sacrifices which he vowed to bring if he was saved (Metsudath David).

before them that fear Him. In the presence of His worshippers, to make his indebtedness to God widely known (Metsudath David).

27. *let...eat.* A votive sacrifice was eaten by the offerer (Lev. vii. 16) and he invites *the humble* to share in it (Metsudath David). Rashi notes the phrase describes the Messianic era when the humble will eat the spoils left by their enemies who denied God (Cf. Kimchi).

may your heart be quickened for ever. He pronounces a blessing upon his guests. They, like him, had suffered; may they be encouraged by what had happened to him and their spirit be forever fortified (Kimchi).

28 All the ends of the earth shall
   remember and turn unto the
   LORD;
   And all the kindreds of the
   nations shall worship before
   Thee.

29 For the kingdom is the LORD's;
   And He is the ruler over the
   nations.

30 All the fat ones of the earth shall
   eat and worship;
   All they that go down to the dust
   shall kneel before Him,
   Even he that cannot keep his soul
   alive.

31 A seed shall serve Him;
   It shall be told of the Lord unto
   the next generation.

32 They shall come and shall declare His righteousness
   Unto a people that shall be born,
   that He hath done it.

28 יִזְכְּרוּ ׀ וְיָשֻׁבוּ אֶל־יְהֹוָה
כָּל־אַפְסֵי־אָרֶץ
וְיִשְׁתַּחֲווּ לְפָנֶיךָ כָּל־מִשְׁפְּחוֹת גּוֹיִם:
29 כִּי לַיהֹוָה הַמְּלוּכָה
וּמֹשֵׁל בַּגּוֹיִם:
30 אָכְלוּ וַיִּשְׁתַּחֲווּ ׀ כָּל־דִּשְׁנֵי־אֶרֶץ
לְפָנָיו יִכְרְעוּ כָּל־יוֹרְדֵי עָפָר
וְנַפְשׁוֹ לֹא חִיָּה:
31 זֶרַע יַעַבְדֶנּוּ
יְסֻפַּר לַאדֹנָי לַדּוֹר:
32 יָבֹאוּ וְיַגִּידוּ צִדְקָתוֹ
לְעַם נוֹלָד כִּי עָשָׂה:

28. The horizon of his outlook has been broadening until it now reaches its limit. He began with 'the fearers of the LORD,' proceeded to 'the seed' of Jacob and Israel, and now envisages all mankind as worshippers of God.

remember. When men serve idols they 'forget' God (ix. 18); in turning from their folly they *remember* Him.

all the kindreds of the nations. In fulfilment of the promise made to Abraham (Gen. xii. 3).

29. *kingdom.* Better, 'kingship.' The universal sovereignty of God is the supreme aspiration of Bible doctrine. Its finest enunciation is the text of Zech. xiv. 9, which concludes every Jewish service.

30. *all the fat ones of the earth.* The sweep of the Psalmist's aspiration is all-embracing. Even they who were arrogant in their prosperity and ignored God will humble themselves before Him (Cf. Kimchi).

shall eat. Hebrew 'have eaten'; the prophetic perfect. According to Kimchi, they will realize that their sustenance is from God. Rashi main-

tains that this verse is convoluted and renders 'they (the humble) shall eat from all the fat of the land and worship, etc.'

all they that go down to the dust. All men without exception, since all are mortal.

even he that cannot keep his soul alive. Explained by Ibn Ezra as referring to the arrogant ones whose spirits will not be fortified by their lifestyle as it was in the case of the humble (verse 27). Rashi understands the verse as alluding to the wicked who, although they have come to recognize God after descending to the grave, will not have their souls revived.

31. *unto the next generation.* Death will not mean the end of God's worship. One generation will receive it as a heritage from its predecessor (Cf. Rashi, Kimchi).

32. *unto a people that shall be born.* The succeeding generation.

that ... done it. That God protects the suffering and releases them from their oppressors, as happened with the Psalmist. This will be the theme transmitted through the ages (Kimchi).

23　　　　　　　　　　　　　　　　　　　　כג

1　A Psalm of David.
　　The LORD is my shepherd; I shall
　　not want.

2　He maketh me to lie down in green
　　　pastures;
　　He leadeth me beside the still
　　　waters.

3　He restoreth my soul;
　　He guideth me in straight paths
　　for His name's sake.

מִזְמוֹר לְדָוִד
יְהֹוָה רֹעִי לֹא אֶחְסָר׃
2 בִּנְאוֹת דֶּשֶׁא יַרְבִּיצֵנִי
עַל־מֵי מְנֻחוֹת יְנַהֲלֵנִי׃
3 נַפְשִׁי יְשׁוֹבֵב
יַנְחֵנִי בְמַעְגְּלֵי־צֶדֶק לְמַעַן שְׁמוֹ׃

THE DIVINE SHEPHERD

THIS Psalm is one of the most precious gems in the treasury of Biblical literature. Its appeal to the human heart has been constant and incalculable. It was composed during one of David's most difficult periods—while on the run from Saul and his men, alone in a desolate forest (1 Sam. xxii). It is dedicated to those who forsake all their worldly comforts and thank God for whatever they have. Their sole aim is to merit spiritual bliss in the World to Come. At first the Psalmist compares himself to a sheep that relies on its shepherd for protection and livelihood. In the last two verses he likens himself to a guest in a home that is God's world. The Targum gives the Psalm a national application as praise to God who fed His people in the wilderness. The Midrash (Shocher Tov) elaborates on this theme.

1. *shepherd*. In a pastoral community the faithful shepherd stood as the personification of tender care and unwearying watchfulness, and men gratefully applied the term to God as the Provider and Protector of His human flock. Its earliest use in this sense was made by Jacob who spoke of *the God Who hath been my shepherd all my life long* (Gen. xlviii. 15 cf. Num. xxvii. 17). The imagery is found in the prophets (Isa. xl. 11; Mic. vii. 14), and frequently in the Psalter.

I shall not want. A simple and perfect expression of calm faith in God's providence.

2. *green pastures*. lit. 'pastures of tender grass.' When the heat of the sun is fierce, the careful shepherd leads his flock to cool meadows (Cant. i. 7).

leadeth. The Hebrew denotes gentle guidance as distinct from forceful driving.

still waters. The beautiful English phrase does not convey the meaning of the Hebrew which is literally 'water of restfulness'—not 'streams where rest can be found,' but placid waters (Ibn Ezra, Kimchi).

3. *He restoreth my soul*. See on xix. 8.

straight paths. Rather lit. as A.V., *paths of righteousness*—the right way, not an easy way (Cf. Malbim).

for His name's sake. God does all this as a demonstration of His essential nature so that it may be known to man (Daath Sofrim).

4. *valley of the shadow of death*. This ex-

4 Yea, though I walk through the
     valley of the shadow of death,
   I will fear no evil,
   For Thou art with me;
   Thy rod and Thy staff, they com-
     fort me.

5 Thou preparest a table before me
     in the presence of mine enemies;
   Thou hast anointed my head with
     oil; my cup runneth over.

6 Surely goodness and mercy shall
     follow me all the days of my life;
   And I shall dwell in the house of
     the LORD for ever.

גַּם כִּי־אֵלֵךְ בְּגֵיא צַלְמָוֶת 4
לֹא־אִירָא רָע כִּי־אַתָּה עִמָּדִי
שִׁבְטְךָ וּמִשְׁעַנְתֶּךָ הֵמָּה יְנַחֲמֻנִי:
תַּעֲרֹךְ לְפָנַי ׀ שֻׁלְחָן נֶגֶד צֹרְרָי 5
דִּשַּׁנְתָּ בַשֶּׁמֶן רֹאשִׁי כּוֹסִי רְוָיָה:
אַךְ ׀ טוֹב וָחֶסֶד יִרְדְּפוּנִי כָּל־יְמֵי חַיָּי 6
וְשַׁבְתִּי בְּבֵית־יְהוָה לְאֹרֶךְ יָמִים:

quisite wording has become part of religious
vocabulary, and one hesitates to interfere with
it. The Hebrew, however, signifies a place
fraught with danger which, on account of its
gloominess, is compared to the grave (Kimchi).
While Targum explains it as a reference to the
exile, Rashi contends that the 'valley' describes the wilderness of Zif where David,
having been betrayed, was hiding from Saul
who was bent on killing him (see 1 Sam. xxiii.
1ff.)

I fear no evil. No evil will befall me—and if I
come face to face with it, I will be saved by an
act of God. Even if I do suffer misfortune, it is
all for the good (Daath Sofrim).

rod. A stick used by a shepherd to control his
flock (Kimchi). Similarly, God finds it necessary to afflict us in order to keep us in line.

staff. A stick to lean upon when he feels the
need to rest (Kimchi).

comfort me. Relieve him of anxiety.

5. The same thought is now conveyed by
means of a different metaphor. A good host
considers it a sacred obligation to ensure the
safety of his guests (cf. Gen. xix.). David is

God's guest and therefore under His protection.

Thou preparest a table before me. God protects him as He did the Israelites in the wilderness.

in the presence of mine enemies. So it is evident to them that he is in God's care and their
plots to injure him must fail. *Enemies* is
strictly 'adversaries,' the same Hebrew word
as in vi. 8.

anointed my head with oil. lit. 'saturated.' I find
solace in the knowledge that my troubles are
only temporary. My anointment as king has
designated me for greatness (Daath Sofrim).

my cup runneth over. God is a bountiful Host
and treats His guest liberally (Sforno).

6. *goodness*. Physical welfare and the provision of his needs.

mercy. Divine love and guardianship.

I shall dwell in the house of the LORD. He will
be privileged to serve in the Temple (Kimchi).

for ever. Hebrew, 'for length of days.' God will
extend his life, and the enjoyment of His favour
will be prolonged (Kimchi).

24

1 A Psalm of David.
The earth is the LORD's, and the
   fulness thereof;
The world, and they that dwell
   therein.

2 For He hath founded it upon the
   seas,
And established it upon the floods.

3 Who shall ascend into the mountain of the LORD?
And who shall stand in His holy
   place?

4 He that hath clean hands, and a
   pure heart;
Who hath not taken My name in
   vain,
And hath not sworn deceitfully.

כד

לְדָוִד מִזְמוֹר
לַיהוָה הָאָרֶץ וּמְלוֹאָהּ
תֵּבֵל וְיֹשְׁבֵי בָהּ׃
2 כִּי־הוּא עַל־יַמִּים יְסָדָהּ
וְעַל־נְהָרוֹת יְכוֹנְנֶהָ׃
3 מִי־יַעֲלֶה בְהַר־יְהוָה
וּמִי־יָקוּם בִּמְקוֹם קָדְשׁוֹ׃
4 נְקִי כַפַּיִם וּבַר־לֵבָב
אֲשֶׁר לֹא־נָשָׂא לַשָּׁוְא נַפְשׁוֹ
וְלֹא נִשְׁבַּע לְמִרְמָה׃

נפשי ק v. 4.

HYMN OF GREETING

THE historical background of the Psalm is described in 2 Sam. vi and 1 Chron. xv. With the defeat of the Jebusites, the city of Jerusalem in its entirety passed into the hands of David. He now had the opportunity of providing a resting place there for the Ark of the Covenant, and the Psalm was composed for the joyous occasion when it was brought from the house of Obed-Edom to the tent which David had prepared for its reception. For this reason it is recited regularly when the Torah scroll is returned to the Ark. According to tradition this Psalm was regularly recited in the Temple on the first day of the week (P. B., p. 80) and was thus chosen to be recited at the conclusion of the morning prayers on the first day of the week.

1-2 LORD OF THE UNIVERSE

1. *the earth is the LORD's.* A noble preface with a deep meaning. Although Zion was His appointed dwelling, His Presence and Sovereignty extend throughout the world. The same thought occurs in the prayer offered at the dedication of Solomon's Temple: *Behold, heaven and the heaven of heavens cannot contain Thee; how much less this house that I have built* (1 Kings viii. 27).

the fulness thereof. All it contains.

world. Inhabited by man (Kimchi).

2. *on seas … floods.* Cf. cxxxvi. 6; Gen. vii. 11. The world was originally covered with a layer of water (Kimchi, Malbim).

3-6 WHO MAY APPROACH GOD

3. *who shall ascend.* Cf. xv. With God's 'dwelling place' having been established in the Temple, it was necessary to define the qualifications of those who were to have access to it. Only those whose ethical records were impeccable were to be considered (Metsudath David).

4. *clean hands.* Unstained by any misdeed or dishonesty.

pure heart. Free of impure thoughts (cf. xviii. 24)

who … in vain. The *kerë* reads *nafshi:* 'Who hath not taken My soul in vain,' which must be understood as a different form of the third commandment, 'My soul' being the equivalent of 'Me, My name' (see on iii. 3). The *kethib* reads *nafsho,* 'who hath not lifted up his soul unto vanity,' i.e. has not striven after aims which have God's disapproval (Kimchi).

5 He shall receive a blessing from
   the LORD,
And righteousness from the God
   of his salvation.

6 Such is the generation of them
   that seek after Him,
That seek Thy face, even Jacob.
                 Selah

7 Lift up your heads, O ye gates,
And be ye lifted up, ye everlast-
   ing doors;
That the King of glory may come in.

8 'Who is the King of glory?'
'The LORD strong and mighty,
The LORD mighty in battle.'

9 Lift up your heads, O ye gates,
Yea, lift them up, ye everlasting
   doors;
That the King of glory may come in.

10 'Who then is the King of glory?'
'The LORD of hosts;
He is the King of glory.'   Selah

5 יִשָּׂא בְרָכָה מֵאֵת יְהֹוָה
וּצְדָקָה מֵאֱלֹהֵי יִשְׁעוֹ:
6 זֶה דּוֹר דֹּרְשָׁו
מְבַקְשֵׁי פָנֶיךָ יַעֲקֹב סֶלָה:
7 שְׂאוּ שְׁעָרִים רָאשֵׁיכֶם
וְהִנָּשְׂאוּ פִּתְחֵי עוֹלָם
וְיָבוֹא מֶלֶךְ הַכָּבוֹד:
8 מִי זֶה מֶלֶךְ הַכָּבוֹד
יְהֹוָה עִזּוּז וְגִבּוֹר
יְהֹוָה גִּבּוֹר מִלְחָמָה:
9 שְׂאוּ שְׁעָרִים רָאשֵׁיכֶם
וּשְׂאוּ פִּתְחֵי עוֹלָם
וְיָבֹא מֶלֶךְ הַכָּבוֹד:
10 מִי הוּא זֶה מֶלֶךְ הַכָּבוֹד
יְהֹוָה צְבָאוֹת
הוּא מֶלֶךְ הַכָּבוֹד סֶלָה:

v. 6. דרשיו ק׳

hath not sworn deceitfully. He does not use his words for the purpose of deception (Hirsch).

5. *righteousness.* The loving care that is evident when one receives his welfare from a benevolent God (Hirsch).

6. *generation.* Type of man; as in xii. 8, xiv. 5 (Cf. Rashi).

seek after Him. Turn to Him for help and guidance (Hirsch).

that seek Thy face. Discipline themselves to be worthy of entrance to Thy presence.

even Jacob. i.e. the seed of Jacob who deserve to be called by his name in consequence of their faithfulness to God.

       7-10   ENTRANCE OF THE ARK

7. The bearers of the Ark are at Zion's gates and the procession is about to enter the city.

lift up your head. In honour of the exalted guest you are about to receive (Kimchi).

everlasting gates. Gates whose holiness are everlasting (Rashi). Portals of the future (Hirsch).

8. *who is the King of glory?* The sentries at the gate are represented as performing their duty of challenging whoever would enter (Kimchi).

mighty in battle. He gave victory to David against the Jebusites.

9. For added impressiveness the invocation and response are repeated.

10. *LORD of Hosts.* LORD of all the heavenly bodies (Ibn Ezra); the Supreme Ruler of the universe and all its creations (Malbim). In contrast to verse 8, no military characteristic is noted, as the Ark would no longer leave its place to go with Israel into battle (Kimchi).

כה

25

1 [A Psalm] of David.
   Unto Thee, O LORD, do I lift up
   my soul.

2 O my God, in Thee have I trusted,
   let me not be ashamed;
   Let not mine enemies triumph
   over me.

3 Yea, none that wait for Thee shall
   be ashamed;
   They shall be ashamed that deal
   treacherously without cause.

4 Show me Thy ways, O LORD;
   Teach me Thy paths.

5 Guide me in Thy truth, and teach
   me;
   For Thou art the God of my salvation;
   For Thee do I wait all the day.

לְדָוִד

אֵלֶיךָ יְהוָה נַפְשִׁי אֶשָּׂא:

2 אֱלֹהַי בְּךָ בָטַחְתִּי אַל־אֵבוֹשָׁה
אַל־יַעַלְצוּ אוֹיְבַי לִי:

3 גַּם כָּל־קֹוֶיךָ לֹא יֵבֹשׁוּ
יֵבֹשׁוּ הַבּוֹגְדִים רֵיקָם:

4 דְּרָכֶיךָ יְהוָה הוֹדִיעֵנִי
אֹרְחוֹתֶיךָ לַמְּדֵנִי:

5 הַדְרִיכֵנִי בַאֲמִתֶּךָ וְלַמְּדֵנִי
כִּי־אַתָּה אֱלֹהֵי יִשְׁעִי
אוֹתְךָ קִוִּיתִי כָּל־הַיּוֹם:

A PRAYER

THIS entire Psalm is the cry of a humble soul in supplication to God. It reflects no special circumstances, although the appeal is intensely personal. In form the Psalm is based upon an alphabetical acrostic, with divergence at three points which will be noted. Two of these irregularities also occur in Ps. xxxiv, which is a companion to this Psalm, but the reason for them cannot be explained with certainty.

1-7 APPEAL FOR PROTECTION, GUIDANCE AND PARDON

1. *do I lift up my soul.* So again lxxxvi. 4, cxliii. 8. The attitude of true prayer, when inner thoughts and emotions are expressed (Hirsch).

2. This verse does not begin with *beth* which is, however, the initial of the second word. It has been suggested that the name of God was not considered to be part of the acrostic, and therefore the verse has the required letter. No known reason has been put forth (Kimchi).

let me not be ashamed. As I would be if the taunt of my enemies were justified, viz. that my trust in God would not help me (Kimchi).

3. He answers the doubt implied in his prayer: he will not be put to shame, because that is never the experience of those who rely upon God and are innocent (Metsudath David).

4. *show me Thy ways.* Cf. Moses' prayer (Exod. xxxiii. 13). To know the *ways* of God is to understand the Divine meaning and purposes of his own life and those happening around him, so that he may order his own conduct accordingly (Malbim).

5. *in Thy truth.* Not the true conception of God's nature (Kimchi), but the true way of life to follow (Ibn Ezra). A verse beginning with the letter *vav* is omitted here and also in xxxiv. It has been suggested that the word *velamdeni* is used for the *vav* but this is not certain (Kimchi).

6 Remember, O Lord, Thy com-
　passions and Thy mercies;
　For they have been from of old.

7 Remember not the sins of my
　youth, nor my transgressions;
　According to Thy mercy remem-
　ber Thou me,
　For Thy goodness' sake, O Lord.

8 Good and upright is the Lord;
　Therefore doth He instruct sinners
　in the way.

9 He guideth the humble in justice;
　And He teacheth the humble His
　way.

10 All the paths of the Lord are
　mercy and truth
　Unto such as keep His covenant
　and His testimonies.

11 For Thy name's sake, O Lord,
　Pardon mine iniquity, for it is
　great.

זְכֹר־רַחֲמֶיךָ יְהוָה וַחֲסָדֶיךָ 6

כִּי מֵעוֹלָם הֵמָּה׃

חַטֹּאות נְעוּרַי וּפְשָׁעַי אַל־תִּזְכֹּר 7

כְּחַסְדְּךָ זְכָר־לִי־אַתָּה

לְמַעַן טוּבְךָ יְהוָה׃

טוֹב־וְיָשָׁר יְהוָה 8

עַל־כֵּן יוֹרֶה חַטָּאִים בַּדָּרֶךְ׃

יַדְרֵךְ עֲנָוִים בַּמִּשְׁפָּט 9

וִילַמֵּד עֲנָוִים דַּרְכּוֹ׃

כָּל־אָרְחוֹת יְהוָה חֶסֶד וֶאֱמֶת 10

לְנֹצְרֵי בְרִיתוֹ וְעֵדֹתָיו׃

לְמַעַן־שִׁמְךָ יְהוָה 11

וְסָלַחְתָּ לַעֲוֹנִי כִּי רַב־הוּא׃

6. *remember.* Since God's nature is constant, He must be merciful to the suffering now as He proved Himself to be in the past.

7. *sins.* Inadvertent errors (see on i. 1), due to youthful indiscretion (Kimchi).

transgressions. Acts of rebellion against God's will in mature age (Kimchi).

for Thy goodness' sake. He pleads that forgiveness should not be dispersed according to the merits of man, but solely for the goodness which God is able to bestow upon all under His sovereignty (Hirsch, Daath Sofrim).

8-14　PRAISE OF GOD

8. *therefore.* A case of cause and effect. Because He is upright, He must necessarily offer guidance to those who stray from the right path. 'The Rabbis deem this one of the great sayings of Scripture. Because God is good, He is *just*; i.e. sinners must suffer the consequences of their misdeeds. And because God is just, He is *good*; i.e. these consequences of men's sins prove in the end to be not vindictive but remedial' (Hertz).

way. Of repentance whereby the sinner may retrace his erring steps. Comment the Rabbis, 'Let him repent and obtain his atonement. My children, what do I ask of you? Seek Me and live' (Midrash).

9. *humble.* See on ix. 13. Here the word has a wider sense. The *humble* are opposite of the arrogant who follow their inclinations wherever they lead them, whereas the former are desirous of making themselves subservient to God. They are anxious for His instruction and He imparts it to them (cf. Daath Sofrim).

justice. Principles of right conduct.

10. *paths of the Lord.* He gives the answer to his petition in verse 4 in terms similar to those proclaimed by God to Moses.

covenant. Made at Sinai (Exod. xix. 5).

testimonies. See on xix. 8.

11. *for Thy name's sake.* I appeal to the Divine attribute of 'mercy and truth' for the expiation of my iniquity.

for it is great. 'Although it is great' (Ibn Ezra).

12 What man is he that feareth the
   LORD?
   Him will He instruct in the way
   that he should choose.

13 His soul shall abide in prosperity;
   And his seed shall inherit the
   land.

14 The counsel of the LORD is with
   them that fear Him;
   And His covenant, to make them
   know it.

15 Mine eyes are ever toward the
   LORD;
   For He will bring forth my feet
   out of the net.

16 Turn Thee unto me, and be
   gracious unto me;
   For I am solitary and afflicted.

17 The troubles of my heart are
   enlarged;
   O bring Thou me out of my dis-
   tresses.

מִי־זֶה הָאִישׁ יְרֵא יְהֹוָה 12
יוֹרֶנּוּ בְּדֶרֶךְ יִבְחָר׃
נַפְשׁוֹ בְּטוֹב תָּלִין 13
וְזַרְעוֹ יִירַשׁ אָרֶץ׃
סוֹד יְהֹוָה לִירֵאָיו 14
וּבְרִיתוֹ לְהוֹדִיעָם׃
עֵינַי תָּמִיד אֶל־יְהֹוָה 15
כִּי־הוּא־יוֹצִיא מֵרֶשֶׁת רַגְלָי׃
פְּנֵה־אֵלַי וְחָנֵּנִי 16
כִּי־יָחִיד וְעָנִי אָנִי׃
צָרוֹת לְבָבִי הִרְחִיבוּ 17
מִמְּצוּקוֹתַי הוֹצִיאֵנִי׃

Because my sin is so grievous, I can only
depend upon the greatness of God for pardon
(Rashi).

12. *way that he should choose.* Being possessed of *fear,* i.e. reverence of God, he becomes amenable to His instruction so that he
learns which is the right path to select for
himself (Ibn Ezra).

13. *prosperity.* His righteousness will be
rewarded in that his soul will find eternal bliss
(Rashi, Hirsch).

his seed shall inherit the land. Transmitting our
heritage and its morals to the future generation
ensures that they will carry on the tradition and
achieve the salvation promised to them on this
earth (Hirsch).

14. *counsel.* More lit. 'secret.' In addition to

material prosperity, the righteous enjoy an
intimate fellowship with the spirit with God.

to make them know it. The covenant made with
those who fear Him bears the promise that He
will reveal His 'Divine Plan' to them and grant
them the ability to understand it (Hirsch).

15-21   HIS PRAYER RESUMED

15. *mine eyes are ever toward the LORD.* As
the source of help when in difficulty.

net. Cf. ix. 16.

16. *turn Thee unto me.* Everything depends
on whether God's face is turned towards him.
Without God there is no way to continue. No
man will come to his aid and he will not have
the strength to remain alive (Hirsch).

solitary. Friendless (Metsudath David). Being

18 See mine affliction and my
   travail;
   And forgive all my sins.

19 Consider how many are mine
   enemies,
   And the cruel hatred wherewith
   they hate me.

20 O keep my soul, and deliver me;
   Let me not be ashamed, for I
   have taken refuge in Thee.

21 Let integrity and uprightness
   preserve me,
   Because I wait for Thee.

22 Redeem Israel, O God,
   Out of all his troubles.

18 רְאֵה עָנְיִי וַעֲמָלִי
וְשָׂא לְכָל־חַטֹּאותָי:
19 רְאֵה־אֹיְבַי כִּי־רָבּוּ
וְשִׂנְאַת חָמָס שְׂנֵאוּנִי:
20 שָׁמְרָה נַפְשִׁי וְהַצִּילֵנִי
אַל־אֵבוֹשׁ כִּי־חָסִיתִי בָךְ:
21 תֹּם־וָיֹשֶׁר יִצְּרוּנִי
כִּי קִוִּיתִיךָ:
22 פְּדֵה אֱלֹהִים אֶת־יִשְׂרָאֵל
מִכֹּל צָרוֹתָיו:

king, I am responsible for the actions of all the people and am, therefore, in need of much grace (Rashi).

17. *troubles of my heart.* Worries and anxieties.

18. The acrostic requires this verse to begin with the letter *koph*; instead it and the next verse both begin with *resh*. Some conjecture that the acrostic is connected in the word *mimetzukothay* which contains both the *tzadey* and the *kuph*. Again, this is not certain.

seen mine affliction. Cf. ix. 14.

forgive. lit. 'lift up,' sin being thought of as a crushing burden. The Psalmist prays to be relieved of this load of sins from the conviction that they are the cause of his sufferings.

19. *cruel hatred.* Unjustified hatred (Rashi). Alternatively, 'hatred of violence'; i.e., they hate me as if I were a person of violence and cruelty (Metsudath David).

20. *keep my soul.* Protect me.

let me not be ashamed. By succumbing to my enemies in spite of reliance upon God's aid. Do not shame me by ignoring me, as I have relied entirely on your aid.

21. *let integrity and uprightness preserve me.* May my trusting heart and the sincerity of my actions prevent me from straying from the right path. As a result, my enemies will be prevented from causing me harm (Ibn Ezra).

wait for Thee. Or, 'place my hope in Thee,' as the Champion of the afflicted.

22 CONCLUDING PETITION

Like xxxiv, the Psalm adds a final verse to the acrostic beginning with the letter *pe*.

redeem Israel. The entire Psalm struck a personal note since his troubles came as a result of his actions as king (Daath Sofrim). Now David adds that he yearns for the redemption of all Israel (Ibn Ezra).

26

לְדָוִד ׀

1 [A Psalm] of David.
 Judge me, O LORD, for I have
  walked in mine integrity,
 And I have trusted in the LORD
  without wavering.

2 Examine me, O LORD, and try me;
 Test my reins and my heart.

3 For Thy mercy is before mine
  eyes;
 And I have walked in Thy truth.

4 I have not sat with men of falsehood;

שָׁפְטֵנִי יְהֹוָה כִּי־אֲנִי בְּתֻמִּי הָלַכְתִּי
וּבַיהֹוָה בָּטַחְתִּי לֹא אֶמְעָד:
2 בְּחָנֵנִי יְהֹוָה וְנַסֵּנִי
צָרְפָה כִלְיוֹתַי וְלִבִּי:
3 כִּי־חַסְדְּךָ לְנֶגֶד עֵינָי
וְהִתְהַלַּכְתִּי בַּאֲמִתֶּךָ:
4 לֹא־יָשַׁבְתִּי עִם־מְתֵי־שָׁוְא

PLEA OF THE UPRIGHT

DAVID's ambition in life was to attain the spiritual heights reached by his forefathers. He asks to
be tested by God so that he may prove his worth. He lists his achievements, which lay claim to
the fact that he has been an ardent follower of God and His precepts. He prays that he may not
suffer the fate of the godless evildoers. He ends with a request for moral support and is confident
that his pleas will not remain unanswered.

1–3 HIS PLEA TO BE JUDGED

1. *judge me.* Judge me so that my uprightness
may be made evident (Kimchi).

integrity. He does not claim never to have
sinned, but he has sincerely endeavoured to
conduct himself in accordance with God's laws
(cf. Hirsch).

without wavering. Under the strain of hard
experience and the mocking of unbelievers.

2. *examine me.* His conscience being clear, he
offers himself to God's penetrating scrutiny.

try me. Submit me to a test. The same verb is
used in *God did try Abraham* (Gen. xxii. 1).

reins ... heart. See on vii. 10.

3. *Thy mercy is before mine eyes.* Because he
ever kept the lovingkindness of God before his
mind, he was deterred from sinning and held to
the true path marked out by Him (Kimchi).

4-8 HIS SELF-VINDICATION

4. *I have not sat.* Recalls i. 1.

men of falsehood. lit. 'men of vanity,' who
pursued worthless aims instead of true ideals.

Neither will I go in with dissemblers.

5 I hate the gathering of evil-doers,
And will not sit with the wicked.

6 I will wash my hands in innocency;
So will I compass Thine altar, O
LORD,

7 That I may make the voice of
thanksgiving to be heard,
And tell of all Thy wondrous
works.

8 LORD, I love the habitation of
Thy house,
And the place where Thy glory
dwelleth.

9 Gather not my soul with sinners,
Nor my life with men of blood;

וְעִם נַעֲלָמִים לֹא אָבוֹא:

5 שָׂנֵאתִי קְהַל מְרֵעִים
וְעִם־רְשָׁעִים לֹא אֵשֵׁב:

6 אֶרְחַץ בְּנִקָּיוֹן כַּפָּי
וַאֲסֹבְבָה אֶת־מִזְבַּחֲךָ יְהוָה:

7 לִשְׁמִעַ בְּקוֹל תּוֹדָה
וּלְסַפֵּר כָּל־נִפְלְאוֹתֶיךָ:

8 יְהוָה אָהַבְתִּי מְעוֹן בֵּיתֶךָ
וּמְקוֹם מִשְׁכַּן כְּבוֹדֶךָ:

9 אַל־תֶּאֱסֹף עִם־חַטָּאִים נַפְשִׁי
וְעִם־אַנְשֵׁי דָמִים חַיָּי:

neither will I go in. Either 'enter their houses,' or a poetically shortened form of the idiom 'go in and come out with,' meaning association. The future tense contrasts with the past of *I have not sat.* The care he had hitherto taken to keep himself undefiled will be maintained by him in the days to come (Daath Sofrim).

dissemblers. lit. 'they who hide themselves,' who conceal their evil intentions behind an outward show of friendliness (Cf. Hirsch).

5. *gathering of evil-doers.* The kind of society he avoids. He unites himself with the *congregations* of God's worshippers (verse 12).

6. *wash my hands.* The priests were required to wash before entering the Tent of Meeting (Exod. xxx. 19f.). He will take care that his hands are unstained by misdeeds (Isa. i. 15f.), so that he is morally pure to bring up offerings (Kimchi).

compass Thine altar. Taking his place among those who offer sacrifices (Kimchi).

7. *voice of thanksgiving to be heard.* In public testimony of God's kindness to him (cf. Kimchi).

wondrous works. As in ix. 2.

8. *I love.* Contrast to *I hate* in verse 5. His delight is to seek communion with God in the Holy Place.

where Thy glory dwelleth. As symbolized by the Ark of the Covenant (see on xxiv. 7). More generally the words may be understood as: the place where man becomes conscious of God's glory.

9-12   HIS PRAYER RENEWED

9. David offers a petition that God not deal too harshly with him even if he is found to be lacking. He prays that since he is diametrically opposed to the evil people in heart and char-

10 אַשֶׁר־בִּידֵיהֶם זִמָּה
וִֽימִינָם מָֽלְאָה שֹּֽׁחַד:
11 וַֽאֲנִי בְּתֻמִּי אֵלֵךְ
פְּדֵנִי וְחָנֵּֽנִי:
12 רַגְלִי עָֽמְדָה בְמִישׁוֹר
בְּמַקְהֵלִים אֲבָרֵךְ יְהֹוָֽה:

acter, God should discriminate between him and them, so that he should not suffer their fate which will result from their sins (cf. Hirsch).

men of blood. Guilty of bloodshed (v. 7).

10. *craftiness.* Evil devices.

bribes. They plot maliciously to pervert justice and to corrupt the path of righteousness and this leads their right hand to be full of bribes (Meiri).

11. *but as for me.* He will have nothing to do with their corrupt methods but persist in his integrity.

I will walk. i.e. I will continue to walk in the path of righteousness, in spite of the severe trials to which my faith in God has been subjected.

redeem me. Deliver me from the fate of the wicked (Metsudath David). Alternatively, following on the previous verse, the meaning may be: the wicked are in a strong position because by bribery they can oppress the weak; I am at

their mercy by refusing to do the same; therefore I appeal to God to release me from danger (cf. Daath Sofrim).

be gracious unto me. Explained in iv. 2, by the addition of *and hear my prayer.*

12. *my foot standeth.* In the certainty that his supplication will be answered, he already sees himself standing *in an even place,* from which dangerous obstacles have been removed, offering thanks to God (cf. Hirsch).

an even place. I have not diverted my steps from following in the path of Your Torah (Meiri). When I shall have found firm footing, I shall have reached the goal of my endeavors (Hirsch).

congregation. Of the righteous (Targum). He will be publicly acknowledge his gratitude (Kimchi).

bless the Lord. For the mercies He displayed to me.

1 [A Psalm] of David.
The Lord is my light and my
salvation; whom shall I fear?
The Lord is the stronghold of my
life; of whom shall I be afraid?

2 When evil-doers came upon me to
eat up my flesh,
Even mine adversaries and my
foes, they stumbled and fell.

3 Though a host should encamp
against me,
My heart shall not fear;
Though war should rise up against
me,
Even then will I be confident.

4 One thing have I asked of the
Lord, that will I seek after:
That I may dwell in the house of
the Lord all the days of my
life,

כז

לְדָוִד ׀ °

יְהוָֹה ׀ אוֹרִי וְיִשְׁעִי מִמִּי אִירָא

יְהוָֹה ° מָעוֹז־חַיַּי מִמִּי אֶפְחָד ׃

2 בִּקְרֹב עָלַי ׀ מְרֵעִים

לֶאֱכֹל אֶת־בְּשָׂרִי

צָרַי וְאֹיְבַי לִי הֵמָּה כָשְׁלוּ וְנָפָלוּ ׃

3 אִם־תַּחֲנֶה עָלַי ׀ מַחֲנֶה לֹא־יִירָא לִבִּי

אִם־תָּקוּם עָלַי מִלְחָמָה

בְּזֹאת אֲנִי בוֹטֵחַ ׃

4 אַחַת ׀ שָׁאַלְתִּי מֵאֵת־יְהוָֹה

אוֹתָהּ אֲבַקֵּשׁ

שִׁבְתִּי בְּבֵית־יְהוָֹה כָּל־יְמֵי חַיַּי

HYMN OF CONFIDENCE

THIS is the third consecutive Psalm which has the prefix *of David* without the word 'mizmor.' It is another personal prayer for help and guidance, which at the same time expresses absolute trust in God and fearlessness from enemies. David's sole ambition is a personal relationship with God and this theme is stressed several times throughout the Psalm (verses 4-6). The composition falls into two distinct divisions. The first half is dedicated to the serenity of those who trust in God while the last verses show concern that without aid from God, his aims cannot be accomplished. In Jewish ritual (P.B., p. 85) this Psalm is recited daily throughout the month of *Elul* and the Ten Days of Penitence as preparation for the advent of the New Year and Day of Atonement. The *adversaries* (verse 12) are metaphorically interpreted as the promptings to sin from which deliverance is sought.

1-3 GOD HIS ALLY

1. *the Lord is my light.* He illuminates the way ahead, guiding me along the correct path of life, and floods my troubled life with brightness enabling me to find solutions to difficult problems (Daath Sofrim).

2. *evil-doers.* Goliath and the Philistines (Midrash Rabba Vayikra xxi. 2).

came upon me. Better, 'draw near against me' to attack.

to eat up my flesh. Like wild beasts devouring their prey (cf. vii. 3, xvii. 12).

stumbled ... fell. Better, 'stumble ... fall'; the prophetic perfect.

3. *even then.* lit. 'in this'; i.e., the conviction expressed in verse 1 (Rashi, Kimchi), or, in the following verse (Ibn Ezra).

4-6 GOD HIS PROTECTOR

4. *one thing.* Above all else.

dwell ... all the days of my life. The language is figurative. He longs is to be a perpetual guest of the Divine Host (see xxiii. 6), and enjoy spiritually rewarding existence wherever he may be (Hirsch).

To behold the graciousness of the
LORD, and to visit early in His
temple.

5 For He concealeth me in His
pavilion in the day of evil;
He hideth me in the covert of His
tent;
He lifteth me up upon a rock.

6 And now shall my head be lifted
up above mine enemies round
about me;
And I will offer in His tabernacle
sacrifices with trumpet-sound;
I will sing, yea, I will sing praises
unto the LORD.

7 Hear, O LORD, when I call with
my voice,
And be gracious unto me, and
answer me.

8 In Thy behalf my heart hath said:
'Seek ye My face';
Thy face, LORD, will I seek.

לַחֲזוֹת בְּנֹעַם־יְהוָה וּלְבַקֵּר בְּהֵיכָלוֹ:

5 כִּי יִצְפְּנֵנִי ׀ בְּסֻכֹּה בְּיוֹם רָעָה
יַסְתִּרֵנִי בְּסֵתֶר אָהֳלוֹ
בְּצוּר יְרוֹמְמֵנִי:

6 וְעַתָּה יָרוּם רֹאשִׁי
עַל אֹיְבַי סְבִיבוֹתַי
וְאֶזְבְּחָה בְאָהֳלוֹ זִבְחֵי תְרוּעָה
אָשִׁירָה וַאֲזַמְּרָה לַיהוָה:

7 שְׁמַע־יְהוָה קוֹלִי אֶקְרָא
וְחָנֵּנִי וַעֲנֵנִי:

8 לְךָ ׀ אָמַר לִבִּי בַּקְּשׁוּ פָנָי
אֶת־פָּנֶיךָ יְהוָה אֲבַקֵּשׁ:

v. 5. בסכו ק׳

---

graciousness. lit. 'pleasantness,' the feeling
of satisfaction which is to be derived from
sincere hospitality.

visit early. Rather, 'contemplate' (see Rashi),
meditate upon the thoughts which will be
aroused in his mind while being there.

temple. See on v. 8.

5. *pavilion*. In x. 9, used as a lion's lair, a
covert. The Tabernacle, though it be a simple
hut, is considered safe shelter for me for it
encompasses His presence even as it sur-
rounds my own person (Hirsch).

evil. Trouble and danger.

rock. A rocky fastness where he is secure from
attáck (Kimchi).

6. *my head be lifted up*. See on iii. 4. With
God as his Helper, he will have more than
protection. Victory will be his over the enemy.

tabernacle. lit. 'tent.'

sacrifices with trumpet-sound. Cf. Num. x. 10.
R.V. *sacrifices of joy* is preferable: sacrifices
accompanied by shouts of triumphant joy (see
xxxiii. 3).

7-14 CALL FOR HELP

7.   The change in tone is unmistakable. After
voicing his implicit trust in God, he is forced by
circumstances to face the realities of his
position. They are such as to induce in him a
mood of prayerfulness.

call with my voice. Cry aloud.

8.   *in Thy behalf*. Hebrew 'to Thee.' The
sense is: in my distress I hear the promptings
of my innermost self, and these are concerned with God Who urges man, when in
trouble, to turn to Him for relief.

9.   *in anger*. Were God to withhold His help,
it could only be understood as a sign of wrath.

9 Hide not Thy face from me;
Put not Thy servant away in
    anger;
Thou hast been my help;
Cast me not off, neither forsake
    me, O God of my salvation.

10 For though my father and my
    mother have forsaken me,
The LORD will take me up.

11 Teach me Thy way, O LORD;
And lead me in an even path,
Because of them that lie in wait
    for me.

12 Deliver me not over unto the will
    of mine adversaries;
For false witnesses are risen up
    against me, and such as breathe
    out violence.

13 If I had not believed to look upon
    the goodness of the LORD
In the land of the living!—

14 Wait for the LORD;
Be strong, and let thy heart take
    courage;
Yea, wait thou for the LORD.

‎9 אַל־תַּסְתֵּר פָּנֶיךָ ׀ מִמֶּנִּי
אַל־תַּט בְּאַף עַבְדֶּךָ עֶזְרָתִי הָיִיתָ
אַל־תִּטְּשֵׁנִי וְאַל־תַּעַזְבֵנִי
אֱלֹהֵי יִשְׁעִי׃
‎10 כִּי־אָבִי וְאִמִּי עֲזָבוּנִי
וַיהוָה יַאַסְפֵנִי׃
‎11 הוֹרֵנִי יְהוָה דַּרְכֶּךָ
וּנְחֵנִי בְּאֹרַח מִישׁוֹר לְמַעַן שׁוֹרְרָי׃
‎12 אַל־תִּתְּנֵנִי בְּנֶפֶשׁ צָרָי
כִּי קָמוּ־בִי עֵדֵי־שֶׁקֶר וִיפֵחַ חָמָס׃
‎13 לוּלֵא הֶאֱמַנְתִּי לִרְאוֹת
בְּטוּב־יְהוָה בְּאֶרֶץ חַיִּים׃
‎14 קַוֵּה אֶל־יְהוָה
חֲזַק וְיַאֲמֵץ לִבֶּךָ
וְקַוֵּה אֶל־יְהוָה׃

Thou hast been my help. In the past he possessed God's favour; he prays that he may have
done nothing to forfeit it now (Kimchi).

10. God's protective care of His creatures is
even more constant than that of parents for
their child. A parallel occurs in Isa. xlix. 15.

take me up. lit. 'gather me,' under His wings to
shield me.

11. *Thy way.* Preserve me in tranquility so
that I may have the time and peace of mind to
engage myself in Your service (Meiri).

12. *false witnesses.* He is the victim of a
campaign of slander with the object of inciting
Saul against him. Doeg the Edomite and the
residents of Ziph are two examples.

breathe out violence. Utter words to injure an
innocent man.

13. The complete thought of the sentence is
'My enemies would have destroyed me had I
not held fast to the faith that I would look upon
the goodness of God in the Next World' (Rashi,
Kimchi). Alternatively, 'If they had not risen
against me, I would have believed that God's
goodness can be experienced during my life on
earth, and not only after my departure from this
earth (Hirsch).

in the land of the living. This world as
against *Sheol* (cf. lii. 7, cxvi. 9) (cf. Hirsch) or
the Next World (Targum, Rashi).

14. *wait for the LORD.* He addresses the words
to himself. He must be patient and not despair
when Divine salvation tarries.

be strong ... take courage. A favourite combination in Hebrew. See xxxi. 25; Deut. xxxi.
7; Joshua i. 6ff.

28

כח

לְדָוִד

1 [A Psalm] of David.
Unto thee, O Lord, do I call;
My Rock, be not Thou deaf unto
    me;
Lest, if Thou be silent unto me,
I become like them that go down
    into the pit.

2 Hear the voice of my supplica-
    tions, when I cry unto Thee,
When I lift up my hands toward
    Thy holy Sanctuary.

3 Draw me not away with the
    wicked,
And with the workers of iniquity;
Who speak peace with their neigh-
    bours,
But evil is in their hearts.

4 Give them according to their
    deeds, and according to the
    evil of their endeavours;
Give them after the work of their
    hands;
Render to them their desert.

אֵלֶיךָ יְהֹוָה אֶקְרָא
צוּרִי אַל־תֶּחֱרַשׁ מִמֶּנִּי
פֶּן־תֶּחֱשֶׁה מִמֶּנִּי
וְנִמְשַׁלְתִּי עִם־יוֹרְדֵי בוֹר׃
2 שְׁמַע קוֹל תַּחֲנוּנַי בְּשַׁוְּעִי אֵלֶיךָ
בְּנָשְׂאִי יָדַי אֶל־דְּבִיר קָדְשֶׁךָ׃
3 אַל־תִּמְשְׁכֵנִי עִם־רְשָׁעִים
וְעִם־פֹּעֲלֵי אָוֶן
דֹּבְרֵי שָׁלוֹם עִם־רֵעֵיהֶם
וְרָעָה בִּלְבָבָם׃
4 תֶּן־לָהֶם כְּפָעֳלָם וּכְרֹעַ מַעַלְלֵיהֶם
כְּמַעֲשֵׂה יְדֵיהֶם תֵּן לָהֶם
הָשֵׁב גְּמוּלָם לָהֶם׃

PRAYER AND THANKSGIVING

This Psalm was written against those two-faced evil doers who pretended to be David's advisers
and covertly plotted malevolence against him.

1-2 INTRODUCTORY APPEAL

1. *Rock.* Hebrew, *tsur.* See on xviii. 3.

deaf. As in the English phrase 'turn a deaf
ear to.'

silent. Irresponsive to my appeal.

pit. The grave. God's silence would mean that
he was in disfavour with Him; and then, although living, he would be as though dead.
This line, repeated in cxliii. 7, is echoed in the
exquisite couplet of Jehudah Halevi:
When far from Thee, I die while yet in life;
But if I cling to Thee I live, though I should die.

2. *lift up my hands.* The gesture of prayer,
symbolizing the offering of the heart (cf. *let us
lift up our heart with our hands unto God in the
heavens,* Lam. iii. 41).

Thy holy Sanctuary. Hebrew, 'to the *debir* of
Thy Sanctuary,' i.e. the innermost part, the
Holy of Holies.

**3-5 MAY HIS FATE NOT BE THAT
OF THE WICKED**

3. *draw me not away.* If I am dragged into
their company, they will influence me with
their evil ideas and I will be condemned like
them. (cf. Rashi, Ibn Ezra).

evil in their hearts. Cf. xii. 3.

4. David did not personally take revenge but
prayed that evil doers receive retribution for
their evil ways. Since they intended to visit
harm on others, return to them their own just
deserts (Hirsch).

5. *works of the Lord.* Better, the 'acts of the
Lord'; i.e., His acts of judgment whereby the

5 Because they give no heed to the
   works of the LORD,
   Nor to the operation of His hands;
   He will break them down and not
   build them up.

6 Blessed be the LORD,
   Because He hath heard the voice
   of my supplications.

7 The LORD is my strength and my
   shield,
   In Him hath my heart trusted,
   And I am helped;
   Therefore my heart greatly re-
   joiceth,
   And with my song will I praise
   Him.

8 The LORD is a strength unto them;
   And He is a stronghold of salvation to His anointed.

9 Save Thy people, and bless Thine
   inheritance;
   And tend them, and carry them
   for ever.

כִּי לֹא יָבִינוּ אֶל־פְּעֻלֹּת יְהֹוָה 5
וְאֶל־מַעֲשֵׂה יָדָיו
יֶהֶרְסֵם וְלֹא יִבְנֵם:
בָּרוּךְ יְהֹוָה 6
כִּי־שָׁמַע קוֹל תַּחֲנוּנָי:
יְהֹוָה עֻזִּי וּמָגִנִּי 7
בּוֹ בָטַח לִבִּי וְנֶעֱזָרְתִּי
וַיַּעֲלֹז לִבִּי וּמִשִּׁירִי אֲהוֹדֶנּוּ:
יְהֹוָה עֹז־לָמוֹ 8
וּמָעוֹז יְשׁוּעוֹת מְשִׁיחוֹ הוּא:
הוֹשִׁיעָה אֶת־עַמֶּךָ 9
וּבָרֵךְ אֶת־נַחֲלָתֶךָ
וּרְעֵם וְנַשְּׂאֵם עַד־הָעוֹלָם:

wicked are given their due punishment
(Metsudath David).

operation of His hands. The marvels of Creation which should direct the mind of man to
such thoughts as are specified in Ps. viii
(Kimchi).

break them down. Cf. Jer. xxiv. 6.

6-7 HIS PRAYER HEARD

6. *blessed be the LORD*. A prophecy—God will
be thanked; deliverance will come (Kimchi).

7. *my strength*. As in the song at the Red Sea
(Exod. xv. 2).

shield. Cf. iii. 4.

greatly rejoiceth. The same word translated
exulteth in Hannah's prayer (1 Sam. ii. 1).

8-9 PRAYER FOR THE PEOPLE

8. The climactic thought is for the people's
welfare (Kimchi).

unto them. Most commentators take the suffix
'*lamo*' as a plural: *them*. Ibn Ezra remarks that
this may be a contraction of the word
'l'ammo,'—to His nation. Hirsch, however,
renders 'the LORD, His is the power which none
is able to overcome.'

His anointed. The king. David refers to himself
in this indirect manner (Kimchi, Meiri).

9. *Thine inheritance*. The community of Israel (cf. *a people of inheritance*, Deut. iv. 20).

tend them. lit. 'shepherd them.' Cf. xxiii. 1.

carry them. As a shepherd carries a tired or
lame sheep (Isa. xl. 11). (Cf. Ibn Ezra).

PSALM XXIX

29

1 A Psalm of David.
> Ascribe unto the LORD, O ye sons
> of might,
> Ascribe unto the LORD glory and
> strength.

2 Ascribe unto the LORD the glory
> due unto His name;
> Worship the LORD in the beauty
> of holiness.

3 The voice of the LORD is upon the
> waters;
> The God of glory thundereth,
> Even the LORD upon many waters.

4 The voice of the LORD is powerful;
> The voice of the LORD is full of
> majesty.

כט

מִזְמוֹר לְדָוִד

הָבוּ לַיהוָה בְּנֵי אֵלִים
הָבוּ לַיהוָה כָּבוֹד וָעֹז:

2 הָבוּ לַיהוָה כְּבוֹד שְׁמוֹ
הִשְׁתַּחֲווּ לַיהוָה בְּהַדְרַת־קֹדֶשׁ:

3 קוֹל יְהוָה עַל־הַמָּיִם
אֵל־הַכָּבוֹד הִרְעִים
יְהוָה עַל־מַיִם רַבִּים:

4 קוֹל־יְהוָה בַּכֹּחַ
קוֹל יְהוָה בֶּהָדָר:

A STORM PICTURE

A THRILLING description of a storm—a verbal symphony in which the shattering peals of thunder, reverberating around the hills, are reproduced in words with realistic effect. The thunderclaps are interpreted as the majestic voice of God. The two opening verses resemble the song David sang while carrying the Holy Ark from the house of Obed-Edom to its permanent sanctuary in Jerusalem (cf. 1 Chron. xvi. 28-29). This Psalm is included in the Sabbath liturgy (P.B., pp. 111, 157). According to the Talmud, (Berachoth 29a) the seven Sabbath-benedictions (P.B., pp. 136-142) correspond to the seven 'voices of the LORD' contained in the Psalm. The Rabbis explains the three closing verses (Tal. Zev. 116a) as referring to the Divine revelation at Mt. Sinai.

1-2 PRELUDE

1. *sons of might.* Hebrew 'sons of the mighty.' The same phrase occurs in lxxxix. 7, where the parallelism shows that the angelic hosts are intended (cf. Targum). They are invoked to join the terrestrial chorus acknowledging God's majesty as revealed in the mighty forces of nature. The Midrash suggests that the allusion is to the Patriarchs who were powerful in their faith.

glory ... strength. Cf. lxviii. 35.

2. *beauty of holiness.* Again in xcvi. 9 where it is used of human worshippers. The Hebrew is best translated 'in holy adornment.' The priests who ministered in the Tabernacle wore *holy garments for splendour and for beauty* (Exod. xxviii. 2); and so all who would wor-

ship God, whether men or angels, must be suitably attired (cf. Tal. Ber 30b).

3–9 THE SEVEN 'VOICES'

3. *voice of the LORD.* Thunder is so designated in xviii. 14.

upon the waters. Either the gathering of waters and storm-clouds in the heavens (xviii. 12), or the sea in the west from which direction the storm usually comes to the Holy Land.

God of glory. Cf. *King of glory* (xxiv. 7ff.).

many waters. Or, 'vast waters.'

4. *powerful ... full of majesty.* lit. 'with power ... with majesty,' a description of the awesome power of God as revealed at Sinai (cf. Rashi).

5. *cedars.* Used to described the princes of

5 The voice of the LORD breaketh
    the cedars;
  Yea, the LORD breaketh in pieces
    the cedars of Lebanon.

6 He maketh them also to skip like
    a calf;
  Lebanon and Sirion like a young
    wild-ox.

7 The voice of the LORD heweth out
    flames of fire.

8 The voice of the LORD shaketh the
    wilderness;
  The LORD shaketh the wilderness
    of Kadesh.

9 The voice of the LORD maketh the
    hinds to calve,
  And strippeth the forests bare;
  And in His temple all say: 'Glory.'

10 The LORD sat enthroned at the
    flood;
  Yea, the LORD sitteth as King for
    ever.

11 The LORD will give strength unto
    His people;
  The LORD will bless His people
    with peace.

5 קוֹל יְהוָה שֹׁבֵר אֲרָזִים
וַיְשַׁבֵּר יְהוָה אֶת־אַרְזֵי הַלְּבָנוֹן׃

6 וַיַּרְקִידֵם כְּמוֹ־עֵגֶל
לְבָנוֹן וְשִׂרְיֹן כְּמוֹ בֶן־רְאֵמִים׃

7 קוֹל־יְהוָה חֹצֵב לַהֲבוֹת אֵשׁ׃

8 קוֹל יְהוָה יָחִיל מִדְבָּר
יָחִיל יְהוָה מִדְבַּר קָדֵשׁ׃

9 קוֹל יְהוָה יְחוֹלֵל אַיָּלוֹת
וַיֶּחֱשֹׂף יְעָרוֹת
וּבְהֵיכָלוֹ כֻּלּוֹ אֹמֵר כָּבוֹד׃

10 יְהוָה לַמַּבּוּל יָשָׁב
וַיֵּשֶׁב יְהוָה מֶלֶךְ לְעוֹלָם׃

11 יְהוָה עֹז לְעַמּוֹ יִתֵּן
יְהוָה יְבָרֵךְ אֶת־עַמּוֹ בַשָּׁלוֹם׃

the nations who considered themselves mighty.
As enemies of the LORD, they are devastated by
His voice as were the Philistines in 1 Samuel vii.
10, 'And God thundered at them with a great
noise.' (Cf. also Isa. xxx. 30, 31) (Rashi).
Lebanon's mountain range in the north of the
Holy Land was famed for its cedars.

6. *maketh them.* The mountains which leap
in terror at the peals of thunder.

Sirion. Ancient name of Mt. Lebanon (see
Deut. iii. 9), the highest mountain in the land.

7. *flames of fire.* The forked lightnings which
shoot through the dark mass of cloud as they
did at Mt. Sinai (Rashi).

8. *wilderness of Kadesh.* (Cf. Num. xx. 16).
One of the names designated to describe the
Sinai desert (Rashi).

9. *hinds to calve.* This actually happens during a violent storm when terror causes animals
to give birth prematurely (cf. Hirsch).

strippeth. Just as trees fall under the battering
of wind and rain (Kimchi), so will the wicked

be stripped of their power and glory (Rashi).

His temple. The heavenly region where the angels, called upon to witness the awe-inspiring
spectacle, unanimously exclaim *Glory* to express their feeling of wonderment (cf. Isa. vi. 3).

10-11   GOD IN HIS MAJESTY

10. The storm having subsided, the Psalmist
meditates upon the phenomenon. It first recalls
to him the deluge which once overwhelmed the
earth (Gen. vi.) (cf. Rashi).

King for ever. As He was the Judge in that
remote period of human history, so is He
always the Judge, holding the fate of the world
in His hand (Rashi).

11. Not only is the infinite might of God
called to mind by such an experience, but also
His graciousness. Though the wicked will be
harshly dealt with, the people of Israel who are
faithful to God will be blessed with peace in the
days of the Messiah (cf. Kimchi). The symphony which had swelled to an ear-shattering
crescendo ends in the softest pianissimo.

30

1 A Psalm; a Song at the Dedication of the House; of David.

2 I will extol Thee, O LORD, for
Thou hast raised me up,
And hast not suffered mine
enemies to rejoice over me.

3 O LORD my God,
I cried unto Thee, and Thou didst
heal me;

4 O LORD, Thou broughtest up my
soul from the nether-world;

מִזְמוֹר שִׁיר־חֲנֻכַּת הַבַּיִת לְדָוִד׃

2 אֲרוֹמִמְךָ יְהוָה כִּי דִלִּיתָנִי
וְלֹא־שִׂמַּחְתָּ אֹיְבַי לִי׃

3 יְהוָה אֱלֹהָי
שִׁוַּעְתִּי אֵלֶיךָ וַתִּרְפָּאֵנִי׃

4 יְהוָה הֶעֱלִיתָ מִן־שְׁאוֹל נַפְשִׁי

THANKSGIVING FOR DELIVERANCE

IF this Psalm is considered apart from the title in the first verse, the theme is akin to that of Psalm VI and the personal character is strongly marked. It is a fervent hymn of gratitude for redemption from a danger which threatened imminent death, possibly a grave illness. It stresses weakness in spiritual matters and contains a plea for the forgiveness of sins, so that one's spirit may be revived. What, then, is its connection with the superscription:—*A Psalm—a Song at the Dedication of the House of David?* These words suggest that although the Psalm contains no reference to the Temple at all, it was composed by David for the future dedication of Solomon's Temple. David's enemies had predicted that his dynasty would not continue because of the incident with Bath-Sheba. When he was prophetically informed that his son Solomon, born from Bath-Sheba, would merit the task of building the Temple and inaugurating it, he knew that he was forgiven, and he then composed this Psalm out of gratitude for the cure for his soul (Kimchi). Later the Psalm was selected for use at the dedication of the Second Temple and subsequently at its rededication by the Maccabees. In addition to being recited daily as an overture to the *pesukei dezimra,* Songs of Praise, a Rabbinical source mentions its recital in connection with kindling of the lights on the Feast of Dedication (*Chanukah*), and the practice remains in the Jewish liturgy (P.B., p. 274).

2-6 GRATITUDE FOR RECOVERY

2. *Thou hast raised me up.* The Hebrew verb is commonly used in connection with drawing water from a well. He had been at the point of death, had descended almost to *Sheol* (verse 4); but God drew him up again and revived his soul.

hast not suffered mine enemies to rejoice. His fate would have gladdened the hearts of his ill wishers. It is interesting to note that for the moment he makes no mention of rejoicing. Since he was not the one chosen to build the Temple, he could not claim to be joyous (Daath Sofrim).

3. *heal.* Probably to be understood as recovery from a spiritual depression and being saved from punishment in the World to Come (Kimchi).

4. *Thou broughtest up my soul from the nether-world.* His condition had been so seri-

Thou didst keep me alive, that I
should not go down to the pit.

5 Sing praise unto the LORD, O ye
His godly ones,
And give thanks to His holy name.

6 For His anger is but for a moment,
His favour is for a life-time;
Weeping may tarry for the night,
But joy cometh in the morning.

7 Now I had said in my security:
'I shall never be moved.'

8 Thou hadst established, O LORD,
in Thy favour my mountain as
a stronghold—
Thou didst hide Thy face; I was
affrighted.

חִיִּיתַנִי מִיָּרְדִי בוֹר׃

5 זַמְּרוּ לַיהוָה חֲסִידָיו
וְהוֹדוּ לְזֵכֶר קָדְשׁוֹ׃

6 כִּי רֶגַע ׀ בְּאַפּוֹ חַיִּים בִּרְצוֹנוֹ
בָּעֶרֶב יָלִין בֶּכִי
וְלַבֹּקֶר רִנָּה׃

7 וַאֲנִי אָמַרְתִּי בְשַׁלְוִי
בַּל־אֶמּוֹט לְעוֹלָם׃

8 יְהוָה בִּרְצוֹנְךָ הֶעֱמַדְתָּה לְהַרְרִי עֹז
הִסְתַּרְתָּ פָנֶיךָ הָיִיתִי נִבְהָל׃

v. 4. מירדי ק׳

ous that he actually thought of himself as
already in *Sheol*; he thanks God for having
brought him up from that dark region.

that I should not go down to the pit. This
translation follows the *kerë*. The *kethib* resembles the phrase in xxviii. 1, and has the
meaning: 'Thou hast revived me from among
them that go down to the pit,' i.e. he was on his
way to the grave with other dying men, but God
spared his life.

5. *sing praise*. As in ix. 12, xxii. 24, he calls
upon all who trust in God to join him in
thanksgiving. His experience was confirmation that ultimately God saves His devoted
from initial drawbacks (Ibn Ezra).

to His holy name. lit. 'to the memorial of His
holiness.' For the identity of 'name' with 'memorial,' cf. Exod. iii. 15. In the recounting of
the favours which He does with man, is thanks
given to His name (Malbim).

6. *His anger ... for a moment*. lit. 'a moment in His anger,' which probably means: in
His anger man undergoes only momentary
suffering, because He is quick to relent

(Kimchi).

His favours are for a life-time. lit. 'life in His
favour'; when man possesses His favour, he
enjoys long life in His presence (Rashi) and
spiritual happiness (xvi. 11).

may tarry for the night. The beautiful rendering does not bring out the force of the original
which is 'comes to lodge in the evening.'
Weeping is likened to a passing traveller who
arrives at dusk to spend the night in a place of
shelter and proceeds on his way in the morning.

but joy cometh in the morning. lit. 'but in the
morning there is a ringing cry of joy.' As soon
as he repented, he was immediately accepted
back into His grace (Metsudath David).

7-11 HE RELATES HIS EXPERIENCE

7. *now I had said*. The subject is emphasized:
'As for me, I (once) said.' He recalls a time
when, like the ungodly, he had been so self-
confident as to think that he could be independent of God's care (cf. x. 6.).

8. *my mountain as a stronghold*. lit. 'strength

9 Unto Thee, O Lord, did I call,
  And unto the Lord I made sup-
      plication:

10 'What profit is there in my blood,
      when I go down to the pit?
    Shall the dust praise Thee? shall
      it declare Thy truth?

11 Hear, O Lord, and be gracious
      unto me;
    Lord, be Thou my helper.'

12 Thou didst turn for me my
      mourning into dancing;
    Thou didst loose my sackcloth,
      and gird me with gladness;

13 So that my glory may sing praise
      to Thee, and not be silent;
    O Lord my God, I will give
      thanks unto Thee for ever.

9 אֵלֶיךָ יְהוָה אֶקְרָא
  וְאֶל־אֲדֹנָי אֶתְחַנָּן׃
10 מַה־בֶּצַע בְּדָמִי בְּרִדְתִּי אֶל־שָׁחַת
   הֲיוֹדְךָ עָפָר הֲיַגִּיד אֲמִתֶּךָ׃
11 שְׁמַע־יְהוָה וְחָנֵּנִי
   יְהוָה הֱיֵה־עֹזֵר לִי׃
12 הָפַכְתָּ מִסְפְּדִי לְמָחוֹל לִי
   פִּתַּחְתָּ שַׂקִּי וַתְּאַזְּרֵנִי שִׂמְחָה׃
13 לְמַעַן ׀ יְזַמֶּרְךָ כָבוֹד וְלֹא יִדֹּם
   יְהוָה אֱלֹהַי לְעוֹלָם אוֹדֶךָּ׃

for my mountain.' Hirsch suggests 'my ascent
to power.' The general sense is: when all was
well with me, I was unconscious of the truth
that the strength and security of which I boasted
had been bestowed upon me by God in His
favour; but I was suddenly brought to a realization of this fact.

Thou didst hide Thy face. He was smitten with
illness, which was a sign that God's favour had
been withdrawn (Malbim).

I was affrighted. The same word as in vi. 3, 4,
11. Awaking to the reality of his position, he
was overcome with terror.

9. *did I call … I made supplication.* The verbs
are in the imperfect mode: I keep on calling …
I make supplication. Or it may signify the
resolve which then came to his heart: (then I
said) *Unto Thee, O Lord, will I call.*

10. *what profit is there in my blood?* What
advantage would God have in slaying me,
seeing that in death man can no longer praise

Him? (Malbim). Alternatively, of what use is
my life on this earth, if I am destined to descend
to *Sheol* instead of receiving a share in the
World to Come (Kimchi). A similar plea was
used by Hezekiah in his illness (Isa. xxxviii.
18f.)

the dust. The grave, as in xxii. 16, 30.

Thy truth. God's faithfulness which is the theme
of the praises offered by the pious.

11. *Lord, be Thou my helper.* Human aid is
of no avail; He alone can restore him to life.
Through suffering he grasped the truth which
had slipped from his mind in the days of well-
being.

12-13 HIS PRAYER ANSWERED

12. He comes to the realization that what was
thought to be a source of sorrow turned out to
be of the most blissful import. The suffering he
had endured prevented his moral stagnation
(Hirsch).

לְמְנַצֵּחַ מִזְמוֹר לְדָוִד:

2 בְּךָ־יְהוָה חָסִיתִי
אַל־אֵבוֹשָׁה לְעוֹלָם
בְּצִדְקָתְךָ פַלְּטֵנִי:

3 הַטֵּה אֵלַי ׀ אָזְנְךָ מְהֵרָה הַצִּילֵנִי
הֱיֵה לִי ׀ לְצוּר־מָעוֹז
לְבֵית מְצוּדוֹת לְהוֹשִׁיעֵנִי:

4 כִּי־סַלְעִי וּמְצוּדָתִי אָתָּה
וּלְמַעַן שִׁמְךָ תַּנְחֵנִי וּתְנַהֲלֵנִי:

5 תּוֹצִיאֵנִי מֵרֶשֶׁת זוּ טָמְנוּ לִי
כִּי אַתָּה מָעוּזִּי:

1 For the **Leader**. A Psalm of David.

2 In Thee, O LORD, have I taken refuge; let me never be ashamed;
Deliver me in Thy righteousness.

3 Incline Thine ear unto me, deliver me speedily;
Be Thou to me a rock of refuge, even a fortress of defence, to save me.

4 For Thou art my rock and my fortress;
Therefore for Thy name's sake lead me and guide me.

5 Bring me forth out of the net that they have hidden for me;
For Thou art my stronghold.

FAITH OF THE PERSECUTED

THE familiar theme of the straits of the innocent is the *motif* of this Psalm. As a Davidic composition it finds its background in the wilderness of Maon (1 Sam. xxiii. 25). The clause *David made haste to get away* (ibid. 26) is comparable to verse 23 of the Psalm, *I said in my haste*. Some verses, however, are not based on any historical event. These were written for the benefit of anyone who might find himself surrounded by enemies and deems it necessary to reaffirm his belief that God can extricate him from any predicament. This Psalm, like others before it, ends with David's thanks to God for having accepted his supplications.

2-9 PRAYER OF FAITH

2. *let me never be ashamed*. See on xxv. 2. The opening of this Psalm is almost identical with that of lxxi.

in Thy righteousness. Being a generous Judge, He vindicates even those who are not entirely deserving (Metsudath David, Malbim).

Incline Thine ear unto me. Finding himself in dire straits, only the speedy intervention of God can help him (Hirsch).

Be Thou to me a rock of refuge, etc. David asks that God serve not only as a rock for temporary refuge, but as a permanent fortress (Daath Sofrim).

4. *lead me and guide me*. Better, 'Thou wilt lead … guide.' This is not a petition but a confident assertion that God will be a fortress to those in danger.

5. *bring me forth*. Here also the rendering should be: 'Thou wilt bring me forth.'

net. Cf. ix. 16, xxv. 15.

6. *unto Thy hand I commit my spirit*. The theme of the concluding lines of the Synagogue hymn, *Adon Olam* (*P.B.*, p. 3). *Spirit* is the breath of life (cxlvi. 4); he entrusts his life into God's keeping.

Thou hast redeemed me. In the past; that is why I put my trust in Thee now (Daath Sofrim).

6 Into Thy hand I commit my spirit;
  Thou hast redeemed me, O Lord,
  Thou God of truth.

7 I hate them that regard lying
  vanities;
  But I trust in the Lord.

8 I will be glad and rejoice in Thy
  lovingkindness;
  For Thou hast seen mine affliction,
  Thou hast taken cognizance of the
  troubles of my soul,

9 And Thou hast not given me over
  into the hand of the enemy;
  Thou hast set my feet in a broad
  place.

10 Be gracious unto me, O Lord,
   for I am in distress;
   Mine eye wasteth away with
   vexation, yea, my soul and my
   body.

11 For my life is spent in sorrow,
   and my years in sighing;
   My strength faileth because of
   mine iniquity, and my bones
   are wasted away.

6 בְּיָדְךָ֘ אַפְקִ֪יד ר֫וּחִ֥י

פָּדִ֖יתָה אוֹתִ֥י יְהֹוָ֗ה אֵ֣ל אֱמֶֽת׃

7 שָׂנֵ֗אתִי הַשֹּׁמְרִ֥ים הַבְלֵי־שָׁ֑וְא

וַ֝אֲנִ֗י אֶל־יְהֹוָ֥ה בָּטָֽחְתִּי׃

8 אָגִ֥ילָה וְאֶשְׂמְחָ֗ה בְּחַ֫סְדֶּ֥ךָ

אֲשֶׁ֣ר רָ֭אִיתָ אֶת־עָנְיִ֑י

יָ֝דַ֗עְתָּ בְּצָר֥וֹת נַפְשִֽׁי׃

9 וְלֹ֣א הִ֭סְגַּרְתַּנִי בְּיַד־אוֹיֵ֑ב

הֶעֱמַ֖דְתָּ בַמֶּרְחָ֣ב רַגְלָֽי׃

10 חָנֵּ֥נִי יְהֹוָה֮ כִּ֤י צַ֫ר־לִ֥י

עָשְׁשָׁ֖ה בְכַ֥עַס עֵינִ֗י נַפְשִׁ֥י וּבִטְנִֽי׃

11 כִּ֤י כָל֣וּ בְיָג֣וֹן חַיַּי֮

וּשְׁנוֹתַ֢י בַּאֲנָ֫חָ֥ה

כָּשַׁ֣ל בַּעֲוֺנִ֣י כֹחִ֑י

וַעֲצָמַ֥י עָשֵֽׁשׁוּ׃

God of truth. Faithful to keep His promises.

7. *lying in vanities.* False gods (Jonah ii. 9 f.), in contrast to the *God of truth* (Rashi).

8. *I will be glad.* Not 'let me be glad,' but an expression of trust.

troubles of my soul. The dangers which surround him, not his spiritual disquiet (cf. Malbim).

9. *in a broad place.* See on iv. 2.

10-19 HIS PRESENT DISTRESS

10. The sharp change of tone at this point is obvious. His faith in God has the effect of heightening his appreciation of the plight he is in. He describes his predicament in poignant words to plead his cause before the Throne of Mercy. The language recalls Ps. vi.

mine eye wasteth away. Cf. vi. 8.

my soul and my body. Suffering has affected him spiritually and physically (Hirsch). Alternatively, 'my soul' means my heart's desire (Kimchi, Metsudath Zion).

11. *signing.* Groaning, as in vi. 7.

mine iniquity. Suffering being generally the consequence of sin, the Psalmist assumes that he has done wrong, although he may be unconscious of it.

12 Because of all mine adversaries I
   am become a reproach,
   Yea, unto my neighbours exceedingly, and a dread to mine
   acquaintance;
   They that see me without flee
   from me.

13 I am forgotten as a dead man out
   of mind;
   I am like a useless vessel.

14 For I have heard the whispering
   of many,
   Terror on every side;
   While they took counsel together
   against me,
   They devised to take away my
   life.

15 But as for me, I have trusted in
   Thee, O LORD;
   I have said: 'Thou art my God.'

16 My times are in Thy hand;
   Deliver me from the hand of mine
   enemies, and from them that
   persecute me.

17 Make Thy face to shine upon
   Thy servant;
   Save me in Thy lovingkindness.

18 O LORD, let me not be ashamed,
   for I have called upon Thee;
   Let the wicked be ashamed, let
   them be put to silence in the
   nether-world.

12 מִכָּל־צֹרְרַי הָיִיתִי חֶרְפָּה
וְלִשְׁכֵנַי ׀ מְאֹד וּפַחַד לִמְיֻדָּעָי
רֹאַי בַּחוּץ נָדְדוּ מִמֶּנִּי׃
13 נִשְׁכַּחְתִּי כְּמֵת מִלֵּב
הָיִיתִי כִּכְלִי אֹבֵד׃
14 כִּי שָׁמַעְתִּי ׀ דִּבַּת רַבִּים
מָגוֹר מִסָּבִיב
בְּהִוָּסְדָם יַחַד עָלַי
לָקַחַת נַפְשִׁי זָמָמוּ׃
15 וַאֲנִי ׀ עָלֶיךָ בָטַחְתִּי יְהוָה
אָמַרְתִּי אֱלֹהַי אָתָּה׃
16 בְּיָדְךָ עִתֹּתָי
הַצִּילֵנִי מִיַּד־אוֹיְבַי וּמֵרֹדְפָי׃
17 הָאִירָה פָנֶיךָ עַל־עַבְדֶּךָ
הוֹשִׁיעֵנִי בְחַסְדֶּךָ׃
18 יְהוָה אַל־אֵבוֹשָׁה כִּי קְרָאתִיךָ
יֵבֹשׁוּ רְשָׁעִים יִדְּמוּ לִשְׁאוֹל׃

12. *reproach.* An object of scorn.

unto my neighbours. With whom he had close
personal contact; even they have been reproached for associating with him (Malbim).

a dread. They fear to acknowledge him in a
friendly manner because it would draw upon
them the displeasure of his powerful enemies
(Malbim).

they that see me without. Casual beholders who
know nothing about him turn away since they
are aware that he is a marked man (Malbim).

13. *forgotten as a dead man.* Nobody cares
about him; he has passed completely out of
mind (Malbim).

useless vessel. lit. 'a perishing vessel,' a broken potsherd which is thrown away.

14. *for I have heard the whispering of many.*
Both clause and the next one formed part of
Jeremiah's plaint (Jer. xx. 10). *Whispering*
means a campaign of slander (Metsudath Zion).

15. *but as for me.* Because men look away
from me, all the more do I look towards God for
safety.

16. *my times.* The varying fortunes of life; all
are under God's control (Rashi).

17. *make Thy face to shine.* Cf. iv. 7.

18. *let me not be ashamed.* The opening prayer
of the Psalm is repeated.

be put to silence. As long as they live, they are
a source of mischief; if brought down to *Sheol*
their power of doing harm will cease.

19 Let the lying lips be dumb,
Which speak arrogantly against
the righteous,
With pride and contempt.

20 Oh how abundant is Thy goodness, which Thou hast laid up
for them that fear Thee;
Which Thou hast wrought for
them that take their refuge in
Thee, in the sight of the sons
of men!

21 Thou hidest them in the covert of
Thy presence from the plot-
tings of man;
Thou concealest them in a pavilion from the strife of tongues.

22 Blessed be the LORD;
For He hath shown me His wondrous lovingkindness in an
entrenched city.

23 As for me, I said in my haste:
'I am cut off from before Thine
eyes';
Nevertheless Thou heardest the
voice of my supplications when
I cried unto Thee.

24 O love the LORD, all ye His godly
ones;
The LORD preserveth the faithful,
And plentifully repayeth him
that acteth haughtily.

25 Be strong, and let your heart
take courage,
All ye that wait for the LORD.

19 תֵּאָלַמְנָה שִׂפְתֵי שָׁקֶר
הַדֹּבְרוֹת עַל־צַדִּיק עָתָק
בְּגַאֲוָה וָבוּז:
20 מָה רַב־טוּבְךָ אֲשֶׁר־צָפַנְתָּ לִּירֵאֶיךָ
פָּעַלְתָּ לַחוֹסִים בָּךְ נֶגֶד בְּנֵי אָדָם:
21 תַּסְתִּירֵם בְּסֵתֶר פָּנֶיךָ מֵרֻכְסֵי־אִישׁ
תִּצְפְּנֵם בְּסֻכָּה מֵרִיב לְשֹׁנוֹת:
22 בָּרוּךְ יְהוָה
כִּי הִפְלִיא חַסְדּוֹ לִי בְּעִיר מָצוֹר:
23 וַאֲנִי אָמַרְתִּי בְחָפְזִי
נִגְרַזְתִּי מִנֶּגֶד עֵינֶיךָ
אָכֵן שָׁמַעְתָּ קוֹל תַּחֲנוּנַי
בְּשַׁוְּעִי אֵלֶיךָ:
24 אֶהֱבוּ אֶת־יְהוָה כָּל־חֲסִידָיו
אֱמוּנִים נֹצֵר יְהוָה
וּמְשַׁלֵּם עַל־יֶתֶר עֹשֵׂה גַאֲוָה:
25 חִזְקוּ וְיַאֲמֵץ לְבַבְכֶם
כָּל־הַמְיַחֲלִים לַיהוָה:

20-25 PRAISE FOR DELIVERANCE

20. After a plaintive interlude, the song of hope and gratitude is resumed.

in the sight of the sons of men. The words are to be connected with *wrought.* God publicly bestows His bounty upon the faithful (Kimchi).

21. *in … Thy presence.* Which affords protection from the evil schemings of man.

pavilion. Cf. xxvii. 5, but here the thought is idealized. No material refuge is meant, but the security of God's Presence.

strife for tongues. Viz. *the whispering of many* (verse 14).

22. *in an entrenched city.* A city under siege; probably an allusion to Keilah which was surrounded by Saul (cf. 1 Sam. xxiii. 11) (Rashi, Malbim).

23. *haste.* Rather, 'alarm.' In a moment of panic he fell into a state of despair. Even then his faith triumphed and he called upon God for help (see introduction).

24. *O love the LORD.* As in xxx. 5, he bids the Godly take heart from his tribulations and the Divine aid which came to him (cf. Kimchi).

repayeth. God's justice reveals itself both in the protection of the good and the condemna-tion of the wicked.

1 [A Psalm] of David. Maschil.
Happy is he whose transgression is
forgiven, whose sin is pardoned

2 Happy is the man unto whom the
LORD counteth not iniquity,
And in whose spirit there is no
guile.

3 When I kept silence, my bones
wore away
Through my groaning all the day
long.

לְדָוִד מַשְׂכִּיל
אַשְׁרֵי נְשׂוּי־פֶּשַׁע כְּסוּי חֲטָאָה׃
2 אַשְׁרֵי־אָדָם לֹא יַחְשֹׁב יְהֹוָה לוֹ עָוֹן
וְאֵין בְּרוּחוֹ רְמִיָּה׃
3 כִּי הֶחֱרַשְׁתִּי בָּלוּ עֲצָמָי
בְּשַׁאֲגָתִי כָּל־הַיּוֹם׃

HAPPINESS OF THE FORGIVEN

A POEM of deep religious and psychological importance. It tells of the serious consequences,
physical and mental, which may follow in the aftermath of sin. The main message is one of
optimism—that forgiveness is available for those who are sincere and show deep sorrow for
their wrongdoings. The highest form of purification is described in verse 2 as being attained
by the man who has been completely vindicated by God. A similar experience is attainable
for all men on the holiest day of the year, Yom Kippur (see Lev. xvi. 30). Many commentators
connect the Psalm with the episode of David and Bath-Sheba. They point to verse 5 in which
David, having admitted his guilt (2 Sam. xii. 13), is assured by Nathan the prophet that his
transgression has been forgiven.

1. *Maschil.* Used in the title of thirteen Psalms.
In form it corresponds to the word in verse 8, *I
will instruct thee*, and has accordingly been
understood as a didactic poem (see Ibn Ezra,
Metsudath David, Tal. Pes. 117a). But such a
definition does not suit all the Psalms which
have the heading. In xlvii. 8 occurs the phrase
Sing ye praises in a skilful song (*maschil*),
which seems to indicate a special kind of
musical instrument which had the power to
stimulate the mind, enabling it to better comprehend what had been heard (Meiri).

happy. See on i. 1.

forgiven. lit. 'lifted up.' Sin is a burden upon
the soul; forgiveness is relief from the load.

pardoned. lit. 'covered,' by his numerous merits, so that the offence is no longer seen by the
Judge for His condemnation (Kimchi).

2 HAPPY IS THE PARDONED SINNER

no guile. An essential qualification for pardon.
The sinner must be filled with genuine remorse
and sincere penitence. But the words are to be
connected with *happy is he* and describe the
blessed state of the man who has rid himself of
every trace of sin and is able to enter into
uninterrupted fellowship with God.

3-4 HIS DISTRESS BEFORE CONFESSION

3. *when I kept silence.* At first he stilled the
voice of conscience which warned him of the
sin he had committed. He refused to acknowledge his guilt even to himself, much less to
God (cf. Rashi).

my bones wore away. The conflict within
himself, coupled with endless worrying, created a disturbed state of mind which affected
his physical condition (cf. Kimchi).

4 For day and night Thy hand was
    heavy upon me;
    My sap was turned as in the
    droughts of summer.   Selah

5 I acknowledged my sin unto Thee,
    and mine iniquity have I not
    hid;
    I said: 'I will make confession
    concerning my transgressions
    unto the LORD'—
    And Thou, Thou forgavest the
    iniquity of my sin.   Selah

6 For this let every one that is
    godly pray unto Thee in a time
    when Thou mayest be found;
    Surely, when the great waters
    overflow, they will not reach
    unto him.

כִּי ׀ יוֹמָם וָלַיְלָה תִּכְבַּד עָלַי יָדֶךָ 4
נֶהְפַּךְ לְשַׁדִּי בְּחַרְבֹנֵי קַיִץ סֶלָה:
חַטָּאתִי אוֹדִיעֲךָ וַעֲוֹנִי לֹא־כִסִּיתִי 5
אָמַרְתִּי אוֹדֶה עֲלֵי פְשָׁעַי לַיהוָה
וְאַתָּה נָשָׂאתָ עֲוֹן חַטָּאתִי סֶלָה:
עַל־זֹאת יִתְפַּלֵּל כָּל־חָסִיד ׀ אֵלֶיךָ 6
לְעֵת מְצֹא
רַק לְשֵׁטֶף מַיִם רַבִּים
אֵלָיו לֹא יַגִּיעוּ:

my groaning. The physical symptoms of his distress were so acute that they forced moans from his lips (Metsudath David).

4. *day and night*. Continuously, without cessation.

Thy hand was heavy upon me. He had the insight to perceive that his suffering was the result of pressure from God to accept the one way of release: confession and repentance.

my sap was turned. His vitality was lowered to vanishing point by the fever which consumed him, as the life-giving moisture is lost to the tree during the drought of a hot summer.

5   HE RESOLVED TO CONFESS

I acknowledged my sin. The tense of the verb depicts the first step in the process of securing pardon. Its literal meaning is: 'I began to make known to Thee.' He was not giving information to God Who knew what he had done; by acknowledging it to Him he acknowledged it to himself. That is the purpose of confession and the first preliminary to forgiveness (Kimchi).

have I not hid. I make no attempt to cover up or excuse my sin but willingly admit that I have done wrong and beg forgiveness for it (Kimchi).

I said. The thought has now become so real to him that he feels he must put it into words (cf. Daath Sofrim).

I will make confession. The final stage is reached in the act of confession prompted by repentance, indicative of the yearning to be cleaned of the stain upon his soul.

and Thou. The subject is emphasized. The sinner having done his part, God was ready to do His as Pardoner.

6   AN EXHORTATION TO OTHERS

for this. Because God had demonstrated through me His readiness to forgive (Kimchi).

in a time when Thou mayest be found. lit. 'at a time of finding.'; i.e., when the mercy of God is most accessible to us (cf. Seek ye the LORD while He may be found, Isa. lv. 6). Alternatively, when he finds an opportune moment, free from other thoughts, he can fully pour out his heart to God (Ibn Ezra).

when the great waters overflow. A symbol of Divine retribution upon the wicked, suggested by the Flood. When this takes place the godly

7 Thou art my hiding-place; Thou
   wilt preserve me from the
   adversary;
   With songs of deliverance Thou
   wilt compass me about.   Selah

8 'I will instruct thee and teach thee
   in the way which thou shalt go;
   I will give counsel, Mine eye being
   upon thee.'

9 Be ye not as the horse, or as the
   mule, which have no understanding;
   Whose mouth must be held in
   with bit and bridle,
   That they come not near unto
   thee.

10 Many are the sorrows of the
   wicked;
   But he that trusteth in the LORD,
   mercy compasseth him about.

11 Be glad in the LORD, and rejoice,
   ye righteous;
   And shout for joy, all ye that are
   upright in heart.

7 אַתָּ֤ה ׀ סֵ֥תֶר לִי֮ מִצַּ֪ר תִּצְּרֵ֫נִי
   רָנֵּ֥י פַלֵּ֑ט תְּס֖וֹבְבֵ֣נִי סֶֽלָה׃

8 אַשְׂכִּ֥ילְךָ֨ ׀ וְֽאוֹרְךָ֗ בְּדֶ֥רֶךְ־ז֥וּ תֵלֵ֑ךְ
   אִיעֲצָ֖ה עָלֶ֣יךָ עֵינִֽי׃

9 אַל־תִּֽהְי֤וּ ׀ כְּס֣וּס כְּפֶרֶד֮ אֵ֪ין הָ֫בִ֥ין
   בְּמֶֽתֶג־וָרֶ֣סֶן עֶדְי֣וֹ לִבְל֑וֹם
   בַּ֝֗ל קְרֹ֣ב אֵלֶֽיךָ׃

10 רַבִּ֥ים מַכְאוֹבִ֗ים לָרָ֫שָׁ֥ע
   וְהַבּוֹטֵ֥חַ בַּֽיהֹוָ֑ה חֶ֝֗סֶד יְסוֹבְבֶֽנּוּ׃

11 שִׂמְח֬וּ בַֽיהֹוָ֣ה וְ֭גִילוּ צַדִּיקִ֑ים
   וְ֝הַרְנִ֗ינוּ כׇּל־יִשְׁרֵי־לֵֽב׃

man who has prayed to God will be like one
standing upon a high rock safe from the waves
which dash against it below (cf. Kimchi).

7   HE APPLIES THE ASSURANCE TO HIMSELF

Thou art my hiding-place. The security which
he had assured to the godly he knows to be his.

Thou wilt preserve me from the adversary. Or,
'Thou wilt guard me from distress.'

with songs of deliverance. All his troubles are
overcome, so that wherever he turns he finds
occasion to sing in gratitude his relief.

8   GOD'S RESPONSE

Here we have the instruction offered by David
which is possibly indicated in the superscription.

Mine eye being upon thee. After what I have
seen with my own eyes, I am ready to advise

you as to the correct path to follow in life
(Kimchi), or, 'I will signal to you with my eyes,'
thus preventing you from going astray (Rashi).

9-11   CONCLUDING MORALIZATION

9.   *which have no understanding.* A contrast
is drawn between man and animal. The latter
has to be put under restraint by means of bit and
bridle, otherwise it runs away and fails to do
the rider's bidding. Man, however, is possessed of understanding, and by its exercise
should voluntarily submit to God's discipline
(cf. Malbim).

10.   *sorrows.* lit. 'pains,' Divine chastisements for their sins.

11.   *be glad in the LORD.* His own experience, which he has related, is not unique. All
the righteous will likewise have occasion to
rejoice.

PSALM XXXIII

33

1 Rejoice in the LORD, O ye righteous,
   Praise is comely for the upright.

2 Give thanks unto the LORD with
   harp,
   Sing praises unto Him with the
   psaltery of ten strings.

3 Sing unto Him a new song;
   Play skilfully amid shouts of joy.

4 For the word of the LORD is upright;
   And all His work is done in faithfulness.

5 He loveth righteousness and justice;
   The earth is full of the lovingkindness of the LORD.

לג

רַנְּנוּ צַדִּיקִים בַּיהוָה
לַיְשָׁרִים נָאוָה תְהִלָּה׃
2 הוֹדוּ לַיהוָה בְּכִנּוֹר
בְּנֵבֶל עָשׂוֹר זַמְּרוּ־לוֹ׃
3 שִׁירוּ לוֹ שִׁיר חָדָשׁ
הֵיטִיבוּ נַגֵּן בִּתְרוּעָה׃
4 כִּי־יָשָׁר דְּבַר־יְהוָה
וְכָל־מַעֲשֵׂהוּ בֶּאֱמוּנָה׃
5 אֹהֵב צְדָקָה וּמִשְׁפָּט
חֶסֶד יְהוָה מָלְאָה הָאָרֶץ׃

SONG OF DELIVERANCE

THE opening verse of this Psalm takes up the call of the last verse in the preceding one. It is throughout a hymn of triumph. It is written in the plural, pointing to a national rather than a personal victory. The circumstance which occasioned its composition is not specified and cannot be determined.

1-3 INTRODUCTORY INVOCATION

1. *rejoice.* Another form of the verb in xxxii. 11, translated *shout for joy.* That is its meaning here (Ibn Ezra).

righteous ... upright. As in xxxii. 11. Only the men of Israel who were faithful to God can fully appreciate His greatness and be able to praise Him sincerely (Kimchi).

2. *harp.* More probably the *kinnor* was a small, portable instrument like the lyre.

psaltery. A larger instrument like the harp is intended. The number of its strings varied; here one with ten strings is mentioned (Targum).

3. *a new song.* God has not only to be praised for past mercies. Fresh manifestations of His supernatural abilities call for new hymns of praise (Malbim).

4-11 WHY PRAISE IS DUE

4. The Psalmist first dwells upon God's moral attributes as grounds for lauding Him.

word. His decrees in the government of the world; they are based upon equity.

in faithfulness. In conformity with the principles of righteousness.

5. *righteousness and justice.* These are the foundations of a stable order of society. When they are faithfully applied peace reigns; their violation leads to strife (see lxxxv. 11; Isa. xxxii. 17).

the earth is full. Repeated in cxix. 64. Kimchi appropriately quotes Jer. ix. 23: *I am the LORD Who exercises mercy, justice, and righteousness in the earth; for in these things I delight.* Man is exhorted to 'imitate God' in this respect

6 By the word of the LORD were the
    heavens made;
  And all the host of them by the
    breath of His mouth.

7 He gathereth the waters of the sea
    together as a heap;
  He layeth up the deeps in store-
    houses.

8 Let all the earth fear the LORD;
  Let all the inhabitants of the world
    stand in awe of Him.

9 For He spoke, and it was;
  He commanded, and it stood.

10 The LORD bringeth the counsel
     of the nations to nought;
   He maketh the thoughts of the
     peoples to be of no effect.

11 The counsel of the LORD stand-
     eth for ever,
   The thoughts of His heart to all
     generations.

12 Happy is the nation whose God
     is the LORD;
   The people whom He hath chosen
     for His own inheritance.

6 בִּדְבַר יְהוָה שָׁמַיִם נַעֲשׂוּ
וּבְרוּחַ פִּיו כָּל־צְבָאָם:

7 כֹּנֵס כַּנֵּד מֵי הַיָּם
נֹתֵן בְּאוֹצָרוֹת תְּהוֹמוֹת:

8 יִירְאוּ מֵיְהוָה כָּל־הָאָרֶץ
מִמֶּנּוּ יָגוּרוּ כָּל־יֹשְׁבֵי תֵבֵל:

9 כִּי הוּא אָמַר וַיֶּהִי
הוּא־צִוָּה וַיַּעֲמֹד:

10 יְהוָה הֵפִיר עֲצַת גּוֹיִם
הֵנִיא מַחְשְׁבוֹת עַמִּים:

11 עֲצַת יְהוָה לְעוֹלָם תַּעֲמֹד
מַחְשְׁבוֹת לִבּוֹ לְדֹר וָדֹר:

12 אַשְׁרֵי הַגּוֹי אֲשֶׁר־יְהוָה אֱלֹהָיו
הָעָם ׀ בָּחַר לְנַחֲלָה לוֹ:

and practise the qualities which distinguish
Him.

6.   Praise is next due to God for His creative
might.

by ... LORD. The heavens made their appearance after *and God said* (Gen. i. 6ff.) (Kimchi).

the host of them. Sun, moon, and stars.

7   HE APPLIES THE ASSURANCE TO OTHERS

The first phrase refers to the history of the
oceans. Upon their creation, they covered the
entire surface of the earth. God then gathered
them into seas, thus forming dry land. They
remain in their position only as a result of
God's command. This leads us to the meaning of the second half of the verse. The seas
are, so to speak, kept in '*vaults in the deep,*'
and though the tides do '*come in,*' they are
never allowed to cover the face of the earth
(Kimchi, Malbim).

8.   *fear the LORD.* At the thought of His majestic works man should be filled with a sense

of reverence.

9.   *He spoke.* The subject is emphatic. God
alone was the Creator of the universe which
came into being as the effect of His word.

stood. The world stood firm and endured
(Metsudath David). Nature can never be
changed (Meiri).

10.   The third reason for praise is His Sovereignty over mankind.

bringeth ... to nought. Man proposes, God
disposes. This is true both of individuals and
nations. When their will clashes with His, it is
His that prevails.

11.   *the counsel of the LORD.* As against *The
counsel of the nations.* Similarly *the thoughts
of His heart* stands in contrast to *the thoughts
of the peoples.*

12-19   HIS CHOSEN PEOPLE

12.   After dealing with God's Kingship over
all nations, the Psalm turns to His relationship

13 The LORD looketh from heaven;
    He beholdeth all the sons of men;

14 From the place of His habitation
    He looketh intently
    Upon all the inhabitants of the
    earth;

15 He that fashioneth the hearts of
    them all,
    That considereth all their doings.

16 A king is not saved by the multi-
    tude of a host;
    A mighty man is not delivered by
    great strength.

17 A horse is a vain thing for safety:
    Neither doth it afford escape by
    its great strength.

18 Behold, the eye of the LORD is
    toward them that fear Him,
    Toward them that wait for His
    mercy;

19 To deliver their soul from death,
    And to keep them alive in famine.

‏מִשָּׁמַיִם הִבִּיט יְהֹוָה‎ 13
‏רָאָה אֶת־כָּל־בְּנֵי הָאָדָם:‎
‏מִמְּכוֹן־שִׁבְתּוֹ הִשְׁגִּיחַ‎ 14
‏אֶל כָּל־יֹשְׁבֵי הָאָרֶץ:‎
‏הַיֹּצֵר יַחַד לִבָּם‎ 15
‏הַמֵּבִין אֶל־כָּל־מַעֲשֵׂיהֶם:‎
‏אֵין הַמֶּלֶךְ נוֹשָׁע בְּרָב־חָיִל‎ 16
‏גִּבּוֹר לֹא־יִנָּצֵל בְּרָב־כֹּחַ:‎
‏שֶׁקֶר הַסּוּס לִתְשׁוּעָה‎ 17
‏וּבְרֹב חֵילוֹ לֹא יְמַלֵּט:‎
‏הִנֵּה עֵין יְהֹוָה אֶל־יְרֵאָיו‎ 18
‏לַמְיַחֲלִים לְחַסְדּוֹ:‎
‏לְהַצִּיל מִמָּוֶת נַפְשָׁם‎ 19
‏וּלְחַיּוֹתָם בָּרָעָב:‎

with the people who acknowledged Him as their God.

inheritance. Cf. xxviii. 9.

13. *looketh from heaven.* From His abode in the distant heavens He surveys all that takes place upon earth.

all the sons of men. Although He is the God of Israel, He is also the King of the whole human race. They may not accept Him as God, but He determines their destiny.

14. *looketh intently.* From this rare verb (again only in Cant. ii. 9 and Isa. xiv. 16) the Rabbinical term *hashgachah,* 'Divine Providence,' is derived. It governs *all the inhabitants of the earth,* from the beginning of time (Malbim).

15. *the hearts of them all.* As the Creator of all men and their *hearts* which dispose their actions, He takes note of how they employ the powers with which He has endowed them.

16. A moral of universal application is drawn from His dealings with Israel. Against His protection the resources of Israel's opponents are powerless (Kimchi).

a king. As, e.g., Pharaoh and his numerous chariots and horsemen (Exod. xiv. 17).

mighty men. The fate of Goliath affords an illustration (Kimchi).

17. *horse.* Cavalry was regarded as a formidable part of an army (cf. xx. 8; Isa. xxxi. 1).

safety. Hebrew 'salvation,' which may here mean *victory* as in Prov. xxi. 31.

escape. The horses upon which so much reliance is place will fail both in attack and retreat (Kimchi).

18. *the eye of the LORD.* The protective eye (Kimchi) Cf. xxxii. 8.

wait. Who continue to hope and do not give way to despair during the period of trial.

20 Our soul hath waited for the LORD;
   He is our help and our shield.

21 For in Him doth our heart re-
      joice,
   Because we have trusted in His
      holy name.

22 Let Thy mercy, O LORD, be
      upon us,
   According as we have waited for
      Thee.

20 נַפְשֵׁנוּ חִכְּתָה לַיהוָה
עֶזְרֵנוּ וּמָגִנֵּנוּ הוּא:
21 כִּי־בוֹ יִשְׂמַח לִבֵּנוּ
כִּי בְשֵׁם קׇדְשׁוֹ בָטָחְנוּ:
22 יְהִי־חַסְדְּךָ יְהוָה עָלֵינוּ
כַּאֲשֶׁר יִחַלְנוּ לָךְ:

19. The two severest national dangers are enumerated: the destructive sword of the invader and famine.

20-22 THE PEOPLE'S RESPONSE

The final section expresses a note of self-confidence.

20. *our soul*. This may mean nothing more than 'we,' but it can also imply the intensity of feeling with which the coming of Divine help was awaited.

hath waited for the LORD. To bring deliverance; and their continued trust has had its reward, as the next verse tells.

our Help and our Shield. The Psalmist recalls the words of the Song of Moses, *Happy art thou, O Israel, who is like unto thee? A people saved by the LORD, the shield of thy help* (Deut. xxxiii. 29). Such an assurance, proved true in past history, kindled an unquenchable hope in the present crisis, and gave them the strength to endure and wait for God's intervention.

21. *in Him doth our heart rejoice*. It is only the realization that He is with us that gives us joy and inspires us in our lives and our endeavours. We have put all our trust exclusively in the blissful truth of His holy name (Hirsch).

trusted in His holy name. To demonstrate the attribute of holiness which is associated with Him; holiness is the essence of His nature from which the qualities of justice and mercy radiate.

22. *let Thy mercy, O LORD, be upon us*. A closing prayer for pity that Israel may have proof of the reality of their confidence by a manifestation of God's love. The petition does not express doubt, but a wish for a speedy demonstration that their hope is well founded.

according as we have waited for Thee. Or, 'hoped for Thee.' Israel learnt the lesson of hopeful trust from the Patriarch Jacob who exclaimed on his death-bed, *I wait for Thy salvation, O LORD* (Gen. xlix. 18).

34

1 [A Psalm] of David; when he changed his demeanour before Abimelech, who drove him away, and he departed.

2 I will bless the LORD at all times; His praise shall continually be in my mouth.

3 My soul shall glory in the LORD; The humble shall hear thereof, and be glad.

4 O magnify the LORD with me, And let us exalt His name together.

5 I sought the LORD, and He answered me, And delivered me from all my fears.

6 They looked unto Him, and were radiant; And their faces shall never be abashed.

לד

לְדָוִד
בְּשַׁנּוֹתוֹ אֶת־טַעְמוֹ לִפְנֵי אֲבִימֶלֶךְ
וַיְגָרֲשֵׁהוּ וַיֵּלַךְ׃
2 אֲבָרֲכָה אֶת־יְהוָה בְּכָל־עֵת
תָּמִיד תְּהִלָּתוֹ בְּפִי׃
3 בַּיהוָה תִּתְהַלֵּל נַפְשִׁי
יִשְׁמְעוּ עֲנָוִים וְיִשְׂמָחוּ׃
4 גַּדְּלוּ לַיהוָה אִתִּי
וּנְרוֹמֲמָה שְׁמוֹ יַחְדָּו׃
5 דָּרַשְׁתִּי אֶת־יְהוָה וְעָנָנִי
וּמִכָּל־מְגוּרוֹתַי הִצִּילָנִי׃
6 הִבִּיטוּ אֵלָיו וְנָהָרוּ
וּפְנֵיהֶם אַל־יֶחְפָּרוּ׃

HYMN OF PRAISE

AN acrostic Psalm resembling XXV in the omission of a verse beginning with *vav* and the addition at the end of a verse with an initial *pe*. The title relates the Psalm to an incident comparable with that narrated in 1 Sam. xxi. 11ff., where, however, the king's name was Achish, not as stated here, Abimelech. The difference in names might easily be accounted for if Abimelech was a dynastic name or a royal title, like 'Agag' among the Amalekites or 'Pharaoh' in Egypt (Rashi). Alternatively, he might have had two different names (Ibn Ezra). According to the Midrash (Shocher Tov) David, having escaped from the hands of Saul, sought refuge among the Philistines who, in turn, sought to avenge the blood of the slain Goliath. He prayed to God that he should appear a madman and, on account of this, Achish, convinced this was not David, spared his life, driving him away instead. In gratitude to God, David composed this Psalm. By making known his personal experience, he also shows the way to salvation. Two themes are stressed; seeking God (verses 5 and 11) and deliverance from troubles (verses 5, 18 and 20). The last verse, which is included in the acrostic, may have been added so that the Psalm should end on a note of encouragement for the faithful.

2. *at all times*. In joy and sorrow.

3. *in the LORD*. Stands first in the verse and is therefore emphatic: in Him alone do I glory as a sure help.

humble. Those, like the Psalmist, who are the victims of the arrogant. When they learn of his experience they will rejoice (Kimchi).

4. *magnify the LORD with me*. The words are addressed to 'the humble' (Kimchi). Man *makes* God *great* by acknowledging and celebrating His greatness (Deut. xxxii. 3), and *exalts* His name by confessing that He is supreme above all.

5. *I sought the LORD*. I begged the LORD to save me (Kimchi).

7 This poor man cried, and the
  LORD heard,
  And saved him out of all his
  troubles.

8 The angel of the LORD encampeth
  round about them that fear
  Him,
  And delivereth them.

9 O consider and see that the LORD
  is good;
  Happy is the man that taketh
  refuge in Him.

10 O fear the LORD, ye His holy
  ones;
  For there is no want to them that
  fear Him.

11 The young lions do lack, and
  suffer hunger;
  But they that seek the LORD want
  not any good thing.

12 Come, ye children, hearken unto
  me;
  I will teach you the fear of the
  LORD.

זֶה עָנִי קָרָא וַיהוָה שָׁמֵעַ 7
וּמִכָּל־צָרוֹתָיו הוֹשִׁיעוֹ:

חֹנֶה מַלְאַךְ־יְהוָה 8
סָבִיב לִירֵאָיו וַיְחַלְּצֵם:

טַעֲמוּ וּרְאוּ כִּי־טוֹב יְהוָה 9
אַשְׁרֵי הַגֶּבֶר יֶחֱסֶה־בּוֹ:

יְראוּ אֶת־יְהוָה קְדֹשָׁיו 10
כִּי־אֵין מַחְסוֹר לִירֵאָיו:

כְּפִירִים רָשׁוּ וְרָעֵבוּ 11
וְדֹרְשֵׁי יְהוָה לֹא־יַחְסְרוּ כָל־טוֹב:

לְכוּ־בָנִים שִׁמְעוּ־לִי 12
יִרְאַת יְהוָה אֲלַמֶּדְכֶם:

6. *they looked.* As often in Hebrew the subject is undefined. It may be expressed in English by: 'They who looked unto Him were illumined.'

A verse beginning with *vav* does not appear at this point.

7. *poor man.* Better, 'afflicted man.' The Psalmist is not referring to himself, but points to an unspecified individual as typical of his class (Malbim).

8. *angel of the LORD.* God's agent in His relations with man, described as *the angel of His presence* (Isa. lxiii. 9), particularly as a protector. Thus Jacob invoked *the angel who hath redeemed me from all evil* (Gen. xlviii. 16). We also hear of *the angel of God who went before the camp of Israel* (Exod. xiv. 19), of an angel appearing to Joshua as *captain of the host of the LORD* (Joshua v. 14), and of an angel protecting Daniel in the lions' den (Dan. vi. 23).

encampeth. Cf. Gen. xxxii. 2f.

9. *consider.* lit. 'taste,' a significant word. More effective than theorizing about God's

goodness is the test of experience. Only by encountering it in one's life can it be really known.

man. Hebrew *geber*, i.e. man in the vigour of life (Malbim in Yair Ohr). Even such as he needs Him as a refuge.

10. *ye Holy ones.* Worthy members of a *holy nation* (Exod. xix. 6) who have obeyed His exhortation, *Ye shall be holy* (Lev. xix. 2).

no want. God is Provider as well as Protector (see xxiii. 1).

11. *young lions.* Kings of the animal world; yet, despite their native strength and agility, they are not always able to provide for themselves (Kimchi).

12. *ye children.* Better, 'sons,' as pupils are often addressed in Proverbs (e.g. ii. 1, iii. 1). Inasmuch as great blessings accrue to the 'fearers' of the LORD, the Psalmist feels the necessity of teaching what *fear* consists of.

the fear of the LORD. Which is *the beginning of knowledge* (Prov. i. 7). The phrase indicates

13 Who is the man that desireth life,
   And loveth days, that he may see
      good therein?

14 Keep thy tongue from evil,
   And thy lips from speaking guile.

15 Depart from evil, and do good;
   Seek peace, and pursue it.

16 The eyes of the LORD are toward
      the righteous,
   And His ears are open unto their
      cry.

17 The face of the LORD is against
      them that do evil,
   To cut off the remembrance of
      them from the earth.

18 ¹They cried, and the LORD heard,
   And delivered them out of all
      their troubles.

19 The LORD is nigh unto them that
   are of a broken heart,

¹That is, the righteous.

13 מִי־הָאִישׁ הֶחָפֵץ חַיִּים
אֹהֵב יָמִים לִרְאוֹת טוֹב:
14 נְצֹר לְשׁוֹנְךָ מֵרָע
וּשְׂפָתֶיךָ מִדַּבֵּר מִרְמָה:
15 סוּר מֵרָע וַעֲשֵׂה־טוֹב
בַּקֵּשׁ שָׁלוֹם וְרָדְפֵהוּ:
16 עֵינֵי יְהוָה אֶל־צַדִּיקִים
וְאָזְנָיו אֶל־שַׁוְעָתָם:
17 פְּנֵי יְהוָה בְּעֹשֵׂי רָע
לְהַכְרִית מֵאֶרֶץ זִכְרָם:
18 צָעֲקוּ וַיהוָה שָׁמֵעַ
וּמִכָּל־צָרוֹתָם הִצִּילָם:
19 קָרוֹב יְהוָה לְנִשְׁבְּרֵי־לֵב

the essence of religion, and it should be noted that the definition which follows is in ethical terms.

13.   *life.* Not just physical existence, but life understood as 'a great and noble calling in which man fulfills the task for which he was called into being'(Hirsch).

loveth days. i.e. length of days, so that good deeds and the will of God can be accomplished all the more (Metsudath David).

good. The Divine bounty of the World to Come, which is the true good (Metsudath David).

14.   *keep thy tongue from evil.* The sins of the tongue are severely denounced, because *death and life are in the power of the tongue* (Prov. xviii. 21). Lying and slander were deemed by the Rabbis to be especially hateful to God. The verse, converted to first person, begins a beautiful meditation included in Jewish liturgy for daily use (*P.B.*, p. 54).

15.   *depart from evil, and do good.* Repeated

in xxxvii. 27. The righteous man must shun evil and also embrace every opportunity to perform good deeds (Hirsch). Cf. *cease to do evil; learn to do well* (Isa. i. 16f.).

seek peace. Create harmony in your relationship with your fellows by removing the wrongs which disturb it.

pursue it. Persist in the attempt to create this peaceful atmosphere even at the risk of personal sacrifice (Hirsch).

16.   *eyes.* See on xxxiii. 18.

17.   *face of the LORD.* His Presence and disposition which may be one of anger, as here, or of blessing, as in the Priestly Benediction (Num. vi. 26).

cut off the remembrance. Cf. ix. 7.

18.   *they cried.* A.J. has a footnote: 'that is, the righteous,' following the LXX which inserts the words. Rashi and Kimchi explain similarly; but Ibn Ezra, while noting this interpretation, comments: when they turn from

And saveth such as are of a contrite spirit.

20 Many are the ills of the righteous,
But the LORD delivereth him out of them all.

21 He keepeth all his bones;
Not one of them is broken.

22 Evil shall kill the wicked;
And they that hate the righteous shall be held guilty.

23 The LORD redeemeth the soul of His servants;
And none of them that take refuge in Him shall be desolate.

וְאֶת־דַּכְּאֵי־רוּחַ יוֹשִׁיעַ׃
20 רַבּוֹת רָעוֹת צַדִּיק
וּמִכֻּלָּם יַצִּילֶנּוּ יְהוָה׃
21 שֹׁמֵר כָּל־עַצְמוֹתָיו
אַחַת מֵהֵנָּה לֹא נִשְׁבָּרָה׃
22 תְּמוֹתֵת רָשָׁע רָעָה
וְשֹׂנְאֵי צַדִּיק יֶאְשָׁמוּ׃
23 פֹּדֶה יְהוָה נֶפֶשׁ עֲבָדָיו
וְלֹא יֶאְשְׁמוּ כָּל־הַחֹסִים בּוֹ׃

their evil and repent. This explanation is favoured by more recent Jewish exegetes (Metsudath David, Hirsch, Daath Sofrim) and harmonizes with Hebraic thought which exalts the power of true repentance.

19. *broken*. By suffering. 'Sorrow purges the human breast of its dross, and, as nothing else, opens the eyes of the soul to spiritual vision and values' (Hertz). The beneficial effects which may ensue from adversity are acknowledged by the Psalmist: *It is good for me that I have been afflicted, in order that I might learn Thy statutes* (cxix. 71). *A broken and contrite heart, O God, Thou wilt not despise* (li. 19).

20. *many are the ills*. The Torah does not promise immunity to the righteous; on the contrary, just because they adhere to the good they are liable to be victimized by the unscrupulous. They have their reward, however, in Divine deliverance (Hirsch).

21. *keepeth all his bones*. Protects his body from physical harm. The blows which fall upon him are grievous and painful, but thanks to God's protection they do not disable him permanently. With His help he is able to recover from them quickly.

22. *evil*. The evil plotted against the righteous will kill the wicked (see vii. 17) (Kimchi); or *evil* denotes adversity and suffering as the punishment of wicked acts, providing a contrast between the two categories: the righteous survive their troubles by the grace of God, whereas the ungodly succumb to them (Daath Sofrim). Commenting on the singular form of the Hebrew, Ibn Ezra remarks that one stroke of *evil* is sufficient to put an end to the wicked, whereas the righteous are able to survive many such blows.

held guilty. By the Judge of the world and receive sentence at His hands (cf. v. 11).

23. An added verse beginning with the letter *pe*.

desolate. Rather, 'held guilty,' same Hebrew word as in the preceding verse (Targum, Ibn Ezra). They will escape the fate of the evildoers. The repetition of the verb in the consecutive verse heightens the contrast between the fate of the rebels against God and those who confide in Him. Such a distinction in their destiny must inevitably follow from His righteousness (cf. Daath Sofrim).

35

1 [A Psalm] of David.
Strive, O Lord, with them that strive with me;
Fight against them that fight against me.

2 Take hold of shield and buckler,
And rise up to my help.

3 Draw out also the spear, and the battle-axe, against them that pursue me;
Say unto my soul: 'I am thy salvation.'

4 Let them be ashamed and brought to confusion that seek after my soul;
Let them be turned back and be abashed that devise my hurt.

5 Let them be as chaff before the wind,

לה

לְדָוִד ׀
רִיבָה יְהֹוָה אֶת־יְרִיבַי
לְחַם אֶת־לֹחֲמָי׃
2 הַחֲזֵק מָגֵן וְצִנָּה
וְקוּמָה בְּעֶזְרָתִי׃
3 וְהָרֵק חֲנִית וּסְגֹר לִקְרַאת רֹדְפָי
אֱמֹר לְנַפְשִׁי יְשֻׁעָתֵךְ אָנִי׃
4 יֵבֹשׁוּ וְיִכָּלְמוּ מְבַקְשֵׁי נַפְשִׁי
יִסֹּגוּ אָחוֹר וְיַחְפְּרוּ חֹשְׁבֵי רָעָתִי׃
5 יִהְיוּ כְּמֹץ לִפְנֵי־רוּחַ

PRAYER WHILE UNDER PERSECUTION

This Psalm should be compared with VII and XXII. It is a cry of distress from David when he was being hunted by Saul (Kimchi), or while fleeing from his rebellious son Absalom (Sforno). Two subjects of his distress are made clear. He is held guilty for crimes he never committed (verses 7 and 11) and he bemoans the fact that the good he has done is being repaid with bad (verse 12).

1-10 APPEAL FOR HELP

1. *strive … fight.* Strive with them before it leads to war. Should it, however, come to that, fight with them (Malbim).

them that strive with me … them that fight against me. lit. 'my antagonists' or 'my adversaries'; 'my attackers' or 'my assailants.' David states that the struggle is one-sided. They are his adversaries; they assail him. He is not fighting them nor does he reciprocate their hostility (Hirsch).

2. *shield a… buckler.* See v. 13. Since his accusers have resorted to violence, he invokes God as his Champion in the fight. In the Scriptures God is named *a man of war* (Exod. xv. 3), but only to help the weak against the ruthless strong.

3. *draw out.* The verb is used to denote drawing a sword from the scabbard (Exod. xv. 9). Similarly the spear was kept in a holder from which it was taken when required.

the battle-axe. The Hebrew may be the imperative of a verb 'close up'; hence A.V. *stop the way* of the enemy (so Rashi, Ibn Ezra). Kimchi suggests that it is a noun signifying an implement of war, and Hirsch specifies it to probably be a defensive 'barrier.'

say unto my soul. Give me the heartening message that Thou wilt help me to victory.

4. *let them be ashamed.* In the complete triumph which God will have secured for the persecuted. Hirsch points out that three different terms are used to describe their embarrassment. While 'busha' denotes humiliation due to frustrated hope, 'klimah' is the painful realization of unworthiness. 'Hefer' expresses the shame felt when unpleasant facts are revealed.

5. *as chaff.* Cf. i. 4. A graphic picture of the complete rout of the enemy.

The angel of the LORD thrusting
them.

6 Let their way be dark and slippery,
The angel of the LORD pursuing
them.

7 For without cause have they hid
for me the pit, even their net,
Without cause have they digged
for my soul.

8 Let destruction come upon him
unawares;
And let his net that he hath hid
catch himself;
With destruction let him fall
therein.

9 And my soul shall be joyful in the
LORD;
It shall rejoice in His salvation.

10 All my bones shall say: 'LORD,
who is like unto Thee,
Who deliverest the poor from him
that is too strong for him,
Yea, the poor and the needy from
him that spoileth him?'

11 Unrighteous witnesses rise up;
They ask me of things that I
know not.

וּמַלְאַךְ יְהוָה דֹּחֶה׃

יְהִי־דַרְכָּם חֹשֶׁךְ וַחֲלַקְלַקֹּת 6
וּמַלְאַךְ יְהוָה רֹדְפָם׃

כִּי־חִנָּם טָמְנוּ־לִי שַׁחַת רִשְׁתָּם 7
חִנָּם חָפְרוּ לְנַפְשִׁי׃

תְּבוֹאֵהוּ שׁוֹאָה לֹא־יֵדָע 8
וְרִשְׁתּוֹ אֲשֶׁר־טָמַן תִּלְכְּדוֹ
בְּשׁוֹאָה יִפָּל־בָּהּ׃

וְנַפְשִׁי תָּגִיל בַּיהוָה 9
תָּשִׂישׂ בִּישׁוּעָתוֹ׃

כָּל עַצְמֹתַי ׀ תֹּאמַרְנָה 10
יְהוָה מִי כָמוֹךָ
מַצִּיל עָנִי מֵחָזָק מִמֶּנּוּ
וְעָנִי וְאֶבְיוֹן מִגֹּזְלוֹ׃

יְקוּמוּן עֵדֵי חָמָס 11
אֲשֶׁר לֹא־יָדַעְתִּי יִשְׁאָלוּנִי׃

---

6. *dark and slippery.* Cf. Jer. xxiii. 12. In their panic to escape they will abandon the roads and paths, and flee down the slippery slopes of the hills darkened by the overhanging trees.

7. *without cause.* The repeated phrase explains the state of his mind and the content of his prayer. Not malice but righteous indignation is his motive.

the pit, even their net. Despite the absence of any violence on my part, they dug a pit and covered it with a net that I should unwittingly fall therein (Kimchi).

8. *upon him.* The singular may point either to the chief enemy, Saul, or to each of his adversaries (Kimchi).

9. *joyful in the LORD.* He will have no doubt to Whom he is indebted for his escape.

10. *all my bones.* In addition to the satisfaction which his 'soul' will enjoy, there will be a grateful sense of relief and thankfulness throughout his bodily frame which had been in danger (cf. Malbim).

poor. Afflicted.

poor and needy. See ix. 19. The Pesiktah explains this verse as referring to the 'good inclination' which is overpowered by the 'evil inclination' robbing man of his good intentions.

11-18 WICKEDNESS OF THE ENEMY

11. *unrighteous witness.* lit. 'witnesses of violence'; they give false testimony to aid the unlawfulness of the persecutor (Hirsch).

ask me of things that I know not. They lay charges against him of which he knows nothing. It seems that David had been accused of

12 They repay me evil for good;
    Bereavement is come to my soul.

13 But as for me, when they were
    sick, my clothing was sack-
    cloth,
    I afflicted my soul with fasting;
    And my prayer, may it return
    into mine own bosom.

14 I went about as though it had
    been my friend or my brother;
    I bowed down mournful, as one
    that mourneth for his mother.

15 But when I halt they rejoice, and
    gather themselves together;
    The abjects gather themselves
    together against me, and those
    whom I know not;
    They tear me, and cease not;

16 With the profanest mockeries of
    backbiting
    They gnash at me with their
    teeth.

יְשַׁלְּמוּנִי רָעָה תַּחַת טוֹבָה 12
שְׁכוֹל לְנַפְשִׁי׃
וַאֲנִי ׀ בַּחֲלוֹתָם לְבוּשִׁי שָׂק 13
עִנֵּיתִי בַצּוֹם נַפְשִׁי
וּתְפִלָּתִי עַל־חֵיקִי תָשׁוּב׃
כְּרֵעַ־כְּאָח לִי הִתְהַלָּכְתִּי 14
כַּאֲבֶל־אֵם קֹדֵר שַׁחוֹתִי׃
וּבְצַלְעִי שָׂמְחוּ וְנֶאֱסָפוּ 15
נֶאֶסְפוּ עָלַי נֵכִים וְלֹא יָדַעְתִּי
קָרְעוּ וְלֹא־דָמּוּ׃
בְּחַנְפֵי לַעֲגֵי מָעוֹג 16
חָרֹק עָלַי שִׁנֵּימוֹ׃

fraud and extortion (Kimchi, Malbim, Daath Sofrim).

12. The *good* he had done is defined in the next two verses.

bereavement is come to my soul. David is the victim of a most heinous crime, a character assassination, which makes him feel as a mother would at the physical destruction of her children (Hirsch). According to Sforno the allusion is to David's son, Absalom, who was killed as a result of his rebellion.

13. *sackcloth.* Worn by mourners and also by penitents (Jonah iii. 8).

afflicted my soul with fasting. To *afflict the soul* is the Hebrew term for a fast (Lev. xvi. 29; Isa. lviii. 3). 'This Hebrew phrase well indicates the spiritual aim of fasting. As the principal source of sin is the gratification of bodily appetites, the fast is to demonstrate to the sinner that man can conquer all physical cravings, that the spirit can always master the body' (Hertz). His thoughts were so completely for the welfare of the attackers when they had

in the past been in distress, that he acted as though he had been praying on his own behalf (Kimchi).

may it return into mine own bosom. As proof of his sincerity, he asks that what he prayed for them may come upon him.

14. *I went about.* i.e. I behaved. He adopted the outward forms of mourning which consisted in neglect of personal appearance by not washing or trimming the hair (2 Sam. xix. 25).

15. *when I halt.* When I stumble and am likely to fall (Hirsch).

and gather themselves together. To rejoice.

the abjects ... I know not. Or, 'And I know not why.' I see no reason for their spite, for I did them no wrong (Kimchi). The Targum, understands the attack to be a campaign of slander; 'who smite me with their words.'

they tear me. Their libelous tongues are like the fangs of a beast of prey tearing his reputation to shreds (cf. Hirsch).

17 Lord, how long wilt Thou look on?
   Rescue my soul from their de-
      structions,
   Mine only one from the lions.

18 I will give Thee thanks in the
      great congregation;
   I will praise Thee among a
      numerous people.

19 Let not them that are wrongfully
      mine enemies rejoice over me;
   Neither let them wink with the
      eye that hate me without a
      cause.

20 For they speak not peace;
   But they devise deceitful matters
      against them that are quiet in
      the land.

21 Yea, they open their mouth wide
      against me;
   They say: 'Aha, aha, our eye hath
      seen it.'

22 Thou hast seen, O LORD; keep
      not silence;
   O Lord, be not far from me.

אֲדֹנָי כַּמָּה תִּרְאֶה 17
הָשִׁיבָה נַפְשִׁי מִשֹּׁאֵיהֶם
מִכְּפִירִים יְחִידָתִי:
אוֹדְךָ בְּקָהָל רָב 18
בְּעַם עָצוּם אֲהַלְלֶךָּ:
אַל־יִשְׂמְחוּ־לִי אֹיְבַי שֶׁקֶר 19
שֹׂנְאַי חִנָּם יִקְרְצוּ־עָיִן:
כִּי לֹא שָׁלוֹם יְדַבֵּרוּ 20
וְעַל רִגְעֵי־אֶרֶץ דִּבְרֵי
מִרְמוֹת יַחֲשֹׁבוּן:
וַיַּרְחִיבוּ עָלַי פִּיהֶם 21
אָמְרוּ הֶאָח הֶאָח רָאֲתָה עֵינֵנוּ:
רָאִיתָה יְהוָה אַל־תֶּחֱרַשׁ 22
אֲדֹנָי אַל־תִּרְחַק מִמֶּנִּי:

---

16. *with the profanest mockeries of backbiting.* The Hebrew is obscure; lit. 'as profane men, mockers for cake,' explained as a comparison with buffoons who indulge in ridicule to earn a meal from their audience (Rashi, Metsudath David). He describes them as unprincipled men who, to curry favour with Saul, make play with his good name and abet the king's plan to destroy him.

17. *look on.* Without intervening (Rashi).

rescue my soul. lit. 'restore my soul' (see on xix. 8).

mine only one. The soul, as in xxii. 21 (Kimchi).

lions. His enemies who are as powerful as wild beasts (cf. lvii. 5).

18. This second section of the Psalm ends like the first (verses 9f.), with a declaration of his readiness to proclaim God's salvation in the event of his foes' defeat.

19-28   HIS FINAL PLEA

19. *wrongfully mine enemies.* lit. 'my enemies (in) falsehood'; they have no just grounds for enmity and so invent false pretexts (Rashi).

wink the eye. To each other in ridiculing me (Kimchi).

21. *open their mouth wide.* A gesture indicative of malicious rejoicing (Hirsch) cf. Isa. lvii. 4.

our eye hath seen it. viz. what we have desired and plotted, his downfall (Kimchi).

22. *Thou hast seen.* He converts their phrase (Ibn Ezra) into a very different sense, as the answer to his plaint *how long wilt Thou look on?* (verse 17) (cf. Daath Sofrim).

keep not silence. As in xxviii. 1. Being the Judge, pronounce the verdict.

be not far from me. See on xxii. 12.

23 Rouse Thee, and awake to my
   judgment,
   Even unto my cause, my God and
   my Lord.

24 Judge me, O LORD my God,
   according to Thy righteousness;
   And let them not rejoice over me.

25 Let them not say in their heart:
   'Aha, we have our desire';
   Let them not say: 'We have swal-
   lowed him up'

26 Let them be ashamed and
   abashed together that rejoice
   at my hurt;
   Let them be clothed with shame
   and confusion that magnify
   themselves against me.

27 Let them shout for joy, and be
   glad, that delight in my right-
   eousness;
   Yea, let them say continually:
   'Magnified be the LORD,
   Who delighteth in the peace of
   His servant.'

28 And my tongue shall speak of
   Thy righteousness,
   And of Thy praise all the day.

הָעִירָה וְהָקִיצָה לְמִשְׁפָּטִי 23
אֱלֹהַי וַאדֹנָי לְרִיבִי׃
שָׁפְטֵנִי כְצִדְקְךָ יְהוָה אֱלֹהָי 24
וְאַל־יִשְׂמְחוּ־לִי׃
אַל־יֹאמְרוּ בְלִבָּם הֶאָח נַפְשֵׁנוּ 25
אַל־יֹאמְרוּ בִּלַּעֲנוּהוּ׃
יֵבֹשׁוּ וְיַחְפְּרוּ ׀ יַחְדָּו 26
שְׂמֵחֵי רָעָתִי
יִלְבְּשׁוּ־בֹשֶׁת וּכְלִמָּה
הַמַּגְדִּילִים עָלָי׃
יָרֹנּוּ וְיִשְׂמְחוּ חֲפֵצֵי צִדְקִי 27
וְיֹאמְרוּ תָמִיד יִגְדַּל יְהוָה
הֶחָפֵץ שְׁלוֹם עַבְדּוֹ׃
וּלְשׁוֹנִי תֶּהְגֶּה צִדְקֶךָ 28
כָּל־הַיּוֹם תְּהִלָּתֶךָ׃

23. *rouse Thee, and awake.* The Psalmist does
not imagine that God is asleep, but rather,
pleads that the attributes of mercy and justice
be roused in support of his cause (Sforno).
Alternatively, awaken the conscience of men,
showing thereby that Your sovereignty does
not sleep or slumber, as they think it does
(Hirsch).

24. *judge me.* Rather, execute justice on my
behalf (Kimchi).

according to Thy righteousness. See on xxxi. 2.

let them not rejoice over me. Because that would
mean the triumph of evil.

25. The plea of verse 4 is repeated and elaborated (cf. xl. 15ff., for a similar petition).

27. *that delight in my righteousness.* Rather

in my vindication (see on iv. 2) (Kimchi).

magnified be the LORD. Who has demonstrated
His justice and might by humbling the arrogant.

peace. Welfare.

His servant. He puts forward his own experience as a shining example of God's care for the
innocent.

28. *shall speak.* The same verb as 'meditate'
in i. 2. Here too it denotes the study of Torah
which necessitates active thinking coupled with
verbal expression (Hirsch).

Thy righteousness. Through the study of Torah, God's righteous ways are recognized
(Daath Sofrim).

all the day. Unceasingly.

36

לו

1 For the Leader. [A Psalm]
of David the servant of the
LORD.

2 Transgression speaketh to the
wicked, methinks—
There is no fear of God before his
eyes.

3 For it flattereth him in his eyes,
Until his iniquity be found, and
he be hated.

4 The words of his mouth are
iniquity and deceit;
He hath left off to be wise, to do
good.

לַמְנַצֵּחַ לְעֶבֶד־יְהֹוָה לְדָוִד׃

נְאֻם־פֶּשַׁע לָרָשָׁע בְּקֶרֶב לִבִּי

אֵין־פַּחַד אֱלֹהִים לְנֶגֶד עֵינָיו׃

כִּי־הֶחֱלִיק אֵלָיו בְּעֵינָיו

לִמְצֹא עֲוֺנוֹ לִשְׂנֹא׃

דִּבְרֵי־פִיו אָוֶן וּמִרְמָה

חָדַל לְהַשְׂכִּיל לְהֵיטִיב׃

DIVINE LOVINGKINDNESS

THE main theme of this Psalm is the attributes of God, particularly His love for His creatures. Its glory is brought into prominence by being set beside the sinfulness of the wicked. The poem begins with a characterization of the godless, but soon turns from their sordidness to extol the goodness of God in language of striking beauty.

1. *the servant of the LORD*. It has been suggested that the sequence of this and the foregoing Psalm was determined by the reference in the latter to *His servant* (xxxv. 27). David is similarly described in the heading of xviii. (cf. Daath Sofrim).

2-5 PORTRAIT OF THE GODLESS

2. *methinks*. lit. 'in the midst of my heart.' The Psalmist tries to penetrate the mental processes of the wicked man in order to account for his evil way of living; he imagines *transgression*, i.e. the evil inclination, inciting the person to sin by assuring him that he need have no fear of being called to account (Rashi).

fear of God. Not the usual phrase denoting reverential awe. The Hebrew means 'dread' inspired by the thought of His condemnation.

before his eyes. Before his mind to deter him from evil conduct.

3. The Hebrew of this verse is somewhat obscure. Several meanings have been attached to it, among them the following: It makes transgression pleasant to his eyes, only so that his transgression be discovered so that he be hated (by God) (Rashi, Metsudath David). Alternatively, in accordance with what he perceives, the LORD has smoothed the path for him to vent his hatred upon anyone who stands in the way of his sinful goals (Hirsch).

4. *iniquity and deceit*. Cf. x. 7. The Psalmist now describes the consequences which follow from the false hypothesis. The first effect is seen in a lying and mischievous tongue.

to be wise. To have the understanding which distinguishes between good and evil and prefers the former.

5 He deviseth iniquity upon his bed;
  He setteth himself in a way that
    is not good;
  He abhorreth not evil.

6 Thy lovingkindness, O LORD, is
    in the heavens;
  Thy faithfulness reacheth unto the
    skies.

7 Thy righteousness is like the
    mighty mountains;
  Thy judgments are like the great
    deep;
  Man and beast Thou preservest,
    O LORD.

8 How precious is Thy lovingkind-
    ness, O God!
  And the children of men take re-
    fuge in the shadow of Thy
    wings.

9 They are abundantly satisfied with
    the fatness of Thy house;

5 אָוֶן ׀ יַחְשֹׁב עַל־מִשְׁכָּבוֹ
יִתְיַצֵּב עַל־דֶּרֶךְ לֹא־טוֹב
רָע לֹא יִמְאָס:
6 יְהֹוָה בְּהַשָּׁמַיִם חַסְדֶּךָ
אֱמוּנָתְךָ עַד־שְׁחָקִים:
7 צִדְקָתְךָ ׀ כְּהַרְרֵי־אֵל
מִשְׁפָּטֶיךָ תְּהוֹם רַבָּה
אָדָם וּבְהֵמָה תוֹשִׁיעַ יְהֹוָה:
8 מַה־יָּקָר חַסְדְּךָ אֱלֹהִים
וּבְנֵי אָדָם בְּצֵל כְּנָפֶיךָ יֶחֱסָיוּן:
9 יִרְוְיֻן מִדֶּשֶׁן בֵּיתֶךָ

---

5. *upon his bed.* A time used by the righteous for wise meditation (see on iv. 5), but
by the wicked for devising base schemes (cf.
Kimchi).

setteth himself. He deliberately selects the
evil way.

he abhorreth not evil. His conscience is so
dulled that it does not instinctively recoil
from wrong-doing.

6-10   THE ATTRIBUTES OF GOD

6. *is in the heavens.* Rashi understands the
verse in a negative light. Because of the
wicked, You have moved your kindness away
from the earth and lifted Your faith out of
reach. Others, however, read this as a description of God's positive qualities. The
Psalmist, unlike the wicked, recognized that
God's kindness fills the world even unto the
heavens (Kimchi). Alternatively, His loving
kindness radiates from the heavens and His

influence on this earth has its source in the
higher spheres (Ibn Ezra, Daath Sofrim).

7. *like the mighty mountains.* lit. 'like the
mountains of God,' symbolizing the idea that
they are immovable and eternal.

like the great deep. Unfathomable and mys-
terious. Likewise, His ways and dealings are
not to be questioned—their purpose is often
hidden from man (Malbim).

man and beast. God cares for all His creatures (cxlv. 9).

8. *precious.* It is man's priceless treasure.

children of men. See on viii. 5. God, the
Father of all, offers His special protection to
man who is imbued with a spiritual soul,
elevating him above other creatures (Malbim).

in the shadow of Thy wings. See on lvii. 2.

9. *the fatness of Thy house.* God is thought
of as a bountiful Host in Whose house the

And Thou makest them drink of
the river of Thy pleasures.

10 For with Thee is the fountain of
life;
In Thy light do we see light.

11 O continue Thy lovingkindness
unto them that know Thee;
And Thy righteousness to the
upright in heart.

12 Let not the foot of pride overtake
me,
And let not the hand of the
wicked drive me away.

13 There are the workers of iniquity
fallen;
They are thrust down, and are
not able to rise.

וַתַּחַל עֲדָנֶיךָ תַשְׁקֵם:

10 כִּי־עִמְּךָ מְקוֹר חַיִּים
בְּאוֹרְךָ נִרְאֶה־אוֹר:

11 מְשֹׁךְ חַסְדְּךָ לְיֹדְעֶיךָ
וְצִדְקָתְךָ לְיִשְׁרֵי־לֵב:

12 אַל־תְּבוֹאֵנִי רֶגֶל גַּאֲוָה
וְיַד־רְשָׁעִים אַל־תְּנִדֵנִי:

13 שָׁם נָפְלוּ פֹּעֲלֵי אָוֶן
דֹּחוּ וְלֹא־יָכְלוּ קוּם:

guests receive an abundance of comforts.

river of Thy pleasures. The knowledge of
God and His ways is compared to delights
which ceaselessly flow in a refreshing stream
(Ibn Ezra). These are no physical enjoyments
but are God endowed pleasures which can be
sensed and enjoyed only by man's spirit
(Hirsch).

10. *fountain of life*. The source of all life
and enlightenment is the Divine Presence.
All of nature derives its vitality from God
alone (Malbim).

in Thy light do we see light. Only by means
of the light which emanates from God is
man able to perceive the more exalted purposes of living. Without it, we would wander
in darkness (Hirsch). Or, the spiritual light is
the source of the physical light by which we
perceive reality (Malbim).

11-13 CONCLUDING PRAYER

11. *continue*. God's lovingkindness is not
a theory, but has been actually experienced
by those who acknowledge Him. The Psalmist therefore prays for its continuance.

12. The petition in this verse must be understood in connection with verses 2ff. He
prays to be spared from the activities of the
transgressors, lest he be driven from his home.

foot of pride. Which ruthlessly tramples upon
the weak.

13. *there are the workers of iniquity fallen*.
In his implicit faith he sees the answer to his
prayer before it has taken place in time. He
points, as it were, to the next world and
exclaims, 'there have they finally met their
end.'

not able to rise. When humbled by God, their
power is broken forever.

37

לֵז

1 [A Psalm] of David.
Fret not thyself because of evil-
doers,
Neither be thou envious against
them that work unrighteousness.

2 For they shall soon wither like
the grass,
And fade as the green herb.

3 Trust in the LORD, and do good;
Dwell in the land, and cherish
faithfulness.

4 So shalt thou delight thyself in
the LORD;
And He shall give thee the petitions of thy heart.

5 Commit thy way unto the LORD;
Trust also in Him, and He will
bring it to pass.

6 And He will make thy righteousness to go forth as the light,
And thy right as the noonday.

לְדָוִד ׀

אַל־תִּתְחַר בַּמְּרֵעִים
אַל־תְּקַנֵּא בְּעֹשֵׂי עַוְלָה׃

2 כִּי כֶחָצִיר מְהֵרָה יִמָּלוּ
וּכְיֶרֶק דֶּשֶׁא יִבּוֹלוּן׃

3 בְּטַח בַּיהוָה וַעֲשֵׂה־טוֹב
שְׁכָן־אֶרֶץ וּרְעֵה אֱמוּנָה׃

4 וְהִתְעַנַּג עַל־יְהוָה
וְיִתֶּן־לְךָ מִשְׁאֲלֹת לִבֶּךָ׃

5 גּוֹל עַל־יְהוָה דַּרְכֶּךָ
וּבְטַח עָלָיו וְהוּא יַעֲשֶׂה׃

6 וְהוֹצִיא כָאוֹר צִדְקֶךָ
וּמִשְׁפָּטֶךָ כַּצָּהֳרָיִם׃

THE PROBLEM OF EVIL

THIS Psalm should be read in connection with Psalm LXXIII and is a sequel to Psalm XXXVI.
It is concerned with the perplexing thoughts aroused by the ascendancy of the wicked and the
seeming triumph of evil. The poet does not go deeply into the question. He is satisfied to
counsel trust. In His own time God punishes the wicked and rewards the just. In structure the
composition is based upon an alphabetical acrostic, with the omission of *ain*, each letter usually
introducing two verses.

1. *fret not thyself.* Because evil-doers
flourish (Rashi, Kimchi).

envious. Of their temporary success. The
verse is repeated in Prov. xxiv. 19.

2. *wither.* Better, 'be cut down.' *Grass* offers a natural simile for what has but a brief
existence (cf. xc. 5f., ciii. 15; Isa. xl. 6ff.).

3. *trust in the LORD.* That He will right
matters giving evil-doers their dues.

and do good. Be not diverted from the path of
righteousness because of the temporary advantages which evil offers.

dwell in the land. The reward for 'doing good'
will be an everlasting serene existence in

your land (Rashi).

cherish. lit. 'feed on.' Let your sustenance be
trust in His faithfulness.

4. *delight thyself in the LORD.* Reliance
upon God will justify itself in spiritual and
material satisfaction.

5. *commit...unto.* lit. 'roll...upon.' Relieve yourself of the burden of anxiety by
placing it upon Him (cf. xxii. 9).

6. *righteousness.* Vindication (cf. Hirsch).
It is now hidden behind a cloud which, when
rolled away, will shine brightly (cf. Job. xi.
15-19.)

as the noonday. When the rays of the sun are

7 Resign thyself unto the Lord,
    and wait patiently for Him;
  Fret not thyself because of him
    who prospereth in his way,
  Because of the man who bringeth
    wicked devices to pass.

8 Cease from anger, and forsake
    wrath;
  Fret not thyself, it tendeth only
    to evil-doing.

9 For evil-doers shall be cut off;
  But those that wait for the Lord
    they shall inherit the land.

10 And yet a little while, and the
    wicked is no more;
  Yea, thou shalt look well at his
    place, and he is not.

11 But the humble shall inherit the
    land,
  And delight themselves in the
    abundance of peace.

12 The wicked plotteth against the
    righteous,
  And gnasheth at him with his
    teeth.

13 The Lord doth laugh at him;
  For He seeth that his day is
    coming.

14 The wicked have drawn out the
    sword, and have bent their
    bow;

7 דּוֹם ׀ לַיהוָֹה וְהִתְחוֹלֵל לוֹ
אַל־תִּתְחַר בְּמַצְלִיחַ דַּרְכּוֹ
בְּאִישׁ עֹשֶׂה מְזִמּוֹת׃

8 הֶרֶף מֵאַף וַעֲזֹב חֵמָה
אַל־תִּתְחַר אַךְ־לְהָרֵעַ׃

9 כִּי־מְרֵעִים יִכָּרֵתוּן
וְקֹוֵי יְהוָֹה הֵמָּה יִירְשׁוּ־אָרֶץ׃

10 וְעוֹד מְעַט וְאֵין רָשָׁע
וְהִתְבּוֹנַנְתָּ עַל־מְקוֹמוֹ וְאֵינֶנּוּ׃

11 וַעֲנָוִים יִירְשׁוּ־אָרֶץ
וְהִתְעַנְּגוּ עַל־רֹב שָׁלוֹם׃

12 זֹמֵם רָשָׁע לַצַּדִּיק
וְחֹרֵק עָלָיו שִׁנָּיו׃

13 אֲדֹנָי יִשְׂחַק־לוֹ
כִּי־רָאָה כִּי־יָבֹא יוֹמוֹ׃

14 חֶרֶב ׀ פָּתְחוּ רְשָׁעִים וְדָרְכוּ קַשְׁתָּם

most brilliant and the light clearest.

7. *resign thyself.* lit. 'be silent,' (Targum), which is explained by *fret not thyself*; remain calm in thy trust (Metsudath David).

8. *cease from anger.* Do not be incensed by the profit of the undeserving (Ibn Ezra), because it may lead to a denial of God's rule in the world and subsequent wrongful acts.

9. *they shall inherit the land.* So again in verses 11, 22, 29, and 34. The wicked schemed to increase their possessions but will lose everything when they are destroyed; the righteous will acquire all that they left behind (cf. Kimchi).

10. *he is not.* Not a trace of him remains.

11. *humble.* They who smarted under the oppression of the sinful (Kimchi).

abundance of peace. Which will ensue after the wicked are cut off (Kimchi).

12. *gnasheth.* Cf. xxxv. 16.

13. *the Lord doth laugh.* In derision, as in ii. 4.

his day. Of retribution, which is preordained by God though its exact time is unknown to man (Hirsch).

14. *sword...bow.* Emblems of violent attack symbolizing the armed might of the

To cast down the poor and
 needy,
To slay such as are upright in the
 way;

15 Their sword shall enter into their
 own heart,
And their bows shall be broken.

16 Better is a little that the righteous
 hath
Than the abundance of many
 wicked.

17 For the arms of the wicked shall
 be broken;
But the LORD upholdeth the
 righteous.

18 The LORD knoweth the days of
 them that are whole-hearted;
And their inheritance shall be for
 ever.

19 They shall not be ashamed in the
 time of evil;
And in the days of famine they
 shall be satisfied.

20 For the wicked shall perish,
And the enemies of the LORD
 shall be as the fat of lambs—
They shall pass away in smoke,
 they shall pass away.

לְהַפִּיל עָנִי וְאֶבְיוֹן
לִטְבוֹחַ יִשְׁרֵי־דָרֶךְ׃
15 חַרְבָּם תָּבוֹא בְלִבָּם
וְקַשְּׁתוֹתָם תִּשָּׁבַרְנָה׃
16 טוֹב מְעַט לַצַּדִּיק
מֵהֲמוֹן רְשָׁעִים רַבִּים׃
17 כִּי זְרוֹעוֹת רְשָׁעִים תִּשָּׁבַרְנָה
וְסוֹמֵךְ צַדִּיקִים יְהוָה׃
18 יוֹדֵעַ יְהוָה יְמֵי תְמִימִם
וְנַחֲלָתָם לְעוֹלָם תִּהְיֶה׃
19 לֹא־יֵבֹשׁוּ בְּעֵת רָעָה
וּבִימֵי רְעָבוֹן יִשְׂבָּעוּ׃
20 כִּי רְשָׁעִים ׀ יֹאבֵדוּ
וְאֹיְבֵי יְהוָה כִּיקַר כָּרִים
כָּלוּ בֶעָשָׁן כָּלוּ׃

wicked as compared with the defenceless
state of their victims.

poor and needy. See on 9:19.

16. *abundance.* lit. 'tumult.' It suggests a
noisy mob clamoring for attention (Hirsch).

17. *arms.* With broken arms they can neither work mischief on others, nor do evil
themselves.

upholdeth. The care of God is their true
strength, supporting them so that they do not
fall.

18. *the days.* The vicissitudes which befall
them day by day; He is not indifferent to their
fate (Hirsch).

for ever. The message of their life's achievements will pass on to their descendants
(Hirsch).

19. *evil.* Misfortune.

days of famine. A common calamity in those
times.

20. *as the fat of lambs.* Burnt upon the altar
as a sacrifice; so will the wicked be consumed. This translation is given in the
Targum, but Rashi has 'like the first rays of
the morning sun shimmering through the
clouds on the horizon,' which do not last.
Accordingly the thought is the same as in
verse 2; the unrighteous will first shine but
later fade away.

they shall pass away, etc. Better, 'they are
consumed; in smoke are they consumed.'
The past tense is used of an action still to take
place as a mark of certainty that it will come
to pass (cf. Daath Sofrim).

21 The wicked borroweth, and
    payeth not;
    But the righteous dealeth grac-
    iously, and giveth.

22 For such as are blessed of Him
    shall inherit the land;
    And they that are cursed of Him
    shall be cut off.

23 It is of the LORD that a man's
    goings are established;
    And He delighteth in his way.

24 Though he fall, he shall not be
    utterly cast down;
    For the LORD upholdeth his hand.

25 I have been young, and now am
    old;
    Yet have I not seen the righteous
    forsaken,
    Nor his seed begging bread.

26 All the day long he dealeth
    graciously, and lendeth;
    And his seed is blessed.

27 Depart from evil, and do good;
    And dwell for evermore.

לֹוֶה רָשָׁע וְלֹא יְשַׁלֵּם 21
וְצַדִּיק חוֹנֵן וְנוֹתֵן׃

כִּי מְבֹרָכָיו יִירְשׁוּ אָרֶץ 22
וּמְקֻלָּלָיו יִכָּרֵתוּ׃

מֵיְהוָה מִצְעֲדֵי־גֶבֶר כּוֹנָנוּ 23
וְדַרְכּוֹ יֶחְפָּץ׃

כִּי־יִפֹּל לֹא־יוּטָל 24
כִּי־יְהוָה סוֹמֵךְ יָדוֹ׃

נַעַר ׀ הָיִיתִי גַּם־זָקַנְתִּי 25
וְלֹא־רָאִיתִי צַדִּיק נֶעֱזָב
וְזַרְעוֹ מְבַקֶּשׁ־לָחֶם׃

כָּל־הַיּוֹם חוֹנֵן וּמַלְוֶה 26
וְזַרְעוֹ לִבְרָכָה׃

סוּר מֵרָע וַעֲשֵׂה־טוֹב 27
וּשְׁכֹן לְעוֹלָם׃

---

21. *the wicked borroweth.* In the reversal of his fortunes he will be in want and forced to borrow, but through lack of means he will never be in a position to repay his debt.

dealeth graciously. In contrast the righteous will have plenty and use their wealth to do acts of charity.

23. *a man's goings are established.* The reference is to the righteous man; his ability to walk steadfastly in his chosen path is granted to him by God. An explanation of verses 23 and 24 is proposed by Hirsch: The direction of man's life has been prescribed by the LORD—and this is the path which is to be desired. Should such a man stumble while on this road, he shall never be cast down entirely for the LORD will help him rise again. The phrase *He delighteth in his way* is ambiguous and may also mean that

God favours the man's way (cf. Kimchi, Metsudath David).

25. The Psalmist gives his personal testimony to the doctrine he is expounding. He does not imply that the righteous man is exempt from privations; the addition of *nor his seed begging bread*, as well as the next verse, indicate clearly what is intended. The righteous man may have to pass through a period of suffering but he is not forsaken by God. Eventually he comes into his own, so that his descendants lack nothing and he has ample means with which to act benevolently towards others.

27. *Depart from evil, and do good.* Repeated from xxxiv. 15.

dwell for evermore. Remain in peaceful possession of your land and bequeath it to your children.

28 For the LORD loveth justice,
And forsaketh not His saints;
They are preserved for ever;
But the seed of the wicked shall
be cut off.

29 The righteous shall inherit the
land,
And dwell therein for ever.

30 The mouth of the righteous
uttereth wisdom,
And his tongue speaketh justice.

31 The law of his God is in his
heart;
None of his steps slide.

32 The wicked watcheth the righteous,
And seeketh to slay him.

33 The LORD will not leave him in
his hand,
Nor suffer him to be condemned
when he is judged.

34 Wait for the LORD, and keep His
way,
And He will exalt thee to inherit
the land;
When the wicked are cut off, thou
shalt see it.

כִּי יְהֹוָה ׀ אֹהֵב מִשְׁפָּט 28
וְלֹא־יַעֲזֹב אֶת־חֲסִידָיו
לְעוֹלָם נִשְׁמָרוּ
וְזֶרַע רְשָׁעִים נִכְרָת׃
צַדִּיקִים יִירְשׁוּ־אָרֶץ 29
וְיִשְׁכְּנוּ לָעַד עָלֶיהָ׃
פִּי־צַדִּיק יֶהְגֶּה חָכְמָה 30
וּלְשׁוֹנוֹ תְּדַבֵּר מִשְׁפָּט׃
תּוֹרַת אֱלֹהָיו בְּלִבּוֹ 31
לֹא תִמְעַד אֲשֻׁרָיו׃
צוֹפֶה רָשָׁע לַצַּדִּיק 32
וּמְבַקֵּשׁ לַהֲמִיתוֹ׃
יְהֹוָה לֹא־יַעַזְבֶנּוּ בְיָדוֹ 33
וְלֹא יַרְשִׁיעֶנּוּ בְּהִשָּׁפְטוֹ׃
קַוֵּה אֶל־יְהֹוָה ׀ וּשְׁמֹר דַּרְכּוֹ 34
וִירוֹמִמְךָ לָרֶשֶׁת אָרֶץ
בְּהִכָּרֵת רְשָׁעִים תִּרְאֶה׃

---

28. *loveth justice*. Cf. xxxiii. 5.

His saints. They who act devoutly and are loyal to His will even beyond required standards.

A verse beginning with *ain* is omitted.

30. *uttereth*. The same verb as *speak* in xxxv. 28 (see commentary).

31. *slide*. From the path of integrity in which he walks firmly.

33. *not leave him in his hand*. Not abandon him to his power.

when he is judged. By judges corrupted by bribery and threats. If he is so condemned, God determines that the unjust verdict is not executed (Kimchi).

34. *thou shalt see it*. If you will 'keep His way,' you will see for yourselves how the Godless have been cut off. Those who have elevated themselves to a higher spiritual plane come to realise how fleeting is the success of the wicked (Hirsch).

35 I have seen the wicked in great
power,
And spreading himself like a leafy
tree in its native soil.

36 But one passed by, and, lo, he
was not;
Yea, I sought him, but he could
not be found.

37 Mark the man of integrity, and
behold the upright;
For there is a future for the man
of peace.

38 But transgressors shall be destroyed together;
The future of the wicked shall
be cut off.

39 But the salvation of the righteous
is of the LORD;
He is their stronghold in the time
of trouble.

40 And the LORD helpeth them, and
delivereth them;
He delivereth them from the
wicked, and saveth them,
Because they have taken refuge
in Him.

35 רָאִיתִי רָשָׁע עָרִיץ
וּמִתְעָרֶה כְּאֶזְרָח רַעֲנָן:

36 וַיַּעֲבֹר וְהִנֵּה אֵינֶנּוּ
וָאֲבַקְשֵׁהוּ וְלֹא נִמְצָא:

37 שְׁמָר־תָּם וּרְאֵה יָשָׁר
כִּי־אַחֲרִית לְאִישׁ שָׁלוֹם:

38 וּפֹשְׁעִים נִשְׁמְדוּ יַחְדָּו
אַחֲרִית רְשָׁעִים נִכְרָתָה:

39 וּתְשׁוּעַת צַדִּיקִים מֵיְהֹוָה
מָעוּזָּם בְּעֵת צָרָה:

40 וַיַּעְזְרֵם יְהֹוָה וַיְפַלְּטֵם
יְפַלְּטֵם מֵרְשָׁעִים וְיוֹשִׁיעֵם
כִּי־חָסוּ בוֹ:

35. *I have seen.* Another personal testimony like that in verse 25.

the wicked in great power. More forcibly, 'the wicked acting the tyrant.'

like a leafy tree. Firmly rooted and apparently full of vitality.

in its native soil. Where it seemed to be an irremoval fixture.

36. *he was not.* See verse 10.

could not be found. He suffered total extinction and not a vestige of him remained.

37. *mark.* lit. 'watch.' Take note of.

there is a future. In the everlasting reward of the World to Come, unlike the wicked man who will suffer everlasting punishment (Meiri).

the man of peace. It is characteristic of the man of integrity that he acts upon the admonition *seek peace and pursue it* (xxxiv. 15), whereas the wicked constantly stir up unrest and strife.

38. *together.* All of them (Hirsch).

future. See on verse 37.

39, 40. The final verses summarize the lesson which the Psalm teaches and the solution to the problem which has been its theme. God is an impregnable citadel, and they who take shelter in it survive the attacks made upon them, however bitter and prolonged.

38

לח

1 A Psalm of David, to make memorial.

2 O LORD, rebuke me not in Thine anger;
Neither chasten me in Thy wrath.

3 For Thine arrows are gone deep into me,
And Thy hand is come down upon me.

4 There is no soundness in my flesh because of Thine indignation;
Neither is there any health in my bones because of my sin.

5 For mine iniquities are gone over my head;
As a heavy burden they are too heavy for me.

מִזְמוֹר לְדָוִד לְהַזְכִּיר׃

2 יְהוָה אַל־בְּקֶצְפְּךָ תוֹכִיחֵנִי
וּבַחֲמָתְךָ תְיַסְּרֵנִי׃

3 כִּי־חִצֶּיךָ נִחֲתוּ בִי
וַתִּנְחַת עָלַי יָדֶךָ׃

4 אֵין־מְתֹם בִּבְשָׂרִי מִפְּנֵי זַעְמֶךָ
אֵין־שָׁלוֹם בַּעֲצָמַי מִפְּנֵי חַטָּאתִי׃

5 כִּי עֲוֺנֹתַי עָבְרוּ רֹאשִׁי
כְּמַשָּׂא כָבֵד יִכְבְּדוּ מִמֶּנִּי׃

A PENITENT'S PRAYER

THE analogy with Psalm VI will at once occur to the reader. The speaker is afflicted with pain and his physical condition causes him searching of heart. He acknowledges that his sufferings are the effect of sin. He therefore offers his prayer in a deeply repentant spirit. David well knew the emotional and physical tribulations that those striving for perfection can undergo. Rashi and others interpret the Psalm as referring to the nation, though the personal note is strongly marked throughout.

1. *to make memorial.* Hebrew *lehazkir,* again in the heading of Ps. lxx. The meaning is to bring the plight of David's suffering (Kimchi) or that of the entire nation (Rashi) to God's remembrance. Kimchi adds that David composed the Psalm for the benefit of anyone who might find himself in dire straits due to a crippling illness, the threats of an enemy, or similar trouble. It was a reminder that such a person could always turn to his Maker and pour out his heart with this prayer. In a similar vein, Hirsch notes that David's intention was to prevent future generations from going as'ray by reminding them how crushing and depressing remorse can be and how unhappy it can make us.

2-9 HIS SUFFERING

2. See vi. 2 with which this verse is identical but for one word.

3. *arrows.* Emblematic of Divine retribution (vii. 14) and descriptive of the spasms of pain which shoot through his body.

Thy hand is come down upon me. With crushing weight (cf. *Thy hand was heavy upon me,* xxxii. 4).

4. *health.* lit. 'peace,' perhaps a fever which prevents him from resting (see vi. 3).

5. *mine iniquities.* The cause of his malady. While in the previous verse the word '*het*' is used, here he mentions '*avon.*' The first word, which is in the singular, applies to an unintentional sin, and in this case may be a reference to the episode of Uriah and Bath-Sheba. The second word, used in the plural, alludes to several deliberate transgressions, such as apportioning the inheritance of Mephi-Bosheth (2 Sam. xix. 30) and the counting of the people of Israel (2 Sam. xxiv. 1) (Kimchi, Malbim).

are gone over my head. Have overwhelmed him like a flood, and he feels that he is sinking in its depths (Kimchi).

6 My wounds are noisome, they fester,
  Because of my foolishness.

7 I am bent and bowed down greatly;
  I go mourning all the day.

8 For my loins are filled with burning;
  And there is no soundness in my flesh.

9 I am benumbed and sore crushed;
  I groan by reason of the moaning of my heart.

10 Lord, all my desire is before Thee;
   And my sighing is not hid from Thee.

11 My heart fluttereth, my strength faileth me;
   As for the light of mine eyes, it also is gone from me.

12 My friends and my companions stand aloof from my plague;
   And my kinsmen stand afar off.

13 They also that seek after my life lay snares for me;
   And they that seek my hurt speak crafty devices,
   And utter deceits all the day.

6 הִבְאִישׁוּ נָמַקּוּ חַבּוּרֹתָי
  מִפְּנֵי אִוַּלְתִּי׃

7 נַעֲוֵיתִי שַׁחֹתִי עַד־מְאֹד
  כָּל־הַיּוֹם קֹדֵר ׀ הִלָּכְתִּי׃

8 כִּי־כְסָלַי מָלְאוּ נִקְלֶה
  וְאֵין מְתֹם בִּבְשָׂרִי׃

9 נְפוּגוֹתִי וְנִדְכֵּיתִי עַד־מְאֹד
  שָׁאַגְתִּי מִנַּהֲמַת לִבִּי׃

10 אֲדֹנָי נֶגְדְּךָ כָל־תַּאֲוָתִי
   וְאַנְחָתִי מִמְּךָ לֹא־נִסְתָּרָה׃

11 לִבִּי סְחַרְחַר עֲזָבַנִי כֹחִי
   וְאוֹר־עֵינַי גַּם־הֵם אֵין אִתִּי׃

12 אֹהֲבַי ׀ וְרֵעַי מִנֶּגֶד נִגְעִי יַעֲמֹדוּ
   וּקְרוֹבַי מֵרָחֹק עָמָדוּ׃

13 וַיְנַקְשׁוּ ׀ מְבַקְשֵׁי נַפְשִׁי
   וְדֹרְשֵׁי רָעָתִי דִּבְּרוּ הַוּוֹת
   וּמִרְמוֹת כָּל־הַיּוֹם יֶהְגּוּ׃

6. *noisome*. Emit foul smelling pus, so that he is an object of horror.

foolishness. Sin is the effect of folly. 'A man does not commit a transgression until a spirit of madness has entered into him' (Talmud Sotah 3a).

7. *bent and bowed*. By the many occurrences of sickness (Kimchi).

I go mourning. He is able to walk about, but his demeanour is that of a mourner.

8. *burning*. Inflammation (Targum).

9. *benumbed*. The same verb as in the phrase *and his heart fainted* (Gen. xlv. 26). The root-meaning is 'to grow cool'; he feels the chill of death creeping over him

moaning of my heart. The moaning for my illness and my suffering emanates from the depths of my heart (Metsudath).

10-15 HIS SUFFERING INTENSIFIED BY FRIENDS AND ENEMIES

10. *my desire*. God alone can fathom his needs (Rashi), and to Him only his heart turns (Ibn Ezra).

my sighing is not hid from Thee. His anguished prayer is addressed to God, and what he longs for is known to Him (cf. Metsudath David).

11. This verse represents the feelings of the troubled man whose mind is confused and who cannot concentrate or think clearly. The eyes, having followed the heart in sin, are also sorely affected (see Num. xv. 39).

12. *plague*. The term is often used of leprosy and he complains that he is treated like a leper.

13. *they that seek my hurt*. His enemies take advantage of his helplessness to scheme

14 But I am as a deaf man, I hear
    not;
   And I am as a dumb man that
    openeth not his mouth.

15 Yea, I am become as a man that
    heareth not,
   And in whose mouth are no
    arguments.

16 For in Thee, O LORD, do I hope;
   Thou wilt answer, O Lord my
    God.

17 For I said: 'Lest they rejoice
    over me;
   When my foot slippeth, they
    magnify themselves against
    me.'

18 For I am ready to halt,
   And my pain is continually be-
    fore me.

19 For I do declare mine iniquity;
   I am full of care because of my
    sin.

20 But mine enemies are strong in
    health;
   And they that hate me wrong-
    fully are multiplied.

21 They also that repay evil for good
   Are adversaries unto me, because
    I follow the thing that is good.

22 Forsake me not, O LORD;
   O my God, be not far from me.

23 Make haste to help me,
   O Lord, my salvation.

his destruction with words calculated to
break him (Kimchi).

14. *as a deaf man.* He ignores their words
and refrains from reacting to them (Kimchi).

15. *no arguments.* To justify himself.

16-23 HIS PLEA TO GOD

16. *in Thee, O LORD, do I hope.* He can expect no mercy from human justice and must
rely solely upon God to stand up for him.

17. *lest they rejoice over me.* Though a
sinner, he is penitent; and he abhors the
thought that his enemies might be able to
gloat that his appeal to God has failed.

my foot slippeth. Through misfortune.

18. *ready to halt.* See on xxxv. 15.

19. *I do declare mine iniquity.* He confesses that his sufferings are deserved as the
punishment of his wrong-doing; but he cannot help comparing his lot with the wicked
who are in sound health.

20. *in health.* Hebrew *chayyim*, 'alive': in
the full vigour of life.

21. *repay evil for good.* The ingratitude of
the men he had benefited is the climax of his
complaint.

22. *forsake me not.* As my friends have
done.

23. *make haste.* Cf. xxii. 20.

39

לט

1 For the Leader, for Jeduthun.
A Psalm of David.

2 I said: 'I will take heed to my
ways,
That I sin not with my tongue;
I will keep a curb upon my mouth,
While the wicked is before me.'

3 I was dumb with silence, I held
my peace, had no comfort;
And my pain was held in check.

4 My heart waxed hot within me;
While I was musing, the fire
kindled;
Then spoke I with my tongue:

לַמְנַצֵּחַ לִידִיתוּן מִזְמוֹר לְדָוִד׃

אָמַרְתִּי אֶשְׁמְרָה דְרָכַי 2
מֵחֲטוֹא בִלְשׁוֹנִי
אֶשְׁמְרָה לְפִי מַחְסוֹם
בְּעֹד רָשָׁע לְנֶגְדִּי׃

נֶאֱלַמְתִּי דוּמִיָּה 3
הֶחֱשֵׁיתִי מִטּוֹב
וּכְאֵבִי נֶעְכָּר׃

חַם־לִבִּי ׀ בְּקִרְבִּי 4
בַּהֲגִיגִי תִבְעַר־אֵשׁ
דִּבַּרְתִּי בִּלְשׁוֹנִי׃

v. l. לידותון ק׳

AN ELEGY

THE resemblance between this Psalm and the preceding one is noticeable. A sufferer in his
distress pleads with God. The language is more restrained and the thought deeper. His
pleading at times leads to an inquiry into the purpose of life.

1. *Jeduthun*. Also in the heading of lxii and
lxxvii. He is mentioned several times in the
Book of Chronicles as a director of the Temple
choir. The title means 'for the leader Jeduthun'
or 'for the leader (to be sung in the style) of
Jeduthun.'

2-4 HIS SILENCE UNDER SUFFERING

2. *I said*. i.e. within my heart; I determined
(Rashi).

take heed to my ways. Keep a strict watch
over his emotions (Rashi).

sin not with tongue. By railing at God for His
apparent injustice when he contrasts his fate
with that of the wicked (Rashi). Similarly Job
sinned not with his lips (ii. 10).

curb. An animal's muzzle (Rashi).

while the wicked is before me. While they
are still in his presence, lest his words,
spoken in their hearing, be an offence to

God (Daath Sofrim).

3. *I held my peace, had no comfort*. lit. 'I
held my peace, from good.' That is, he maintained silence and so denied himself even the
good things in life, i.e. the study of Torah
(Targum, Rashi). An alternative rendering is
that of A.V., *even from good*, i.e. he did not
even speak words to which no exception
could be taken (Kimchi, Ibn Ezra, Malbim).

my pain … in check. The more probable
translation is: 'but my pain was stirred,' intensified all the more by stifling the words which
sprang to his lips (cf. Hirsch) or, because of his
abstinence from Torah study (Rashi).

4. *my heart waxed hot*. With the heat of his
emotion.

the fire kindled. It blazed into flame; he could
no longer restrain himself and had to break
his silence (Malbim, Hirsch).

5 'LORD, make me to know **mine end**,
  And the measure of **my days**, what
    it is;
  Let me know how **short-lived I
    am.**

6 Behold, **Thou hast made my days
    as hand-breadths**;
  And mine age is as nothing before
    Thee;
  Surely every man at his best estate
    is altogether vanity.   Selah

7 Surely man walketh as a mere
    semblance;
  Surely for vanity they are in tur-
    moil;
  He heapeth up riches, and
    knoweth not who shall gather
    them.

8 And now, Lord, what wait I for?
  My hope, it is in Thee.

9 Deliver me from all my transgres-
    sions;
  Make me not the reproach of the
    base.

5 הוֹדִיעֵנִי יְהוָֹה ׀ קִצִּי

וּמִדַּת יָמַי מַה־הִיא

אֵדְעָה מֶה־חָדֵל אָנִי:

6 הִנֵּה טְפָחוֹת ׀ נָתַתָּה יָמַי

וְחֶלְדִּי כְאַיִן נֶגְדֶּךָ

אַךְ כָּל־הֶבֶל כָּל־אָדָם נִצָּב סֶלָה:

7 אַךְ־בְּצֶלֶם ׀ יִתְהַלֶּךְ־אִישׁ

אַךְ־הֶבֶל יֶהֱמָיוּן

יִצְבֹּר וְלֹא־יֵדַע מִי־אֹסְפָם:

8 וְעַתָּה מַה־קִּוִּיתִי אֲדֹנָי

תּוֹחַלְתִּי לְךָ הִיא:

9 מִכָּל־פְּשָׁעַי הַצִּילֵנִי

חֶרְפַּת נָבָל אַל־תְּשִׂימֵנִי:

5-7   HE ASKS FOR SELF-KNOWLEDGE

5. *make ... mine end.* A similar question is
asked by Job (vi. 11). It is not his wish to
know the end of his days, as this could hardly
have troubled him so deeply. More likely, it
is a desire to find out whether his existence
has any purpose at all; "what is the 'goal'
toward which life is directed?" (Hirsch). Alternatively, it is a wish to know how much
longer he will live and if he will have the time
to heal, as he cannot continue if no end to his
pain is imminent (Rashi, Kimchi).

what it is. How brief and fleeting life is.

how short-lived I am. What a transient creature I am.

6. *hand-breadths.* A small measure, the
sixth of a cubit. His lifetime consists of a few
such brief spaces.

mine age. My term of earthly existence.

at his best estate. lit. 'when standing firm,' in
his fullest vitality. Even then he is nothing
but *vanity*, 'a vapour,' something devoid of
substance.

7. *walketh as a mere semblance.* Or 'goeth
to and fro like a phantom.' There is nothing
solid about him.

they ... in turmoil. They worry and trouble
themselves over things without permanence.
The abstract ideas expressed are illustrated
by a concrete example. Man toils to pile up a
store of wealth, but he cannot be sure that he
will be the one to make use of it (cf. Hirsch).

8-12   HIS PRAYER FOR RELIEF

8. *and now.* Introduces a change in the line
of argument.

what wait I for? In view of the estimate of
life just given, what goal can I have before
me? The answer comes at once: he rests his
future in God (Hirsch).

9. *from ... transgressions.* Which are the
source of his bodily pain and mental anguish.
His sins are a barrier between himself and
God's desire to heal him (Kimchi).

the base. Hebrew *nabal*, the word used in xiv.
1. Those who acted on the thought 'there is

10 I am dumb, I open not my
    mouth;
    Because Thou hast done it.
11 Remove Thy stroke from off me;
    I am consumed by the blow of
    Thy hand.
12 With rebukes dost Thou chasten
    man for iniquity,
    And like a moth Thou makest
    his beauty to consume away;
    Surely every man is vanity.
                 Selah
13 Hear my prayer, O Lord, and
    give ear unto my cry;
    Keep not silence at my tears;
    For I am a stranger with Thee,
    A sojourner, as all my fathers
    were.
14 Look away from me, that I may
    take comfort,
    Before I go hence, and be no
    more.'

10 נֶאֱלַמְתִּי לֹא אֶפְתַּח־פִּי
כִּי אַתָּה עָשִׂיתָ:
11 הָסֵר מֵעָלַי נִגְעֶךָ
מִתִּגְרַת יָדְךָ אֲנִי כָלִיתִי:
12 בְּתוֹכָחוֹת עַל־עָוֹן יִסַּרְתָּ אִישׁ
וַתֶּמֶס כָּעָשׁ חֲמוּדוֹ
אַךְ הֶבֶל כָּל־אָדָם סֶלָה:
13 שִׁמְעָה תְפִלָּתִי יְהוָה
וְשַׁוְעָתִי הַאֲזִינָה
אֶל־דִּמְעָתִי אַל־תֶּחֱרַשׁ
כִּי גֵר אָנֹכִי עִמָּךְ
תּוֹשָׁב כְּכָל־אֲבוֹתָי:
14 הָשַׁע מִמֶּנִּי וְאַבְלִיגָה
בְּטֶרֶם אֵלֵךְ וְאֵינֶנִּי:

no God.' He does not wish to be the taunt of such degraded men, which he would be if no proof of Divine help were forthcoming (Kimchi).

10. *I am dumb*. This may signify that he makes no retort to the scoffers, conscious that what has befallen him was ordained by God (Kimchi). Or, connected with what follows, it is the expression of his resolve to cease his questioning of God and submit to His judgment (Hirsch).

11. *by the blow of Thy hand*. More lit. 'by the hostility of Thy hand' (Rashi).

12. *with rebukes*. He confirms his belief that man's iniquity is followed by chastening reproofs from God (cf. Rashi).

like a moth. Symbolic of destructive power (cf. Isa. i. 9; Hosea v. 12).

his beauty. Better, 'his desirable things,' (cf. Hirsch) a reference either to his monetary possessions (Metsudath), or to his body and his physical strength (Rashi, Ibn Ezra, Kimchi).

13-14   THE FINAL PLEA

13. *hear my prayer*. For pardon and renewed health.

at my tears. 'From the day the Temple was destroyed, the gates of prayer were locked; but although the gates of prayer were locked, the gates of tears remained unlocked' (Talmud B.M. 59a).

stranger...sojourner. Unlike natives possessing the rights of citizenship, the forefathers were dependant upon the tolerance of the people among whom they temporarily resided. The Psalmist thought of himself as a temporary dweller upon earth, and appealed to God to make his stay bearable.

14. *look away from me*. Usually the petition is for God to look towards the suppliant and show favour to him. But here, the Psalmist asks that the hand of God which causes suffering shall be turned away from him, so that he may strengthen himself (Rashi).

take comfort. More lit. 'recover his strength' (Rashi, see Hirsch).

40

לַמְנַצֵּחַ לְדָוִד ° מִזְמוֹר:

2 קַוֹּה קִוִּיתִי יְהֹוָה
וַיֵּט אֵלַי וַיִּשְׁמַע שַׁוְעָתִי:

3 וַיַּעֲלֵנִי ׀ מִבּוֹר שָׁאוֹן מִטִּיט הַיָּוֵן
וַיָּקֶם עַל־סֶלַע רַגְלַי כּוֹנֵן אֲשֻׁרָי:

4 וַיִּתֵּן בְּפִי ׀ שִׁיר חָדָשׁ
תְּהִלָּה לֵאלֹהֵינוּ
יִרְאוּ רַבִּים וְיִירָאוּ וְיִבְטְחוּ בַּיהֹוָה:

5 אַשְׁרֵי הַגֶּבֶר אֲשֶׁר־שָׂם יְהֹוָה מִבְטַחוֹ
וְלֹא־פָנָה אֶל־רְהָבִים וְשָׂטֵי כָזָב:

1 For the Leader. A Psalm of David.

2 I waited patiently for the LORD;
And He inclined unto me, and heard my cry.

3 He brought me up also out of the tumultuous pit, out of the miry clay;
And He set my feet upon a rock, He established my goings.

4 And He hath put a new song in my mouth, even praise unto our God;
Many shall see, and fear,
And shall trust in the LORD.

5 Happy is the man that hath made the LORD his trust,
And hath not turned unto the arrogant, nor unto such as fall away treacherously.

PRAISE AND PRAYER

A DISTINCT break occurs at the end of verse 12. The first part consists of a hymn of praise for past deliverance, while the second is a petition for aid in present danger. David is confident, however, that God will deliver him as in the past. He points out that he has always striven to apply his own understanding of God's ways for purposes of spiritual ennoblement as well as for the edification of his people. Thus, while in the midst of his suffering, he is filled with Divine inspiration (Hirsch). A notable feature is that verses 14-18 appear separately as Ps lxx.

2-4 HIS TRUST IN GOD REWARDED

2. *He inclined unto me.* He approached to effect my rescue; or, it may be an abbreviated form of the phrase *incline Thine ear unto me* (xxxi. 3) to hearken to my prayer.

3. *the tumultuous pit.* Metsudath Zion has 'a dark pit' but Rashi renders 'pit of roaring waters.' All the phrases in the verse are to be understood figuratively and are explained in the Talmud (Eruv. 19a) as being Scriptural idioms used to describe Gehinom.

miry clay. Swamps indicate his feeling of doom. He was in a position where escape seemed impossible (Malbim).

set ... upon a rock. When Divine help reached him, he no longer languished in a watery pit but felt that he stood upon solid rock.

established my goings. Better, 'made firm my steps' (cf. xxxvii. 23); he no longer slithered in a morass.

4. *a new song.* See on xxxiii. 3.

shall see, and fear. They will reflect upon his deliverance and be filled with awe at God's saving power (cf. Kimchi).

5-6 HAPPINESS OF THE TRUSTFUL

5. *a man.* Hebrew, *geber*. See on xxxiv. 9.

hath not turned. To obtain security by compromising with the *arrogant* who at first inspire trust, but when needed turn out to be treacherous (Hirsch).

such as fall away treacherously. Rather, 'such as fall away to falsehood'; they who rely

6 Many things hast Thou done, O
    Lord my God,
  Even Thy wondrous works, and
    Thy thoughts toward us;
  There is none to be compared
    unto Thee!
  If I would declare and speak of
    them,
  They are more than can be told.

7 Sacrifice and meal-offering Thou
    hast no delight in;
  Mine ears hast Thou opened;
  Burnt-offering and sin-offering
    hast Thou not required.

8 Then said I: 'Lo, I am come
  With the roll of a book which is
    prescribed for me;

9 I delight to do Thy will, O my God;
  Yea, Thy law is in my inmost
    parts.'

10 I have preached righteousness in
    the great congregation,
  Lo, I did not refrain my lips;
  O Lord, Thou knowest.

6 רַבּוֹת עָשִׂיתָ ׀ אַתָּה ׀ יְהוָה אֱלֹהַי
נִפְלְאֹתֶיךָ וּמַחְשְׁבֹתֶיךָ אֵלֵינוּ
אֵין ׀ עֲרֹךְ אֵלֶיךָ אַגִּידָה וַאֲדַבֵּרָה
עָצְמוּ מִסַּפֵּר׃

7 זֶבַח וּמִנְחָה ׀ לֹא־חָפַצְתָּ
אָזְנַיִם כָּרִיתָ לִּי
עוֹלָה וַחֲטָאָה לֹא שָׁאָלְתָּ׃

8 אָז אָמַרְתִּי הִנֵּה־בָאתִי
בִּמְגִלַּת־סֵפֶר כָּתוּב עָלָי׃

9 לַעֲשׂוֹת־רְצוֹנְךָ אֱלֹהַי חָפָצְתִּי
וְתוֹרָתְךָ בְּתוֹךְ מֵעָי׃

10 בִּשַּׂרְתִּי צֶדֶק ׀ בְּקָהָל רָב
הִנֵּה שְׂפָתַי לֹא אֶכְלָא
יְהוָה אַתָּה יָדָעְתָּ׃

upon what proves to be false, instead of God Who is sure (Kimchi).

6. Translate: 'Abundantly hast Thou wrought, even Thou, O Lord, my God, Thy wondrous works and Thy plans towards us' (cf. Hirsch). This is in contrast to the broken reeds to which others had resorted for safety; and so the Psalmist continues with the exclamation that God is incomparable as a Helper.

7-9 HOW GRATITUDE IS BEST DISPLAYED

7. To understand this section, it should be prefaced with the question, 'How can I thank God for His wondrous works toward me?' The first part of the answer is clearly influenced by 1 Sam. xv. 22.

mine ears hast Thou opened. lit. 'pierced,' so that they are not stopped up and he is able to hear the declaration of God's will and thank Him for His favours. Obedience to His law is superior to sacrifice (Kimchi).

hast Thou not required. The inference is not to be drawn that the service of the altar was contrary to Divine ordinance. The offerings were part of His worship, but not independent of a sense of duty toward Him and moral self improvement. To the question, *What doth the Lord require of thee?* Scripture answers: *To walk in all His ways and to love Him* (Deut. x. 12; cf. also Micah vi. 8) (see Hirsch. See also Hirsch on Gen. iv. 3, Lev. x. 1).

8. *then said I.* When his ears had been opened to an understanding of God's message (Malbim, Hirsch).

lo, I am come. Equal to 'behold, here am I,' denoting his readiness to obey.

the roll of a book. A book in the form of a scroll, viz. the Torah of Moses (Kimchi).

9. *I delight.* Obedience is not prompted by dread of God's punishment or expectation of a reward. It is his joy to do God's will.

my inmost parts. lit. 'my bowels,' the seat of emotion which controls action.

10-12 PUBLIC TESTIMONY

10. *preached.* Announced publicly. He had

11 I have not hid Thy righteousness
within my heart;
I have declared Thy faithfulness
and Thy salvation;
I have not concealed Thy mercy
and Thy truth from the great
congregation.

12 Thou, O Lord, wilt not withhold
Thy compassions from me;
Let Thy mercy and Thy truth
continually preserve me.

13 For innumerable evils have compassed me about,
Mine iniquities have overtaken
me, so that I am not able to
look up;
They are more than the hairs of
my head, and my heart hath
failed me.

14 Be pleased, O Lord, to deliver
me;
O Lord, make haste to help me.

15 Let them be ashamed and
abashed together

11 צִדְקָתְךָ לֹא־כִסִּיתִי ׀ בְּתוֹךְ לִבִּי
אֱמוּנָתְךָ וּתְשׁוּעָתְךָ אָמָרְתִּי
לֹא־כִחַדְתִּי חַסְדְּךָ וַאֲמִתְּךָ
לְקָהָל רָב:
12 אַתָּה יְהֹוָה לֹא־תִכְלָא רַחֲמֶיךָ מִמֶּנִּי
חַסְדְּךָ וַאֲמִתְּךָ תָּמִיד יִצְּרוּנִי:
13 כִּי אָפְפוּ־עָלַי ׀ רָעוֹת עַד־אֵין מִסְפָּר
הִשִּׂיגוּנִי עֲוֹנֹתַי וְלֹא־יָכֹלְתִּי לִרְאוֹת
עָצְמוּ מִשַּׂעֲרוֹת רֹאשִׁי
וְלִבִּי עֲזָבָנִי:
14 רְצֵה יְהֹוָה לְהַצִּילֵנִי
יְהֹוָה לְעֶזְרָתִי חוּשָׁה:
15 יֵבֹשׁוּ וְיַחְפְּרוּ ׀ יַחַד

not been satisfied to benefit from God's
mercy, but his longing had been to induce
others to recognize it too (Kimchi).

the great congregation. Cf. xxii. 26, xxxv.
18.

11. He proclaimed the Divine attributes of
righteousness, faithfulness, mercy and truth
to as many as possible of his fellowmen.

12. *withhold.* The same verb as *refrain* in
verse 10. As he had not refrained from proclaiming to others the merciful qualities of
God, he feels sure that God will not refrain
from continuing to display them towards
him. He is still in need of them as the next
section proceeds to tell (Daath Sofrim).

13-18 PLEA FOR HELP

13. *for.* The reason of his hope in verse 12.

Many afflictions have descended upon him;
he is surrounded by them on all sides.

mine iniquities have overtaken me. The
consequences of his sins have come upon
him. Only that can explain the dangerous
plight he is in (Kimchi).

look up. Better, 'see.' But I was originally
blind to the fact that my sins were the cause
of my suffering (Malbim).

my heart. My courage (Metsudath).

14. *be pleased.* lit. 'have the will.' As it had
been his delight to do God's will (verse 9), so
may it be His will to fulfil his wish.

make haste to help me. The same phrase as in
xxxviii. 23, but with the order of the words
inverted.

15. Almost a verbal repetition of xxxv. 4.

That seek after my soul to sweep
    it away;
Let them be turned backward
    and brought to confusion
That delight in my hurt.

16 Let them be appalled by reason
    of their shame
That say unto me: 'Aha, aha.'

17 Let all those that seek Thee re-
    joice and be glad in Thee;
Let such as love Thy salvation
    say continually:
'The LORD be magnified.'

18 But, as for me, that am poor and
    needy,
The Lord will account it unto
    me;
Thou art my help and my de-
    liverer;
O my God, tarry not.

מְבַקְשֵׁי נַפְשִׁי לִסְפּוֹתָהּ

יִסֹּגוּ אָחוֹר וְיִכָּלְמוּ חֲפֵצֵי רָעָתִי׃

16 יָשֹׁמּוּ עַל־עֵקֶב בָּשְׁתָּם

הָאֹמְרִים לִי הֶאָח ׀ הֶאָח׃

17 יָשִׂישׂוּ וְיִשְׂמְחוּ ׀ בְּךָ כָּל־מְבַקְשֶׁיךָ

יֹאמְרוּ תָמִיד יִגְדַּל יְהוָה

אֹהֲבֵי תְּשׁוּעָתֶךָ׃

18 וַאֲנִי ׀ עָנִי וְאֶבְיוֹן

אֲדֹנָי יַחֲשָׁב־לִי

עֶזְרָתִי וּמְפַלְטִי אַתָּה

אֱלֹהַי אַל־תְּאַחַר׃

---

16.   *appalled.* Following Rashi, or 'desolate' according to Kimchi as the verb is translated in Lam. i. 16. In lxx. 4 there is a different reading, viz. *let them be turned back.*

shame. Their discomfiture at the annulment of their plans to destroy him.

aha, aha. As in xxxv. 21, 25 (Malbim).

17.   The verse bears a close resemblance to xxxv. 27.

love Thy salvation. Which he had been active in preaching (verse 11).

the LORD be magnified. As the proved Champion of the afflicted against their ruthless opponents.

18.   *poor.* Afflicted (see on ix. 19). Whereas the helplessness of a man attracts the unwelcome attentions of the arrogant and increases his sufferings, it is the cause for God to take pity upon him and come to his rescue.

account it unto me. Better, 'will take thought of me,' will consider his suffering (Rashi). The verb is connected with the root from which *thoughts* (verse 6) is derived.

tarry not. Considering his great need; another form of his prayer *make haste to help me* (verse 14). Daniel similarly prayed, O LORD, *attend and do, defer not.* (Dan. ix. 19). "Why prolong my suffering if at any rate I am eventually to be redeemed by You—my only source of help (cf. Daath Sofrim).

41

מא

1 For the Leader. A Psalm of
David.

2 Happy is he that considereth the
poor;
The LORD will deliver him in the
day of evil.

3 The LORD preserve him, and keep
him alive, let him be called
happy in the land;
And deliver not Thou him unto
the greed of his enemies.

4 The LORD support him upon the
bed of illness;
Mayest Thou turn all his lying
down in his sickness.

לַמְנַצֵּחַ מִזְמוֹר לְדָוִד:

2 אַשְׁרֵי מַשְׂכִּיל אֶל־דָּל
בְּיוֹם רָעָה יְמַלְּטֵהוּ יְהוָה:

3 יְהוָה יִשְׁמְרֵהוּ וִיחַיֵּהוּ
יֹאשַׁר בָּאָרֶץ
וְאַל־תִּתְּנֵהוּ בְּנֶפֶשׁ אֹיְבָיו:

4 יְהוָה יִסְעָדֶנּוּ עַל־עֶרֶשׂ דְּוָי
כָּל־מִשְׁכָּבוֹ הָפַכְתָּ בְחָלְיוֹ:

v. 3. וֹאשַׁר ק'

A SUFFERER'S PRAYER

ANOTHER Psalm relating to a time when physical suffering was aggravated by mental
uneasiness over the machinations of enemies. In particular one man whom he considered
a close friend had proved traitorous. His main objective is not to complain about his
physical suffering, but to ensure that his enemies receive their due for their treachery. It
is not clear whether the Psalm was composed during an illness and the opening verses were
said in the hope of a happier future, or if it was written later as a narrative of what had
occurred in the past. This Psalm constitutes the climax to the first book of PSALMS and
it is for this reason that the final verse takes the form of an appreciation to God for accepting
the prayer of the Psalmist.

2-4 BLESSEDNESS OF THE BENEVOLENT

2. *considereth.* lit. 'dealeth wisely with.'
'It is not written, "Blessed is he that giveth to
the poor." It refers to a man who considers
how the meritorious act can best be carried
out' (Talmud). He takes thought of the most
effective way to help the person in need (cf.
Kimchi, Metsudath).

poor. The Hebrew signifies 'feeble,' not necessarily a poor man; it here applies to one
enfeebled in health (Tal. Ned. 40a).

evil. Trouble.

3. *the LORD preserve him.* Although this
rendering as a prayer is possible, it can also
be understood as a future assurance. The
Psalmist describes the happy consequences
which follow such considerate behaviour (cf.
Daath Sofrim).

keep him alive. Revive him should he fall
sick.

let him be called happy. Rather, 'he shall be
accounted happy' by reason of the good
fortune which God will bestow upon him.

greed. Hebrew 'soul,' i.e. desire. Let not his
enemies accomplish their will to his undoing
(Ibn Ezra).

4. *the LORD support him.* Render 'will support him,' whose bed, which is primarily for
rest, has turned into a place of toil (Meiri).

*mayest Thou turn all his lying down in his
sickness.* lit. 'all his lying down Thou hast
changed in his sickness'; the prophetic perfect. The verse is explained by Rashi and
Kimchi as 'all his peace and tranquility
have been disturbed by the severity of his
illness.'

5 As for me, I said: 'O Lord, be
   gracious unto me;
   Heal my soul; for I have sinned
   against Thee.'

6 Mine enemies speak evil of me:
   'When shall he die, and his name
   perish?'

7 And if one come to see me, he
   speaketh falsehood;
   His heart gathereth iniquity to
   itself;
   When he goeth abroad, he speaketh of it.

8 All that hate me whisper together
   against me,
   Against me do they devise my
   hurt:

9 'An evil thing cleaveth fast unto
   him;
   And now that he lieth, he shall
   rise up no more.'

אֲנִי אָמַרְתִּי יְהוָה חָנֵּנִי 5
רְפָאָה נַפְשִׁי כִּי־חָטָאתִי לָךְ:
אוֹיְבַי יֹאמְרוּ רַע לִי 6
מָתַי יָמוּת וְאָבַד שְׁמוֹ:
וְאִם־בָּא לִרְאוֹת שָׁוְא יְדַבֵּר 7
לִבּוֹ יִקְבָּץ־אָוֶן לוֹ
יֵצֵא לַחוּץ יְדַבֵּר:
יַחַד עָלַי יִתְלַחֲשׁוּ כָּל־שֹׂנְאָי 8
עָלַי יַחְשְׁבוּ רָעָה לִי:
דְּבַר־בְּלִיַּעַל יָצוּק בּוֹ 9
וַאֲשֶׁר שָׁכַב לֹא־יוֹסִיף לָקוּם:

5-10 THE MALICE OF HIS ENEMIES

5. After a general introduction he deals
with his own case as one who has endeavoured
to live up to the ideal he described.

heal my soul. If the soul is healed by forgiveness for his sins, then the body will be able to
regain its former strength (Kimchi).

I have sinned. He confesses, knowing that
suffering is punishment of transgression.

6. *speak evil of me.* Wish me harm in longing for my death.

his name perish. They hope for the extinction
of all his family.

7. *if one come.* lit. 'if he come,' viz. one of
his enemies (Kimchi).

he speaketh falsehood. He tells me that he
hopes for my recovery, but I know his words
are false.

gathereth iniquity. Or, 'mischief.' He de-

scribes the hypocrite who, while visiting the
sick and still in his presence, gathers material
upon which hatred may feed, and then joins
his associates outside to expend his mean and
spiteful soul (Rashi, Kimchi).

speaketh of it. He gives utterance to his malicious thoughts (Rashi).

8. *whisper together.* A realistic picture of
the ill-wishers discussing his condition and
hoping for the worst.

devise my hurt. Better, 'imagine evil for me.'
They plot how to precipitate my death
(Malbim). Alternatively, 'imagine evil for
me' i.e. they wish that bad happenings will
overcome me (Metsudath David).

9. *an evil thing cleaveth fast unto him.* lit.
'a thing of *Belial* (see on xviii. 5) is poured
out upon him.' A heinous crime has been the
cause of his illness (Metsudath David).

lieth. On a bed of final sickness as a penalty
(Metsudath David).

10 Yea, mine own familiar friend, in whom I trusted, who did eat of my bread,
Hath lifted up his heel against me.

11 But Thou, O Lᴏʀᴅ, be gracious unto me, and raise me up,
That I may requite them.

12 By this I know that Thou delightest in me,
That mine enemy doth not triumph over me.

13 And as for me, Thou upholdest me because of mine integrity,
And settest me before Thy face for ever.

14 Blessed be the Lᴏʀᴅ, the God of Israel,
From everlasting and to everlasting.
Amen, and Amen.

10 נַם־אִישׁ שְׁלוֹמִי ׀ אֲשֶׁר־בָּטַחְתִּי בוֹ
אוֹכֵל לַחְמִי הִגְדִּיל עָלַי עָקֵב׃
11 וְאַתָּה יְהֹוָה חָנֵּנִי וַהֲקִימֵנִי
וַאֲשַׁלְּמָה לָהֶם׃
12 בְּזֹאת יָדַעְתִּי כִּי־חָפַצְתָּ בִּי
כִּי לֹא־יָרִיעַ אֹיְבִי עָלָי׃
13 וַאֲנִי בְּתֻמִּי תָּמַכְתָּ בִּי
וַתַּצִּיבֵנִי לְפָנֶיךָ לְעוֹלָם׃
14 בָּרוּךְ יְהֹוָה ׀ אֱלֹהֵי יִשְׂרָאֵל
מֵהָעוֹלָם וְעַד־הָעוֹלָם
אָמֵן ׀ וְאָמֵן׃

10. *mine own familiar friend.* lit.'the man of my peace'; our relations were of the friendliest.

who did eat of my bread. Just as the host had obligations to protect his guest, so was the guest in honour bound not to injure his host.

lifted up his heel. To trip me up and bring about my fall.

11–13 HIS PRAYER CONTINUED

11. *but Thou.* My true Friend, in contrast to the false.

raise me up. And so belie their hope, *he shall rise up no more* (verse 9).

that I may requite them. To avoid the impression of vindictiveness which the phrase suggests, Kimchi quotes the comment of the famous Jewish scholar, Saadia: 'I will requite them good for evil.' This view is supported by the Midrash (Schocher Tov) which quotes Psalms xxxv. 13 where David showed concern for the plight of his enemies. Kimchi

and Sforno maintain that David was, as king, required to protect his honour and it was, therefore, within his right to pray that he may be given the opportunity to punish the traitors as they deserved.

12. *triumph.* lit. 'shout in exultation.'

13. *integrity.* In spite of his sin. The doctrine that to err is human is certainly Scriptural (Eccles. vii. 20), but the sinner who acknowledges his fault and repents of it preserves his *integrity*.

settest me before Thy face for ever. As against the enemies' hope that his name would perish (verse 6), he is confident that he and his descendants would be privileged to stand in His presence to serve Him.

14 CLOSING DOXOLOGY

The climax of the Psalm, forming to a close Book I (Malbim). Each of the other Books is similarly concluded.

amen. Truly; response to the doxology.

מב

לַמְנַצֵּחַ מַשְׂכִּיל לִבְנֵי־קֹרַח׃
2 כְּאַיָּל תַּעֲרֹג עַל־אֲפִיקֵי־מָיִם
כֵּן נַפְשִׁי תַעֲרֹג אֵלֶיךָ אֱלֹהִים׃
3 צָמְאָה נַפְשִׁי לֵאלֹהִים לְאֵל חָי
מָתַי אָבוֹא וְאֵרָאֶה פְּנֵי אֱלֹהִים׃
4 הָיְתָה־לִּי דִמְעָתִי לֶחֶם יוֹמָם וְלַיְלָה

42

1 For the Leader; Maschil of the sons of Korah.

2 As the hart panteth after the water brooks,
So panteth my soul after Thee, O God.

3 My soul thirsteth for God, for the living God:
'When shall I come and appear before God?'

4 My tears have been my food day and night,

LAMENT OF AN EXILE

THE subject matter of this and the next Psalm is one (Kimchi Ps. xliii. 5) and it is to be noted that XLIII is the only Psalm in Book II which has no superscription. In the Psalm we have a pathetic lament representing Israel in exile longing for redemption and the Temple Service. A feature of the Psalm is the greater length of the verses, which is distinctive of the *Kinah* or plaintive style, the best illustration of which is the Book of Lamentations.

1. *Maschil.* See on xxxii. 1.

of the sons of Korah. Again in the headings of xliv-xlix, lxxxv, lxxxvii, lxxxviii. Korah perished in the abortive revolt against Moses, but *the sons of Korah died not* (Num. xxvi. 11). We read of *Korahites* among the Levitical choristers in the Temple (2 Chron. xx. 19). The words of the title may indicate that the Psalms enumerated were composed by this family (Rashi); or they form part of a collection composed by David which used to be chanted by them (Meiri).

2-3 HIS YEARNING
FOR COMMUNION WITH GOD

2. *hart.* Though the verb is feminine, the noun, in the masculine form, refers to the species as a whole (Daath Sofrim). No more vivid a simile could be imagined: a hind, faint in the desert with thirst, hears springs of water flow, yet, tragically, the life giving waters are out of its reach. It offers a most striking analogy to Israel, who may realise that God watches over them but, because of their sufferings in exile, lack the spiritual refreshment to draw close to Him (Hirsch).

3. *thirsteth.* An especially telling image in the sun-scorched Middle–East where water is held to be very precious. It is used again in lxiii. 2; Amos viii. 11; Isa. lv. 1.

living God. The God Who is *the fountain of living waters* (Jer. ii. 13, xvii. 13), which alone can satisfy the thirst of the true believer.

appear before God. The technical phrase for a pilgrimage to the Temple (lxxxiv. 8; Exod. xxiii. 17).

4-6 DISTRESSED BY PAST MEMORIES

4. *my tears have been my food.* Anguish of spirit had driven from him all desire to eat (cf. lxxx. 6, cii. 5) (Rashi).

they say. He had been forced to leave his homeland and was dwelling among heathens. They taunted him with the question *Where is thy God?* This distressed him because it implied that He was powerless to aid those who had faith in Him (cf. Kimchi).

While they say unto me all the day: 'Where is thy God?'

5 These things I remember, and pour out my soul within me,
How I passed on with the throng, and led them to the house of God,
With the voice of joy and praise, a multitude keeping holyday.

6 Why art thou cast down, O my soul?
And why moanest thou within me?
Hope thou in God; for I shall yet praise Him
For the salvation of His countenance.

7 O my God, my soul is cast down within me;
Therefore do I remember Thee from the land of Jordan,
And the Hermons, from the hill Mizar.

בֵּאמֹר אֵלַי כָּל־הַיּוֹם אַיֵּה אֱלֹהֶיךָ׃

5 אֵלֶּה אֶזְכְּרָה וְאֶשְׁפְּכָה עָלַי נַפְשִׁי
כִּי אֶעֱבֹר בַּסָּךְ
אֶדַּדֵּם עַד־בֵּית אֱלֹהִים
בְּקוֹל־רִנָּה וְתוֹדָה הָמוֹן חוֹגֵג׃

6 מַה־תִּשְׁתּוֹחֲחִי נַפְשִׁי וַתֶּהֱמִי עָלָי
הוֹחִלִי לֵאלֹהִים כִּי־עוֹד אוֹדֶנּוּ
יְשׁוּעוֹת פָּנָיו׃

7 אֱלֹהַי עָלַי נַפְשִׁי תִשְׁתּוֹחָח
עַל־כֵּן אֶזְכָּרְךָ מֵאֶרֶץ יַרְדֵּן
וְחֶרְמוֹנִים מֵהַר מִצְעָר׃

5. The form of the verbs suggests the translation: 'These things I would remember as I pour out…how I was wont to pass on…leading them in procession to the house of God.' In exile the recollection of that happy scene clings to him.

a multitude keeping holyday. Or, 'a pilgrim throng.'

6 THE HOPEFUL REFRAIN

He addresses a rebuke to his soul which drooped under the depressing effect of his memories. The verse is a refrain which is repeated in verse 12 and xliii. 5.

cast down. Bowed like one who is mourning.

hope thou in God. Wait patiently for Him to send help (Rashi).

the salvation of His countenance. See verse 12 where 'His' countenance becomes 'My' countenance. Here the meaning is that 'He alone will deliver me from exile.' Cf. Exodus xxxiii. 15 (Meiri).

7-8 HIS PLIGHT DESCRIBED

7. *my soul is cast down.* The hopefulness of

the refrain passes away, and he acknowledges that he is in the depth of depression as the consequence of finding himself beyond the frontiers of Zion.

I remember Thee. Far from the thought that God will leave him in the land of exile, a return home to the Temple is constantly in his mind.

the land of Jordan, and the Hermons. The location is in the north, on the eastern side of the Jordan which has its source in the Hermon mountain-range. The plural may refer to its three peaks.

the hill Mizar. lit. 'a young hill': this alludes to Mt. Sinai which is low compared to the other peaks around it (Rashi). Some suggest it as a reference to an area of low hills in the Hermon before they rise to a peak (cf. Hirsch).

8. *deep calleth unto deep.* The scenery around him becomes suggestive of the troubles which have descended upon him. The melting snows from the peaks of Hermon form thunderous waterfalls; to these are added

8 Deep calleth unto deep at the voice
   of Thy cataracts;
  All Thy waves and Thy billows
   are gone over me.

9 By day the LORD will command
   His lovingkindness,
  And in the night His song shall be
   with me,
  Even a prayer unto the God of my
   life.

10 I will say unto God my Rock:
   'Why hast Thou forgotten me?
  Why go I mourning under the
   oppression of the enemy?'

11 As with a crushing in my bones,
   mine adversaries taunt me;
  While they say unto me all the
   day: 'Where is thy God?'

12 Why art thou cast down, O my
   soul?
  And why moanest thou within
   me?
  Hope thou in God; for I shall yet
   praise Him,
  The salvation of my countenance,
   and my God.

8 תְּהוֹם־אֶל־תְּהוֹם קוֹרֵא
לְקוֹל צִנּוֹרֶיךָ
כָּל־מִשְׁבָּרֶיךָ וְגַלֶּיךָ עָלַי עָבָרוּ׃

9 יוֹמָם ׀ יְצַוֶּה יְהֹוָה ׀ חַסְדּוֹ
וּבַלַּיְלָה שִׁירֹה עִמִּי
תְּפִלָּה לְאֵל חַיָּי׃

10 אוֹמְרָה ׀ לְאֵל סַלְעִי לָמָה שְׁכַחְתָּנִי
לָמָּה־קֹדֵר אֵלֵךְ בְּלַחַץ אוֹיֵב׃

11 בְּרֶצַח ׀ בְּעַצְמוֹתַי חֵרְפוּנִי צוֹרְרָי
בְּאָמְרָם אֵלַי כָּל־הַיּוֹם
אַיֵּה אֱלֹהֶיךָ׃

12 מַה־תִּשְׁתּוֹחֲחִי ׀ נַפְשִׁי
וּמַה־תֶּהֱמִי עָלָי
הוֹחִילִי לֵאלֹהִים כִּי־עוֹד אוֹדֶנּוּ
יְשׁוּעֹת פָּנַי וֵאלֹהָי׃

the rapids of the Jordan. This display of the
forces guided by the hand of God make him
think of the waters of tribulation which are
overwhelming him.

waves...billows. Again in Jonah ii. 4. The
words are connected with a stormy sea. He
feels himself to be 'at sea' with numerous
troubles that are his lot. Only with God's help
is he able to withstand them (Daath Sofrim).

9.   Just as he knows that God directs the
mighty flow of waters around him, so does
the conviction deepen in him that He is directing the flood of troubles and will see that
he is not drowned in them.

by day...and in the night. Constantly.

will command His lovingkindness. If appearances lead to the belief that God's love
has been withdrawn, He will, as it were, order
it to become again operative.

His song. Song of praise to God (Midrash,
Kimchi).

prayer. The essence of prayer is an opportunity for man to acknowledge that his day to
day sustenance and his continued existence
are thanks to the kindness of his Creator
(Daath Sofrim).

10.   *I ... unto God.* I will address myself to
the God of my life and to the Rock of my
salvation, and urge upon Him the soul's
insistent question; For what purpose hast
Thou forsaken me? Why must I suffer the
oppression of my foe? The apparent apathy is
in contradiction to all he knew of God
(Hirsch).

11.   *a crushing in my bones.* Their mocking
words affect him so deeply that he feels
physical pain.

12.   *the salvation ... countenance.* lit. 'sal-
vations.' The plural points to the many acts of
Providence by which he had benefited in the
past. He still hopes that God will bring ultimate salvation in his own life (Kimchi).

43

שָׁפְטֵנִי אֱלֹהִים וְרִיבָה רִיבִי
מִגּוֹי לֹא־חָסִיד
מֵאִישׁ מִרְמָה וְעַוְלָה תְפַלְּטֵנִי:
כִּי־אַתָּה אֱלֹהֵי מָעוּזִּי לָמָה זְנַחְתָּנִי 2
לָמָּה־קֹדֵר אֶתְהַלֵּךְ בְּלַחַץ אוֹיֵב:
שְׁלַח־אוֹרְךָ וַאֲמִתְּךָ הֵמָּה יַנְחוּנִי 3
יְבִיאוּנִי אֶל־הַר־קָדְשְׁךָ
וְאֶל־מִשְׁכְּנוֹתֶיךָ:

1 Be Thou my judge, O God, and
   plead my cause against an ungodly nation;
   O deliver me from the deceitful
   and unjust man.

2 For Thou art the God of my
   strength; why hast Thou cast
   me off?
   Why go I mourning under the
   oppression of the enemy?

3 O send out Thy light and Thy
   truth; let them lead me;
   Let them bring me unto Thy holy
   mountain, and to Thy dwelling-
   places;

PRAYER OF AN EXILE

A SUPPLEMENT to XLII. Note the occurrence of the refrain at the end.

1-2 PLEA FOR VINDICATION

be Thou my judge. Also the opening cry of xxvi.

plead my cause. For I am not able to plead for myself (Kimchi).

an ungodly nation. lit. 'from a nation not pious,' a heathen people which knows not the ways of God. He had suffered from their oppression, as stated in xlii. 10.

deceitful and unjust man. No particular individual is meant. *Man* is to be understood collectively: men who practise deceit and lawlessness.

2. *God of my strength.* Render 'God of my protection.' How is it, then, that I am defenceless against my enemies?

cast me off. lit. 'rejected.' His previous question, *Why hast Thou forgotten me?* (xlii. 10) assumes a much stronger form. As no response had come to his prayer, he begins to feel that he is not merely forgotten by God but rejected by Him (Daath Sofrim).

why go I mourning? Repeated from xlii. 10, with a different and more emphatic form of the verb (as in xxxv. 14), meaning 'walk about by myself.'

3-4 HE PRAYS TO RETURN HOME

3. *Thy light and Thy truth.* An immediate recoil ensues after he had given expression to the fearful thought that God had abandoned him. Whatever be the explanation for the continuance of his sufferings, the fact remains that God is enthroned in heaven and favours *light* as against the darkness of evil and *truth* over deceit. Let Him send them forth from His Presence as guiding angels and they will lead him back home from the land of exile.

Thy holy mountain. As in xv. 1, to be understood literally as Mount Zion on which the Temple stood.

dwelling-places. The plural may refer to the various courtyards that will feature in the third Temple (Ibn Ezra).

4 Then will I go unto the altar of
  God, unto God, my exceeding
  joy;
  And praise Thee upon the harp,
  O God, my God.

5 Why art thou cast down, O my
  soul?
  And why moanest thou within me?
  Hope thou in God; for I shall yet
  praise Him,
  The salvation of my countenance,
  and my God.

וְאָבוֹאָה ׀ אֶל־מִזְבַּח אֱלֹהִים 4
אֶל־אֵל שִׂמְחַת גִּילִי
וְאוֹדְךָ בְכִנּוֹר אֱלֹהִים אֱלֹהָי:
מַה־תִּשְׁתּוֹחֲחִי ׀ נַפְשִׁי 5
וּמַה־תֶּהֱמִי עָלָי
הוֹחִילִי לֵאלֹהִים כִּי־עוֹד אוֹדֶנּוּ
יְשׁוּעֹת פָּנַי וֵאלֹהָי:

4. *then will I go.* Better, 'that I may come'
(cf. xlii. 3).

unto God. The sacrifice upon the altar was
not an end in itself but the means of establish-
ing communion with God. He is the ultimate
goal towards which the Psalmist longs to
make his way.

my exceeding joy. lit. 'the gladness of my
joy,' the Source of all that gladdens my life.

praise Thee. Or 'thank Thee,' for my signal
deliverance and restoration. Praising God
'upon the harp' is an allusion to the new
praise that will be occasioned by the return to
the Temple (Meiri). In exile *we hung our harps
upon willows*, for *How shall we sing the* LORD'*s
song in a foreign land?* But upon our return
home we will *praise Thee upon the harp* (See
Ps. cxxxvii) (Yaavetz).

harp. See on xxxiii. 2.

5 CLOSING REFRAIN

Repeated for the third time; but though the
words remain the same, they are now sung on
a new note. They ring with triumphant hope
and certainty (Daath Sofrim).

44

1 For the Leader; [a Psalm] of the
    sons of Korah. Maschil.

2 O God, we have heard with our
    ears, our fathers have told us;
    A work Thou didst in their days,
    in the days of old.

3 Thou with Thy hand didst drive
    out the nations, and didst plant
    them in;
    Thou didst break the peoples, and
    didst spread them abroad.

4 For not by their own sword did
    they get the land in possession,
    Neither did their own arm save
    them;

מד

לַמְנַצֵּחַ לִבְנֵי־קֹרַח מַשְׂכִּיל:

2 אֱלֹהִים ׀ בְּאָזְנֵינוּ שָׁמַעְנוּ
אֲבוֹתֵינוּ סִפְּרוּ־לָנוּ
פֹּעַל פָּעַלְתָּ בִימֵיהֶם בִּימֵי קֶדֶם:

3 אַתָּה ׀ יָדְךָ גּוֹיִם הוֹרַשְׁתָּ וַתִּטָּעֵם
תָּרַע לְאֻמִּים וַתְּשַׁלְּחֵם:

4 כִּי לֹא בְחַרְבָּם יָרְשׁוּ־אָרֶץ
וּזְרוֹעָם לֹא־הוֹשִׁיעָה לָּמוֹ

A NATIONAL PRAYER OF INTERCESSION

WE clearly have in this Psalm the cry of a nation in distress and not a personal lament. The
mention of *our hosts* (verse 10) as having been unaided by God points to a time of defeat on
the battlefield. Another reference which has to be noted is the impassioned declaration in
verses 18-23 that the nation had been faithful to God and was suffering for His sake. It seems
to be generally accepted that the Psalm portrays the events that occurred during the period of
exile. The allusion to the voice of the blasphemer (verse 17) recalls what is narrated of
Sennacherib king of Assyria, in Isa. xxxvii. 6, 23. Verses 10-22 are especially applicable to
the last part of the exile which began after the destruction of the Second Temple and are
pertinent even to the most recent past and, indeed, even to the present day (Hirsch). The Psalm
depicts Israel as a nation that remains loyal, whatever the circumstances, to their God and His
law (verses 18-23), and ends with the hope that this will merit the final redemption.

2-4   GOD'S HELP IN THE PAST

2. *our fathers have told us.* Knowledge of
the past was kept alive by the instruction
given by parents to their children (cf. Exod.
x. 2; Deut. vi. 20f., xxxii 7). The addition of
in their days shows that *fathers* here means
their forefathers who passed through the wilderness to Canaan. The tradition was handed
down from generation to generation (cf.
Kimchi).

3. *Thou with Thy hand.* The acquisition of
the Land of Promise was achieved by God's
might, not the valour of Israel's army
(Kimchi). The Divine verdict passed upon
Canaan was no exception. Such judgment is
executed on any state once the measure of its

sin has been filled to capacity and the time
has come for its dismissal from the stage of
history (Hirsch).

didst plant them. Our ancestors (Targum,
Rashi etc.).

didst spread them abroad. As a direct consequence of their wickedness, the nations were
banished from the land.

4. *save them.* Better, 'give them victory.'

But Thy right hand, and Thine arm. The right
hand that saved Israel and the arm that
chastised the Canaanites (Hirsch).

the light of Thy countenance. The favour
which God displays towards them and for
which the priests prayed on their behalf (Num.
vi. 25).

But Thy right hand, and Thine
arm, and the light of Thy
countenance,
Because Thou wast favourable
unto them.

5 Thou art my King, O God;
Command the salvation of Jacob.

6 Through Thee do we push down
our adversaries;
Through Thy name do we tread
them under that rise up against
us.

7 For I trust not in my bow,
Neither can my sword save me.

8 But Thou hast saved us from our
adversaries,
And hast put them to shame that
hate us.

9 In God have we gloried all the day,
And we will give thanks unto Thy
name for ever.   Selah

10 Yet Thou hast cast off, and
brought us to confusion;
And goest not forth with our
hosts.

כִּי־יְמִינְךָ וּזְרוֹעֲךָ וְאוֹר פָּנֶיךָ
כִּי רְצִיתָם׃

5 אַתָּה־הוּא מַלְכִּי אֱלֹהִים
צַוֵּה יְשׁוּעוֹת יַעֲקֹב׃

6 בְּךָ צָרֵינוּ נְנַגֵּחַ
בְּשִׁמְךָ נָבוּס קָמֵינוּ׃

7 כִּי לֹא בְקַשְׁתִּי אֶבְטָח
וְחַרְבִּי לֹא תוֹשִׁיעֵנִי׃

8 כִּי הוֹשַׁעְתָּנוּ מִצָּרֵינוּ
וּמְשַׂנְאֵינוּ הֱבִישׁוֹתָ׃

9 בֵּאלֹהִים הִלַּלְנוּ כָל־הַיּוֹם
וְשִׁמְךָ לְעוֹלָם נוֹדֶה סֶלָה׃

10 אַף־זָנַחְתָּ וַתַּכְלִימֵנוּ
וְלֹא־תֵצֵא בְּצִבְאוֹתֵינוּ׃

Thou ... unto them. Not even Israel's merit earned them Divine aid; it was the effect of God's choice of them (cf. Malbim).

5-9 The nation's trust in God

5. *my King.* The Psalmist regards himself as the nation's spokesman (see Daath Sofrim).

command. As the King He has the prerogative of safeguarding the people.

salvation. The word is plural, and either means 'victories' (as in verse 4) or complete deliverance.

6. *through Thee.* As in the past with their ancestors, so in the present do they have to depend upon His help to overcome their foes.

push down. The common meaning of the verb is 'to gore' with horns, and it is used symbolically for defeating an enemy (cf. Deut. xxxiii. 17; 1 Kings xxii. 11) (cf. Kimchi, Metsudath Zion).

through Thy name. An elaborated form of

'through Thee'; If we are not deserving of God's direct assistance, let us at least merit the aid of an angel who comes in the name of the Lord, to help destroy those who rise against us (Malbim).

7. *bow...sword.* The same thought as in xx. 8, xxxiii. 16, and in view of the connection to Isa. xxxvii. 6, 23, see 2 Kings xix.

8. *thou hast saved us.* In past crises; hence our confidence now.

9. *have we gloried.* When victory was ours.

10-17 The nation's desperate plight

10. *yet.* The conjunction marks the contrast between what happened previously and what is happening in the present.

Thou hast cast off. Same word as in xliii. 2.

confusion. Better, 'and disgraced us,' i.e. You made us aware of our unworthiness (Hirsch), and abandoned us, withholding the aid which was granted to our forefathers.

goest not forth. To lead the *hosts* to victory.

11 Thou makest us to turn back
  from the adversary;
And they that hate us spoil at
  their will.

12 Thou hast given us like sheep to
  be eaten;
And hast scattered us among the
  nations.

13 Thou sellest Thy people for small
  gain,
And hast not set their prices high.

14 Thou makest us a taunt to our
  neighbours,
A scorn and a derision to them
  that are round about us.

15 Thou makest us a byword among
  the nations,
A shaking of the head among the
  peoples.

16 All the day is my confusion
  before me,
And the shame of my face hath
  covered me,

17 For the voice of him that taunteth
  and blasphemeth;

11 תְּשִׁיבֵנוּ אָחוֹר מִנִּי־צָר
וּמְשַׂנְאֵינוּ שָׁסוּ לָמוֹ:

12 תִּתְּנֵנוּ כְּצֹאן מַאֲכָל
וּבַגּוֹיִם זֵרִיתָנוּ:

13 תִּמְכֹּר־עַמְּךָ בְלֹא־הוֹן
וְלֹא־רִבִּיתָ בִּמְחִירֵיהֶם:

14 תְּשִׂימֵנוּ חֶרְפָּה לִשְׁכֵנֵינוּ
לַעַג וָקֶלֶס לִסְבִיבוֹתֵינוּ:

15 תְּשִׂימֵנוּ מָשָׁל בַּגּוֹיִם
מְנוֹד־רֹאשׁ בַּלְאֻמִּים:

16 כָּל־הַיּוֹם כְּלִמָּתִי נֶגְדִּי
וּבֹשֶׁת פָּנַי כִּסָּתְנִי:

17 מִקּוֹל מְחָרֵף וּמְגַדֵּף

11. *at their will.* lit. 'for themselves,' to their hearts' content with none to prevent them.

12. *like the sheep to be eaten.* Many have been slain by the enemy (see verse 23).

scattered us. Where many of us were forced to be slaves (verse 13).

13. *for small gain.* Lit. 'for a low price,' as though they were of very little value despite their being *Thy people.*

and hast not set their prices high. More accurately, 'and Thou hast not gained by their price.' God, so to speak, gave them away for nothing and derived no profit from the transaction. This mode of speech concerning God does not imply irreverence. Rather, it points out the severity of collective punishment which leads to His nation's degradation. Even so, Israel did not bow under the pressure and

always hoped that their suffering would see better times (Daath Sofrim).

14. Cf. lxxix. 4.

neighbours. Such as the people of Edom, Ammon and Moab who always rejoiced over Israel's misfortunes.

15. *byword.* The theme of derisive songs.

nations. More distant peoples.

a shaking of the head. See on xxii. 8.

16. *shame of my face.* The overpowering sense of humiliation was evident in their faces.

covered me. Cf. *let them be clothed with shame and confusion.* (xxxv. 26).

17. *for the voice.* i.e. because of the voice.

by reason of. Or, 'because of the face of'; their malicious, gloating faces.

By reason of the enemy and the
revengeful.

18 All this is come upon us; yet have
we not forgotten Thee,
Neither have we been false to
Thy covenant.

19 Our heart is not turned back,
Neither have our steps declined
from Thy path;

20 Though Thou hast crushed us
into a place of jackals,
And covered us with the shadow
of death.

21 If we had forgotten the name of
our God,
Or spread forth our hands to a
strange god;

22 Would not God search this out?
For He knoweth the secrets of
the heart.

23 Nay, but for Thy sake are we
killed all the day;
We are accounted as sheep for
the slaughter.

מִפְּנֵי אוֹיֵב וּמִתְנַקֵּם:

18 כָּל־זֹאת בָּאַתְנוּ וְלֹא שְׁכַחֲנוּךָ
וְלֹא־שִׁקַּרְנוּ בִּבְרִיתֶךָ:

19 לֹא־נָסוֹג אָחוֹר לִבֵּנוּ
וַתֵּט אֲשֻׁרֵינוּ מִנִּי אָרְחֶךָ:

20 כִּי דִכִּיתָנוּ בִּמְקוֹם תַּנִּים
וַתְּכַס עָלֵינוּ בְצַלְמָוֶת:

21 אִם־שָׁכַחְנוּ שֵׁם אֱלֹהֵינוּ
וַנִּפְרֹשׂ כַּפֵּינוּ לְאֵל זָר:

22 הֲלֹא אֱלֹהִים יַחֲקָר־זֹאת
כִּי־הוּא יֹדֵעַ תַּעֲלֻמוֹת לֵב:

23 כִּי־עָלֶיךָ הֹרַגְנוּ כָל־הַיּוֹם
נֶחְשַׁבְנוּ כְּצֹאן טִבְחָה:

18-23 ISRAEL REMAINS FAITHFUL TO GOD

18. *yet have we not forgotten Thee.* The reason for this cruel visitation cannot be that Israel has been disloyal to God.

false to Thy covenant. In Lev. xxvi. 14ff. and Deut. xxviii. 15ff. dire punishments were foretold if Israel broke the covenant with God. Those afflictions had overtaken them, although they had been faithful to the covenant.

19. *turned back.* From following Him.

20. *crushed us into a place of jackals.* The cruelty and the rage of the peoples among whom Thou hast dispersed us has crushed us as wild beasts crush lesser beings (Hirsch).

shadow of death. Thick darkness of exile (Kimchi) (see on xxiii. 4).

21. *spread forth our hands.* In prayer.

22. *would not God search this out?* He is all-knowing and would have been aware of the people's faithlessness if they had been guilty of it (Kimchi). Conscious of this fact, they protested their innocence because they were guiltless, not trying to hide any wrongs they had committed which could justify their disaster.

23. *for Thy sake.* They protested that far from suffering because of disloyalty, they were attacked for the reason that they were God's people who kept to His appointed paths. All the more inexplicable, therefore, was their hard fate, and all the more urgently should His help come to them.

24 Awake, why sleepest Thou, O
     Lord?
   Arouse Thyself, cast not off for
     ever.

25 Wherefore hidest Thou Thy face,
   And forgettest our affliction and
     our oppression?

26 For our soul is bowed down to
     the dust;
   Our belly cleaveth unto the
     earth.

27 Arise for our help,
   And redeem us for Thy mercy's
     sake.

עוּרָה ׀ לָמָּה תִישַׁן ׀ אֲדֹנָי 24
הָקִיצָה אַל־תִּזְנַח לָנֶצַח:
לָמָּה־פָנֶיךָ תַסְתִּיר 25
תִּשְׁכַּח עָנְיֵנוּ וְלַחֲצֵנוּ:
כִּי שָׁחָה לֶעָפָר נַפְשֵׁנוּ 26
דָּבְקָה לָאָרֶץ בִּטְנֵנוּ:
קוּמָה עֶזְרָתָה לָּנוּ 27
וּפְדֵנוּ לְמַעַן חַסְדֶּךָ:

24-27 CRY FOR DELIVERANCE

24. *why sleepest Thou?* This cannot be understood literally for in a calmer moment the Psalmist testifies: "He that keepeth Israel doth neither slumber nor sleep" (cxxi. 4). However, when His nation suffers constant persecution, it appears to mankind as if God is oblivious to their cries; as if He were 'asleep' (cf. Ibn Ezra).

25. *hidest Thou Thy face.* In apparent indifference to Thy people's distressful situation (Kimchi).

forgettest. i.e. why dost Thou act as though Thou hast forgotten our plight by not hastening to our rescue?

26. *our soul is bowed down to the dust.* They were utterly humiliated.

cleaveth unto the earth. Crushed and helpless at the feet of the enemy (cf. cxix. 25 where the Psalmist may have had this verse in mind).

27. *arise.* See on iii. 8.

for Thy mercy's sake. Or, 'for the sake of Thy lovingkindness.'

This concluding phrase indicates that the painful experience of the people had not induced in them a disbelief in God. What troubled them was an inability to understand His ways. They still had faith in Him in spite of what had taken place and appealed to His attribute of love as their hope for redemption from their desperate condition.

מה

45

1 For the Leader; upon Shoshannim; [a Psalm] of the sons of
   Korah. Maschil. A Song of
   loves.
2 My heart overfloweth with a
   goodly matter;
   I say: 'My work is concerning a
   king';
   My tongue is the pen of a ready
   writer.
3 Thou art fairer than the children of
   men;
   Grace is poured upon thy lips;
   Therefore God hath blessed thee
   for ever.

לַמְנַצֵּחַ עַל־שֹׁשַׁנִּים לִבְנֵי־קֹרַח

מַשְׂכִּיל שִׁיר יְדִידֹת׃

2 רָחַשׁ לִבִּי ׀ דָּבָר טוֹב

אֹמֵר אָנִי מַעֲשַׂי לְמֶלֶךְ

לְשׁוֹנִי עֵט ׀ סוֹפֵר מָהִיר׃

3 יָפְיָפִיתָ מִבְּנֵי אָדָם

הוּצַק חֵן בְּשִׂפְתוֹתֶיךָ

עַל־כֵּן בֵּרַכְךָ אֱלֹהִים לְעוֹלָם׃

A 'ROYAL MARRIAGE' SONG

AT first glance this composition seems to be no more than a wedding song, celebrating the marriage of a king to his princess, containing praise for the groom, an exhortation to the bride, and a prayer for the happiness of the union. Several profound interpretations have been ascribed to the Psalm. Ibn Ezra understands the 'king' as referring to David or, as Targum and Kimchi, to the Messiah, and the 'marriage' as an allusion to his redemption of Israel. Rashi explains the song as dedicated to Torah scholars who are acclaimed as kings (Prov. viii., 15; Git. 62a). The scholar's partner is the nation of Israel who, to survive, must heed the words of its elders who are its true spiritual leaders. According to Malbim, the 'king' is the mind and the soul that rule the rest of the body. The 'queen' represents the senses which must be trained to accept instruction from the brain that is their 'master' (verse 12) and knows how best to utilise the various parts of the body for good.

1. *upon Shoshannim.* lit. 'roses'; a direction that the poem was to be sung with a musical instrument so named (cf. the headings of LX and LXXX) (Meiri, Kimchi).

a song of loves. God's love for His Messiah.

2 A PRELUDE

overfloweth. This is the only place where the verb occurs. As a noun it means a reptile and the root meaning is to move or stir (Hirsch). Translate: 'my heart is stirred with a choice subject,' or 'with beautiful words,' the singular noun being used collectively. He cannot allow the happy occasion to pass without recording the emotional song which it aroused within him.

my work. My poem, which etymologically means 'work.'

my tongue is. His tongue will express all the thoughts of his mind (Malbim).

3-10 PRAISE OF THE BRIDEGROOM

3. *thou art fairer.* It is thought appropriate that a king should have physical beauty above that of commoners (cf. Daath Sofrim).

grace is poured upon thy lips. His speech is gracious.

therefore. These outward qualities which all can see are an indication that the king has been blessed by God, and the favour will assuredly rest upon him eternally.

4 Gird thy sword upon thy thigh, O
      mighty one,
   Thy glory and thy majesty.

5 And in thy majesty prosper, ride
      on,
   In behalf of truth and meekness
      and righteousness;
   And let thy right hand teach thee
      tremendous things.

6 Thine arrows are sharp—
   The peoples fall under thee—
   [They sink] into the heart of the
      king's enemies.

7 Thy throne given of God is for
      ever and ever;
   A sceptre of equity is the sceptre
      of thy kingdom.

8 Thou hast loved righteousness,
      and hated wickedness;
   Therefore God, thy God, hath
      anointed thee

חֲגֽוֹר־חַרְבְּךָ֣ עַל־יָרֵ֑ךְ גִּבּ֑וֹר 4
הֽוֹדְךָ֗ וַהֲדָרֶֽךָ׃
וַהֲדָרְךָ֨ ׀ צְלַ֬ח רְכַ֗ב 5
עַֽל־דְּבַר־אֱ֭מֶת וְעַנְוָה־צֶ֑דֶק
וְתוֹרְךָ֖ נוֹרָא֣וֹת יְמִינֶֽךָ׃
חִצֶּ֗יךָ שְׁנ֫וּנִ֥ים עַ֭מִּים תַּחְתֶּ֣יךָ יִפְּל֑וּ 6
בְּ֝לֵ֗ב אֽוֹיְבֵ֥י הַמֶּֽלֶךְ׃
כִּסְאֲךָ֣ אֱ֭לֹהִים עוֹלָ֣ם וָעֶ֑ד 7
שֵׁ֥בֶט מִ֝ישֹׁ֗ר שֵׁ֣בֶט מַלְכוּתֶֽךָ׃
אָהַ֣בְתָּ צֶּדֶק֮ וַתִּשְׂנָ֫א רֶ֥שַׁע 8
עַל־כֵּ֤ן ׀ מְשָׁחֲךָ֡ אֱלֹהִ֬ים אֱלֹהֶ֗יךָ

4.   *O mighty one.* Or, 'O warrior hero.' According to Rashi this is a cry to fight for the cause of Torah. Literally, it is a call to the king to prove his might with his sword.

thy glory and thy majesty. By the power of the sword your glory will be verified; i.e. the Messiah will lead us to victory in the final battle against the wicked (Kimchi).

5.   *prosper, ride on.* Real glory is attained not by might and the sword but by defending truth and uprightness (Metsudath David, Malbim).

in behalf of. To champion the cause of right which, as God's anointed, he has the duty to defend (cf. Hirsch).

thy right hand. Emblem of power, with him as with God (cf. xliv. 4).

teach ... things. God's acts are said to be *tremendous*, i.e. awe-inspiring (cvi. 22, cxlv. 6). Similarly the king's battle prowess will reveal that he had been endowed with the power to perform deeds of valour which inspire fear.

6.   The word 'fall' refers not only to 'the peoples' but also to the 'arrows.' Rashi takes the second line as an interjection, so that 'thine arrows etc.' is connected to 'in the heart etc.'

7.   *thy throne given of God.* This follows the rendering of Metsudath David, as the literal translation 'Thy throne O God' does not suit the context. Many commentators translate 'Elohim' as judge (Rashi, Hirsch) and, accordingly, the verse refers to the mortal king in his role as ruler. Another interpretation is proposed by Ibn Ezra; 'Thy throne is (the throne of) God. Cf. 1 Chron. xxix: 23, 'and Solomon sat on the throne of the Lord.'

for ever and ever. The king's dynasty will endure into the distant future (cf. the promise in 2 Sam. vii. 16).

sceptre. The emblem of regal power which the king exercises to show that law and order are not dependent on the whims of the people. It represents a system they are duty bound to obey that which they are commanded, especially since the system is based on fairness and equality for all concerned (Daath Sofrim).

8.   *hath anointed thee.* Oil was the symbol of joy (Isa. lxi. 3) and the Psalmist intends that God, by anointing the Messiah as His king, will elevate him above others and generate universal joy (Kimchi).

With the oil of gladness above thy fellows.

9 Myrrh, and aloes, and cassia are all thy garments;
Out of ivory palaces stringed instruments have made thee glad.

10 Kings' daughters are among thy favourites;
At thy right hand doth stand the queen in gold of Ophir.

11 'Hearken, O daughter, and consider, and incline thine ear;
Forget also thine own people, and thy father's house;

12 So shall the king desire thy beauty;
For he is thy lord; and do homage unto him.

13 And, O daughter of Tyre, the richest of the people
Shall entreat thy favour with a gift.'

שֶׁמֶן שָׂשׂוֹן מֵחֲבֵרֶךָ׃

9 מֹר־וַאֲהָלוֹת קְצִיעוֹת כָּל־בִּגְדֹתֶיךָ
מִן־הֵיכְלֵי שֵׁן מִנִּי שִׂמְּחוּךָ׃

10 בְּנוֹת מְלָכִים בְּיִקְּרוֹתֶיךָ
נִצְּבָה שֵׁגַל לִימִינְךָ בְּכֶתֶם אוֹפִיר׃

11 שִׁמְעִי־בַת וּרְאִי וְהַטִּי אָזְנֵךְ
וְשִׁכְחִי עַמֵּךְ וּבֵית אָבִיךְ׃

12 וְיִתְאָו הַמֶּלֶךְ יָפְיֵךְ
כִּי־הוּא אֲדֹנַיִךְ וְהִשְׁתַּחֲוִי־לוֹ׃

13 וּבַת־צֹר בְּמִנְחָה
פָּנַיִךְ יְחַלּוּ עֲשִׁירֵי עָם׃

9. *all thy garments.* The 'bridegroom' is attired in garments heavily perfumed with costly spices (Rashi). Kimchi reads the verse as metaphorically referring to the good character traits that a person is meant to acquire.

ivory palaces. Palaces inlaid with ivory from which the 'bridegroom' will go forth to meet his 'bride' (Malbim).

stringed instruments … thee glad. A more correct rendering would be 'more than palaces of ivory, will those which come from Me gladden you' (Rashi)—the word 'minni' being a shortened form of 'mimenni,' from me. Others translate the word as being an emphatic form of the word 'that' (cf. Judges v. 14) and render 'from ivory palaces which verily do gladden thee' (Kimchi, Hirsch).

10. *thy favourites.* Better, thy precious ones. This follows Ibn Ezra and Kimchi. The verse portrays the esteem in which the king was held by the neighbouring rulers, who were honoured to offer their daughters to him in marriage. Rashi maintains that the word is derived from the verb 'to visit' meaning 'the daughters of kings are among those who come to visit.' The Targum renders 'come to visit you and show you honour.'

gold of Ophir. Famed as the choicest specimen of the precious metal (1 Kings ix. 28). There are varying opinions as to the location of Ophir. Some suggest Arabia or India.

11-13 ADDRESS TO THE BRIDE

11. *O daughter.* The 'daughter' may allude to each of those mentioned in the previous verse (Kimchi) or to the nation of Israel [called the 'daughter of Judah' (Lam. ii. 6)] (Targum, Rashi).

forget also thine own people. The bride comes from a foreign nation where idols are worshipped. This might suggest the wife of David (Ibn Ezra) or Solomon who married Maacha of Geshur and the daughter of Pharaoh, respectively, though this is questionable (Hirsch). Read in its messianic context, it is a call to the nations to identify with the cause of the Messiah and not with the intrigues of his opponents (Metsudath David).

12. *so shall the king desire thy beauty.* As her reward for loyalty to the king's interests, the marriage will be a happy union and she will retain his affection.

14 All glorious is the king's daughter
   within the palace;
   Her raiment is of chequer work
   inwrought with gold.

15 She shall be led unto the king on
   richly woven stuff;
   The virgins her companions in
   her train being brought unto
   thee.

16 They shall be led with gladness
   and rejoicing;
   They shall enter into the king's
   palace.

17 Instead of thy fathers shall be thy
   sons,
   Whom thou shalt make princes
   in all the land.

18 I will make thy name to be
   remembered in all generations;
   Therefore shall the peoples praise
   thee for ever and ever.

כָּל־כְּבוּדָּה בַת־מֶלֶךְ פְּנִימָה 14
מִמִּשְׁבְּצוֹת זָהָב לְבוּשָׁהּ׃
לִרְקָמוֹת תּוּבַל לַמֶּלֶךְ 15
בְּתוּלוֹת אַחֲרֶיהָ רֵעוֹתֶיהָ
מוּבָאוֹת לָךְ׃
תּוּבַלְנָה בִּשְׂמָחֹת וָגִיל 16
תְּבֹאֶינָה בְּהֵיכַל מֶלֶךְ׃
תַּחַת אֲבֹתֶיךָ יִהְיוּ בָנֶיךָ 17
תְּשִׁיתֵמוֹ לְשָׂרִים בְּכָל־הָאָרֶץ׃
אַזְכִּירָה שִׁמְךָ בְּכָל־דֹּר וָדֹר 18
עַל־כֵּן עַמִּים יְהוֹדֻךָ לְעֹלָם וָעֶד׃

he is thy Lord. Like his subjects she must
serve him and work for his welfare.

do homage unto him. lit. 'bow down to him,'
be obedient.

13. *O daughter of Tyre, the richest of the
people.* More correct would be 'and the richest of nations.' Not only the inhabitants of
Tyre but also the affluent of other nations will
bring their gifts (cf. Kimchi). Those who
adopt the hypothesis that the bridegroom is
Solomon (Malbim) or a Torah scholar (Rashi),
translate: 'and the daughter of Tyre shall seek
thy favour with a gift, yea, the richest among
nations.' Tyre is singled out as the wealthiest
of the neighbouring nations who will all
bring gifts to the new 'queen.'

14-16 DESCRIPTION OF THE BRIDE

14. *all glorious.* Based on this verse, the
sages taught that the true glory for the modest
woman is within the privacy of her home
(Shavuoth 30a; see also Maimonides Mishneh
Torah, Laws Pertaining to Women 13:11, and
cf. Hirsch).

15. *on richly woven stuff.* The Hebrew
word is connected with *weaver in colours*
(Exodus xxvi. 36). Here it signifies 'embroi-

dered work' and alludes to her garments. The
idea presented is that she does not need this
finery to satisfy her vanity, but only to en-
hance the honour of the king (cf. Hirsch).

her companions. The bridesmaids who follow her in the procession.

16. *gladness and rejoicing.* The bride is
conducted to her groom to the accompaniment of music and dancing.

17-18 CONCLUDING ADDRESS TO THE KING

17. *instead of thy fathers.* The messianic
dynasty created by illustrious ancestors will
not end with him but will be assured a distinguished future through his male offspring
(cf. Kimchi).

in all the land. Better, *in all the earth* (R.V.).
His kingdom will extend by the subjugation
of other peoples over whom his sons will
rule.

18. *I will make thy name to be remembered.* The speaker is the Psalmist. His
songs of praise will preserve the king's
memory for generations unborn, and other
nations besides his own will hold his name in
honour.

1 For the Leader; [a Psalm] of the
   sons of Korah; upon Alamoth.
   A Song.

2 God is our refuge and strength,
   A very present help in trouble.

3 Therefore will we not fear, though
   the earth do change,
   And though the mountains be
   moved into the heart of the seas;

4 Though the waters thereof roar and
   foam,
   Though the mountains shake at
   the swelling thereof.   Selah

לַמְנַצֵּחַ לִבְנֵי־קֹרַח
עַל־עֲלָמוֹת שִׁיר׃
2 אֱלֹהִים לָנוּ מַחֲסֶה וָעֹז
עֶזְרָה בְצָרוֹת נִמְצָא מְאֹד׃
3 עַל־כֵּן לֹא־נִירָא בְּהָמִיר אָרֶץ
וּבְמוֹט הָרִים בְּלֵב יַמִּים׃
4 יֶהֱמוּ יֶחְמְרוּ מֵימָיו
יִרְעֲשׁוּ־הָרִים בְּגַאֲוָתוֹ סֶלָה׃

GOD THE NATION'S STRONGHOLD

THIS and the next two Psalms which form a closely connected group are of common Korahic
authorship and originated in the same historical event. They both tell of a grievous national
danger which had been overcome by the mercy of God. Ibn Ezra cites an opinion that the
occasion which inspired the three Psalms was the invasion of the land by Sennacherib's army.
However, he and many others are of the opinion that the Psalms speak of future times,
particularly of the days leading to the coming of the Messiah.

1. *Alamoth.* A clue to the definition of this word is 1 Chron. xv. 20f., *with psalteries set to Alamoth...with harps on the Sheminith* (for the latter, see on vi. 1), which seems to indicate that the former were instruments with high pitched tones.

2-4 UNSHAKABLE CONFIDENCE IN GOD

2. *God is our refuge.* The hypothesis that the Psalm relates to the Messianic era is strengthened by the noticeable resemblance between this phrase and the prophecy of Joel (iv. 16) where he details the events to occur in those times.

a very present help in trouble. lit. 'a help in straits has He been found exceedingly,' the words implying that we are frequently in straits because of our bad choice of action (Sforno).

3. *though the earth do change.* Secure in the stronghold of God, those within it have no cause for fear though the earth be overturned by a mighty convulsion of nature and the mountains disappear in the sea (cf. Isa. li. 6f.). A Hebraic way of saying: whatever may happen.

4. An elaboration of the thought contained in the preceding verse.

5 There is a river, the streams where-
   of make glad the city of God,
  The holiest dwelling-place of the
   Most High.

6 God is in the midst of her, she
   shall not be moved;
  God shall help her, at the approach of morning.

7 Nations were in tumult, kingdoms
   were moved;
  He uttered His voice, the earth
   melted.

8 The LORD of hosts is with us;
  The God of Jacob is our high
   tower.   Selah

9 Come, behold the works of the
   LORD,
  Who hath made desolations in the
   earth.

5 נָהָר פְּלָגָיו יְשַׂמְּחוּ עִיר־אֱלֹהִים
  קְדֹשׁ מִשְׁכְּנֵי עֶלְיוֹן:

6 אֱלֹהִים בְּקִרְבָּהּ בַּל־תִּמּוֹט
  יַעְזְרֶהָ אֱלֹהִים לִפְנוֹת בֹּקֶר:

7 הָמוּ גוֹיִם מָטוּ מַמְלָכוֹת
  נָתַן בְּקוֹלוֹ תָּמוּג אָרֶץ:

8 יְהוָה צְבָאוֹת עִמָּנוּ
  מִשְׂגָּב־לָנוּ אֱלֹהֵי יַעֲקֹב סֶלָה:

9 לְכוּ־חֲזוּ מִפְעֲלוֹת יְהוָה
  אֲשֶׁר־שָׂם שַׁמּוֹת בָּאָרֶץ:

5-8 Joy of God's Presence

5. *there is a river.* In contrast to the storm-swept ocean, the Psalmist thinks of God as a river with tributaries whose waters fertilize the country and give refreshment to its inhabitants. The protection of God, figured as a river, is found in Isa. viii. 6, xxxiii. 21.

the city of God. Zion (cf. xlviii. 2, 9; Isa. lx. 14).

holiest dwelling-place of the Most High. lit. 'holiness of the dwelling-places of the Most High'; for the plural, see on xliii. 3. The failure of the Assyrian siege of Jerusalem, if this is the reference, was interpreted as a demonstration that God had chosen it as His abode (see on verse 6).

6. *God is in the midst of her.* Cf. Isa. xii. 6; so long as that remains true no human power can avail against the holy city.

at the approach of morning. After the dark night of peril God's deliverance becomes apparent at dawn. There may be an allusion to what is narrated in Isa. xxxvii. 36, *and when men arose early in the morning, behold, they (the Assyrians) were all dead corpses.*

7. *were in tumult...were moved.* These verbs were used of the waters and mountains (verses 3f.): and as they who take refuge in God pass unscathed through nature's upheavals, so do they come safely through the upheavals of war. (cf. Daath Sofrim).

He uttered His voice. He thundered and the whole universe dissolved in fear.

8. *the LORD of hosts is with us.* A reminiscence of the name Immanuel, *God is with us* (Isa. vii. 14, viii. 8, 10). For the Divine name, see on xxiv. 10).

God of Jacob. The God Who redeemed the Patriarch from all his troubles.

is our high tower. Cf. the use of the verb from which the noun is derived in xx. 2, *the name of the God of Jacob set thee up on high.*

9-11 Lesson of the Crisis

9. *come, behold.* The Psalmist calls upon all nations to take note of what occurred and to draw a moral (Malbim).

10 He maketh wars to cease unto the
    end of the earth;
    He breaketh the bow, and cutteth
       the spear in sunder;
    He burneth the chariots in the
       fire.

11 'Let be, and know that I am God;
    I will be exalted among the
       nations,
    I will be exalted in the earth.'

12 The LORD of hosts is with us;
    The God of Jacob is our high
       tower.   Selah

10 מַשְׁבִּית מִלְחָמוֹת עַד־קְצֵה הָאָרֶץ
קֶשֶׁת יְשַׁבֵּר וְקִצֵּץ חֲנִית
עֲגָלוֹת יִשְׂרֹף בָּאֵשׁ׃

11 הַרְפּוּ וּדְעוּ כִּי־אָנֹכִי אֱלֹהִים
אָרוּם בַּגּוֹיִם אָרוּם בָּאָרֶץ׃

12 יְהוָה צְבָאוֹת עִמָּנוּ
מִשְׂגָּב־לָנוּ אֱלֹהֵי יַעֲקֹב סֶלָה׃

hath made desolations. As noted, according to most commentators this is a portrayal of things to come and not merely a description of the events of the time. To effect a final salvation, the wicked nations of the world must perish and the resulting devastation, caused primarily by war, will be vast.

10. *maketh war to cease*. Just as the haughty Assyrians had been crushed by the hand of God, so the hope is voiced that the desolation mentioned in the previous verse will culminate in permanent ruin for the aggressors and be followed by everlasting world-wide peace (cf. Isa. ii. 4) (Kimchi, Hirsch).

breaketh the bow. The language is doubtless suggested by the scene of the battle-field strewn with broken weapons and burnt vehicles. All implements of war are to be rendered useless by God. For a similar declaration, cf. Ezek. xxxix. 3 and Zech. ix. 10.

chariots. Not the usual word for war-chariots, but elsewhere meaning 'wagons.' The Targum, as well as the LXX, understood these as weapons and translated 'shields.' In 1 Sam. xvii. 20, xxvi. 7 a cognate word is used for 'baggage-wagons' of an army or *barricade*.

11. *let be*. Rather, 'desist,' from warlike adventures to win supremacy. God is supreme and decides the destinies of nations.

I will be exalted in the earth. The thought underlying this phrase becomes the subject of the next Psalm.

12. The Psalm is impressively ended with the repetition of the refrain of verse 8 which strikes its dominant key-note.

47

1 For the Leader; a Psalm of the sons of Korah.

2 O clap your hands, all ye peoples;
Shout unto God with the voice of triumph.

3 For the LORD is most high, awful;
A great King over all the earth.

4 He subdueth peoples under us,
And nations under our feet.

5 He chooseth our inheritance for us,
The pride of Jacob whom He loveth. Selah

6 God is gone up amidst shouting,
The LORD amidst the sound of the horn.

7 Sing praises to God, sing praises;
Sing praises unto our King, sing praises.

מז

לַמְנַצֵּחַ לִבְנֵי־קֹרַח מִזְמוֹר׃

2 כָּל־הָעַמִּים תִּקְעוּ־כָף
הָרִיעוּ לֵאלֹהִים בְּקוֹל רִנָּה׃

3 כִּי־יְהוָה עֶלְיוֹן נוֹרָא
מֶלֶךְ גָּדוֹל עַל־כָּל־הָאָרֶץ׃

4 יַדְבֵּר עַמִּים תַּחְתֵּינוּ
וּלְאֻמִּים תַּחַת רַגְלֵינוּ׃

5 יִבְחַר־לָנוּ אֶת־נַחֲלָתֵנוּ
אֶת גְּאוֹן יַעֲקֹב אֲשֶׁר־אָהֵב סֶלָה׃

6 עָלָה אֱלֹהִים בִּתְרוּעָה
יְהוָה בְּקוֹל שׁוֹפָר׃

7 זַמְּרוּ אֱלֹהִים זַמֵּרוּ
זַמְּרוּ לְמַלְכֵּנוּ זַמֵּרוּ׃

GOD THE KING

A POEM on the theme of xlvi. 11, *I will be exalted in the earth.* It foretells the time when the nations will recognize God as the Omnipotent Ruler of all living beings (cf. Malbim). The Psalm is recited in the Synagogue before the sounding of the *Shofar* (ram's horn) on the New Year, a day when the liturgy dwells upon the thought of God's universal Sovereignty.

2-5 A CALL TO THE NATIONS

2. *clap your hands...shout.* The demonstrations which greeted a king when he ascended the throne (cf. 1 Sam. x. 24; 2 Kings xi. 12) are called for from the peoples on the acknowledgment of God as the supreme Ruler of the universe.

3. *awful.* Awe-inspiring.

4. *subdueth.* A general truth is enunciated, demonstrated in known victories.

5. *our inheritance.* The Holy land.

the pride of Jacob. The inheritance in which Israel takes pride as a gift from God. According to some this is a specific reference to the Temple in Jerusalem (cf. Kimchi).

whom He loveth. That love was demonstrated in the bestowal of the inheritance (cf. lxxxvii. 2).

6-7 PRAISE THE KING

6. *God is gone up.* The prophecy mentioned in xlvi. 11 is realized and amidst much fanfare God is declared the Almighty (Kimchi).

amidst the sound of the horn. Acclaiming, as it were, His triumph. Some commentators associate this with the blast of the 'great horn' mentioned in Isa. xxvii. 13 (Sforno).

7. *sing praises.* The Hebrew verb is the root of *mizmor*, Psalm, and is used of vocal praise (cf. Hirsch).

8 For God is the King of all the
 earth;
 Sing ye praises in a skilful song.

9 God reigneth over the nations;
 God sitteth upon His holy throne.

10 The princes of the peoples are
 gathered together,
 The people of the God of
 Abraham;
 For unto God belong the shields
 of the earth;
 He is greatly exalted.

כִּי מֶלֶךְ כָּל־הָאָרֶץ אֱלֹהִים 8
זַמְּרוּ מַשְׂכִּיל׃
מָלַךְ אֱלֹהִים עַל־גּוֹיִם 9
אֱלֹהִים יָשַׁב ׀ עַל־כִּסֵּא קָדְשׁוֹ׃
נְדִיבֵי עַמִּים ׀ נֶאֱסָפוּ 10
עַם אֱלֹהֵי אַבְרָהָם
כִּי לֵאלֹהִים מָגִנֵּי־אֶרֶץ
מְאֹד נַעֲלָה׃

8-9 GOD IS ENTHRONED

8. *King of all the earth.* This is the great
truth proclaimed in the Psalm; hence the call
to *all ye peoples* (verse 2) to unite in acknowledging His Kingship.

a skilful song. See on xxxii. 1.

9. *reigneth...sitteth.* Translate 'hath become King...hath taken His seat' (cf. Hirsch).
The Psalmist describes the effect of the victory. God had been King of the earth before
but His sovereignty was recognized only by
Israel. Now He establishes Himself as supreme ruler of all nations (cf. Kimchi) and
subsequently takes His place on the throne
whence He administers dominion over the
affairs of the world (Metsudath David).

10 HIS KINGSHIP ACKNOWLEDGED

The verse is in the prophetic mood, looking
forward to a scene which is depicted as actually happening.

princes of the peoples. The representatives of
all nations are assembled to pay homage to
the Supreme King (Ibn Ezra).

the people of the God of Abraham. The sense
required is 'together with the people of the
God of Abraham,' and the LXX supplies the
preposition 'with.' Another possibility is to
understand the word 'to become' before 'the
people' (Ibn Ezra). The mention of Abraham
links the prophecy of the future with the
promise of the past that he was to become
father of a multitude of nations (Gen. xvii. 4).
It was with the awareness that as the first
among the nations it must lead all the other
peoples back to God that Israel assumed its
role in the history of the world (Hirsch).

the shields of the earth. Designation for
kings and princes (*rulers*, Hosea iv. 18); although themselves governors, they are under
His sway (Kimchi).

He is greatly exalted. Or, 'He has become
greatly exalted,' as the sequel to what has
taken place. God's exultation results from
recognition of Him by all peoples. It is one of
the dominant notes struck in the Psalter and
truly expresses the ultimate aim of Israel's
religion.

48

מח

1 A Song; a Psalm of the sons of
   Korah.

2 Great is the LORD, and highly to
     be praised,
   In the city of our God, His holy
     mountain,

3 Fair in situation, the joy of the
     whole earth;
   Even mount Zion, the uttermost
     parts of the north,
   The city of the great King.

4 God in her palaces
   Hath made Himself known for a
     stronghold.

שִׁיר מִזְמוֹר לִבְנֵי־קֹרַח:

2 גָּדוֹל יְהֹוָה וּמְהֻלָּל מְאֹד
בְּעִיר אֱלֹהֵינוּ הַר־קָדְשׁוֹ:

3 יְפֵה נוֹף מְשׂוֹשׂ כָּל־הָאָרֶץ
הַר־צִיּוֹן יַרְכְּתֵי צָפוֹן
קִרְיַת מֶלֶךְ רָב:

4 אֱלֹהִים בְּאַרְמְנוֹתֶיהָ
נוֹדַע לְמִשְׂגָּב:

THE DELIVERANCE OF ZION

IN the last of this trilogy of Psalms the restoration of Jerusalem as God's spiritual dwelling place is celebrated. As 'the city of the great King' it will become the centre of worship for
all the nations who will come to acknowledge God as the Almighty. This brings to mind the
verse in Isa. ii. 2ff. 'And it shall come to pass in the end of the days...'

2-4 GOD IN THE MIDST OF ZION

2. *highly to be praised.* By all the peoples.

city of our God. The city He chose for the site
of the Temple.

His holy mountain. Strictly speaking this is
the Temple Mount, but it is here applied to
Jerusalem as a whole.

3. *fair in situation.* Its location is ideal and
its setting so beautiful that its very appearance shows it to be a place upon which the
rest of the land looks with delight (Hirsch).
Kimchi points out that the climate of Jerusalem is exceptional in that anyone can adapt to
it without harmful effect. Indeed, even the ill
go there to benefit from its invigorating air.

joy of the whole earth. The centre from which
radiates the true knowledge of God which is
a source of blessing to all who accept it. In
i. 2, it is described as *the perfection of
beauty,* and both descriptions are recalled
in Lam. ii. 15.

the uttermost parts of the north. This phrase

occurs again in Isaiah (xiv. 13) and Ezekiel
(xxxviii. 6, 15 and xxxix. 2) to indicate the
remote and inaccessible regions. Its use here
is variously explained, but the simplest interpretation is to understand the second half of
the verse as giving an account of Jerusalem in
its two main divisions: Mount Zion, i.e.
Moriah, which lies to the northeast, and the
city proper which is at its foot.

city. Hebrew *kiryah* (not the word in verse 2),
used also in Isa. xxxiii. 20. This word occurs
in poetical and prophetical diction.

great King. Better 'king,' as the reference is
to a mortal monarch, either David or the
Messiah (Redak). Its imposing position and
natural beauty indicate that it is the home of
a great and mighty king (cf. Daath Sofrim).

4. *palaces.* Again mentioned in verse 14;
the noble buildings which would have been
plundered and burnt by the invaders had
God's Presence not been within them
(Kimchi).

stronghold. The word translated *high tower*
in xlvi. 8, 12.

5 For, lo, the kings assembled themselves,
   They came onward together.

6 They saw, straightway they were
   amazed;
   They were affrighted, they hasted
   away.

7 Trembling took hold of them
   there,
   Pangs, as of a woman in travail.

8 With the east wind
   Thou breakest the ships of Tarshish.

9 As we have heard, so have we seen
   In the city of the LORD of hosts, in
   the city of our God—
   God establish it for ever.   Selah

10 We have thought on Thy lovingkindness, O God,
   In the midst of Thy temple.

כִּי־הִנֵּה הַמְּלָכִים נוֹעֲדוּ 5
עָבְרוּ יַחְדָּו׃
הֵמָּה רָאוּ כֵּן תָּמָהוּ 6
נִבְהֲלוּ נֶחְפָּזוּ׃
רְעָדָה אֲחָזָתַם שָׁם 7
חִיל כַּיּוֹלֵדָה׃
בְּרוּחַ קָדִים 8
תְּשַׁבֵּר אֳנִיּוֹת תַּרְשִׁישׁ׃
כַּאֲשֶׁר שָׁמַעְנוּ כֵּן רָאִינוּ 9
בְּעִיר יְהוָה־צְבָאוֹת בְּעִיר אֱלֹהֵינוּ
אֱלֹהִים יְכוֹנְנֶהָ עַד־עוֹלָם סֶלָה׃
דִּמִּינוּ אֱלֹהִים חַסְדֶּךָ 10
בְּקֶרֶב הֵיכָלֶךָ׃

5-9   DEFEAT OF THE BESIEGERS

5. *kings.* Before the coming of the Messiah, the leaders of the world's nations will gather in a combined attempt to conquer Jerusalem.

came onward. Rather, 'passed over,' the frontier.

6. *they saw.* God's presence in the holy city.

they hasted away. In their fright and astonishment.

7. The verse is reminiscent of Exod. xv. 14.

8. *with the east wind.* Metaphorical language borrowed from the storm at sea is employed to describe the rout of the invading army. *East wind* as a symbol of destructive power is found in Isa. xxvii. 8; Jer. xviii. 17; Job xxvii. 21. There may also be a recollection of the east wind which parted the water of the Red Sea and saved Israel from the Egyptians (Exod. xiv. 21) (cf. Rashi).

ships of Tarshish. As in Isa. ii. 16, a symbol of great size and strength. Tarshish (see Jonah i. 3) is identified with Tartessus in southwest Spain or more probably a location in Asia Minor (see Ezek. xxvii. 12). It was a major seaport and its fleets were among the largest of the age (Kimchi).

9. *as we have heard.* The wondrous acts God performed on behalf of Israel and the prophecies for the future.

so we have seen. The fulfillment of these prophecies.

God establish it for ever. This may be understood as an assurance for the future and as a prayerful exclamation (Daath Sofrim).

10-15   MEDITATION UPON THE EVENT

10. *we ... thought on.* The Hebrew verb means 'to compare'; i.e. form the picture in one's mind. So the meaning: 'We have (until now) only been able to ponder about Your acts of kindness without actually witnessing them' (Hirsch). Alternatively, the word means 'to hope' and the phrase would be rendered: "we have always yearned for Your kindness, O God" (Rashi).

11 As is Thy name, O God,
So is Thy praise unto the ends of
the earth;
Thy right hand is full of righteousness.

12 Let mount Zion be glad,
Let the daughters of Judah re-
joice,
Because of Thy judgments.

13 Walk about Zion, and go round
about her;
Count the towers thereof.

14 Mark ye well her ramparts,
Traverse her palaces;
That ye may tell it to the genera-
tion following.

15 For such is God, our God, for
ever and ever;
He will guide us eternally.

11 כְּשִׁמְךָ ׀ אֱלֹהִים כֵּן תְּהִלָּתְךָ
עַל־קַצְוֵי־אֶרֶץ
צֶדֶק מָלְאָה יְמִינֶךָ׃
12 יִשְׂמַח ׀ הַר־צִיּוֹן
תָּגֵלְנָה בְּנוֹת יְהוּדָה
לְמַעַן מִשְׁפָּטֶיךָ׃
13 סֹבּוּ צִיּוֹן וְהַקִּיפוּהָ
סִפְרוּ מִגְדָּלֶיהָ׃
14 שִׁיתוּ לִבְּכֶם ׀ לְחֵילָה
פַּסְּגוּ אַרְמְנוֹתֶיהָ
לְמַעַן תְּסַפְּרוּ לְדוֹר אַחֲרוֹן׃
15 כִּי זֶה ׀ אֱלֹהִים אֱלֹהֵינוּ עוֹלָם וָעֶד
הוּא יְנַהֲגֵנוּ עַל־מוּת׃

11. *Thy name.* God's repute as a mighty Deliverer.

so is Thy praise. The recognition of God's act of deliverance celebrated in hymns of praise.

right hand. His Power which is exercised to defend the right and humble the arrogant.

12. The verse is adapted in xcvii. 8. *Daughters of Judah* are the towns and villages surrounding Jerusalem (Ibn Ezra) which were also imperilled by the invaders and would have been overrun.

judgments. Passed upon the enemy, resulting in their defeat.

13. *count the towers thereof.* Cf. Isa. xxxiii.18. A call to the nations to take note of Zion's splendid structures and the magnificent towers which surround her (Kimchi). Alternatively, a command to those rebuilding the city to calculate the number of towers needed for fortifications (Rashi).

14. *mark ye well.* lit. 'set your heart to,' attend to the city's ramparts to ascertain that they are structurally sound and are capable of

withstanding an enemy assault.

tell it. As proof of the claim which is made of God.

15. *such is God.* lit. 'this is God,' Saviour of Zion and Israel when they are endangered.

for ever and ever. He will be eternally the same.

He. Emphatic in the Hebrew. He and none other.

eternally. Hebrew 'al-muth' lit. 'upon death.' Here the sense is 'until death' (Kimchi). Rashi, following Targum, reads it as one word 'almuth,' the Hebrew for youth, and renders 'He will guide us like young children,' i.e. with extreme caution. Meiri, using the same word, understands it to mean: 'He will lead us on in eternal youth,' i.e. we will not weaken even in old age. Hirsch translates literally 'above death' and interprets the verse as meaning 'God will lead us beyond mortality, making us immortal among the nations.' Rashi cites Menachem who understands 'almuth' as stemming from the root 'olam' and meaning 'for ever and ever.'

49　　　　　　　　　　　　　　　　　　　מט

1 For the Leader; a Psalm of the
　sons of Korah.

2 Hear this, all ye peoples;
　Give ear, all ye inhabitants of the
　　world,

3 Both low and high,
　Rich and poor together.

4 My mouth shall speak wisdom,
　And the meditation of my heart
　　shall be understanding.

5 I will incline mine ear to a parable;
　I will open my dark saying upon
　　the harp.

למנצח לבני־קרח מזמור׃

2 שמעו־זאת כל־העמים
האזינו כל־ישבי חלד׃

3 גם־בני אדם גם־בני־איש
יחד עשיר ואביון׃

4 פי ידבר חכמות
והגות לבי תבונות׃

5 אזה למשל אזני
אפתח בכנור חידתי׃

DEATH THE LEVELLER

THE link between this Psalm and the group of three that precedes it is that they are alike
addressed to *all ye peoples*. The latter called upon mankind to acknowledge God's Kingship; this one deals with a problem which exercises the mind of all thinking persons and
should be read in connection with LXXIII. Wealth is unequally distributed: some possess
more than others and derive from it power and authority over the poor. This seemingly
unfair arrangement must be due to Divine ordering; so how is it to be explained? The
solution which the Psalmist puts forward is that the might of wealth is limited. It cannot
ward off the oncoming of death, and at its advent the rich are reduced to the same level as
the poor. If that truism were borne in mind, wealth would not breed insolent pride; and in
that thought the poor in their disability may hope for the ultimate triumph of right. The
Psalm has been appointed for recital in a Jewish house of mourning (P.B., p. 322).

2-5　EXHORTATORY INTRODUCTION

2. *all ye peoples*. A question of universal
interest and application is to be discussed.

world. Hebrew, *cheled* as in xvii. 14, man's
temporary place of abode (cf. Rashi). The
choice of the word prepares the readers for
the theme of the Psalm.

3. *both low and high*. Hebrew, 'both ye sons
of *adam* (i.e. men generally) and ye sons of
ish (i.e. men of higher station, see on iv. 3).'
The message is for all people, and also for all
sections of human society, especially the
well-to-do (Hirsch).

rich and poor. The *rich* were to derive a so-
bering, and the *poor* a comforting lesson from

what they are about to hear (cf. Hirsch).

4. *wisdom...understanding*. Wisdom refers to the teachings of wisdom as explicitly
given, while understanding refers to the
inferences that are to be drawn from the
former (Hirsch).

5. *incline mine ear*. To receive instruction
from God which comes in the form of a
parable, i.e. an oracular utterance in poetical
style (cf. Num. xxiii. 7).

dark saying. The Hebrew is used for 'a rid-
dle' and also, as here, for a pronouncement
upon an enigmatic problem.

upon the harp. To the accompaniment of
string music.

6 Wherefore should I fear in the
   days of evil,
   When the iniquity of my supplanters compasseth me about,

7 Of them that trust in their wealth,
   And boast themselves in the multitude of their riches?

8 No man can by any means redeem
   his brother,
   Nor give to God a ransom for
   him—

9 For too costly is the redemption
   of their soul,
   And must be let alone for ever—

10 That he should still live alway,
   That he should not see the pit.

11 For he seeth that wise men die,
   The fool and the brutish to-
   gether perish,
   And leave their wealth to others.

6 לָמָּה אִירָא בִּימֵי רָע
אֲוֹן עֲקֵבַי יְסוּבֵּנִי:
7 הַבֹּטְחִים עַל־חֵילָם
וּבְרֹב עָשְׁרָם יִתְהַלָּלוּ:
8 אָח לֹא־פָדֹה יִפְדֶּה אִישׁ
לֹא־יִתֵּן לֵאלֹהִים כָּפְרוֹ:
9 וְיֵקַר פִּדְיוֹן נַפְשָׁם
וְחָדַל לְעוֹלָם:
10 וִיחִי־עוֹד לָנֶצַח
לֹא יִרְאֶה הַשָּׁחַת:
11 כִּי יִרְאֶה חֲכָמִים יָמוּתוּ
יַחַד כְּסִיל וָבַעַר יֹאבֵדוּ
וְעָזְבוּ לַאֲחֵרִים חֵילָם:

6-13   WEALTH AND DEATH

6. *days of evil.* Man's existence is considered evil in that his days are wasted in pursuit
of wealth that has no value for him in the
world to come (Kimchi).

my supplanters. Better '[which I trod upon]
with my heels.'

7. *trust in their wealth.* As the righteous
have faith in God for their support, so the rich
put their trust in wealth as the means of
obtaining security.

8. *redeem his brother.* One thing cannot be
bought off at a price, and that is, redemption
from the final end which comes to all men.
Not even a *brother*, one to whom the rich man
is attached by close kinship or intimate
friendship, can be saved from natural death
by the power of money. If he cannot do this
for a brother, how much less for himself! (Ibn
Ezra)

ransom. The Psalmist has in mind, and uses
the language of, the law of Exod. xxi. 30.

9. *too costly.* It is beyond the means of a
wealthy man to offer a 'ransom' to save his
friend's life when God had decreed his death
(Metsudath David).

and must be let alone for ever. It were useless
to think of attempting such an impossible
transaction (Metsudath David). This verse is
parenthetical, and verse 10 continues verse 8.

10. *see the pit.* Experience death; as in xvi.

11. *he seeth.* It must be obvious to the
wealthy that death comes to all men, whatever their character or status (Metsudath
David).

wise men die. Wisdom, which is far superior
to riches, does not bring exemption from
death.

perish. The verb suggests that all trace of
them is lost. On the other hand, wise men *die*,
their lives comes to an end, but their souls
live on (Rashi).

leave their wealth to others. At death, class
distinction based upon material possessions,

12 Their inward thought is, that
    their houses shall continue for
    ever,
    And their dwelling-places to all
    generations;
    They call their lands after their
    own names.

13 But man abideth not in honour;
    He is like the beasts that perish.

14 This is the way of them that are
    foolish,
    And of those who after them
    approve their sayings.   Selah

15 Like sheep they are appointed for
    the nether-world;
    Death shall be their shepherd;
    And the upright shall have
    dominion over them in the
    morning;
    And their form shall be for the
    nether-world to wear away,
    That there be no habitation for it.

16 But God will redeem my soul
    from the power of the nether-
    world;
    For He shall receive me.   Selah

קִרְבָּם בָּתֵּימוֹ ׀ לְעוֹלָם 12
מִשְׁכְּנֹתָם לְדוֹר וָדֹר
קָרְאוּ בִשְׁמוֹתָם עֲלֵי אֲדָמוֹת׃
וְאָדָם בִּיקָר בַּל־יָלִין 13
נִמְשַׁל כַּבְּהֵמוֹת נִדְמוּ׃
זֶה דַרְכָּם כֵּסֶל לָמוֹ 14
וְאַחֲרֵיהֶם ׀ בְּפִיהֶם יִרְצוּ סֶלָה׃
כַּצֹּאן ׀ לִשְׁאוֹל שַׁתּוּ מָוֶת יִרְעֵם 15
וַיִּרְדּוּ בָם יְשָׁרִים ׀ לַבֹּקֶר
וְצוּרָם לְבַלּוֹת שְׁאוֹל מִזְּבֻל לוֹ׃
אַךְ־אֱלֹהִים יִפְדֶּה־נַפְשִׁי מִיַּד־שְׁאוֹל 16
כִּי יִקָּחֵנִי סֶלָה׃

 v. 15. וצורם ק'

---

at once ceases, 'In the hour of man's departure from the world neither silver nor gold
nor jewels accompany him, but only Torah
and good deeds (Aboth).

12. *their ... thought is.* They imagine themselves living with their worldly possessions
forever. Some read the word *kivrom*, Hebrew
for 'their grave,' and render: 'Their grave will
be their home for evermore'; i.e. they shall not
be resurrected (Talmud M.K. 9b).

13. *but man abideth not in honour.* Better,
'so man in (his) splendour abideth not.' All
that he prided himself on, his accumulation
of land and other forms of property, avails
him nothing. Physically his end is the same as
that of cattle (Kimchi).

    14-21   VANITY OF WEALTH: TRIUMPH
          OF THE UPRIGHT

14. *foolish.* Foolishly self-confident.

approve their sayings. lit. 'find pleasure in
their mouth,' adopt the same attitude as their

predecessors. They, too, will meet with a like
fate (Kimchi).

15. *like sheep.* Their wealth cannot save
them for descent to Sheol and are like sheep
in a pen destined for slaughter (Kimchi).

the upright. Who had been the victims of
their lawlessness, then triumph over them.

in the morning. The mornings of resurrection
after the sleep of death (cf. Daniel xii. 2.)
According to Rashi the word is used metaphorically of the light of deliverance after the
darkness of exile (see on xlvi. 6).

their form. The soul of the wicked is doomed
to waste away in the nether world, *Gehinom*
(Rashi).

16. *redeem my soul.* An allusion to the
doctrine of immortality of the soul (Malbim,
Metsudath David). According to Rashi, the
Psalmist expresses his confidence that, unlike the foolish who rely upon their wealth to

17 Be not thou afraid when one
   waxeth rich,
   When the wealth of his house is
   increased;

18 For when he dieth he shall carry
   nothing away;
   His wealth shall not descend
   after him.

19 Though while he lived he blessed
   his soul:
   'Men will praise thee, when thou
   shalt do well to thyself';

20 It shall go to the generation of
   his fathers;
   They shall never see the light.

21 Man that is in honour understandeth not;
   He is like the beasts that perish.

אַל־תִּירָא כִּי־יַעֲשִׁר אִישׁ 17
כִּי־יִרְבֶּה כְּבוֹד בֵּיתוֹ:
כִּי לֹא בְמוֹתוֹ יִקַּח הַכֹּל 18
לֹא־יֵרֵד אַחֲרָיו כְּבוֹדוֹ:
כִּי־נַפְשׁוֹ בְּחַיָּיו יְבָרֵךְ 19
וְיוֹדֻךָ כִּי־תֵיטִיב לָךְ:
תָּבוֹא עַד־דּוֹר אֲבוֹתָיו 20
עַד־נֵצַח לֹא יִרְאוּ־אוֹר:
אָדָם בִּיקָר וְלֹא יָבִין 21
נִמְשַׁל כַּבְּהֵמוֹת נִדְמוּ:

save them from the perils which endanger
life, he will be protected by God from a
premature death. Accordingly the verse gives
the answer to the question in verse 6,
wherefore should I fear in the days of evil?
He has no reason to fear, being under Divine
protection.

from the power of the nether-world. lit. 'from
the hand of Sheol,' i.e. from coming under its
sway through the incidence of death (Rashi).

He shall receive me. God will rescue me from
peril. The verb is the same as that rendered
took in xviii. 17.

17. *be not thou afraid.* Having learnt the
lesson himself, he exhorts others to adopt it
(Kimchi).

wealth. lit. 'glory,' the magnificence which
wealth can provide.

18. For the thought, cf. Job i. 21; Eccles. v. 14.

19. *while he lived.* lit. 'in his life'; having
had his portion with which he was satisfied
during his lifetime.

he blessed his soul. Congratulated himself on
his prosperity and power.

men will praise thee. Render, '(but) men will
praise *thee* when thou doest good' (Rashi).

20. *it shall go.* The subject is *his soul* in the
preceding verse (Kimchi, Ibn Ezra).

to the generation of his fathers. An idiom for
'dying,' as in *he was gathered unto his fathers.*

they shall never see. Better, 'who shall never
see.' For him, as for them, the darkness of
Sheol will be everlasting (Rashi, Ibn Ezra).

21. A repetition of verse 13 with the substitution of *understandeth not* for 'abideth not;'
the phrase employed here strikingly emphasizes the moral of the Psalm. There is nothing
sinful in being rich, and a wealthy man may
be as righteous as, or better than, a poor man.
When, however, he glories only in material
prosperity and fails to appreciate the value of
spiritual and moral virtues, he lacks the understanding of life with its God-given purpose and sublime opportunities. His existence is merely animal and he perishes like the
beast.

50

נ

1 A Psalm of Asaph.
  God, God, the Lord, hath spoken,
    and called the earth
  From the rising of the sun unto
    the going down thereof.

2 Out of Zion, the perfection of
    beauty,
  God hath shined forth.

מִזְמוֹר לְאָסָף
אֵל ׀ אֱלֹהִים יְהֹוָה דִּבֶּר וַיִּקְרָא־אָרֶץ
מִמִּזְרַח־שֶׁמֶשׁ עַד־מְבֹאוֹ:
מִצִּיּוֹן מִכְלַל־יֹפִי 2
אֱלֹהִים הוֹפִיעַ:

ISRAEL ARRAIGNED

The subject of this Psalm is one which is treated by several of the prophets, viz. the faulty conception of religion held by the people. For some it consisted in nothing more than the bringing of sacrifices; others pretended to be faithful to God's commands but in private violated them. A court scene is described in which God acts as Plaintiff and Judge with Israel as the defendant. Their faults are exposed and they are sharply rebuked for the manner in which they have conducted their lives (verses 15-22). At the same time, the true aim of religion is taught. Those who are sincere in their dealings with both man and God will behold His presence while the corrupt of this world, be they of Israel or of other nations, will perish.

1-6 GOD APPEARS AS JUDGE

1. *Psalm of Asaph.* A group of eleven Psalms (LXXIII-LXXXIII) bears this title in addition to this one. Asaph, endowed with a prophetic spirit (cf. 1 Chron. xxv. 2) was a contemporary of David. Being famous for his skill as a composer, he was one of those selected to superintend the musical arrangements when the Ark was brought to Jerusalem (1 Chron. xvi. 4ff.), and he is mentioned elsewhere in connection with Temple music. There is a difference of opinion on the identity of Asaph. Rabbi Jochanan opines that he was one of the three sons of Korah who was privileged to be the sole composer of songs, besides working in collaboration with his brothers. Rav disputes this, citing evidence that Asaph lived in a later era (Midrash Song of Songs).

God, God, the Lord. Hebrew *kel Elohim Adonai*, representing the Deity in three aspects: the Mighty One, the Judge, the Gracious One. The combination is also found in

Joshua xxii. 22. In the call to the earth to hear His revelation, God's will, particularly as regards the attitude to be taken by Israel, is laid clear and obvious before us (Hirsch).

hath spoken. In His summons to Israel to appear in judgment.

called the earth. To attend the tribunal and learn the lesson which was to be derived from the proceedings. Although the delinquencies of Israel are to be tried, God is concerned with all mankind and desires that they should understand His will. So all receive the call to be present, from one end of the earth to the other.

2. *out of Zion.* The abode of the Shechinah whence Torah goes forth to the world.

perfection of beauty. See on xlviii. 3.

God hath shined forth. As the sun illumines the earth, so does God bring light to the human mind and soul (cf. lxxx. 2, xciv. 1). The passage in Deut. xxxiii. 2 seems to have been in the Psalmist's mind.

3 Our God cometh, and doth not
   keep silence;
   A fire devoureth before Him,
   And round about Him it stormeth
   mightily.

4 He calleth to the heavens above,
   And to the earth, that He may
   judge His people:

5 'Gather My saints together unto
   Me;
   Those that have made a covenant
   with Me by sacrifice.'

6 And the heavens declare His
   righteousness;
   For God, He is judge.   Selah

7 'Hear, O My people, and I will
   speak;
   O Israel, and I will testify against
   thee:
   God, thy God, am I.

3 יָבֹא אֱלֹהֵינוּ וְאַל־יֶחֱרַשׁ
   אֵשׁ־לְפָנָיו תֹּאכֵל
   וּסְבִיבָיו נִשְׂעֲרָה מְאֹד׃

4 יִקְרָא אֶל־הַשָּׁמַיִם מֵעָל
   וְאֶל־הָאָרֶץ לָדִין עַמּוֹ׃

5 אִסְפוּ־לִי חֲסִידָי
   כֹּרְתֵי בְרִיתִי עֲלֵי־זָבַח׃

6 וַיַּגִּידוּ שָׁמַיִם צִדְקוֹ
   כִּי־אֱלֹהִים שֹׁפֵט הוּא סֶלָה׃

7 שִׁמְעָה עַמִּי וַאֲדַבֵּרָה
   יִשְׂרָאֵל וְאָעִידָה בָּךְ
   אֱלֹהִים אֱלֹהֶיךָ אָנֹכִי׃

3. *doth not keep silent.* He will no longer tolerate the continued harassment of His people (Rashi, Kimchi, Metsudath David).

fire. The fire of God's wrath will be turned in vengeance against Israel's enemies (Kimchi).

4. *heavens...earth.* Commonly named as witnesses to Divine action (cf. Deut. xxxii. 1; Isa. i. 2).

5. *My saints.* Hebrew *chasidai*; those people of Israel who, in complete selflessness (*chessed*), devote themselves to the fulfilment of God's will. Being spiritually closer to God, they enjoy a privileged relationship with Him and will be gathered to serve as witnesses as He passes judgment upon others (Hirsch).

those that have made. lit. 'the makers of.' Each generation of Israel, as it were, renews the covenant which was originally made at Sinai. The obligation then undertaken is transmitted from parent to child.

by sacrifice. In the first instance the cov-enant had been ratified by the offering of sacrifices (Exod. xxiv. 5ff.). The phrase can also mean 'in the matter of sacrifice' (so Ibn Ezra), which formed part of God's worship as prescribed by Him but which had been abused by the people.

6. *the heavens declare His righteousness.* As the trial is about to open, the Psalmist depicts the heavens, which had been witness to history, testifying that the proceedings will be in strict fairness since God, Whose attribute is righteousness, presides as Judge.

7-15   ABOVE SACRIFICES HE DEMANDS
            GRATITUDE AND TRUST

7. *testify against thee.* Again in lxxxi. 9, where the Hebrew is translated *I will admonish thee*. That is its meaning here, the purpose of the convention being reformative' rather than punitive.

God, thy God. The relationship between God and the people is stressed to indicate that He gave them His law and He alone has the right to decide how it is to be interpreted in action.

8 I will not reprove thee for thy
  sacrifices;
And thy burnt-offerings are continually before Me.

9 I will take no bullock out of thy
  house,
Nor he-goats out of thy folds.

10 For every beast of the forest is
  Mine,
And the cattle upon a thousand
  hills.

11 I know all the fowls of the mountains;
And the wild beasts of the field
  are Mine.

12 If I were hungry, I would not tell
  thee;
For the world is Mine, and the
  fulness thereof.

13 Do I eat the flesh of bulls,
Or drink the blood of goats?

14 Offer unto God the sacrifice of
  thanksgiving;
And pay thy vows unto the Most
  High;

8 לֹא עַל־זְבָחֶיךָ אוֹכִיחֶךָ
וְעוֹלֹתֶיךָ לְנֶגְדִּי תָמִיד׃
9 לֹא־אֶקַּח מִבֵּיתְךָ פָר
מִמִּכְלְאֹתֶיךָ עַתּוּדִים׃
10 כִּי־לִי כָל־חַיְתוֹ־יָעַר
בְּהֵמוֹת בְּהַרְרֵי־אָלֶף׃
11 יָדַעְתִּי כָּל־עוֹף הָרִים
וְזִיז שָׂדַי עִמָּדִי׃
12 אִם־אֶרְעַב לֹא־אֹמַר לָךְ
כִּי־לִי תֵבֵל וּמְלֹאָהּ׃
13 הַאוֹכַל בְּשַׂר אַבִּירִים
וְדַם עַתּוּדִים אֶשְׁתֶּה׃
14 זְבַח לֵאלֹהִים תּוֹדָה
וְשַׁלֵּם לְעֶלְיוֹן נְדָרֶיךָ׃

8. *I will not reprove thee.* Or, 'not concerning thy sacrifices do I reprove thee.' God
proffers no charge that they had been negli-
gent in the duty of bringing the ordained
sacrifices. They had done so regularly; and
yet they had failed to win His approval
(Hirsch).

9. *I will take no bullock.* The absurdity of
the popular view that God needs the animals
offered to Him is forcibly exposed. An earthly
king takes from his subjects whatever he
wants with or without their consent. Not so
God Who takes nothing from man; on the
contrary, all that man claims to own belongs
in reality to Him (Kimchi).

10. *a thousand hills.* The Hebrew may be
translated 'upon mountains of thousands,'
where thousands of cattle graze (Rashi).

11. *wild beasts of the field.* The phrase is
repeated in lxxx. 14, where it is rendered *that
which moveth in the field*, all the creeping
things, corresponding to Gen. i. 24.

12. *if I were hungry.* The biting sarcasm of
these two verses effectively disposes of the
idea that, in the religious worship of Israel,
sacrifices are 'food of God.'

world is Mine. Cf. xxiv. 1, lxxxix. 12.

14. *the sacrifice of thanksgiving.* If worship begins and ends with the offerings of
animals, it is futile. The sacrifice must be
accompanied by an acknowledgement that
we sincerely appreciate and are most grateful
for the love and care that God has shown for
us (Cf. Sforno, Hirsch).

pay thy vows. An allusion to the offering
consequent upon a vow (Lev. vii. 16); but
that is not the only kind of vow to God which
man should make and loyally fulfil.

15 And call upon Me in the day of
 trouble;
 I will deliver thee, and thou shalt
 honour Me.'

16 But unto the wicked God saith:
 'What hast thou to do to declare
 My statutes,
 And that thou hast taken My
 covenant in thy mouth?

17 Seeing thou hatest instruction,
 And castest My words behind
 thee.

18 When thou sawest a thief, thou
 hadst company with him,
 And with adulterers was thy
 portion.

19 Thou hast let loose thy mouth
 for evil,
 And thy tongue frameth deceit.

20 Thou sittest and speakest against
 thy brother;
 Thou slanderest thine own
 mother's son.

15 וְֽקָרָאֵנִי בְּיוֹם צָרָה
אֲחַלֶּצְךָ וּֽתְכַבְּדֵֽנִי׃
16 וְלָרָשָׁע ׀ אָמַר אֱלֹהִים
מַה־לְּךָ לְסַפֵּר חֻקָּי
וַתִּשָּׂא בְרִיתִי עֲלֵי־פִֽיךָ׃
17 וְאַתָּה שָׂנֵאתָ מוּסָר
וַתַּשְׁלֵךְ דְּבָרַי אַחֲרֶֽיךָ׃
18 אִם־רָאִיתָ גַנָּב וַתִּרֶץ עִמּוֹ
וְעִם מְנָאֲפִים חֶלְקֶֽךָ׃
19 פִּיךָ שָׁלַחְתָּ בְרָעָה
וּלְשׁוֹנְךָ תַּצְמִיד מִרְמָה׃
20 תֵּשֵׁב בְּאָחִיךָ תְדַבֵּר
בְּבֶן־אִמְּךָ תִּתֶּן־דֹּֽפִי׃

---

15. *call upon Me.* An offering of words in earnest prayer will prove acceptable to Him.

honour Me. Because of the answer which He gives to such prayer.

16-21 HYPOCRITES DENOUNCED

16. *declare My statutes.* Speak of them as though accepted as rules of living.

taken My covenant in thy mouth. Profess to have agreed to the terms of the covenant.

17. *instruction.* Hebrew *musar*, discipline, moral restraint. In late Hebrew it is the term for 'ethics.' It is the ultimate purpose of the Torah to curb man's desires, whereas the wicked give full rein to them.

castest My words behind thee. To be out of sight and mind, because they forbid what the wicked long to do. The words refer to all the other commandments laid down in the Torah besides the aforementioned *instructions* (laws involving other people) and *statutes* (Kimchi).

18. *thou hadst company with him.* lit. 'thou didst delight to be with him.'

thy portion. Immorality was condoned in others and also practised by those who professed to accept the covenant.

19. Sins of the tongue were committed instead of being carefully guarded against (xxxiv. 14).

20. *sittest and speakest.* The act of slander was calculated and deliberate.

brother. The following phrase *thine own mother's son* shows that the word is to be understood as referring to a paternal brother (Kimchi). Not even the closest blood tie was a safeguard against the spread of calumny.

21 These things hast thou done, and
    should I have kept silence?
  Thou hadst thought that I was
    altogether such a one as thyself;
  But I will reprove thee, and set
    the cause before thine eyes.

22 Now consider this, ye that forget
    God,
  Lest I tear in pieces, and there be
    none to deliver.

23 Whoso offereth the sacrifice of
    thanksgiving honoureth Me;
  And to him that ordereth his way
    aright
  Will I show the salvation of God.'

21 אֵלֶּה עָשִׂיתָ ׀ וְהֶחֱרַשְׁתִּי
דִּמִּיתָ הֱיוֹת־אֶהְיֶה כָמוֹךָ
אוֹכִיחֲךָ וְאֶעֶרְכָה לְעֵינֶיךָ׃
22 בִּינוּ־נָא זֹאת שֹׁכְחֵי אֱלוֹהַּ
פֶּן־אֶטְרֹף וְאֵין מַצִּיל׃
23 זֹבֵחַ תּוֹדָה יְכַבְּדָנְנִי
וְשָׂם דֶּרֶךְ אַרְאֶנּוּ בְּיֵשַׁע אֱלֹהִים׃

21. *and should I have kept silence?* The
rendering 'and I kept silent' is to be preferred. The meaning is: For a long time I
allowed these men to behave thus, without
punishing them. Man is granted free will to
do as he chooses. Only later does God take
him to account (Daath Sofrim).

that I was altogether such a one as thyself.
Rather 'that I should be,' etc., taking no
account of such misdeeds as though they
were consistent with the acceptance of the
covenant. The evil-doer debases his conception of God to make it suit his foul
purposes, and pretends that He would act in
like manner and so does not disapprove of
his deeds. God's silence is interpreted as
acquiescence (cf. Eccles. viii. 11).

and set the cause. Better, 'I will set (them) in
order:' enumerate them in the indictment and
impose a penalty for each of them (Kimchi).

    22-23 FINAL EXHORTATION

22. *forget God.* See on ix. 18.

I tear in pieces. Like a lion; the same imagery
in Hosea v. 14.

23. In a fine conclusion the Psalmist declares the true principles of religion. It is not
the one who brings sacrifices alone who does
honour to God. It is the one who, with the
sacrifices, brings a penitent heart and acknowledges the goodness of the Creator. He
is the one who truly honours Him (Rashi).

whoso offereth. An abbreviation of verses
13f., summarizing the lesson of the Psalm.
The sinner is urged to repent to avoid the
punishment which must follow on guilt, but
more especially that he may have the joy of
bringing a thanksgiving sacrifice as a token
of reconciliation with God and so have part in
His salvation.

ordereth his way aright. lit. 'ordereth a way,'
viz. in conformity with God's will.

salvation of God. Since God is the Speaker,
we should expect 'My salvation'; but a change
in grammatical person of this kind is common in Hebrew.

נא

לַמְנַצֵּחַ מִזְמוֹר לְדָוִד: בְּבוֹא־אֵלָיו

2 נָתָן הַנָּבִיא כַּאֲשֶׁר־בָּא אֶל־בַּת־שָׁבַע:

3 חָנֵּנִי אֱלֹהִים כְּחַסְדֶּךָ
כְּרֹב רַחֲמֶיךָ מְחֵה פְשָׁעָי:

4 הֶרֶב כַּבְּסֵנִי מֵעֲוֹנִי
וּמֵחַטָּאתִי טַהֲרֵנִי:

5 כִּי־פְשָׁעַי אֲנִי אֵדָע
וְחַטָּאתִי נֶגְדִּי תָמִיד:

6 לְךָ לְבַדְּךָ וְהָרַע

ק׳ הרב v. 4.

51

1 For the Leader. A Psalm of David; 2 when Nathan the prophet came unto him, after he had gone in to Bath-sheba.

3 Be gracious unto me, O God, according to Thy mercy;
According to the multitude of Thy compassions blot out my transgressions.

4 Wash me thoroughly from mine iniquity,
And cleanse me from my sin.

5 For I know my transgressions;
And my sin is ever before me.

6 Against Thee, Thee only, have I sinned,

A PENITENT'S CRY

AMONG the outpourings of the human heart agonized by the consciousness of sin, this Psalm stands pre-eminent. David was being called to account for the incident with Bath-Sheba. Nathan, the prophet, was sent to draw David's attention to the seriousness of his transgression and to picture for him the full extent of the destruction which he had brought upon himself and his house. Since David instantly realized how gravely he had sinned, Nathan was able to advise him that the LORD would spare him from severe punishment to the extent that he would not die, his dynasty would continue and he would have the opportunity to create a better future for himself in his lifetime. However, his misdeeds had given cause for the wicked to scoff at God. David would, therefore, have to atone for his guilt by suffering disaster so that the scoffers would know that such behaviour does not go unpunished. It was on the basis of this theme that the Psalm was composed (Hirsch).

2. *Nathan the prophet.* See 2 Sam. xii.

3-14 PRAYER FOR PARDON

3. *be gracious unto me.* David used this phrase in 2 Sam. xii. 22. The possibility of forgiveness is dependent upon God's graciousness. Sin is rebellion against Him and He bestows a favour upon the rebel by accepting his repentance.

blot out. Erase the record from the book in which man's actions are entered; or discharge the indebtedness which is incurred by guilt.

4. *wash me thoroughly.* Sin leaves a stain upon the soul which pardon removes.

cleanse me. 'Me' being 'my soul' which has

been tainted by sin. Furthermore, purify my body which has become impure through my wrongdoing (Malbim).

5. *I know.* The subject is emphatic. God, of course, was aware of what he had done; now he is himself fully alive to the heinousness of his act. This acknowledgment of guilt is the first essential step in repentance (see on xxxii. 5).

my sin is ever before me. Occasioning distress of mind and body. If Ps. xxxii. is also connected with this episode, the symptoms are there described in detail.

6. *against Thee, Thee only.* The words agree with David's admission, *I have sinned against the LORD* (2 Sam. xii. 13). Similarly Joseph

And done that which is evil in Thy
   sight;
That Thou mayest be justified
   when Thou speakest,
And be in the right when Thou
   judgest.

7 Behold, I was brought forth in
   iniquity,
And in sin did my mother con-
   ceive me.

8 Behold, Thou desirest truth in the
   inward parts;
Make me, therefore, to know
   wisdom in mine inmost heart.

9 Purge me with hyssop, and I shall
   be clean;
Wash me, and I shall be whiter
   than snow.

10 Make me to hear joy and gladness;
That the bones which Thou hast
   crushed may rejoice.

וְהָרַע בְּעֵינֶיךָ עָשִׂיתִי
לְמַעַן תִּצְדַּק בְּדָבְרֶךָ
תִּזְכֶּה בְשָׁפְטֶךָ׃
7 הֵן־בְּעָווֹן חוֹלָלְתִּי
וּבְחֵטְא יֶחֱמַתְנִי אִמִּי׃
8 הֵן־אֱמֶת חָפַצְתָּ בַטֻּחוֹת
וּבְסָתֻם חָכְמָה תוֹדִיעֵנִי׃
9 תְּחַטְּאֵנִי בְאֵזוֹב וְאֶטְהָר
תְּכַבְּסֵנִי וּמִשֶּׁלֶג אַלְבִּין׃
10 תַּשְׁמִיעֵנִי שָׂשׂוֹן וְשִׂמְחָה
תָּגֵלְנָה עֲצָמוֹת דִּכִּיתָ׃

exclaimed: *How then can I do this great wickedness and sin against God?* (Gen. xxxix. 9). Even though Uriah was the victim of his sin, it was God's word that was transgressed and only He can be the one to forgive (Rashi). Hirsch adds that these words show that David's misdeeds were a violation of the spirit rather than of the letter of the legal code (cf. Tal. Sab. 56b). Nevertheless, his actions were a result of temptation and were considered grievous crimes in the eyes of God. Though he had no legal need to ask forgiveness of Uriah, who rightfully had been condemned to death anyway (cf. Tal. ibid), he was considered guilty for his innermost motives (cf. Hirsch).

when Thou speakest. In pronouncing sentence and punishment upon the convicted sinner.

7. *I was brought forth in iniquity.* The thought of this verse is not that the marital act is sinful or that the child inherits sin. It is a way of expressing the idea that the human being is naturally prone to err. The Psalmist does not make this plea in self-excuse but as urging the essential need for God's clemency (Maharal).

8. *truth in the inward parts.* Man must be perfectly sincere with himself, his fellows and God, Who condemns self-deception, as well as the deception of others. The Rabbis urged the necessity of man being 'inwardly the same as outwardly.'

wisdom. See on xlix. 4.

9. *purge me with hyssop.* As one defiled by contact with the dead (Num. xix. 6), or a *metzora* (Lev. xiv. 4), was cleansed of his impurity by the use of hyssop in the act of sprinkling, so he prays to be figuratively purified in the same way.

wash me. To remove every befouling stain. The verb is used of washing a dirty garment (cf. verse 4).

whiter than snow. Similarly in Isa. i. 18.

10. *make me to hear joy.* By the ceremony of purification they who had been excluded from the life of the community and participation in religious worship were restored to these privileges. In like manner the sinner, who had been granted Divine pardon, finds the barrier removed which prevented his enjoyment of communion with God. The *joy* and *gladness* are of the spiritual order.

.11 Hide Thy face from my sins,
And blot out all mine iniquities.

12 Create me a clean heart, O God;
And renew a stedfast spirit within me.

13 Cast me not away from Thy presence;
And take not Thy holy spirit from me.

14 Restore unto me the joy of Thy salvation;
And let a willing spirit uphold me.

15 Then will I teach transgressors Thy ways;
And sinners shall return unto Thee.

16 Deliver me from bloodguiltiness, O God, Thou God of my salvation;
So shall my tongue sing aloud of Thy righteousness.

11 הַסְתֵּר פָּנֶיךָ מֵחֲטָאָי
וְכָל־עֲוֹנֹתַי מְחֵה:

12 לֵב טָהוֹר בְּרָא־לִי אֱלֹהִים
וְרוּחַ נָכוֹן חַדֵּשׁ בְּקִרְבִּי:

13 אַל־תַּשְׁלִיכֵנִי מִלְּפָנֶיךָ
וְרוּחַ קָדְשְׁךָ אַל־תִּקַּח מִמֶּנִּי:

14 הָשִׁיבָה לִי שְׂשׂוֹן יִשְׁעֶךָ
וְרוּחַ נְדִיבָה תִסְמְכֵנִי:

15 אֲלַמְּדָה פֹשְׁעִים דְּרָכֶיךָ
וְחַטָּאִים אֵלֶיךָ יָשׁוּבוּ:

16 הַצִּילֵנִי מִדָּמִים ׀
אֱלֹהִים אֱלֹהֵי תְּשׁוּעָתִי
תְּרַנֵּן לְשׁוֹנִי צִדְקָתֶךָ:

bones which Thou hast crushed. An idiom expressing the effect of grief, pain or a troubled conscience (cf. xxxviii. 9, xlii. 11).

11. *hide Thy face.* A sin is more commonly said to receive atonement by being 'covered over' by God, so that it is no longer seen by Him. Here the same result is asked for by God turning His gaze from it.

12. *create me a clean heart.* As an earnest expression of his wish to repent fully, he begs for a new heart, which will repel every debased thought or desire (Kimchi).

a stedfast spirit. Which stands firm in the moment of temptation.

13. *cast me not away from Thy presence.* Like a courtier who incurs his king's displeasure and is banished from his presence, a sinner is excluded from the Presence of God.

take not Thy holy spirit from me. It is related that *the spirit of the LORD had departed from Saul* (1 Sam. xvi. 14), with the result that he degenerated. David, perhaps recalling that example, begs that it may not happen to him.

14. *the joy of Thy salvation.* He longs to have again the joyful sense of God's saving help lost through guilt.

a willing spirit uphold me. So that he may not fall again he asks to be supported by a spirit which freely and willingly responds to the right.

15-19   HIS RESOLVES FOR THE FUTURE

15. *then will I teach.* The relief and happiness which will come to him as the effect of pardon will be so intense that he will be impelled to communicate his experience to others and induce them to follow his example (cf. Metsudath).

sinners shall return unto Thee. His testimony will bring them the assurance that they need not perish in their sin, because God receives the penitent (Kimchi).

16. *bloodguiltiness.* David conspired the death of Uriah and he prays that he should not die by the blood-producing sword as a punishment for this (Rashi).

Thy righteousness. The leniency that God had shown David seeing that he was truly penitent (cf. Malbim).

17 O Lord, open Thou my lips;
   And my mouth shall declare Thy
   praise.
18 For Thou delightest not in
   sacrifice, else would I give it;
   Thou hast no pleasure in burnt-
   offering.
19 The sacrifices of God are a
   broken spirit;
   A broken and a contrite heart,
   O God, Thou wilt not despise.
20 Do good in Thy favour unto
   Zion;
   Build Thou the walls of Jerusalem.
21 Then wilt Thou delight in the
   sacrifices of righteousness, in
   burnt-offering and whole offering;
   Then will they offer bullocks
   upon Thine altar.

17 אֲדֹנָי שְׂפָתַי תִּפְתָּח
וּפִי יַגִּיד תְּהִלָּתֶךָ:
18 כִּי ׀ לֹא־תַחְפֹּץ זֶבַח וְאֶתֵּנָה
עוֹלָה לֹא תִרְצֶה:
19 זִבְחֵי אֱלֹהִים רוּחַ נִשְׁבָּרָה
לֵב־נִשְׁבָּר וְנִדְכֶּה
אֱלֹהִים לֹא תִבְזֶה:
20 הֵיטִיבָה בִרְצוֹנְךָ אֶת־צִיּוֹן
תִּבְנֶה חוֹמוֹת יְרוּשָׁלָ͏ִם:
21 אָז תַּחְפֹּץ זִבְחֵי־צֶדֶק עוֹלָה וְכָלִיל
אָז יַעֲלוּ עַל־מִזְבַּחֲךָ פָרִים:

17. *open Thou my lips*. The Divine spirit had left him since his wrongdoing, as he was no longer worthy of it. If God forgives him, this spirit would return to him enabling him once again to declare the praises of God as he had done in the past (see Kimchi).

18. *delightest not in sacrifice*. The teaching of i. 8ff. is here applied.

Thou hast no pleasure in burnt-offering. The verb is used in its technical sense: 'Thou wouldst not give acceptance to a burnt-offering,' as the price of forgiveness.

19. *the sacrifices of God*. Which are acceptable to Him.

a broken spirit. In which obstinacy and pride have been suppressed by humility. The Midrash finely points out that a fractured limb disqualifies an animal as a sacrifice, whereas a *broken spirit* in man was approved by God.

20-21 PRAYER FOR TEMPLE'S RESTORATION

It has been suggested by a Spanish sage that these concluding verses were added by a Babylonian exile, entreating God to rebuild Jerusalem. He put forward this idea since it was not yet known, at this point of David's life, that Zion would be the site of the Temple.

It is equally probable, however, that David composed the verses prophetically (Ibn Ezra).

20. *do good…unto Zion*. Which had suffered the ravages of an invading army; repair the damage.

build … Jerusalem. Indeed, David's son, Solomon, supplied a protecting wall to the city (1 Kings iii. 1) (Daath Sofrim). However, *banah* often means 'rebuild, repair' as well as 'build,' and that appears to be its intention here.

21. *then wilt Thou delight in*. As against the declaration in verse 18; but now the sacrifices are described as *of righteousness* (cf. iv. 6), brought in a right spirit and with a proper motive (Kimchi).

whole offering. The meal offering which, like the burnt offering, was completely consumed by fire (Ibn Ezra, Metsudath David). Others, based on Talmud Yoma (26a), identify it with the burnt offering (cf. 1 Sam. vii. 9). According to this, the two words *olah* and *kalil* are synonymous (Kimchi). When the Jewish people live in harmony and thus attract Divine favour and protection, then the sacrifices will attain their full worth and be seen as a symbolic expression of their desire to serve God in the correct way (Hirsch).

נב

לַמְנַצֵּחַ מַשְׂכִּיל לְדָוִד: בְּבוֹא דּוֹאֵג

2 הָאֲדֹמִי וַיַּגֵּד לְשָׁאוּל וַיֹּאמֶר לוֹ
בָּא דָוִד אֶל־בֵּית אֲחִימֶלֶךְ:

3 מַה־תִּתְהַלֵּל בְּרָעָה הַגִּבּוֹר
חֶסֶד אֵל כָּל־הַיּוֹם:

4 הַוּוֹת תַּחְשֹׁב לְשׁוֹנֶךָ
כְּתַעַר מְלֻטָּשׁ עֹשֵׂה רְמִיָּה:

5 אָהַבְתָּ רָּע מִטּוֹב
שֶׁקֶר מִדַּבֵּר צֶדֶק סֶלָה:

52

1 For the Leader. Maschil of David;
2 when Doeg the Edomite came
and told Saul, and said unto
him: 'David is come to the
house of Ahimelech.'

3 Why boastest thou thyself of evil,
O mighty man?
The mercy of God endureth con-
tinually.

4 Thy tongue deviseth destruction;
Like a sharp razor, working deceitfully.

5 Thou lovest evil more than good;
Falsehood rather than speaking
righteousness.   Selah

AN EVILDOER'S DOOM

THE background of the Psalm is plain. A person, rich and influential, had been abusing his position to work mischief. In particular he had ruined innocent persons with his slanderous tongue. One of his victims foretells his downfall and the triumph of those he had injured. The ascription identifies the villain with Doeg who was not only the head of the Sanhedrin, but also an important official in Saul's household and wielded much influence. To gain the king's favour for his own advantage he played the role of informer and committed many brutal murders. He is denounced by David as a prototype of one who is willing to spread slander and fabricate stories to destroy his rivals. The consequences of his treachery is mentioned in verse 7. David composed this Psalm as a warning to others not to follow this course.

1. *Maschil.* See on xxxii. 1.

2. *Doeg the Edomite.* See 1 Sam. xxi., xxii.

3-7 DENUNCIATION OF THE OPPRESSOR

3. *why boastest thou?* He not only does evil, but prides himself in it; thus displaying an utter lack of scruple. Of what avail will it be to him, since opposed to his scheming stands the eternal love of God for the upright? The whole theme of the Psalm is stated in this opening verse.

O mighty man. Here meant to signify not only mighty in strength, but also in Torah (Rashi, Kimchi). The statement is addressed in an ironic vein as his act of treachery was anything but heroic (see Midrash Shocher Tov, Hirsch).

God. Hebrew *el,* 'the Powerful,' in comparison with Whose might the power of the strongest man is as nothing.

4. *thy tongue deviseth destruction.* As often in the Psalms, the vice of slander is condemned. Doeg's tongue certainly brought *destruction* upon many.

like a sharp razor. His tongue is compared to a sharp knife with which, if not used carefully, he may harm himself (Hirsch).

working deceitfully. Or, 'O thou worker of deceit.'

5. *lovest evil more than good.* And so rejects the good and prefers what is evil, deliberately ignoring the counsel of xxxiv. 15, *depart from evil, and do good,* which is immediately preceded by *keep thy tongue from evil, and thy lips from speaking guile.*

speaking righteousness. Using the faculty of speech for promoting justice (cf. *speaking peace to all his seed,* Esther x. 3).

6 Thou lovest all devouring words,
The deceitful tongue.

7 God will likewise break thee for
ever,
He will take thee up, and pluck
thee out of thy tent,
And root thee out of the land of
the living.   Selah

8 The righteous also shall see, and
fear,
And shall laugh at him:

9 'Lo, this is the man that made not
God his stronghold;
But trusted in the abundance of
his riches,
And strengthened himself in his
wickedness.'

10 But as for me, I am like a leafy
olive-tree in the house of God;

‎6 אָהַבְתָּ כָל־דִּבְרֵי־בָלַע
‎לְשׁוֹן מִרְמָה:
‎7 גַּם־אֵל יִתָּצְךָ לָנֶצַח
‎יַחְתְּךָ וְיִסָּחֲךָ מֵאֹהֶל
‎וְשֵׁרֶשְׁךָ מֵאֶרֶץ חַיִּים סֶלָה:
‎8 וְיִרְאוּ צַדִּיקִים וְיִירָאוּ
‎וְעָלָיו יִשְׂחָקוּ:
‎9 הִנֵּה הַגֶּבֶר לֹא־יָשִׂים אֱלֹהִים מָעוּזּוֹ
‎וַיִּבְטַח בְּרֹב עָשְׁרוֹ יָעֹז בְּהַוָּתוֹ:
‎10 וַאֲנִי כְּזַיִת רַעֲנָן בְּבֵית אֱלֹהִים

---

6. *devouring words*. lit. 'words of swallowing,' which cause an innocent person to be engulfed. The word is employed in this sense in xxxv. 25.

7. *God*. Hebrew *el* as in verse 3. His might will *break* the mischievous activities of a slanderer. This man may imagine his position unassailable, but God will shatter it *forever* so that it cannot be restored.

take thee up. The verb is ordinarily used of picking up burning coal from a hearth. He may think himself secure under the king's patronage, but he will be snatched up and carried off.

pluck thee out of thy tent. Render him homeless by forcing him into banishment (cf. Metsudath Zion, Metsudath David).

root thee out of the land of the living. He will be like a tree uprooted from the soil and doomed to perish. His fate is to be contrasted

with that of the righteous in verse 10.

8-11   SECURITY OF THE RIGHTEOUS

8. *fear*. Translate 'be filled with awe.' The sight of God's retributive justice will render them awe-struck.

laugh at him. Use the taunting words of verse 9. Rejoicing at the calamity of one's enemy is condemned in the holy scriptures (see Job xxxi. 29; Prov. xxiv. 17), but the downfall of the wicked, as an illustration and proof of the government of God, must be welcomed with joy by the righteous (cf. Rashi).

9. *man*. Hebrew *geber*, 'man in his vigour,' cognate with *gibbor*, 'mighty man' in verse 3.

trusted in the abundance of his riches. Cf. xlix. 7.

wickedness. The noun signifies the havoc done to a person through treachery (Malbim).

I trust in the mercy of God for
ever and ever.

11 I will give Thee thanks for ever,
because Thou hast done it;
And I will wait for Thy name,
for it is good, in the presence
of Thy saints.

בְּטַחְתִּי בְחֶסֶד־אֱלֹהִים עוֹלָם וָעֶד:
11 אוֹדְךָ לְעוֹלָם כִּי עָשִׂיתָ
וַאֲקַוֶּה שִׁמְךָ כִי־טוֹב נֶגֶד חֲסִידֶיךָ:

10. *as for me*. The Psalmist refers to himself, not only personally, but also as the
spokesman of the righteous.

leafy olive-tree. Unlike the wicked man who
withers away, he is compared to a flourishing
olive tree which remains evergreen throughout its lifetime (Kimchi) (cf. the thought of
Ps. i, where the righteous are likened to a tree
that withstands storms, and the wicked to
chaff, which is easily blown away).

in the house of God. In contrast to the wicked
man who is plucked out of His tent, i.e. the
Tabernacle (Targum), the righteous man is a
welcome guest in God's house. The words
'tent' and 'house' may also refer to places of
learning (cf. Tal. San. 106b). Doeg was prevented from disseminating Torah because of
his wickedness. David, on the other hand,
hopes that he will succeed in understanding
God's ways through the study of His law (cf.
Daath Sofrim).

mercy of God. The word *Elohim* is used referring to God as a dispenser of judgment
albeit with leniency.

for ever and ever. As long as I continue to
live.

11. *Thou hast done it*. See on xxii. 32 where
the Hebrew verb is similarly employed.

I will wait for Thy name. In addition to
praising God for what He had just done, he
will look forward to future demonstrations of
God's nature as the Protector of the righteous
(Malbim). Difficult though the times were
for David, he nevertheless showed utmost
faith and patience in waiting for the salvation
of God. He sincerely believes that anything
that befell him would ultimately turn out to
be for the good (Daath Sofrim).

saints. The Israelites who are loyal to God
(see on iv. 4).

53
נג

1 For the Leader; upon Mahalath.
Maschil of David.

2 The fool hath said in his heart:
'There is no God';
They have dealt corruptly, and
have done abominable iniquity;
There is none that doeth good.

3 God looked forth from heaven
upon the children of men,
To see if there were any man of
understanding, that did seek
after God.

4 Every one of them is unclean, they
are together become impure;
There is none that doeth good, no,
not one.

לַמְנַצֵּחַ עַל־מָחֲלַת מַשְׂכִּיל לְדָוִד׃

אָמַר נָבָל בְּלִבּוֹ אֵין אֱלֹהִים 2
הִשְׁחִיתוּ וְהִתְעִיבוּ עָוֶל
אֵין עֹשֵׂה־טוֹב׃
אֱלֹהִים מִשָּׁמַיִם הִשְׁקִיף 3
עַל־בְּנֵי־אָדָם
לִרְאוֹת הֲיֵשׁ מַשְׂכִּיל
דֹּרֵשׁ אֶת־אֱלֹהִים׃
כֻּלּוֹ סָג יַחְדָּו נֶאֱלָחוּ 4
אֵין עֹשֵׂה־טוֹב
אֵין גַּם־אֶחָד׃

A LATER VERSION OF PSALM XIV

THIS Psalm is virtually the same as XIV. The name of God is changed to *Elohim,* the more frequent designation in Book II, and there are other variants which will be noted; the passages in common to both versions will be left without comment. Rashi, Meiri, and Metsudath David are of the opinion that the two Psalms describe the destruction of the first and second Temples, respectively. This Psalm follows the previous one as a reminder that those who attempt to destroy Israel will eventually suffer the fate of Doeg. Malbim suggests that this Psalm is a revised form of Psalm XIV, i.e. Psalm XIV was originally composed when David was saved from the hands of his enemies, but was later changed to suit the circumstances surrounding the defeat of Sannecherib (see verse 6).

1. The form of the superscription has been changed. In XIV it is simply *For the Leader. Of David.* Here it is amplified by the addition of *upon Mahalath* (lit. 'sickness'), perhaps an abbreviation of *Mahalath Leannoth* in lxxxviii., the name of a musical instrument (Meiri), and of *Maschil* (see on xxxii. 1).

2. *and have done abominable iniquity.* Replaces 'they have done abominably.'

3. *God.* Instead of *the LORD.* The substitution throughout the Psalm emphasizes that Divine judgment will be meted out upon the nations before Israel is liberated.

4. *every one of them is unclean.* Hebrew *kullo sag;* in XIV, *they are all corrupt (hakkol sar).* Both verbs have much the same meaning, but *sag* is used especially of backsliding and is therefore more emphatic.

5 'Shall not the workers of iniquity
know it,
Who eat up My people as they eat
bread,
And call not upon God?'

6 There are they in great fear, where
no fear was;
For God hath scattered the bones
of him that encampeth against
thee;
Thou hast put them to shame, because God hath rejected them.

7 Oh that the salvation of Israel
were come out of Zion!
When God turneth the captivity of
His people,
Let Jacob rejoice, let Israel be
glad.

ה הֲלֹא יָדְעוּ פֹּעֲלֵי אָוֶן
אֹכְלֵי עַמִּי אָכְלוּ לֶחֶם
אֱלֹהִים לֹא קָרָאוּ:
ו שָׁם ׀ פָּחֲדוּ פַחַד לֹא־הָיָה פָחַד
כִּי־אֱלֹהִים פִּזַּר עַצְמוֹת חֹנָךְ
הֱבִשֹׁתָה כִּי־אֱלֹהִים מְאָסָם:
ז מִי יִתֵּן מִצִּיּוֹן יְשֻׁעוֹת יִשְׂרָאֵל
בְּשׁוּב אֱלֹהִים שְׁבוּת עַמּוֹ
יָגֵל יַעֲקֹב יִשְׂמַח יִשְׂרָאֵל:

5. Apart from the difference in the Divine name, the only variant is the omission of *all* before *the workers*.

6. In this verse we have an almost complete re-wording of xiv. 5f., and Metsudath David maintains that this verse was altered to describe the overthrow of Sannecherib's army.

where no fear was. A difficult verse. Malbim renders 'there they feared God greatly and consequently had no fear of Sannecherib and his military might.'

the bones. The bodies of the invaders which remained unburied (Rashi) (cf. the threat of desolation in Ezek. vi. 5, *I will scatter your bones round about your altars*). For the body not to receive an honourable burial is a dreadful thought. The mercy of the Hebraic legislation is particularly evident in the law that the body of a criminal must not be allowed to hang on a gibbet but has to be interred the same day (Deut. xxi. 23).

Thou hast put them to shame. Inflicted defeats upon them by an act of God, not by Israel's superior might. They had said, *There is no God*, and the falsity of the utterance had been proved by their downfall at His hands.

rejected. By their defeat God manifested His abhorrence of those who attack Israel.

7. *salvation*. Here the word is plural, to express the more intensive idea of complete salvation (Daath Sofrim).

נד

למנצח בנגינת משכיל לדוד׃
2 בבוא הזיפים ויאמרו לשאול
הלא דוד מסתתר עמנו׃
3 אלהים בשמך הושיעני
ובגבורתך תדינני׃
4 אלהים שמע תפלתי
האזינה לאמרי־פי׃
5 כי זרים ׀ קמו עלי
ועריצים בקשו נפשי
לא שמו אלהים לנגדם סלה׃

1 For the Leader; with string-
   music. Maschil of David; 2
   when the Ziphites came and
   said to Saul: 'Doth not David
   hide himself with us?'

3 O God, save me by Thy name,
   And right me by Thy might.

4 O God, hear my prayer;
   Give ear to the words of my mouth.

5 For strangers are risen up against
      me,
   And violent men have sought after
      my soul;
   They have not set God before
      them.   Selah

A PRAYER WHILE IN PERIL

THE poem resembles many earlier ones in being a cry for help by one who was in imminent danger of death from pitiless enemies. The title connects it with Saul's persecution of David. A difficulty is, however, created by the mention of *strangers* in verse 5 which normally indicates non-Israelites, a reference which does not fit into that episode. But the meaning of the word will be considered in the notes.

2. *Ziphites*. See 1 Sam. xxiii. 19ff.

3-5 HIS PERIL

3. *by Thy name*. In Thy character a Savior of the pitiable (Malbim).

right me. lit. 'judge me,' vindicate me.

by Thy might. R.V. *in Thy might* is preferable. He petitions God because He possesses the might to judge fairly.

5. *strangers*. Often this word refers to foreign enemies (cf. Ibn Ezra); but against this interpretation three points are to be noted: (1) the *strangers* may be the Ziphites, who though *strangers* unrelated to Saul, betrayed David, as Metsudath David and Malbim suggest; (2) *zar* is also used of an Israelite of another family (Deut. xxv. 5), or a non-priest and non-Levite (Lev. xxii. 12; Num. i. 51). Its root meaning implies 'difference,' and the word may simply indicate that his attackers are men who had no dealings with him and, therefore, had no cause to harm him (Kimchi, Hirsch). (3) Instead of our reading, as well as that of LXX, of *zarim*, Targum reads *zedim*, 'the proud,' as does the verse quoted in lxxxvi. 14, which sheds light on the intended connotation of the word.

violent men. If *strangers* are the Ziphites, or possibly the inhabitants of Keilah who were of Canaanite origin, *violent men* would be Saul and his followers (Malbim).

have not set God before them. The thought that He punishes evil and violence should have deterred them; but they refused to let it weigh with them.

6 Behold, God is my helper;
The Lord is for me as the upholder of my soul.

7 He will requite the evil unto them
that lie in wait for me;
Destroy Thou them in Thy truth.

8 With a freewill-offering will I
sacrifice unto Thee;
I will give thanks unto Thy name,
O Lord, for it is good.

9 For He hath delivered me out of
all trouble;
And mine eye hath gazed upon
mine enemies.

הֵנֵּה אֱלֹהִים עֹזֵר לִי 6
אֲדֹנָי בְּסֹמְכֵי נַפְשִׁי׃
יָשׁוֹב הָרַע לְשֹׁרְרָי 7
בַּאֲמִתְּךָ הַצְמִיתֵם׃
בִּנְדָבָה אֶזְבְּחָה־לָּךְ 8
אוֹדֶה שִּׁמְךָ יְהוָה כִּי־טוֹב׃
כִּי מִכָּל־צָרָה הִצִּילָנִי 9
וּבְאֹיְבַי רָאֲתָה עֵינִי׃

v. 7. ישיב ק׳

6-9 HIS CONFIDENCE IN DIVINE AID

6. *God is my helper.* His previous experience leaves no doubt in his mind that he has God's aid. Hence his confidence that God is at his side, even though those who attempted to help him, such as Ahimelech and the priests of Nob, felt the fury of Saul's wrath and even paid with their lives (Hirsch).

as the upholder of my soul. The Hebrew is idiomatic and is more accurately reproduced by the translation 'is of them that uphold my soul' (Kimchi, Malbim). Hirsch comments that the mere fact that there remain people who are courageous enough to help him, is evidence that God lavishes care on him for being dedicated to His service.

7. *he will requite the evil.* This is the rendering of the *kerë*, the *kethib* means 'the evil will return to.'

in Thy truth. In faithfulness to Thy character as Judge (cf. Metsudath David).

8. *a freewill-offering.* A token of sincere gratitude; but more probably the Hebrew is to be translated 'with a free will,' in a spirit of glad relief (Kimchi).

it is good. i.e. Thy name is good (as in lii. 11), not 'giving thanks' is good. There may be a reference back to verse 3, *save me by Thy name*, and the fulfilment of that petition.

9. *hath delivered me...hath gazed.* The verbs are prophetic perfect. To 'gaze upon' one's enemies is to be an uninvolved witness to their downfall by God's hands (Malbim). The sudden change to the third person, *he hath delivered*, immediately after *Thy name, O Lord*, is in accordance with Hebrew idiom.

לַמְנַצֵּחַ בִּנְגִינֹת מַשְׂכִּיל לְדָוִד׃

2 הַאֲזִינָה אֱלֹהִים תְּפִלָּתִי
וְאַל־תִּתְעַלַּם מִתְּחִנָּתִי׃

3 הַקְשִׁיבָה לִּי וַעֲנֵנִי
אָרִיד בְּשִׂיחִי וְאָהִימָה׃

4 מִקּוֹל אוֹיֵב מִפְּנֵי עָקַת רָשָׁע
כִּי־יָמִיטוּ עָלַי אָוֶן
וּבְאַף יִשְׂטְמוּנִי׃

5 לִבִּי יָחִיל בְּקִרְבִּי
וְאֵימוֹת מָוֶת נָפְלוּ עָלָי׃

6 יִרְאָה וָרַעַד יָבֹא בִי
וַתְּכַסֵּנִי פַּלָּצוּת׃

1 For the Leader; with string-music. Maschil of David.

2 Give ear, O God, to my prayer;
And hide not Thyself from my supplication.

3 Attend unto me, and answer me;
I am distraught in my complaint, and will moan;

4 Because of the voice of the enemy,
Because of the oppression of the wicked;
For they cast mischief upon me;
And in anger they persecute me.

5 My heart doth writhe within me;
And the terrors of death are fallen upon me.

6 Fear and trembling come upon me,
And horror hath overwhelmed me.

TREACHERY DENOUNCED

A MAN who had been betrayed by a close friend opens his heart in this Psalm. The victim of base treachery, he turns to God in supplication. He first pleads for His help, then describes his situation, and finally asserts his conviction that God will intervene. Tradition concurs that the Psalm is connected with Absalom's rebellion; the 'familiar friend' (verse 14) is named as Ahitophel in the Targum and in *Ethics of the Fathers* (vi. 3). Having once been a companion and close confidant of the king, Ahitophel was responsible for inciting David's son, Absalom, to plot against his own father. Disillusioned, David is forced to flee Jerusalem, and in despair wonders if, after having been betrayed by such an intimate friend (verses 13-15, 21-22), there remains any mortal who can be trusted. Consequently, his conclusion is to place all hope in God alone (verses 17 and 23). So strong are his feelings, that twice in the Psalm (verses 16 and 24) he wishes that his enemy meet with untimely death and destruction, a wish that was indeed realised (2 Sam. xvii. 23).

2-9 HIS CRY OF DISTRESS

2. *hide not Thyself.* Cf. x. 1.

3. *distraught.* Others render 'I lament' (Rashi, Kimchi) (cf. Gen. xxvii. 40), or 'I control' (my emotions) (see Rashi, Daath Sofrim). This agitation must find an outlet in sound, as one who moans in physical pain.

4. *voice of the enemy.* Which slanders and threatens him.

oppression. The rare Hebrew word conveys the idea of crushing pressure.

cast mischief. Better, 'they burden me with guilt,' charging me with crimes of which I am innocent (Hirsch).

5. *terrors of death.* The fear that he was their target for death (Kimchi).

6. *come upon me.* lit. 'enter into me,' and take possession of me.

horror hath overwhelmed me. Same language as in Ezek. vii. 18.

7 And I said: 'Oh that I had wings
      like a dove!
   Then would I fly away, and be at
      rest.

8 Lo, then would I wander far off,
   I would lodge in the wilderness.
                                Selah

 9 I would haste me to a shelter
   From the stormy wind and
      tempest.'

10 Destroy, O Lord, and divide
      their tongue;
   For I have seen violence and
      strife in the city.

11 Day and night they go about it
      upon the walls thereof;
   Iniquity also and mischief are in
      the midst of it.

12 Wickedness is in the midst
      thereof;
   Oppression and guile depart
      not from her broad place.

7 וָאֹמַר מִי־יִתֶּן־לִּי אֵבֶר כַּיּוֹנָה
   אָעוּפָה וְאֶשְׁכֹּנָה׃
8 הִנֵּה אַרְחִיק נְדֹד
   אָלִין בַּמִּדְבָּר סֶלָה׃
9 אָחִישָׁה מִפְלָט לִי
   מֵרוּחַ סֹעָה מִסָּעַר׃
10 בַּלַּע אֲדֹנָי פַּלַּג לְשׁוֹנָם
   כִּי־רָאִיתִי חָמָס וְרִיב בָּעִיר׃
11 יוֹמָם וָלַיְלָה יְסוֹבְבֻהָ עַל־חוֹמֹתֶיהָ
   וְאָוֶן וְעָמָל בְּקִרְבָּהּ׃
12 הַוּוֹת בְּקִרְבָּהּ
   וְלֹא־יָמִישׁ מֵרְחֹבָהּ תֹּךְ וּמִרְמָה׃

7. *dove*. Which makes its home *in the clefts of the rock, in the covert of the cliff* (Cant. ii. 14), away from human habitation (cf. Kimchi, Metsudath David).

be at rest. lit. 'dwell,' in quietness and security. David longs for a calm life which is denied him, because his sense of duty as king compels him to remain in the capital. He fled only when a violent death threatened him.

8. *lodge in the wilderness*. He would gladly exchange the luxuries of the palace for a bare tent in the solitude of the desert.

9. *stormy wind and tempest*. The turmoil which rages in the city.

10-16 DENUNCIATION OF HIS BETRAYER

Recollection of the unjust treatment received from a bosom friend rouses him to righteous indignation and his language grows bitter. This person had been the instigator of the men who plotted against him, and he begs that God will give him and them their deserts.

10. *destroy*. Better, 'confuse.' He asks that God should break up their unity by dividing their counsels and so throw them into confusion (Kimchi), (Cf. 2 Sam. xv. 31). Perhaps he had in mind the history of Babel.

11. *they go about it*. Like watchmen, they are always on the alert to prevent the enemy from attacking the city from without, not realising that they harbor the greatest peril to their welfare within their own walls (Hirsch). According to most others, however, the subject of the verb is 'violence and strife.'

12. *wickedness*. lit. 'destructions,' as in lii. 4. Perhaps 'treacherous plots' best reproduces the meaning.

her broad place. The public square where civic business is transacted (Kimchi).

13. *it was not an enemy*. In this and the next verses the tenses should be changed to the present. He heaps his reproaches upon an

13 For it was not an enemy that
    taunted me,
Then I could have borne it;
Neither was it mine adversary
    that did magnify himself
    against me,
Then I would have hid myself
    from him.

14 But it was thou, a man mine
    equal,
My companion, and my familiar
    friend;

15 We took sweet counsel together,
In the house of God we walked
    with the throng.

16 May He incite death against
    them,
Let them go down alive into the
    nether-world;
For evil is in their dwelling, and
    within them.

17 As for me, I will call upon God;
And the Lord will save me.

18 Evening, and morning, and at
    noonday, will I complain, and
    moan;
And He hath heard my voice.

כִּי לֹא־אוֹיֵב יְחָרְפֵנִי וְאֶשָּׂא 13
לֹא־מְשַׂנְאִי עָלַי הִגְדִּיל
וְאֶסָּתֵר מִמֶּנּוּ:
וְאַתָּה אֱנוֹשׁ כְּעֶרְכִּי 14
אַלּוּפִי וּמְיֻדָּעִי:
אֲשֶׁר יַחְדָּו נַמְתִּיק סוֹד 15
בְּבֵית אֱלֹהִים נְהַלֵּךְ בְּרָגֶשׁ:
יַשִּׁימָוֶת ׀ עָלֵימוֹ 16
יֵרְדוּ שְׁאוֹל חַיִּים
כִּי־רָעוֹת בִּמְגוּרָם בְּקִרְבָּם:
אֲנִי אֶל־אֱלֹהִים אֶקְרָא 17
וַיהוָה יוֹשִׁיעֵנִי:
עֶרֶב וָבֹקֶר וְצָהֳרַיִם 18
אָשִׂיחָה וְאֶהֱמֶה
וַיִּשְׁמַע קוֹלִי:

v. 16. ישיא מות ק׳

individual who is the prime instigator and, to
make matters far worse, one formerly a trusted
and intimate friend.

14. *mine equal.* lit. 'like my valuation,' of
equal status.

companion. With whom I constantly associated.

15. *sweet counsel together.* There is a pathetic touch in the wording which reveals
how deeply wounded David was by this
betrayal. They were so friendly that they
shared confidences, and went together to
worship and study.

16. *may He incite death against them.* This
follows Rashi. Alternatively (Kimchi), 'may
He command that death overtake them.' Both
follow the *kerë* reading as two words; the
kethib means: 'may desolations be upon
them.'

go down alive. Let them perish suddenly,

while in good health, so that it be made
obvious to all that their death is an assured
mark of Divine visitation (Metsudath
David).

and within them. There is no *and* in the Hebrew, which either means 'within them' or
'in their midst.' They live in an atmosphere
of evil.

17-22   GOD THE VINDICATOR

17. *God.* The Deity as Judge.

the Lord. God in His aspect of graciousness
and mercy.

18. *evening, and morning.* Evening is
mentioned first, as in Gen. i., as the beginning of the day.

complain, and moan. Repeating the words of
verse 3. He will pray incessantly until he
receives a response from God.

He hath heard. The prophetic perfect.

19 He hath redeemed my soul in
     peace so that none came nigh
     me;
   For they were many that strove
     with me.

20 God shall hear, and humble
     them,
   Even He that is enthroned of
     old,   Selah
   Such as have no changes,
   And fear not God.

21 He hath put forth his hands
     against them that were at peace
     with him;
   He hath profaned his covenant.

22 Smoother than cream were the
     speeches of his mouth,
   But his heart was war;
   His words were softer than oil,
   Yet were they keen-edged
     swords.

23 Cast thy burden upon the LORD,
     and He will sustain thee;

פָּדָה בְשָׁלוֹם נַפְשִׁי מִקְּרָב־לִי 19
כִּי־בְרַבִּים הָיוּ עִמָּדִי:
יִשְׁמַע אֵל וְיַעֲנֵם 20
וְיֵשֵׁב קֶדֶם סֶלָה
אֲשֶׁר אֵין חֲלִיפוֹת לָמוֹ
וְלֹא יָרְאוּ אֱלֹהִים:
שָׁלַח יָדָיו בִּשְׁלֹמָיו 21
חִלֵּל בְּרִיתוֹ:
חָלְקוּ מַחְמָאֹת פִּיו וּקְרָב־לִבּוֹ 22
רַכּוּ דְבָרָיו מִשֶּׁמֶן וְהֵמָּה פְתִחוֹת:
הַשְׁלֵךְ עַל־יְהֹוָה יְהָבְךָ 23
וְהוּא יְכַלְכְּלֶךָ

19. *He hath redeemed.* Likewise the prophetic perfect.

came nigh me. To accomplish their evil intentions.

that strove. Not represented in the Hebrew
but to be understood from the context.

20. *and humble them.* So Kimchi and
Metsudath David render. Ibn Ezra renders
'and cause them (my enemies) to suffer.'

enthroned of old. As King and Judge of the
world. The Psalmist bases his confidence
upon the past record of Divine judgments.
The occurrence of *Selah* in the middle of a
verse is uncommon; it is found also in lvii. 4.
(Cf. Targum —'forever').

such as have no changes. An obscure phrase.
The most probable interpretation is: these
men have enjoyed an unbroken series of

successes with no setbacks, and consequently
are uninfluenced by the thought of death and
eventual retribution (cf. Rashi).

21. *he hath put forth.* The Psalmist's mind
again reverts to his treacherous friend whom,
in his outraged feelings, he once more singles
out for mention.

covenant. Of friendship, and this made his
act the more despicable.

22. *smoother.* Cf. v. 10, *they make smooth
their tongue.*

his heart was war. 'Heart' and 'war' become
identified as one entity. Similarly *I am prayer*
(cix. 4).

swords. Deadly weapons.

23-24 THE LESSON OF THE EPISODE

23. *cast thy burden.* Either an assurance

He will never suffer the righteous
to be moved.

24 But Thou, O God, wilt bring
them down into the nethermost
pit;
Men of blood and deceit shall
not live out half their days;
But as for me, I will trust in Thee.

לֹא־יִתֵּן לְעוֹלָם מוֹט לַצַּדִּיק:
24 וְאַתָּה אֱלֹהִים ׀ תּוֹרִדֵם לִבְאֵר שַׁחַת
אַנְשֵׁי דָמִים וּמִרְמָה
לֹא־יֶחֱצוּ יְמֵיהֶם
וַאֲנִי אֶבְטַח־בָּךְ:

which he gives himself, or an exhortation to
others to learn from his experience (Kimchi).
There are times when no man can be trusted
(Daath Sofrim).

to be moved. The constant boast of evil-doers
is that they will never be moved (x. 6).
Actually it is true only of the righteous under
Providence. Less probable is the rendering:
'He will not suffer the righteous to be moved
for ever.'

24. *bring them down*. Thinking finally of
retribution, he foretells the end of all the
mischief-workers, not only of the betrayer.
This fate awaits them because they persist in
their malicious designs. Scriptural doctrine
has consistently stressed the saving power of
repentance, of which thought and emphatic
expressions are to be found in Gen iv. 7 and
Ezek. xviii. 23.

nethermost pit. Rather, 'well of destruction'
(Hirsch).

men of blood. i.e. men seeking the blood of
others; would-be murderers.

shall not live out half their days. As the mark
of God's favour is *length of days*, so the sign
of His displeasure is a premature end. The
Hebrew is literally, 'they shall not halve their
days' (cf. Jer. xvii. 11, *In the midst of his days*
(literally, in the half of his days) *he shall leave
them*).

I will trust in Thee. Though I pray that my
enemies will not live out their days, I am
confident that I will live to see the end of my
allotted number of days (Ibn Ezra). Interesting to note is that Ahitophel died at age
thirty-three, less than half of a normal lifespan
(cf. Ps. xc. 10), and David lived exactly
seventy years (cf. Tal. San. 106b).

נו

לַמְנַצֵּחַ ׀ עַל־יוֹנַת אֵלֶם רְחֹקִים
לְדָוִד מִכְתָּם
בֶּאֱחֹז אֹתוֹ פְלִשְׁתִּים בְּגַת:

2 חָנֵּנִי אֱלֹהִים כִּי־שְׁאָפַנִי אֱנוֹשׁ
כָּל־הַיּוֹם לֹחֵם יִלְחָצֵנִי:

3 שָׁאֲפוּ שׁוֹרְרַי כָּל־הַיּוֹם
כִּי־רַבִּים לֹחֲמִים לִי מָרוֹם:

4 יוֹם אִירָא אֲנִי אֵלֶיךָ אֶבְטָח:

5 בֵּאלֹהִים אֲהַלֵּל דְּבָרוֹ

56

1 For the Leader; upon Jonath-
elem-rehokim. [A Psalm] of
David; Michtam; when the
Philistines took him in Gath.

2 Be gracious unto me, O God, for
man would swallow me up;
All the day he fighting oppresseth
me.

3 They that lie in wait for me would
swallow me up all the day;
For they are many that fight
against me, O Most High,

4 In the day that I am afraid,
I will put my trust in Thee.

5 In God—I will praise His word—

FAITH TRIUMPHANT

THIS Psalm and the one following it form a pair, similar in structure, theme and style. They are a beautiful expression of the confidence in God which overcomes present fear. David's adventure with the Philistines at Gath and the circumstances suit the thought and wording. The Targum interprets the title 'upon Jonath,' etc., as alluding to the people of Israel, giving the Psalm a national interpretation. Indeed, David's life personified the history of Israel. He was forced to wander from land to land and was constantly hiding from fear of being caught.

1. *upon Jonath-elem-rehokim.* The meaning is 'the silent dove of them that are distant.' It is paraphrased by the Targum, 'Concerning the community of Israel likened to a silent dove, when they are far from their cities and repent and praise the LORD of the universe'; and by the LXX, 'For the people removed far from the Sanctuary.' Alternatively, it is the name of an instrument (Meiri) to whose accompaniment the Psalm was sung.

Michtam. See on xvi. 1.

Philistines ... in Gath. See 1 Sam. xxi. 11ff.

2-5 PRAYER WHILE IN DISTRESS

2. *be gracious unto me, O God.* The opening phrase also of LI, LVII.

man. Hebrew *enosh*, a frail, mortal creature, who would presumptuously challenge the will of *Elohim*, the Creator and Ruler of the world.

swallow me up. Or, 'grasp greedily for me' (Hirsch); again in verse 3.

all the day. Without ceasing. Used again in verses 3, 6.

he fighting. The Psalmist's antagonist.

3. *O Most High.* Hebrew is *marom*, not the usual *elyon* (e.g. lvii. 3). It occurs in xcii. 9, *but Thou, O LORD, art on high.* There is uncertainty whether it is to be understood here as an epithet of God. It is so accepted by Targum and Rashi but Ibn Ezra translates, 'but they are many that fight for me in the celestial spheres,' i.e., the angels who were commanded to protect him.

4. *I am afraid.* David fled to Gath *for fear of Saul* (1 Sam. xxi. 11).

5. *His word.* God's promise to make David king (Kimchi, Malbim). He is confident that

In God do I trust, I will not be
   afraid;
What can flesh do unto me?

6 All the day they trouble mine
   affairs;
All their thoughts are against me
   for evil.

7 They gather themselves together,
   they hide themselves,
They mark my steps;
According as they have waited
   for my soul.

8 Because of iniquity cast them out;
In anger bring down the peoples,
   O God.

9 Thou hast counted my wanderings;
Put Thou my tears into Thy
   bottle;
Are they not in Thy book ?

בֵּאלֹהִים בָּטַחְתִּי לֹא אִירָא

מַה־יַּעֲשֶׂה בָשָׂר לִי:

6 כָּל־הַיּוֹם דְּבָרַי יְעַצֵּבוּ

עָלַי כָּל־מַחְשְׁבֹתָם לָרָע:

7 יָגוּרוּ ׀ יִצְפּוֹנוּ הֵמָּה עֲקֵבַי יִשְׁמֹרוּ

כַּאֲשֶׁר קִוּוּ נַפְשִׁי:

8 עַל־אָוֶן פַּלֶּט־לָמוֹ

בְּאַף עַמִּים ׀ הוֹרֵד אֱלֹהִים:

9 נֹדִי סָפַרְתָּה אָתָּה

שִׂימָה דִמְעָתִי בְנֹאדֶךָ

הֲלֹא בְּסִפְרָתֶךָ:

v. 7. יצפונו ק'

---

he will have cause to acknowledge (that is the
meaning of the Hebrew for *praise*) the
fulfilment of that promise.

flesh. A mere mortal being. In the repetition
of the refrain (verse 12), *adam*, 'man,' is
substituted; *adam*:'an earth-born creature'
(see on viii. 5).

6-12 THE PRAYER CONTINUED

6. *they trouble mine affairs.* Better, 'they
cause me to utter words of pain'. (Rashi,
Hirsch). Alternatively, 'that fact about me
(that I trust in God) causes them to pain me'
(Ibn Ezra).

7. *they gather... together.* Cf. xxxv. 15.

they hide themselves. Lying in wait to trap
him. This follows the *kerë*; the *kethib* means
'they set an ambush' (Kimchi).

mark my steps. Follow his trail like a hunter
following the track of an animal.

waited for my soul. Sought an opportunity to
kill him (Kimchi).

8. *because of iniquity cast them out.* A

doubtful translation; more probably 'for (their
iniquity) shall there be escape for them?'
God being the Judge, they cannot escape
punishment (Kimchi).

bring down the peoples. When God has cause
to be angry, not only individuals but even
whole nations will fear Him, for they too
will He cast down from their high places
(Hirsch).

9. *my wanderings.* The many occasions
when he was forced to leave home to evade
the pursuers (Metsudath David).

my tears into Thy bottle. He prays that the
tears which he shed in his anguish shall not
evaporate but be preserved as a reminder of
what he had suffered and bring forth Divine
vengeance (Metsudath David). The verse
brings to mind the words of the Talmud
(B.M. 59a) 'Yet though the gates of prayer
are locked, the gates of tears are not.'

are they not in Thy book? All his sufferings
are, so to speak, recorded in God's book of
remembrance (cf. Mal. iii. 16) (Kimchi).

10 Then shall mine enemies turn
  back in the day that I call;
  This I know, that God is for me.

11 In God—I will praise His word—
  In the LORD—I will praise His
  word—

12 In God do I trust, I will not be
  afraid;
  What can man do unto me?

13 Thy vows are upon me, O God;
  I will render thank-offerings unto
  Thee.

14 For Thou hast delivered my soul
  from death;
  Hast Thou not delivered my feet
  from stumbling?
  That I may walk before God in
  the light of the living.

10 אָז יָשׁוּבוּ אוֹיְבַי אָחוֹר בְּיוֹם אֶקְרָא
זֶה יָדַעְתִּי כִּי־אֱלֹהִים לִי׃

11 בֵּאלֹהִים אֲהַלֵּל דָּבָר
בַּיהוָה אֲהַלֵּל דָּבָר׃

12 בֵּאלֹהִים בָּטַחְתִּי לֹא אִירָא
מַה־יַּעֲשֶׂה אָדָם לִי׃

13 עָלַי אֱלֹהִים נְדָרֶיךָ
אֲשַׁלֵּם תּוֹדֹת לָךְ׃

14 כִּי הִצַּלְתָּ נַפְשִׁי מִמָּוֶת
הֲלֹא רַגְלַי מִדֶּחִי
לְהִתְהַלֵּךְ לִפְנֵי אֱלֹהִים
בְּאוֹר הַחַיִּים׃

10. *turn back.* Defeated, their plans thwarted.

this I know. Inspired by the certainty that God is helping him, there is no doubt in his mind of the final outcome.

11. *God ... LORD.* The two Divine names denote God in His aspect of justice and mercy respectively. With this variant, and also *man* instead of *flesh*, this and the next verse are a refrain repeated from verse 5.

13-14 HIS VOW OF THANKSGIVING

13. *Thy vows are upon me.* The meaning is, the vows I have made to Thee are obligatory upon me to fulfil. Vows are obligations assumed in the hour of distress to be discharged in the time of relief (Kimchi, Ibn Ezra).

thank-offerings. The symbol of the gratitude which then fills the heart. These, in addition to vows undertaken during exile on condition that deliverance was forthcoming (Kimchi).

14. *Thou hast delivered.* The prophetic perfect.

hast Thou not delivered? Not a question seeking information, but an emphatic declaration of what has happened (Kimchi).

walk before God. In conformity with His will, leading a righteous life (Gen. xvii. 1).

in the light of the living. Possibly 'in the light of life,' the life of Torah and its precepts (Kimchi) in the Holy Land (Rashi, Ibn Ezra) illuminated by the Divine Presence, in contrast to the darkness of Sheol.

1 For the Leader; Al-tashheth. [A Psalm] of David; Michtam; when he fled from Saul, in the cave.

לַמְנַצֵּחַ אַל־תַּשְׁחֵת לְדָוִד מִכְתָּם בְּבָרְחוֹ מִפְּנֵי־שָׁאוּל בַּמְּעָרָה:

2 Be gracious unto me, O God, be gracious unto me,
For in Thee hath my soul taken refuge;
Yea, in the shadow of Thy wings will I take refuge,
Until calamities be overpast.

חָנֵּנִי אֱלֹהִים וְחָנֵּנִי
כִּי בְךָ חָסָיָה נַפְשִׁי
וּבְצֵל־כְּנָפֶיךָ אֶחְסֶה
עַד יַעֲבֹר הַוּוֹת:

3 I will cry unto God Most High;
Unto God that accomplisheth it for me.

אֶקְרָא לֵאלֹהִים עֶלְיוֹן
לָאֵל גֹּמֵר עָלָי:

4 He will send from heaven, and save me,
When he that would swallow me up taunteth;   Selah

יִשְׁלַח מִשָּׁמַיִם וְיוֹשִׁיעֵנִי
חֵרֵף שֹׁאֲפִי סֶלָה

CONFIDENCE IN DANGER

THE similarity between this and the preceding Psalm is apparent. External conditions and the poet's state of mind are the same in both. As indicated by the heading, the Psalm was occasioned by Saul's persecution of David which effected the cry of distress accompanied by its underlying note of certainty in ultimate triumph.

1. *Al-tashheth.* lit. 'destroy not.' Again in the next two Psalms and LXXV.

in the cave. These Psalms were composed by David while he was on the brink of being apprehended by Saul as narrated in 1 Sam. xxiv.(Rashi).

2-6 PRAYER IN PERSECUTION

2. *in… Thy wings.* Cf. xxxvi. 8. As a young bird flies instinctively for protection to the cover of its mother's wings when it senses danger, so the Psalmist's soul turns spontaneously to God as a refuge in time of peril.

calamities. Which threaten his 'destruction' (as the same word is translated in lii. 4). The verb *be overpast* suggests the idea of a destructive storm.

3. *God Most High.* The Judge and the Ruler of the world Whose prerogative is to ad-minister justice.

unto God. Hebrew *el*, 'the Mighty one,' Who has the power of executing His will.

that accomplisheth it. The object is unspecified. He accomplishes whatever He has promised to do (Metsudath David).

4. *He will send … Selah.* The word *Selah* is unusual in the middle of the verse (see lv. 20). Malbim maintains that it indicates that the first part of the verse is parenthesized and reads thus: 'those who desire to swallow me up taunt me by saying that there is no natural way in which I can be saved. It would be necessary for God Himself to descend from heaven in order to deliver me from my present state, and that they consider highly unlikely. But I say that God shall indeed send forth His mercy and His truth to save me.'

God shall send forth His mercy
and His truth.

5 My soul is among lions, I do lie
down among them that are
aflame;
Even the sons of men, whose
teeth are spears and arrows,
And their tongue a sharp sword.

6 Be Thou exalted, O God, above
the heavens;
Thy glory be above all the earth.

7 They have prepared a net for my
steps,
My soul is bowed down;
They have digged a pit before me,
They are fallen into the midst
thereof themselves.   Selah

8 My heart is stedfast, O God, my
heart is stedfast;
I will sing, yea, I will sing praises.

יִשְׁלַח אֱלֹהִים חַסְדּוֹ וַאֲמִתּוֹ׃

5 נַפְשִׁי ׀ בְּתוֹךְ לְבָאִם
אֶשְׁכְּבָה לֹהֲטִים
בְּנֵי־אָדָם שִׁנֵּיהֶם חֲנִית וְחִצִּים
וּלְשׁוֹנָם חֶרֶב חַדָּה׃

6 רוּמָה עַל־הַשָּׁמַיִם אֱלֹהִים
עַל כָּל־הָאָרֶץ כְּבוֹדֶךָ׃

7 רֶשֶׁת ׀ הֵכִינוּ לִפְעָמַי
כָּפַף נַפְשִׁי
כָּרוּ לְפָנַי שִׁיחָה
נָפְלוּ בְתוֹכָהּ סֶלָה׃

8 נָכוֹן לִבִּי אֱלֹהִים נָכוֹן לִבִּי
אָשִׁירָה וַאֲזַמֵּרָה׃

His mercy and His truth. Compassion for the
weak and eagerness to relieve the innocent
who suffer wrong are His attributes, and
these will be revealed by Him on the present
occasion.

5. *my soul.* Equals 'I' or 'my life.'

lions. Descriptive of savage and pitiless enemies (cf. vii. 3, x. 9f.) (Metsudath David).

I do lie down. According to Ibn Ezra and
Hirsch these words are connected to the previous phrase as well as to the following word.

among them that are aflame. The Ziphites (so
Rashi) in whose hearts is a blazing hatred and
a burning desire to slander me.

whose teeth. Continuing the simile of *lions.*

a sharp sword. Cf. lii. 4.

6. The refrain of the Psalm, repeated at the
end.

be Thou exalted. By proving Thyself the
Judge of mankind, the Vindicator of the
innocent.

7-12   STEDFASTNESS WHILE UNDER TRIAL

7. The structure of the Psalm is identical
with that of LVI. The second half is parallel
to the first, repeating the account of danger
and following it with a statement of the
certain coming of deliverance.

my soul is bowed down. Being human, he feels
the effects of their pursuit despite his trust in
God; but that trust saves him from the utter
despair which leads to surrender.

they are fallen. The prophetic perfect. That,
he is sure, is what will happen (Kimchi).

8. *my heart is stedfast.* In li. 12, the prayer
had been that God *renew a stedfast spirit
within me.*

9 Awake, my glory; awake, psaltery
    and harp;
  I will awake the dawn.
10 I will give thanks unto Thee, O
     Lord, among the peoples;
  I will sing praises unto Thee
     among the nations.
11 For Thy mercy is great unto the
     heavens,
  And Thy truth unto the skies.
12 Be Thou exalted, O God, above
     the heavens;
  Thy glory be above all the earth.

עוּרָה כְבוֹדִי 9

עוּרָה הַנֵּבֶל וְכִנּוֹר

אָעִירָה שָּׁחַר:

אוֹדְךָ בָעַמִּים ׀ אֲדֹנָי 10

אֲזַמֶּרְךָ בַּלְאֻמִּים:

כִּי־גָדֹל עַד־שָׁמַיִם חַסְדֶּךָ 11

וְעַד־שְׁחָקִים אֲמִתֶּךָ:

רוּמָה עַל־שָׁמַיִם אֱלֹהִים 12

עַל כָּל־הָאָרֶץ כְּבוֹדֶךָ:

9. *awake, my glory.* As in vii. 6, xvi. 9, xxx.
13, *glory* signifies the soul as the Divine
element in man. The Psalmist calls on his
soul to bestir itself to sing of the deliverance
which will be his (Metsudath David).

psaltery and harp. The instruments are personified and summoned to be ready to accompany the songs of praise (Kimchi).

I will awake the dawn. This may be understood metaphorically 'will anticipate the
dawn of a new era in which my monarchy
will come to be recognized' (Malbim). More
literally, 'I will awake [in] the dawn.' A
harp hung above David's couch, and when
the North wind touched its strings at midnight, producing sweet music, he arose to
occupy himself with the study of Torah
(Ber. 3b, 4a).

10. *give thanks unto Thee ... among the
peoples.* Publicly and far and wide will he
proclaim the reality of God's deliverance.
David, despite being persecuted and hunted,
can still find the pride in himself to declare,
'Thou hast chosen me to be Thy servant and
to sing praises unto Thee amongst the peoples
and nations. Allow me to broadcast my experiences amongst all society so that Thy greatness will be acknowledged by all human
powers' (Hirsch).

11. *for.* This verse explains the urge for
the action announced in the previous verse.
The Divine mercy and truth are so extensive
as to be a connecting link between heaven
and earth, and all mankind should unite in
praise of God in recognition of this blessing
(cf. cviii. 5).

mercy ... skies. The confidence expressed in
verse 4 has been proved by the Psalmist's
experience.

heavens ... skies. See on xxxvi. 6.

58

1 For the Leader; Al-tashheth.
   [A Psalm] of David; Michtam.

2 Do ye indeed speak as a righteous
   company?
   Do ye judge with equity the sons
   of men?

3 Yea, in heart ye work wickedness;
   Ye weigh out in the earth the
   violence of your hands.

4 The wicked are estranged from
   the womb;
   The speakers of lies go astray as
   soon as they are born.

5 Their venom is like the venom of a
   serpent;
   They are like the deaf asp that
   stoppeth her ear;

נח

לַמְנַצֵּחַ אַל־תַּשְׁחֵת
לְדָוִד מִכְתָּם:
2 הַאֻמְנָם אֵלֶם צֶדֶק תְּדַבֵּרוּן
מֵישָׁרִים תִּשְׁפְּטוּ בְּנֵי אָדָם:
3 אַף־בְּלֵב עוֹלֹת תִּפְעָלוּן
בָּאָרֶץ חֲמַס יְדֵיכֶם תְּפַלֵּסוּן:
4 זֹרוּ רְשָׁעִים מֵרָחֶם
תָּעוּ מִבֶּטֶן דֹּבְרֵי כָזָב:
5 חֲמַת־לָמוֹ כִּדְמוּת חֲמַת־נָחָשׁ
כְּמוֹ־פֶתֶן חֵרֵשׁ יַאְטֵם אָזְנוֹ:

UNJUST JUDGES CONDEMNED

A VEHEMENT denunciation of corrupt judges is the theme of this outspoken poem. In spirit it
is true to the supreme importance which is attached to the impartial administration of justice
by the Pentateuch and the Prophets. Placed between Psalms LVII and LIX, commentators
explains that it has a connection with David's personal life. More specifically, it is maintained
that the persons referred to are Abner and other supporters of Saul who unlawfully sided with
the king in his condemnation of David as a rebel. A point of importance is here made which
must be borne in mind when assessing the moral standard of the speaker in his imprecations
upon the men he censures. He may forgive injury done to himself; but he has no right to feel
lenient towards those who are guilty of flagrant injustice to others.

2-6 THE JUDGES ARRAIGNED

2. *do ye indeed speak?* When pronouncing
judgment in a suit. The answer implied is 'no.'

as a righteous company. The translation of
the obscure word *elem* by *company* is based
upon Kimchi. Rashi interprets: *do ye indeed
in silence speak righteousness?* They are
silent when they ought to speak words of
condemnation.

3. *in heart ye work wickedness.* Scheming
to pervert the course of justice.

ye weigh out. Cf. *let me be weighed in a just
balance* (Job. xxxi. 6). Scales are an instrument for fair dealing, but these men employed them for the purpose of doing violence to the innocent. They claimed that their

evil judgments were a result of fair considerations, when in fact their perverted minds
were incapable of producing favourable ver-
dicts (cf. Rashi, Kimchi).

4. *the wicked.* Descriptive of these corrupt
judges.

are estranged. From the principles of equity
which should control the exercise of their
authority.

from the womb. They were born with this
inclination to evil and it has become in-
grained in their nature through repeated exercise (Kimchi).

5. *their venom.* The words which fall from
their lips are deadly like a snake's poison
(Kimchi).

6 Which hearkeneth not to the voice
    of charmers,
  Or of the most cunning binder of
    spells.

7 Break their teeth, O God, in their
    mouth;
  Break out the cheek-teeth of the
    young lions, O LORD.

8 Let them melt away as water that
    runneth apace;
  When he aimeth his arrows, let
    them be as though they were cut
    off.

9 Let them be as a snail which melt-
    eth and passeth away;
  Like the untimely births of a
    woman, that have not seen the
    sun.

10 Before your pots can feel the
    thorns,
  He will sweep it away with a
    whirlwind, the raw and the
    burning alike.

11 The righteous shall rejoice when
    he seeth the vengeance;
  He shall wash his feet in the
    blood of the wicked.

12 And men shall say: 'Verily there
    is a reward for the righteous;
  Verily there is a God that judgeth
    in the earth.'

אֲשֶׁר לֹא־יִשְׁמַע 6
לְקוֹל מְלַחֲשִׁים
חוֹבֵר חֲבָרִים מְחֻכָּם:
אֱלֹהִים הֲרָס־שִׁנֵּימוֹ בְּפִימוֹ 7
מַלְתְּעוֹת כְּפִירִים נְתֹץ ׀ יְהוָה:
יִמָּאֲסוּ כְמוֹ־מַיִם יִתְהַלְּכוּ־לָמוֹ 8
יִדְרֹךְ חִצּוֹ כְּמוֹ יִתְמֹלָלוּ:
כְּמוֹ שַׁבְּלוּל תֶּמֶס יַהֲלֹךְ 9
נֵפֶל אֵשֶׁת בַּל־חָזוּ שָׁמֶשׁ:
בְּטֶרֶם יָבִינוּ סִּירֹתֵיכֶם אָטָד 10
כְּמוֹ־חַי כְּמוֹ־חָרוֹן יִשְׂעָרֶנּוּ:
יִשְׂמַח צַדִּיק כִּי־חָזָה נָקָם 11
פְּעָמָיו יִרְחַץ בְּדַם הָרָשָׁע:
וְיֹאמַר אָדָם אַךְ־פְּרִי לַצַּדִּיק 12
אַךְ יֵשׁ־אֱלֹהִים שֹׁפְטִים בָּאָרֶץ:

חציו ק׳   v. 8.

like the deaf asp that stoppeth her ear. Against
the voice of the charmer (cf. Jer. viii. 17); so
these judges are deaf to the whisperings of
conscience (Metsudath David).

7. *break their teeth.* Render them incapable of doing harm.

young lions. Ferocious enemies.

8. *as water that runneth apace.* He is
thinking of water which does not stay in one
place, but runs in different directions.

when he aimeth. Kimchi notes this is not a
reference to God but when one of these
wicked men shoots at a victim, may the
arrows be blunted and become harmless.

9. *which melteth and passeth away.* Alluding to the popular belief that the slimy trail
which the snail leaves in its track is the
dissolution of its substance (Sforno).

the … births. Stillborn children (cf. Rashi).

10. *before … the thorns.* Derived from what
happens when thorns are used as fuel to cook
meat. Before the time it takes for the pot to
feel the effect of the burning thorns; i.e.,
while the meat is yet uncooked (Kimchi).

the raw … alike. A better translation: 'just as
it (the meat) is yet raw, so will the anger
(come hurriedly) and sweep them away.'
God's wrath will manifest itself suddenly
while the wicked are unprepared (Kimchi).

11. *vengeance.* Retribution from God.

wash his feet. This need not be understood literally, since nowhere in the Psalm is the physical
killing of the wicked called for (Hirsch).

12. *a reward for the righteous.* In the ultimate triumph of right over evil.

that judgeth. The verb is plural, which is
unusual with *Elohim* as the subject, if it refers
to God (see Kimchi).

59

1 For the Leader; Al-tashheth. [A
  Psalm] of David; Michtam;
  when Saul sent, and they watched
  the house to kill him.

2 Deliver me from mine enemies, O
  my God;
  Set me on high from them that
  rise up against me.

3 Deliver me from the workers of
  iniquity,
  And save me from the men of
  blood.

4 For, lo, they lie in wait for my
  soul;
  The impudent gather themselves
  together against me;
  Not for my transgression, nor for
  my sin, O LORD.

5 Without my fault, they run and
  prepare themselves;
  Awake Thou to help me, and
  behold.

נט

לַמְנַצֵּחַ אַל־תַּשְׁחֵת לְדָוִד
מִכְתָּם בִּשְׁלֹחַ שָׁאוּל
וַיִּשְׁמְרוּ אֶת־הַבַּיִת לַהֲמִיתוֹ׃
הַצִּילֵנִי מֵאֹיְבַי ׀ אֱלֹהָי 2
מִמִּתְקוֹמְמַי תְּשַׂגְּבֵנִי׃
הַצִּילֵנִי מִפֹּעֲלֵי אָוֶן 3
וּמֵאַנְשֵׁי דָמִים הוֹשִׁיעֵנִי׃
כִּי הִנֵּה אָרְבוּ לְנַפְשִׁי 4
יָגוּרוּ עָלַי עַזִּים
לֹא־פִשְׁעִי וְלֹא־חַטָּאתִי יְהוָה׃
בְּלִי־עָוֹן יְרֻצוּן וְיִכּוֹנָנוּ 5
עוּרָה לִקְרָאתִי וּרְאֵה׃

PRAYER IN DANGER

A COMPANION to the previous two Psalms, it runs on similar lines and has the same historical
background. The occasion is identified as *when Saul sent, and they watched the house to kill
him.* David's wife, Michal, helped him escape and it was then that he composed the Psalm
(Meiri). In the course of the Psalm David turns his attention to the enemies of Israel and asks
that God should humble them, too.

1. *when Saul sent.* See 1 Sam. xix. 11.

2-6 GOD'S HELP INVOKED

2. *set me on high.* See on xx. 2.

3. *the men of blood.* Thirsting for my life.

4. *they lie in wait for my soul.* Better, 'they
have been lying in wait for my life.' For some
time they had prepared plans in secret; now
they had grown *impudent,* brazen, and
openly *gather themselves together* to execute them.

not for my transgression. He protests his in-

nocence of the charges they bring against him.

5. *without my fault.* Hebrew, 'without fault'
on my part.

awake Thou. Cf. *why sleepest Thou?* (xliv. 24).

to help me. lit. 'to meet me' with help.

6. *God of hosts.* See on xxiv. 10.

all the nations. Here David lays aside his own
interests and expands his prayer to include a
judgment on all the enemies of Israel. There
is a connection, however. If violence and
tyranny were tolerated amongst the chosen

6 Thou therefore, O Lord God of
    hosts, the God of Israel,
  Arouse Thyself to punish all the
    nations;
  Show no mercy to any iniquitous
    traitors. Selah

7 They return at evening, they howl
    like a dog,
  And go round about the city.

8 Behold, they belch out with their
    mouth;
  Swords are in their lips:
  'For who doth hear?'

9 But Thou, O Lord, shalt laugh at
    them;
  Thou shalt have all the nations in
    derision.

10 Because of his strength, I will
     wait for Thee;
   For God is my high tower.

11 The God of my mercy will come
     to meet me;
   God will let me gaze upon mine
     adversaries.

6 וְאַתָּה יְהוָה־אֱלֹהִים צְבָאוֹת
אֱלֹהֵי יִשְׂרָאֵל
הָקִיצָה לִפְקֹד כָּל־הַגּוֹיִם
אַל־תָּחֹן כָּל־בֹּגְדֵי אָוֶן סֶלָה׃

7 יָשׁוּבוּ לָעֶרֶב יֶהֱמוּ כַכָּלֶב
וִיסוֹבְבוּ עִיר׃

8 הִנֵּה ׀ יַבִּיעוּן בְּפִיהֶם
חֲרָבוֹת בְּשִׂפְתוֹתֵיהֶם
כִּי־מִי שֹׁמֵעַ׃

9 וְאַתָּה יְהוָה תִּשְׂחַק־לָמוֹ
תִּלְעַג לְכָל־גּוֹיִם׃

10 עֻזּוֹ אֵלֶיךָ אֶשְׁמֹרָה
כִּי־אֱלֹהִים מִשְׂגַּבִּי׃

11 אֱלֹהֵי חַסְדּוֹ יְקַדְּמֵנִי
אֱלֹהִים יַרְאֵנִי בְשֹׁרְרָי׃

v. 11. חסדי ק׳

---

people, it would imply that such behaviour is
Divinely sanctioned and human society would
become corrupt and unbearable. For the sake
of a better world, those dishonest ones
amongst us (in David's case the marauding
henchmen of Saul) must be brought to Divine
justice (Hirsch). Some maintain that Saul and
his supporters are compared to 'others nations': just as God shows no pity for the
oppressors of Israel, so should He not favour
the wicked elements in Israel (Metsudath
David; cf. Rashi).

7-8 THE ENEMIES DESCRIBED

7. *they return at evening.* An allusion to the
rotating guards whom Saul commissioned to
guard David's house and who are likened to
dogs that howl upon awakening (Kimchi).

8. *they belch out with their mouth.* The
guards are depicted as having poured forth
a stream of malicious words which are as

deadly as swords (lvii. 5).

for who doth hear? They believe that David
cannot hear them talking outside his house.
Alternatively they persuade themselves that
God does not hear their criminal speech
(Kimchi, Metsudath David).

9-10 GOD WILL INTERVENE

9. *but Thou.* The retort to their question 'for
who doth hear?' They will make a mockery
of themselves as God will undoubtedly foil
their evil plans (Kimchi).

shalt laugh at them. Cf. ii. 4.

10. A refrain repeated with variations in
verse 18 (see note.)

11-14 FATE OF THE WICKED

11. *the God of my mercy.* So the *kerĕ*: the
kethib means 'my God shall come to meet me
with His mercy.'

12 Slay them not, lest my people
     forget,
   Make them wander to and fro by
     Thy power, and bring them
     down,
   O Lord our shield.

13 For the sin of their mouth, and
     the words of their lips,
   Let them even be taken in their
     pride,
   And for cursing and lying which
     they speak.

14 Consume them in wrath, con-
     sume them, that they be no
     more;
   And let them know that God
     ruleth in Jacob,
   Unto the ends of the earth.
                              Selah

אַל־תַּהַרְגֵם ׀ פֶּן־יִשְׁכְּחוּ עַמִּי 12
הֲנִיעֵמוֹ בְחֵילְךָ וְהוֹרִידֵמוֹ
מָגִנֵּנוּ אֲדֹנָי:
חַטֹּאת־פִּימוֹ דְּבַר־שְׂפָתֵימוֹ 13
וְיִלָּכְדוּ בִגְאוֹנָם
וּמֵאָלָה וּמִכַּחַשׁ יְסַפֵּרוּ:
כַּלֵּה בְחֵמָה כַּלֵּה וְאֵינֵמוֹ 14
וְיֵדְעוּ כִּי־אֱלֹהִים מֹשֵׁל בְּיַעֲקֹב
לְאַפְסֵי הָאָרֶץ
סֶלָה:

12. *slay them not.* The Psalmist does not pray that his enemies may suffer a cruel, lingering punishment, that he may gloat over their pain; but that their decline from power be gradual so that God's judgment of them may serve as a visible monument to all Israel. A swift and complete destruction, though momentarily awesome, will leave no impact and will soon be forgotten (cf. Rashi, Kimchi).

make them wander to and fro. Drive them from their homes and degrade them from their position of influence to wander about as outcasts, that they become far and wide visible proof of God's condemnation (Metsudath David).

bring them down. From their position of wealth and power.

our shield. The Psalmist speaks not only for himself but for the whole community. He is concerned with more than his own danger, and thinks also of the effect upon the entire nation when such lawless men are its leaders. Hence the reference to *my people* (cf. Daath Sofrim).

13. *for the sin of their mouth.* lit. 'the word of their lips (is) the sin of their mouth'; i.e., every word uttered constitutes a misuse of the gift of speech (Hirsch).

taken in their pride. Let their self-assurance be the means of their downfall, and the defiant question, *for who doth hear?* receive an answer which convincingly demonstrates that there is One that heareth (Ibn Ezra).

14. *consume them.* The repetition of the verb indicates the urgency of the supplication. Another example is to be found in lvii. 2.

that they be no more. No contradiction is to be discerned with the prayer *slay them not.* He does not presume to suggest to God how they are to be punished. After they have served as a living example of Divine retribution, God—so he prays—will adopt measures that they be incapable of ever again working mischief (cf. Daath Sofrim).

let them know. Better, 'let it be known (lit. let men know) unto the ends of the earth that God ruleth.' The Psalmist desires that his

15 And they return at evening, they
    howl like a dog,
    And go round about the city;

16 They wander up and down to
    devour,
    And tarry all night if they have
    not their fill.

17 But as for me, I will sing of Thy
    strength;
    Yea, I will sing aloud of Thy
    mercy in the morning;
    For Thou hast been my high
    tower,
    And a refuge in the day of my
    distress.

18 O my strength, unto Thee will I
    sing praises;
    For God is my high tower, the
    God of my mercy.

וַיָשֻׁבוּ לָעֶרֶב יֶהֱמוּ כַכָּלֶב 15
וִיסוֹבְבוּ עִיר׃
הֵמָּה יְנוּעוּן לֶאֱכֹל 16
אִם־לֹא יִשְׂבְּעוּ וַיָּלִינוּ׃
וַאֲנִי ׀ אָשִׁיר עֻזֶּךָ 17
וַאֲרַנֵּן לַבֹּקֶר חַסְדֶּךָ
כִּי־הָיִיתָ מִשְׂגָּב לִי
וּמָנוֹס בְּיוֹם צַר־לִי׃
עֻזִּי אֵלֶיךָ אֲזַמֵּרָה 18
כִּי־אֱלֹהִים מִשְׂגַּבִּי אֱלֹהֵי חַסְדִּי׃

v. 16. יניעון ק׳

personal salvation shall yield a truth which
gains universal recognition.

15-18   THEIR FATE COMPARED WITH HIS OWN

15. Repeats verse 7 for the purpose of making the contrast between what will happen to
them and to him.

16. *they wander.* The subject is emphasized in the Hebrew, and so is *but as for me*
in the next verse.

to devour. The object to be understood is the
Psalmist himself.

tarry all night. The whole night is spent in
search of their prey and it passes without their
having their fill. Their quest fails.

17. *Thy strength.* Which frustrated their plot
and enabled me to survive the persistent and
determined attempts upon my life (cf. Hirsch).

in the morning. When he finds himself safe
and sound after the night spent by his enemies in their hunt of him (Rashi).

high tower...refuge. David's use of such
similes of God at the close of the Psalm is a
revelation of his state of mind, the sense of
relief he feels, now that the danger is over and
he has come through his ordeal unscathed.
What other protection, except that which is
from God, could have secured his safety in so
acute a time of danger? The second half of the
verse seems to be an echo of xviii. 3.

18. See verse 10 where strength is attributed to Saul. Here, David looks to the future
when the power shall have been transferred
to him. On that day he will rejoice in his
newly gained might, and acknowledge it as a
gift from God's bounty by proclaiming that
God alone is his exaltation (Hirsch).

60

1 For the Leader; upon Shushan Eduth; Michtam of David, to teach; 2when he strove with Aram-naharaim and with Aram-zobah, and Joab returned, and smote of Edom in the Valley of Salt twelve thousand.

1 For the Leader; upon Shushan Eduth; Michtam of David, to teach; 2when he strove with Aram-naharaim and with Aram-zobah, and Joab returned, and smote of Edom in the Valley of Salt twelve thousand.

3 O God, Thou hast cast us off, Thou hast broken us down; Thou hast been angry; O restore us.

4 Thou hast made the land to shake, Thou hast cleft it; Heal the breaches thereof; for it tottereth.

לַמְנַצֵּחַ עַל־שׁוּשַׁן עֵדוּת מִכְתָּם

2 לְדָוִד לְלַמֵּד: בְּהַצּוֹתוֹ ׀ אֶת אֲרַם נַהֲרַיִם וְאֶת־אֲרַם צוֹבָה וַיָּשָׁב יוֹאָב וַיַּךְ אֶת־אֱדוֹם בְּגֵיא־מֶלַח שְׁנֵים עָשָׂר אָלֶף:

3 אֱלֹהִים זְנַחְתָּנוּ פְרַצְתָּנוּ אָנַפְתָּ תְּשׁוֹבֵב לָנוּ:

4 הִרְעַשְׁתָּה אֶרֶץ פְּצַמְתָּהּ רְפָה שְׁבָרֶיהָ כִי־מָטָה:

IN THE SHADOW OF DEFEAT

A TIME of national humiliation is mirrored in this composition. At the campaign's outset the army had suffered a reverse. The Psalm reveals the humbled mood of the people, hoping that God would retrieve their fortunes and turn defeat into victory. The title points to the Aramite and Edomite wars in which David was engaged and a particular incident is singled out which, however, tells of success rather than failure. The Psalm was probably composed immediately before this exploit which turned the scales.

1. *upon Shushan Eduth.* lit. 'lily of testimony,' with which the titles of XLV, LXIX and LXXX are to be compared. It perhaps indicates the name of a musical instrument (Meiri).

to teach. Cf. 2 Sam. i. 18. The direction perhaps means that the poem was to be taught to the Temple singers to publicize God's mercy in bringing David's army to victory after near defeat (Ibn Ezra).

2. *Aram-naharaim.* 'Syria of the two rivers,' the land between the Euphrates and Chaboras.

Aram-zobah. Country to the northeast of Damascus between the Orontes and Euphrates. They are mentioned in 1 Chron. xix. 6, as having combined against David.

Valley of Salt. Situated in the Dead Sea region. In 2 Sam. viii. 13 it is recorded: *And David got him a name when he returned from smiting the Arameans in the Valley of Salt, even eighteen thousand men.* Cf. 1 Chron. xviii. 12. A threefold discrepancy appears:

Here, the success is ascribed to Joab, whereas in Chronicles Abishai is named as general; the numbers also differ, and the vanquished nation is named here as Edom. In order to establish harmony between the Psalm and Chronicles, both Rashi and Kimchi explain that Edom and Aram joined forces against Israel. Hence, the enemy is called by one name or the other. Initially, Abishai led a force which killed six thousand enemy troops. Joab took over (Psalms) and killed an additional twelve thousand but Abishai, who began the campaign, is credited with all eighteen thousand (Chron.). In Sam., it is related that David, the commander of the Israelite army, earned himself a name for masterminding the plan to conquer the enemy forces.

3–5 NATIONAL DISASTER

3. *Thou hast cast us off.* Cf. xliv. 10. Defeat indicated the withdrawal of God's favour and help, in the same way that victory was understood to be the effect of His aid.

broken us down. lit. 'made a breach in us,' so

5 Thou hast made Thy people to
   see hard things;
   Thou hast made us to drink the
   wine of staggering.

6 Thou hast given a banner to them
   that fear Thee,
   That it may be displayed because
   of the truth.   Selah

7 That Thy beloved may be delivered,
   Save with Thy right hand, and
   answer me.

8 God spoke in His holiness, that I
   would exult;
   That I would divide Shechem,
   and mete out the valley of
   Succoth.

9 Gilead is mine, and Manasseh is
   mine;

5 הִרְאִיתָ עַמְּךָ קָשָׁה
הִשְׁקִיתָנוּ יַיִן תַּרְעֵלָה׃

6 נָתַתָּה לִּירֵאֶיךָ נֵּס לְהִתְנוֹסֵס
מִפְּנֵי קֹשֶׁט סֶלָה׃

7 לְמַעַן יֵחָלְצוּן יְדִידֶיךָ
הוֹשִׁיעָה יְמִינְךָ וַעֲנֵנִי׃

8 אֱלֹהִים ׀ דִּבֶּר בְּקָדְשׁוֹ אֶעְלֹזָה
אֲחַלְּקָה שְׁכֶם
וְעֵמֶק סֻכּוֹת אֲמַדֵּד׃

9 לִי גִלְעָד ׀ וְלִי מְנַשֶּׁה

that we are exposed to the assaults of the
attackers.

4. *made the land to shake.* The Psalmist
compares the country in defeat to what happens during an earthquake: the land trembles,
the walls of buildings are split asunder and
crash to the ground.

heal the breaches. Repair the devastation
caused by the invaders.

5. *wine of staggering.* Again in Isa. li. 17,
22; Jer. xxv. 15ff., where it is defined as *the
cup of My fury.* As a person is overcome by
drink and reels in his stupefaction, so the
nation, having been made to drain the cup of
His displeasure, staggers helplessly.

6–10   HOPE OF VICTORY

6. *a banner to them that fear Thee.* In the
darkness of the nation's humiliation, the
Psalmist perceives a ray of hope by reflecting
upon the past. God had summoned Israel,
who acknowledged His Sovereignty, to His
service, and, so to speak, presented them
with the banner of His cause, which they
were to hold aloft for the purpose of guiding
other peoples to His truth (cf. Hirsch).

7. *that Thy beloved may be delivered.* By
recognizing Israel as His standard-bearers
He had displayed His love for them. Upon

that fact the Psalmist bases his plea.

save. Or, 'grant victory.'

Thy right hand. See on xvii. 7.

8.   The remainder of the Psalm occurs again
as the second half of CVIII.

God spoke in His holiness. He made a
promise through His prophets (Metsudath
David), the guarantee being His attribute of
holiness which rules out any possibility of
the pledge remaining unfulfilled. Elsewhere
God is said to swear by his holiness (lxxxix.
36; Amos iv. 2).

that I would exult. This translation follows
Kimchi, Meiri, and Metsudath David in un-
derstanding 'I' to be David, who relates that
God's word proved to be true since he was
given rule over all of Israel, including those
areas who attempted to deny his sovereignty.
The places mentioned in this verse were in
Ephraim where Ish-Bosheth had failed in his
attempt to set up a kingdom (see 2 Sam. ii.)
(Kimchi).

Shechem. Representing the territory west of
the Jordan, and *Succoth* the land on the east
side.

9.   *Gilead.* In the land of Bashan which was
inhabited by part of the tribe of Manasseh.

190

Ephraim also is the defence of my
head;
Judah is my sceptre.

10 Moab is my washpot;
Upon Edom do I cast my shoe;
Philistia, cry aloud because of
me!

11 Who will bring me into the fortified city?
Who will lead me unto Edom?

12 Hast not Thou, O God, cast us
off?
And Thou goest not forth, O
God, with our hosts.

13 Give us help against the adversary;
For vain is the help of man.

14 Through God we shall do
valiantly;
For He it is that will tread down
our adversaries.

וְאֶפְרַיִם מָעוֹז רֹאשִׁי
יְהוּדָה מְחֹקְקִי:
10 מוֹאָב ׀ סִיר רַחְצִי
עַל־אֱדוֹם אַשְׁלִיךְ נַעֲלִי
עָלַי פְּלֶשֶׁת הִתְרוֹעָעִי:
11 מִי יֹבִלֵנִי עִיר מָצוֹר
מִי נָחַנִי עַד־אֱדוֹם:
12 הֲלֹא־אַתָּה אֱלֹהִים זְנַחְתָּנוּ
וְלֹא־תֵצֵא אֱלֹהִים בְּצִבְאוֹתֵינוּ:
13 הָבָה־לָּנוּ עֶזְרָת מִצָּר
וְשָׁוְא תְּשׁוּעַת אָדָם:
14 בֵּאלֹהִים נַעֲשֶׂה־חָיִל
וְהוּא יָבוּס צָרֵינוּ:

Ephraim and *Judah*. The verse refers to the
areas that were involved in the uprising but
later submitted to David's rule; Judah is
mentioned as the tribe that gave him support
by recognizing his authority (Kimchi).

my sceptre. Alluding to Jacob's blessing in
Gen. xlix. 10 (cf. Rashi). The *sceptre* is the
emblem of ruling power, and it was in Judah's
capital, Jerusalem, that the seat of government was located. In verses 9f. *mine* and *my*
still refer to David.

10. *Moab is my washpot*. As in the preceding verses, David gains control over the
countries here designated and reduces them
to an abject state. Moab had planned to destroy Israel (Num. xxii) but it will become
like a basin in which the conqueror washes
his feet or his utensils, degraded to menial
service (cf. Kimchi).

upon Edom do I cast my shoe. Perhaps an
allusion to the casting of a shoe over a piece
of land as a symbolic act of taking possession
(Malbim). An alternative translation is given
by Rashi, 'upon Edom shall I cast my *lock*' i.e.,

they will be held in my tight grip. According
to Metsudath David, 'I will fetter their feet
with iron chains.' No mention is made here of
the Aramitic lands, as it was David's intention to annex them to Israel (Hirsch).

cry aloud. Proclaiming God as Victor.

11-14 GOD'S HELP ESSENTIAL

11. The extreme difficulty of the task
confronting David is voiced in this verse.
Edom was a strong foe living in a mountainous region which made an expedition haz-
ardous.

the fortified city. Edom's capital was Petra,
approached through precipitous mountains
(cf. Obadiah 3).

12. If the present circumstances were to
continue, it would be impossible to make the
attempt.

13. *vain is the help of man*. To rely upon his
own resources would be inadequate for the
accomplishment of the task.

14. *through God*. Only with His aid is victory possible and certain.

61

פא

1 For the Leader; with string-music. [A Psalm] of David.

2 Hear my cry, O God;
   Attend unto my prayer.

3 From the end of the earth will I
   call unto Thee, when my heart
   fainteth;
   Lead me to a rock that is too high
   for me.

4 For Thou hast been a refuge for
   me,
   A tower of strength in the face of
   the enemy.

5 I will dwell in Thy Tent for ever;
   I will take refuge in the covert of
   Thy wings.   Selah

6 For Thou, O God, hast heard my
   vows;
   Thou hast granted the heritage of
   those that fear Thy name.

לַמְנַצֵּחַ עַל־נְגִינַת לְדָוִד׃

2 שִׁמְעָה אֱלֹהִים רִנָּתִי
   הַקְשִׁיבָה תְּפִלָּתִי׃

3 מִקְצֵה הָאָרֶץ אֵלֶיךָ אֶקְרָא
   בַּעֲטֹף לִבִּי
   בְּצוּר־יָרוּם מִמֶּנִּי תַנְחֵנִי׃

4 כִּי־הָיִיתָ מַחְסֶה לִי
   מִגְדַּל־עֹז מִפְּנֵי אוֹיֵב׃

5 אָגוּרָה בְאָהָלְךָ עוֹלָמִים
   אֶחֱסֶה בְסֵתֶר כְּנָפֶיךָ סֶּלָה׃

6 כִּי־אַתָּה אֱלֹהִים שָׁמַעְתָּ לִנְדָרָי
   נָתַתָּ יְרֻשַּׁת יִרְאֵי שְׁמֶךָ׃

A PRAYER IN EXILE

A PETITION to God for restoration is offered while away from home. It has been suggested that David composed it during the campaign against Aram (Metsudath David) or while being pursued by Saul (Malbim).

2–4 APPEAL FOR HELP

2. *my cry.* See on xvii. I. *Rinah, cry* denotes a lament during difficult times, while *tefilah* is the *prayer* offered during the times of success (Malbim).

3. *from the end of the earth.* Better, 'of the land.' Either a reference to the land of the Philistines where David sought refuge from Saul (Kimchi) or to the northern borders where the war with Aram was being fought (Metsudath David).

a rock that is too high for me. A place of refuge inaccessible to him if he has to depend upon his own efforts, and only to be reached with God's guidance and aid (Rashi).

4. *Thou hast been a refuge for me.* As so often in this type of Psalm, recollection of past favours is made the ground of a plea for present assistance.

5-6 CONFIDENCE IN GOD

5. *I will dwell in Thy Tent for ever.* The words may be understood as a prayer: 'let me dwell…let me take refuge.' *Tent* is understood as a reference to the Tabernacle or to the 'hall of study,' which brings to mind David's quest (xvii. 4): 'that I may dwell in the house of the LORD all the days of my life' (Daath Sofrim).

covert of Thy wings. See on lvii. 2.

6. *hast heard.* The verbs in the verse may be prophetic perfect, written when David was in exile (Kimchi), or past, when he was returning to Jerusalem after recapturing the cities of Israel from Aram (cf. Rashi).

my vows. Which formed part of his supplication to God, but they are not specified. Doubtless they expressed his resolve to show gratitude for his safe return (Kimchi).

7 Mayest Thou add days unto the
   king's days!
   May his years be as many generations!

8 May he be enthroned before God
   for ever!
   Appoint mercy and truth, that they
   may preserve him.

9 So will I sing praise unto Thy
   name for ever,
   That I may daily perform my
   vows.

7 יָמִים עַל־יְמֵי־מֶלֶךְ תּוֹסִיף
שְׁנוֹתָיו כְּמוֹ־דֹר וָדֹר:
8 יֵשֵׁב עוֹלָם לִפְנֵי אֱלֹהִים
חֶסֶד וֶאֱמֶת מַן יִנְצְרֻהוּ:
9 כֵּן ׀ אֲזַמְּרָה שִׁמְךָ לָעַד
לְשַׁלְּמִי נְדָרַי יוֹם ׀ יוֹם:

Thou hast granted the heritage. Heritage is a common designation for the land of Israel. Here David acknowledges that, with his return, he will be allowed to enjoy the spiritual legacy which had been promised to his people (Ibn Ezra). More specifically, he asks for the privilege of serving in the Holy Temple where all stand in awe in God's presence (Kimchi).

7-8 HOPES FOR THE KING'S FUTURE

7. *unto the king's days.* David is speaking of himself in the third person, because he thinks of his kingly office, not of himself as an individual. It is also possible that his prayer is for all future kings, that they live their full lifespan and not perish while at the zenith of their career, leaving the country without a responsible leader (Daath Sofrim).

may his years be as many generations! lit. 'generation and generation.' Two generations (Kimchi). Or, 'as any generation,' e.g. an unshortened seventy years (Metsudath David). Perhaps, *may the years he yet lives equal in number the many generations which will follow in his dynasty!* So that if the words are not a petition—*may* is not in the Hebrew— David avows his assurance given

him by God through Nathan the prophet: *Thy house and thy kingdom shall be made sure for ever before thee; thy throne shall be established for ever* (2 Sam. vii. 16).

8. *before God.* In the enjoyment of His favour.

for ever. For his whole life.

mercy and truth. May they be his guardian angels! (cf. lvii. 4). In the light of Prov. xx. 28, *mercy and truth preserve the king*, the supplication may be that God will help him and his descendants to display these virtues during their successive reigns, so that the dynasty may deserve to endure.

9 HIS GRATITUDE TO GOD

9. *so will I sing praise.* The sudden change to the first person is not uncommon, and its occurrence here suits the interpretation of verses 7f. as David speaking of himself.

my vows. As in verse 6. The Targum gives the Psalm a national application, referring it to the Jews' captivity and paraphrases: 'Then will I praise Thy name for all eternity when I pay my vows in the day of Israel's redemption and in the day when King Messiah is consecrated to become ruler.'

1 For the Leader; for Jeduthun.
   A Psalm of David.

2 Only for God doth my soul wait in
   stillness;
   From Him cometh my salvation.

3 He only is my rock and my salvation,
   My high tower, I shall not be
   greatly moved.

4 How long will ye set upon a man,
   That ye may slay him, all of you,
   As a leaning wall, a tottering
   fence?

5 They only devise to thrust him
   down from his height, delighting in lies;
   They bless with their mouth, but
   they curse inwardly.   Selah

THE ONE SURE REFUGE

THEME and phraseology are familiar. Circumstances of distress are described in which the poet
turns to God as the only safe haven from the storm raging around him. There are no specific
details in the Psalm which point to a definite period. Rashi describes the Psalm as depicting
the nation of Israel in exile.

1. *for Jeduthun.* See on xxxix. 1.

2-5 THE ONLY SALVATION IN DISTRESS

2. *only.* Hebrew *ach* is a distinctive word in
this Psalm occurring six times and striking its
keynote. To God alone, and to nobody else,
he turns in the hour of need (Hirsch).

stillness. Humble resignation and quiet confidence.

3. *rock.* For the various terms in the verse
as applied to God, cf. xviii. 3.

greatly moved. As a weak mortal he cannot
but react to the pressure of adverse circumstances and be moved; but his trust in God
saves him from being *greatly* disturbed and
overwhelmed by a feeling of hopelessness.

4. *how long will ye set upon a man?* Addressed to his persecutors in indignation at

their unjust treatment, also perhaps suggesting the futility of their efforts to plot against
(so Rashi) one who is upheld by God. The
Hebrew verb occurs only here and Hirsch
maintains that its root meaning is 'to strike
terror in a person with menacing cries.'

as a leaning wall. The subject is the one who
persecutes and the verse is better rendered
'may you (eventually) all be slain (and live
your lives in fear) like a leaning wall and a
tottering fence'; i.e. on the brink of destruction (Kimchi, Metsudath David).

5. *from his height.* His exalted position as
king.

delighting in lies. e.g. the allegation that
David neglected his duty and an aggrieved
person had no chance of redress (2 Sam. xv.
2ff.) (cf. Metsudath David).

6 Only for God wait thou in stillness,
   my soul;
  For from Him cometh my hope.

7 He only is my rock and my salvation,
  My high tower, I shall not be
   moved.

8 Upon God resteth my salvation
   and my glory;
  The rock of my strength, and my
   refuge, is in God.

9 Trust in Him at all times, ye
   people;
  Pour out your heart before Him;
  God is a refuge for us.   Selah

10 Men of low degree are vanity,
   and men of high degree are a
   lie;
  If they be laid in the balances,
   they are together lighter than
   vanity.

אַ֤ךְ לֵֽאלֹהִ֗ים דּ֭וֹמִּי נַפְשִׁ֑י 6
כִּֽי־מִ֝מֶּ֗נּוּ תִּקְוָתִֽי׃

אַךְ־ה֣וּא צ֭וּרִי וִישׁוּעָתִ֑י 7
מִ֝שְׂגַּבִּ֗י לֹ֣א אֶמּֽוֹט׃

עַל־אֱ֭לֹהִים יִשְׁעִ֣י וּכְבוֹדִ֑י 8
צוּר־עֻזִּ֥י מַ֝חְסִ֗י בֵּֽאלֹהִֽים׃

בִּטְח֘וּ ב֤וֹ בְכָל־עֵ֨ת ׀ עָ֗ם 9
שִׁפְכֽוּ־לְפָנָ֥יו לְבַבְכֶ֑ם
אֱלֹהִ֖ים מַחֲסֶה־לָּ֣נוּ סֶֽלָה׃

אַ֤ךְ ׀ הֶ֥בֶל בְּנֵֽי־אָדָם֮ כָּזָ֪ב בְּנֵ֫י־אִ֥ישׁ 10
בְּמֹאזְנַ֥יִם לַעֲל֑וֹת
הֵ֝֗מָּה מֵהֶ֥בֶל יָֽחַד׃

they bless with their mouth. They who pretended to be loyal to the throne and glorified the king with their words but had very different sentiments buried in their hearts (Metsudath David).

6-9 TRUST IN GOD REPEATED

6f. The acknowledgment of his faith which he had proclaimed in verse 2 as a guiding principle of his life he now addresses to his soul to fortify it in a testing time.

7. *shall not be moved.* The omission of *greatly* in this repetition of verse 3 is significant. Now that a trial of his faith has come upon him his self-confidence has grown stronger (Daath Sofrim).

8. *upon God.* The issue rests with Him.

glory. His regal dignity.

9. *ye people.* The words may be addressed to David's adherents (see 2 Sam. xvii. 2), whose faith was not as firm as his and who may have been wavering (Daath Sofrim). Alternatively, the verse is an exhortation to

Israel in general to trust in God and never give up hope of redemption (Kimchi).

10-13 GROUNDS FOR CONFIDENCE

10. The translation fails to reproduce the important introductory *ach*: 'nothing but vanity are men.'

men of low degree...high degree. The Hebrew is the same as in xlix. 3, *both low and high* (see note); but here the meaning is that all types of men, even those who figure in life, are worthless compared to God.

vanity. Something unsubstantial; lit. 'breath,' or a 'vapour.'

a lie. The wealth and influence which distinguished them from the lower class were without stability and could easily be swept away.

if they be laid in the balances. Hebrew 'in the balances to go up,' i.e. on the scales they register no weight and the pan ascends.

together lighter than vanity. The sense being that all men together are worth less than

11   אַל־תִּבְטְחוּ בְעֹשֶׁק

וּבְגָזֵל אַל־תֶּהְבָּלוּ

חַיִל ׀ כִּי־יָנוּב אַל־תָּשִׁיתוּ לֵב:

12 אַחַת ׀ דִּבֶּר אֱלֹהִים

שְׁתַּיִם־זוּ שָׁמָעְתִּי

כִּי עֹז לֵאלֹהִים:

13 וּלְךָ־אֲדֹנָי חָסֶד

כִּי־אַתָּה תְשַׁלֵּם לְאִישׁ כְּמַעֲשֵׂהוּ:

11 Trust not in oppression,
    And put not vain hope in robbery;
    If riches increase, set not your
      heart thereon.

12 God hath spoken once,
    Twice have I heard this:
    That strength belongeth unto
      God;

13 Also unto Thee, O Lord, be-
      longeth mercy;
    For Thou renderest to every man
      according to his work.

---

nothingness (Ibn Ezra, Kimchi). Alternatively, 'they are equal *to* vanity' (Rashi).

11. *trust not in oppression.* As the means of gaining an unworthy end. Instead, *trust in Him at all times* (verse 9). If your aims are worthy and have His sanction, He may be depended upon to bring them to fruition.

put not vain hope in robbery. Better, 'become not vain in robbery,' as in Job xxvii. 12. Ill-gotten gains will yield no permanent advantage.

set not your heart thereon. Therefore if you see ill-gotten *riches increase* in the possession of evil men, do not be envious of such fortune and be not tempted to imitate their example (Metsudath David).

12. *once, twice.* An idiom signifying repetition (Kimchi).

have I heard this. Together with all Israel. The doctrine he proclaims is not his own invention, but the teaching of God which has been communicated repeatedly through the prophets (Kimchi).

strength belongeth unto God. Consequently His Will always decides the outcome, and the resources of men are powerless to resist it. This is the foundation upon which rests confidence in Him (Kimchi). The fate which has overtaken his adversaries demonstrated how well-grounded such trust is.

13. *mercy.* To 'render to every man according to his work' is a mark of love, as, through his punishment, he will understand the nature of the offense and this will lead him to repentance (Metsudath David). The Hebrew may be rendered '*like* his work.' God's punishment is not strictly measure for measure but only part of what one fully deserves (Rashi).

Thou renderest ... work. The idea of this clause is found in Prov. xxiv. 12.

63

1 A Psalm of David, when he was
   in the wilderness of Judah.

2 O God, Thou art my God, earnestly will I seek Thee;
   My soul thirsteth for Thee, my
   flesh longeth for Thee,
   In a dry and weary land, where no
   water is.

3 So have I looked for Thee in the
   sanctuary,
   To see Thy power and Thy glory.

4 For Thy lovingkindness is better
   than life;
   My lips shall praise Thee.

5 So will I bless Thee as long as I
   live;
   In Thy name will I lift up my
   hands.

6 My soul is satisfied as with
   marrow and fatness;

סג

מִזְמוֹר לְדָוִד בִּהְיוֹתוֹ
בְּמִדְבַּר יְהוּדָה:
2 אֱלֹהִים אֵלִי אַתָּה אֲשַׁחֲרֶךָ
צָמְאָה לְךָ נַפְשִׁי כָּמַהּ לְךָ בְשָׂרִי
בְּאֶרֶץ צִיָּה וְעָיֵף בְּלִי־מָיִם:
3 כֵּן בַּקֹּדֶשׁ חֲזִיתִךָ
לִרְאוֹת עֻזְּךָ וּכְבוֹדֶךָ:
4 כִּי־טוֹב חַסְדְּךָ מֵחַיִּים
שְׂפָתַי יְשַׁבְּחוּנְךָ:
5 כֵּן אֲבָרֶכְךָ בְחַיָּי
בְּשִׁמְךָ אֶשָּׂא כַפָּי:
6 כְּמוֹ חֵלֶב וָדֶשֶׁן תִּשְׂבַּע נַפְשִׁי

AN EXILE'S LONGING

THE superscripture explicitly reveals this Psalm's origin as a disturbed period of David's career, his flight from Saul into the wilderness. In this Psalm David tells of the longing for the Sanctuary which consumed him, and the consolation he found in meditation upon God during his banishment from home.

1. *in the wilderness of Judah.* See 1 Sam. xvii. 5.

2-5 YEARNING FOR THE SANCTUARY

2. *soul … flesh.* Cf. xlii 2f. The whole of him thirsts for the intimate communion which he had experienced in the Sanctuary.

in a dry and weary land. Descriptive of the wilderness where thirst is more readily created than satisfied. As the traveller there pines for water, so the Psalmist yearns for the spiritual refreshment which only God can provide.

3. *so have I looked for Thee.* Better, 'so have I contemplated Thee.' He recalls his feelings in the past when he was able to gratify them. How much more intense have they grown in his present circumstances when he is ex- cluded from the holy place!

4. He gives another reason to be returned. Having so often known the reality of His loving kindness, the desire to offer Him praises has become the real purpose of his life, more precious than existence. But he longs to offer them not in a wilderness, but in the Holy Temple (cf. Metsudath David).

5. *bless Thee.* Acknowledging God's love.

lift up my hands. See on xxviii. 2.

6-8 REMEMBRANCE OF PAST MERCIES

6. *my soul is satisfied.* As the hunger of the body can be satisfied with choice ani- mal food, the soul of the Psalmist even in the barren wilderness is fed by Divine grace. For this spiritual meal he is impelled, as in the past, to utter words of thanksgiving (Hirsch).

And my mouth doth praise Thee
　with joyful lips;

7 When I remember Thee upon my
　　couch,
　And meditate on Thee in the
　　night-watches.

8 For Thou hast been my help,
　And in the shadow of Thy wings
　　do I rejoice.

9 My soul cleaveth unto Thee;
　Thy right hand holdeth me fast.

10 But those that seek my soul, to
　　　destroy it,
　Shall go into the nethermost
　　parts of the earth.

11 They shall be hurled to the power
　　of the sword;
　They shall be a portion for foxes.

12 But the king shall rejoice in God;
　Every one that sweareth by Him
　　shall glory;
　For the mouth of them that speak
　　lies shall be stopped.

וּשְׂפָתֵי רְנָנוֹת יְהַלֶּל־פִּי:

7 אִם־זְכַרְתִּיךָ עַל־יְצוּעָי
בְּאַשְׁמֻרוֹת אֶהְגֶּה־בָּךְ:

8 כִּי־הָיִיתָ עֶזְרָתָה לִּי
וּבְצֵל כְּנָפֶיךָ אֲרַנֵּן:

9 דָּבְקָה נַפְשִׁי אַחֲרֶיךָ
בִּי תָּמְכָה יְמִינֶךָ:

10 וְהֵמָּה לְשׁוֹאָה יְבַקְשׁוּ נַפְשִׁי
יָבֹאוּ בְּתַחְתִּיּוֹת הָאָרֶץ:

11 יַגִּירֻהוּ עַל־יְדֵי־חָרֶב
מְנָת שֻׁעָלִים יִהְיוּ:

12 וְהַמֶּלֶךְ יִשְׂמַח בֵּאלֹהִים
יִתְהַלֵּל כָּל־הַנִּשְׁבָּע בּוֹ
כִּי יִסָּכֵר פִּי דוֹבְרֵי־שָׁקֶר:

7.　*upon my couch.* In the stillness of the
night when thoughts crowd into the mind
(Kimchi).

night-watches. Of which there were three
according to the Israelite division of the night
(cf. Tal. Ber. 3a) (Kimchi).

8.　*shadow of Thy wings.* See on lvii. 2.

　　9-12　His fate and his persecutors'

9.　*my soul cleaveth unto Thee.* The term
cleaving to God is common in Deut., e.g. iv.
4, x. 20, xxx. 20.

Thy right hand holdeth me fast. God's response to man's cleaving to Him.

10.　No malice enters into his thoughts of
what is to happen to his opponents. As
God's right hand upholds the righteous, His
justice demands that there should be dis-
crimination against the wicked who will
accordingly feel the destructive power of
that same right hand.

nethermost parts of the earth. The location of
Sheol.

11.　*the power of the sword.* The weapon
which they intended to use against the innocent will be the implement of justice, and by
it they will be destroyed.

a portion for foxes. Or 'jackals,' which will
devour their unburied bodies. Not to receive
honourable burial is a thought of horror.

12.　*the king.* Alluding to himself, though
Saul still reigned, since he was already
anointed by the prophet (Rashi).

that sweareth by Him. Connected with serving God (Deut. vi. 13, x. 20). Those worthy of
taking an oath in His name; i.e. they who are
honest and God fearing, will also rejoice in
God (Kimchi).

that speak lies. Deceiving men by oaths
sworn in the name of God which they falsify
in act (Kimchi). They will be reduced to
silence in Sheol.

64   סד

1 For the Leader. A Psalm **of** David.

2 Hear my voice, O God, in my complaint;
Preserve my life from the terror of the enemy.

3 Hide me from the council of evil-doers;
From the tumult of the workers of iniquity;

4 Who have whet their tongue like **a** sword,
And have aimed their arrow, **a** poisoned word;

5 That they may shoot in secret places at the blameless;
Suddenly do they shoot at him, and fear not.

6 They encourage one another in **an** evil matter;
They converse of laying snares secretly;
They ask, who would see them.

לַמְנַצֵּחַ מִזְמוֹר לְדָוִד׃

2 שְׁמַע־אֱלֹהִים קוֹלִי בְשִׂיחִי
מִפַּחַד אוֹיֵב תִּצֹּר חַיָּי׃

3 תַּסְתִּירֵנִי מִסּוֹד מְרֵעִים
מֵרִגְשַׁת פֹּעֲלֵי אָוֶן׃

4 אֲשֶׁר שָׁנְנוּ כַחֶרֶב לְשׁוֹנָם
דָּרְכוּ חִצָּם דָּבָר מָר׃

5 לִירֹת בַּמִּסְתָּרִים תָּם
פִּתְאֹם יֹרֻהוּ וְלֹא יִירָאוּ׃

6 יְחַזְּקוּ־לָמוֹ דָּבָר רָע
יְסַפְּרוּ לִטְמוֹן מוֹקְשִׁים
אָמְרוּ מִי יִרְאֶה־לָּמוֹ׃

DIVINE JUDGMENT

IN his sufferings at the hands of unscrupulous men, David, after enumerating their evil deeds, utters his conviction that God will judge and condemn them. The language resembles that of earlier Psalms which tell of Saul's persecution.

2-7 PRAYER FOR PROTECTION

2. *preserve*. This verb, as well as *hide* in verse 3, is in the imperfect mood, which may be rendered by the imperative particularly in a prayer. The meaning is 'raise me high above any fear of the enemy; preserve my life and my spiritual vigour in the midst of all the dangers that surround me' (Hirsch).

terror of the enemy. i.e. Saul, who was seeking his life (Kimchi).

3. *council ... tumult*. Secret plotting and open assault (Malbim, Hirsch). The verbs connected with these nouns occur in ii. 1f.

4. *tongue like a sword*. Cf. lv. 22, lvii. 5 and for *aimed their arrow*, lviii. 8.

a poisoned word. lit. 'a bitter word, or matter.' The phrase *evil matter* in verse 6 suggests the meaning here to be 'a serious matter,' a deadly scheme.

5. *in secret places*. Cf. x. 8, xvii. 12.

fear not. Neither God nor man.

6. *encourage*. lit. 'strengthen.'

who would see them. God will take no notice of their proceedings (x. 11) (Kimchi).

7. *search out*. Better, 'devise'; and con-

7 They search out iniquities, they
 have accomplished a diligent
 search;
 Even in the inward thought of
 every one, and the deep heart.

8 But God doth shoot at them with
 an arrow suddenly;
 Thence are their wounds.

9 So they make their own tongue a
 stumbling unto themselves;
 All that see them shake the head.

10 And all men fear;
 And they declare the work of
 God,
 And understand His doing.

11 The righteous shall be glad in the
 LORD, and shall take refuge in
 Him;
 And all the upright in heart shall
 glory.

יַחְפְּשׂוּ עוֹלֹת 7
תַּמְנוּ חֵפֶשׂ מְחֻפָּשׂ
וְקֶרֶב אִישׁ וְלֵב עָמֹק:
וַיֹּרֵם אֱלֹהִים חֵץ 8
פִּתְאוֹם הָיוּ מַכּוֹתָם:
וַיַּכְשִׁילוּהוּ עָלֵימוֹ לְשׁוֹנָם 9
יִתְנֹדְדוּ כָּל־רֹאֵה בָם:
וַיִּירְאוּ כָּל־אָדָם 10
וַיַּגִּידוּ פֹּעַל אֱלֹהִים
וּמַעֲשֵׂהוּ הִשְׂכִּילוּ:
יִשְׂמַח צַדִּיק בַּיהוָה וְחָסָה בוֹ 11
וְיִתְהַלְלוּ כָּל־יִשְׁרֵי־לֵב:

tinue: 'we have perfected (they say) a carefully planned scheme; it has been thought out
so profoundly that no man can improve upon
it' (Kimchi).

8-11 GOD WILL THWART THE SCHEMERS

8. The translation follows the M.T. ac-
cents. The sentence could be punctuated
differently, 'but God shall shoot at them
with an arrow; suddenly shall they be
wounded'; and Kimchi upholds the combination of both renderings by connecting the
word 'suddenly' to both clauses. He also
remarks that the verbs are prophetic perfect
as is usual in this kind of Psalm, and that the
verse connotes that what the schemers intended to do to their victim (cf. verse 5),
God will do to them.

9. *a stumbling unto themselves*. They, not
he, will be ruined by their mischievous talk.

shake the head. Scornfully (see on xxii. 8).

10. A lesson of universal import would be
learnt from the outcome of the episode, that
in the end righteousness triumphs because
there is a God Who judges the world.

and all men fear. Possibly meant to be a contrast to *and fear not* (verse 5). When there is
no fear of God in men's hearts, they lack
moral restraint, behave violently, and the
innocent suffer. Now, the Psalmist hopes, all
mankind will be controlled by such *fear*, and
as a consequence unrighteous conduct will
be avoided.

declare the work of God. Confess that His
will decides human issues, and accordingly
act so as to have His approval.

11. *shall be glad*. Enjoying security.

shall glory. In the victory of right over wrong
(lxiii. 12).

65

סה

1 For the Leader. A Psalm. A Song of David.

2 Praise waiteth for Thee, O God, in Zion;
And unto Thee the vow is performed.

3 O Thou that hearest prayer,
Unto Thee doth all flesh come.

4 The tale of iniquities is too heavy for me;
As for our transgressions, Thou wilt pardon them.

5 Happy is the man whom Thou choosest, and bringest near,
That he may dwell in Thy courts;

לַמְנַצֵּחַ מִזְמוֹר לְדָוִד שִׁיר׃

2 לְךָ דֻמִיָּה תְהִלָּה אֱלֹהִים בְּצִיּוֹן
וּלְךָ יְשֻׁלַּם־נֶדֶר׃

3 שֹׁמֵעַ תְּפִלָּה
עָדֶיךָ כָּל־בָּשָׂר יָבֹאוּ׃

4 דִּבְרֵי עֲוֹנֹת גָּבְרוּ מֶנִּי
פְּשָׁעֵינוּ אַתָּה תְכַפְּרֵם׃

5 אַשְׁרֵי ׀ תִּבְחַר וּתְקָרֵב יִשְׁכֹּן חֲצֵרֶיךָ

A HARVEST HYMN

A SONG of praise to God for the prospect of an abundant harvest is the subject of the Psalm. It may also be a song of thanks for rains which came after a drought. It was common for the people to bring offerings which had been promised during the dry weather (see verse 2) in the hope that God would send rain. The Psalmist alludes to a particular incident when the nation was delivered from disaster. This may refer to the three year famine that took place during David's reign (2 Sam. xxi. 1). Ibn Ezra suggests that it was not composed by David but by a chorister for the occasion of the building of Solomon's Temple.

2-5 PRAISE TO GOD IN THE TEMPLE

2. *praise waiteth for Thee.* Cf. xxxvii. 7. Praise waits for God in Zion where the people gather to pay homage and bring sacrifices (Ibn Ezra). Rashi renders 'silence is your praise, O God,' meaning that since any attempt to expand upon God's virtues is futile, since these are infinite, to do so is considered an affront to His unique totality and completeness.

vow. Perhaps to be understood collectively as 'vows,' promises made during the time of stress.

3. *Thou that hearest prayer.* Salvation in the form of rains (Malbim).

doth all flesh come. More lit. 'shall all flesh come.' The Psalmist believes that the moral of what had happened would have widespread acceptance. God being acknowledged as a Hearer of prayer, the whole of mankind will eagerly look to Him. The picture of Zion as the rallying point of humanity and the Temple as a house of prayer for all is found in Isa. ii. 2ff., lvi. 7, lxvi. 23; 1 Kings viii. 41ff. (cf. Kimchi).

4. *tale of iniquities.* Sin creates a barrier between man and God (Isa. lix. 2). The Psalmist, on his own and on the people's behalf (note '*our* transgressions'), therefore, first makes confession of sin and prays for pardon.

5. *the man whom Thou choosest.* Those individuals who, in each generation, God has singled out to be the leaders of His people.

dwell to Thy courts. If the author was a chorister (see introduction), this is a direct reference to the Holy Temple. If David composed the Psalm, he is alluding to places of worship (cf. Daath Sofrim).

the goodness of Thy house. The spiritual

May we be satisfied with the goodness of Thy house,
The holy place of Thy temple!

6 With wondrous works dost Thou
   answer us in righteousness,
   O God of our salvation;
   Thou the confidence of all the
   ends of the earth,
   And of the far distant seas;

7 Who by Thy strength settest fast
   the mountains,
   Who art girded about with might;

8 Who stillest the roaring of the
   seas, the roaring of their waves,
   And the tumult of the peoples;

9 So that they that dwell in the
   uttermost parts stand in awe of
   Thy signs;
   Thou makest the outgoings of the
   morning and evening to rejoice.

10 Thou hast remembered the earth,
   and watered her, greatly enrich
   ing her,

נִשְׂבְּעָה בְּטוּב בֵּיתֶךָ קְדֹשׁ הֵיכָלֶךָ:

6 נוֹרָאוֹת ׀ בְּצֶדֶק תַּעֲנֵנוּ אֱלֹהֵי יִשְׁעֵנוּ
מִבְטָח כָּל־קַצְוֵי־אֶרֶץ
וְיָם רְחֹקִים:

7 מֵכִין הָרִים בְּכֹחוֹ
נֶאְזָר בִּגְבוּרָה:

8 מַשְׁבִּיחַ ׀ שְׁאוֹן יַמִּים
שְׁאוֹן גַּלֵּיהֶם וַהֲמוֹן לְאֻמִּים:

9 וַיִּירְאוּ ׀ יֹשְׁבֵי קְצָוֹת מֵאוֹתֹתֶיךָ
מוֹצָאֵי בֹקֶר וָעֶרֶב תַּרְנִין:

10 פָּקַדְתָּ הָאָרֶץ ׀ וַתְּשֹׁקְקֶהָ
רַבַּת תַּעְשְׁרֶנָּה

refreshment which the Sanctuary offered (Ibn
Ezra).

6-9   GOD'S AWE-INSPIRING DEEDS

6. *wondrous works*. Rather, 'works arous-
ing awe,' alluding to the discomfiture of the
hostile enemy (Rashi).

in righteousness. A nation's salvation is not
due to favouritism by God but to repentance
for sins and a return to His ways (Ibn Ezra).

confidence. From being the God of *our salvation*, He will become the trust of all peoples.

7. *mountains*. Confidence in God as the
Vindicator of justice is based upon His infinite might as demonstrated by His creation of
the universe. Mountains typify solid matter
which he fashioned according to His will (cf.
Hirsch).

girded about with might. Cf. xciii. 1.

8. *seas*. Denoting the other part of the universe which is likewise under His control.

tumult of the peoples. Or 'multitude of nations.' He is Master of the physical world, but
also of its inhabitants (cf. Ibn Ezra).

9. *Thy signs*. Proofs of Divine power.

outgoings of the morning and evening. The
regular rising and setting of the sun fosters a
sense of security and brings mankind to sing
joyfully on these occasions (Metsudath
David).

10-14   THANKSGIVING FOR THE HARVEST

All that has gone before in the Psalm is a
prelude to its real theme which is now stated.

10. *remembered*. lit. 'visited,' used of God's
intervention for a benign purpose (cf. Gen.
xxi. 1; Exod. xiii. 19). Here it refers to His
sending the rains in their season and so assuring an abundant harvest.

river of God. Perhaps a poetical phrase for
rain which descends from a heavenly source.

her. The earth, which is fem. in Hebrew (Ibn
Ezra).

With the river of God that is full
    of water;
Thou preparest them corn, for so
    preparest Thou her.

11 Watering her ridges abundantly,
    Settling down the furrows there-
    of,
    Thou makest her soft with
    showers;
    Thou blessest the growth thereof.

12 Thou crownest the year with Thy
    goodness;
    And Thy paths drop fatness.

13 The pastures of the wilderness
    do drop;
    And the hills are girded with joy.

14 The meadows are clothed with
    flocks;
    The valleys also are covered over
    with corn;
    They shout for joy, yea, they
    sing.

פֶּלֶג אֱלֹהִים מָלֵא מָיִם
תָּכִין דְּגָנָם כִּי־כֵן תְּכִינֶהָ׃

11 תְּלָמֶיהָ רַוֵּה נַחֵת גְּדוּדֶהָ
בִּרְבִיבִים תְּמֹגְגֶנָּה
צִמְחָהּ תְּבָרֵךְ׃

12 עִטַּרְתָּ שְׁנַת טוֹבָתֶךָ
וּמַעְגָּלֶיךָ יִרְעֲפוּן דָּשֶׁן׃

13 יִרְעֲפוּ נְאוֹת מִדְבָּר
וְגִיל גְּבָעוֹת תַּחְגֹּרְנָה׃

14 לָבְשׁוּ כָרִים הַצֹּאן
וַעֲמָקִים יַעַטְפוּ־בָר
יִתְרוֹעֲעוּ אַף־יָשִׁירוּ׃

11. The verse graphically describes the effect which the *former rain* of late autumn and winter (Deut. xi. 14) has upon the soil.

ridges. The soil had been ploughed up and the seed scattered; but men's labour needs the heaven-sent rain if a bountiful harvest is to ensue.

furrows. The deep furrows between the ridges caused by the plough. They need to be secure so that the rain flows along and thoroughly moistens the seed.

12. *Thou crownest.* Better, 'Thou hast crowned,' with beautiful crops (Metsudath David).

Thy paths drop fatness. A bold image of God passing over the land and sprinkling blessed rain which ensured a rich harvest.

13. *wilderness.* Hebrew *midbar* does not always denote barren soil, but may signify open tracts of country as distinct from cultivated land, to which cattle are driven for pasture. Here, too, the effects of the rains are noticeable (Malbim).

do drop. viz. with *fatness.*

hills. With vines and trees growing on their slopes.

14. *clothed with flocks.* They are so numerous that their wool appears to form a garment over the meadows.

they shout for joy. Cf. xcvi. 12.

66

סו

1 For the Leader. A Song, a
  Psalm.
  Shout unto God, all the earth;

2 Sing praises unto the glory of His
  name;
  Make His praise glorious.

3 Say unto God: 'How tremendous
  is Thy work!
  Through the greatness of Thy
  power shall Thine enemies
  dwindle away before Thee.

4 All the earth shall worship Thee,
  And shall sing praises unto Thee;
  They shall sing praises to Thy
  name.'   Selah

5 Come, and see the works of God;
  He is terrible in His doing toward
  the children of men.

6 He turned the sea into dry land;
  They went through the river on
  foot;
  There let us rejoice in Him!

לַמְנַצֵּחַ שִׁיר מִזְמוֹר
הָרִיעוּ לֵאלֹהִים כָּל־הָאָרֶץ:
2 זַמְּרוּ כְבוֹד־שְׁמוֹ
שִׂימוּ כָבוֹד תְּהִלָּתוֹ:
3 אִמְרוּ לֵאלֹהִים מַה־נּוֹרָא מַעֲשֶׂיךָ
בְּרֹב עֻזְּךָ יְכַחֲשׁוּ־לְךָ אֹיְבֶיךָ:
4 כָּל־הָאָרֶץ ׀ יִשְׁתַּחֲווּ לְךָ וִיזַמְּרוּ־לָךְ
יְזַמְּרוּ שִׁמְךָ סֶלָה:
5 לְכוּ וּרְאוּ מִפְעֲלוֹת אֱלֹהִים
נוֹרָא עֲלִילָה עַל־בְּנֵי אָדָם:
6 הָפַךְ יָם ׀ לְיַבָּשָׁה
בַּנָּהָר יַעַבְרוּ בְרָגֶל
שָׁם נִשְׂמְחָה־בּוֹ:

SONG OF DELIVERANCE

A PAEAN for a safe ending to a national crisis rings through this Psalm. It lacks the data which make it possible to determine the occasion with any degree of certainty. Malbim maintains that it was written by King Mannasseh, son of King Hezekiah, who was captured by the Assyrians and was sent to Babylon. He entreated God and his prayers were answered. He returned to Jerusalem where he offered sacrifices in thanks for his salvation. Meiri suggests that the Psalm was originally composed at the time of the exodus from Egypt and was later adapted by David. A peculiarity of the Psalm is the use of the plural up to the end of verse 12 and the subsequent change to the singular.

1-4 CALL TO MANKIND TO PRAISE GOD

1. *shout unto God.* More fully in xlvii. 1, *shout unto God with the voice of triumph.*

all the earth. The kingdom of God will be acknowledged even by other nations who will perceive the wonders that He wrought for Israel (Kimchi).

2. *sing praises.* More lit. 'celebrate in song the glory of His name,' the revelation of His glorious Being in recent events.

make His praise glorious. Proclaim His praise in terms of glory.

3. *tremendous.* Awe-inspiring (see lxv. 6).

dwindle away. Better, 'because of the greatness of Thy power thine enemies feign [homage] to Thee' (Hirsch).

4. *all the earth shall worship Thee.* Cf. Hezekiah's prayer (Isa. xxxvii. 20).

5-7 GOD'S MIGHTY DEEDS

5. *terrible.* Exciting awe.

toward. lit. 'over,' denoting His superior might as compared with human strength.

6. *turned the sea into dry land.* At the exodus from Egypt (see introduction).

the river on foot. The crossing of the Jordan (Targum, Kimchi).

7 Who ruleth by His might for ever;
His eyes keep watch upon the
nations;
Let not the rebellious exalt themselves.   Selah

8 Bless our God, ye peoples,
And make the voice of His praise
to be heard;

9 Who hath set our soul in life,
And suffered not our foot to be
moved.

10 For Thou, O God, hast tried us;
Thou hast refined us, as silver is
refined.

11 Thou didst bring us into the
hold;
Thou didst lay constraint upon
our loins.

12 Thou hast caused men to ride
over our heads;
We went through fire and
through water;
But Thou didst bring us out unto
abundance.

7 מָשֵׁל בִּגְבוּרָתוֹ ׀ עוֹלָם
עֵינָיו בַּגּוֹיִם תִּצְפֶּינָה
הַסּוֹרְרִים ׀ אַל־יָרוּמוּ לָמוֹ סֶלָה׃

8 בָּרְכוּ עַמִּים ׀ אֱלֹהֵינוּ
וְהַשְׁמִיעוּ קוֹל תְּהִלָּתוֹ׃

9 הַשָּׂם נַפְשֵׁנוּ בַּחַיִּים
וְלֹא־נָתַן לַמּוֹט רַגְלֵנוּ׃

10 כִּי־בְחַנְתָּנוּ אֱלֹהִים
צְרַפְתָּנוּ כִּצְרָף־כָּסֶף׃

11 הֲבֵאתָנוּ בַמְּצוּדָה
שַׂמְתָּ מוּעָקָה בְמָתְנֵינוּ׃

12 הִרְכַּבְתָּ אֱנוֹשׁ לְרֹאשֵׁנוּ
בָּאנוּ־בָאֵשׁ וּבַמַּיִם
וַתּוֹצִיאֵנוּ לָרְוָיָה׃

v. 7. ירומו ק׳

there let us rejoice in Him! As the Israelites
did on those occasions, so should mankind
continue to look back upon those memorable
events and rejoice in them, because they are
the pattern of God's working in the destinies
of people.

7. *for ever.* God Who manifested His might
in those far-off days still rules and will continue to rule until the end of time.

upon the nations. In the past God had dealt
leniently with the nations but in the future He
will deal strictly with them and punish them
according to their deeds (Kimchi).

rebellious. They had suffered no setbacks
and consequently defied God and made Israel an object of their aggression. Cf. what
was said of Sannecherib: *Yea, thou hast lifted
up thine eyes on high, even against the Holy
One of Israel* (Isa. xxxvii. 23).

8-12 THANKSGIVING FOR DELIVERANCE

8. *ye peoples.* Conscious of Israel's mission to the world, the Psalmist can call upon

the nations to acknowledge God for the miraculous ways with which He has preserved
His people (Rashi, Kimchi).

9. *to be moved.* To stumble and fall before
the enemy (Metsudath David).

10. *tried us.* As precious metal is tested and
purified in the refiner's crucible, Israel was
made to pass through the fires of suffering,
and issued from the ordeal cleansed through
repentance of the dross (Rashi).

11. *the hold.* i.e. cage. They were isolated
from the rest of the world leaving them open
to attack yet without protection (Hirsch).

lay constraint. A weight of trouble, which
well-nigh crushed them, was imposed upon
the nation.

12. *men.* Hebrew *enosh* (see on viii. 5).

ride over our heads. The lowest level of
people were given the right to control Israel's
destiny (Hirsch).

through fire and through water. Symbol of
terrible suffering.

13 I will come into Thy house with
    burnt-offerings,
  I will perform unto Thee my
    vows,

14 Which my lips have uttered,
  And my mouth hath spoken,
    when I was in distress.

15 I will offer unto Thee burnt-
    offerings of fatlings,
  With the sweet smoke of rams;
  I will offer bullocks with goats.
               Selah

16 Come, and hearken, all ye that
    fear God,
  And I will declare what He hath
    done for my soul.

17 I cried unto Him with my mouth,
  And He was extolled with my
    tongue.

18 If I had regarded iniquity in my
    heart,
  The Lord would not hear;

19 But verily God hath heard;
  He hath attended to the voice of
    my prayer.

20 Blessed be God,
  Who hath not turned away my
    prayer, nor His mercy from
    me.

אָב֣וֹא בֵיתְךָ֣ בְעוֹל֑וֹת 13
אֲשַׁלֵּ֖ם לְךָ֣ נְדָרָֽי׃
אֲשֶׁר־פָּצ֥וּ שְׂפָתָ֑י 14
וְדִבֶּר־פִּ֝֗י בַּצַּר־לִֽי׃
עֹ֥לוֹת מֵיחִ֣ים אַעֲלֶה־לָּךְ֮ 15
עִם־קְטֹ֪רֶת אֵ֫ילִ֥ים
אֶעֱשֶׂ֣ה בָקָ֣ר עִם־עַתּוּדִ֣ים סֶֽלָה׃
לְכֽוּ־שִׁמְע֣וּ וַ֭אֲסַפְּרָה 16
כָּל־יִרְאֵ֣י אֱלֹהִ֑ים
אֲשֶׁ֖ר עָשָׂ֣ה לְנַפְשִֽׁי׃
אֵלָ֥יו פִּֽי־קָרָ֑אתִי 17
וְ֝רוֹמַ֗ם תַּ֣חַת לְשׁוֹנִֽי׃
אָ֭וֶן אִם־רָאִ֣יתִי בְלִבִּ֑י 18
לֹ֖א יִשְׁמַ֣ע ׀ אֲדֹנָֽי׃
אָ֭כֵן שָׁמַ֣ע אֱלֹהִ֑ים 19
הִ֝קְשִׁ֗יב בְּק֣וֹל תְּפִלָּתִֽי׃
בָּר֥וּךְ אֱלֹהִ֑ים 20
אֲשֶׁ֥ר לֹֽא־הֵסִ֘יר תְּפִלָּתִ֥י
וְ֝חַסְדּ֗וֹ מֵאִתִּֽי׃

unto abundance. As distinct from the privations which had been endured.

13-15 THE KING DISCHARGES HIS VOWS

13. *I will come into Thy house.* The
Psalmist speaks as the head of the nation who
acts on its behalf (cf. Ibn Ezra).

my vows. Cf. lxv. 2.

14. *which my lips have uttered.* lit.
'wherewith my lips opened' to utter the words
of promise.

16-20 HIS TESTIMONY TO GOD'S AID

16. *all ye that fear God.* A reference to the
proselytes (Rashi) who have been led to
worship Him by appreciating His words
(Daath Sofrim).

what He hath done for my soul. For my life
when it was in peril.

17. *and He was extolled* …. More lit. 'and
high praise was under my tongue.' Prayer
was mingled with praise because He would
answer immediately (Hirsch).

18. *iniquity in my heart.* He made every
effort to be innocent of any iniquity, lest God
not hear his prayer.

20. *blessed be God.* I would understand if
God would not answer my prayer, since I
am undeserving. However, He overlooked
my shortcomings and showed me much
mercy by treating me as if I were righteous
(Malbim).

67

1 For the Leader; with string-music. A Psalm, a Song.

2 God be gracious unto us, and bless us;
May He cause His face to shine toward us;   Selah

3 That Thy way may be known upon earth,
Thy salvation among all nations.

4 Let the peoples give thanks unto Thee, O God;
Let the peoples give thanks unto Thee, all of them.

סז

לַמְנַצֵּחַ בִּנְגִינֹת
מִזְמוֹר שִׁיר׃
אֱלֹהִים יְחָנֵּנוּ וִיבָרְכֵנוּ 2
יָאֵר פָּנָיו אִתָּנוּ סֶלָה׃
לָדַעַת בָּאָרֶץ דַּרְכֶּךָ 3
בְּכָל־גּוֹיִם יְשׁוּעָתֶךָ׃
יוֹדוּךָ עַמִּים ׀ אֱלֹהִים 4
יוֹדוּךָ עַמִּים כֻּלָּם׃

UNIVERSAL PRAISE OF GOD

IT is possible to connect this Psalm with LXV as a hymn of thanksgiving for an abundant harvest which followed the long famine during David's reign. But the mention of the earth's produce, if it is to be so understood, is limited to a phrase in verse 7. The main theme is the summons to all the peoples of the earth to pay homage to God. In the Jewish liturgy the Psalm is appointed by many congregations for recital at the termination of the Sabbath (P.B., p. 211). It is also customary to recite this Psalm during the forty nine days between Passover and Shavuoth after the counting of the Omer. Meiri suggests that the Psalm was composed with the ingathering of the exiles in mind. People will come to understand God's ways and God's system of justice. They will see God's salvation, will be filled with a sense of happiness and will come to praise and to thank God. The traditional association of the Sabbath's end with this Psalm supports the usually accepted interpretation of verse 7; but another has been proposed which will be noted below.

2-3 RECOGNITION OF GOD
THROUGH ISRAEL

2. The verse is based upon the Priestly Benediction (Num. vi. 24f.). (Rashbam). In place of *shine upon*, the preposition here is *toward*, lit. 'with.'

3. *that Thy way may be known upon earth.* An emphatic formulation of the thought which appeared in the two preceding Psalms. God's gracious dealing with Israel will be the means of turning all peoples towards Him (Kimchi).

4-5 MAY ALL MANKIND
ACKNOWLEDGE HIM

4. *let the peoples give thanks.* In recognition of His mercies to them.

5. *judge.* Rule over them, which means in effect the reign of righteousness in which they will enjoy peace and happiness.

lead the nations. The verb is used of God guiding Israel through the wilderness to the land of promise (lxxviii. 14); the same guidance is at the disposal of all peoples if, like Israel, they accept Him as their God.

67. 5

5 O let the nations be glad and sing
    for joy;
  For Thou wilt judge the peoples
    with equity,
  And lead the nations upon earth.
                    Selah

6 Let the peoples give thanks unto
    Thee, O God;
  Let the peoples give thanks unto
    Thee, all of them.

7 The earth hath yielded her in-
    crease;
  May God, our own God, bless us.

8 May God bless us;
  And let all the ends of the earth
    fear Him.

5 יִשְׂמְחוּ וִירַנְּנוּ לְאֻמִּים
כִּי־תִשְׁפֹּט עַמִּים מִישֹׁר
וּלְאֻמִּים ׀ בָּאָרֶץ תַּנְחֵם סֶלָה:

6 יוֹדוּךָ עַמִּים ׀ אֱלֹהִים
יוֹדוּךָ עַמִּים כֻּלָּם:

7 אֶרֶץ נָתְנָה יְבוּלָהּ
יְבָרְכֵנוּ אֱלֹהִים אֱלֹהֵינוּ:

8 יְבָרְכֵנוּ אֱלֹהִים
וְיִירְאוּ אוֹתוֹ כָּל־אַפְסֵי־אָרֶץ:

6-8   THE EFFECT OF ALLEGIANCE
TO GOD

6.   A repetition of verse 4, but possibly with a change of meaning. If the verse is a refrain, it should more appropriately be connected with the previous section; but the introduction of *Selah* suggests that a new paragraph begins here.

6-8.   Hirsch notes that the Psalm is divided into three sections, divided by the word *Selah*, describing three stages of man's recognition of God. The first relates to the recognition of God by the Jewish people who alone obey His command. The worship of God will then spread to the other nations, and their rulers will submit to the Supreme Authority. In the third and final section the people themselves will render homage to God without the need of an intermediary. In this way, the message of verse 7 can be understood. It does not necessarily mean 'vegetation' but (figuratively) 'product.' That all the nations will come to praise God for His moral governing of the world, is the highest 'product' of the whole life on earth. The development of the earth will have achieved its ultimate purpose. Cf. Psalm lxxxv. 12 'truth springeth out of the earth.' Then we shall reach the goal of our mission among the nations, by preaching that God is served through obedience and not only through 'belief.' For this God shall bless us, and the rest of the world will come to fear Him and obey his will (Hirsch).

68

1 For the Leader. A Psalm of David, a Song.

2 Let God arise, let His enemies be scattered;
And let them that hate Him flee before Him.

3 As smoke is driven away, so drive them away;
As wax melteth before the fire,
So let the wicked perish at the presence of God.

4 But let the righteous be glad, let them exult before God;
Yea, let them rejoice with gladness.

5 Sing unto God, sing praises to His name;
Extol Him that rideth upon the skies, whose name is the LORD;
And exult ye before Him.

סח

לַמְנַצֵּחַ לְדָוִד מִזְמוֹר שִׁיר:

2 יָקוּם אֱלֹהִים יָפוּצוּ אוֹיְבָיו
וְיָנוּסוּ מְשַׂנְאָיו מִפָּנָיו:

3 כְּהִנְדֹּף עָשָׁן תִּנְדֹּף
כְּהִמֵּס דּוֹנַג מִפְּנֵי־אֵשׁ
יֹאבְדוּ רְשָׁעִים מִפְּנֵי אֱלֹהִים:

4 וְצַדִּיקִים יִשְׂמְחוּ
יַעַלְצוּ לִפְנֵי אֱלֹהִים
וְיָשִׂישׂוּ בְשִׂמְחָה:

5 שִׁירוּ לֵאלֹהִים זַמְּרוּ שְׁמוֹ
סֹלּוּ לָרֹכֵב בָּעֲרָבוֹת
בְּיָהּ שְׁמוֹ וְעִלְזוּ לְפָנָיו:

GOD'S VICTORIES

WHILE this Psalm is one of the most magnificent of all (Ibn Ezra) in its forceful sweep of thought and language, the commentators are in disagreement on the events which occasioned it. The Targum and others connect it with the revelation at Sinai or the exodus from Egypt. If we look for an occasion in the lifetime of David, it might allude to the occasions when he triumphed in victories over Aram-Zobah and Aram Damascus, Moab, Edom and Philistia (2 Sam. viii.) (Malbim). It has also been suggested (Kimchi) that it refers to the future downfall of Sennacherib's army in the days of Hezekiah. Meiri contends that, more probably, it is a prophecy relating to the battle of Gog and Magog which will lead to the coming of the Messiah. Whatever the reason for its composition, it takes the form of a triumphant march proclaiming the kingship of God over the earth.

2-7 ADVENT OF GOD AND ITS EFFECTS

2. *let God arise.* An adaptation of Israel's ancient watchword (Num. x. 35).

3. *smoke.* Cf. xxxvii. 20; Hosea xiii. 3.

wax. Cf. xcvii. 5; Micah i. 4.

4. *let the righteous be glad.* Whereas the manifestation of God will bring destruction upon the wicked, to the righteous it will offer cause for rejoicing in the establishment of equity.

5. *extol Him.* So the traditional rendering of the verb (Rashi, Ibn Ezra, Kimchi). An alternative translation is 'cast up a high way for Him,' for which there is a parallel in Isa. xl. 3 'straighten out in the wilderness a highway for our God,' in which God is pictured as a saving warrior riding his chariot through the desert to meet the enemy in battle (Malbim).

rideth upon the skies. This translation follows Targum and most commentators, that *ba'aravoth* denotes the highest of the heavens where God 'sits' astride His throne. Malbim has 'through the deserts,' following R.V. Hirsch suggests that the noun is derived from the Hebrew 'arava' meaning 'barrenness,' and the word allegorically describes

6 A father of the fatherless, and a
  judge of the widows,
  Is God in His holy habitation.

7 God maketh the solitary to dwell
  in a house;
  He bringeth out the prisoners into
  prosperity;
  The rebellious dwell but in a
  parched land.

8 O God, when Thou wentest forth
  before Thy people,
  When Thou didst march through
  the wilderness;   Selah

9 The earth trembled, the heavens
  also dropped at the presence of
  God;
  Even yon Sinai trembled at the
  presence of God, the God of
  Israel.

10 A bounteous rain didst Thou
   pour down, O God;
   When Thine inheritance was
   weary, Thou didst confirm it.

6 אֲבִי יְתוֹמִים וְדַיַּן אַלְמָנוֹת
אֱלֹהִים בִּמְעוֹן קָדְשׁוֹ:
7 אֱלֹהִים ׀ מוֹשִׁיב יְחִידִים ׀ בַּיְתָה
מוֹצִיא אֲסִירִים בַּכּוֹשָׁרוֹת
אַךְ־סוֹרְרִים שָׁכְנוּ צְחִיחָה:
8 אֱלֹהִים בְּצֵאתְךָ לִפְנֵי עַמֶּךָ
בְּצַעְדְּךָ בִישִׁימוֹן סֶלָה:
9 אֶרֶץ רָעָשָׁה ׀ אַף־שָׁמַיִם נָטְפוּ
מִפְּנֵי אֱלֹהִים
זֶה סִינַי מִפְּנֵי אֱלֹהִים אֱלֹהֵי יִשְׂרָאֵל:
10 גֶּשֶׁם נְדָבוֹת תָּנִיף אֱלֹהִים
נַחֲלָתְךָ וְנִלְאָה אַתָּה כוֹנַנְתָּהּ:

the state where man is searching for some meaning that he cannot easily find.

the Lord. Hebrew *Jah*, chosen in allusion to Exod. xv. 2.

6. *fatherless ... widows*. See on x. 14.

His holy habitation. Heaven (Deut. xxvi. 15).

7. The verse may be understood as a reference to the Divine act of matchmaking in which individuals are brought together to become family units. The union's success, however, depends on the couple (see Tal. Sotah 2a, Yalkut); or it can be interpreted as a specific reference to the first time that, as a nation, Israel experienced God, thus forming an introduction to the historical retrospect which follows. In that case the *solitary* are the Israelites in Egypt for whom He secured a *house* in Canaan, and the *rebellious* are the Egyptians whose land was devastated by the plagues.

8-19   THE PAST REVIEWED

8. The exodus from Egypt and conquest of Canaan are the roots from which the tree of Israel's history grew, and provide the beginning of the survey wherein God's dealings with His people are signally revealed. Verses 8f. are adapted from Judges v. 4f.

Thou wentest forth. To guide the people through the trackless wilderness in a pillar of cloud by day and a pillar of fire by night (Exod. xiii. 21) (Targum).

Selah. There God demonstrated that it is His way that for every distress there is deliverance (Rashi).

9. *the earth trembled.* See on xviii. 8.

heavens also dropped. Thunder and lightning were followed by heavy rainstorms (Hirsch) (lxxvii. 18).

Sinai trembled. Cf. Exod. xix. 18.

the God of Israel. It was at Sinai that the covenant between God and Israel was contracted.

10. *a bounteous rain.* Best understood figuratively as the abundance of gifts which were provided for them at the giving of the Law at Sinai (Hirsch). Rashi refers to actual rain in the time of need.

11 Thy flock settled therein;
  Thou didst prepare in Thy good-
    ness for the poor, O God.

12 The Lord giveth the word;
  The women that proclaim the
    tidings are a great host.

13 Kings of armies flee, they flee;
  And she that tarrieth at home
    divideth the spoil.

14 When ye lie among the sheep-
    folds,
  The wings of the dove are
    covered with silver,
  And her pinions with the shim-
    mer of gold.

15 When the Almighty scattereth
    kings therein,
  It snoweth in Zalmon.

16 A mountain of God is the moun-
    tain of Bashan;
  A mountain of peaks is the moun-
    tain of Bashan.

חַיָּתְךָ יָשְׁבוּ־בָהּ 11
תָּכִין בְּטוֹבָתְךָ לֶעָנִי אֱלֹהִים:
אֲדֹנָי יִתֶּן־אֹמֶר 12
הַמְבַשְּׂרוֹת צָבָא רָב:
מַלְכֵי צְבָאוֹת יִדֹּדוּן יִדֹּדוּן 13
וּנְוַת־בַּיִת תְּחַלֵּק שָׁלָל:
אִם־תִּשְׁכְּבוּן בֵּין שְׁפַתַּיִם 14
כַּנְפֵי יוֹנָה נֶחְפָּה בַכֶּסֶף
וְאֶבְרוֹתֶיהָ בִּירַקְרַק חָרוּץ:
בְּפָרֵשׂ שַׁדַּי מְלָכִים בָּהּ 15
תַּשְׁלֵג בְּצַלְמוֹן:
הַר־אֱלֹהִים הַר־בָּשָׁן 16
הַר גַּבְנֻנִּים הַר־בָּשָׁן:

when Thine inheritance was weary. A nation
which was weary from past sufferings had
first to be spiritually revived in preparation
for the acceptance of Torah (Hirsch). Rashi
interprets the phrase to mean that on occasions when the drought afflicted God's land,
God made it firm by sending rain.

11. *flock.* The uncommon Hebrew word
chayyah occurs again in 2 Sam. xxiii. 13,
where it means 'congregation' (Rashi) and
is translated *troop.* In Arabic it means a clan
consisting of persons sharing the same
blood.

poor. A reference to the condition of the
Israelites when they were wandering in the
desert (see Rashi).

12. *the* LORD *giveth the word.* For the subjection of the inhabitants of Canaan, and
victory ensued.

the women that proclaim. An army's triumph
was celebrated by the women in song (Ibn
Ezra) (cf. verse 26; Exod. xv. 20; 1 Sam.
xviii. 6).

13. *kings of armies.* The word for armies is
the same as in the phrase LORD *of hosts.* Their

military prowess is of no avail against His
might.

she ... at home. Whilst its enemies will be
expelled and will flee, the nation of Israel
(the dweller of the land) will divide the spoils
(Rashi).

14. *when ... among the sheepfolds.* Better,
'between borders.' (Malbim) (cf. Judges v.
16) or 'among the vessels' (Metsudoth, Ibn
Ezra). Israel is compared to a dove that is
covered with silver but has golden pinions;
i.e. it seeks only peace, but if attacked while
dwelling within its own borders, it will prove
its strength by striking out at the enemy with
'indestructible wings' (Malbim).

15. *snoweth in Zalmon.* Better, 'with
darkness.' The word *zalmon* does not refer to
a particular place but is associated with darkness (cf. 'tzalmaveth' xxiii. 4). The meaning
here is that the enemy will be overcome with
disaster. Continuing the theme of the previous verse, Malbim explains that the nation of
Israel will merit God's help and be able to
spread its wings over the enemy and bring
their armies under its control by showering
them with 'heavy snow.'

17 Why look ye askance, ye moun-
    tains of peaks,
   At the mountain which God hath
    desired for His abode?
   Yea, the Lord will dwell therein
    for ever.

18 The chariots of God are myriads,
    even thousands upon thou-
    sands;
   The Lord is among them, as in
    Sinai, in holiness.

19 Thou hast ascended on high,
    Thou hast led captivity
    captive;
   Thou hast received gifts among
    men,
   Yea, among the rebellious also,
    that the Lord God might
    dwell there.

20 Blessed be the Lord, day by day
   He beareth our burden,
   Even the God who is our salva-
    tion.   Selah

17 לָמָּה ׀ תְּרַצְּדוּן הָרִים גַּבְנֻנִּים
הָהָר חָמַד אֱלֹהִים לְשִׁבְתּוֹ
אַף־יְהוָה יִשְׁכֹּן לָנֶצַח:
18 רֶכֶב אֱלֹהִים רִבֹּתַיִם
אַלְפֵי שִׁנְאָן
אֲדֹנָי בָם סִינַי בַּקֹּדֶשׁ:
19 עָלִיתָ לַמָּרוֹם ׀ שָׁבִיתָ שֶּׁבִי
לָקַחְתָּ מַתָּנוֹת בָּאָדָם
וְאַף סוֹרְרִים לִשְׁכֹּן ׀ יָהּ אֱלֹהִים:
20 בָּרוּךְ אֲדֹנָי יוֹם ׀ יוֹם יַעֲמָס־לָנוּ
הָאֵל יְשׁוּעָתֵנוּ סֶלָה:

16. The Psalm now tells of the selections of Mount Sinai and Mount Zion in preference to the loftier mountains (Metsudath David).

a mountain of God. The Bashan is known for its lushness and its imposing appearance. Sinai and Zion are compared to it because of their importance (Metsudath David).

a mountain of peaks. The Hebrew *gavnunim* is associated with the root word *gavoah*, tall or high (Rashi).

17. *look ye askance.* The verb occurs only here; its meaning is to eye with envious hostility. For God's choice of Zion cf. cxxxii. 13f. (cf. Rashi).

18. *the chariots of God.* He is imagined as entering His chosen abode with an innumerable retinue.

thousands upon thousands. A thousand twice over; i.e., two thousand (Ibn Ezra). Others render 'thousands of angels' (cf. Targum, Rashi).

as in Sinai, in holiness. Since there is nothing in the Hebrew corresponding to *as in*, the preferable translation is 'Sinai is in the sanctuary'; i.e. now Mount Sinai is no longer to be sought in the wilderness but may be found within the sanctuary which God has caused human hands to erect for Him (Hirsch).

19. A symbolical picture of the climax of the campaign, revealing God in the triumph of His might.

Thou hast ascended on high. The subject may be God who allowed foreign nations to invade Israel by remaining aloof in His heavenly abode (Kimchi). Targum and Rashi see the subject to be Moses who, on behalf of Israel, ascended Mount Sinai to 'capture' the Torah from the hands of the angels.

received gifts among men. According to Kimchi the meaning is, 'You (God) took from men the gifts that had belonged to them, i.e. the land of Judea and its spiritual advantages. According to the interpretation of Targum and Rashi the verse means 'you (Moses) brought the Torah as a gift for humanity.'

rebellious. According to Kimchi the 'rebellious' are the gentile kings who sought to dwell in the sanctuary of the Lord.

21 God is unto us a God of deliverances;
   And unto GOD the Lord belong
   the issues of death.

22 Surely God will smite through
   the head of His enemies,
   The hairy scalp of him that goeth
   about in his guiltiness.

23 The Lord said: 'I will bring back
   from Bashan,
   I will bring them back from the
   depths of the sea;

24 That thy foot may wade through
   blood,
   That the tongue of thy dogs may
   have its portion from thine
   enemies.'

25 They see Thy goings, O God,
   Even the goings of my God, my
   King, in holiness.

26 The singers go before, the
   minstrels follow after,
   In the midst of damsels playing
   upon timbrels:

הָאֵל ׀ לָנוּ אֵל לְמוֹשָׁעוֹת 21
וְלֵיהוִה אֲדֹנָי לַמָּוֶת תּוֹצָאוֹת:
אַךְ־אֱלֹהִים יִמְחַץ רֹאשׁ אֹיְבָיו 22
קָדְקֹד שֵׂעָר מִתְהַלֵּךְ בַּאֲשָׁמָיו:
אָמַר אֲדֹנָי מִבָּשָׁן אָשִׁיב 23
אָשִׁיב מִמְּצֻלוֹת יָם:
לְמַעַן ׀ תִּמְחַץ רַגְלְךָ בְּדָם 24
לְשׁוֹן כְּלָבֶיךָ מֵאֹיְבִים מִנֵּהוּ:
רָאוּ הֲלִיכוֹתֶיךָ אֱלֹהִים 25
הֲלִיכוֹת אֵלִי מַלְכִּי בַקֹּדֶשׁ:
קִדְּמוּ שָׁרִים אַחַר נֹגְנִים 26
בְּתוֹךְ עֲלָמוֹת תּוֹפֵפוֹת:

that the LORD. That is not the Hebrew. Rashi
understands instead 'nevertheless.' The spirit
of God remains with His people even when
they rebel.

20-24 GOD THE DELIVERER

20. The events of the past, just narrated,
teach a lesson for the present and future.

He beareth our burden. lit., 'he carrieth for
us' (cf. the same verb in Isa. xlvi. 3, *that are
borne* by God) (cf. Midrash Rabbah, Shemoth
xxv. 9). Targum translates 'He burdens us,'
meaning He adds to our duties and provides
new challenges.

even the God who is our salvation. Or, more
simply, 'God is our salvation.'

21. *deliverances.* The plural, as in xliv. 5,
indicates many decisive, acts of salvation.

the issues of death. The various methods of
death which God inflicts on our enemies
(Rashi).

22. *the hairy scalp.* Cf. *the long-haired
heads of the enemy* (Deut. xxxii. 42). This

probably describes the bold appearance of
the enemy. He walks haughtily, unperturbed
by his guilt and the presence of a God Who is
watching him (Hirsch).

guiltiness. Defiance of God.

23. *I will bring back.* The enemies from
Bashan and the coasts of the Dead Sea who
escaped from their lands will be brought back
to their countries (Malbim).

24. *wade through blood.* lit. 'split' through
blood. Cf. Judges v. 26. Your feet will wade
through the blood of those slain on the battle-
fields (Rashi).

25-28 PROCESSION TO THE TEMPLE

25. The Psalmist now visualizes events lying in the future when the people will offer
their thanks to God for guiding them safely
out of danger.

they see Thy goings. Israel is fully aware of
the ways in which they have been led (Ibn
Ezra) and of God's dealings with their enemies (Kimchi).

27 'Bless ye God in full assemblies,
   Even the Lord, ye that are from
     the fountain of Israel.'

28 There is Benjamin, the youngest,
   ruling them,
   The princes of Judah their
     council,
   The princes of Zebulun, the
     princes of Naphtali.

29 Thy God hath commanded thy
   strength;
   Be strong, O God, Thou that
     hast wrought for us

30 Out of Thy temple at Jerusalem,
   Whither kings shall bring pre-
     sents unto Thee.

31 Rebuke the wild beast of the
   reeds,
   The multitude of the bulls, with
     the calves of the peoples

27 בְּמַקְהֵלוֹת בָּרְכוּ אֱלֹהִים
אֲדֹנָי מִמְּקוֹר יִשְׂרָאֵל:

28 שָׁם בִּנְיָמִן ׀ צָעִיר רֹדֵם
שָׂרֵי יְהוּדָה רִגְמָתָם
שָׂרֵי זְבֻלוּן שָׂרֵי נַפְתָּלִי:

29 צִוָּה אֱלֹהֶיךָ עֻזֶּךָ
עוּזָּה אֱלֹהִים זוּ פָּעַלְתָּ לָּנוּ:

30 מֵהֵיכָלֶךָ עַל־יְרוּשָׁלִָם
לְךָ יוֹבִילוּ מְלָכִים שָׁי:

31 גְּעַר חַיַּת קָנֶה
עֲדַת אַבִּירִים ׀ בְּעֶגְלֵי עַמִּים

my King. By means of victory He has confirmed His Kingship over Israel.

in holiness. He is the Holy one, His ways are
absolute and inviolate (Hirsch).

26. *damsels playing upon timbrels*. The
Psalmist has in mind the example of Miriam
and other Israelite women who celebrated
the deliverance at the Red Sea (Exod. xv. 20).

27. The verse gives the burden of the
people's song.

full assemblies. The fem. form of the noun
translated *congregations* in xxvi. 12 (see
note).

the … Israel. 'The source of Israel' viz. the
Patriarch Jacob (cf. xxii. 24) (Metsudath
David) from whom are descended those who
bless God for His wondrous ways (Kimchi).

28. Four tribes of different natures figure in
this verse. Benjamin, the youngest, represents the weakest among them. Even they
will have the strength to rule over their enemies. Judah, the strongest, stands for the
spiritual leaders of the nation, whose task it is
to ward off *rigmatham*, the 'stones' (rather
than *council*) that threaten to shatter the life
of the community. Zebulun consisted of trad-
ers and Naphtali had the gift of oratory. All

four types, in the spirit of communal activity
and observance of the law, have contributed
to counteract the disintegrating forces of the
exile (Hirsch).

29-32   APPEAL TO GOD

29. *thy God … thy strength*. Addressed to
Israel who has learnt that the power which
brought victory in the past was derived from
God. Upon that consciousness a prayer for
the future is grounded (Daath Sofrim).

be strong. Disclose that strength again in the
contingencies still to be met (Daath Sofrim).

30. *out of Thy temple*. The words belong to
the preceding verse, as the absence of the full
stop in the translation indicates. From the
abode of His Presence in Jerusalem may He
manifest His wondrous deeds (cf. Malbim).

bring presents. Tribute, in acknowledgment
of submission (cf. lxxvi. 12) (Hirsch).

31. *the wild beast of the reeds*. Rashi
maintains that this refers to (descendants of)
Ishmael who is compared to the wild boar.

*multitude of the bulls, with the calves of the
peoples*. Better, 'amongst the peoples.' The
bulls represent the most powerful nations,
while those with lesser influence and experience are likened to *calves* (Rashi, Hirsch).

Every one submitting himself
  with pieces of silver;
He hath scattered the peoples
  that delight in war!

32 Nobles shall come out of Egypt;
  Ethiopia shall hasten to stretch
  out her hands unto God.

33 Sing unto God, ye kingdoms of
  the earth;
  O sing praises unto the Lord;
                          Selah

34 To Him that rideth upon the
  heavens of heavens, which are
  of old;
  Lo, He uttereth His voice, a
  mighty voice.

35 Ascribe ye strength unto God;
  His majesty is over Israel,
  And His strength is in the skies.

36 Awful is God out of thy holy
  places;
  The God of Israel, He giveth
  strength and power unto the
  people;
  Blessed be God.

מְתְרַפֵּס בְּרַצֵּי־כָסֶף
בִּזַּר עַמִּים קְרָבוֹת יֶחְפָּצוּ:
32 יֶאֱתָיוּ חַשְׁמַנִּים מִנִּי מִצְרָיִם
כּוּשׁ תָּרִיץ יָדָיו לֵאלֹהִים:
33 מַמְלְכוֹת הָאָרֶץ שִׁירוּ לֵאלֹהִים
זַמְּרוּ אֲדֹנָי סֶלָה:
34 לָרֹכֵב בִּשְׁמֵי שְׁמֵי־קֶדֶם
הֵן יִתֵּן בְּקוֹלוֹ קוֹל עֹז:
35 תְּנוּ עֹז לֵאלֹהִים
עַל־יִשְׂרָאֵל גַּאֲוָתוֹ
וְעֻזּוֹ בַּשְּׁחָקִים:
36 נוֹרָא אֱלֹהִים מִמִּקְדָּשֶׁיךָ
אֵל יִשְׂרָאֵל הוּא נֹתֵן עֹז
וְתַעֲצֻמוֹת לָעָם
בָּרוּךְ אֱלֹהִים:

*every one submitting himself with pieces of
silver.* Better, 'which will submit,' the reference being to the 'bulls' who, though they
outdo their fellow nations in cunning and
power, will cower for the sake of money and
exploit the disunity among other nations for
their own ends. The Psalmist prays that they
be deterred from their dastardly deeds (Hirsch).

He hath scattered. Prophetic perfect. God will
break up the peoples whose pursuits are warlike, disturbing the peace of the world.

32. *Egypt; Ethiopia.* The effect of God's
triumph will be that even a land like Egypt,
traditionally hostile to Israel, will send am-
bassadors to negotiate for peace; and a powerful nation like the Ethiopians (Isa. xviii.)
will appeal to be allowed to come under
God's Sovereignty (Tal. Pes. 118b).

33-36 LET ALL JOIN IN HIS PRAISE

33. *sing unto God.* Proclaiming His supremacy.

34. *to Him that rideth.* See verse 5. Here
God rides upon the highest heavens, created
in the beginning of time, as the eternal and
supreme Ruler of the universe (cf. Kimchi).

He uttereth His voice. See on xlvi. 7.

a mighty voice. Cf. xxix. 4, *The voice of the
Lord is powerful.*

35. *ascribe.* Testify to His infinite might
which controls the fate of all peoples (Hirsch).

His majesty is over Israel. Protecting the
nation from attackers (Kimchi).

His strength is in the skies. As Ruler of the
entire universe.

36. *awful is God.* Better, 'awe-inspiring is
God out of thy Sanctuary.' Spoken to Israel
and affirming that from His dwelling-place
in their midst, He performs deeds which
arouse awe throughout the earth (Kimchi).

the people. Israel.

69

מט

1 For the Leader; upon Shoshannim.   [A Psalm] of David.

2 Save me, O God;
  For the waters are come in even
    unto the soul.

3 I am sunk in deep mire, where
    there is no standing;
  I am come into deep waters, and
    the flood overwhelmeth me.

4 I am weary with my crying; my
    throat is dried;
  Mine eyes fail while I wait for my
    God.

5 They that hate me without a cause
    are more than the hairs of my
    head;
  They that would cut me off, being
    mine enemies wrongfully, are
    many;
  Should I restore that which I
    took not away?

לַמְנַצֵּחַ עַל־שֹׁשַׁנִּים לְדָוִד׃

2 הוֹשִׁיעֵנִי אֱלֹהִים

כִּי בָאוּ מַיִם עַד־נָפֶשׁ׃

3 טָבַעְתִּי בִּיוֵן מְצוּלָה וְאֵין מָעֳמָד

בָּאתִי בְמַעֲמַקֵּי־מַיִם

וְשִׁבֹּלֶת שְׁטָפָתְנִי׃

4 יָגַעְתִּי בְקָרְאִי נִחַר גְּרוֹנִי

כָּלוּ עֵינַי מְיַחֵל לֵאלֹהָי׃

5 רַבּוּ מִשַּׂעֲרוֹת רֹאשִׁי שֹׂנְאַי חִנָּם

עָצְמוּ מַצְמִיתַי אֹיְבַי שֶׁקֶר

אֲשֶׁר לֹא־גָזַלְתִּי אָז אָשִׁיב׃

PRAYER OF THE PERSECUTED

A DEEPLY pathetic human document is presented by this Psalm. A devout servant of God is undergoing cruel treatment and feels that his sufferings are due to his religious loyalty. He pleads with God for relief and, in burning indignation, begs that retribution come upon his persecutors. His faith remains firm through the ordeal and he looks to the future with confidence. There are several passages in the Psalm which point to the fact that it was written as a prophetic vision that foretold of the era when Israel would be in captivity. Indeed, the Midrash understands the Psalm as relating to the Babylonian exile. In collective singular, the downtrodden outcasts describe their woeful sufferings, while, at the same time, begging for the mercy of God. In the closing verses they affirm their faith in Him by triumphantly proclaiming His praises in a sincere song of devotion. The parallels between this Psalm and the book of Jeremiah are frequent and striking.

1. *upon Shoshannim.* See on xlv. 1.

2-7 APPEAL FOR HELP

2. *the waters.* He feels himself drowning in a sea of troubles.

even unto the soul. Endangering his life.

3. *deep mire.* Figurative of instability. Instead of treading firm soil, he is like one stepping through a morass in which he might be engulfed.

the flood overwhelmeth me. The fast-flowing current of hostility sweeps him off his feet.

4. *weary.* Cf. vi. 7. He is spent with physical exhaustion from praying to God for relief.

5. *should I restore that which I took not away?* Or, 'what I took not away, that I must restore.' A proverbial expression for the exactions made upon him by his oppressors on the pretext that they are executing justice (cf. Kimchi).

6 O God, Thou knowest my folly;
And my trespasses are not hid
from Thee.

7 Let not them that wait for Thee be
ashamed through me, O Lord
GOD of hosts;
Let not those that seek Thee be
brought to confusion through
me, O God of Israel.

8 Because for Thy sake I have borne
reproach;
Confusion hath covered my face.

9 I am become a stranger unto my
brethren,
And an alien unto my mother's
children.

10 Because zeal for Thy house hath
eaten me up,
And the reproaches of them that
reproach Thee are fallen upon
me.

11 And I wept with my soul fasting,
And that became unto me a
reproach.

אֱלֹהִים אַתָּה יָדַעְתָּ לְאִוַּלְתִּי ‎6
וְאַשְׁמוֹתַי מִמְּךָ לֹא־נִכְחָדוּ:

אַל־יֵבֹשׁוּ בִי ׀ קוֶֹיךָ ‎7
אֲדֹנָי יְהוִה צְבָאוֹת
אַל־יִכָּלְמוּ בִי מְבַקְשֶׁיךָ
אֱלֹהֵי יִשְׂרָאֵל:

כִּי־עָלֶיךָ נָשָׂאתִי חֶרְפָּה ‎8
כִּסְּתָה כְלִמָּה פָנָי:

מוּזָר הָיִיתִי לְאֶחָי ‎9
וְנָכְרִי לִבְנֵי אִמִּי:

כִּי־קִנְאַת בֵּיתְךָ אֲכָלָתְנִי ‎10
וְחֶרְפּוֹת חוֹרְפֶיךָ נָפְלוּ עָלָי:

וָאֶבְכֶּה בַצּוֹם נַפְשִׁי ‎11
וַתְּהִי לַחֲרָפוֹת לִי:

---

6. *my folly.* See on xxxviii. 6. The sufferer here does not, as the Psalmist frequently does, plead complete innocence. In part his trials are punishment for the sins which resulted from foolishness (Hirsch).

7. *through me.* Although not altogether free from guilt, he is known to be a fearer of God; so if no response comes to his prayers, others who look to Him for help in times of trouble may lose confidence.

LORD God of hosts … God of Israel. It was God, the LORD of all living things, that caused Israel to be scattered among the nations so that they become a wandering reminder to the world of the existence of God and the relationship that man should have to Him (Hirsch).

8-13 HE SUFFERS IN GOD'S CAUSE

8. *for Thy sake.* See Jer. xv. 15 for the same plea.

confusion hath covered my face. Cf. xliv. 16.

9. *a stranger unto my brethren.* His kinsfolk have betrayed and ill-treated him, ignoring the relationship between them.

my mother's children. Common motherhood was the strongest of blood ties (l. 20), but it did not help him.

10. *zeal for Thy house.* They saw the love that God showed Israel when the Temple existed, and became envious of them (Rashi). If the Psalm bemoans the exile, the meaning would be 'they despise me for the longing I have to rebuild the Temple' (Hirsch).

reproaches. They who scoff at God pour their scorn upon His servant who believes in Him (Malbim), as they scorned the prophet who spoke in His name (Jer. xx. 8).

11. *I wept.* He wept and fasted, but they only reviled him for it (Malbim).

12 I made sackcloth also my garment,
   And I became a byword unto
   them.

13 They that sit in the gate talk of
   me;
   And I am the song of the drunkards.

14 But as for me, let my prayer be
   unto Thee, O LORD, in an
   acceptable time;
   O God, in the abundance of Thy
   mercy,
   Answer me with the truth of Thy
   salvation.

15 Deliver me out of the mire, and
   let me not sink;
   Let me be delivered from them
   that hate me, and out of the
   deep waters.

16 Let not the waterflood overwhelm me,
   Neither let the deep swallow me
   up;
   And let not the pit shut her
   mouth upon me.

17 Answer me, O LORD, for Thy
   mercy is good;
   According to the multitude of
   Thy compassions turn Thou
   unto me.

18 And hide not Thy face from Thy
   servant;
   For I am in distress; answer me
   speedily.

12 וָאֶתְּנָה לְבוּשִׁי שָׂק
וָאֱהִי לָהֶם לְמָשָׁל:

13 יָשִׂיחוּ בִי יֹשְׁבֵי שָׁעַר
וּנְגִינוֹת שׁוֹתֵי שֵׁכָר:

14 וַאֲנִי תְפִלָּתִי־לְךָ יְהוָה עֵת רָצוֹן
אֱלֹהִים בְּרָב־חַסְדֶּךָ
עֲנֵנִי בֶּאֱמֶת יִשְׁעֶךָ:

15 הַצִּילֵנִי מִטִּיט וְאַל־אֶטְבָּעָה
אִנָּצְלָה מִשֹּׂנְאַי וּמִמַּעֲמַקֵּי־מָיִם:

16 אַל־תִּשְׁטְפֵנִי שִׁבֹּלֶת מַיִם
וְאַל־תִּבְלָעֵנִי מְצוּלָה
וְאַל־תֶּאְטַר־עָלַי בְּאֵר פִּיהָ:

17 עֲנֵנִי יְהוָה כִּי־טוֹב חַסְדֶּךָ
כְּרֹב רַחֲמֶיךָ פְּנֵה אֵלָי:

18 וְאַל־תַּסְתֵּר פָּנֶיךָ מֵעַבְדֶּךָ
כִּי־צַר־לִי מַהֵר עֲנֵנִי:

12. *byword.* Subject of derision (Kimchi).

13. *sit in the gate.* Since the gateway of the city was built into the wall and afforded shade, men collected there to do business and converse. His name is on their lips at these gatherings.

I am the song of the drunkards. lit. 'the songs of the drunkards (are about me)' (cf. Lam. iii. 14).

14-19 PRAYER FOR DELIVERANCE

14. *in an acceptable time.* In a time when God is disposed to respond (cf. Isa. xlix 8).

with the truth of Thy salvation. With a demonstration of the reality of the Divine aid.

15. *mire … waters.* The prayer relates to his condition as described in verse 3 (Malbim).

16. *waterflood.* See verse 3.

pit. See lv. 24.

17. *turn Thou unto me.* Opposite of 'hiding the face' against which he prays in the next verse.

18. *from Thy servant.* Not a term of abjectness, but a self-description as one in the service of God.

19 Draw nigh unto my soul, and
    redeem it;
    Ransom me because of mine
    enemies.

20 Thou knowest my reproach, and
    my shame, and my confusion;
    Mine adversaries are all before
    Thee.

21 Reproach hath broken my heart;
    and I am sore sick;
    And I looked for some to show
    compassion, but there was
    none;
    And for comforters, but I found
    none.

22 Yea, they put poison into my
    food;
    And in my thirst they gave me
    vinegar to drink.

23 Let their table before them be-
    come a snare;
    And when they are in peace, let
    it become a trap.

19 קָרְבָה אֶל־נַפְשִׁי גְאָלָהּ
לְמַעַן אֹיְבַי פְּדֵנִי:
20 אַתָּה יָדַעְתָּ חֶרְפָּתִי
וּבָשְׁתִּי וּכְלִמָּתִי
נֶגְדְּךָ כָּל־צוֹרְרָי:
21 חֶרְפָּה ׀ שָׁבְרָה לִבִּי וָאָנוּשָׁה
וָאֲקַוֶּה לָנוּד וָאַיִן
וְלַמְנַחֲמִים וְלֹא מָצָאתִי:
22 וַיִּתְּנוּ בְּבָרוּתִי רֹאשׁ
וְלִצְמָאִי יַשְׁקוּנִי חֹמֶץ:
23 יְהִי־שֻׁלְחָנָם לִפְנֵיהֶם לְפָח
וְלִשְׁלוֹמִים לְמוֹקֵשׁ:

19. *because of mine enemies.* Who will gloat, if I perish, and account for my fate by imputing to God inability to save (Kimchi).

20-22 HIS SUFFERINGS RETOLD

20. *my reproach.* The reproach I endure from the taunters.

shame ... confusion. In the apparent justification of their mocking words while God fails to intervene on his behalf.

are all before Thee. He implies: I am not merely telling Thee of them; they are in Thy sight and Thou seest the injury they do me.

21. *broken my heart.* Cf. Jer. xxiii. 9.

there was none. Abandoned by all human friends and solitary, upon God alone can he rely for comfort.

22. The language of the verse is figurative. The sense is like 'they added salt to my wounds.' More than failing to sympathize with me, they aggravated my hard lot (Metsudath David).

food. A special word, *baruth,* is employed meaning the meal supplied to a mourner by sympathetic friends. Its use emphasizes their sadistic conduct.

23-29 HE IMPRECATES HIS ENEMIES

23. The thought of their despicable behaviour and his unjust sufferings overrides the barriers of restraint, and in fiery indignation he begs of God not to let them go unpunished. Divine justice cannot permit such villainies to pass uncondemned.

let their table before them become a snare. He prays that just as he had been mistreated by them (verse 22) so may they suffer at the hands of others, thus becoming the victims of treacherous plots (cf. Daath Sofrim).

when they are in peace. Better, 'and let their peace' i.e. may their wish to remain composed and tranquil be frustrated. Let them, too, suffer anxiety and misfortune (Rashi, Metsudath David).

24 Let their eyes be darkened, that
    they see not;
    And make their loins continually
      to totter.

25 Pour out Thine indignation upon
    them,
    And let the fierceness of Thine
      anger overtake them.

26 Let their encampment be deso-
    late;
    Let none dwell in their tents.

27 For they persecute him whom
    Thou hast smitten;
    And they tell of the pain of those
      whom Thou hast wounded.

28 Add iniquity unto their iniquity;
    And let them not come into
    Thy righteousness.

29 Let them be blotted out of the
    book of the living,
    And not be written with the
    righteous.

30 But I am afflicted and in pain;

24 תֶּחְשַׁכְנָה עֵינֵיהֶם מֵרְאוֹת
וּמָתְנֵיהֶם תָּמִיד הַמְעַד:
25 שְׁפָךְ־עֲלֵיהֶם זַעְמֶךָ
וַחֲרוֹן אַפְּךָ יַשִּׂיגֵם:
26 תְּהִי־טִירָתָם נְשַׁמָּה
בְּאָהֳלֵיהֶם אַל־יְהִי יֹשֵׁב:
27 כִּי־אַתָּה אֲשֶׁר־הִכִּיתָ רָדָפוּ
וְאֶל־מַכְאוֹב חֲלָלֶיךָ יְסַפֵּרוּ:
28 תְּנָה־עָוֹן עַל־עֲוֹנָם
וְאַל־יָבֹאוּ בְּצִדְקָתֶךָ:
29 יִמָּחוּ מִסֵּפֶר חַיִּים
וְעִם צַדִּיקִים אַל־יִכָּתֵבוּ:
30 וַאֲנִי עָנִי וְכוֹאֵב

---

24. *their eyes*. Which gloated over my agonies.

their loins. Regarded as a seat of strength. They had abused their superiority of power; may they be reduced in status (Kimchi).

25. For the language, cf. lxxix. 6; Jer. x. 25.

26. *desolate*. Let their palaces lose their value, so becoming worthless (Daath Sofrim)

27. *they persecute him whom Thou hast smitten*. The heinousness of their conduct is pointed out in this verse. Without authorization from God, they vented their malice upon one whom He was chastening, and selected as the victim of their savagery a nation that could not defend itself because it was under God's displeasure (cf. Rashi, Metsudath David).

they tell of the pain. They ascribe iniquities to Israel in addition to the lesser ones of which they are actually guilty, iniquities which the accusers commit (Hirsch).

28. *add iniquity*. They devise false tales to explain God punishing Israel (Hirsch).

into Thy righteousness. May they never participate in the Divine graciousness which brings forgiveness to penitent sinners.

29. *the book of the living*. The image is of an annual register in which are entered the names of those who have gained God's grace and earned the gift of life. To be excluded from that book was equivalent to receiving a death sentence (see Tal. R.H. 16b).

30-37 DELIVERANCE AWAITS ISRAEL

30. A preferable translation is: 'But as for me, [who am] afflicted and in pain, Thy salvation, O God, shall set me up on high' (Hirsch). He contrasts his future with what, he prayed, would be the fate of his enemies.

Let Thy salvation, O God, set me
up on high.

31 I will praise the name of God
with a song,
And will magnify Him with
thanksgiving.

32 And it shall please the LORD
better than a bullock
That hath horns and hoofs.

33 The humble shall see it, and be
glad;
Ye that seek after God, let your
heart revive.

34 For the LORD hearkeneth unto
the needy,
And despiseth not His prisoners.

35 Let heaven and earth praise Him,
The seas, and every thing that
moveth therein.

36 For God will save Zion, and
build the cities of Judah;
And they shall abide there, and
have it in possession.

37 The seed also of His servants
shall inherit it;
And they that love His name
shall dwell therein.

יְשׁוּעָתְךָ אֱלֹהִים תְּשַׂגְּבֵנִי׃

31 אֲהַלְלָה שֵׁם־אֱלֹהִים בְּשִׁיר
וַאֲגַדְּלֶנּוּ בְתוֹדָה׃

32 וְתִיטַב לַיהֹוָה מִשּׁוֹר פָּר
מַקְרִן מַפְרִיס׃

33 רָאוּ עֲנָוִים יִשְׂמָחוּ
דֹּרְשֵׁי אֱלֹהִים וִיחִי לְבַבְכֶם׃

34 כִּי־שֹׁמֵעַ אֶל־אֶבְיוֹנִים יְהֹוָה
וְאֶת־אֲסִירָיו לֹא בָזָה׃

35 יְהַלְלוּהוּ שָׁמַיִם וָאָרֶץ
יַמִּים וְכָל־רֹמֵשׂ בָּם׃

36 כִּי אֱלֹהִים יוֹשִׁיעַ צִיּוֹן
וְיִבְנֶה עָרֵי יְהוּדָה
וְיָשְׁבוּ שָׁם וִירֵשׁוּהָ׃

37 וְזֶרַע עֲבָדָיו יִנְחָלוּהָ
וְאֹהֲבֵי שְׁמוֹ יִשְׁכְּנוּ־בָהּ׃

---

31. *I will praise.* To express thanksgiving
for salvation.

32. *than a bullock.* A maturing bullock
(Hirsch). R.V., following Kimchi, renders *an
ox* (and/or) *a bullock.* For the thought, cf. l.
9ff., li. 18f.

that hath horns and hoofs. The necessary
qualifications to be possessed by an animal
fit for a sacrifice. Horns were the sign of
maturity, and the cloven hoof was a mark of
a *clean* animal (Lev. xi. 3).

33. Cf. xxii. 27. While the arrogant will
perish, the humble shall rejoice in surviving
(Kimchi) to witness the successful outcome
of my prayers (Metsudath David). Those
who have never given up hope, but sought
God, will be able to take heart and hope for

a final redemption.

34. *His prisoners.* The exiled Israelites
whom He allowed to be sent as captives to
Babylon.

35. *let heaven and earth praise Him.* For the
coming redemption of Zion. (cf. Isa. xliv.
23).

36. *build.* i.e. rebuilt the cities which were
left in ruins by the Babylonians.

37. The language is reminiscent of Isa.
lxv. 9.

they that love His name. They that have
cherished the name of God and have remained loyal to His ideals even during the
difficult days of exile, will receive the home
and the peace which was denied them by the
rest of the world (Hirsch).

1 For the Leader. [A Psalm] of
David; to make memorial.

2 O God, to deliver me,
O LORD, to help me, make haste.

3 Let them be ashamed and abashed
That seek after my soul;
Let them be turned backward and
brought to confusion
That delight in my hurt.

4 Let them be turned back by reason
of their shame
That say: 'Aha, aha.'

5 Let all those that seek Thee rejoice and be glad in Thee;
And let such as love Thy salvation say continually:
'Let God be magnified.'

6 But I am poor and needy;
O God, make haste unto me;
Thou art my help and my de-
liverer;
O LORD, tarry not.

לַמְנַצֵּחַ לְדָוִד לְהַזְכִּיר: 1

אֱלֹהִים לְהַצִּילֵנִי 2

יְהוָה לְעֶזְרָתִי חוּשָׁה:

יֵבֹשׁוּ וְיַחְפְּרוּ מְבַקְשֵׁי נַפְשִׁי 3

יִסֹּגוּ אָחוֹר וְיִכָּלְמוּ חֲפֵצֵי רָעָתִי:

יָשׁוּבוּ עַל־עֵקֶב בָּשְׁתָּם 4

הָאֹמְרִים הֶאָח וְהֶאָח:

יָשִׂישׂוּ וְיִשְׂמְחוּ בְּךָ כָּל־מְבַקְשֶׁיךָ 5

וְיֹאמְרוּ תָמִיד יִגְדַּל אֱלֹהִים

אֹהֲבֵי יְשׁוּעָתֶךָ:

וַאֲנִי עָנִי וְאֶבְיוֹן 6

אֱלֹהִים חוּשָׁה־לִּי

עֶזְרִי וּמְפַלְטִי אַתָּה

יְהוָה אַל־תְּאַחַר:

A CRY FOR HELP

THIS Psalm is a reproduction of xl. 14-18 with an occasional change of the Divine name to *Elohim* and a few textual alterations. Malbim suggests that David composed Psalm XL while hiding from Saul and that he wrote this Psalm in his latter years while fleeing from Absalom. This is supported by the fact that the following Psalm makes two references to David's old age (verses 9, 18).

1.   *to make memorial.* See on xxxviii. 1.

2.   *O God, to deliver me.* In XL the text has *be pleased, O LORD, to deliver me.* Here both verbs are governed by *make haste,* and in its revised form the prayer sounds a note of greater urgency.

3.   In XL *together* is added after *abashed,* and *to sweep away* after *my soul.*

4.   *let them be turned back.* In XL the reading is: *let them be appalled.* The two Hebrew verbs are the same except for one letter. Perhaps the change was made to suit the circumstances. The phrase speaks of enemies such as Shim'ei, who were out to slander and embarrass David

(Malbim). The implication is, let them suffer a taste of their own medicine (cf. Rashi, Daath Sofrim).

5.   The only changes are the substitution of *God* for *the LORD,* the addition of *and* before *let such as love,* and a slightly different Hebrew word for *salvation.*

6.   *O God, make haste unto me.* In XL *the LORD will account it unto me,* altered into a form of a prayer to meet a desperate situation. This time, instead of confidence, David expresses a call of need, giving the whole Psalm a more plaintive tone.

my help. The Hebrew word is used here in its feminine form.

71

1 In thee, O Lord, have I taken
   refuge;
   Let me never be ashamed.

2 Deliver me in Thy righteousness,
   and rescue me;
   Incline Thine ear unto me, and
   save me.

3 Be Thou to me a sheltering rock,
   whereunto I may continually
   resort,
   Which Thou hast appointed to
   save me;
   For Thou art my rock and my
   fortress.

4 O my God, rescue me out of the
   hand of the wicked,
   Out of the grasp of the unrighteous and ruthless man.

5 For Thou art my hope;
   O Lord God, my trust from my
   youth.

עא

בְּךָֽ־יְהוָה חָסִיתִי
אַל־אֵבוֹשָׁה לְעוֹלָם:
2 בְּצִדְקָתְךָ תַּצִּילֵנִי וּתְפַלְּטֵנִי
הַטֵּה־אֵלַי אָזְנְךָ וְהוֹשִׁיעֵנִי:
3 הֱיֵה לִי לְצוּר מָעוֹן
לָבוֹא תָּמִיד צִוִּיתָ לְהוֹשִׁיעֵנִי
כִּי־סַלְעִי וּמְצוּדָתִי אָתָּה:
4 אֱלֹהַי פַּלְּטֵנִי מִיַּד רָשָׁע
מִכַּף מְעַוֵּל וְחוֹמֵץ:
5 כִּי־אַתָּה תִקְוָתִי
אֲדֹנָי יְהוִה מִבְטַחִי מִנְּעוּרָי:

PRAYER IN OLD AGE

No superscription heads this Psalm as it is a continuation of the previous one (Hirsch). It was
a prayer offered by David who, having had to suffer many trials, was still undergoing
hardships from relentless enemies. His confidence remained in God to Whom he addressed
his petition. The personal note predominates, but at times the thoughts turn to the needs of his
people (cf. Meiri). Repeatedly drawing upon the other Psalms in voicing his feelings, David's
prayer is a fervent request for the ability to achieve meaningful accomplishments even in his
late stage in life, thereby crowning his magnificent career with good deeds.

1-3 HIS TRUST IN GOD

This section is based upon xxxi 1-3.

1. *let me never be ashamed.* In the eyes of
ill-wishers through the prayer remaining unanswered.

2. *in Thy righteousness.* Being a righteous
God, He supports the good when they are
assailed by the wicked.

incline Thine ear. See on xxxi. 3.

3. *a sheltering rock.* lit. 'a rock of habitation (*maon*)'—a rock in which shelter can be
found. In xxxi. 3, the reading is a *rock of
refuge* (*maoz*). By now adopting *maon*, the

Psalmist may have had in mind *Lord, Thou
hast been our dwelling-place* (maon) *in all
generations* (xc. 1).

my rock. Hebrew *sela* (see on xviii. 3).

4-13 APPEAL FOR DELIVERANCE

4. *ruthless man.* To be understood collec-
tively, the verse refers to a corrupt state of
society where justice did not protect the weak
(Hirsch). Alternatively, 'wicked' refers to
Absalom and 'ruthless' to his adviser,
Ahitophel (Kimchi).

5. This and the next verses are paraphrased
from xxii. 10f.

6 Upon Thee have I stayed myself
  from birth;
  Thou art He that took me out of
  my mother's womb;
  My praise is continually of Thee.

7 I am as a wonder unto many;
  But Thou art my strong refuge.

8 My mouth shall be filled with Thy
  praise,
  And with Thy glory all the day.

9 Cast me not off in the time of old
  age;
  When my strength faileth, forsake
  me not.

10 For mine enemies speak concerning me,
   And they that watch for my soul
   take counsel together,

11 Saying: 'God hath forsaken him;
   Pursue and take him; for there is
   none to deliver.'

12 O God, be not far from me;
   O my God, make haste to help
   me.

13 Let them be ashamed and
   consumed that are adversaries
   to my soul;
   Let them be covered with reproach and confusion that seek
   my hurt.

6 עָלֶיךָ נִסְמַכְתִּי מִבֶּטֶן
מִמְּעֵי אִמִּי אַתָּה גוֹזִי
בְּךָ תְהִלָּתִי תָמִיד׃
7 כְּמוֹפֵת הָיִיתִי לְרַבִּים
וְאַתָּה מַחֲסִי־עֹז׃
8 יִמָּלֵא פִי תְּהִלָּתֶךָ
כָּל־הַיּוֹם תִּפְאַרְתֶּךָ׃
9 אַל־תַּשְׁלִיכֵנִי לְעֵת זִקְנָה
כִּכְלוֹת כֹּחִי אַל־תַּעַזְבֵנִי׃
10 כִּי־אָמְרוּ אוֹיְבַי לִי
וְשֹׁמְרֵי נַפְשִׁי נוֹעֲצוּ יַחְדָּו׃
11 לֵאמֹר אֱלֹהִים עֲזָבוֹ
רִדְפוּ וְתִפְשׂוּהוּ כִּי־אֵין מַצִּיל׃
12 אֱלֹהִים אַל־תִּרְחַק מִמֶּנִּי
אֱלֹהַי לְעֶזְרָתִי חִישָׁה׃
13 יֵבֹשׁוּ יִכְלוּ שֹׂטְנֵי נַפְשִׁי
יַעֲטוּ חֶרְפָּה וּכְלִמָּה מְבַקְשֵׁי רָעָתִי

v. 12. חושה ק׳

---

from my youth. In old age he looks back upon his life and sees the hand of God upholding him.

6. *He that took me.* Hebrew *gozi,* but in xxii. 10, *gochi.* The meaning is uncertain, and 'You drew me' (Rashi), or 'You cut or separated me' (Malbim) have been suggested.

7. *as a wonder.* Like the suffering servant of God in Isa. lii. 14, men stared at him appalled, wondering how one so righteous should be made to endure such hardships; but his trust in God as his *strong refuge* continued unshaken.

8. While onlookers marvelled at his sufferings, in the midst of them he is able to extol God's glory.

9. *cast me not off.* Cf. *cast me not away*

from Thy presence (li. 13).

in ... old age. With advancing years his physical strength declines, exposing him all the more to the attacks of the wicked. Greater, then, becomes his need of God's support.

10. For this and the next verses, cf. iii. 3, xli. 8, lvi. 7.

12. *be not far from me.* Cf. xxxv. 22.

make haste to help me. Cf. xl. 14.

13. *consumed.* Derived from xxxv. 4; but instead of *brought to confusion* (*yikholmu*) the verb here is *yikhlu* (a difference of one letter omitted), for which cf. xxxvii. 20.

adversaries to my soul. Opponents threatening me with death. In xxxv. 4 the text has *that seek after my soul.*

14 But as for me, I will hope con-
    tinually,
    And will praise Thee yet more
    and more.

15 My mouth shall tell of Thy
    righteousness,
    And of Thy salvation all the day;
    For I know not the numbers
    thereof.

16 I will come with Thy mighty
    acts, O Lord God;
    I will make mention of Thy
    righteousness, even of Thine
    only.

17 O God, Thou hast taught me
    from my youth;
    And until now do I declare Thy
    wondrous works.

18 And even unto old age and hoary
    hairs, O God, forsake me not;
    Until I have declared Thy
    strength unto the next genera-
    tion,
    Thy might to every one that is to
    come;

19 Thy righteousness also, O God,
    which reacheth unto high
    heaven;
    Thou who hast done great things,
    O God, who is like unto Thee?

14 וַאֲנִי תָּמִיד אֲיַחֵל
וְהוֹסַפְתִּי עַל־כָּל־תְּהִלָּתֶךָ׃
15 פִּי ׀ יְסַפֵּר צִדְקָתֶךָ
כָּל־הַיּוֹם תְּשׁוּעָתֶךָ
כִּי לֹא יָדַעְתִּי סְפֹרוֹת׃
16 אָבוֹא בִּגְבֻרוֹת אֲדֹנָי יְהוִֹה
אַזְכִּיר צִדְקָתְךָ לְבַדֶּךָ׃
17 אֱלֹהִים לִמַּדְתַּנִי מִנְּעוּרָי
וְעַד־הֵנָּה אַגִּיד נִפְלְאוֹתֶיךָ׃
18 וְגַם עַד־זִקְנָה ׀ וְשֵׂיבָה
אֱלֹהִים אַל־תַּעַזְבֵנִי
עַד־אַגִּיד זְרוֹעֲךָ לְדוֹר
לְכָל־יָבוֹא גְּבוּרָתֶךָ׃
19 וְצִדְקָתְךָ אֱלֹהִים עַד־מָרוֹם
אֲשֶׁר־עָשִׂיתָ גְדֹלוֹת
אֱלֹהִים מִי כָמוֹךָ׃

covered with reproach. Cf. xxxv. 26.

14-16 HIS STEDFAST HOPE IN GOD

14. *but as for me.* Marking the contrast between his future and the fate which he is sure
is in store for his adversaries.

15. *Thy salvation.* The manifestation of Thy
righteousness.

I know not the numbers thereof. Cf. xl .6.

16. *I will come.* Into the Sanctuary to offer
thanksgiving for God's *mighty acts* of deliverance.

even of Thine only. As the only Saviour.

17-20 THE LESSON OF HIS LONG LIFE

17. *Thou hast taught me.* God has been his

Teacher because of his willingness to be a
pupil (cf. *and all thy children shall be taught
of the Lord,* Isa. liv. 13).

Thy wondrous works. Which reveal His attributes as experienced in the affairs of men.

18. *Thy strength.* lit. 'Thy arm,' the power
which sustains the weak and humbles the
ruthless strong.

the next generation. So Ibn Ezra. Lit. 'to a
generation.' Kimchi renders 'to the present
generation.'

19. *Thy righteousness,* etc. Cf. xxxvi. 6,
lvii. 11.

who is like unto Thee? Cf. xxxv. 10; Exod.
xv. 11.

20 Thou, who hast made me to see
    many and sore troubles,
    Wilt quicken me again, and bring
    me up again from the depths
    of the earth.

21 Thou wilt increase my greatness,
    And turn and comfort me.

22 I also will give thanks unto Thee
    with the psaltery,
    Even unto Thy truth, O my God,
    I will sing praises unto Thee with
    the harp,
    O Thou Holy One of Israel.

23 My lips shall greatly rejoice when
    I sing praises unto Thee;
    And my soul, which Thou hast
    redeemed.

24 My tongue also shall tell of Thy
    righteousness all the day;
    For they are ashamed, for they
    are abashed, that seek my hurt.

20 אֲשֶׁר הִרְאִיתַנוּ ׀ צָרוֹת רַבּוֹת וְרָעוֹת
תָּשׁוּב תְּחַיֵּנוּ
וּמִתְּהֹמוֹת הָאָרֶץ תָּשׁוּב תַּעֲלֵנִי׃
21 תֶּרֶב ׀ וְּגְדֻלָּתִי
וְתִסֹּב תְּנַחֲמֵנִי׃
22 גַּם־אֲנִי ׀ אוֹדְךָ בִכְלִי־נֶבֶל
אֲמִתְּךָ אֱלֹהָי
אֲזַמְּרָה לְךָ בְכִנּוֹר קְדוֹשׁ יִשְׂרָאֵל׃
23 תְּרַנֵּנָּה שְׂפָתַי כִּי אֲזַמְּרָה־לָּךְ
וְנַפְשִׁי אֲשֶׁר פָּדִיתָ׃
24 גַּם־לְשׁוֹנִי כָּל־הַיּוֹם תֶּהְגֶּה צִדְקָתֶךָ
כִּי־בֹשׁוּ כִי־חָפְרוּ מְבַקְשֵׁי רָעָתִי׃

v. 20. הראיתני ק׳   v. 20. תחייני ק׳   v. 20. תעלני ק׳

---

20. *made me to see.* As also with *quicken me* and *bring me up*, the *kethib* reads 'us.' M.T. makes it a personal profession of faith; in the alternative the Psalmist is the spokesman of the nation whose plight is comparable with his own (Kimchi).

from the depths of the earth. Where Sheol is located; equals: from the very gates of destruction.

21. *Thou wilt increase.* In its restored greatness the nation will surpass any honour it enjoyed in previous times (Kimchi).

comfort. Cf. Isa. xl. 1 where Divine comfort is the forerunner of redemption from captivity.

22. *I also will give thanks.* Together with

the rest of the nation when this happy consummation is effected.

Thy truth. When God has proved Himself true to His promises.

Holy One of Israel. Commonly used of God in Isaiah, but in the Psalter only lxxviii. 41, lxxxix. 19. Even though the nation contained some sinners and rebels, David makes it clear that Israel sanctifies the name of God on earth making Him known as the Holy One of Israel (Daath Sofrim).

23. *and my soul.* His entire being will join in the exultation which will be aroused by the Divine act of redemption.

24. *my tongue.* See on xxxv. 28.

they are ashamed. Cf. xxxv. 4, 26, xl. 15.

1 [A Psalm] of Solomon.
  Give the king Thy judgments, O
  God,
  And Thy righteousness unto the
  king's son;

2 That he may judge Thy people
  with righteousness,
  And Thy poor with justice.

3 Let the mountains bear peace to
  the people,
  And the hills, through righteousness.

4 May he judge the poor of the
  people,

GOD'S IDEAL KING

THE superscription reads *le-Shelemoh* which is generally understood as not 'of' or 'by' but 'concerning Solomon.' A.V. adopted this view and rendered *for Solomon;* but the Targum translates '(composed) by Solomon.' Most commentators subscribe to the former suggestion maintaining that David wrote the Psalm near the end of his days, to communicate to his successor, Solomon, the status and qualifications of the king as the representative of God in the governing of the people. As God is righteous and the Defender of the weak, so must the national ruler be. It presents an ideal of justice as the foundation of a nation's happiness and stability. David's wish is that his son will be able to master a perfect society resembling the age of the Messiah. Indeed, Jewish tradition attached a Messianic interpretation to the Psalm which appears in the Targum, and also in the Talmud which understood verse 17 as 'may his (the Messiah's) name be Yinon as long as the sun.' The language is prayerful which supports the reading of the Psalm as an ideal to be realized in the future.

1-7 THE RIGHTEOUS KING

1. *give the king Thy judgments*. The prayer is founded upon the doctrine that *judgment is God's* (Deut. i. 17), and He has laid down the right principles of government. The request made of God is recalled by the wording (1 Kings. iii. 9).

the king's son. The same person as 'the king,' who is himself the rightful heir of the preceding monarch (Rashi).

2. *Thy poor*. The poor among Thy people. Under a corrupt system the rich had the advantage by their ability to bribe judges; here the strictly impartial administration of justice to all is demanded.

3. *mountains ... hills*. A similar expression is found in Isa. iv. 12 *the mountains and the hills shall break forth in glad song*. The land is pictured as having human traits, announcing peace and prosperity throughout the land.

4. *the poor of the people*. Not synonymous with *Thy poor* in verse 2. In the earlier verse the meaning is, poor in worldly possessions as part of the natural order decreed by God. Here the reference is to those who are poor as the victims of injustice on the part of their fellow citizens (Hirsch).

And save the children of the
needy,
And crush the oppressor.

5 They shall fear Thee while the sun
endureth,
And so long as the moon, throughout all generations.

6 May he come down like rain upon
the mown grass,
As showers that water the earth.

7 In his days let the righteous flourish,
And abundance of peace, till the
moon be no more.

8 May he have dominion also from
sea to sea,
And from the River unto the ends
of the earth.

9 Let them that dwell in the wilderness bow before him;
And his enemies lick the dust.

יוֹשִׁיעַ לִבְנֵי אֶבְיוֹן
וִידַכֵּא עוֹשֵׁק:
⁵ יִירָאוּךָ עִם־שָׁמֶשׁ
וְלִפְנֵי יָרֵחַ דּוֹר דּוֹרִים:
⁶ יֵרֵד כְּמָטָר עַל־גֵּז
כִּרְבִיבִים זַרְזִיף אָרֶץ:
⁷ יִפְרַח־בְּיָמָיו צַדִּיק
וְרֹב שָׁלוֹם עַד־בְּלִי יָרֵחַ:
⁸ וְיֵרְדְּ מִיָּם עַד־יָם
וּמִנָּהָר עַד־אַפְסֵי־אָרֶץ:
⁹ לְפָנָיו יִכְרְעוּ צִיִּים
וְאֹיְבָיו עָפָר יְלַחֵכוּ:

---

the children of the needy. Whose position is
jeopardized by the poverty of the parents.

oppressor. The man whose wealth is employed to exploit those who cannot protect
themselves.

5. *they shall fear Thee.* When the subjects
see the judgments of God applied, and derive
therefrom the blessings of peace and security, they will be led to reverence Him as the
source of their happy condition.

6. *like rain.* The verse may have been suggested by the effect produced by a righteous
king as described in 2 Sam. xxiii. 4. After the
grass has been mown, the soil needs rain for
fertility. Similarly, the king's subjects will
eagerly drink his words of wisdom (Malbim).

that water. Better, 'moistening'; an unusual
word is employed.

7. *let the righteous flourish.* Cf. the

righteous shall flourish like the palm-tree
(xcii. 13).

8-14   MAY HIS DOMINION EXTEND
TO ALL

In the hope, voiced in this section, that the
king's rule may grow world-wide, there is no
thought of his personal aggrandizement; but
rather that the blessings which he bestowed
upon his own people may be enjoyed by all.

8. *from sea to sea.* Repeated in Zech ix. 10.
The *River* is the Euphrates, the eastern geographical boundary familiar to the Hebrews
(Alshich). The phrase really covers the whole
of the then known world.

9. *dwell in the wilderness.* Nomadic tribes
(Kimchi) which normally resent any system
of control.

lick the dust. Lie prostrate before him in
submission with their faces touching the
ground.

10 The kings of Tarshish and of the
   isles shall render tribute;
   The kings of Sheba and Seba
   shall offer gifts.

11 Yea, all kings shall prostrate
   themselves before him;
   All nations shall serve him.

12 For he will deliver the needy
   when he crieth;
   The poor also, and him that hath
   no helper.

13 He will have pity on the poor and
   needy,
   And the souls of the needy he
   will save.

14 He will redeem their soul from
   oppression and violence,
   And precious will their blood be
   in his sight;

15 That they may live, and that he
   may give them of the gold of
   Sheba,
   That they may pray for him con-
   tinually,
   Yea, bless him all the day.

16 May he be as a rich cornfield in
   the land upon the top of the
   mountains;

10 מַלְכֵי תַרְשִׁישׁ וְאִיִּים

מִנְחָה יָשִׁיבוּ

מַלְכֵי שְׁבָא וּסְבָא

אֶשְׁכָּר יַקְרִיבוּ׃

11 וְיִשְׁתַּחֲווּ־לוֹ כָל־מְלָכִים

כָּל־גּוֹיִם יַעַבְדוּהוּ׃

12 כִּי־יַצִּיל אֶבְיוֹן מְשַׁוֵּעַ

וְעָנִי וְאֵין־עֹזֵר לוֹ׃

13 יָחֹס עַל־דַּל וְאֶבְיוֹן

וְנַפְשׁוֹת אֶבְיוֹנִים יוֹשִׁיעַ׃

14 מִתּוֹךְ וּמֵחָמָס יִגְאַל נַפְשָׁם

וְיֵיקַר דָּמָם בְּעֵינָיו׃

15 וִיחִי וְיִתֶּן־לוֹ מִזְּהַב שְׁבָא

וְיִתְפַּלֵּל בַּעֲדוֹ תָמִיד

כָּל־הַיּוֹם יְבָרֲכֶנְהוּ׃

16 יְהִי פִסַּת־בַּר בָּאָרֶץ בְּרֹאשׁ הָרִים

---

10. *Tarshish.* See on xlviii. 8.

the isles. The Mediterranean coast.

Sheba. Southeast part of Arabia, a country of great wealth.

Seba. Gen. x. 7. Josephus identified it with the capital of Meroe in Ethiopia.

11. This hope was verified in Solomon's reign (1 Kings v. i).

12. *he will deliver the needy.* The king's supremacy will not result from military conquests, but from voluntary submission by other peoples who place themselves under his fatherly care (cf. Kimchi).

13. *the poor.* See on xli. 2.

souls. Lives; so again in the next verse.

14. *precious.* He will not hold a human life cheap; it will be protected as something of high value.

15-17 PRAYERS ON THE KING'S BEHALF

15. *that they may live.* Translate rather 'so may he (the king) live.' With this is to be compared *long live the king* (1 Sam. x. 24), the origin of the phrase 'God save the king.'

that he may give them. Rather 'He (God) will give to him … and He will pray' i.e. bless him (Rashi).

gold of Sheba. See 1 Kings iii. 13.

16. *may he be as a rich cornfield.* Render, instead, 'may there be abundance of corn.'

upon the top of the mountains. May the growth be so abundant that it will spread up the sides of the mountains to the summit (Tal. Keth. 111b).

יִרְעַשׁ כַּלְּבָנוֹן פִּרְיוֹ
וְיָצִיצוּ מֵעִיר כְּעֵשֶׂב הָאָרֶץ:
17 יְהִי שְׁמוֹ לְעוֹלָם
לִפְנֵי־שֶׁמֶשׁ יִנּוֹן שְׁמוֹ
וְיִתְבָּרְכוּ בוֹ כָּל־גּוֹיִם יְאַשְּׁרוּהוּ:
18 בָּרוּךְ יְהוָה אֱלֹהִים אֱלֹהֵי יִשְׂרָאֵל
עֹשֵׂה נִפְלָאוֹת לְבַדּוֹ:
19 וּבָרוּךְ שֵׁם כְּבוֹדוֹ לְעוֹלָם
וְיִמָּלֵא כְבוֹדוֹ אֶת־כָּל־הָאָרֶץ
אָמֵן וְאָמֵן:
20 כָּלּוּ תְפִלּוֹת דָּוִד בֶּן־יִשָׁי:

ינון ק' v. 17

May his fruit rustle like Lebanon;
And may they blossom out of the
city like grass of the earth.

17 May his name endure for ever;
May his name be continued as
long as the sun;
May men also bless themselves
by him;
May all nations call him happy.

18 Blessed be the LORD God, the
God of Israel,
Who only doeth wondrous things;

19 And blessed be His glorious
name for ever;
And let the whole earth be filled
with His glory.
Amen, and Amen.

20 The prayers of David the son of
Jesse are ended.

---

may his fruit rustle like Lebanon. May the cornstalks be tall and thick so that the sound of the wind sweeping through them will sound like the rustling of cedars on Mount Lebanon (Kimchi).

may they blossom. They, the inhabitants. May they be as numerous as the blades of grass (Kimchi) (cf. the description of the population during the reign of Solomon, 1 Kings iv. 20).

17. *may his name be continued.* lit. 'may his name produce issue.' May his dynasty endure as long as the sun exists (Kimchi).

bless themselves by him. Or, 'in him' (cf. the promises to Abraham and Isaac, Gen. xii. 3, xxii. 18, xxvi. 4).

18-29 CONCLUDING DOXOLOGY

These verses are not part of the Psalm, but praise of God appended to each Book of the Psalter (Kimchi).

19. *Amen, and Amen.* The response of the congregation.

20 EDITORIAL NOTE

The Rabbis (Tal. Pes. 117b) maintained that the Hebrew word *kolu* is actually a contraction of two words, *kol elu*, meaning 'all these,' meaning that the entire book of Psalms was edited by David, although several Psalms were composed by others, such as Asaph and the sons of Korah. It is accordingly interesting to note that Rashi, who interpreted the Psalm as David's prayers on behalf of his son, suggests as an alternate possibility that we have here an illustration of the Rabbinical principle of exegesis, that the Scriptures do not necessarily follow a chronological order, and the Psalm with its concluding verse was the last of David's compositions written when he nominated Solomon as his successor (1 Kings i. 30).

73

PSALM LXXIII

1 A Psalm of Asaph.
Surely God is good to Israel,
Even to such as are pure in heart.

2 But as for me, my feet were almost
gone;
My steps had well nigh slipped.

3 For I was envious at the arrogant,
When I saw the prosperity of the
wicked.

4 For there are no pangs at their
death,
And their body is sound.

עג

מִזְמוֹר לְאָסָף
אַךְ טוֹב לְיִשְׂרָאֵל אֱלֹהִים
לְבָרֵי לֵבָב:

2 וַאֲנִי כִּמְעַט נָטוּי רַגְלָי
כְּאַיִן שֻׁפְּכָה אֲשֻׁרָי:

3 כִּי־קִנֵּאתִי בַּהוֹלְלִים
שְׁלוֹם רְשָׁעִים אֶרְאֶה:

4 כִּי אֵין חַרְצֻבּוֹת לְמוֹתָם
וּבָרִיא אוּלָם:

v. 2. שפכו ק׳   v. 2. נטיו ק׳

TRIAL OF FAITH

THE outspoken confession of a man whose faith had been sorely tested is narrated in this intensely human document. His mind was deeply perturbed by the sight of wicked men triumphing and flourishing. All seemed to be well with them. Their defiance of God brought them no set-back, whereas the righteous suffered. In his distress of spirit he betook himself to the Sanctuary, and there his faith was restored. The assurance then came to him that Divine retribution was a reality. In subject matter the Psalm is akin to XXXVII, XLIX, XCIV.

1-2 INTRODUCTORY STATEMENT

1. In this verse the writer summarizes at the outset the conclusion to which he came after passing through a period of doubt, created by the problem of the ungodly lording it over the virtuous.

Asaph. See on l.1.

surely. The Hebrew particle strikes the note of certainty (Kimchi, Malbim). Despite appearances to the contrary, God is naught but good, and does differentiate between the good and the bad, deciding their ultimate fate (Metsudath David).

good. Gracious.

to Israel. This must mean, not the people as a whole, but such as are true to their covenant with Him (Metsudath David).

pure in heart. The essential qualification for admittance to His Presence (xxiv. 4).

2. Here are stated the circumstances which occasioned the Psalmist's meditation.

as for me. When, under the strain of trial, his faith weakened.

my feet were almost gone. Indicating the nearness of total collapse; or, on the basis of xliv. 19, we may render: 'my feet had almost turned aside' (from the right path).

slipped. Cf. xvii. 5.

3-9 PROSPERITY OF THE WICKED

3. *envious.* Of their success (xxxvii. 1).

arrogant. Same Hebrew word as *boasters* in v. 6. Their offensive talk is described in verses 8f.

prosperity. lit. 'peace'; stability and flourishing condition.

4. *no pangs at their death.* Although their life had been vile, they have a peaceful end.

5 In the trouble of man they are not;
   Neither are they plagued like men.

6 Therefore pride is as a chain about
   their neck;
   Violence covereth them as a garment.

7 Their eyes stand forth from fatness;
   They are gone beyond the imagi-
   nations of their heart.

8 They scoff, and in wickedness
   utter oppression;
   They speak as if there were none
   on high.

9 They have set their mouth against
   the heavens,
   And their tongue walketh through
   the earth.

10 Therefore His people return
   hither;
   And waters of fulness are drained
   out by them.

5 בַּעֲמַל אֱנוֹשׁ אֵינֵמוֹ
וְעִם־אָדָם לֹא יְנֻגָּעוּ:
6 לָכֵן עֲנָקַתְמוֹ גַאֲוָה
יַעֲטָף־שִׁית חָמָס לָמוֹ:
7 יָצָא מֵחֵלֶב עֵינֵמוֹ
עָבְרוּ מַשְׂכִּיּוֹת לֵבָב:
8 יָמִיקוּ וִידַבְּרוּ בְרָע עֹשֶׁק
מִמָּרוֹם יְדַבֵּרוּ:
9 שַׁתּוּ בַשָּׁמַיִם פִּיהֶם
וּלְשׁוֹנָם תִּהֲלַךְ בָּאָרֶץ:
10 לָכֵן וִישִׁיב עַמּוֹ הֲלֹם
וּמֵי מָלֵא יִמָּצוּ לָמוֹ:

v. 10. ישוב ק׳

---

sound. No ailments, regarded by the pious as visitations from God, afflict them.

5. *trouble.* The Hebrew word occurs in *Man is born unto trouble, as the sparks fly upward* (Job. v. 7). The wicked, seem to escape that fate, and the troubles that leave them untouched do come upon men who seek to be loyal to God's ways (cf. Targum).

man. Hebrew *enosh*, and *men* is *adam* (see on viii. 5).

plagued. The verb means *smitten* by God (cf. Isa liii. 4). In contrast to the wicked, the Psalmist says of himself, *all the day have I been plagued* (verse 14).

6. *therefore.* Because they have been immune from the hard lot which other men experience (Rashi).

a chain. They display their insolent pride as though it were an adornment (Metsudath David, Malbim).

violence. Lawlessness (cf. Gen. vi. 11) had become part of their regular equipment.

7. *fatness.* Physical well-being.

they are gone. After God fulfilled their desires in a manner surpassing the imaginings of their hearts, they began to mock and blaspheme, as the succeeding verses describe (Midrash Shocher Tov).

8. *on high.* Hirsch renders 'they speak [down] from above.' Their speech is even more pernicious than their acts. They speak as if they were on high, as if whatever they had done was only just and proper.

9. *the heavens* i.e. God Who dwells above; they blaspheme and defy Him. They pass judgment on all things and on all people and, in general, they act as if they were the masters of the universe.

10-11   EVIL EFFECTS OF THE WICKED

10. *His people return hither.* The behaviour of the wicked had a corrupting influence upon many Israelites who were drawn to copy their evil example and adopt their manner of thought and speech (Rashi).

water of fulness. The influenced Israelites thoroughly imbibed the pernicious ideas and sayings of the blasphemers (Metsudath David). For the metaphor in a good sense, cf. 'drink their (the wise men's) words with thirst' (Aboth).

11 And they say: 'How doth God
    know?
    And is there knowledge in the
    Most High?'

12 Behold, such are the wicked;
    And they that are always at ease
    increase riches.

13 Surely in vain have I cleansed my
    heart,
    And washed my hands in inno-
    cency;

14 For all the day have I been
    plagued,
    And my chastisement came every
    morning.

15 If I had said: 'I will speak thus,'
    Behold, I had been faithless to
    the generation of Thy children.

16 And when I pondered how I
    might know this,
    It was wearisome in mine eyes;

11 וַיֹּאמְרוּ אֵיכָה יָדַע־אֵל
וְיֵשׁ דֵּעָה בְעֶלְיוֹן׃
12 הִנֵּה־אֵלֶּה רְשָׁעִים
וְשַׁלְוֵי עוֹלָם הִשְׂגּוּ־חָיִל׃
13 אַךְ־רִיק זִכִּיתִי לְבָבִי
וָאֶרְחַץ בְּנִקָּיוֹן כַּפָּי׃
14 וָאֱהִי נָגוּעַ כָּל־הַיּוֹם
וְתוֹכַחְתִּי לַבְּקָרִים׃
15 אִם־אָמַרְתִּי אֲסַפְּרָה כְמוֹ
הִנֵּה דוֹר בָּנֶיךָ בָגָדְתִּי׃
16 וָאֲחַשְּׁבָה לָדַעַת זֹאת
עָמָל הִיא בְעֵינָי׃

הוא ק׳ v. 16.

11. *they say.* The subject is still the Israelites who had been seduced from their loyalty
to God.

how doth God know? What men do on earth,
so that He punishes evil and rewards good
(Metsudath David). (Cf. x. 4, 11, 13 and see
xiv. 1).

12-14 THE PSALMIST'S REFLECTION

12. After recounting the harmful effect of
the wicked upon other Israelites, he records
his own reactions.

such … wicked. Prosperous and in the ascen-
dant although they rebel against God (Rashi).

and they … at ease. Hirsch renders 'and always contented they attain might in great
measure.'

13. *in vain.* No such happy lot has befallen
the Psalmist as he sees the evil-doers enjoying (Kimchi).

washed … in innocency. See on xxvi. 6.

14. *all the day.* Constantly.

plagued. See on verse 5.

chastisement. Though I am chastised for no
apparent misdeeds, I search my actions and

strengthen my fear of God, while the arch-
sinners continue with their misdeeds and are
nevertheless successful (Malbim).

15-17 BAFFLED BY THE PROBLEM

15. *I will speak thus.* If he gave public expression to his doubts, his words would have
undermined the faith of his brethren
(Metsudath David).

Thy children. They who were not nominal
Israelites, but faithful to the will of their
Father in heaven.

16. *and when I pondered.* Although I feared
to give public expression to these perplexing
doubts, I nevertheless pondered the matter in
my own mind (Kimchi).

know this. Understand the meaning of the
phenomena which disturbed him.

wearisome. lit. 'laborious toil,' difficult and
beyond his powers (Hirsch).

17. *sanctuary.* The Hebrew is plural, to
connote the wise priests, 'the repositories of
holiness' (Ibn Ezra) as well as the Temple
(Metsudath David). Or, he entered his
thoughts into the realm of the angels (Kimchi).
There he found the solution to his problem.

17 Until I entered into the sanctuary
   of God,
   And considered their end.

18 Surely Thou settest them in
   slippery places;
   Thou hurlest them down to utter
   ruin.

19 How are they become a desolation in a moment!
   They are wholly consumed by
   terrors.

20 As a dream when one awaketh,
   So, O Lord, when Thou arousest
   Thyself, Thou wilt despise
   their semblance.

21 For my heart was in a ferment,
   And I was pricked in my reins.

22 But I was brutish, and ignorant;
   I was as a beast before Thee.

17 עַד־אָבוֹא אֶל־מִקְדְּשֵׁי־אֵל
אָבִינָה לְאַחֲרִיתָם:
18 אַךְ בַּחֲלָקוֹת תָּשִׁית לָמוֹ
הִפַּלְתָּם לְמַשּׁוּאוֹת:
19 אֵיךְ הָיוּ לְשַׁמָּה כְרָגַע
סָפוּ תַמּוּ מִן־בַּלָּהוֹת:
20 כַּחֲלוֹם מֵהָקִיץ
אֲדֹנָי בָּעִיר ׀ צַלְמָם תִּבְזֶה:
21 כִּי יִתְחַמֵּץ לְבָבִי
וְכִלְיוֹתַי אֶשְׁתּוֹנָן:
22 וַאֲנִי־בַעַר וְלֹא אֵדָע
בְּהֵמוֹת הָיִיתִי עִמָּךְ:

their end. Ultimately the wicked are over-thrown (Rashi). He must look beyond their present happy state to a time when God brings condemnation upon them. Ibn Ezra submits that the holy priests in the Temple and the scholars of Israel taught him that man was not brought to this world to enjoy its temporal pleasures, to be a king or to be wealthy, but to strive that his final lot be good, viz. that he earns the final reward for the souls of the righteous (cf. Kimchi).

18-20 FATE OF THE WICKED

18. *slippery places.* They have no firm foothold; their position is insecure and they will fall (cf. xxxv. 6).

utter ruin. The Hebrew occurs again only in lxxiv. 3.

terrors. Calamities which terrify them.

20. *as a dream.* The prosperity of the evil-doers is likened to a dream which vanishes when the sleep is over; it, too, does not endure (Kimchi).

arousest Thyself. To execute judgment (see Targum). (Cf. *rouse Thee, and awake to my*

judgment, xxxv. 23).

their semblance. Cf. xxxix. 7. All their prosperity is a sham, a mere counterfeit of reality, external without substance; and God rates it at its true value (Meiri).

21-22 HE ADMITS HIS FORMER ERROR

21. After the light had come to him, he acknowledged how wrong had been his previous criticism of Divine Providence, and attributed it to his troubled state of mind (Kimchi, Metsudath David).

heart. Mind.

in a ferment. lit. 'grew sour, became embittered,' when he brooded over his trials and contrasted the happy condition of the wicked.

I was pricked. The Hebrew suggests: I felt stinging pains.

reins. See on vii. 10.

22. *brutish and ignorant.* The words occur again in a similar connection in xcii. 7f.

as a beast. Like an animal which is controlled by emotions and not by reason (see Ibn Ezra, Kimchi).

23 Nevertheless I am continually
   with Thee;
   Thou holdest my right hand.
24 Thou wilt guide me with Thy
   counsel,
   And afterward receive me with
   glory.
25 Whom have I in heaven but
   Thee?
   And beside Thee I desire none
   upon earth.
26 My flesh and my heart faileth;
   But God is the rock of my heart
   and my portion for ever.
27 For, lo, they that go far from
   Thee shall perish;
   Thou dost destroy all them that
   go astray from Thee.
28 But as for me, the nearness of
   God is my good;
   I have made the Lord GoD my
   refuge,
   That I may tell of all Thy works.

23 וַאֲנִי תָמִיד עִמָּךְ
אָחַזְתָּ בְּיַד־יְמִינִי׃
24 בַּעֲצָתְךָ תַנְחֵנִי
וְאַחַר כָּבוֹד תִּקָּחֵנִי׃
25 מִי־לִי בַשָּׁמָיִם
וְעִמְּךָ לֹא־חָפַצְתִּי בָאָרֶץ׃
26 כָּלָה שְׁאֵרִי וּלְבָבִי
צוּר־לְבָבִי וְחֶלְקִי אֱלֹהִים לְעוֹלָם׃
27 כִּי־הִנֵּה רְחֵקֶיךָ יֹאבֵדוּ
הִצְמַתָּה כָּל־זוֹנֶה מִמֶּךָּ׃
28 וַאֲנִי קִרְבַת אֱלֹהִים לִי־טוֹב
שַׁתִּי בַּאדֹנָי יֱהוִֹה מַחְסִי
לְסַפֵּר כָּל־מַלְאֲכוֹתֶיךָ׃

23-26 HIS TRUST IN GOD RETURNS

23. *I am continually with Thee.* Since I am
always with Thee, cling to Thee and to Thy
service, constantly occupied with the knowledge of Thee, I merited Thy aid to attain
understanding (Kimchi).

holdest my right hand. Cf. lxiii. 9.

24. *guide me with Thy counsel.* Just as Your
counsel has guided and aided me (till now),
so may You always guide me with Your
counsel and teach me all the days of my life
(Kimchi).

afterward receive me with glory. Better, 'take
me to Glory' (Rashi). The word is meant in
the same sense as *took* in Gen. xlviii. 1 and
Exod. xiv. 6, viz. lead a person to an appointed destination.

25. *but Thee.* Not in the Hebrew, but to be
understood from *beside Thee*. The sense is:
having God as his Helper, he needs nobody
else (Metsudath David).

26. *my flesh and my heart.* My physical
powers and mental aspirations (see Rashi,
Ibn Ezra).

rock of my heart. Upon Him my mind can rest
securely.

portion. See on xvi. 5.

27-28 FATE OF THE WICKED AND HIS FATE

27. *go far from Thee.* Estrange themselves
from God by their evil thoughts and actions
(Ibn Ezra).

28. *nearness of God.* Union with Him in
worship. The Hebrew may also be rendered:
'to draw near to God,' which gives the contrast to the wicked in the preceding verse who
go far from Him (Ibn Ezra).

my good. The source of happiness and well-
being.

tell of all Thy works. Others pass through
agonies of doubt as he had done. It will be his
mission to announce to them the relief which
had come to him.

עד

74

1 Maschil of Asaph.
Why, O God, hast Thou cast us
off for ever ?
Why doth Thine anger smoke
against the flock of Thy pasture?

2 Remember Thy congregation,
which Thou hast gotten of old,
Which Thou hast redeemed to be
the tribe of Thine inheritance;
And mount Zion, wherein Thou
hast dwelt.

3 Lift up Thy steps because of the
perpetual ruins,
Even all the evil that the enemy
hath done in the sanctuary.

מַשְׂכִּיל לְאָסָף
לָמָה אֱלֹהִים זָנַחְתָּ לָנֶצַח
יֶעְשַׁן אַפְּךָ בְּצֹאן מַרְעִיתֶךָ:
2 זְכֹר עֲדָתְךָ ׀ קָנִיתָ קֶּדֶם
גָּאַלְתָּ שֵׁבֶט נַחֲלָתֶךָ
הַר־צִיּוֹן זֶה ׀ שָׁכַנְתָּ בּוֹ:
3 הָרִימָה פְעָמֶיךָ לְמַשֻּׁאוֹת נֶצַח
כָּל־הֵרַע אוֹיֵב בַּקֹּדֶשׁ:

A NATIONAL LAMENT

THE agony of the nation in a shattering disaster finds voice in this moving Psalm. After witnessing the destruction of the Temple and holy city, the people feel themselves forsaken by God and implore His mercy. Hirsch points out the didactic element of the Psalm. 'This Psalm teaches us how to gather confidence in eventual redemption in the very act of reflecting on our present state of utter "Churban" (destruction) and "Galuth" (dispersion).'

1-3 APPEAL TO GOD

1. *Maschil*. See on xxxii. 1.

cast us off. Only in the thought that God had utterly rejected Israel could an explanation be found of the dire calamity which had befallen them (cf. Lam v. 20) (cf. Kimchi, Metsudath David, Malbim).

anger smoke. Evidence of His burning wrath (Lam. ii. 3f.).

flock of Thy pasture. God is frequently pictured as the Shepherd of Israel. As such they had the right to look to Him for protection; but He had apparently left them exposed to the ravages of the enemy (cf. Hirsch).

2. *remember*. Israel's appeal in the present is based upon past history in which is recorded the special relationship God established with the people (Malbim).

Thy congregation. The community which God had chosen to be His witnesses to the world.

gotten … redeemed. The verbs were suggested by the phrases in the song at the Red Sea (Exod. xv. 13, 16).

tribe of Thine inheritance. Again in Jer. x. 16. *Tribe* stands for *nation. Tribe* is singular to denote the singular unity of the entire nation in their trust in God when they left Egypt. For the conception of God selecting Israel as His *inheritance*, cf. Deut. xxxii. 7ff.

and mount Zion. Also governed by the verb *remember*. On God's choice of this mountain as His abode, cf. lxviii. 17.

3. *lift up Thy steps*. Hasten to intervene and to lay desolate forever, the enemy who has done evil in the sanctuary (Meiri).

evil. The enemy was determined to destroy the very sanctity of the sanctuary (Sforno). Here the verse speaks of serious damage to the edifice, and the next section describes it in detail.

4 Thine adversaries have roared in
the midst of Thy meeting-place;
They have set up their own signs
for signs.

5 It seemed as when men wield
upwards
Axes in a thicket of trees.

6 And now all the carved work
thereof together
They strike down with hatchet
and hammers.

7 They have set Thy sanctuary on
fire;
They have profaned the dwelling-
place of Thy name even to the
ground.

8 They said in their heart: 'Let us
make havoc of them altogether';
They have burned up all the meeting-places of God in the land.

4 שָׁאֲגוּ צֹרְרֶיךָ בְּקֶרֶב מוֹעֲדֶךָ
שָׂמוּ אוֹתֹתָם אֹתוֹת:
5 יִוָּדַע כְּמֵבִיא לְמָעְלָה
בִּסְבָךְ־עֵץ קַרְדֻּמּוֹת:
6 וְעֵת פִּתּוּחֶיהָ יָּחַד
בְּכַשִּׁיל וְכֵילַפּוֹת יַהֲלֹמוּן:
7 שִׁלְחוּ בָאֵשׁ מִקְדָּשֶׁךָ
לָאָרֶץ חִלְּלוּ מִשְׁכַּן־שְׁמֶךָ:
8 אָמְרוּ בְלִבָּם
נִינָם יָחַד
שָׂרְפוּ כָל־מוֹעֲדֵי־אֵל בָּאָרֶץ:

וְעַתָּה ק' v. 6.

4-9 HAVOC IN THE TEMPLE

4. *Thine adversaries*. The enemies of Israel are the enemies of God, proved by the
devastation of the Sanctuary at their hands.
Hirsch adds 'not as our foes but as Thy own
enemies did they roar into the Holy of Holies.'

roared. The Temple courts resounded with
the shouts of the attackers who thought they
had vanquished Thee (Hirsch) (cf. Isa v. 29;
Jer. ii. 15).

Thy meeting–place. The Temple (Rashi,
Kimchi); also in Lam. ii. 6. The Tabernacle
too, was described as *tent of meeting*.

signs. In Num. ii. 2, the word is rendered
ensigns, military banners with distinctive
emblems. The enemy planted them within
the Temple to mark their conquest (cf.
Malbim). The signs were put up not only to
signify a political victory but as a symbol of
the triumph of paganism over Judaism.

5. The soldiers hacked the woodwork of
the holy building like lumbermen felling
trees in a forest.

6. *carved work*. The walls were orna-
mented with *carved figures of cherubim and
palm-trees and open flowers* (1 Kings vi. 29).

7. *set Thy sanctuary on fire*. This was done
by Nebuchadnezzar's chief of the army (2
Kings xxv. 9).

even to the ground. They *broke down the walls
of Jerusalem* (2 Kings xxv. 10), and so profaned the city which God had chosen as the
habitation of His name (Deut. xii. 11).

8. *make havoc of them*. Better, 'suppress
them' (Ibn Ezra), and this they purposed to
do *altogether*, i.e. completely. Not satisfied
with destroying the Temple, they proceeded
to burn *all the meeting-places of God in the
land* (Metsudath David). Hirsch, following
Targum, renders *ninam* as 'their descendants.' Malbim understands the verse as the
enemies' descendants boasting that even after their ancestors destroyed the Sanctuary
they themselves continued the city's destruction even further.

9 We see not our signs;
    There is no more any prophet;
    Neither is there among us any that
       knoweth how long.

10 How long, O God, shall the
      adversary reproach?
    Shall the enemy blaspheme Thy
      name for ever ?

11 Why withdrawest Thou Thy
      hand, even Thy right hand?
    Draw it out of Thy bosom and
      consume them.

12 Yet God is my King of old,
    Working salvation in the midst
      of the earth.

9 אֹתוֹתֵינוּ לֹא־רָאִינוּ
אֵין־עוֹד נָבִיא
וְלֹא־אִתָּנוּ יֹדֵעַ עַד־מָה:
10 עַד־מָתַי אֱלֹהִים יְחָרֶף צָר
יְנָאֵץ אוֹיֵב שִׁמְךָ לָנֶצַח:
11 לָמָּה תָשִׁיב יָדְךָ וִימִינֶךָ
מִקֶּרֶב חוֹקְךָ כַלֵּה:
12 וֵאלֹהִים מַלְכִּי מִקֶּדֶם
פֹּעֵל יְשׁוּעוֹת בְּקֶרֶב הָאָרֶץ:

חיקך ק׳   v. 11.

---

9. *our signs*. It is historically impossible to interpret this as the distinctive observances of religion, such as the Sabbath (called a *sign* in Exod. xxxi. 13, 17) and festivals. Most commentators understand the 'signs' as those of redemption from the long exile.

no more any prophet. To tell us when the redemption will take place (Kimchi). Moreover, says Hirsch, 'we no longer have in our midst a prophet who, imbued with the spirit of God and with His word upon his lips, might teach us how to see the present in its proper perspective and tell us what we might rightfully expect of the future.'

how long. Would the Temple service be suspended and the exile continue.

10-11   APPEAL TO GOD RENEWED

10. *how long*. Since no prophet is able to supply the information, the question is addressed to God.

reproach. Act contemptuously towards God and the Temple.

11. *withdrawest*. Only because God had

remained passive could this disaster happen (cf. Malbim).

right hand. Symbol of power (cf. Exod. xv.6).

draw it out. There is nothing in the Hebrew corresponding to this. The Text is abrupt: 'from the midst of Thy bosom! destroy!' and eloquently conveys the deep emotion of the speaker.

12-17   THE MIGHT OF GOD

From their bitter experience the people did not think that God *could* not have spared them, but that He *would* not. They never doubted His power.

12. *yet God is my King*. In spite of what has happened, Israel utters its conviction that He Who became the nation's Ruler in the remote past had not abdicated (cf. Hirsch).

salvation. Hebrew is plural, 'performing acts of salvation.'

in the midst of the earth. As in Exod. viii. 18. the demonstration of Divine might served the purpose of making His name

13 Thou didst break the sea in pieces
   by Thy strength;
   Thou didst shatter the heads
   of the sea-monsters in the
   waters.

14 Thou didst crush the heads of
   leviathan,
   Thou gavest him to be food to
   the folk inhabiting the wilderness.

15 Thou didst cleave fountain and
   brook;
   Thou driedst up ever-flowing
   rivers.

16 Thine is the day, Thine also the
   night;
   Thou hast established luminary
   and sun.

17 Thou hast all set the borders of
   the earth;
   Thou hast made summer and
   winter.

18 Remember this, how the enemy
   hath reproached the LORD,

אַתָּה פוֹרַרְתָּ בְעׇזְּךָ יָם ‏13.
שִׁבַּרְתָּ רָאשֵׁי תַנִּינִים
עַל־הַמָּיִם:

אַתָּה רִצַּצְתָּ רָאשֵׁי לִוְיָתָן ‏14
תִּתְּנֶנּוּ מַאֲכָל לְעָם לְצִיִּים:

אַתָּה בָקַעְתָּ מַעְיָן וָנָחַל ‏15
אַתָּה הוֹבַשְׁתָּ נַהֲרוֹת אֵיתָן:

לְךָ יוֹם אַף־לְךָ לָיְלָה ‏16
אַתָּה הֲכִינוֹתָ מָאוֹר וָשָׁמֶשׁ:

אַתָּה הִצַּבְתָּ כָּל־גְּבוּלוֹת אָרֶץ ‏17
קַיִץ וָחֹרֶף אַתָּה יְצַרְתָּם:

זְכׇר־זֹאת אוֹיֵב חֵרֵף יְהֹוָה ‏18

known to all nations (Kimchi).

13. *Thou.* Here and in the following verses, the subject is emphatic: Thou and no one else.

the sea. The Red Sea during the exodus.

sea-monsters. This and *leviathan* (verse 14) are symbolic representation of Egypt (Ezek. xxix. 3) (Kimchi), figured as a land sprawling across the Nile.

14. *heads.* Plural, referring to the rulers, officers and heads of the Egyptians (Kimchi, Metsudath David, Malbim).

to be food. The reference is to the drowned Egyptians when their bodies were washed on to the shore.

the folk. Better, nomads. The Israelites who were destined to be a nation of wanderers through the wilderness (Hirsch).

15. *cleave fountain and brook.* The meaning is: God split rocks to produce a flow of water for the thirsting people (lxxviii. 15f.; Exod. xvii. 6; Num. xx. 8).

ever-flowing rivers. Better, *rivers of antiquity* or *mighty rivers*. The allusion is to the Jordan River.

16. *Thine.* Thou art the Creator of (Metsudath David).

luminary and sun. The moon (Gen. i. 16) and sun (Ibn Ezra, Metsudath David); or perhaps the first word is collective: 'luminaries, and in particular the sun.'

17. *borders.* The geographical features, such as rivers and mountains, which often become national frontiers.

18-23 CONCLUDING PRAYER

18. *reproached.* As in verse 10.

And how **a** base people **have**
blasphemed Thy name.

19 O deliver not the soul of Thy
turtledove unto the wild beast;
Forget not the life of Thy poor
for ever.

20 Look upon the covenant;
For the dark places of the land
are full of the habitations of
violence.

21 O let not the oppressed turn back
in confusion;
Let the poor and needy praise
Thy name.

22 Arise, O God, plead Thine own
cause;
Remember Thy reproach all the
day at the hand of the base
man.

23 Forget not the voice of Thine
adversaries,
The tumult of those that rise up
against Thee which ascendeth
continually.

וְעַם־נָבָל נִאֲצוּ שְׁמֶֽךָ׃

19 אַל־תִּתֵּן לְחַיַּת נֶפֶשׁ תּוֹרֶךָ
חַיַּת עֲנִיֶּיךָ אַל־תִּשְׁכַּח לָנֶֽצַח׃

20 הַבֵּט לַבְּרִית
כִּי מָלְאוּ מַחֲשַׁכֵּי־אֶרֶץ
נְאוֹת חָמָס׃

21 אַל־יָשֹׁב דַּךְ נִכְלָם
עָנִי וְאֶבְיוֹן יְהַלְלוּ שְׁמֶֽךָ׃

22 קוּמָה אֱלֹהִים רִיבָה רִיבֶךָ
זְכֹר חֶרְפָּתְךָ מִנִּי־נָבָל כָּל־הַיּֽוֹם׃

23 אַל־תִּשְׁכַּח קוֹל צֹרְרֶיךָ
שְׁאוֹן קָמֶיךָ עֹלֶה תָמִֽיד׃

---

a base people. Rendered *a vile nation* in Deut.
xxxii. 21.

19. *turtledove.* The innocent, defenceless
bird exposed to attacks by birds of prey
(Hirsch).

20. *the covenant.* Contracted between God
and Israel (Lev. xxvi. 44, 45) (Hirsch).

dark places of the land. Not literally areas in
which Israelites hid from the invader, but
those dark and gloomy places to which the
Israelites have been exiled.

full of the habitations of violence. In these
places of exile brutal acts have made their
home, and they offer no security to those who
seek shelter in them.

21. *turn back.* When they pray to God for
succour (Rashi).

in confusion. Because their petition received
no answer.

poor. Afflicted.

praise. Have reason to praise for the aid
which God had granted them.

22. *plead thine own cause.* The Psalmist
views the catastrophe from the standpoint
not only of the people's sufferings, but also
of the effect it must produce upon God's
repute in the world (cf. Kimchi).

the base man. The Hebrew is collective,
'base men,' who belong to *a base people*
(verse 18).

23. *voice.* The sounds uttered by God's
adversaries who *roared in the midst of Thy
meeting-place* (verse 4) (Ibn Ezra).

ascendeth. To heaven in defiance.

עה

75

1 For the Leader; Al-tashheth.
  A Psalm of Asaph, a Song.

2 We give thanks unto Thee, O God,
  We give thanks, and Thy name is
    near;
  Men tell of Thy wondrous works.

3 'When I take the appointed time,
  I Myself will judge with equity.

4 When the earth and all the in-
    habitants thereof are dissolved,
  I Myself establish the pillars of it.'
    Selah

5 I say unto the arrogant: 'Deal not
    arrogantly';
  And to the wicked: 'Lift not up
    the horn.'

לַמְנַצֵּחַ אַל־תַּשְׁחֵת

מִזְמוֹר לְאָסָף שִׁיר:

2 הוֹדִינוּ לְּךָ ׀ אֱלֹהִים הוֹדִינוּ

וְקָרוֹב שְׁמֶךָ סִפְּרוּ נִפְלְאוֹתֶיךָ:

3 כִּי אֶקַּח מוֹעֵד

אֲנִי מֵישָׁרִים אֶשְׁפֹּט:

4 נְמֹגִים אֶרֶץ וְכָל־יֹשְׁבֶיהָ

אָנֹכִי תִכַּנְתִּי עַמּוּדֶיהָ סֶּלָה:

5 אָמַרְתִּי לַהוֹלְלִים אַל־תָּהֹלּוּ

וְלָרְשָׁעִים אַל־תָּרִימוּ קָרֶן:

THE NATION'S GRATITUDE

THE mood changes abruptly as we pass from the foregoing Psalm to the present one. Here is a song of thanksgiving for deliverance from peril. It may be compared with XLVI-XLVIII which, according to some, tell of the defeat of the Assyrian invasion of Judea by Sannecherib, and possibly relates to the same incident (cf. Ibn Ezra, Malbim on xlvi. 1). The LXX has the title, 'A Song concerning the Assyrians.'

1. *Al-tashheth.* See on lvii. 1.

2 ISRAEL THANKS GOD

2. *Thy name is near.* God had revealed His 'nearness' to the Israelite people by the humiliating defeat He inflicted upon the enemy.

men tell. Better, 'told.' A reference to prophets of old who always told the wonders of Your name (Ibn Ezra).

3-4 GOD UPHOLDS THE MORAL ORDER

God is the Speaker and announces His will. He bides His time and chooses His moment to intervene against the aggressor.

3. *take.* Select.

the appointed time. Rashi understands this phrase as a reference to the holidays when the nation of Israel indulges not in ribaldness and silliness but sings songs of praise and gratitude to God.

I Myself. Hebrew 'I,' meaning that 'once I choose the proper time, then I will come forth as 'ani' (I Who judge the world and its state of affairs decisively, by My might), and I shall *judge with equity* (Hirsch).

with equity. Justice triumphs when God discharges His office as Judge of the world.

4. *dissolved.* When human society appears to be at the point of collapse, because its foundation—which is righteousness—has been undermined, God strengthens it again. Rashi suggests that this verse is a reference to the time of the revelation at Mount Sinai: when all the world was dissolved in fear of destruction, Israel accepted the Torah and kept the world intact.

5-6 WARNING TO THE ARROGANT

5. *lift not up the horn.* Do not behave like horned animals which toss their heads defiantly because of confidence in their strength. Targum translates *keren* as pride.

6 Lift not up your horn on high;
  Speak not insolence with a haughty
    neck.

7 For neither from the east, nor
    from the west,
  Nor yet from the wilderness,
    cometh lifting up.

8 For God is judge;
  He putteth down one, and lifteth
    up another.

9 For in the hand of the LORD there
    is a cup, with foaming wine, full
    of mixture,
  And He poureth out of the same;
  Surely the dregs thereof, all the
    wicked of the earth shall drain
    them, and drink them.

10 But as for me, I will declare for
    ever,
  I will sing praises to the God of
    Jacob.

11 All the horns of the wicked also
    will I cut off;
  But the horns of the righteous
    shall be lifted up.

6 אַל־תָּרִימוּ לַמָּרוֹם קַרְנְכֶם
תְּדַבְּרוּ בְצַוָּאר עָתָק׃
7 כִּי לֹא מִמּוֹצָא וּמִמַּעֲרָב
וְלֹא מִמִּדְבַּר הָרִים׃
8 כִּי־אֱלֹהִים שֹׁפֵט
זֶה יַשְׁפִּיל וְזֶה יָרִים׃
9 כִּי כוֹס בְּיַד־יְהוָה וְיַיִן
חָמַר מָלֵא מֶסֶךְ וַיַּגֵּר מִזֶּה
אַךְ־שְׁמָרֶיהָ יִמְצוּ יִשְׁתּוּ
כֹּל רִשְׁעֵי־אָרֶץ׃
10 וַאֲנִי אַגִּיד לְעֹלָם
אֲזַמְּרָה לֵאלֹהֵי יַעֲקֹב׃
11 וְכָל־קַרְנֵי רְשָׁעִים אֲגַדֵּעַ
תְּרוֹמַמְנָה קַרְנוֹת צַדִּיק׃

6. *a haughty neck*. Which thrusts the head
upward as a gesture of insolent pride. If you
assert yourself above your fellow men because of your contempt of the Law, you
actually set yourself above God Himself by
presuming to despise Him and to trample His
Law underfoot (Hirsch).

7-9   MAN'S FATE IN GOD'S HANDS

7. *the wilderness*. At the south of the Holy
Land. The north is not mentioned because it
was considered by the ancients to be a region
of darkness (cf. Malbim).

cometh lifting up. From no point of the compass should men seek allies to establish their
superiority over others, because the issue is
ultimately decided by God (Hirsch).

8. *putteth down ... lifteth up*. Cf. cxlvii. 6;
1 Sam. ii. 7.

9. *cup*. In which is *wine of staggering* (see
on lx. 5), rendering those who drink it mentally and physically helpless.

mixture. Mixed precisely in those propor-
tions, the effect being to make the drink more
enticing (Metsudath David).

drain. Cf. Isa. li. 17, where the same image is
used of Israel who had drunk deep of the cup
of God's wrath.

10-11   TRIUMPH OF THE RIGHTEOUS

10. *as for me*. The Psalmist as his people's
spokesman.

declare. The object to be understood is *Thy
wondrous works* (as in verse 2).

for ever. As long as he lives.

11. *horns*. The instrument of aggressive
and destructive power (cf. verse 5).

will I cut off. The Psalmist as the representative of the peoples speaks with the confidence that God is Israel's Ally in the campaign against wickedness.

righteous. i.e. Israel (Rashi, Kimchi).

76

עו

1 For the Leader; with string-music.
A Psalm of Asaph, a Song.

2 In Judah is God known;
His name is great in Israel.

3 In Salem also is set His tabernacle,
And His dwelling-place in Zion.

4 There He broke the fiery shafts of
the bow;
The shield, and the sword, and
the battle.   Selah

5 Glorious art Thou and excellent,
coming down from the mountains of prey.

לַמְנַצֵּחַ בִּנְגִינֹת
מִזְמוֹר לְאָסָף שִׁיר:
2 נוֹדָע בִּיהוּדָה אֱלֹהִים
בְּיִשְׂרָאֵל גָּדוֹל שְׁמוֹ:
3 וַיְהִי בְשָׁלֵם סֻכּוֹ
וּמְעוֹנָתוֹ בְצִיּוֹן:
4 שָׁמָּה שִׁבַּר רִשְׁפֵי־קָשֶׁת
מָגֵן וְחֶרֶב וּמִלְחָמָה סֶלָה:
5 נָאוֹר אַתָּה אַדִּיר מֵהַרְרֵי־טָרֶף:

GOD TRIUMPHANT

THIS Psalm is a companion and sequel to the preceding and arose out of the same circumstances. The theme is common in the Psalter: the defeat of Israel's foe is a glorification of
God's name.

1. *with string-music.* See on iv. 1.

2-4 GOD'S VICTORY IN ZION

2. *is God known.* He has gained renown as
the result of the overthrow of the Assyrian
army.

great. It has become magnified by the proof
of His invincible might.

Israel. Here a synonym of *Judah*, and the
names do not refer to the two divisions of the
nation.

3. *Salem.* The older form of Jerusalem,
which means 'the city of Salem' (Gen. xiv.
18).

tabernacle. The Hebrew means a covered-
over place, and is the usual word for a lion's
den. Perhaps the Psalmist intends to describe
God as the lion of Judah, breaking forth from
His lair, seizing His prey (cf. Sforno).

4. *there.* At the boundary of Jerusalem did
the defeat of the invader take place (Metsudath

David, Malbim).

fiery shafts. Poetically descriptive of the
lightning speed of the arrows (Rashi).

and the battle. Explained as the equivalent of
war-equipment in general (Ibn Ezra). It may
perhaps signify the plan of the campaign
which was completely upset by God's intervention.

5-7 THE ENEMY'S COLLAPSE

5. *Glorious.* lit. 'illuminated,' clearly recognized.

Glorious art Thou and excellent. Better,
'Glorious art Thou, more unique in might
than the mountains of prey.'

excellent. Majestic in power.

coming down from the mountains of prey.
There is nothing in the text to correspond
with *coming down*, and the verb to be supplied may be 'returning,' i.e. coming back
from the hills on which He had treated the

6 The stout-hearted are bereft of
sense, they sleep their sleep;
And none of the men of might
have found their hands.

7 At Thy rebuke, O God of Jacob,
They are cast into a dead sleep,
the riders also and the horses.

8 Thou, even Thou, art terrible;
And who may stand in Thy sight
when once Thou art angry?

9 Thou didst cause sentence to be
heard from heaven;
The earth feared, and was still,

10 When God arose to judgment,
To save all the humble of the
earth.   Selah

11 Surely the wrath of man shall
praise Thee;

6 אֶשְׁתּוֹלְלוּ ׀ אַבִּירֵי לֵב נָמוּ שְׁנָתָם
וְלֹא־מָצְאוּ כָל־אַנְשֵׁי־חַיִל יְדֵיהֶם:

7 מִגַּעֲרָתְךָ אֱלֹהֵי יַעֲקֹב
נִרְדָּם וְרֶכֶב וָסוּס:

8 אַתָּה ׀ נוֹרָא אַתָּה
וּמִי־יַעֲמֹד לְפָנֶיךָ מֵאָז אַפֶּךָ:

9 מִשָּׁמַיִם הִשְׁמַעְתָּ דִּין
אֶרֶץ יָרְאָה וְשָׁקָטָה:

10 בְּקוּם־לַמִּשְׁפָּט אֱלֹהִים
לְהוֹשִׁיעַ כָּל־עַנְוֵי־אֶרֶץ סֶלָה:

11 כִּי־חֲמַת אָדָם תּוֹדֶךָּ

Assyrian host as prey.

6. *stout-hearted.* The swaggering soldiers whose boastful speech is recounted in Isa. x. 12ff.

are bereft of sense. Or, 'are despoiled.' Instead of departing with rich loot, they are themselves plundered of their possessions (cf. Kimchi).

sleep their sleep. i.e. the sleep from which there is no awaking (xiii. 4). They lay dead on the battlefield (Hirsch).

have found their hands. Strength to resist the fate which God decreed for them (Rashi).

7. *Thy rebuke.* The soldiers did not lie down to sleep. It was fear that resulted from Thy rebuke that cast them into deep slumber (Malbim).

cast into a dead sleep. The root usually denotes a state of coma induced by God (as in Gen. ii. 21).

riders. Hebrew 'chariots'; charioteers are intended (cf. Hirsch).

horses. So lit., but the meaning is horsemen.

8-10 JUDGMENT FROM HEAVEN

8. *terrible.* Awe-inspiring.

when once Thou art angry. lit. 'from then Thine anger.' For the idiom, cf. the Hebrew of Jer. xliv. 18; Ruth ii. 7.

9. *sentence.* viz. the defeat of the invading army (see Isa. xxxvii. 33ff.) (Rashi).

from heaven. Where His throne of judgment is established (cf. Ibn Ezra).

feared. Was awe-struck at the discomfiture of a widely dreaded military power (Rashi).

and was still. In amazement at the unexpected happening.

10. *all the humble of the earth.* Represented by Israel (Kimchi).

11-13 HOMAGE TO GOD

11. *the wrath of man.* Exemplified by aggressive attacks upon weaker neighbours, like the onslaught of Assyria upon Israel (cf. Kimchi, Malbim).

The residue of wrath shalt Thou
gird upon Thee.

12 Vow, and pay unto the LORD your
God;
   Let all that are round about Him
   bring presents unto Him that
   is to be feared;

13 He minisheth the spirit of princes;
   He is terrible to the kings of the
   earth.

שְׁאֵרִית חֵמֹת תַּחְגֹּר׃
12 נִדֲרוּ וְשַׁלְּמוּ לַיהוָה אֱלֹהֵיכֶם
כָּל־סְבִיבָיו יֹבִילוּ שַׁי לַמּוֹרָא׃
13 יִבְצֹר רוּחַ נְגִידִים
נוֹרָא לְמַלְכֵי־אָרֶץ׃

shall praise Thee. Such acts of brutality are contrary to the will of God, and result in His passing judgment upon them. The sequel, therefore, becomes an occasion for God being praised as the all-powerful Judge (cf. Rashi).

the residue of wrath. Rashi suggests two possibilities: 1) when the wicked shall see Thy judgment over Thy enemies, they will restrain the residue of their wrath against Thee; 2) The unspent wrath of mortal avengers Thou wilt gird upon Thyself.

12. *vow, and pay*. i.e. fulfil in the hour of victory the vows made in the time of danger.

all that are round about Him. The nations bordering on Judea (Kimchi).

presents. Better, *tribute*. see lxviii. 30. It is recorded in 2 Chron. xxxii. 23 that *many* (viz. surrounding nations) *brought gifts unto the*

LORD *to Jerusalem*, after the defeat of Sannecherib.

unto Him that is to be feared. lit. 'to the object of reverence' (cf. Isa. viii. 13, *let Him be your fear, and let Him be your dread*). The triumph of Israel should have its sequel in universal allegiance to Him Who willed it and made it happen (cf. Kimchi).

13. *minisheth*. Rather, 'cut off,' but the meaning will depend upon the interpretation of *spirit*. Some take it to mean their boastful spirit, pride; the sense is then: God will humble the arrogant rulers (Targum, Rashi, Kimchi). *Spirit* may also indicate the breath of life, vitality; and if this is adopted here, the idea is that God will cut short the life of such rulers.

terrible. God makes Himself feared by kings when they note what He had done to so powerful and dreaded a monarch as Sannecherib.

עז

לַמְנַצֵּחַ עַל־יְדוּתוּן לְאָסָף מִזְמוֹר׃

2 קוֹלִי אֶל־אֱלֹהִים וְאֶצְעָקָה
קוֹלִי אֶל־אֱלֹהִים וְהַאֲזִין אֵלָי׃

3 בְּיוֹם צָרָתִי אֲדֹנָי דָּרָשְׁתִּי
יָדִי ׀ לַיְלָה נִגְּרָה וְלֹא תָפוּג
מֵאֲנָה הִנָּחֵם נַפְשִׁי׃

4 אֶזְכְּרָה אֱלֹהִים וְאֶהֱמָיָה
אָשִׂיחָה ׀ וְתִתְעַטֵּף רוּחִי סֶלָה׃

5 אָחַזְתָּ שְׁמֻרוֹת עֵינָי
נִפְעַמְתִּי וְלֹא אֲדַבֵּר׃

6 חִשַּׁבְתִּי יָמִים מִקֶּדֶם
שְׁנוֹת עוֹלָמִים׃

—————
v. 1. ק׳ ידותון

77

1 For the Leader; for Jeduthun.
A Psalm of Asaph.

2 I will lift up my voice unto God,
and cry;
I will lift up my voice unto God,
that He may give ear unto me.

3 In the day of my trouble I seek the
Lord;
With my hand uplifted, [mine eye]
streameth in the night without
ceasing;
My soul refuseth to be comforted.

4 When I think thereon, O God, I
must moan;
When I muse thereon, my spirit
fainteth.   Selah

5 Thou holdest fast the lids of mine
eyes;
I am troubled, and cannot speak.

6 I have pondered the days of old,
The years of ancient times.

A CRY OF AFFLICTION

In this Psalm of deep anguish, the writer gives voice to the feelings of the people in a time of national eclipse. The occasion is in all probability the anticipated Babylonian captivity, and the *motif* has points of resemblance with the prayer in Habakkuk iii.

1. *Jeduthun.* See on lxii. 1.

2-4 HIS DISTURBED SPIRIT

2. *I will lift up my voice.* With impressive brevity the text in both clauses is simply 'my voice.' The meaning is 'aloud unto God I cry,' or 'hark! unto God I cry.'

3. *With my hand* etc. The text actually reads only 'My hand [at] night.' A better rendering is offered by Hirsch: 'but my hand melted away into the night without ceasing.' I was unable to acquire the spiritual and moral energy which I needed to soar up to God (cf. Ezek. i. 3). Indeed, my strength failed perceptibly, and ebbed away into the night of suffering which was round about me. Ibn Ezra totally rejects the notion of substituting mine eye for *my hand* as a fundamental error.

4. *when I think thereon, O God.* Preferably: 'when I would remember God.' In his tragic plight, his thoughts turn inevitably towards God, but it only results in disturbing his mind.

when I muse thereon. In meditation and prayer (cf. lv. 18).

5-10 QUESTIONS WHICH HAUNT HIM

5. *Thou holdest fast.* God prevents his eyelids from closing so that he is unable to sleep. He therefore spends the night brooding.

troubled. Mentally, perplexed by the thoughts which crowded into his mind during the sleepless night. The verb may also mean 'I was stunned.'

cannot speak. The bewildering ideas which occur to him relative to his people's tragedy (cf. Sforno).

6. The past history of Israel was reviewed by him with its many illustrations of God's providential care (Rashi).

7 In the night I will call to remembrance my song;
   I will commune with mine own
   heart;
   And my spirit maketh diligent
   search:

8 'Will the Lord cast off for ever?
   And will He be favourable no
   more?

9 Is His mercy clean gone for ever?
   Is His promise come to an end for
   evermore?

10 Hath God forgotten to be
   gracious?
   Hath He in anger shut up His
   compassions?'   Selah

11 And I say: 'This is my weakness,
   That the right hand of the Most
   High could change.

12 I will make mention of the deeds
   of the LORD;
   Yea, I will remember Thy
   wonders of old.

13 I will meditate also upon all Thy
   work,
   And muse on Thy doings.'

14 O God, Thy way is in holiness;
   Who is a great god like unto God?

7 אֶזְכְּרָה נְגִינָתִי בַּלָּיְלָה
עִם־לְבָבִי אָשִׂיחָה וַיְחַפֵּשׂ רוּחִי:
8 הַלְעוֹלָמִים יִזְנַח ׀ אֲדֹנָי
וְלֹא־יֹסִיף לִרְצוֹת עוֹד:
9 הֶאָפֵס לָנֶצַח חַסְדּוֹ
גָּמַר אֹמֶר לְדֹר וָדֹר:
10 הֲשָׁכַח חַנּוֹת אֵל
אִם־קָפַץ בְּאַף רַחֲמָיו סֶלָה:
11 וָאֹמַר חַלּוֹתִי הִיא
שְׁנוֹת יְמִין עֶלְיוֹן:
12 אֶזְכִּיר מַעַלְלֵי־יָהּ
כִּי־אֶזְכְּרָה מִקֶּדֶם פִּלְאֶךָ:
13 וְהָגִיתִי בְכָל־פָּעֳלֶךָ
וּבַעֲלִילוֹתֶיךָ אָשִׂיחָה:
14 אֱלֹהִים בַּקֹּדֶשׁ דַּרְכֶּךָ
מִי־אֵל גָּדוֹל כֵּאלֹהִים:

v. 12. אזכור ק'

7. *night*. Figurative of the period of the nation's darkness in exile (Rashi, Kimchi).

I will call to remembrance. Omit *will* here and also before *commune*. He recalls, by contrast, the song of praise he had occasion to offer to God in happier times (Rashi, Kimchi).

commune. Over the questions which he formulates in the next verses.

8. *for ever*. Not *netsach*, the usual Hebrew word in such a connection, but *olamim*, the same one used in verse 6 for *ancient times*. A comparison is thereby drawn between future 'ages' and those of the past.

be favourable. The withdrawal of His favour alone accounts for the disaster, and only in its restoration is there hope of nation revival.

9. The implied suggestion is repudiated in cv. 8.

10. *to be gracious*. The attribute which He had proclaimed as His (Exod. xxxiv. 6) (cf. Malbim).

11-16 MEMORY OF THE EXODUS

11. *and I say*. In refutation of the suggestion contained in the previous verses.

this is my weakness. The cause of all my mental and spiritual distress is that I dare to imagine that God is capable of such a change of purpose with respect to Israel (cf. Malbim).

12. *I will make mention*. This rendering follows the *kethib*; the *kerē* is to be translated: 'I will remember.'

LORD. Hebrew *Jah* (Exod. xv. 2).

14. *Thy way*. God's dealings and goals.

who is a great god. Recalling Exod. xv. 11. A preferable translation is: 'where is there a power as great as God is?' (Hirsch).

15 Thou art the God that doest
    wonders;
    Thou hast made known Thy
        strength among the peoples.

16 Thou hast with Thine arm re-
    deemed Thy people,
    The sons of Jacob and Joseph.
                       Selah

17 The waters saw Thee, O God;
    The waters saw Thee, they were
        in pain;
    The depths also trembled.

18 The clouds flooded forth waters;
    The skies sent out a sound;
    Thine arrows also went abroad.

19 The voice of Thy thunder was in
    the whirlwind;
    The lightnings lighted up the
        world;
    The earth trembled and shook.

20 Thy way was in the sea,
    And Thy path in the great waters,
    And Thy footsteps were not
    known.

21 Thou didst lead Thy people like
    a flock,
    By the hand of Moses and Aaron.

15 אַתָּה הָאֵל עֹשֵׂה פֶלֶא
דוֹדַעְתָּ בָעַמִּים עֻזֶּךָ׃
16 גָּאַלְתָּ בִּזְרוֹעַ עַמֶּךָ
בְּנֵי־יַעֲקֹב וְיוֹסֵף סֶלָה׃
17 רָאוּךָ מַּיִם ׀ אֱלֹהִים
רָאוּךָ מַּיִם יָחִילוּ
אַף יִרְגְּזוּ תְהֹמוֹת׃
18 זֹרְמוּ מַיִם ׀ עָבוֹת
קוֹל נָתְנוּ שְׁחָקִים
אַף־חֲצָצֶיךָ יִתְהַלָּכוּ׃
19 קוֹל רַעַמְךָ ׀ בַּגַּלְגַּל
הֵאִירוּ בְרָקִים תֵּבֵל
רָגְזָה וַתִּרְעַשׁ הָאָרֶץ׃
20 בַּיָּם דַּרְכֶּךָ וּשְׁבִילְךָ בְּמַיִם רַבִּים
וְעִקְּבוֹתֶיךָ לֹא נֹדָעוּ׃
21 נָחִיתָ כַצֹּאן עַמֶּךָ
בְּיַד־מֹשֶׁה וְאַהֲרֹן׃

15.   *that doest wonders.* From Exod. xv. 11.

made known Thy strength. As the overthrow of Pharaoh and his host. Tanchuma (cxxxii. 8) has *strength* as a reference to Divine Law.

among the peoples. See Exod. xv. 14f.

16.   *with Thine arm redeemed.* Cf. Exod. xiii. 16.

the sons of Jacob and Joseph. Similarly, *the house of Jacob* and *the house of Joseph* (Obad. verse 18) together denote the entire people of Israel. Joseph was the father of Ephraim and Manasseh, the ancestors of the leading tribes in the N. Kingdom.

     17-24   THE MIRACLES AT THE RED SEA

17.   *the waters saw Thee.* For the personification of the waters, cf. cxiv. 3.

18.   *clouds.* We have here, as in xviii. 8ff., a poetical elaboration of the scene.

sound. Of thunder.

arrows. Flashes of lightning (Ibn Ezra) (cf. Hab. iii. 11.).

19.   *whirlwind.* Better, 'rumbling,' of the chariot in which God is represented as riding (Hab. iii. 8).

20.   *footsteps were not known.* God's victorious progression is so rapid that its traces cannot be perceived at the time; only its after-effects are evident.

21.   *by the hand of Moses and Aaron.* The miracles at the Red Sea served to instill into the Israelite, for all time, the certainty that Moses and Aaron had indeed been sent by God to be their leaders (Hirsch). The abrupt ending of the Psalm strengthens the impression upon the reader of God's Providence.

78

עח

1 Maschil of Asaph.
Give ear, O my people, to my
teaching;
Incline your ears to the words of
my mouth.

מַשְׂכִּיל לְאָסָף
הַאֲזִינָה עַמִּי תּוֹרָתִי
הַטּוּ אָזְנְכֶם לְאִמְרֵי־פִי׃

2 I will open my mouth with a
parable;
I will utter dark sayings concerning days of old.

2 אֶפְתְּחָה בְמָשָׁל פִּי
אַבִּיעָה חִידוֹת מִנִּי־קֶדֶם׃

3 That which we have heard and
known,
And our fathers have told us,

3 אֲשֶׁר שָׁמַעְנוּ וַנֵּדָעֵם
וַאֲבוֹתֵינוּ סִפְּרוּ־לָנוּ׃

4 We will not hide from their
children,
Telling to the generation to come
the praises of the LORD,
And His strength, and His wondrous works that He hath done.

4 לֹא נְכַחֵד ׀ מִבְּנֵיהֶם לְדוֹר אַחֲרוֹן
מְסַפְּרִים תְּהִלּוֹת יְהֹוָה
וֶעֱזוּזוֹ וְנִפְלְאֹתָיו אֲשֶׁר עָשָׂה׃

5 For He established a testimony in
Jacob,
And appointed a law in Israel,
Which He commanded our fathers,
That they should make them
known to their children;

5 וַיָּקֶם עֵדוּת ׀ בְּיַעֲקֹב
וְתוֹרָה שָׂם בְּיִשְׂרָאֵל
אֲשֶׁר צִוָּה אֶת־אֲבוֹתֵינוּ
לְהוֹדִיעָם לִבְנֵיהֶם׃

LESSON OF ISRAEL'S HISTORY

A DIDACTIC Psalm, bringing home to the people a warning which was writ large in their annals.
It reveals the Israelites' eternal mission to inspire all future generations to loyal obedience to
God and His Divine Law. A survey is made of the historical moments of deliverance and
decline from the days of Moses to David, hailing the election of David as the beginning of a
new and better future for the nation. The Psalmist points out the dire consequences suffered
when 'Ephraim' fails to learn from history that God is the sole source of their good fortune,
and concludes with the poetic description of the Divine shepherd choosing David, the
Judahite, to be the father of the dynasty that would lead the nation to be ever mindful of their
eternal bond to God.

1-8 PURPOSE OF THE PSALM

1. *Maschil.* See on xxxii. 1.

teaching. Hebrew *Torah.* This is its true signification, the idea of 'law' is secondary.

2. *parable ... dark sayings.* See on xlix. 5.

concerning days of old. What the past has to
teach the present and future generations.

4. *from their children.* The children of our
forebears; our brethren who have not received instruction in Torah. To those who

know not their link in the historic chain of
Torah tradition, it is incumbent upon us to
transmit this knowledge, and not to hide it
from them. They, in turn, will tell it to their
children till the entire generation to come will
be telling the praises of the LORD (Kimchi).

praises. Deeds which called forth praise.

wondrous works. See on lxxi. 17.

5. *testimony.* viz. the duty of a father to
instruct his children in their national annals,

6 That the generation to come might
   know them, even the children
   that should be born;
  Who should arise and tell them to
   their children,

7 That they might put their confi-
   dence in God,
  And not forget the works of God,
  But keep His commandments;

8 And might not be as their fathers,
  A stubborn and rebellious generation;
  A generation that set not their
   heart aright,
  And whose spirit was not stedfast
   with God.

9 The children of Ephraim were as
   archers handling the bow,
  That turned back in the day of
   battle.

6 לְמַעַן יֵדְעוּ ׀ דּוֹר אַחֲרוֹן בָּנִים יִוָּלֵדוּ
יָקֻמוּ וִיסַפְּרוּ לִבְנֵיהֶם:
7 וְיָשִׂימוּ בֵאלֹהִים כִּסְלָם
וְלֹא יִשְׁכְּחוּ מַעַלְלֵי־אֵל
וּמִצְוֹתָיו יִנְצֹרוּ:
8 וְלֹא יִהְיוּ ׀ כַּאֲבוֹתָם
דּוֹר סוֹרֵר וּמֹרֶה
דּוֹר לֹא־הֵכִין לִבּוֹ
וְלֹא־נֶאֶמְנָה אֶת־אֵל רוּחוֹ:
9 בְּנֵי־אֶפְרַיִם נוֹשְׁקֵי רוֹמֵי־קָשֶׁת
הָפְכוּ בְּיוֹם קְרָב:

which bear evidence to God's special relationship with His people (cf. Exod. x. 2, xii. 26f., xiii. 8, 14).

make them known. The object is that *which we have heard and known* (verse 3).

6. The verse may be differently punctuated as follows: 'That the generation to come might know (them), (and) children yet to be born should arise and tell (them) to their children.' The succeeding generations are to form an unbroken medium for the transmission of this knowledge.

7. *confidence.* So Ibn Ezra and Kimchi. A.V. renders it 'hope' in accordance with Targum.

the works of God. The deeds He wrought for Israel.

but keep His commandments. A familiarity with history has always been regarded by Jews as a powerful factor in moulding the religious thought of the young and inducing in them a sense of loyalty to God and to their people. All the events of early Jewish history revealing the hand of God in Jewish destiny had as their purpose to train Jews to acquire

unshakeable faith … not only to fulfill [the commandments] but also to see that they are passed on to future generations.

8. *stubborn and rebellious.* The adjectives are taken from the *stubborn and rebellious son, that will not hearken to the voice of his father, or the voice of his mother, and though they chasten him, will not hearken unto them* (Deut. xxi. 18). A parallel is drawn between such a perverse child and a perverse generation of Israelites disobedient to their heavenly Father.

set not their heart aright. But allowed it to stray after heathenish worship and practices.

not stedfast. lit. 'not faithful,' easily seduced from the ways of God.

9-16 WHAT HAPPENED IN EGYPT

9. A difficult verse, explained by a tradition, based on 1 Chron. vii. 21, that the Ephraimites did not wait for God's act of redemption, but left Egypt on their own. They then came into collision with the men of Gath who refused to sell them cattle, suffering defeat in the ensuing battle with heavy losses.

10 They kept not the covenant of
   God,
   And refused to walk in His law;

11 And they forgot His doings,
   And His wondrous works that He
   had shown them.

12 Marvellous things did He in the
   sight of their fathers,
   In the land of Egypt, in the field
   of Zoan.

13 He cleaved the sea, and caused
   them to pass through;
   And He made the waters to stand
   as a heap.

14 By day also He led them with a
   cloud,
   And all the night with a light of
   fire.

15 He cleaved rocks in the wilderness,
   And gave them drink abundantly
   as out of the great deep.

16 He brought streams also out of
   the rock,
   And caused waters to run down
   like rivers.

17 Yet went they on still to sin
   against Him,
   To rebel against the Most High
   in the desert.

18 And they tried God in their heart
   By asking food for their craving.

10 לֹא שָׁמְרוּ בְּרִית אֱלֹהִים
וּבְתוֹרָתוֹ מֵאֲנוּ לָלֶכֶת:

11 וַיִּשְׁכְּחוּ עֲלִילוֹתָיו
וְנִפְלְאוֹתָיו אֲשֶׁר הֶרְאָם:

12 נֶגֶד אֲבוֹתָם עָשָׂה פֶלֶא
בְּאֶרֶץ מִצְרַיִם שְׂדֵה־צֹעַן:

13 בָּקַע יָם וַיַּעֲבִירֵם
וַיַּצֶּב־מַיִם כְּמוֹ־נֵד:

14 וַיַּנְחֵם בֶּעָנָן יוֹמָם
וְכָל־הַלַּיְלָה בְּאוֹר אֵשׁ:

15 יְבַקַּע צֻרִים בַּמִּדְבָּר
וַיַּשְׁקְ כִּתְהֹמוֹת רַבָּה:

16 וַיּוֹצִא נוֹזְלִים מִסָּלַע
וַיּוֹרֶד כַּנְּהָרוֹת מָיִם:

17 וַיּוֹסִיפוּ עוֹד לַחֲטֹא־לוֹ
לַמְרוֹת עֶלְיוֹן בַּצִּיָּה:

18 וַיְנַסּוּ־אֵל בִּלְבָבָם
לִשְׁאָל־אֹכֶל לְנַפְשָׁם:

12. *in the field of Zoan.* The district of
Zoan, the ancient capital of Egypt. There is
a passing allusion to the plagues, which are
detailed in verses 43ff.

13. *cleaved.* The verb used in Exod.
xiv. 16.

stand as a heap. From Exod. xv. 8.

14. Cf. Exod. xiii. 21.

15. *cleaved rocks.* At Rephidim (Exod.
xvii. 6).

great deep. The subterranean stores of water
(xxxiii. 7; Gen. vii. 11).

16. *out of the rock.* At Kadesh (Num. xx.
8ff.).

17-31 MURMURINGS FOR FOOD AND DRINK

17. *rebel.* Their acts of disobedience were
a revolt against God's Sovereignty (Malbim).

desert. Not the common word, but one meaning 'parched land.'

18. *tried.* By their doubts of Him which
resulted in constant murmuring (cf. Malbim).

by asking food. As though He would not have
provided for their needs without their clamour.

for their craving. lit. 'for their soul,' which
may mean 'for their appetite' or just 'for
themselves.'

19. *prepare a table.* For the phrase, cf.
xxiii. 5.

19 Yea, they spoke against God;
　　They said: 'Can God prepare a
　　　table in the wilderness?

20 Behold, He smote the rock, that
　　　waters gushed out,
　　And streams overflowed;
　　Can He give bread also?
　　Or will He provide flesh for His
　　　people?'

21 Therefore the Lord heard, and
　　　was wroth;
　　And a fire was kindled against
　　　Jacob,
　　And anger also went up against
　　　Israel;

22 Because they believed not in God,
　　And trusted not in His salvation.

23 And He commanded the skies
　　　above,
　　And opened the doors of heaven;

24 And He caused manna to rain
　　　upon them for food,
　　And gave them of the corn of
　　　heaven.

25 Man did eat the bread of the
　　　mighty;
　　He sent them provisions to the
　　　full.

וַיְדַבְּרוּ בֵּאלֹהִים אָמְרוּ 19
הֲיוּכַל אֵל לַעֲרֹךְ שֻׁלְחָן בַּמִּדְבָּר׃
הֵן הִכָּה־צוּר וַיָּזוּבוּ מַיִם 20
וּנְחָלִים יִשְׁטֹפוּ
הֲגַם־לֶחֶם יוּכַל תֵּת
אִם־יָכִין שְׁאֵר לְעַמּוֹ׃
לָכֵן שָׁמַע יְהֹוָה וַיִּתְעַבָּר 21
וְאֵשׁ נִשְּׂקָה בְיַעֲקֹב
וְגַם־אַף עָלָה בְיִשְׂרָאֵל׃
כִּי לֹא הֶאֱמִינוּ בֵּאלֹהִים 22
וְלֹא בָטְחוּ בִּישׁוּעָתוֹ׃
וַיְצַו שְׁחָקִים מִמָּעַל 23
וְדַלְתֵי שָׁמַיִם פָּתָח׃
וַיַּמְטֵר עֲלֵיהֶם מָן לֶאֱכֹל 24
וּדְגַן־שָׁמַיִם נָתַן לָמוֹ׃
לֶחֶם אַבִּירִים אָכַל אִישׁ 25
צֵידָה שָׁלַח לָהֶם לָשֹׂבַע׃

20. The presentation of the circumstances is poetical rather than historical. In fact, food was supplied (Exod. xvi. 8, 12; Num. xi. 31ff.) before water (Exod. xvii. 6; Num. xx. 8ff.).

21. *a fire … kindled*. Allusion to Num. xi. 1ff.

anger also went up. Like smoke from a blaze (xviii. 9).

22. *believed not*. Cf. Num. xiv. 11.
His salvation. To allow them to enter the promised land without warfare (Kimchi).

23. *doors of heaven*. A similar use of *windows in heaven* occurs in 2 Kings vii. 2, 19; Mal. iii. 10.

24. *manna to rain*. Borrowing the language of Exod. xvi. 4, *I will cause to rain bread from heaven for you*.

corn of heaven. So described because of its resemblance to seeds (Exod. xvi. 31).

25. *man*. So lit., but the sense of the word here is 'each one,' as Exod. xvi. 18.

bread of the mighty. The angels are described as *mighty in strength* (ciii. 20), and tradition says manna was their food (so Targum).

26 He caused the east wind to set
   forth in heaven;
   And by His power He brought
   on the south wind.

27 He caused flesh also to rain upon
   them as the dust,
   And winged fowl as the sand of
   the seas;

28 And He let it fall in the midst of
   their camp,
   Round about their dwellings.

29 So they did eat, and were well
   filled;
   And He gave them that which
   they craved.

30 They were not estranged from
   their craving,
   Their food was yet in their
   mouths,

31 When the anger of God went up
   against them,
   And slew of the lustiest among
   them,
   And smote down the young men
   of Israel.

32 For all this they sinned still,
   And believed not in His wondrous works.

33 Therefore He ended their days as
   a breath,
   And their years in terror.

34 When He slew them, then they
   would inquire after Him,
   And turn back and seek God
   earnestly.

26 יַסַּע קָדִים בַּשָּׁמָיִם
וַיְנַהֵג בְּעֻזּוֹ תֵימָן׃

27 וַיַּמְטֵר עֲלֵיהֶם כֶּעָפָר שְׁאֵר
וּכְחוֹל יַמִּים עוֹף כָּנָף׃

28 וַיַּפֵּל בְּקֶרֶב מַחֲנֵהוּ
סָבִיב לְמִשְׁכְּנֹתָיו׃

29 וַיֹּאכְלוּ וַיִּשְׂבְּעוּ מְאֹד
וְתַאֲוָתָם יָבִא לָהֶם׃

30 לֹא־זָרוּ מִתַּאֲוָתָם
עוֹד אָכְלָם בְּפִיהֶם׃

31 וְאַף אֱלֹהִים עָלָה בָהֶם
וַיַּהֲרֹג בְּמִשְׁמַנֵּיהֶם
וּבַחוּרֵי יִשְׂרָאֵל הִכְרִיעַ׃

32 בְּכָל־זֹאת חָטְאוּ־עוֹד
וְלֹא־הֶאֱמִינוּ בְּנִפְלְאוֹתָיו׃

33 וַיְכַל־בַּהֶבֶל יְמֵיהֶם
וּשְׁנוֹתָם בַּבֶּהָלָה׃

34 אִם־הֲרָגָם וּדְרָשׁוּהוּ
וְשָׁבוּ וְשִׁחֲרוּ־אֵל׃

26. *east … south.* The two words are separated to secure the parallelism which is a
feature of Hebrew poetry. The direction from
which the quails came was southeast.

27. *flesh … winged fowl.* Cf. Exod. xvi. 13;
Num. xi. 31.

30. *not estranged from.* They were still in-
dulging in the object of their lust when punishment befell them (Num. xi. 33).

31. *lustiest.* Strongest, in the prime of life
(Kimchi).

32-39 STILL THE LESSON WAS NOT LEARNT

33. *breath.* Their life ended in nothingness,
inasmuch as they failed to reach the goal of
their wandering, the promised land (Ibn
Ezra).

terror. Defined in Lev. xxvi. 16, as *consumption and fever.*

34. *slew them.* When God caused some of
them to die, the people were moved to repent.
This repentance, however, was not sincere,
as seen in verses 36, 37.

35. *God was their Rock.* In Him alone was
security to be found.

Most High God. The combination *el elyon*
occurs again only in Gen. xiv. 18ff.

35 And they remembered that God
    was their Rock,
    And the Most High God their
    Redeemer.

36 But they beguiled Him with their
    mouth,
    And lied unto Him with their
    tongue.

37 For their heart was not stedfast
    with Him,
    Neither were they faithful in His
    covenant.

38 But He, being full of compassion,
    forgiveth iniquity, and destroy-
    eth not;
    Yea, many a time doth He turn
    His anger away,
    And doth not stir up all His
    wrath.

39 So He remembered that they
    were but flesh;
    A wind that passeth away, and
    cometh not again.

40 How oft did they rebel against
    Him in the wilderness,
    And grieve Him in the desert!

41 And still again they tried God,
    And set bounds to the Holy One
    of Israel.

35 וַיִּזְכְּרוּ כִּי־אֱלֹהִים צוּרָם
וְאֵל עֶלְיוֹן גֹּאֲלָם:

36 וַיְפַתּוּהוּ בְּפִיהֶם
וּבִלְשׁוֹנָם יְכַזְּבוּ־לוֹ:

37 וְלִבָּם לֹא־נָכוֹן עִמּוֹ
וְלֹא נֶאֶמְנוּ בִּבְרִיתוֹ:

38 וְהוּא רַחוּם ׀
יְכַפֵּר עָוֺן וְלֹא־יַשְׁחִית
וְהִרְבָּה לְהָשִׁיב אַפּוֹ
וְלֹא־יָעִיר כָּל־חֲמָתוֹ:

39 וַיִּזְכֹּר כִּי־בָשָׂר הֵמָּה
רוּחַ הוֹלֵךְ וְלֹא יָשׁוּב:

40 כַּמָּה יַמְרוּהוּ בַמִּדְבָּר
יַעֲצִיבוּהוּ בִּישִׁימוֹן:

41 וַיָּשׁוּבוּ וַיְנַסּוּ אֵל
וּקְדוֹשׁ יִשְׂרָאֵל הִתְווּ:

36. *beguiled.* No sincere motive prompted them in their return to God. They thought they could deceive Him with their words of flattery (cf. Isa. xxix. 13), and so their protestations of regret and loyalty were only lies (cf. Tosephta Bava Kama 7:3).

37. *their heart was not stedfast.* It is the heart that determines conduct; therefore the Rabbis insisted, 'The All-merciful demands the heart.'

38. *full of compassion, forgiveth iniquity.* Cf. Exod. xxxiv. 6f.

all His wrath. In which case He would have brought the national career of Israel to an end. Cf. Deut. ix. 19.

39. *but flesh.* Mortal beings and liable to err (Rashi, Kimchi).

a wind that passeth away. Man's death ne-

cessitates that while still alive God grants him forgiveness (Kimchi).

40-55 PAST MERCIES RECALLED

40. The same thought to introduce a fresh section as in verse 17.

grieve. Cf. Gen. vi. 6; Isa. lxiii. 10.

41. *set bounds to.* Ascribed limitations to God's power (Ibn Ezra). Hirsch adds: 'they confined His might or His will to certain definite areas. They conceived special "compartments" of living and achievement, which they regarded either as beyond the scope of His power, or else as beneath the province of His concern or will.'

Holy One of Israel. See on lxxi. 22.

42. *His hand.* His might which He directed to their rescue and protection.

42 They remembered not His hand,
Nor the day when He redeemed
them from the adversary.

43 How He set His signs in Egypt,
And His wonders in the field of
Zoan;

44 And turned their rivers into
blood,
So that they could not drink their
streams.

45 He sent among them swarms of
flies, which devoured them;
And frogs, which destroyed them.

46 He gave also their increase unto
the caterpillar,
And their labour unto the locust.

47 He destroyed their vines with
hail,
And their sycomore-trees with
frost.

48 He gave over their cattle also to
the hail,
And their flocks to fiery bolts.

42 לֹא־זָכְרוּ אֶת־יָדוֹ
יוֹם אֲשֶׁר־פָּדָם מִנִּי־צָר:

43 אֲשֶׁר־שָׂם בְּמִצְרַיִם אֹתוֹתָיו
וּמוֹפְתָיו בִּשְׂדֵה־צֹעַן:

44 וַיַּהֲפֹךְ לְדָם יְאֹרֵיהֶם
וְנֹזְלֵיהֶם בַּל־יִשְׁתָּיוּן:

45 יְשַׁלַּח בָּהֶם עָרֹב וַיֹּאכְלֵם
וּצְפַרְדֵּעַ וַתַּשְׁחִיתֵם:

46 וַיִּתֵּן לֶחָסִיל יְבוּלָם
וִיגִיעָם לָאַרְבֶּה:

47 יַהֲרֹג בַּבָּרָד גַּפְנָם
וְשִׁקְמוֹתָם בַּחֲנָמַל:

48 וַיַּסְגֵּר לַבָּרָד בְּעִירָם
וּמִקְנֵיהֶם לָרְשָׁפִים:

---

adversary. Pharaoh.

43. *His signs ... His wonders.* The ten plagues. Only six, or possibly seven, are enumerated in the next verses; nor is the historical order followed.

field of Zoan. As in verse 12.

44. *their rivers.* In the singular *yĕor* is only used of the Nile; the plural denotes that river with its tributary canals.

could not drink. Exod. vii. 18. The first plague.

45. *swarms of flies.* The fourth plague (Exod. viii. 20).

frogs. The second plague (Exod. viii. 1).

46. *their increase.* The produce of their land.

caterpillar. The Hebrew is a word for locust, perhaps in the pupa stage.

locust. The eighth plague (Exod. x. 4).

47. *hail.* The seventh plague (Exod. ix. 18).

sycamore-trees. Very common in Egypt, its wood is used for mummy cases.

frost. The Hebrew, *hanamal*, occurs nowhere else. Ibn Ezra and Saadya, cited by Kimchi, suggest crushing hailstones, and this makes for a parallelism (Hirsch). Rashi however, renders it a type of locust.

48. *their cattle also to the hail.* The injury to the cattle is specifically mentioned in Exod. ix. 19, 25.

fiery bolts. Lightning flashes which accompany a hailstorm (see Exod. ix. 24) (Hirsch); but in Hab iii. 5 they are said to be connected with *pestilence* and may mean 'fever, inflammation' (cf. Deut. xxxii. 24).

49. *sent forth.* As the climax of the demonstration of Divine anger. Kimchi sees this verse as a collective reference to the

49 He sent forth upon them the
fierceness of His anger,
Wrath, and indignation, and
trouble,
A sending of messengers of evil.

50 He levelled a path for His anger;
He spared not their soul from
death,
But gave their life over to the
pestilence;

51 And smote all the first-born in
Egypt,
The first-fruits of their strength
in the tents of Ham;

52 But He made His own people to
go forth like sheep,
And guided them in the wilderness like a flock.

53 And He led them safely, and they
feared not;
But the sea overwhelmed their
enemies.

54 And He brought them to His
holy border,
To the mountain, which His
right hand had gotten.

49 יְשַׁלַּח־בָּ֨ם ׀ חֲר֬וֹן אַפּ֗וֹ
עֶבְרָ֣ה וָזַ֣עַם וְצָרָ֑ה
מִ֝שְׁלַ֗חַת מַלְאֲכֵ֥י רָעִֽים׃
50 יְפַלֵּ֥ס נָתִ֗יב לְאַ֫פּ֥וֹ
לֹא־חָשַׂ֣ךְ מִמָּ֣וֶת נַפְשָׁ֑ם
וְ֝חַיָּתָ֗ם לַדֶּ֥בֶר הִסְגִּֽיר׃
51 וַיַּ֥ךְ כָּל־בְּכ֗וֹר בְּמִצְרָ֑יִם
רֵאשִׁ֥ית א֝וֹנִ֗ים בְּאָהֳלֵי־חָֽם׃
52 וַיַּסַּ֣ע כַּצֹּ֣אן עַמּ֑וֹ
וַֽיְנַהֲגֵ֥ם כַּ֝עֵ֗דֶר בַּמִּדְבָּֽר׃
53 וַיַּנְחֵ֣ם לָ֭בֶטַח וְלֹ֣א פָחָ֑דוּ
וְאֶת־א֝וֹיְבֵיהֶ֗ם כִּסָּ֥ה הַיָּֽם׃
54 וַ֭יְבִיאֵם אֶל־גְּב֣וּל קָדְשׁ֑וֹ
הַר־זֶ֝֗ה קָנְתָ֥ה יְמִינֽוֹ׃

plagues not specifically enumerated (see on
verse 43).

50. *levelled a path.* God created a path free
of obstructions for His anger (Kimchi).

their soul. Equals 'them.' He no longer spared
their lives as He did when He decimated their
cattle by pestilence (Hirsch).

to the pestilence. The cognate word for 'deber'
in Arabic signifies 'death,' and *deber* has a
similar meaning in Rabbinic Hebrew.

51. *first-fruits of their strength.* The first-
born (cf. Gen. xlix. 3).

Ham. Ancestor of Mizraim, i.e. Egypt
(Gen. x. 6).

52. *made...to go forth.* More lit. 'He caused
... to journey by stages,' the common word

used in the wandering from Egypt to Canaan.
He appointed the halting places for them.

53. *they feared not.* In accordance with the
exhortation, *fear ye not* (Exod. xiv. 13),
whereas the Egyptians were panic-stricken
(Exod. xiv. 25).

54. *border.* Besides 'frontier,' the Hebrew
word also signifies 'a delimited piece of land.'
Here the meaning is 'to His holy land' (Hirsch).

mountain. Better, 'mountain land,' Canaan,
as in Deut. iii. 25 (Hirsch). Another possibility, 'Temple Mount' (so Ibn Ezra, Kimchi,
Malbim).

55. *allotted them.* i.e. their land.

an inheritance by line. So render Metsudath
David and Hirsch. Or perhaps 'as the portion

55 He drove out the nations also
    before them,
  And allotted them for an inherit-
    ance by line,
  And made the tribes of Israel to
    dwell in their tents.

56 Yet they tried and provoked God,
    the Most High,
  And kept not His testimonies;

57 But turned back, and dealt treach-
    erously like their fathers;
  They were turned aside like a
    deceitful bow.

58 For they provoked Him with
    their high places,
  And moved Him to jealousy with
    their graven images.

59 God heard, and was wroth,
  And He greatly abhorred Israel;

60 And He forsook the tabernacle of
    Shiloh,
  The tent which He had made to
    dwell among men;

61 And delivered His strength into
    captivity,
  And His glory into the adver-
    sary's hand.

55 וַיְגָרֶשׁ מִפְּנֵיהֶם ׀ גּוֹיִם

וַֽיַּפִּילֵם בְּחֶבֶל נַחֲלָה

וַיַּשְׁכֵּן בְּאָהֳלֵיהֶם שִׁבְטֵי יִשְׂרָאֵל׃

56 וַיְנַסּוּ וַיַּמְרוּ אֶת־אֱלֹהִים עֶלְיוֹן

וְעֵדוֹתָיו לֹא שָׁמָרוּ׃

57 וַיִּסֹּגוּ וַיִּבְגְּדוּ כַּאֲבוֹתָם

נֶהְפְּכוּ כְּקֶשֶׁת רְמִיָּה׃

58 וַיַּכְעִיסוּהוּ בְּבָמוֹתָם

וּבִפְסִילֵיהֶם יַקְנִיאוּהוּ׃

59 שָׁמַע אֱלֹהִים וַיִּתְעַבָּר

וַיִּמְאַס מְאֹד בְּיִשְׂרָאֵל׃

60 וַיִּטֹּשׁ מִשְׁכַּן שִׁלוֹ

אֹהֶל שִׁכֵּן בָּאָדָם׃

61 וַיִּתֵּן לַשְּׁבִי עֻזּוֹ

וְתִפְאַרְתּוֹ בְיַד־צָר׃

(or, territory) of inheritance'; it passed into Israel's possession.

56-64 MORE REVOLT AND PUNISHMENT

56. *God, the Most High. Elohim elyon*, with which compare *el elyon* in verse 35.

testimonies. See on xix. 8.

57. *like their fathers*. The Israelites who witnessed God's wondrous works in the conquest of Canaan proved as forgetful of Him as did their fathers who had been redeemed by Him from Egypt.

a deceitful bow. From which the arrows fail to hit the target (again Hos. vii. 16).

58. *high places*. Idolatrous altars.

to jealousy. Like a man who will not tolerate a rival, God demands that He alone must be

worshipped (Exod. xx. 5). Only by whole-hearted devotion can He be served at all.

59. *greatly abhorred*. Better, 'utterly rejected.' He permitted the land to be overrun by a neighbouring people, the Philistines.

60. *forsook the tabernacle of Shiloh*. So that the ark was captured by the Philistines.

61. *His strength*. Abbreviated from *the ark of Thy strength* (cxxxii. 8).

His glory. Cf. *the glory is departed from Israel* (1 Sam. iv. 21).

62. *unto the sword*. Cf. 1 Sam. iv. 2, 10.

His inheritance. The people of Israel (see on xxviii. 9).

62 He gave His people over also
   unto the sword;
   And was wroth with His inheritance.

63 Fire devoured their young men;
   And their virgins had no marriage-song.

64 Their priests fell by the sword;
   And their widows made **no**
   lamentation.

65 Then the Lord awaked as one
   asleep,
   Like a mighty man recovering
   from wine.

66 And He smote His adversaries
   backward;
   He put upon them a perpetual
   reproach.

67 Moreover He abhorred the tent
   of Joseph,
   And chose **not** the tribe of
   Ephraim;

וַיַּסְגֵּר לַחֶרֶב עַמּוֹ 62
וּבְנַחֲלָתוֹ הִתְעַבָּר׃
בַּחוּרָיו אָכְלָה־אֵשׁ 63
וּבְתוּלֹתָיו לֹא הוּלָּלוּ׃
כֹּהֲנָיו בַּחֶרֶב נָפָלוּ 64
וְאַלְמְנֹתָיו לֹא תִבְכֶּינָה׃
וַיִּקַץ כְּיָשֵׁן ׀ אֲדֹנָי 65
כְּגִבּוֹר מִתְרוֹנֵן מִיָּיִן׃
וַיַּךְ־צָרָיו אָחוֹר 66
חֶרְפַּת עוֹלָם נָתַן לָמוֹ׃
וַיִּמְאַס בְּאֹהֶל יוֹסֵף 67
וּבְשֵׁבֶט אֶפְרַיִם לֹא בָחָר׃

63. *fire.* Figurative of the devastation of
war (Kimchi).

had no marriage-song. They stayed unmar-
ried through the slaughter of the men who
might have been their husbands (Rashi, Ibn
Ezra) and the other priests accompanying the
ark (Kimchi).

64. *priests fell.* e.g. Hophni and Phinehas
(1 Sam. iv. 11) (Rashi, Ibn Ezra, Kimchi) and
the other priests accompanying the ark
(Kimchi).

their widows made no lamentation. Also in
Job xxvii. 15. The havoc wrought was so
heavy and widespread, that in the state of
panic and anxiety widows had no thought to
bewail their dead husbands. Rashi has this
refer to Phineas' wife who, having heard the
tragic news, was seized by premature birth
pangs and died at childbirth, thus never
mourning her husband's death.

65-66   GOD PITIED HIS ERRING PEOPLE

65. *as one asleep.* Cf. xliv. 24. During the
period of national distress, God had been
passive like a sleeper; at length He roused
Himself to activity on their behalf.

recovering. The verb is of uncertain meaning; probably 'as a mighty man overcome by
wine (awakes, so He awoke)' (Targum).

66. *smote His adversaries.* Alluding to the
defeats of the Philistines by Saul and David.

a perpetual reproach. A reverse on the
battlefield from which they never recovered.

67-69   CHOICE OF ZION FOR THE TEMPLE

67. *abhorred.* Rejected, as in verse 59.

the tent of Joseph. The temporary Sanctuary
at Shiloh, which was in the territory of
Ephraim, son of Joseph (Rashi). Even after
its recapture, the ark was never restored in
Shiloh, but travelled from place to place with
its Sanctuary and finally was brought to

68 But chose the tribe of Judah,
The mount Zion which He loved.

69 And He built His sanctuary like
the heights,
Like the earth which He hath
founded for ever.

70 He chose David also His servant,
And took him from the sheepfolds;

71 From following the ewes that
give suck He brought him,
To be shepherd over Jacob His
people, and Israel His inheritance.

72 So he shepherded them according to the integrity of his
heart;
And led them by the skilfulness
of his hands.

68 וַיִּבְחַר אֶת־שֵׁבֶט יְהוּדָה
אֶת־הַר צִיּוֹן אֲשֶׁר אָהֵב:

69 וַיִּבֶן כְּמוֹ־רָמִים מִקְדָּשׁוֹ
כְּאֶרֶץ יְסָדָהּ לְעוֹלָם:

70 וַיִּבְחַר בְּדָוִד עַבְדּוֹ
וַיִּקָּחֵהוּ מִמִּכְלְאֹת צֹאן:

71 מֵאַחַר עָלוֹת הֱבִיאוֹ
לִרְעוֹת בְּיַעֲקֹב עַמּוֹ
וּבְיִשְׂרָאֵל נַחֲלָתוֹ:

72 וַיִּרְעֵם כְּתֹם לְבָבוֹ
וּבִתְבוּנוֹת כַּפָּיו יַנְחֵם:

Jerusalem by David (Kimchi).

68. *tribe of Judah.* In whose territory the Holy City was located. Ibn Ezra already sees in the mention of this tribe an allusion to David, born in Bethlehem, a Judahite town.

mount Zion. Here denotes Jerusalem. For its selection, see lxviii. 17.

69. *heights ... earth.* The mountains and the earth represent that which is fixed and enduring; so He intended the Temple to be (Kimchi, Metsudath David). God is said to have *built His sanctuary* (see Isa. xlv. 12, xlviii. 13) and so did He build His sanctuary with His 'two hands' (see Exod. xv. 17) (Rashi).

70-72 CHOICE OF DAVID AS KING

70. *His servant.* A title of distinction applied to those selected by God for His purposes. It is

used of David in 2 Sam. iii. 18, vii. 5, 8.

71. *to be shepherd over Jacob.* Cf. *thou shalt feed* (lit. shepherd) *My people Israel* (2 Sam. v. 2). His charge of the flock was a training for his kingship when he had the responsibility of caring for the welfare of the people. The Rabbis made a similar remark of Moses, who also was a shepherd (Exod. iii. 1) when God called him to become Israel's leader (Hirsch).

Israel His inheritance. See verse 62.

72. *the integrity of his heart.* Cf. *as David thy father walked, in integrity of heart* (1 Kings ix. 4).

skilfulness. lit. 'understanding'; he acted with discernment.

1 A Psalm of Asaph.
  O God, the heathen are come into
    Thine inheritance;
  They have defiled Thy holy
    temple;
  They have made Jerusalem into
    heaps.

2 They have given the dead bodies
    of Thy servants to be food unto
    the fowls of the heaven,
  The flesh of Thy saints unto the
    beasts of the earth.

3 They have shed their blood like
    water
  Round about Jerusalem, with none
    to bury them.

4 We are become a taunt to our
    neighbours,
  A scorn and derision to them that
    are round about us.

5 How long, O Lord, wilt Thou be
    angry for ever?

מִזְמוֹר לְאָסָף
אֱלֹהִים בָּאוּ גוֹיִם ׀ בְּנַחֲלָתֶךָ
טִמְּאוּ אֶת־הֵיכַל קָדְשֶׁךָ
שָׂמוּ אֶת־יְרוּשָׁלַם לְעִיִּים׃
2 נָתְנוּ אֶת־נִבְלַת עֲבָדֶיךָ
מַאֲכָל לְעוֹף הַשָּׁמָיִם
בְּשַׂר חֲסִידֶיךָ לְחַיְתוֹ־אָרֶץ׃
3 שָׁפְכוּ דָמָם ׀ כַּמַּיִם
סְבִיבוֹת יְרוּשָׁלַם וְאֵין קוֹבֵר׃
4 הָיִינוּ חֶרְפָּה לִשְׁכֵנֵינוּ
לַעַג וָקֶלֶס לִסְבִיבוֹתֵינוּ׃
5 עַד־מָה יְהֹוָה תֶּאֱנַף לָנֶצַח

PRAYER IN NATIONAL DISASTER

This Psalm is a companion to LXXIV and emanates from the same dark situation, the destruction of Jerusalem and the Temple by the Babylonians. Tractate Sopherim xviii. 3 appoints this Psalm and CXXXVII for recital on the ninth of Ab, the fast day which is the anniversary of the calamitous event.

1-4 THE DISASTER DESCRIBED

1. *the heathen.* lit. 'nations,' Gentile peoples.

Thine inheritance. The Holy Land.

defiled. Before destroying it (cf. lxxiv. 4ff.).

heaps. Of ruins.

2. *servants … saints.* Terms applied to Israel as the people of God's covenant. Hirsch makes a salient point by stating that 'however grievously the people of Israel may have sinned against God [to have deserved destruction], they were still "servants" and "saints" compared to the nations to which they had succumbed' (cf. Tal. San. 47a).

3. *with none to bury them.* Such treatment of the dead is regarded with the utmost horror. The corpse of an executed criminal must be given decent burial (Deut. xxi. 23); and even a High Priest who is a Nazirite, and so doubly precluded from defiling himself by such contact, had the obligation of attending to the proper disposal of the dead body when there was nobody else to do so (see Shulhan Aruch, Yoreh Deah 374:1).

4. Almost a verbal repetition of xliv. 14.

5-8 CRY OF DISTRESS

5. *how long … for ever?* The clause really contains two questions: How long? Will it be for ever?

How long will Thy jealousy burn
like fire?

6 Pour out Thy wrath upon the
nations that know Thee not,
And upon the kingdoms that call
not upon Thy name.

7 For they have devoured Jacob,
And laid waste his habitation.

8 Remember not against us the
iniquities of our forefathers;
Let Thy compassions speedily
come to meet us;
For we are brought very low.

9 Help us, O God of our salvation,
for the sake of the glory of Thy
name;
And deliver us, and forgive our
sins, for Thy name's sake.

10 Wherefore should the nations
say: 'Where is their God?'

תִּבְעַר כְּמוֹ־אֵשׁ קִנְאָתֶֽךָ׃

6 שְׁפֹךְ חֲמָֽתְךָ אֶל־הַגּוֹיִם
אֲשֶׁר לֹא־יְדָעֽוּךָ
וְעַל־מַמְלָכוֹת
אֲשֶׁר בְּשִׁמְךָ לֹא קָרָֽאוּ׃

7 כִּי אָכַל אֶת־יַעֲקֹב
וְאֶת־נָוֵהוּ הֵשַֽׁמּוּ׃

8 אַל־תִּזְכָּר־לָנוּ עֲוֺנֹת רִאשֹׁנִים
מַהֵר יְקַדְּמֽוּנוּ רַחֲמֶיךָ
כִּי דַלּוֹנוּ מְאֹד׃

9 עׇזְרֵנוּ אֱלֹהֵי יִשְׁעֵנוּ
עַל־דְּבַר כְּבוֹד־שְׁמֶךָ
וְהַצִּילֵנוּ וְכַפֵּר עַל־חַטֹּאתֵינוּ
לְמַעַן שְׁמֶֽךָ׃

10 לָמָּה יֹאמְרוּ הַגּוֹיִם אַיֵּה אֱלֹהֵיהֶם

Thy jealousy. See on lxxviii. 58.

6. With this and the following verse cf. Jer.
x. 25.

upon the nations that know Thee not. Better,
'toward.' 'Let Thy anger smite those nations
who have not recognized Thy hand in the
fateful decrees which Thou hast caused them
to carry out upon us ... to whom it never
occurred that they were only tools in Thy
hand ... .'(Hirsch).

8. *the iniquities of our forefathers.* The view
of some moderns, that the phrase means 'our
former iniquities,' is mentioned and rejected
by Ibn Ezra. We have here the thought explicitly expressed in Lam. v. 7, *Our fathers
have sinned, and are not; and we have borne
their iniquities.* It is the doctrine of Exod. xx.
5, in the sense that children suffer for their

fathers' sins when they retain the evil deeds
of their fathers (see on Exod. xx. 5).

come to meet us. Cf. lix. 11

brought very low. Same root as *poor* in xli. 2.
Here it may signify both enfeebled in strength
and impoverished.

9-12 PRAYER FOR HELP

9. *for the sake of the glory of Thy name.* A
frequent plea to God in prayer. If the
suppliant's sins are so heavy as not to deserve
a response, the appeal is made on the ground
of God's honour which is compromised, since
Israel's fate is bound up therewith.

10. *wherefore should the nations say.* So
pleaded Moses after the sin of the Golden
Calf (Exod. xxxii. 12) and the affair of the
spies (Num. xiv. 13ff.). Cf. also cxv. 2.

Let the avenging of Thy servants' blood that is shed
Be made known among the
nations in our sight.

11 Let the groaning of the prisoner
come before Thee;
According to the greatness of
Thy power set free those that
are appointed to death;

12 And render unto our neighbours
sevenfold into their bosom
Their reproach, wherewith they
have reproached Thee, O
Lord.

13 So we that are Thy people and
the flock of Thy pasture
Will give Thee thanks for ever;
We will tell of Thy praise to all
generations.

יִוָּדַע בַּגּוֹיִם לְעֵינֵינוּ
נִקְמַת דַּם־עֲבָדֶיךָ הַשָּׁפוּךְ:
11 תָּבוֹא לְפָנֶיךָ אֶנְקַת אָסִיר
כְּגֹדֶל זְרוֹעֲךָ הוֹתֵר בְּנֵי תְמוּתָה:
12 וְהָשֵׁב לִשְׁכֵנֵינוּ
שִׁבְעָתַיִם אֶל־חֵיקָם
חֶרְפָּתָם אֲשֶׁר חֵרְפוּךָ אֲדֹנָי:
13 וַאֲנַחְנוּ עַמְּךָ וְצֹאן מַרְעִיתֶךָ
נוֹדֶה לְּךָ לְעוֹלָם
לְדֹר וָדֹר נְסַפֵּר תְּהִלָּתֶךָ:

v. 10. בגוים ק׳

---

avenging ... blood. Cf. Deut. xxxii. 43. It
should be noted that the call for Divine retribution is not motivated by the desire to see
the persecutors suffer, but that it should be
known how God upholds the cause of their
victims and executes justice upon earth.

in our sight. May this happen soon; do not
defer it.

11. Cf. cii. 21.

the prisoner. Israel in captivity. Ibn Ezra
comments that Israel in exile is likened unto
a prisoner in jail.

those that are appointed to death. lit. 'sons of
death.' It may mean 'condemned to die' (1
Sam. xx. 31, xxvi. 16), and also as here 'those
enduring a living death of exile' (cf. Kimchi).

12. *our neighbours.* Who gloated over our
misfortune instead of showing sympathy.

sevenfold. Cf. Gen. iv. 15. See on xii. 7.

into their bosom. An allusion to the thoughts
in their hearts (Alshich).

their reproach. It is not a reproach to Thee.
The slighting remarks about Israel's God is a
reproach to themselves.

they have reproached Thee. They made
slighting remarks about Israel's God as being
powerless to help His people.

13 HOPE FOR THE FUTURE

After God executes retribution, Israel, his
nation, will praise Him.

flock of Thy pasture. As in lxxiv. 1.

tell of Thy praise. That is Israel's appointed
mission (Isa. xliii. 21). 'Let each generation
deem it its task to bequeath to its descendants
the memory of the manifestation of the mighty
acts of God' (Hirsch).

80

פ

1 For the Leader; upon Shoshannim. A testimony. A Psalm of
Asaph.

2 Give ear, O Shepherd of Israel,
Thou that leadest Joseph like a
flock;
Thou that art enthroned upon the
cherubim, shine forth.

3 Before Ephraim and Benjamin and
Manasseh, stir up Thy might,
And come to save us.

4 O God, restore us;
And cause Thy face to shine, and
we shall be saved.

לַמְנַצֵּחַ אֶל־שֹׁשַׁנִּים
עֵדוּת לְאָסָף מִזְמוֹר:
2 רֹעֵה יִשְׂרָאֵל הַאֲזִינָה
נֹהֵג כַּצֹּאן יוֹסֵף
יֹשֵׁב הַכְּרוּבִים הוֹפִיעָה:
3 לִפְנֵי אֶפְרַיִם וּבִנְיָמִן וּמְנַשֶּׁה
עוֹרְרָה אֶת־גְּבוּרָתֶךָ
וּלְכָה לִישֻׁעָתָה לָּנוּ:
4 אֱלֹהִים הֲשִׁיבֵנוּ
וְהָאֵר פָּנֶיךָ וְנִוָּשֵׁעָה:

PRAYER FOR ISRAEL'S RESTORATION

ALTHOUGH it is clear that this prayer concerns itself with a time of national straits, the exact
reference is a matter of varying opinions. Rashi sees it as an allusion to three periods of exile:
the Babylonian, the Greek and the Roman. Malbim suggests that it was composed in the time
of Ezra and Nehemiah, when they returned from the Babylonian exile to rebuild the Temple,
and their enemies threatened to thwart their plans by doing battle with them. Impoverished
and in a dire position, they composed this prayer contrasting their return from Babylon with
the exodus from Egypt. Hirsch develops the idea that it is a Psalm written for the generations
of Israel in exile.

1. *upon Shoshannim.* See on lx. 1.

    2-4 THE PEOPLE'S CRY FOR HELP

2. *Shepherd of Israel.* God to Whom Israel is *the flock of His pasture* (lxxiv. 1, lxxix.
13). *Israel* is best understood as the whole
nation, not the Northern Kingdom only.

Joseph. The Psalmist is concerned about
the future of the northern Kingdom which
seceded from the rule of Judah and Benjamin and was called Joseph and Ephraim
(Kimchi).

enthroned upon the cherubim. For *cherubim*,
see on xviii. 11. The phrase is associated with
the ark of the covenant (1 Sam. iv. 4; 2 Sam.
vi. 2) which accompanied the people in their
journey through the wilderness.

shine forth. See on l, 2.

3. *Ephraim, Benjamin, Manasseh.* In Num.

ii. 18 these three tribes, united by their common descent from Rachel, are mentioned as
encamping together on the western side.
Hirsch contends that 'it is clear that the names
of Ephraim and Manasseh are intended to
represent the shattered kingdom of the ten
tribes … The connection of Ephraim with
Benjamin, however, is somewhat obscure.
Benjamin was the only tribe to adhere to
Judah and to share its fate … Perhaps the
intent is to state that Ephraim and Manasseh
long to be reunited with Benjamin so that,
together once again under one banner and
near the Sanctuary of God, they may follow
the guidance of Divine Omnipotence.'

stir up. lit. 'arouse, awaken,' as though God's
might had been dormant.

4. A refrain, recurring in verses 8, 20.

restore us. Probably a reminiscence of

5 O Lord God of hosts,
How long wilt Thou be angry
against the prayer of Thy
people?

6 Thou hast fed them with the
bread of tears,
And given them tears to drink in
large measure.

7 Thou makest us a strife unto our
neighbours;
And our enemies mock as they
please.

8 O God of hosts, restore us;
And cause Thy face to shine, and
we shall be saved.

9 Thou didst pluck up a vine out
of Egypt;
Thou didst drive out the nations,
and didst plant it.

10 Thou didst clear a place before
it,
And it took deep root, and filled
the land.

5 יְהוָה אֱלֹהִים צְבָאוֹת
עַד־מָתַי עָשַׁנְתָּ בִּתְפִלַּת עַמֶּךָ׃
6 הֶאֱכַלְתָּם לֶחֶם דִּמְעָה
וַתַּשְׁקֵמוֹ בִּדְמָעוֹת שָׁלִישׁ׃
7 תְּשִׂימֵנוּ מָדוֹן לִשְׁכֵנֵינוּ
וְאֹיְבֵינוּ יִלְעֲגוּ־לָמוֹ׃
8 אֱלֹהִים צְבָאוֹת הֲשִׁיבֵנוּ
וְהָאֵר פָּנֶיךָ וְנִוָּשֵׁעָה׃
9 גֶּפֶן מִמִּצְרַיִם תַּסִּיעַ
תְּגָרֵשׁ גּוֹיִם וַתִּטָּעֶהָ׃
10 פִּנִּיתָ לְפָנֶיהָ
וַתַּשְׁרֵשׁ שָׁרָשֶׁיהָ
וַתְּמַלֵּא־אָרֶץ׃

Ephraim's prayer in Jer. xxxi. 18, *Turn Thou
me, and I shall be turned*, amplified later into
*Turn Thou us unto Thee, O Lord, and we shall
be turned; renew our days as of old* (Lam. v.
21). From the root is derived the Hebrew
religious key-word *teshubah*, 'repentance.'
The appeal is for God to help the exiled tribes
to repent, as the essential preliminary to their
restoration.

cause Thy face to shine. Cf. iv. 7; Num.
vi. 26.

5-8 THE PEOPLE'S DESPERATE PLIGHT

5. *O Lord God of hosts*. As in lix. 6 (see on
xxiv. 10).

be angry. lit. 'smoke,' as in lxxiv. 1.

against the prayer. The idea may be that
expressed in Lam. iii. 44, *Thou hast covered
Thyself with a cloud* (here, of smoking wrath),
so that no prayer can pass through. Alternatively the preposition may signify 'notwithstanding' instead of *against*. Meiri sug-

gests 'how long will the prayer be considered
by You as smoke; for accepted prayer is
considered as incense' (see cxli. 2).

bread of tears. Cf. xlii. 4, cii. 10.

in large measure. lit. 'third,' perhaps of an
ephah. Again only in Isa. xl. 12.

7. *a strife*. An object of strife, in that
neighbouring nations fight to seize Israel's
land.

mock. At the people's distress.

9-14 THE PRESENT AND PAST CONTRASTED

9. *pluck up a vine*. Better, *broughtest a vine*
(Sforno followed by R.V.). The same verb as
in lxxviii. 52. Jacob compared Joseph to a
fruitful vine (Gen. xlix. 22), and the vine is a
common figure for Israel (Hos. x. 1; Isa. v.
1ff.; Jer. ii. 21).

drive out ... plant. Cf. xliv. 3.

10. *clear a place*. As the vine-grower prepares the soil by removing stones, etc., so

11 The mountains were covered
    with the shadow of it,
    And the mighty cedars with the
    boughs thereof.

12 She sent out her branches unto
    the sea,
    And her shoots unto the River.

13 Why hast Thou broken down her
    fences,
    So that all they that pass by the
    way do pluck her?

14 The boar out of the wood doth
    ravage it,
    That which moveth in the field
    feedeth on it.

15 O God of hosts, return, we be-
    seech Thee;
    Look from heaven, and behold,
    and be mindful of this vine,

16 And of the stock which Thy right
    hand hath planted,

11 כִּסּוּ הָרִים צִלָּהּ
וַעֲנָפֶיהָ אַרְזֵי־אֵל:
12 תְּשַׁלַּח קְצִירֶהָ עַד־יָם
וְאֶל־נָהָר יוֹנְקוֹתֶיהָ:
13 לָמָּה פָּרַצְתָּ גְדֵרֶיהָ
וְאָרוּהָ כָּל־עֹבְרֵי דָרֶךְ:
14 יְכַרְסְמֶנָּה חֲזִיר מִיָּעַר
וְזִיז שָׂדַי יִרְעֶנָּה:
15 אֱלֹהִים צְבָאוֹת שׁוּב נָא
הַבֵּט מִשָּׁמַיִם וּרְאֵה
וּפְקֹד גֶּפֶן זֹאת:
16 וְכַנָּה אֲשֶׁר־נָטְעָה יְמִינֶךָ

God made Canaan free of its inhabitants for the settlement of Israel.

11. *mountains.* 'Mountain land,' as in lxxviii. 54.

mighty cedars. lit. 'Cedars of God,' which may mean the cedars planted by Him. The verse describes the Israelites' spreading out over the entire country, from the hilly region in the south to the Lebanons with their cedars in the north (cf. Meiri).

12. The two remaining points of the compass are here mentioned: the Mediterranean on the west, and the Euphrates on the east (lxxii. 8) (Rashi).

13. Cf. lxxxix. 41f. The *fences* set up to protect the vine against trespassers are comparable to the frontiers which are the country's natural defences. This idea is also expressed in Isa. v. 5. Kimchi explains this verse as describing God's having removed His protection from them, leaving them at the mercy of the nations (see Deut. xxxi. 17).

14. As wild animals gnaw the grapes and tender shoots, so the land has been desolated by enemies.

that which moveth in the field. See L. 11.

15-20 RENEWAL OF PRAYER

15. *return … look.* Hebrew idiom for 'look again.'

16. *and of the stock.* Another possible translation is: 'and protect (or, maintain) that which Thy right hand hath planted' (cf. Meiri).

And the branch that Thou
madest strong for Thyself.

17 It is burned with fire, it is cut
down;
They perish at the rebuke of Thy
countenance.

18 Let Thy hand be upon the man
of Thy right hand,
Upon the son of man whom
Thou madest strong for Thyself.

19 So shall we not turn back from
Thee;
Quicken Thou us, and we will
call upon Thy name.

20 O Lord God of hosts, restore us;
Cause Thy face to shine, and we
shall be saved.

וְעַל־בֵּן אִמַּצְתָּה לָּךְ׃
שְׂרֻפָה בָאֵשׁ כְּסוּחָה 17
מִגַּעֲרַת פָּנֶיךָ יֹאבֵדוּ׃
תְּהִי־יָדְךָ עַל־אִישׁ יְמִינֶךָ 18
עַל־בֶּן־אָדָם אִמַּצְתָּ לָּךְ׃
וְלֹא־נָסוֹג מִמֶּךָּ 19
תְּחַיֵּנוּ וּבְשִׁמְךָ נִקְרָא׃
יְהוָה אֱלֹהִים צְבָאוֹת הֲשִׁיבֵנוּ 20
הָאֵר פָּנֶיךָ וְנִוָּשֵׁעָה׃

the branch. lit. 'son,' in allusion to *Israel is
My son* (Exod. iv. 22).

Thou madest strong. By Divine nurture and
protection.

17. *it is burned.* The subject of the verb
refers to the vine (the Holy Land) which is
treated as of no other use than to be chopped
for fuel. This verse is a continuation of the
prayer begun in verse 15 'be mindful of this
vine' … which is now being 'burned with
fire' (cf. Meiri, Ibn Ezra).

they perish. The metaphor is now translated
into plain language: the people are threatened with annihilation.

18. *Thy hand be upon.* As a cover and shield.

the man of Thy right hand. i.e. the people Thy
right hand planted (verse 16) in the land.

son of man. lit. 'son of *adam*' (see on viii. 5),
a frail earth-born mortal who would not have
grown to manhood unless *Thou madest* (him)
strong for Thyself (repeated from verse 16).

19. *not turn back.* If God sends His salvation, the people vow never to be disloyal to
Him again. Rashi interprets this phrase as
'cause us not to turn away from Thee.'

quicken. Revive, viz. the life of the nation.
Rashi suggests 'revive us from exile,' while
Sforno notes that the revival of the nation is
via the study of Torah.

call upon Thy name. Acknowledge allegiance to God.

20. In this final repetition of the refrain
'Lord' is added to 'God of hosts' as a refer-
ence to the previous verse 'and we will call
Thy name' (Ibn Ezra).

81

1 For the Leader; upon the Gittith.
  [A Psalm] of Asaph.

2 Sing aloud unto God our strength;
  Shout unto the God of Jacob.

3 Take up the melody, and sound
    the timbrel,
  The sweet harp with the psaltery.

4 Blow the horn at the new moon,
  At the full moon for our feast-day.

5 For it is a statute for Israel,
  An ordinance of the God of Jacob.

פא

לַמְנַצֵּחַ עַל־הַגִּתִּית לְאָסָף׃

2 הַרְנִינוּ לֵאלֹהִים עוּזֵּנוּ
הָרִיעוּ לֵאלֹהֵי יַעֲקֹב׃

3 שְׂאוּ־זִמְרָה וּתְנוּ־תֹף
כִּנּוֹר נָעִים עִם־נָבֶל׃

4 תִּקְעוּ בַחֹדֶשׁ שׁוֹפָר
בַּכֶּסֶה לְיוֹם חַגֵּנוּ׃

5 כִּי חֹק לְיִשְׂרָאֵל הוּא
מִשְׁפָּט לֵאלֹהֵי יַעֲקֹב׃

A FESTIVAL MEDITATION

The Talmud makes several references to this Psalm, all of which connect it with the New Year. In Tractate Rosh Hashanah 8a, verse 4 is cited as evidence that at the beginning of the year sentence is passed as to what will take place throughout the entire year. Verses 4 and 6 are quoted to support the statement that on the New Year, Joseph was released from prison (ibid. 11 a, b). The idea that the Hebrews' bondage in Egypt ceased on the New Year is backed up with verse 7 (ibid. 11b), and thus the connection of God's redemption of His people from the Egyptian bondage, in verses 6ff., with the Psalm's initial focus on the New Year. The sounding of the Shofar (verse 4), in addition to announcing the New Year and the coronation of God, also proclaims freedom from servitude (cf. Lev. xxv. 9, 10).

1. *Gittith.* See on viii. 1.

2-6 SUMMONS TO OBSERVE THE FESTIVAL

2. *shout.* Raise your voices in praise.

3. *psaltery.* A stringed instrument.

4. *horn.* Hebrew *shofar*, ram's horn.

at the new moon. This cannot refer to the blowing at each new moon (Num. x. 10) because on that occasion silver trumpets, and not the *shofar*, were sounded. The first day of the seventh month, however, was marked by *blowing* (the shofar) (Num. xxix. 1), and observed *as a memorial proclaimed with the blast* (of the shofar) (Lev. xxiii. 24). Ibn Ezra, however, maintains that it can refer also to each new moon, for on that occasion the *shofar* too, was blown. The use of the word *hodesh* as a reference to the New Year is an allusion to the word *hadesh* (meaning new or renewal) from the same root, and suggests

that the New Year is the time for the renewal of one's deeds (Midrash Shocher Tov).

at the full moon. lit. veiling [of the moon]; so, Hirsch. While all other holy days occur later in the month, at the full moon, only the New Year occurs at the beginning of the month, when the moon is still 'covered' (R.H. 8a). Most commentators render 'at the time appointed' (cf. Prov. VII).

feast-day. Hebrew *chag*, a pilgrimage-festival to Jerusalem, of which there were three: Passover, Pentecost and Tabernacles (Deut. xvi. 16). The word *chag* is usually used with particular reference to the feast of Tabernacles, which indeed occurs in the same month as the New Year. Meiri renders *blow the Shofar at the new moon, at the appointed time of that month in which our feast day occurs.*

5. *it ... God of Jacob.* The horn is blown by

6 He appointed it in Joseph for a
    testimony,
When He went forth against the
    land of Egypt.
The speech of one that I knew not
    did I hear:

7 'I removed his shoulder from the
    burden;
His hands were freed from the
    basket.

8 Thou didst call in trouble, and
    I rescued thee;
I answered thee in the secret place
    of thunder;
I proved thee at the waters of
    Meribah.   Selah

9 Hear, O My people, and I will
    admonish thee:
O Israel, if thou wouldest hearken
    unto Me!

10 There shall no strange god be in
    thee;
Neither shalt thou worship any
    foreign god.

6 עֵדוּת ׀ בִּיהוֹסֵף שָׂמוֹ
בְּצֵאתוֹ עַל־אֶרֶץ מִצְרָיִם
שְׂפַת לֹא־יָדַעְתִּי אֶשְׁמָע׃

7 הֲסִירוֹתִי מִסֵּבֶל שִׁכְמוֹ
כַּפָּיו מִדּוּד תַּעֲבֹרְנָה׃

8 בַּצָּרָה קָרָאתָ וָאֲחַלְּצֶךָּ
אֶעֶנְךָ בְּסֵתֶר רַעַם
אֶבְחָנְךָ עַל־מֵי מְרִיבָה
סֶלָה׃

9 שְׁמַע עַמִּי וְאָעִידָה בָּךְ
יִשְׂרָאֵל אִם־תִּשְׁמַע לִי׃

10 לֹא־יִהְיֶה בְךָ אֵל זָר
וְלֹא תִשְׁתַּחֲוֶה לְאֵל נֵכָר׃

statute from the God of Jacob, Who had redeemed his descendants from Egypt.

6. *it*. This could refer either to the institu-
tion of the New Year, the new moon or to the
blowing of the horn (see Hirsch).

Joseph. Not the N. Kingdom as in lxxx. 2, but
a synonym of Israel (Hirsch, cf. Ibn Ezra).

when He went forth. To bring the tenth plague
upon the Egyptians (Exod. xi. 4) (Hirsch, cf.
Kimchi).

7-8 GOD'S REDEMPTIVE ACTS

7. *his shoulder*. The shoulder of the toiling
Israelite bent under the Egyptian burden.

basket. Rather, 'pot,' in which they were
forced to cook for their masters (Rashi), or, as
Targum and most commentators, 'oven,' in
which they made bricks.

8. *Thou didst call*. For Israel's appeal to
God and His decision to aid them, cf. Exod.
ii. 23f.

in the secret place of thunder. The Divine
abode was thought of as being in *thick clouds
of the skies* from which He thundered (xviii.
12ff.). Rashi paraphrases *you called to Me in
secret between Me and you; and I answered
you in thunderous noise; that is, I manifested
mighty acts and wonders publicly*.

waters of Meribah. cf. lxxviii. 20; Exod.
xvii.7; Num. xx. 13.

9-11 THE FUNDAMENTAL LESSON

9. *hear, O My people*. Note the similar
language in Deut. vi. 4 and xi. 13.

10. The teaching of the second commandment, the corollary of the great historical fact
enshrined in the first commandment.

11 I am the LORD thy God,
Who brought thee up out of the
land of Egypt;
Open thy mouth wide, and I will
fill it.

12 But My people hearkened not to
My voice;
And Israel would none of Me.

13 So I let them go after the stub-
bornness of their heart,
That they might walk in their
own counsels.

14 Oh that My people would
hearken unto Me,
That Israel would walk in My
ways!

15 I would soon subdue their
enemies,
And turn My hand against their
adversaries.

16 The haters of the LORD should
dwindle away before Him;
And their punishment should
endure for ever.

17 They should also be fed with the
fat of wheat;
And with honey out of the rock
would I satisfy thee.'

אָנֹכִי ׀ יְהֹוָה אֱלֹהֶיךָ 11
הַמַּעַלְךָ מֵאֶרֶץ מִצְרָיִם
הַרְחֶב־פִּיךָ וַאֲמַלְאֵהוּ׃
וְלֹא־שָׁמַע עַמִּי לְקוֹלִי 12
וְיִשְׂרָאֵל לֹא־אָבָה לִי׃
וָאֲשַׁלְּחֵהוּ בִּשְׁרִירוּת לִבָּם 13
יֵלְכוּ בְּמוֹעֲצוֹתֵיהֶם׃
לוּ עַמִּי שֹׁמֵעַ לִי 14
יִשְׂרָאֵל בִּדְרָכַי יְהַלֵּכוּ׃
כִּמְעַט אוֹיְבֵיהֶם אַכְנִיעַ 15
וְעַל־צָרֵיהֶם אָשִׁיב יָדִי׃
מְשַׂנְאֵי יְהֹוָה יְכַחֲשׁוּ־לוֹ 16
וִיהִי עִתָּם לְעוֹלָם׃
וַיַּאֲכִילֵהוּ מֵחֵלֶב חִטָּה 17
וּמִצּוּר דְּבַשׁ אַשְׂבִּיעֶךָ׃

---

11. *open thy mouth wide.* God not only rescued Israel from slavery but provided their wants; He will continue to do so abundantly as long as the people are faithful to Him. It is unnecessary to go to strange gods for one's needs, when God is able to give all that every man can wish. (Sforno).

12-13 ISRAEL'S DISLOYALTY

12. *would none of Me.* lit. 'was unwilling towards Me.'

13. *I let them go.* God does not compel obedience but leaves it to man's choice, because without the exercise of free will, morality loses all meaning. 'All is in the hands of God except the fear of God' is the Rabbinic formulation of this principle (Tal. Ber. 33b). Man is warned that evil is destruc-

tive; if he persists in ignoring that truth, God does not hinder his proceeding along the road of ruin.

14-17 GOD'S APPEAL TO ISRAEL

15. *turn My hand.* From punishing Israel and direct it against their enemies (Rashi).

16. *dwindle away.* Better, 'come cringing' as in xviii. 45, lxvi. 3.

17. *they should also be fed.* lit. 'and He (God) will feed him (Israel).' The translation of A.J. avoids the awkwardness in English, but not so much in Hebrew, of the change in person in *I satisfy thee.* (Cf. Ibn Ezra).

fat of wheat. The richest ears of corn. Both this and the next phrase, *honey out of the rock,* are taken form Deut. xxxii. 13f.

82

1 A Psalm of Asaph.
  God standeth in the congregation
    of God;
  In the midst of the judges He
    judgeth:

2 'How long will ye judge unjustly,
  And respect the persons of the
    wicked ?   Selah

3 Judge the poor and fatherless;

פב

מִזְמוֹר לְאָסָף
אֱלֹהִים נִצָּב בַּעֲדַת־אֵל
בְּקֶרֶב אֱלֹהִים יִשְׁפֹּט׃
2 עַד־מָתַי תִּשְׁפְּטוּ־עָוֶל
וּפְנֵי רְשָׁעִים תִּשְׂאוּ־סֶלָה׃
3 שִׁפְטוּ־דַל וְיָתוֹם

CORRUPT JUDGES ARRAIGNED

THE interpretation of the Psalm depends upon the meaning attached to the word *Elohim* in its second occurrence in verse 1. The Targum renders it 'judges' and it was thus understood by the medieval commentator Rashi. Accordingly, God, the Supreme Judge, calls the administrators of justice in Israel to account for failing to discharge their office equitably. As an alternative, *Elohim* is interpreted as 'angels' (so Ibn Ezra). In support of the first reading of the Psalm is the close parallel to the scene found in Isa. iii. 14f., and the same circumstances as in LVIII.

1. GOD THE JUDGE OF JUDGES

1. *God.* Elohim, the heavenly Judge.

standeth. The verb is not the usual one denoting the opposite of sitting. It conveys the idea of Israel taking up a position for a solemn purpose, as in Deut. xxix 9, to ratify the covenant.

in the congregation of God. Hebrew *el;* an assembly convened by the All-powerful.

the judges. Hebrew *elohim.* In Exod. xxi. 6, xxii. 7, 8, 27; 1 Sam. ii. 25, the word occurs in a judicial connection; and on the principle that *the judgment is God's* (Deut. i. 17), the men who administer justice are considered to be His agents. They exercise a Godly function, and as such have His name attached to them. (cf. Kimchi, Sforno).

2-4 GOD'S INDICTMENT
OF THEIR PARTIALITY

2. *respect the persons.* They contravened the basic rule: *Thou shalt not respect the person of the poor, nor favour the person of the mighty; but in righteousness shalt thou judge thy neighbour* (Lev xix. 15). The scales of justice must be held evenly, without bias in favour of the poor, since a verdict against the richer party to the suit would not be an inconvenience, and certainly without partiality to the influencial from fear of consequences to the judge or as the result of bribery (cf. Rashi, Sforno).

3. *judge.* The verbs in the two verses indicate the duty of a judge which has not been carried out by the men whom God now indicts.

poor. Hebrew *dal* (see on xli. 2).

fatherless. Without a father to protect him, his interests are endangered and he is likely to become a victim of the unscrupulous.

Do justice to the afflicted and
destitute.

4 Rescue the poor and needy;
Deliver them out of the hand of
the wicked.

5 They know not, neither do they
understand;
They go about in darkness;
All the foundations of the earth
are moved.

6 I said: Ye are godlike beings,
And all of you sons of the Most
High.

7 Nevertheless ye shall die like men,
And fall like one of the princes.'

8 Arise, O God, judge the earth;
For Thou shalt possess all the
nations.

עָנִי וָרָשׁ הַצְדִּיקוּ׃

4 פַּלְּטוּ־דַל וְאֶבְיוֹן
מִיַּד רְשָׁעִים הַצִּילוּ׃

5 לֹא יָדְעוּ וְלֹא יָבִינוּ
בַּחֲשֵׁכָה יִתְהַלָּכוּ
יִמּוֹטוּ כָּל־מוֹסְדֵי אָרֶץ׃

6 אֲנִי אָמַרְתִּי אֱלֹהִים אַתֶּם
וּבְנֵי עֶלְיוֹן כֻּלְּכֶם׃

7 אָכֵן כְּאָדָם תְּמוּתוּן
וּכְאַחַד הַשָּׂרִים תִּפֹּלוּ׃

8 קוּמָה אֱלֹהִים שָׁפְטָה הָאָרֶץ
כִּי־אַתָּה תִנְחַל בְּכָל־הַגּוֹיִם׃

do justice to. The Hebrew is best rendered by
'vindicate.'

afflicted. A helpless man in the grip of an
exploiter.

destitute. Being poor in the material sense, he
lacks friends to support him. These categories are particularly dependent upon a strictly
impartial system of justice.

4. *rescue.* Since they cannot escape by
their own means, the aid of the courts must be
at their disposal.

5-7 THEIR CONDEMNATION

5. *know ... understand.* Unlike king
Solomon who prayed, *Give Thy servant
therefore an understanding heart to judge
Thy people* (1 Kings iii. 9), the accused judges
showed in practice that they lacked the essential qualification.

go about in darkness. Morally as well as in-
tellectually, and so are quite unfit for their
sacred duty. Kimchi and Ibn Ezra note that
the judges go about in darkness because the
bribes that they took 'blinded' them (see
Exod. xxiii. 8 and Deut. xvi. 19).

foundations ... moved. Human society is undermined when the cause of justice is corrupted; for 'by three things is the world

preserved: by truth, by judgement and by
peace' (Aboth) (Metsudath David).

6. *I said.* The subject is emphatic: 'I, God,
Who entrusted you with this function.'

godlike beings. Hebrew *elohim,* men invested with a Divine prerogative (Sforno).

sons of the Most High. It was therefore incumbent upon them to conform to their
Father's will.

7. *ye shall die like men.* As ordinary men
suffer capital punishment when they incur it,
so will you receive at My hands the sentence
of death for condemning the innocent (Ibn
Ezra). Your dignified title gives you no immunity, but increases your liability.

fall like one of the princes. Even princes have
judgement passed upon them by God; so will
you (cf. Ibn Ezra).

8 THE PSALMIST'S APPEAL TO GOD

judge the earth. Because human judges are
unreliable, he pleads that God should act as
Judge over all peoples, not only Israel
(Kimchi, Metsudath David).

shalt possess. All nations being God's possession, He being their Maker, He has the
right to rule and judge them (Metsudath
David).

83

1 A Song, a Psalm of Asaph.

2 O God, keep not Thou silence;
Hold not Thy peace, and be not
still, O God.

3 For, lo, Thine enemies are in an
uproar;
And they that hate Thee have
lifted up the head.

4 They hold crafty converse against
Thy people,
And take counsel against Thy
treasured ones.

5 They have said: 'Come, and let us
cut them off from being a
nation;
That the name of Israel may be no
more in remembrance.'

פג

שִׁיר מִזְמוֹר לְאָסָף:

2 אֱלֹהִים אַל־דֳּמִי־לָךְ
אַל־תֶּחֱרַשׁ וְאַל־תִּשְׁקֹט אֵל:

3 כִּי־הִנֵּה אוֹיְבֶיךָ יֶהֱמָיוּן
וּמְשַׂנְאֶיךָ נָשְׂאוּ רֹאשׁ:

4 עַל־עַמְּךָ יַעֲרִימוּ סוֹד
וְיִתְיָעֲצוּ עַל־צְפוּנֶיךָ:

5 אָמְרוּ לְכוּ וְנַכְחִידֵם מִגּוֹי
וְלֹא־יִזָּכֵר שֵׁם־יִשְׂרָאֵל עוֹד:

NATIONAL PRAYER FOR DIVINE AID

A COALITION menaces the people's existence. The nations plan to wipe out the very name of Israel. Confronted by a military force of overwhelming strength, Israel invokes the intervention of God. He is besought to do to these aggressors what He had done to Israel's enemies in the past. Extreme non-traditionalists, who suggest the occasion to be the onslaught of Antiochus in the Maccabean age, ignore that there was then no confederation of nations involved. Meiri asserts that this Psalm is related to the wars during the reign of Jehoshaphat (2 Chron. xx) when a confederation of Seir, Ammon, Moab and mercenaries from other nations attacked Israel.

2-6 CRY FOR HELP IN DANGER

2. *keep not Thou silence.* The Hebrew is much stronger, being lit. 'let there be no rest to Thee'; do not be inactive. The wording corresponds to *give Him no rest* (Isa. lxii. 7).

hold not Thy peace. When intervention is urgently required to save us from destruction.

3. *Thine enemies.* As throughout the Psalter, an attack upon Israel is an attack upon the cause which God had committed to them (cf. Hirsch).

are in an uproar. The verb denotes the clamour made by the gathering of a large crowd (cf. Kimchi).

lifted up the head. In defiant arrogance.

4. *hold crafty converse.* They meet to devise plans for the carrying out of their purpose (cf. Kimchi).

against Thy people. Hence the obligation rests upon God not to remain passive in the crisis.

Thy treasured ones. lit. 'Thy hidden ones,' those whom God hides in His covert as a protection from danger (cf. xxvii. 5, xxxi. 21) (Kimchi).

5. The extreme peril in which the nation stood is forcibly conveyed in the words of the schemers. The necessity for God's help is therefore imperative, if the dastardly aims are not to be accomplished.

6 For they have consulted together
  with one consent;
  Against Thee do they make a covenant;

7 The tents of Edom and the Ish-
  maelites;
  Moab, and the Hagrites;

8 Gebal, and Ammon, and Amalek;
  Philistia with the inhabitants of
  Tyre;

9 Assyria also is joined with them;
  They have been an arm to the
  children of Lot.   Selah

10 Do Thou unto them as unto
  Midian;
  As to Sisera, as to Jabin, at the
  brook Kishon;

11 Who were destroyed at En-dor;
  They became as dung for the
  earth.

6 כִּי נוֹעֲצוּ לֵב יַחְדָּו
עָלֶיךָ בְּרִית יִכְרֹתוּ׃
7 אָהֳלֵי אֱדוֹם וְיִשְׁמְעֵאלִים
מוֹאָב וְהַגְרִים׃
8 גְּבָל וְעַמּוֹן וַעֲמָלֵק
פְּלֶשֶׁת עִם־יֹשְׁבֵי צוֹר׃
9 גַּם־אַשּׁוּר נִלְוָה עִמָּם
הָיוּ זְרוֹעַ לִבְנֵי־לוֹט סֶלָה׃
10 עֲשֵׂה־לָהֶם כְּמִדְיָן
כְּסִיסְרָא כְיָבִין בְּנַחַל קִישׁוֹן׃
11 נִשְׁמְדוּ בְעֵין־דֹּאר
הָיוּ דֹּמֶן לָאֲדָמָה׃

6. *against Thee.* See on verse 3. (See also Midrash Shocher Tov).

7-9 THE ALLIANCE AGAINST ISRAEL

7. *tents.* i.e. tent-dwellers (Metsudath David).

Edom, etc. The peoples enumerated, dwelling in the south, were the traditional enemies of Israel. The Hagarites inhabited the land east of Gilead on the other side of the Jordan (1 Chron. v. 10).

8. *Gebal.* North of Edom.

Ammon and Amalek. Israel's inveterate foes.

Philistia...Tyre. On the Mediterranean coast. They are both denounced for hostile conduct to Israel (Amos i. 6, 9).

9. *Assyria.* The destroyer of the N. Kingdom.

an arm. Cf. Isa. xxxiii. 2. They lent assistance to the alliance.

children of Lot. Moabites and Ammonites (Deut. ii. 9, 19). Despite their blood-con- nection with Israel, they were leaders of the confederacy.

10-19 PRAYER FOR THEIR OVERTHROW

As always in the Psalter, the depth of feeling aroused by persecution springs from more than the agonies of the afflicted; righteous indignation is also a motive of the protest, inasmuch as an attack by the pitiless strong upon the weak is rebellion against the rule of God in the world.

10. *Midian.* Routed by Gideon (Judges vii. 19ff.).

Sisera ... Jabin. Overthrown by Barak and Deborah (Judges iv. 12ff.).

the brook Kishon. Judges v. 21

11. *En-dor.* The village is not named in connection with the campaign; but it was located near Taanach and Megiddo (Joshua xvii. 11) where intense fighting took place (Judges v. 19).

as dung for the earth. The corpses lay on the ground unburied.

12 Make their nobles like Oreb and
    Zeeb,
  And like Zebah and Zalmunna
    all their princes;

13 Who said: 'Let us take to our-
    selves in possession
  The habitations of God.'

14 O my God, make them like the
    whirling dust;
  As stubble before the wind.

15 As the fire that burneth the forest,
  And as the flame that setteth the
    mountains ablaze;

16 So pursue them with Thy
    tempest,
  And affright them with Thy
    storm.

17 Fill their faces with shame;
  That they may seek Thy name,
    O Lord.

18 Let them be ashamed and
    affrighted for ever;
  Yea, let them be abashed and
    perish;

19 That they may know that it is
    Thou alone whose name is the
    Lord,
  The Most High over all the earth.

12 שִׁיתֵמוֹ נְדִיבֵמוֹ כְּעֹרֵב וְכִזְאֵב
וּכְזֶבַח וּכְצַלְמֻנָּע כָּל־נְסִיכֵמוֹ׃
13 אֲשֶׁר אָמְרוּ נִירֲשָׁה לָּנוּ
אֵת נְאוֹת אֱלֹהִים׃
14 אֱלֹהַי שִׁיתֵמוֹ כַגַּלְגַּל
כְּקַשׁ לִפְנֵי־רוּחַ׃
15 כְּאֵשׁ תִּבְעַר־יָעַר
וּכְלֶהָבָה תְּלַהֵט הָרִים׃
16 כֵּן תִּרְדְּפֵם בְּסַעֲרֶךָ
וּבְסוּפָתְךָ תְבַהֲלֵם׃
17 מַלֵּא פְנֵיהֶם קָלוֹן
וִיבַקְשׁוּ שִׁמְךָ יְהוָה׃
18 יֵבֹשׁוּ וְיִבָּהֲלוּ עֲדֵי־עַד
וְיַחְפְּרוּ וְיֹאבֵדוּ׃
19 וְיֵדְעוּ כִּי־אַתָּה שִׁמְךָ יְהוָה לְבַדֶּךָ
עֶלְיוֹן עַל־כָּל־הָאָרֶץ׃

12. *Oreb and Zeeb*. Midianite princes
(Judges vii. 25).

Zebah and Zalmunna. Kings of Midian
(Judges viii. 5ff.).

13. *who said*. The subject is the nations
mentioned in verses 7ff., and the words that
follow summarize the purpose of their con-
sultation (Rashi).

the habitations of God. The land of Canaan
which He had allotted to Israel (Kimchi).

14. *like the whirling dust*. Again in Isa. xvii.
13, where the phrase is amplified by *before
the storm*.

as stubble. Or, *chaff* (i. 4).

15. *forest*. The fire that burns the forest is
all consuming because of the close clusters of

trees (Metsudath David).

mountains. What grows upon their slopes.

16. *tempest ... storm*. Descriptive of Divine wrath sweeping irresistibly along.

17. *shame*. When their cherished hopes are
frustrated; but, adds the Psalmist, may their
humiliation create within them a feeling of
contrition so that instead of being God's
'enemies,' they seek to know Him and submit to His will (Hirsch).

18. If the hope that they will repent is
unfulfilled, then let their disgrace be everlasting and may they perish. The world will
be well rid of them.

19. Not in vindictiveness is their destruction prayed for, but to demonstrate that God's
rule is supreme in the world.

84

לַמְנַצֵּחַ עַל־הַגִּתִּית
לִבְנֵי־קֹרַח מִזְמוֹר:

1 For the Leader; upon the Gittith.
    A Psalm of the sons of Korah.

2 מַה־יְּדִידוֹת מִשְׁכְּנוֹתֶיךָ
יְהוָה צְבָאוֹת:

2 How lovely are Thy tabernacles,
    O LORD of hosts!

3 נִכְסְפָה וְגַם־כָּלְתָה ׀ נַפְשִׁי
לְחַצְרוֹת יְהוָה
לִבִּי וּבְשָׂרִי יְרַנְּנוּ אֶל־אֵל־חָי:

3 My soul yearneth, yea, even pineth
        for the courts of the LORD;
    My heart and my flesh sing for
        joy unto the living God.

4 גַּם־צִפּוֹר ׀ מָצְאָה בַיִת
וּדְרוֹר ׀ קֵן ׀ לָהּ
אֲשֶׁר־שָׁתָה אֶפְרֹחֶיהָ
אֶת־מִזְבְּחוֹתֶיךָ יְהוָה צְבָאוֹת
מַלְכִּי וֵאלֹהָי:

4 Yea, the sparrow hath found a
        house, and the swallow a nest
        for herself,
    Where she may lay her young;
    Thine altars, O LORD of hosts,
    My King, and my God—

5 אַשְׁרֵי יוֹשְׁבֵי בֵיתֶךָ
עוֹד יְהַלְלוּךָ סֶּלָה:

5 Happy are they that dwell in Thy
        house,
    They are ever praising Thee.
                                    Selah

6 אַשְׁרֵי אָדָם עוֹז־לוֹ בָךְ
מְסִלּוֹת בִּלְבָבָם:

6 Happy is the man whose strength
        is in Thee;
    In whose heart are the highways.

JOY IN THE SANCTUARY

AT this point the Asaph Psalms end, and some more Korahite Psalms appear. In its intense love for the communion with God which is to be experienced in the Sanctuary, this Psalm is a companion to the Korahite Psalm xlii; but whereas in the latter we had the lament of one to whom adverse circumstances had denied that privilege, now we hear the joyous tones of a pilgrim who recounts his deep happiness in standing once more within the sacred precincts. The Psalm does not specify the occasion. Kimchi offers two suggestions: 1) the Psalm was composed by David, who having fled from Saul to the land of the Philistines, expressed his yearning for the sanctuary; 2) He relates the longing of all Jews for the return to Israel and the Sanctuary. Indeed the words are more than personal; they echo the sentiments of every religious soul in the Diaspora.

1. *Gittith.* See on viii. 1.

sons of Korah. See on xlii. 1.

    2-5 HIS YEARNING FOR THE TEMPLE

2. *tabernacles.* lit. 'dwelling-places'; for the plural, see on xliii. 3.

3. *yearneth … pineth.* Better, 'yearned … pined,' expressing his emotion when he was away from the Temple.

4. *Thine altars.* The rendering of A.J. fol-lows Hirsch and supposes that words have to be supplied after *my God* to complete the sentence. It is preferable to understand *eth* as Targum does, 'with, by,' and fill in '(thus do I find my resting-place) by Thine altars' (cf. Metsudath David).

5. *dwell in Thy house.* He envies those who spend their lives in God's Service.

    6-8 HAPPINESS IN GOD'S WORSHIP

6. *highways.* viz. to Zion, longing for the

7 Passing through the valley of Baca
  they make it a place of springs;
  Yea, the early rain clotheth it with
  blessings.

8 They go from strength to strength,
  Every one of them appeareth
  before God in Zion.

9 O Lord God of hosts, hear my
  prayer;
  Give ear, O God of Jacob. Selah

10 Behold, O God our shield,
  And look upon the face of Thine
  anointed.

11 For a day in Thy courts is better
  than a thousand;
  I had rather stand at the threshold of the house of my God,
  Than to dwell in the tents of
  wickedness.

12 For the Lord God is a sun and a
  shield;
  The Lord giveth grace and
  glory;
  No good thing will He withhold
  from them that walk uprightly.

13 O Lord of hosts,
  Happy is the man that trusteth in
  Thee.

עֹבְרֵי ׀ בְּעֵמֶק הַבָּכָא
מַעְיָן יְשִׁיתוּהוּ
גַּם־בְּרָכוֹת יַעְטֶה מוֹרֶה:
8 יֵלְכוּ מֵחַיִל אֶל־חָיִל
יֵרָאֶה אֶל־אֱלֹהִים בְּצִיּוֹן:
9 יְהוָה אֱלֹהִים צְבָאוֹת
שִׁמְעָה תְפִלָּתִי
הַאֲזִינָה אֱלֹהֵי יַעֲקֹב סֶלָה:
10 מָגִנֵּנוּ רְאֵה אֱלֹהִים
וְהַבֵּט פְּנֵי מְשִׁיחֶךָ:
11 כִּי טוֹב־יוֹם בַּחֲצֵרֶיךָ מֵאָלֶף
בָּחַרְתִּי הִסְתּוֹפֵף בְּבֵית אֱלֹהַי
מִדּוּר בְּאָהֳלֵי־רֶשַׁע:
12 כִּי שֶׁמֶשׁ ׀ וּמָגֵן יְהוָה אֱלֹהִים
חֵן וְכָבוֹד יִתֵּן יְהוָה
לֹא יִמְנַע־טוֹב לַהֹלְכִים בְּתָמִים:
13 יְהוָה צְבָאוֹת
אַשְׁרֵי אָדָם בֹּטֵחַ בָּךְ:

road to the Temple (Ibn Ezra).

7. *passing.* Pilgrims to Jerusalem (cf.
Kimchi).

valley of Baca. The last word means the
balsam-tree which thrives in dry places. A
waterless valley thickly planted with these
trees was so named and lay on the route to
Jerusalem (Kimchi). In the eyes of the pilgrims, religiously exalted, it was converted
into *place of springs* (cf. Hirsch).

clotheth it with blessings. When the pilgrims
traversed the arid glen, they dug in the sand
to find water (Kimchi).

9-13   PRAYER IN THE TEMPLE

10. *O God our shield.* Although God is referred to as a *shield* in verse 12, a better parallelism is obtained by: 'Behold, O God, our
shield,' viz. the king, defined by *Thine
anointed.* Thus, they offer prayer for the

welfare of their sovereign whose protection
they enjoy en route to the Temple (Ibn Ezra).

11. *than a thousand.* i.e. days elsewhere
(Rashi).

stand at the threshold. As a suppliant.

12. *a sun.* God provides the pilgrims with
sunny weather. But where the sun produces
harmful effects, He acts as *a shield* (Ibn Ezra).
Sforno compares the sun's light to intellectual radiance, with which God granted brilliance of mind to the pilgrims who came to
the Temple, allowing them to understand the
depths and wonders of the Torah. The expression equals 'my light' (xxvii. 1).

13. Ibn Ezra sees happiness as based upon
the every *good thing* of verse 12. Kimchi holds
that it is a reference to undiminished faith and
hope of release from exile and return to
Temple life.

85

1 For the Leader. A Psalm of the
sons of Korah.

2 LORD, Thou hast been favourable
unto Thy land,
Thou hast turned the captivity of
Jacob.

3 Thou hast forgiven the iniquity
of Thy people,
Thou hast pardoned all their sin.
Selah.

4 Thou hast withdrawn all Thy
wrath;
Thou hast turned from the fierceness of Thine anger.

5 Restore us, O God of our salvation,
And cause Thine indignation toward us to cease.

פה

לַמְנַצֵּחַ לִבְנֵי־קֹרַח מִזְמוֹר:

2 רָצִיתָ יְהוָה אַרְצֶךָ
שַׁבְתָּ שְׁבוּת יַעֲקֹב:

3 נָשָׂאתָ עֲוֹן עַמֶּךָ
כִּסִּיתָ כָל־חַטָּאתָם סֶלָה:

4 אָסַפְתָּ כָל־עֶבְרָתֶךָ
הֱשִׁיבוֹתָ מֵחֲרוֹן אַפֶּךָ:

5 שׁוּבֵנוּ אֱלֹהֵי יִשְׁעֵנוּ
וְהָפֵר כַּעַסְךָ עִמָּנוּ:

---

v. 2. שבית ק׳

PRAYER OF RETURNED EXILES

THE reactions of the captives from Babylon who had come back to the homeland are vividly mirrored in this Psalm. Depressed by the scene of desolation which confronted them and the magnitude of reconstruction, they pray that the Divine anger which had sanctioned the national disaster may be wholly withdrawn so they they can look to the future with confidence. A reply comes to their petition, a heartening assurance that all will be well.

2-4 GOD'S FORGIVENESS

2. *favourable unto Thy land.* A reference to the return of the Jewish people from the Babylon exile to Judea to establish the second Temple (Ibn Ezra, Kimchi, Malbim).

turned the captivity. See on liii. 7, but here the phrase alludes to the end of the exile.

3. *forgiven.* lit. 'lifted up,' as though it were a crushing burden upon the people (cf. xxxviii. 5). When God forgives, he 'lifts away' the iniquity of the sinner.

4. *withdrawn.* Heb. 'gathered in,' and the effects of that wrath are no longer felt by them.

fierceness of … anger. Aroused by Israel's lapses which resulted in the captivity.

5-8 PRAYER FOR RESTORATION

5. *restore us.* To our former national glory. An alternative rendering is 'return to us.' Rashi reads both meanings in the abnormal form of the Hebrew: 'return to us and restore us.'

cause Thine indignation … to cease. lit. 'annul Thine indignation,' that it no longer provokes Thee.

6 Wilt Thou be angry with us for
 ever?
 Wilt Thou draw out Thine anger
 to all generations?

7 Wilt Thou not quicken us again,
 That Thy people may rejoice in
 Thee?

8 Show us Thy mercy, O Lord,
 And grant us Thy salvation.

9 I will hear what God the Lord
 will speak;
 For He will speak peace unto His
 people, and to His saints;
 But let them not turn back to
 folly.

10 Surely His salvation is nigh them
 that fear Him;
 That glory may dwell in our land.

11 Mercy and truth are met together;
 Righteousness and peace have
 kissed each other.

6 הַלְעוֹלָם תֶּאֱנַף־בָּנוּ
 תִּמְשֹׁךְ אַפְּךָ לְדֹר וָדֹר:
7 הֲלֹא־אַתָּה תָּשׁוּב תְּחַיֵּנוּ
 וְעַמְּךָ יִשְׂמְחוּ־בָךְ:
8 הַרְאֵנוּ יְהוָה חַסְדֶּךָ
 וְיֶשְׁעֲךָ תִּתֶּן־לָנוּ:
9 אֶשְׁמְעָה מַה־יְדַבֵּר הָאֵל וְהוָה
 כִּי יְדַבֵּר שָׁלוֹם אֶל־עַמּוֹ
 וְאֶל־חֲסִידָיו
 וְאַל־יָשׁוּבוּ לְכִסְלָה:
10 אַךְ קָרוֹב לִירֵאָיו יִשְׁעוֹ
 לִשְׁכֹּן כָּבוֹד בְּאַרְצֵנוּ:
11 חֶסֶד־וֶאֱמֶת נִפְגָּשׁוּ
 צֶדֶק וְשָׁלוֹם נָשָׁקוּ:

6. *be angry … for ever.* To punish us constantly (Sforno).

7. *Thou.* Emphatic in the Hebrew. 'Thou
Who madest us such a promise through the
prophets' (Rashi).

quicken. Revive, as in lxxx. 19.

9-14   ASSURANCE FOR THE FUTURE

9. *I will hear.* The speaker is the Psalmist
who listens for the answer which God gives
to the people's supplication (Ibn Ezra).

God. Hebrew *el*, the All-powerful Whose
might to fulfil His purpose is not limited.

He will speak peace. Work for their welfare.
It was said of Mordecai, *seeking the good of
his people and speaking peace to all his seed*
(Esther x. 3)

and to His saints. Better, 'even to His saints,'
identical with *His people.* For the meaning of

chasid, see on iv. 4. Kimchi understands *His
saints* to be the peoples who turned to Judaism at the return of the exiles, who are warned
not to *not turn back to folly.*

10. *glory.* God's glorious Presence will once
again be visible when they will indeed fear
Him, for the fear of God prevents sin (Hirsch).

11. *mercy and truth.* The Divine salvation
is dependent upon human co-operation. When
truth is spoken in the land, it receives the
blessing of God's *mercy* (Rashi).

righteousness and peace. The thought that
peace, in the broader sense of well-being in
addition to harmony, is the fruit of *righteousness,* is prominent in the Bible and
Rabbinical literature. In the Bible, the most
impressive enunciation of the doctrine is
found in Isa. xxxii. 17. In Rabbinical literature, there is the forceful declaration: 'The

12 Truth springeth out of the earth;
And righteousness hath looked down from heaven.

13 Yea, the LORD will give that which is good;
And our land shall yield her produce.

14 Righteousness shall go before Him,
And shall make His footsteps a way.

אֱמֶת מֵאֶרֶץ תִּצְמָח 12
וְצֶדֶק מִשָּׁמַיִם נִשְׁקָף:
גַּם־יְהוָה יִתֵּן הַטּוֹב 13
וְאַרְצֵנוּ תִּתֵּן יְבוּלָהּ:
צֶדֶק לְפָנָיו יְהַלֵּךְ 14
וְיָשֵׂם לְדֶרֶךְ פְּעָמָיו:

sword comes into the world for the delay of justice and for the perversion of justice' (Aboth).

kissed each other. Formed a mutual alliance.

12. A restatement of the previous verse. When men plant the seed of *truth* so that it grows luxuriantly in the land, there is a harvest of *righteousness* sent from heaven.

earth … heaven. The earth is mentioned first, because moral reformation must begin with man; having begun on earth, it receives impetus from the help which comes from heaven (Kimchi).

13. *that which is good*. The rain essential for a fruitful season (Rashi, Ibn Ezra). Perhaps the sense is more general: prosperity will be the accompaniment of a high standard of national morality. Such a statement would fully accord with the connection between virtuous conduct and physical well-being, both with the individual and the community (cf. Lev. xxvi. 3ff.; Deut. xxviii) (cf. Hirsch).

14. *shall go before Him*. If Israel is loyal to God, He will guide the nation to greatness. 'First righteousness must precede Him on earth; then will He, God, also prepare Himself for the re-entry of His glory upon earth' (Hirsch). (Cf. Isa. lviii. 8, where the words are used of Israel).

shall make His footsteps a way. The Hebrew is obscure. Rashi's interpretation seems the simplest: 'and He shall make His footsteps for a way' to be followed by His children. God marks out the path for Israel to traverse, leading to salvation and happiness. Otherwise the subject is *righteousness*, which is pictured as a herald clearing a way for God's advent, Who brings with Him safety and happiness for the nation (Malbim).

86

פו

1 A Prayer of David.
  Incline Thine ear, O LORD, and
    answer me;
  For I am poor and needy.

2 Keep my soul, for I am godly;
  O Thou my God, save Thy servant
    that trusteth in Thee.

3 Be gracious unto me, O Lord;
  For unto Thee do I cry all the day.

4 Rejoice the soul of Thy servant;
  For unto Thee, O Lord, do I lift
    up my soul.

5 For Thou, Lord, art good, and
    ready to pardon,
  And plenteous in mercy unto all
    them that call upon Thee.

6 Give ear, O LORD, unto my prayer;
  And attend unto the voice of my
    supplications.

7 In the day of my trouble I call
    upon Thee;
  For Thou wilt answer me.

תְּפִלָּה לְדָוִד
הַטֵּה־יְהוָה אָזְנְךָ עֲנֵנִי
כִּי־עָנִי וְאֶבְיוֹן אָנִי:
שָׁמְרָה נַפְשִׁי כִּי־חָסִיד אָנִי 2
הוֹשַׁע עַבְדְּךָ אַתָּה אֱלֹהַי
הַבּוֹטֵחַ אֵלֶיךָ:
חָנֵּנִי אֲדֹנָי 3
כִּי־אֵלֶיךָ אֶקְרָא כָּל־הַיּוֹם:
שַׂמֵּחַ נֶפֶשׁ עַבְדֶּךָ 4
כִּי־אֵלֶיךָ אֲדֹנָי נַפְשִׁי אֶשָּׂא:
כִּי־אַתָּה אֲדֹנָי טוֹב וְסַלָּח 5
וְרַב־חֶסֶד לְכָל־קֹרְאֶיךָ:
הַאֲזִינָה יְהוָה תְּפִלָּתִי 6
וְהַקְשִׁיבָה בְּקוֹל תַּחֲנוּנוֹתָי:
בְּיוֹם צָרָתִי אֶקְרָאֶךָ 7
כִּי תַעֲנֵנִי:

A CRY FOR HELP

THE title *A Prayer* is an index to the contents of the Psalm. It is largely made up of quotations from the Psalter and other parts of the Bible, indicating that the author drew on the Scriptures for the compilation of a liturgical poem. No particular circumstance seems to have been responsible for the composition; rather is it to be regarded as a meditation to be used by anyone in time of trouble (cf. Hirsch).

1-5 PLEA FOR A HEARING

1. *incline Thine ear.* A common introductory formula in supplication (xvii. 6, xxxi. 3).

poor and needy. Cf. xl. 18.

2. *keep my soul.* Cf. xxv. 20.

godly. Hebrew *chasid*, one who loves God and is therefore deserving of His love.

3. *be gracious unto me.* Cf. lvii. 2.

do I cry. Cf. lvii 3.

4. *rejoice the soul.* With deliverance from its present agony (cf. xc. 15).

unto Thee, O LORD, etc. Quoted from xxv. 1.

5. Based on Exod. xxxiv. 6.

6-10 CONFIDENT OF A RESPONSE

6. *give ear … prayer.* From lv. 2.

attend … supplications. Cf. cxxx. 2.

7. Cf. lxxvii. 3.

8 There is none like unto Thee
   among the gods, O Lord;
And there are no works like Thine.

9 All nations whom Thou hast made
   shall come and prostrate themselves before Thee, O Lord;
And they shall glorify Thy name.

10 For Thou art great, and doest
   wondrous things;
Thou art God alone.

11 Teach me, O LORD, Thy way,
   that I may walk in Thy truth;
Make one my heart to fear Thy
   name.

12 I will thank Thee, O Lord my
   God, with my whole heart;
And I will glorify Thy name for
   evermore.

13 For great is Thy mercy toward
   me;
And Thou hast delivered my
   soul from the lowest nether-
   world.

14 O God, the proud are risen up
   against me,

8 אֵין־כָּמוֹךָ בָאֱלֹהִים ׀ אֲדֹנָי
וְאֵין כְּמַעֲשֶׂיךָ׃
9 כָּל־גּוֹיִם ׀ אֲשֶׁר עָשִׂיתָ
יָבוֹאוּ ׀ וְיִשְׁתַּחֲווּ לְפָנֶיךָ אֲדֹנָי
וִיכַבְּדוּ לִשְׁמֶךָ׃
10 כִּי־גָדוֹל אַתָּה וְעֹשֵׂה נִפְלָאוֹת
אַתָּה אֱלֹהִים לְבַדֶּךָ׃
11 הוֹרֵנִי יְהוָה ׀ דַּרְכֶּךָ אֲהַלֵּךְ בַּאֲמִתֶּךָ
יַחֵד לְבָבִי לְיִרְאָה שְׁמֶךָ׃
12 אוֹדְךָ ׀ אֲדֹנָי אֱלֹהַי בְּכָל־לְבָבִי
וַאֲכַבְּדָה שִׁמְךָ לְעוֹלָם׃
13 כִּי־חַסְדְּךָ גָּדוֹל עָלָי
וְהִצַּלְתָּ נַפְשִׁי מִשְּׁאוֹל תַּחְתִּיָּה׃
14 אֱלֹהִים ׀ זֵדִים קָמוּ עָלַי

---

8. *none like unto Thee.* From Exod. xv. 11, and Deut. iii. 24.

9. Cf. Isa. xxiv. 15. The verse expresses the culminating hope in Jewish thought, the union of all mankind under the Sovereignty of God, which figures prominently in the liturgy (cf. especially P.B., pp. 76f.)

10. *doest wondrous things.* Cf. lxxii. 18, lxxvii. 14f.

Thou art God alone. Cf. lxxxiii. 19.

    11-13 PRAYER FOR GUIDANCE

11. *teach me, O LORD, Thy way.* From xxvii. 11.

walk in Thy truth. Cf. xxvi. 3.

make one my heart. Cf. Jer. xxxii. 39. The

petition is for a heart entirely concentrated upon God, and not distracted by other desires (Meiri).

12. *I will thank Thee.* Cf. ix. 2.

with my whole heart. For which he prayed in the previous verse.

for evermore. During the remainder of his life.

13. *great is Thy mercy.* Cf. lvii. 11.

Thou hast delivered. Cf. lvi. 14.

the lowest nether-world. The depths of Sheol. A similar phrase occurs in Deut. xxxii. 22.

    14-17 PRAYER FOR PROTECTION

14. Almost verbatim from liv. 5.

And the company of violent men
    have sought after my soul,
And have not set Thee before
    them.
15 But Thou, O Lord, art a God full
    of compassion and gracious,
    Slow to anger, and plenteous in
    mercy and truth.
16 O turn unto me, and be gracious
    unto me;
    Give Thy strength unto Thy
    servant,
And save the son of Thy hand-
    maid.
17 Work in my behalf a sign for
    good;
    That they that hate me may see
    it, and be put to shame,
Because Thou, LORD, hast helped
    me, and comforted me.

וַעֲדַת עָרִיצִים
בִּקְשׁוּ נַפְשִׁי
וְלֹא שָׂמוּךָ לְנֶגְדָּם:
15 וְאַתָּה אֲדֹנָי אֵל־רַחוּם וְחַנּוּן
אֶרֶךְ אַפַּיִם וְרַב־חֶסֶד וֶאֱמֶת:
16 פְּנֵה אֵלַי וְחָנֵּנִי
תְּנָה־עֻזְּךָ לְעַבְדֶּךָ
וְהוֹשִׁיעָה לְבֶן־אֲמָתֶךָ:
17 עֲשֵׂה־עִמִּי אוֹת לְטוֹבָה
וְיִרְאוּ שֹׂנְאַי וְיֵבֹשׁוּ
כִּי־אַתָּה יְהוָה עֲזַרְתַּנִי וְנִחַמְתָּנִי:

15. Quoted from Exod. xxxiv. 6. The Psalmist draws a comparison between the heartlessness of his enemies and the graciousness of God (Hirsch). Relying upon the Divine clemency, he takes courage to offer the prayer which follows, although conscious of his unworthiness (Kimchi).

16. *turn unto me, and be gracious unto me.* Quotation from xxv. 16.

servant ... son of Thy handmaid. Again in cxvi. 16. One who, by his free will, has chosen to be Your servant and, having been born to a mother who was Your humble handmaid, has it in his nature to serve You (Malbim).

17. *a sign.* A visible manifestation of Divine favour.

for good. i.e. for my benefit.

they that hate me ... Thou. Since there is nothing corresponding to *it* in the text, another translation may be: 'that they that hate me may see and be ashamed that Thou.' The pronoun is emphatic; the recognition that it was God and no one else Who has rescued him from their hands, may have the effect of filling his persecutors with shame and remorse.

be put to shame. Cf. xxxv. 4.

1 A Psalm of the sons of Korah;
  a Song.
  His foundation is in the holy
  mountains.

2 The Lord loveth the gates of
  Zion
  More than all the dwellings of
  Jacob.

3 Glorious things are spoken of
  Thee,
  O city of God.   Selah

לִבְנֵי־קֹרַח מִזְמוֹר שִׁיר
יְסוּדָתוֹ בְּהַרְרֵי־קֹדֶשׁ:

2 אֹהֵב יְהוָה שַׁעֲרֵי צִיּוֹן
מִכֹּל מִשְׁכְּנוֹת יַעֲקֹב:

3 נִכְבָּדוֹת מְדֻבָּר בָּךְ
עִיר הָאֱלֹהִים סֶלָה:

ZION THE WORLD CENTRE

THIS brief Psalm is one of the most remarkable in the Psalter. Both in tone and outlook its
character is prophetic, in the sense that it proclaims the hope of a universal Kingdom of God
with Zion as its metropolis. It is an amplification of lxxxvi. 9, and as such was placed next in
order. Kimchi suggests that this Psalm, in praise of Zion, was composed either by David, who
gave it to the sons of Korah to sing, or by the sons of Korah themselves. The purpose of the
Psalm is to praise Zion, not only as the respected place of wisdom, but also as the region of
holiness (Meiri). 'The foundation of this song rests upon the mountains of the Sanctuary. It
is based upon and springs from those ideals that are nurtured and taught in God's sanctuary'
(Hirsch).

1-3 ZION THE CITY OF GOD

1. *His foundation.* The style of the Psalm
is oracular and therefore terse. The meaning is: the city which He founded. For the
thought, cf. Isa. xiv. 32. According to all the
classical commentators, however, it should
be rendered 'whose foundation'; the Psalm's
foundation is the mountains of Zion and
Jerusalem.

in the holy mountains. Better, 'concerning
the holy mountains,' i.e. of Zion and
Jerusalem (Rashi). Cf. *the mountains of Zion*
(cxxxiii. 3). Jerusalem was situated on a
high elevation (over 800 feet above sea
level), and the surrounding hills partook of

the sanctity with which the city was invested.

2. *gates of Zion.* A poetical phrase for the
city itself (cf. cxxii. 2). The Psalmist may be
thinking especially of the gates through which
the nations will stream to worship God.

all the dwellings. All the other towns inhabited by Israelites.

3. *glorious things.* Referring to the utter-
ances, such as: *Out of Zion shall go forth the
law, and the word of the Lord from Jerusalem* (Isa. ii. 3), or *Fair in situation, the joy of
the whole earth; even Mount Zion* (xlviii. 3).

city of God. The city selected by Him as His
abode (xlvi. 5, xlviii. 2).

4 'I will make mention of Rahab
and Babylon as among them
that know Me;
Behold Philistia, and Tyre, with
Ethiopia;
This one was born there.'

5 But of Zion it shall be said: 'This
man and that was born in her;
And the Most High Himself doth
establish her.'

6 The LORD shall count in the register of the peoples:
'This one was born there.' Selah

7 And whether they sing or dance
All my thoughts are in thee.

4 אַזְכִּיר ׀ רַהַב וּבָבֶל לְיֹדְעָי
הִנֵּה פְלֶשֶׁת וְצֹר עִם־כּוּשׁ
זֶה יֻלַּד־שָׁם׃

5 וּלְצִיּוֹן ׀ יֵאָמַר
אִישׁ וְאִישׁ יֻלַּד־בָּהּ
וְהוּא יְכוֹנְנֶהָ עֶלְיוֹן׃

6 יְהוָה יִסְפֹּר בִּכְתוֹב עַמִּים
זֶה יֻלַּד־שָׁם סֶלָה׃

7 וְשָׁרִים כְּחֹלְלִים
כָּל־מַעְיָנַי בָּךְ׃

4-6 ZION THE METROPOLIS
OF THE KINGDOM OF GOD

4. The speaker is God announcing that the powerful nations which had warred against Israel will bring gifts to Zion (cf. Isa. lxvi. 20) (Rashi).

Rahab. Poetical name of Egypt. It means 'the haughty, arrogant,' or was the name of a sea-monster in an ancient myth to which that country was likened (cf. Isa. li. 9).

Babylon. Even the nation which had destroyed Jerusalem and the Temple will be included.

that know Me. Acknowledge Me as the Most High and serve me.

Philistia, and Tyre. Coupled in lxxxiii. 8, as antagonists of Israel.

Ethiopia. Included because of the prophecy in Isa. xviii. 7.

this one. Reference to the exiles who will be returned to Zion by each of the peoples named (see on Isa. xxvii. 12, xlix. 7-12, lx. 4ff., lxvi. 12).

5. *this man and that.* The Talmud (Keth. 75a) explains this statement as a reference to 'both he who was born therein and he who looks forward to seeing it.'

doth establish her. Or, 'shall establish her' (cf. the prayer, *God establish it* (the city of God) *for ever,* xlviii. 9).

6. *shall count in the register.* Better, 'shall reckon when He registers.' In registering the deeds of the nations throughout the period of the Jewish exile, God will not count as one of them those Jews who were lost among the nations by assimilation or by force, and will declare *this one was born there* (in Zion) (cf. Isa. lxvi. 21ff.) (Rashi).

7 UNIVERSAL REJOICING

7. *whether they sing ... in thee.* Render, 'and singers and dancers alike (chant), "All my fountains are in Thee."' The last line may mean: in Zion are all my thoughts and hopes (Metsudath David) or the wellsprings of my heart from whence flow songs of praise to Thee (Kimchi). Dancing was an expression of religious fervour (cf. cxlix. 3, cl. 4). The verse alludes to the era of exultation and happiness which would be ushered in when Zion will be acknowledged as the city of God.

88

פח

1 A Song, a Psalm of the sons of Korah; for the Leader; upon Mahalath Leannoth. Maschil of Heman the Ezrahite.

2 O LORD, God of my salvation, What time I cry in the night before Thee,

3 Let my prayer come before Thee, Incline Thine ear unto my cry.

4 For my soul is sated with troubles, And my life draweth nigh unto the grave.

שִׁיר מִזְמוֹר לִבְנֵי קֹרַח
לַמְנַצֵּחַ עַל־מָחֲלַת לְעַנּוֹת
מַשְׂכִּיל לְהֵימָן הָאֶזְרָחִי:
2 יְהוָה אֱלֹהֵי יְשׁוּעָתִי
יוֹם־צָעַקְתִּי בַלַּיְלָה נֶגְדֶּךָ:
3 תָּבוֹא לְפָנֶיךָ תְּפִלָּתִי
הַטֵּה אָזְנְךָ לְרִנָּתִי:
4 כִּי־שָׂבְעָה בְרָעוֹת נַפְשִׁי
וְחַיַּי לִשְׁאוֹל הִגִּיעוּ:

A CRY FROM THE DEPTHS

THE whole of the Psalm is enshrouded in gloom, and in this respect it differs from others (e.g. VII, XXII, XXXI) which tell of bitter personal suffering. No gleam of light or hope breaks through the plaint. The author prays for relief without any mention of its coming or even its expectation. The Targum explains the Psalm as relating to Israel in captivity, and it is similarly interpreted by Rashi. It is narrated with an intense personal note either as a portrayal of the suffering of the national body of Israel or as a description of each individual wanderer in exile.

1. *a song.* Hirsch addresses the unusual use of the term in a Psalm expressing bitter pain. He explains 'that which seems to us a complaint' as really the theme of the 'song,' dedicated to God who grants us the ability to win spiritual 'victory over crushing pain.'

upon Mahalath Leannoth. Cf. the title of liii. ; lit. 'sickness to afflict,' i.e. concerning one's pain in exile and love-sickness for Zion (Rashi), or simply the name of a melody (cf. Kimchi).

Maschil. See on xxxii. 1.

Heman the Ezrahite. A director of the Temple music, of uncertain identity. In 1 Chron. ii. 6, a Heman is mentioned among the sons of Zerah, a Judahite. A Korahite Heman is named in 1 Chron. vi. 18 and xv. 17, 19 who, together with Asaph and Ethan, was appointed to take charge of the instrumental music. This may be the man intended.

A reference occurs to a Heman, coupled with Ethan the Ezrahite, as a person of great wisdom (1 Kings v. 11), and there may well have been two Hemans and two Ethans.

2-3 APPEAL FOR GOD'S HEARING

2. *God of my salvation.* In the midst of his agonies he clings to faith in God as the only source from which his salvation can come.

what time I cry in the night. lit. 'by day I cried in the night before Thee,' which can only mean: I cried in the daytime (and my cry continues) into the night. A.V. and R.V. *I have cried day and night* is a paraphrase.

3. *cry.* See on xvii. 1.

4-6 HIS EXTREME STRAITS

4. *draweth nigh.* Better, 'hath drawn nigh'; he is at the point of death.

5. *go down into the pit.* Cf. xxviii. 1.

5 I am counted with them that go
   down into the pit;
  I am become as a man that hath
   no help;

6 Set apart among the dead,
  Like the slain that lie in the
   grave,
  Whom Thou rememberest no
   more;
  And they are cut off from Thy
   hand.

7 Thou hast laid me in the nethermost pit,
  In dark places, in the deeps.

8 Thy wrath lieth hard upon me,
  And all Thy waves Thou pressest
   down.   Selah

9 Thou hast put mine acquaintance
   far from me;
  Thou hast made me an abomination unto them;
  I am shut up, and I cannot come
   forth.

נֶחְשַׁבְתִּי עִם־יוֹרְדֵי בוֹר 5
הָיִיתִי כְּגֶבֶר אֵין־אֱיָל׃
בַּמֵּתִים חָפְשִׁי 6
כְּמוֹ חֲלָלִים ׀ שֹׁכְבֵי קֶבֶר
אֲשֶׁר לֹא זְכַרְתָּם עוֹד
וְהֵמָּה מִיָּדְךָ נִגְזָרוּ׃
שַׁתַּנִי בְּבוֹר תַּחְתִּיּוֹת 7
בְּמַחֲשַׁכִּים בִּמְצֹלוֹת׃
עָלַי סָמְכָה חֲמָתֶךָ 8
וְכָל־מִשְׁבָּרֶיךָ עִנִּיתָ סֶּלָה׃
הִרְחַקְתָּ מְיֻדָּעַי מִמֶּנִּי 9
שַׁתַּנִי תוֹעֵבוֹת לָמוֹ
כָּלֻא וְלֹא אֵצֵא׃

help. Or, 'strength'; he is inert like a dead man (Rashi).

6.   *set apart among the dead*. lit. 'among the dead I am free,' i.e. apart from the living and reckoned among the dead. The word is used in 2 Chron. xxvi. 21 of the leper king Uzziah who was confined *in a house set apart*.

slain … grave. Not a separate grave which can be identified and serves as a memorial to the dead person, but the kind of large trench in which the corpses of the slain on the battlefield are heaped for burial.

Thou rememberest no more. In my current state of exile, I am likened unto slain corpses who lie in the grave, who Thou hast not yet remembered to resurrect. So am I, for whom Thou hast not yet remembered to bring salvation (Metsudath David).

cut off from Thy hand. i.e. from Thy saving power (cf. *I am cut off from before Thine eyes*, xxxi. 23).

     7-9   GOD'S WRATH IS UPON HIM

7.   *Thou hast laid me*. In his desperate plight he thinks of himself as already departed from the world.

the nethermost pit. Cf. *the lowest nether-world* (Sheol) (lxxxvi. 13), located in the depths of the earth.

dark places. Darkness of Sheol (cxliii. 3).

the deeps. The Hebrew usually denotes the sea-depths; here it is Sheol.

8.   *Thy wrath*. Demonstrated by the pains inflicted upon him.

all Thy waves. Cf. *all Thy waves and Thy billows are gone over me* (xlii. 8).

pressest down. To overwhelm me.

9.   *mine acquaintance*. Better, 'mine intimate friends.' With this verse which describes the condition of a leper, cf. xxxi. 12.

abomination. The Hebrew is plural with an intensive force: an utter abomination. Kimchi observes that the personal suffering in exile has prevented each person from being con-

10 Mine eye languisheth by reason
   of affliction;
   I have called upon Thee, O LORD,
   every day,
   I have spread forth my hands
   unto Thee.

11 Wilt Thou work wonders for the
   dead ?
   Or shall the shades arise and give
   Thee thanks?   Selah

12 Shall Thy mercy be declared in
   the grave?
   Or Thy faithfulness in destruction?

13 Shall Thy wonders be known in
   the dark?
   And Thy righteousness in the
   land of forgetfulness?

14 But as for me, unto Thee, O LORD,
   do I cry,
   And in the morning doth my
   prayer come to meet Thee.

15 LORD, why castest Thou off my
   soul?
   Why hidest Thou Thy face from
   me?

עֵינִי דָאֲבָה מִנִּי־עֹנִי 10
קְרָאתִיךָ יְהוָה בְּכָל־יֹום
שִׁטַּחְתִּי אֵלֶיךָ כַפָּי:
הֲלַמֵּתִים תַּעֲשֶׂה־פֶּלֶא 11
אִם־רְפָאִים יָקוּמוּ ׀ יֹודוּךָ סֶּלָה:
הַיְסֻפַּר בַּקֶּבֶר חַסְדֶּךָ 12
אֱמוּנָתְךָ בָּאֲבַדֹּון:
הֲיִוָּדַע בַּחֹשֶׁךְ פִּלְאֶךָ 13
וְצִדְקָתְךָ בְּאֶרֶץ נְשִׁיָּה:
וַאֲנִי ׀ אֵלֶיךָ יְהוָה שִׁוַּעְתִּי 14
וּבַבֹּקֶר תְּפִלָּתִי תְקַדְּמֶךָּ:
לָמָה יְהוָה תִּזְנַח נַפְשִׁי 15
תַּסְתִּיר פָּנֶיךָ מִמֶּנִּי:

cerned with the plight of the other. This resulted in friends becoming distant from each
other as if they were mutual abominations.

10-13   WILL NOT GOD RELIEVE
        HIM ERE IT IS TOO LATE?

10.   *mine eyes languisheth*. The sufferings
of his mind and body are visible in the look of
his eyes (cf. vi. 8, xxxi. 10).

spread forth. In supplication.

11.   Unless God soon answers his prayer,
he will be dead (cf. Ibn Ezra, Metsudath
David).

work wonders for the dead. God's marvellous acts are of no purpose for the dead (cxv.
17) (Ibn Ezra, Kimchi).

shades. lit. 'weak, helpless ones'; the powerless dead.

give Thee thanks. That is man's prerogative
only when he is living (cf. *the dead praise not
the LORD*, cxv. 17).

12.   *mercy … faithfulness*. These Divine
attributes (lxxxix. 2) can only be experienced
by living men, and they alone are able to
praise God for having received them.

destruction. Hebrew *Abaddon*, 'place of
perishing,' another name of Sheol (Tal. Erub.
19a).

13.   *dark*. Sheol, the home of darkness (cf.
verse 7).

land of forgetfulness. Another description of
Sheol: where one is forgotten (Kimchi).

14-19   HIS PRAYER RENEWED

14.   *as for me*. Unlike the dead who are
incapable of praying, he still has the breath of
life within him, and so he persists in his
supplication (Kimchi, Malbim).

in the morning. As soon as he awakes (v. 4).

15.   *my soul*. Equals 'me.'

hidest Thou Thy face. See on xiii. 2.

16 I am afflicted and at the point of
    death from my youth up;
  I have borne Thy terrors, I am
    distracted.

17 Thy fierce wrath is gone over me;
  Thy terrors have cut me off.

18 They came round about me like
    water all the day;
  They compassed me about to-
    gether.

19 Friend and companion hast Thou
    put far from me,
  And mine acquaintance into
    darkness.

עָנִי אֲנִי וְגֹוֵעַ מִנֹּעַר 16
נָשָׂאתִי אֵמֶיךָ אָפוּנָה:
עָלַי עָבְרוּ חֲרוֹנֶיךָ 17
בִּעוּתֶיךָ צִמְּתֻתוּנִי:
סַבּוּנִי כַמַּיִם כָּל־הַיּוֹם 18
הִקִּיפוּ עָלַי יָחַד:
הִרְחַקְתָּ מִמֶּנִּי אֹהֵב וָרֵעַ 19
מְיֻדָּעַי מַחְשָׁךְ:

16. *from my youth up*. He has borne his affliction from youth.

Thy terrors. Afflictions which terrify.

I am distracted. The Hebrew root occurs nowhere else and its meaning is uncertain. The sense required by the context is, 'I would like to turn aside from Thy fears which terrify me on all sides.'

17. *Thy fierce wrath*. The Hebrew is plural, 'Thy streams of fiery wrath.'

is gone over me. i.e. 'overwhelmed me' (cf. xlii. 8 quoted on verse 8).

Thy terrors. 'Thine alarming, overwhelming deeds.' Not the same Hebrew word as in the previous verse; again only in Job vi. 4.

have cut me off. Better, 'have made an end of me.'

18. *like water*. He is sinking under God's wrathful visitations like a man drowning in the waters.

all the day. He suffers continuously, without respite.

19. *friend and companion*. To whom he had a right to look for help in his desperate plight. He repeats his complaint of verse 9 as he ends his tale of woe. A similar lament was made by Job in the time of his suffering (Job xix. 13ff.).

put far from me. In consequence of the ravages of his suffering he is avoided by his friends (see on verse 9).

and mine acquaintance into darkness. Perhaps, 'my intimate friends are darkness.' Abandoned by all, he is solitary and has only his dark surroundings to associate with. So ends this pathetic story of agony, without any expression of hope. Nevertheless, although the note of hopefulness is not struck in the concluding verse, it may be implied in the conviction which pervades the Psalm that the sufferer is all the time in the hands of God. If He smote, He can and may heal.

PSALM LXXXIX

89

1 Maschil of Ethan the Ezrahite.

2 I will sing of the mercies of the
   LORD for ever;
   To all generations will I make
   known Thy faithfulness with
   my mouth.

3 For I have said: 'For ever is
   mercy built;
   In the very heavens Thou dost
   establish Thy faithfulness.

4 I have made a covenant with My
   chosen,
   I have sworn unto David My
   servant:

5 For ever will I establish thy seed,
   And build up thy throne to all
   generations.'   Selah

פט

מַשְׂכִּיל לְאֵיתָן הָאֶזְרָחִי׃

2 חַסְדֵי יְהוָה עוֹלָם אָשִׁירָה
לְדֹר וָדֹר ׀ אוֹדִיעַ אֱמוּנָתְךָ בְּפִי׃

3 כִּי־אָמַרְתִּי עוֹלָם חֶסֶד יִבָּנֶה
שָׁמַיִם ׀ תָּכִן אֱמוּנָתְךָ בָהֶם׃

4 כָּרַתִּי בְרִית לִבְחִירִי
נִשְׁבַּעְתִּי לְדָוִד עַבְדִּי׃

5 עַד־עוֹלָם אָכִין זַרְעֶךָ
וּבָנִיתִי לְדֹר־וָדוֹר כִּסְאֲךָ סֶלָה׃

MEDITATION IN NATIONAL ADVERSITY

Two divisions are clearly marked in the Psalm, with the break at verse 39. The first section
deals with the past in which the two attributes of God, mercy and faithfulness, were
abundantly demonstrated in His relation with Israel. In particular the promise to David, that
his throne would endure for ever, is recalled. The second section paints its dark picture of the
nation's vicissitudes and the overthrow of the kingdom by a triumphant enemy. So glaring is
the contrast between the promise and its frustration, that the Psalmist gives utterance to his
perplexity in forceful language, and finally prays that God will remember His people in their
adversity.

1. *Ethan the Ezrahite.* See on lxxxviii. 1.

2-5 THEME OF THE PSALM

2. *mercies.* Hebrew *chesed;* God's acts of
love wrought for Israel out of His goodness.
This is the meaning of the word throughout
the Psalm.

faithfulness. In implementing His promises
(cf. Malbim).

with my mouth. Publicly.

3. *for I have said.* After reflecting upon the
national past, the Psalmist detects certain
outstanding lessons, and these he proceeds to
state.

for ever is mercy built. Notwithstanding the
tragic condition of Israel at the moment,
God's *chesed* is an eternal structure rearing
itself from earth to heaven.

4f. God's covenant with David is to be the
principal *motif* of the Psalm (verses 20ff.); so
the Psalmist reproduces a summary of the
promise which God had made to the king
early in his reign (2 Sam. vii).

6 So shall the heavens praise Thy
   wonders, O LORD,
   Thy faithfulness also in the
   assembly of the holy ones.

7 For who in the skies can be compared unto the LORD,
   Who among the sons of might can
   be likened unto the LORD,

8 A God dreaded in the great council of the holy ones,
   And feared of all them that are
   round about Him ?

9 O LORD God of hosts,
   Who is a mighty one, like unto
   Thee, O LORD?
   And Thy faithfulness is round
   about Thee.

10 Thou rulest the proud swelling
   of the sea;
   When the waves thereof arise,
   Thou stillest them.

11 Thou didst crush Rahab, as one
   that is slain;
   Thou didst scatter Thine enemies
   with the arm of Thy strength.

6 וְיוֹדוּ שָׁמַיִם פִּלְאֲךָ יְהוָה

אַף־אֱמוּנָתְךָ בִּקְהַל קְדֹשִׁים:

7 כִּי מִי בַשַּׁחַק יַעֲרֹךְ לַיהוָה

יִדְמֶה לַיהוָה בִּבְנֵי אֵלִים:

8 אֵל נַעֲרָץ בְּסוֹד־קְדֹשִׁים רַבָּה

וְנוֹרָא עַל־כָּל־סְבִיבָיו:

9 יְהוָה אֱלֹהֵי צְבָאוֹת

מִי־כָמוֹךָ חֲסִין יָהּ

וֶאֱמוּנָתְךָ סְבִיבוֹתֶיךָ:

10 אַתָּה מוֹשֵׁל בְּגֵאוּת הַיָּם

בְּשׂוֹא גַלָּיו אַתָּה תְשַׁבְּחֵם:

11 אַתָּה דִכִּאתָ כֶחָלָל רָהַב

בִּזְרוֹעַ עֻזְּךָ פִּזַּרְתָּ אוֹיְבֶיךָ:

6-15 GOD'S ATTRIBUTES RECOUNTED

6. See on xix. 2.

Thy wonders. The Hebrew is singular and
probably is not collective. It denotes the
scheme of the constant revolution of the
planets. This continuous precise motion is a
manifestation of a prime mover, and is a
cause for praise (Kimchi).

holy ones. Parallel to *heavens*, the angels
(Kimchi). The same juxtaposition occurs in
Job xv. 15.

7. *who in the skies.* Other peoples worship
the heavenly bodies as deities; but how can
these be compared unto God! (cf. Ibn Ezra).

sons of might. See on xxix. 1.

8. *dreaded in the great council.* Perhaps,
'dreaded in the council of the holy ones
greatly.' The angels constitute a council in
heaven (Jer. xxiii. 18, 22) over which God is
undisputed Ruler. Alshich makes reference
to the dread of the fiery angels (seraphim)

who gather to herald the supreme degree of
God's holiness (see on Isa. vi. 2ff.).

9. *O LORD.* Hebrew *Jah*, the Divine name
used at the overthrow of Pharaoh (Exod. xv.
2), and the question *Who is like unto Thee?*
recalls the song at the Red Sea (Exod. xv. 11).

round about Thee. Loyalty to His promises
enwraps Him and will not separate from Him
(Metsudath David).

10. In this and the following verses, *Thou*
and *Thine* are emphatic in the Hebrew. Of
God only can these statements be made.

proud swelling of the sea. 'The sea's water
would, by their turbulent nature, sweep over
the earth. God in His mercy has 'set a boundary which they should not pass over' (Meiri)
(cf. civ. 9, Jer. v. 22).

11. *Rahab.* Egypt (see on lxxxvii. 4).

scatter Thine enemies. Cf. the prayer in the
wilderness: *Rise up, O LORD, and let Thine
enemies be scattered* (Num. x. 35).

12 Thine are the heavens, Thine also
the earth;
The world and the fulness thereof, Thou hast founded them.

13 The north and the south, Thou
hast created them;
Tabor and Hermon rejoice in
Thy name.

14 Thine is an arm with might;
Strong is Thy hand, and exalted
is Thy right hand.

15 Righteousness and justice are the
foundation of Thy throne;
Mercy and truth go before Thee.

16 Happy is the people that know
the joyful shout;
They walk, O LORD, in the light
of Thy countenance.

17 In Thy name do they rejoice all
the day;
And through Thy righteousness
are they exalted.

18 For Thou art the glory of their
strength;
And in Thy favour our horn is
exalted.

לְךָ שָׁמַיִם אַף־לְךָ אָרֶץ 12
תֵּבֵל וּמְלֹאָהּ אַתָּה יְסַדְתָּם:
צָפוֹן וְיָמִין אַתָּה בְרָאתָם 13
תָּבוֹר וְחֶרְמוֹן בְּשִׁמְךָ יְרַנֵּנוּ:
לְךָ זְרוֹעַ עִם־גְּבוּרָה 14
תָּעֹז יָדְךָ תָּרוּם יְמִינֶךָ:
צֶדֶק וּמִשְׁפָּט מְכוֹן כִּסְאֶךָ 15
חֶסֶד וֶאֱמֶת יְקַדְּמוּ פָנֶיךָ:
אַשְׁרֵי הָעָם יֹדְעֵי תְרוּעָה 16
יְהוָה בְּאוֹר־פָּנֶיךָ יְהַלֵּכוּן:
בְּשִׁמְךָ יְגִילוּן כָּל־הַיּוֹם 17
וּבְצִדְקָתְךָ יָרוּמוּ:
כִּי־תִפְאֶרֶת עֻזָּמוֹ אָתָּה 18
וּבִרְצוֹנְךָ תָּרִים קַרְנֵנוּ:

v. 18. תרום ק'

---

12. Cf. xxiv. 1f.

13. *north and the south.* The world from
one end to the other.

Tabor and Hermon. The two most prominent
mountains in Israel, named as the most impressive natural features of the country.

rejoice in Thy name. They joyfully testify to
the infinite greatness of the Creator.

14. *exalted.* Not only is God all-powerful
but He demonstrates His might in the affairs
of men. The words in the verse, *arm, hand,
right hand*, occur in the song at the Red Sea.

15. *righteousness ... throne.* Repeated in
xcvii. 2. *Justice* is *righteousness* in practice.
God's Sovereignty does not rest upon His
might but upon His ethical attributes.

go before Thee. According to this translation,
mercy and *truth* are represented as God's
forerunners or heralds, preceding His manifestations in the world. The verb may also be
rendered 'attend Thy presence'; they wait

upon Him to obey His commands (Kimchi).

16-19 ISRAEL AS GOD'S PEOPLE

16. *the joyful shout.* Hebrew *teruah*, which
is employed of sounding trumpets of the
shofar, acclaiming a king, and the happy
cries of pilgrims on the festivals, which Israel, as God's people, has been privileged to
know (cf. Metsudath David).

the light of Thy countenance. In accordance
with the Priestly Benediction: *The LORD make
His face to shine upon thee, and be gracious
unto thee* (Num. vi. 25).

17. *in Thy name.* In His essence as revealed
in His dealings with Israel (cf. Hirsch).

are they exalted. Israel's eminence is the effect of God's fulfilment of His covenant.

18. *the glory of their strength.* The Power
in which they glory (xliv. 6ff.).

our horn is exalted. See on lxxv. 5. Here the
meaning is: we can raise our heads resolutely
when opposed by enemies. The translation

19 For of the LORD is our shield;
And of the Holy One of Israel is
our king.

20 Then Thou spokest in vision to
Thy godly ones,
And saidst: 'I have laid help
upon one that is mighty;
I have exalted one chosen out of
the people.

21 I have found David My servant;
With My holy oil have I anointed
him;

22 With whom My hand shall be
established;
Mine arm also shall strengthen
him.

23 The enemy shall not exact from
him;
Nor the son of wickedness afflict
him.

24 And I will beat to pieces his
adversaries before him,
And smite them that hate him.

19 כִּי לַיהוָה מָגִנֵּנוּ

וְלִקְדוֹשׁ יִשְׂרָאֵל מַלְכֵּנוּ:

20 אָז דִּבַּרְתָּ בְחָזוֹן לַחֲסִידֶיךָ

וַתֹּאמֶר שִׁוִּיתִי עֵזֶר עַל־גִּבּוֹר

הֲרִימוֹתִי בָחוּר מֵעָם:

21 מָצָאתִי דָּוִד עַבְדִּי

בְּשֶׁמֶן קָדְשִׁי מְשַׁחְתִּיו:

22 אֲשֶׁר יָדִי תִּכּוֹן עִמּוֹ

אַף־זְרוֹעִי תְאַמְּצֶנּוּ:

23 לֹא־יַשִּׁיא אוֹיֵב בּוֹ

וּבֶן־עַוְלָה לֹא יְעַנֶּנּוּ:

24 וְכַתּוֹתִי מִפָּנָיו צָרָיו

וּמְשַׂנְאָיו אֶגּוֹף:

follows the *kerë* which is supported by the LXX; the Targum follows the *kethib*, 'Thou wilt raise our horn on high.' As for the change of *their* to *our*, Hirsch notes that it is to indicate that this pledge (verse 16ff.) is first and foremost to Israel.

19. *our shield*. The king, as the protector of the people (see on lxxxiv. 10). He is *of the LORD*, designated by Him as the occupant of the throne.

the Holy One of Israel. See on lxxi. 22. The mention of the *king* is the link with the next section.

20-38 THE COVENANT WITH DAVID

20. *then*. On the occasion narrated in 2 Sam. vii and referring back to verses 4f. of this Psalm (Kimchi).

in vision. Cf. 2 Sam. vii. 17.

Thy godly ones. Hebrew *chasid*; The people of Israel (see on lxxix. 2). Some MSS., however, read the singular (*chasid' cha* rather than *chasidecha*), which would allude to Samuel the prophet (Kimchi, Metsudath David) or

perhaps Nathan the prophet who was active in the episode. Rashi explains the plural as a reference to Nathan and Gad the seer.

I have laid help upon. In appointing David as king, God conferred upon him the aid of which he would stand in need.

one that is mighty. David had proved his prowess against the Philistines.

21. *found*. Discovered as the man best fitted for the throne (cf. Ibn Ezra).

David My servant. Cf. lxxviii. 70.

holy oil. Cf. Exod. xxx. 25.

anointed. See on ii. 2. For David's anointing, cf. 1 Sam. xvi. 13.

22. *shall be established*. God's help will be fixed to him, i.e. never fail him (cf. Ibn Ezra).

23. *exact from him*. As a usurer exacts interest from a debtor. Meiri translates the verb as 'beguile' (see Gen. iii. 13). No enemy will beguile him to forsake Thy service.

nor the son … afflict him. Again in 2 Sam. vii. 10, where the words refer to Israel.

25 But My faithfulness and My
  mercy shall be with him;
  And through My name shall his
  horn be exalted.

26 I will set his hand also on the sea,
  And his right hand on the rivers.

27 He shall call unto Me: Thou art
  my Father,
  My God, and the rock of my
  salvation.

28 I also will appoint him first-born,
  The highest of the kings of the
  earth.

29 For ever will I keep for him My
  mercy,
  And My covenant shall stand fast
  with him.

30 His seed also will I make to
  endure for ever,
  And his throne as the days of
  heaven.

31 If his children forsake My law,
  And walk not in Mine ordinances;

32 If they profane My statutes,
  And keep not My commandments;

33 Then will I visit their transgression with the rod,
  And their iniquity with strokes.

25 וֶאֱמוּנָתִי וְחַסְדִּי עִמּוֹ
וּבִשְׁמִי תָּרוּם קַרְנוֹ:
26 וְשַׂמְתִּי בַיָּם יָדוֹ
וּבַנְּהָרוֹת יְמִינוֹ:
27 הוּא יִקְרָאֵנִי אָבִי אָתָּה
אֵלִי וְצוּר יְשׁוּעָתִי:
28 אַף־אָנִי בְּכוֹר אֶתְּנֵהוּ
עֶלְיוֹן לְמַלְכֵי־אָרֶץ:
29 לְעוֹלָם אֶשְׁמוֹר־לוֹ חַסְדִּי
וּבְרִיתִי נֶאֱמֶנֶת לוֹ:
30 וְשַׂמְתִּי לָעַד זַרְעוֹ
וְכִסְאוֹ כִּימֵי שָׁמָיִם:
31 אִם־יַעַזְבוּ בָנָיו תּוֹרָתִי
וּבְמִשְׁפָּטַי לֹא יֵלֵכוּן:
32 אִם־חֻקֹּתַי יְחַלֵּלוּ
וּמִצְוֹתַי לֹא יִשְׁמֹרוּ:
33 וּפָקַדְתִּי בְשֵׁבֶט פִּשְׁעָם
וּבִנְגָעִים עֲוֹנָם:

---

25. *but.* Rather, 'and.'

horn be exalted. See on verse 18.

26. *hand.* Power, dominion.

the sea. The Mediterranean on the west.

the rivers. The Euphrates and its eastern tributaries. The terms set the maximum limits of
the Israelite kingdom (cf. lxxii. 8, lxxx. 12).

27. *my Father.* The promise made of
Solomon (2 Sam. vii. 14) is applied to David
(cf. ii. 7, of God's anointed).

my God, etc. Cf. xviii. 3; Deut. xxxii. 15.

28. *first-born.* Chief among the kings

(Meiri). The term used of Israel (Exod. iv.
22) holds good also of its monarch.

29. *for ever.* The promise is made not only
to David personally, but is extended to the
dynasty which he will found (2 Sam. vii. 16).

30. *as the days of heaven.* Eternally (cf.
Deut. xi. 21).

31. *children.* i.e. the descendants who will
succeed to the throne.

33. *rod … strokes.* Quoted from 2 Sam. vii.
14. As a father chastises a disobedient child,
God will inflict punishment upon them.

34 But My mercy will I not break
off from him,
Nor will I be false to My faithfulness.

35 My covenant will I not profane,
Nor alter that which is gone out
of My lips.

36 Once have I sworn by My holi-
ness:
Surely I will not be false unto
David;

37 His seed shall endure for ever,
And his throne as the sun before
Me.

38 It shall be established for ever as
the moon;
And be stedfast as the witness in
the sky.'   Selah

39 But Thou hast cast off and re-
jected,
Thou hast been wroth with
Thine anointed.

40 Thou hast abhorred the covenant
of Thy servant;
Thou hast profaned his crown
even to the ground.

34 וְחַסְדִּי לֹא־אָפִיר מֵעִמּוֹ
וְלֹא־אֲשַׁקֵּר בֶּאֱמוּנָתִי:
35 לֹא־אֲחַלֵּל בְּרִיתִי
וּמוֹצָא שְׂפָתַי לֹא אֲשַׁנֶּה:
36 אַחַת נִשְׁבַּעְתִּי בְקָדְשִׁי
אִם־לְדָוִד אֲכַזֵּב:
37 זַרְעוֹ לְעוֹלָם יִהְיֶה
וְכִסְאוֹ כַשֶּׁמֶשׁ נֶגְדִּי:
38 כְּיָרֵחַ יִכּוֹן עוֹלָם
וְעֵד בַּשַּׁחַק נֶאֱמָן סֶלָה:
39 וְאַתָּה זָנַחְתָּ וַתִּמְאָס
הִתְעַבַּרְתָּ עִם־מְשִׁיחֶךָ:
40 נֵאַרְתָּה בְּרִית עַבְדֶּךָ
חִלַּלְתָּ לָאָרֶץ נִזְרוֹ:

34. The penalty will not take the extreme form of repudiating the promise which had been made to David (Meiri).

35. *profane.* A covenant is a sacred under-taking; to violate it is to profane what is holy.

gone out of My lips. Used of a vow (Num. XXX. 13).

36. *once.* i.e. once and for all time (cf. Targum).

sworn. Cf. verse 4.

by My holiness. See on lx. 8.

37. *endure for ever.* Cf. verses 5, 30.

throne. The kingship.

as the sun. Equals *while the sun endureth* (lxxii. 5, 17) (cf. Kimchi).

38. *and be stedfast … sky.* The witness is the sun or moon whose durability testifies to

the permanence of David's throne. There is however, no *as* in the Hebrew, and the clause may be rendered: 'and the witness in the sky (i.e. God) is faithful.' Since His word is pledged, there is certainty that the throne will endure (cf. Rashi).

39-46   CONTRAST WITH THE PRESENT

39. *but Thou.* Emphatic in Hebrew. Al-though actual conditions are so very different from the ideal promised by God, it is still He Who has ordained the calamities. Whatever change may have taken place, the same *Thou* is guiding the nation's destiny.

40. *abhorred.* Or, 'spurned.'

Thy servant. The last reigning monarch in the line of David (cf. Rashi on verse 39).

profaned … to the ground. Cf. lxxiv. 7, where used regarding the Temple.

41 Thou hast broken down all his
      fences;
   Thou hast brought his strong-
      holds to ruin.

42 All that pass by the way spoil
      him;
   He is become a taunt to his
      neighbours.

43 Thou hast exalted the right hand
      of his adversaries;
   Thou hast made all his enemies
      to rejoice.

44 Yea, Thou turnest back the edge
      of his sword,
   And hast not made him to stand
      in the battle.

45 Thou hast made his brightness to
      cease,
   And cast his throne down to the
      ground.

46 The days of his youth hast Thou
      shortened;
   Thou hast covered him with
      shame.   Selah

47 How long, O LORD, wilt Thou
      hide Thyself for ever?
   How long shall Thy wrath burn
      like fire?

41 פָּרַצְתָּ כָל־גְּדֵרֹתָיו

שַׂמְתָּ מִבְצָרָיו מְחִתָּה׃

42 שַׁסֻּהוּ כָּל־עֹבְרֵי דָרֶךְ

הָיָה חֶרְפָּה לִשְׁכֵנָיו׃

43 הֲרִימוֹתָ יְמִין צָרָיו

הִשְׂמַחְתָּ כָּל־אוֹיְבָיו׃

44 אַף־תָּשִׁיב צוּר חַרְבּוֹ

וְלֹא הֲקֵמֹתוֹ בַּמִּלְחָמָה׃

45 הִשְׁבַּתָּ מִטָּהֳרוֹ

וְכִסְאוֹ לָאָרֶץ מִגַּרְתָּה׃

46 הִקְצַרְתָּ יְמֵי עֲלוּמָיו

הֶעֱטִיתָ עָלָיו בּוּשָׁה סֶלָה׃

47 עַד־מָה יְהוָה תִּסָּתֵר לָנֶצַח

תִּבְעַר כְּמוֹ־אֵשׁ חֲמָתֶךָ׃

---

41. *Thou hast broken down all his fences.*
Cf. lxxx. 13. What happened to the land is
described as happening to the king, whose
duty is to maintain the frontiers against attack
(cf. Malbim).

42. *all that pass by the way spoil him.* Again
cf. lxxx. 13, with a different verb.

a taunt to his neighbours. Cf. lxxix. 4.

44. *turnest back.* In the act of striking, the
edge is turned away from the enemy and fails
to wound him (cf. Rashi).

45. *brightness.* The brilliance of his throne,
now darkened by national eclipse (cf. Kimchi,
Metsudath David).

cast ... to the ground. Or, 'overthrown.'

46. *days of his youth.* Referring to the
comparative brevity of David's dynasty (Ibn
Ezra) or to the limited period of 'youth' or
good days in David's rule (Kimchi). It could
perhaps be an allusion to the last kings of the
Davidic dynasty (cf. Malbim).

47-52   PLEA FOR CLEMENCY

47. Repeated with slight variation from
lxxix 5.

48 O remember how short my time
　　is;
　　For what vanity hast Thou
　　created all the children of men!

49 What man is he that liveth and
　　shall not see death,
　　That shall deliver his soul from
　　the power of the grave? Selah

50 Where are Thy former mercies,
　　O Lord,
　　Which Thou didst swear unto
　　David in Thy faithfulness?

51 Remember, Lord, the taunt of
　　Thy servants;
　　How I do bear in my bosom [the
　　taunt of] so many peoples;

52 Wherewith Thine enemies have
　　taunted, O LORD,
　　Wherewith they have taunted
　　the footsteps of Thine
　　anointed.

53 Blessed be the LORD for ever-
　　more.
　　Amen, and Amen.

זְכָר־אֲנִי מֶה־חָלֶד ‎48
עַל־מַה־שָּׁוְא בָּרָאתָ
כָל־בְּנֵי־אָדָם:
מִי גֶבֶר יִחְיֶה וְלֹא יִרְאֶה־מָּוֶת ‎49
יְמַלֵּט נַפְשׁוֹ מִיַּד־שְׁאוֹל סֶלָה:
אַיֵּה וַחֲסָדֶיךָ הָרִאשֹׁנִים וַאֲדֹנָי ‎50
נִשְׁבַּעְתָּ לְדָוִד בֶּאֱמוּנָתֶךָ:
זְכֹר אֲדֹנָי חֶרְפַּת עֲבָדֶיךָ ‎51
שְׂאֵתִי בְחֵיקִי כָּל־רַבִּים עַמִּים:
אֲשֶׁר חֵרְפוּ אוֹיְבֶיךָ וַיהוָה ‎52
אֲשֶׁר חֵרְפוּ עִקְּבוֹת מְשִׁיחֶךָ:
בָּרוּךְ יְהוָה לְעוֹלָם ‎53
אָמֵן וְאָמֵן:

---

48. *how short my time is*. Hebrew, 'what a fleeting thing I am.' Inasmuch as his term of life is brief, he prays that God will bring redemption to Israel speedily so that he may be alive to see it (cf. Kimchi, Metsudath David).

for what vanity ... men. If he will not live to see the final redemption, then life is for naught (cf. Malbim).

49. *grave*. Hebrew *Sheol*. The Psalmist shares the mortality common to all men. May God remember that and hasten the end of the captivity! (cf. Ibn Ezra).

50. *Thy former mercies*. That you swore to David.

swear. In closing the Psalm the author reverts to its opening thought (verse 4).

51. *taunt of Thy servants*. The mocking reproaches hurled at Israel in his time of adversity, that God was unwilling to save him (cf. Kimchi).

bosom. See on lxxiv. 11.

[*the taunt of*] *so many peoples*. Hebrew, 'all that many peoples,' an obscure clause which can only be made intelligible by assuming that *the taunt of* qualifies both halves of the verse.

52. *footsteps ... anointed*. A reference to the long wait for the Messiah because of which Israel was taunted by those claiming he would never come (Kimchi).

53.　CLOSING DOXOLOGY

The verse is not a part of the Psalm, but the usual form of ending a Book of the Psalter (Kimchi, Ibn Ezra).

PSALM XC

1 A Prayer of Moses the man of
   God.
   Lord, Thou hast been our dwel-
   ling-place in all generations.

2 Before the mountains were
   brought forth,
   Or ever Thou hadst formed the
   earth and the world,
   Even from everlasting to everlasting, Thou art God.

תְּפִלָּה לְמֹשֶׁה אִישׁ־הָאֱלֹהִים
אֲדֹנָי מָעוֹן אַתָּה הָיִיתָ לָּנוּ
בְּדֹר וָדֹר׃
2 בְּטֶרֶם ׀ הָרִים יֻלָּדוּ
וַתְּחוֹלֵל אֶרֶץ וְתֵבֵל
וּמֵעוֹלָם עַד־עוֹלָם אַתָּה אֵל׃

MAN'S BREVITY, GOD'S ETERNITY

IN sublime language this Psalm dwells upon the transitory character of man's existence, but in no pessimistic mood. If life is brief, its moments are precious and must not be wasted in vain pursuits. The swift passing of his stay upon earth would render it meaningless and purpose-less, were it not that God is everlasting and under Him is man's abiding dwelling-place. The Psalm is entitled *A Prayer of Moses*, and Rashi notes that it corresponds to the blessings bestowed by Moses in Deut. xxxiii. Rashi further comments that the first eleven Psalms which open the fourth book of Psalms were all authored by Moses.

1-6 GOD IMMORTAL, MAN MORTAL

1. *the man of God.* Moses is so named in Deut. xxxiii. 1, but the description is also applied to other prophets (see Sifri, ibid.)

our dwelling-place. 'A place of shelter to hide under Your wings' (Meiri). (cf. Deut. xxxiii.27).

in all generations. lit. 'in a generation and a generation.' God had proved Himself a dwelling-place not spasmodically, but in one generation after another.

2. *the mountains.* Cf. *the ancient mountains* (Deut. xxxiii. 15).

Thou hadst formed. The Hebrew verb is the normal one for the birth of a child, and it is used in *thou (Israel) didst forget God that bore thee* (Deut. xxxii. 18).

world. Hebrew *tebel*, the part of the earth inhabited by man (cf. xxiv. 1).

from everlasting to everlasting. Before time was and after time shall cease (cf. Meiri).

3 Thou turnest man to contrition;
　And sayest: 'Return, ye children
　　of men.'

4 For a thousand years in Thy sight
　Are but as yesterday when it is
　　past,
　And as a watch in the night.

5 Thou carriest them away as with a
　　flood; they are as a sleep;
　In the morning they are like grass
　　which groweth up.

6 In the morning it flourisheth, and
　　groweth up;
　In the evening it is cut down, and
　　withereth.

7 For we are consumed in Thine
　　anger,
　And by Thy wrath are we hurried
　　away.

תָּשֵׁב אֱנוֹשׁ עַד־דַּכָּא 3
וַתֹּאמֶר שׁוּבוּ בְנֵי־אָדָם׃
כִּי אֶלֶף שָׁנִים בְּעֵינֶיךָ 4
כְּיוֹם אֶתְמוֹל כִּי יַעֲבֹר
וְאַשְׁמוּרָה בַלָּיְלָה׃
זְרַמְתָּם שֵׁנָה יִהְיוּ 5
בַּבֹּקֶר כֶּחָצִיר יַחֲלֹף׃
בַּבֹּקֶר יָצִיץ וְחָלָף 6
לָעֶרֶב יְמוֹלֵל וְיָבֵשׁ׃
כִּי־כָלִינוּ בְאַפֶּךָ 7
וּבַחֲמָתְךָ נִבְהָלְנוּ׃

3. *contrition*. On this interpretation *return* means: 'unto Me, the Judge of the human spirit. God, the unchanging, is the refuge of changing and erring man' (Hertz, following Rashi). The Hebrew translated *contrition* also has the significance of 'dust' (lit. crumbled to powder) and Ibn Ezra connects the verse with *dust thou art and unto dust shalt thou return* (Gen. iii. 19). The word for *man* (*enosh*) denotes the human being in his frailty (see on viii. 5). Accordingly the verse contrasts the fate of man, which is to revert to dust, with God's deathlessness.

4. *a thousand years*. Continuing the thought of the previous verse, the Psalmist proclaims that time has no meaning with God. In the estimation of man a thousand years is a vast stretch of time; in God's estimation it is like a day which has already gone—not in the sense that the hours drag slowly by and in retrospect appears so short. Nay, it is less even than that, the Psalmist continues, it is like a night-watch (see on lxiii. 7), of which the sleeper takes no reck-oning and which has vanished on his waking.

5. *Thou carriest...flood*. The same verb as in lxxvii. 18, *the clouds flooded forth waters*. As a sudden storm sweeps away a hut or a tent, so is man's life brought to a sudden end (cf. Kimchi).

they are as a sleep. lit. 'they are a sleep,' they are in a sleeping condition, viz. in the sleep of death (see on lxxvi.6).

in the morning...up. The line is elaborated in the next verse.

like grass. Cf. ciii. 15f.

6. Cf. xxxvii.2.

7-12 THE EFFECT OF DIVINE WRATH

7. *we are consumed*. The shortness of human life and the troubles which fill it are the effect of sin which kindles God's anger, as proved by the experience of the people of Israel (cf. Meiri).

are we hurried away. To an untimely end. The Hebrew may mean 'dismayed,' filled with apprehension at God's judgments.

8 Thou hast set our iniquities before
  Thee,
  Our secret sins in the light of Thy
  countenance.

9 For all our days are passed away
  in Thy wrath;
  We bring our years to an end as
  a tale that is told.

10 The days of our years are threescore years and ten,
  Or even by reason of strength
  four-score years;
  Yet is their pride but travail and
  vanity;
  For it is speedily gone, and we fly
  away.

11 Who knoweth the power of
  Thine anger,
  And Thy wrath according to the
  fear that is due unto Thee?

12 So teach us to number our days,
  That we may get us a heart of
  wisdom.

8 שַׁתָּ עֲוֺנֹתֵינוּ לְנֶגְדֶּךָ
עֲלֻמֵנוּ לִמְאוֹר פָּנֶיךָ׃
9 כִּי כָל־יָמֵינוּ פָּנוּ בְעֶבְרָתֶךָ
כִּלִּינוּ שָׁנֵינוּ כְמוֹ־הֶגֶה׃
10 יְמֵי־שְׁנוֹתֵינוּ בָהֶם שִׁבְעִים שָׁנָה
וְאִם בִּגְבוּרֹת שְׁמוֹנִים שָׁנָה
וְרָהְבָּם עָמָל וָאָוֶן
כִּי־גָז חִישׁ וַנָּעֻפָה׃
11 מִי־יוֹדֵעַ עֹז אַפֶּךָ
וּכְיִרְאָתְךָ עֶבְרָתֶךָ׃
12 לִמְנוֹת יָמֵינוּ כֵּן הוֹדַע
וְנָבִא לְבַב חָכְמָה׃

v. 8. שתה ק׳

---

8. *set our iniquities before Thee.* For them to be judged; God has not hidden them from His sight (Metsudath David).

secret sins. They may be concealed or hidden within us, but God brings them into light for punishment.

9. *are passed away.* Better, 'decline' (towards evening). The hours of sunlight seem shortened and the dusk early in its oncoming as the effect of His wrath.

as a tale that is told. Rather, 'as a sigh' (Targum, 'as a breath') which passes the lips so quickly and reveals a feeling of weariness.

10. *threescore years and ten.* Against the Mosaic authorship of the Psalm it is urged that Moses exceeded the age of a hundred. The answer to the objection is that Moses here makes a reference to the majority of people (Kimchi). Meiri opines that Moses herewith prophesies about future generations (cf. Tosaphoth, Tractate Yeb. 64b).

by reason of strength. i.e. more than average vitality.

travail. The same word as in *man is born unto trouble* (Job v. 7).

vanity. Rather, 'wretchedness'.

and we fly away. Cf. *he* (man) *shall fly away as a dream* (Job xx. 8).

11. *who knoweth.* How few are they who appreciate the intensity of Divine wrath which is aroused by sinfulness, so that it induces within them a sense of awe deterring them from wrong-doing!

12. *so.* With a full understanding of the consequences which follow the spending of life's opportunities in unworthy ways.

to ... days. Realizing how few they are, and then they will be so employed that 'each tomorrow finds us farther than to-day'.

a heart of wisdom. The same thought as in Moses's exhortation: *if they were wise, they would understand this, they would discern their latter end* (Deut. xxxii. 29).

13 Return, O LORD; now long?
And let it repent Thee concerning Thy servants.

14 O satisfy us in the morning with
Thy mercy;
That we may rejoice and be glad
all our days.

15 Make us glad according to the
days wherein Thou hast afflicted us,
According to the years wherein
we have seen evil.

16 Let Thy work appear unto Thy
servants,
And Thy glory upon their
children.

17 And let the graciousness of the
Lord our God be upon us;
Establish Thou also upon us the
work of our hands;
Yea, the work of our hands
establish Thou it.

13 שׁוּבָה יְהוָה עַד־מָתָי
וְהִנָּחֵם עַל־עֲבָדֶיךָ׃
14 שַׂבְּעֵנוּ בַבֹּקֶר חַסְדֶּךָ
וּנְרַנְּנָה וְנִשְׂמְחָה בְּכָל־יָמֵינוּ׃
15 שַׂמְּחֵנוּ כִּימוֹת עִנִּיתָנוּ
שְׁנוֹת רָאִינוּ רָעָה׃
16 יֵרָאֶה אֶל־עֲבָדֶיךָ פָעֳלֶךָ
וַהֲדָרְךָ עַל־בְּנֵיהֶם׃
17 וִיהִי נֹעַם אֲדֹנָי אֱלֹהֵינוּ עָלֵינוּ
וּמַעֲשֵׂה יָדֵינוּ כּוֹנְנָה עָלֵינוּ
וּמַעֲשֵׂה יָדֵינוּ כּוֹנְנֵהוּ׃

13-17 PRAYER FOR
RETURN OF GOD'S FAVOR

13. *return.* i.e. from Thine anger (as in vi. 5).

how long? Wilt Thou be angry? (Metsudath David).

let it repent Thee. God's 'change of attitude' is spoken of in Scripture in anthropomorphic terms (cf. Nachmanides and Ibn Ezra on Gen. vi. 6).

Thy servants. The people of Israel (cf. Deut. xxxii. 36).

14. *in the morning.* Meiri and Metsudath David explain this phrase as 'every morning.' Others take it to mean: after the night of trouble (cf. xxx. 6). This would refer to the dawn of the final redemption (Rashi, Kimchi). 'Morning' is also interpreted as the time of youth. Hence: if Thou satisfy us with Thy mercy in our youth, then we will rejoice and

be glad all our days (Meiri, Ibn Ezra, Malbim).

rejoice. Hebrew 'sing in ringing tones.'

15. *according to the days.* When restored to God's favour, may their happiness be proportionate to the wretchedness they had endured during the time that His anger burned against them (Malbim).

evil. Adversity.

16. *Thy work.* The working of God's Providence. May He make this evident in His dealings with His people.

glory. Or, 'majesty.' Let Israel have a demonstration of the Divine splendour as revealed in God's saving power.

17. *graciousness.* lit. 'pleasantness,' favour.

the work of our hands. Our daily tasks.

yea, the work ... it. A repetition of the phrase for emphasis.

צא

יֹשֵׁב בְּסֵתֶר עֶלְיוֹן
בְּצֵל שַׁדַּי יִתְלוֹנָן:
2 אֹמַר לַיהוָה מַחְסִי וּמְצוּדָתִי
אֱלֹהַי אֶבְטַח־בּוֹ:
3 כִּי הוּא יַצִּילְךָ מִפַּח יָקוּשׁ
מִדֶּבֶר הַוּוֹת:
4 בְּאֶבְרָתוֹ יָסֶךְ לָךְ
וְתַחַת־כְּנָפָיו תֶּחְסֶה
צִנָּה וְסֹחֵרָה אֲמִתּוֹ:

91

1 O thou that dwellest in the covert
　of the Most High,
And abidest in the shadow of the
　Almighty;

2 I will say of the LORD, who is my
　refuge and my fortress,
My God, in whom I trust,

3 That He will deliver thee from the
　snare of the fowler,
And from the noisome pestilence.

4 He will cover thee with His
　pinions,
And under His wings shalt thou
　take refuge;
His truth is a shield and a buckler.

SECURITY IN GOD

MANY commentators regard this Psalm with its confident tone as a pendant to XC to correct its gloomy reflection upon man's life. Indeed, as noted above, Moses was evidently the author of the whole series from XC to C, so that its not infrequent resemblances to Deut. xxxii. are to be expected (Rashi). Nevertheless, the Targum explains the poem as a dialogue between David and Solomon. The former begins at verse 2, Solomon responds at verse 9, and God addresses the angels at verse 10.

1-2 DIVINE PROTECTION

1. *O thou,* etc. Render: 'He that dwelleth in the covert of the Most High abideth in the shadow of the Almighty.'

covert. lit. 'secret hiding-place' (cf. xxvii. 5).

shadow. The image is of a mother-bird sheltering her young beneath her wings (cf. verse 4, and *hide me in the shadow of Thy wings,* xvii. 8).

Almighty. This appellation, like Most High, indicates God's power to provide the refuge.

2. *who is my refuge.* Better, 'He is my refuge,' and substitute a full stop for the comma at the end of the verse.

3-4 GOD THE DELIVERER

3. *that He.* Better, 'indeed He'; the pronoun is emphatic in the Hebrew.

the snare of the fowler. Traps laid by adversaries (again cxxiv. 7).

and from the noisome pestilence. Render perhaps, 'from a violent death,' lit. 'from death of destruction.' For this sense of *deber,* see lxxviii. 50.

4. *He will cover thee.* For the elaboration of the figure, see Deut. xxxii. 11.

His truth. Fidelity to His promised word.

shield. See on v. 13.

buckler. lit. 'that which goes round' as a protection.

5 Thou shalt not be afraid of the
    terror by night,
  Nor of the arrow that flieth by day;

6 Of the pestilence that walketh in
    darkness,
  Nor of the destruction that wast-
    eth at noonday.

7 A thousand may fall at thy side,
  And ten thousand at thy right
    hand;
  It shall not come nigh thee.

8 Only with thine eyes shalt thou
    behold,
  And see the recompense of the
    wicked.

9 For thou hast made the LORD who
    is my refuge,
  Even the Most High, thy habita-
    tion.

10 There shall no evil befall thee,
   Neither shall any plague come
     nigh thy tent.

5 לֹא־תִירָא מִפַּחַד לָיְלָה
מֵחֵץ יָעוּף יוֹמָם:
6 מִדֶּבֶר בָּאֹפֶל יַהֲלֹךְ
מִקֶּטֶב יָשׁוּד צָהֳרָיִם:
7 יִפֹּל מִצִּדְּךָ ׀ אֶלֶף
וּרְבָבָה מִימִינֶךָ
אֵלֶיךָ לֹא יִגָּשׁ:
8 רַק בְּעֵינֶיךָ תַבִּיט
וְשִׁלֻּמַת רְשָׁעִים תִּרְאֶה:
9 כִּי־אַתָּה יְהֹוָה מַחְסִי
עֶלְיוֹן שַׂמְתָּ מְעוֹנֶךָ:
10 לֹא־תְאֻנֶּה אֵלֶיךָ רָעָה
וְנֶגַע לֹא־יִקְרַב בְּאָהֳלֶךָ:

5-8 IMMUNITY FROM ATTACK

5. *terror by night.* A sudden onslaught in
the dark (cf. Cant. iii. 8).

arrow ... day. An assault by foes in the daytime. The language may be metaphorical and
allude to secret and open antagonism.

6. *pestilence.* The verse personifies nature's
dangers to life.

in darkness. A plague was more virulent in
the absence of the sun which had healing
effects (Mal. iii. 20).

destruction. The word is found in Deut. xxxii.
24, where the parallel has *fiery bolts*. It would
therefore seem to be a menace to life which is
connected with the sun's heat (cf. Ibn Ezra).

7. *thousand ... ten thousand.* Cf. Deut. xxxii.
30, Jud. xx. 10, and 1 Sam. xviii. 7. Kimchi
interprets this as protection in the time of
war.

8. As happened at the Red Sea (Exod. xiv.
13, 31).

9-13 THE REWARD OF TRUST

9. Render, 'for thou (the righteous servant
of God) hast said, "the LORD is my refuge";
even the Most High hast thou (the righteous
servant of God) made thy habitation' (Kimchi,
Ibn Ezra).

10. *evil.* Adversity, as in xc. 15.

plague. lit. 'stroke,' affliction.

11 For He will give His angels
    charge over thee,
    To keep thee in all thy ways.

12 They shall bear thee upon their
    hands,
    Lest thou dash thy foot against a
    stone.

13 Thou shalt tread upon the lion
    and asp;
    The young lion and the serpent
    shalt thou trample under feet.

14 'Because he hath set his love upon
    Me, therefore will I deliver
    him;
    I will set him on high, because
    he hath known My name.

15 He shall call upon Me, and I will
    answer him;
    I will be with him in trouble;
    I will rescue him, and bring him
    to honour.

16 With long life will I satisfy him,
    And make him to behold My
    salvation.'

כִּי מַלְאָכָיו יְצַוֶּה־לָּךְ 11
לִשְׁמָרְךָ בְּכָל־דְּרָכֶיךָ:
עַל־כַּפַּיִם יִשָּׂאוּנְךָ 12
פֶּן־תִּגֹּף בָּאֶבֶן רַגְלֶךָ:
עַל־שַׁחַל וָפֶתֶן תִּדְרֹךְ 13
תִּרְמֹס כְּפִיר וְתַנִּין:
כִּי בִי חָשַׁק וַאֲפַלְּטֵהוּ 14
אֲשַׂגְּבֵהוּ כִּי־יָדַע שְׁמִי:
יִקְרָאֵנִי וְאֶעֱנֵהוּ 15
עִמּוֹ־אָנֹכִי בְצָרָה
אֲחַלְּצֵהוּ וַאֲכַבְּדֵהוּ:
אֹרֶךְ יָמִים אַשְׂבִּיעֵהוּ 16
וְאַרְאֵהוּ בִּישׁוּעָתִי:

11. *He will give His angels charge.* Cf. Gen. xxiv. 7, 40; Exod. xxiii. 20. On the basis of this verse, the Talmud taught that two ministering angels accompany a man through life to testify about his conduct before the heavenly tribunal after death (Tal. Hag. 16a).

in all thy ways. i.e. in the varied activities of life.

12. *dash ... stone.* Come to harm; cf. Prov. iii. 23, where the parallel is *walk in thy way securely.*

13. The animals and reptiles are symbols of deadly dangers, the lion represents an open attack and the serpents underhand scheming.

14-16 DIVINE ASSURANCE

Now God speaks to the angels (Ibn Ezra).

14. *hath set his love upon Me.* lit. 'hath clung affectionately to Me.' Used of God's attitude to Israel in Deut. vii. 7, x. 15. God's love at once responds to man's love of Him.

set him on high. Above the reach of his foes, as in xx. 2.

known My name. See on ix. 11.

15. Cf. l. 15.

16. *long life.* lit. 'length of days,' the reward promised for faithfulness to God's will (Exod. xx. 12; Deut. xxx. 20).

will I satisfy him. i.e. I will grant him a satisfying long life.

My salvation. God's Providence working in human affairs. Cf. l. 23; for illustration see Job xlii. 12-17.

92

מִזְמוֹר שִׁיר לְיוֹם הַשַּׁבָּת:

2 טוֹב לְהֹדוֹת לַיהוָה
וּלְזַמֵּר לְשִׁמְךָ עֶלְיוֹן:

3 לְהַגִּיד בַּבֹּקֶר חַסְדֶּךָ
וֶאֱמוּנָתְךָ בַּלֵּילוֹת:

4 עֲלֵי־עָשׂוֹר וַעֲלֵי־נָבֶל
עֲלֵי הִגָּיוֹן בְּכִנּוֹר:

1 A Psalm, a Song. For the sabbath
day.

2 It is a good thing to give thanks
unto the LORD,
And to sing praises unto Thy
name, O Most High;

3 To declare Thy lovingkindness in
the morning,
And Thy faithfulness in the night
seasons,

4 With an instrument of ten strings,
.and with the psaltery;
With a solemn sound upon the
harp.

THE SABBATH HYMN

THE title occurs in the Targum in the form: 'A Psalm and song which Adam uttered on the Sabbath day,' in accordance with the tradition that it was composed by him on the first Sabbath of creation. Its association with the holy day was recognized in the Temple where it was chanted by the Levites each Sabbath; but why was it selected for that occasion? Rashi comments that it speaks of 'the world to come which is an unending Sabbath.' We may suggest another relationship of the Psalm to the Sabbath. The Levites lived in a world wherein *workers of iniquity do flourish*, bringing hardship and anxiety upon the righteous. How, in such circumstances, could they sing praises to God for His goodness? Their minds were beset by the perplexing problem on reconciling the facts of life with Divine Providence. On the hallowed day, man's spiritual nature is heightened and fortified, and his vision rendered clearer. He then views the situation with a more optimistic outlook. The contrast between the transitory character of the material and the permanence of the spiritual is borne in upon him. His eyes are turned away from the physical world, with its cares and trials, to the world which is ever radiant with the glory of God. Exalted by so glorious a vision, he is able to sing His praises even before the wicked are overthrown (cf. Malbim and Hirsch on verses 3-5).

2-4 THANKSGIVING DUE TO GOD

2. *a good thing*. Right and proper.

Thy name, O Most High. Thy character as supreme Ruler of the universe.

3. *morning ... night seasons*. Suitable times of the day in which to direct thoughts to God, before the round of duty begins and after it has ended. Rashi interprets 'morning' as an allusion to the period of redemption, and 'night' as the period of exile, adding the perceptive comment that even during the torment of exile it is right and proper to believe that God will keep His promise (of redemption).

4. *psaltery*. See on xxxiii. 2.

a solemn sound. Hebrew *higgaion* (see on ix. 17).

5 For Thou, Lord, hast made me
glad through Thy work;
I will exult in the works of Thy
hands.

6 How great are Thy works, O Lord!
Thy thoughts are very deep.

7 A brutish man knoweth not,
Neither doth a fool understand
this.

8 When the wicked spring up as the
grass,
And when all the workers of iniquity do flourish;
It is that they may be destroyed
for ever.

9 But Thou, O Lord, art on high
for evermore.

10 For, lo, Thine enemies, O Lord,
For, lo, Thine enemies shall
perish;
All the workers of iniquity shall
be scattered.

כִּי שִׂמַּחְתַּנִי יְהוָה בְּפָעֳלֶךָ 5
בְּמַעֲשֵׂי יָדֶיךָ אֲרַנֵּן׃
מַה־גָּדְלוּ מַעֲשֶׂיךָ יְהוָה 6
מְאֹד עָמְקוּ מַחְשְׁבֹתֶיךָ׃
אִישׁ־בַּעַר לֹא יֵדָע 7
וּכְסִיל לֹא־יָבִין אֶת־זֹאת׃
בִּפְרֹחַ רְשָׁעִים ׀ כְּמוֹ־עֵשֶׂב 8
וַיָּצִיצוּ כָּל־פֹּעֲלֵי אָוֶן
לְהִשָּׁמְדָם עֲדֵי־עַד׃
וְאַתָּה מָרוֹם לְעֹלָם יְהוָה׃ 9
כִּי הִנֵּה אֹיְבֶיךָ ׀ יְהוָה 10
כִּי־הִנֵּה אֹיְבֶיךָ יֹאבֵדוּ
יִתְפָּרְדוּ כָּל־פֹּעֲלֵי אָוֶן׃

5-8 GOD'S WORK

5. *glad.* A response has come from God to
the prayer offered in xc. 15f.

Thy work. The working of Divine Providence,
as in xc. 16.

I will exult. Hebrew 'sing in ringing tones,' as
xc. 14.

works. A different word; 'acts' of salvation
which have been recently wrought for the
people.

6. *works.* Again 'acts' as in the previous
verse.

thoughts. Cf. My *thoughts are not your
thoughts … as the heavens are higher than
the earth … My thoughts are higher than
your thoughts* (Isa. lv. 8f.). God's designs in
the universe, in allowing the wicked to triumph for a while, are *very deep*, beyond man's
comprehension.

7. *brutish man.* Cf. lxxiii. 22. One in whom
animal instincts overrule the spiritual element.

fool. Who lacks understanding and perception.

this. viz. the truth stated in the next verse.

8. *destroyed for ever.* Their temporary ascendancy followed by their final downfall is
intended to teach a salutary lesson.

9-12 THE WICKED PERISH

9. *art on high.* Pronouncing judgment; for
that reason retribution descends upon the
evil-doers, and the righteous are vindicated.

10. *Thine enemies.* Hirsch points out that
both the *enemies* and *workers of iniquity* are
the Lord's enemies, since they are foes of
God's kingdom on earth.

shall be scattered. The Hebrew may signify
'shall scatter themselves,' cease to be a compact powerful body and break up.

11 But my horn hast Thou exalted
   like the horn of the wild-ox;
   I am anointed with rich oil.

12 Mine eye also hath gazed on them
   that lie in wait for me,
   Mine ears have heard my desire
   of the evil-doers that rise up
   against me.

13 The righteous shall flourish like
   the palm-tree;
   He shall grow like a cedar in
   Lebanon.

14 Planted in the house of the LORD,
   They shall flourish in the courts
   of our God.

15 They shall still bring forth fruit
   in old age;
   They shall be full of sap and
   richness;

16 To declare that the LORD is upright,
   My Rock, in whom there is no
   unrighteousness.

11 וַתָּרֶם כִּרְאֵים קַרְנִי
בַּלֹּתִי בְּשֶׁמֶן רַעֲנָן:
12 וַתַּבֵּט עֵינִי בְּשׁוּרָי
בַּקָּמִים עָלַי מְרֵעִים
תִּשְׁמַעְנָה אָזְנָי:
13 צַדִּיק כַּתָּמָר יִפְרָח
כְּאֶרֶז בַּלְּבָנוֹן יִשְׂגֶּה:
14 שְׁתוּלִים בְּבֵית יְהוָה
בְּחַצְרוֹת אֱלֹהֵינוּ יַפְרִיחוּ:
15 עוֹד יְנוּבוּן בְּשֵׂיבָה
דְּשֵׁנִים וְרַעֲנַנִּים יִהְיוּ:
16 לְהַגִּיד כִּי־יָשָׁר יְהוָה
צוּרִי וְלֹא־עֲלָתָה בּוֹ:

עולתה ק׳ v. 16.

---

11. *horn.* See on lxxv. 6.

wild-ox. See on xxii. 22.

anointed with rich oil. A figure of speech for gladness (cf. xxiii. 5, xlv. 8) (cf. Kimchi).

12. *mine eye ... gazed.* With satisfaction at their defeat (cf. liv. 9).

have heard my desire. Hebrew 'have heard' the cries of dismay from the overthrown foes. Kimchi explains it as 'I have seen and have heard that which I had desired'.

13-16 THE RIGHTEOUS TRIUMPH

13. · *the palm-tree.* Admired for its stature and erectness (Cant. vii. 8).

cedar in Lebanon. See on xxix. 5.

14. *planted in the house of the LORD.* Like the trees which flourish when their roots are imbedded in rich soil, the righteous derive their sustenance from the Temple and there-fore grow luxuriantly.

15. *in old age.* Like the palm which is known sometimes to live for 200 years and still produce fruit, Israel, although an ancient people, will retain its vigour because its youth is constantly renewed. Kimchi notes this as a reference to the vigorous rejuvenation of Israel at the time of the Messiah. Rashi and others explain the verse as applying to the righteous individuals who remain intellectu-ally fruitful and full of richness in old age, as opposed to the *brutish man* and *fool* (verse 7) who becomes unsettled and unclear.

full of sap and richness. Like the olive (Judges ix. 9). The righteous are likened to *a leafy olive-tree* (lii. 10).

16. The verse is based on Deut. xxxii. 4.

to declare. By their prosperous condition they will be witnesses to God's just rule in the world (cf. Kimchi, Hirsch).

93

1 The LORD reigneth; He is clothed
   in majesty;
   The LORD is clothed, He hath
   girded Himself with strength;
   Yea, the world is established, that
   it cannot be moved.

2 Thy throne is established of old;
   Thou art from everlasting.

3 The floods have lifted up, O LORD,
   The floods have lifted up their
   voice;
   The floods lift up their roaring.

4 Above the voices of many waters,
   The mighty breakers of the sea,
   The LORD on high is mighty.

5 Thy testimonies are very sure,
   Holiness becometh Thy house,
   O LORD, for evermore.

צג

יְהֹוָה מָלָךְ גֵּאוּת לָבֵשׁ
לָבֵשׁ יְהֹוָה עֹז הִתְאַזָּר
אַף־תִּכּוֹן תֵּבֵל בַּל־תִּמּוֹט:
2 נָכוֹן כִּסְאֲךָ מֵאָז מֵעוֹלָם אָתָּה:
3 נָשְׂאוּ נְהָרוֹת יְהֹוָה
נָשְׂאוּ נְהָרוֹת קוֹלָם
יִשְׂאוּ נְהָרוֹת דָּכְיָם:
4 מִקֹּלוֹת מַיִם רַבִּים
אַדִּירִים מִשְׁבְּרֵי־יָם
אַדִּיר בַּמָּרוֹם יְהֹוָה:
5 עֵדֹתֶיךָ נֶאֶמְנוּ מְאֹד
לְבֵיתְךָ נַאֲוָה־קֹּדֶשׁ
יְהֹוָה לְאֹרֶךְ יָמִים:

GOD THE KING

THIS Psalm inaugurates a group ending with C (but omitting XCIV) which has as its theme
the enthronement of God as King of the universe. The classic commentators gave these Psalms
a Messianic interpretation as relating to a reformed world in the future. Hirsch adds that this
Psalm is a direct continuation of Psalm XCII for it sings of an era when all mankind will
recognize and declare that the LORD is upright, in Whom there is no unrighteousness. Meiri
sees this Psalm as reference to Creation and, especially, to the day when the earth was revealed
as a result of the gathering of the waters. The LXX has the title, 'For the day before the
Sabbath,' conforming to the statement in the Talmud (R.H. 31a) that the Psalm was chanted
in the Temple by the Levites each Friday.

1. *reigneth*. Better, 'hath become King.' In
Messiah's days, it will be declared that His
apparently interrupted reign has resumed
(Metsudath David).

is clothed. Rather, 'hath robed Himself.'

girded Himself with strength. To uphold the
cause of righteousness.

the ... established. When His kingdom will
be recognized, the world will rejoice (Rashi).

2. *of old*. His kingship goes back to the
beginning of time.

3. *floods*. lit. 'rivers.' As a tidal wave inun-
dates the surrounding country, heathen

powers attempt to overrun Israel (cf. Rashi).

4. *voices*. Better, 'thunderings.'

is mighty. The Hebrew includes the idea of
glory as well as power.

5. *testimonies*. See on xix. 8. God's Kingdom is governed by moral laws which are
very sure, firmly established and unchange-
able like Himself. God's might is always
associated with the idea of holiness.

very sure. Hirsch renders 'infinitely faithful.'

Thy house. May refer to the Temple or Zion
as a whole. Under God's rule it will no more
be desecrated.

צד

אֵל־נְקָמוֹת יְהוָֹה
אֵל נְקָמוֹת הוֹפִיעַ:

2 הִנָּשֵׂא שֹׁפֵט הָאָרֶץ
הָשֵׁב גְּמוּל עַל־גֵּאִים:

3 עַד־מָתַי רְשָׁעִים ׀ יְהוָֹה
עַד־מָתַי רְשָׁעִים יַעֲלֹזוּ:

4 יַבִּיעוּ יְדַבְּרוּ עָתָק
יִתְאַמְּרוּ כָּל־פֹּעֲלֵי אָוֶן:

1 O LORD, Thou God to whom
vengeance belongeth,
Thou God to whom vengeance
belongeth, shine forth.

2 Lift up Thyself, Thou Judge of
the earth;
Render to the proud their recompense.

3 LORD, how long shall the wicked,
How long shall the wicked exult?

4 They gush out, they speak arrogancy;
All the workers of iniquity bear
themselves loftily.

PLEA FOR DIVINE JUDGMENT

THE tone, style, and matter of this Psalm contrast sharply with the preceding and succeeding Psalms. Far from God's Sovereignty being acknowledged and in force over the earth, a state of moral chaos prevails in which justice is denied to those who need its protection most. Perhaps in this very idea is its place within the group to be explained. XCIII described the future: this Psalm dwells upon the present which discloses so different a state of things; the following Psalms resume the joyful note because of unshakable assurance in the ultimate realization of the ideal. Who are the oppressors and the oppressed? According to one interpretation foreign nations are acting ruthlessly against Israel; others hold that lawless Israelites deal unjustly with their brethren. The latter is the view here adopted.

1-2 THE SUPREME JUDGE INVOKED

1. *Thou … whom vengeance belongeth.* lit. 'God of vengeances,' the plural of intensity, i.e. God of great vengeance, or God Who avenges thoroughly. We must not associate any idea of vindictiveness with the word *vengeance;* it rather comes close to the word 'retribution' (cf. *vengeance is Mine, and rec-ompense* (lit. payment) … *the LORD will judge His people,* Deut. xxxii. 35f.). 'The moment we recognize righteousness to be an essential quality of the Divine Nature, it is impossible to overlook the penal activity of the Divine government. A righteous God cannot con-done sin, crime and inhumanity. When the righteous were oppressed, and the wicked triumphant, the Psalmists deemed it not only allowable, but their sacred duty, to pray for the destruction of insolent rulers who poi-soned the foundations of justice and crushed the poor, the widow and the orphan' (Hertz).

shine forth. See on l. 2.

2. *lift up Thyself.* Assert Thy supremacy as the Judge of man (cf. vii. 7).

Judge of the earth. Cf. Gen xviii. 25.

render … recompense. As in xxviii. 4.

proud. Men who vaunt themselves in their high station and use it ruthlessly.

3-7 THE OPPRESSORS DESCRIBED

3. *how long.* The question does not imply that God cannot put an end to their deeds of violence, but wonders why He defers the exercise of His power.

4. *gush out.* Same verb translated *belch out* (lix. 8); they pour forth a stream of arrogant words.

speak arrogancy. Again in xxxi. 19, where the verb is amplified by *with pride and con-tempt.*

5 They crush Thy people, O Lord,
  And afflict Thy heritage.

6 They slay the widow and the
    stranger,
  And murder the fatherless.

7 And they say: 'The Lord will not
    see,
  Neither will the God of Jacob give
    heed.'

8 Consider, ye brutish among the
    people;
  And ye fools, when will ye under-
    stand?

9 He that planted the ear, shall He
    not hear?
  He that formed the eye, shall He
    not see?

10 He that instructeth nations, shall
    not He correct,
   Even He that teacheth man
    knowledge?

11 The Lord knoweth the thoughts
    of man,
   That they are vanity.

עַמְּךָ יְהוָה יְדַכְּאוּ 5
וְנַחֲלָתְךָ יְעַנּוּ:
אַלְמָנָה וְגֵר יַהֲרֹגוּ 6
וִיתוֹמִים יְרַצֵּחוּ:
וַיֹּאמְרוּ לֹא יִרְאֶה־יָּהּ 7
וְלֹא־יָבִין אֱלֹהֵי יַעֲקֹב:
בִּינוּ בֹּעֲרִים בָּעָם 8
וּכְסִילִים מָתַי תַּשְׂכִּילוּ:
הֲנֹטַע אֹזֶן הֲלֹא יִשְׁמָע 9
אִם־יֹצֵר עַיִן הֲלֹא יַבִּיט:
הֲיֹסֵר גּוֹיִם הֲלֹא יוֹכִיחַ 10
הַמְלַמֵּד אָדָם דָּעַת:
יְהוָה יֹדֵעַ מַחְשְׁבוֹת אָדָם 11
כִּי־הֵמָּה הָבֶל:

5. *Thy people.* The minority, by their oppressive government, keep the whole of Israel in subjection.

Thy heritage. A synonym of Israel.

6. Widows and orphans are always mentioned as those who particularly suffer when
the ruling class is corrupt. Here the *stranger*
is included among the victims, in violation of
the commandment which ordains fair treatment for him (Exod. xxii. 20).

7. *the Lord.* Hebrew *Jah.* In their pride these
evil men presume to believe that God, who
rescued the Israelites from the tyrant Pharaoh, will overlook their tyrannous acts.

will not see. Cf. x. 11.

8-11 THE OPPRESSORS' BELIEF REFUTED

8. *brutish…fools.* Cf. xcii. 7. Only persons
who lack perception and understanding, and
are enslaved by their animal instincts, would
question whether God is aware of what is
done on earth.

9. Maimonides, in *Guide for the Perplexed*
(vol. 3, Ch. xix) states: 'In the case of everyone who makes any instrument, it is clear that
unless he had a conception of the work to be
done with that instrument, he would be unable to make it. For instance, unless a smith
had a conception and an understanding of
sewing, he would not make a needle in the
form which alone permits performing the
acts of sewing… If the meaning of apprehension of the sense of sight is hidden from Him
and He does not know it, how did He bring
into existence this instrument, which is disposed for visual apprehension?' Rashi renders this verse: 'Is it conceivable that God
Who planted the ear shall not Himself listen
to the anguished cries of His nation?'

10. *instructeth nations.* If God Who has
endowed heathens with a moral sense holds
them to account, will He omit to do so with
any members of the community of Israel to
whom He committed the Torah!

even He that teacheth. The meaning is: shall

12 Happy is the man whom Thou
    instructest, O LORD,
    And teachest out of Thy law;

13 That Thou mayest give him rest
    from the days of evil,
    Until the pit be digged for the
    wicked.

14 For the LORD will not cast off
    His people,
    Neither will He forsake His
    inheritance.

15 For right shall return unto
    justice,
    And all the upright in heart shall
    follow it.

16 Who will rise up for me against
    the evil-doers?
    Who will stand up for me against
    the workers of iniquity?

17 Unless the LORD had been my
    help,
    My soul had soon dwelt in
    silence.

18 If I say: 'My foot slippeth,'
    Thy mercy, O LORD, holdeth me
    up.

12 אַשְׁרֵי הַגֶּבֶר אֲשֶׁר־תְּיַסְּרֶנּוּ יָּהּ
וּמִתּוֹרָתְךָ תְלַמְּדֶנּוּ:

13 לְהַשְׁקִיט לוֹ מִימֵי רָע
עַד יִכָּרֶה לָרָשָׁע שָׁחַת:

14 כִּי לֹא־יִטֹּשׁ יְהוָה עַמּוֹ
וְנַחֲלָתוֹ לֹא יַעֲזֹב:

15 כִּי־עַד־צֶדֶק יָשׁוּב מִשְׁפָּט
וְאַחֲרָיו כָּל־יִשְׁרֵי־לֵב:

16 מִי־יָקוּם לִי עִם־מְרֵעִים
מִי־יִתְיַצֵּב לִי עִם־פֹּעֲלֵי אָוֶן:

17 לוּלֵי יְהוָה עֶזְרָתָה לִּי
כִּמְעַט שָׁכְנָה דוּמָה נַפְשִׁי:

18 אִם־אָמַרְתִּי מָטָה רַגְלִי
חַסְדְּךָ יְהוָה יִסְעָדֵנִי:

He that teacheth man knowledge Himself
lack knowledge!

11. *the thoughts*. This is the climax of the
refutation: God knows more than man's acts;
He can read their unspoken thoughts.

that. Better, 'for.' *They* is masc. and may not
refer to *thoughts* (a fem. word) but to *man*.
Against the eternal God, the human being is
momentary and unsubstantial (xxxix. 6).

12-15   JUSTICE FOR THE RIGHTEOUS

12. *happy is the man*. With this verse cf.
cxix. 71, *It is good for me that I have been
afflicted, in order that I might learn Thy
statutes*. The sufferings the human being is
called upon to endure may be accepted as
God's method of disciplining and instructing
him in an understanding of Divine Providence. If he accepts the experience in that
spirit, happy is he! (cf. Tal. Ber. 5a).

Thy law. Used in a general sense of God's
self-revelation of His Will to man.

13. *give him rest*. This does not mean, make
him physically secure, but mentally reassured. A good parallel for the use of the verb
is: *Be quiet, fear not, neither let thy heart be
faint* (Isa. vii. 4). The man who has accepted
God's instruction will not lose heart or faith
in the days of trial, because he is convinced
that a day of reckoning will come.

pit be digged. Cf. vii. 16, lvii 7.

14. It is unthinkable that God would abandon Israel to a lawless ruling class.

15. *justice*. Hebrew *mishpat*, i.e. the administration of law; it will again be governed
by equity.

16-19   SECURITY IN GOD

16. *rise up for me*. As my champion. The

19 When my cares are many within
   me,
   Thy comforts delight my soul.

20 Shall the seat of wickedness have
   fellowship with Thee,
   Which frameth mischief by
   statute?

21 They gather themselves together
   against the soul of the righteous,
   And condemn innocent blood.

22 But the LORD hath been my high
   tower,
   And my God the rock of my
   refuge.

23 And He hath brought upon them
   their own iniquity,
   And will cut them off in their
   own evil;
   The LORD our God will cut them
   off.

19 בְּרֹב שַׂרְעַפַּי בְּקִרְבִּי
תַּנְחוּמֶיךָ יְשַׁעַשְׁעוּ נַפְשִׁי׃
20 הַיְחָבְרְךָ כִּסֵּא הַוּוֹת
יֹצֵר עָמָל עֲלֵי־חֹק׃
21 יָגוֹדּוּ עַל־נֶפֶשׁ צַדִּיק
וְדָם נָקִי יַרְשִׁיעוּ׃
22 וַיְהִי־יְהוָה לִי לְמִשְׂגָּב
וֵאלֹהַי לְצוּר מַחְסִי׃
23 וַיָּשֶׁב עֲלֵיהֶם ׀ אֶת־אוֹנָם
וּבְרָעָתָם יַצְמִיתֵם
יַצְמִיתֵם יְהוָה אֱלֹהֵינוּ׃

implied answer is: God alone (cf. Kimchi).

17. *silence.* Of the grave (cxv. 17).

18. *if I say.* To myself, I think (Ibn Ezra).

my foot slippeth. See on xxxviii. 17.

19. *cares.* lit. 'dividing (distracting) thoughts.'

delight my soul. By creating in the heart a sense of calm.

20-23 UNJUST RULERS DOOMED

20. *seat of wickedness.* lit. 'throne of destructions,' the judiciary which schemes the exploitation of the weak instead of upholding their rights.

have fellowship with Thee. Can the seat of falsehood be associated with Thee? (Targum)

frameth mischief by statute. Under the cloak of legal enactments they work their mischievous plans. They act unjustly, although legally, because their laws are unjust (Malbim).

21. *gather themselves.* Conspire together. Rashi renders: 'they attack (make inroads upon) the life of the righteous.'

22. *hath been.* The tense may be what grammarians call the perfect of certainty: 'will surely be.'

high tower ... rock of my refuge. Cf. xviii. 3.

23. *He ... brought ... them.* Also the perfect of certainty: 'He will bring upon them (cf. Kimchi).

in their own evil. By means of evil which they thought to do to the innocent they will themselves perish (cf. *let them fall by their own counsels,* v. 11, *his mischief shall return upon his own head,* vii. 17).

The LORD ... will cut them off. 'Whatever machinations they will attempt in order to attain their goals will come to a standstill by virtue of the fact that the LORD is our God' (Hirsch).

95   צה

1 O come, let us sing unto the Lord;
  Let us shout for joy to the Rock of
    our salvation.

2 Let us come before His presence
    with thanksgiving,
  Let us shout for joy unto Him
    with psalms.

3 For the Lord is a great God,
  And a great King above all gods;

לְכוּ נְרַנְּנָה לַיהוָה
נָרִיעָה לְצוּר יִשְׁעֵנוּ׃
2 נְקַדְּמָה פָנָיו בְּתוֹדָה
בִּזְמִרוֹת נָרִיעַ לוֹ׃
3 כִּי אֵל גָּדוֹל יְהוָה
וּמֶלֶךְ גָּדוֹל עַל־כָּל־אֱלֹהִים׃

CALL TO ISRAEL TO WORSHIP

This Psalm calls on the experiences of the people of Israel in the wilderness after their exodus from Egypt, to prepare all generations for the sojourn through future exiles. They are called to observe God as the supreme being, and are summoned to observe Him as Israel's God. The Psalm concludes with an exhortation that disobedience of God can cause Israel to forfeit its future. Kimchi and Sforno say that this Psalm will be sung at the advent of the Messiah during the ingathering of the exiles. At the end of the sixteenth and beginning of the seventeenth century, Psalms xcv-xcix and xxix were included by the Kabbalists of Safed in the liturgy for the inauguration of the Sabbath. Midrash Shocher Tov connects the Psalm with Sabbath in another way. Verse 7 reads: 'For He is our God … today if you would but hearken to His voice,' and the Midrash comments: 'If Israel would observe even one single Sabbath properly, deliverance would ensue forthwith.'

1-2 INVOCATION TO PRAISE GOD

1. *O come.* lit. 'go.' The word is used as a term of urging and encouraging one to 'come along' (cf. Isa. i. 18). Meiri sees the Psalmist encouraging the populace to leave their erroneous beliefs and serve God with song, happiness and a glad heart.

sing. With voices joyfully ringing.

shout … Rock of our salvation. (cf. lxxxix. 27). Joyful shouting occurs when the king comes amongst his people (cf. 1 Sam. iv. 5, x. 24) (Malbim).

2. *with thanksgiving.* Our song will be with words of thanksgiving (Ibn Ezra; cf. Jonah ii. 10).

3-5 BECAUSE HE IS SUPREME

3. *great King.* The implication is that He is almighty and has the ability to change nature according to His will (Meiri).

above all gods. The words cannot bear the interpretation that the Psalmist believed in the reality of other deities, because it would be inconsistent with xcvi. 5, *all the gods of the peoples are things of nought.* The reference, therefore, must be to the angels (cf. Ibn Ezra).

4 In whose hand are the depths of
   the earth;
   The heights of the mountains are
   His also.

5 The sea is His, and He made it;
   And His hands formed the dry
   land.

6 O come, let us bow down and bend
   the knee;
   Let us kneel before the LORD our
   Maker;

7 For He is our God,
   And we are the people of His
   pasture, and the flock of His
   hand.
   To-day, if ye would but hearken
   to His voice!

8 'Harden not your heart, as at
   Meribah,
   As in the day of Massah in the
   wilderness;

אֲשֶׁר בְּיָדוֹ מֶחְקְרֵי־אָרֶץ 4
וְתוֹעֲפוֹת הָרִים לוֹ:
אֲשֶׁר־לוֹ הַיָּם וְהוּא עָשָׂהוּ 5
וְיַבֶּשֶׁת יָדָיו יָצָרוּ:
בֹּאוּ נִשְׁתַּחֲוֶה וְנִכְרָעָה 6
נִבְרְכָה לִפְנֵי־יְהוָה עֹשֵׂנוּ:
כִּי הוּא אֱלֹהֵינוּ 7
וַאֲנַחְנוּ עַם מַרְעִיתוֹ וְצֹאן יָדוֹ
הַיּוֹם אִם־בְּקֹלוֹ תִשְׁמָעוּ:
אַל־תַּקְשׁוּ לְבַבְכֶם כִּמְרִיבָה 8
כְּיוֹם מַסָּה בַּמִּדְבָּר:

---

4. *in whose hand.* Under divine control is
the whole universe, from its foundations in
the unexplorable depths to the summits of
unscalable mountains.

5. The verse may also be rendered: 'To
Whom belong the sea—it was He that made
it—and the dry land (which) His hands
formed.'

6-7 BECAUSE HE IS ISRAEL'S GOD

6. Not only in recognition of God as the
Creator of the universe are the Israelites
summoned to worship Him; there is an additional reason, viz. His declaring them his
own nation (Malbim).

bow down. Better, 'Prostrate ourselves' upon
the ground in homage (Kimchi, Metsudath
David).

bend the knee. Better, 'bow.' A posture of
fealty to Israel's King (Kimchi, Metsudath
David).

kneel. To go on one's knees.

our Maker. The Maker of the Israelite nation
(cf. Deut. xxxii. 6, 15).

7. *the people of His pasture.* Cf. lxxiv. 1,
lxxix. 13.

the flock of His hand. Under His charge and
tended by Him.

to-day … voice. Ibn Ezra asserts that 'to-day'
modifies 'come let us bow down … ' (verse
6): If you have it within your hearts to hearken
unto His voice, then cast yourselves down
before Him, to-day! Kimchi renders 'that
day' and sees these words as an introduction
to the admonition that follows in verses 8-11:
'Hearken unto His voice and we (became)
the flock of His hand that day (He released us
from bondage); and He will continue to be
your God if you do not try Him as did your
fathers.' Malbim approaches this last section
of our verse as the key to understanding the

9 When your fathers tried Me,
  Proved Me, even though they saw
    My work.
10 For forty years was I wearied
    with that generation,
  And said: It is a people that do
    err in their heart,
  And they have not known My
    ways;
11 Wherefore I swore in My wrath,
  That they should not enter into
    My rest.'

9 אֲשֶׁר נִסּוּנִי אֲבוֹתֵיכֶם
בְּחָנוּנִי גַּם־רָאוּ פָעֳלִי:
10 אַרְבָּעִים שָׁנָה ׀ אָקוּט בְּדוֹר
וָאֹמַר עַם תֹּעֵי לֵבָב הֵם
וְהֵם לֹא־יָדְעוּ דְרָכָי:
11 אֲשֶׁר־נִשְׁבַּעְתִּי בְאַפִּי
אִם־יְבֹאוּן אֶל־מְנוּחָתִי:

difference between the recognition of God because He is supreme as described in verses 1-5, and the recognition of God because He is the God of Israel. His connection with Israel as their God is something that depends on their free choice. This acceptance of Him as their God is renewed every day if they hearken unto His voice.

8-11 WARNING AGAINST DISOBEDIENCE

8. God is now the speaker.

Meribah ... Massah. When Israel murmured at the lack of water (Exod. xvii. 1ff.; Num. xx. 1ff.).

9. *tried Me.* In their lack of faith, to see whether I would provide water for them.

proved Me. Tested Me, doubting my ability to supply their want.

they saw My work. In Egypt and at the Red Sea where God's infinite might had been abundantly displayed. *Work* means Divine Providence, as in xc. 16, xcii. 5. In spite of these wonderful demonstrations of His might and care, so recently witnessed by them, they

had not yet learned to put their trust in Him.

10. *was I wearied.* The Hebrew is much stronger: 'was I disgusted' (cf. Targum, Ibn Ezra).

with that generation. lit. 'with a generation,' i.e. a generation of Israelites of the type described in the continuation of the verse. A *generation* represents a period of forty years; and so the phrase really means that throughout the interval between the departure from Egypt and the arrival at the boundary of Canaan, the whole people had all the time acted in this unworthy manner.

do err in their heart. lit. 'wanderers of heart,' fickle-minded.

have not known My ways. They failed to learn how God acted with them.

11. *I swore.* Cf. Num. xiv. 21ff.

My rest. The land of promise, the resting-place after their journey through the wilderness (cf. cxxxii. 14 and Deut. xii. 9, *for ye are not as yet come to the rest and to the inheritance, which the* LORD *your God giveth thee*).

96   צו

1 O sing unto the LORD a new song;
Sing unto the LORD, all the earth.

2 Sing unto the LORD, bless His name;
Proclaim His salvation from day to day.

3 Declare His glory among the nations,
His marvellous works among all the peoples.

4 For great is the LORD, and highly to be praised;
He is to be feared above all gods.

5 For all the gods of the peoples are things of nought;
But the LORD made the heavens.

שִׁירוּ לַיהוָה שִׁיר חָדָשׁ
שִׁירוּ לַיהוָה כָּל־הָאָרֶץ:
2 שִׁירוּ לַיהוָה בָּרְכוּ שְׁמוֹ
בַּשְּׂרוּ מִיּוֹם־לְיוֹם יְשׁוּעָתוֹ:
3 סַפְּרוּ בַגּוֹיִם כְּבוֹדוֹ
בְּכָל־הָעַמִּים נִפְלְאוֹתָיו:
4 כִּי גָדוֹל יְהוָה וּמְהֻלָּל מְאֹד
נוֹרָא הוּא עַל־כָּל־אֱלֹהִים:
5 כִּי כָּל־אֱלֹהֵי הָעַמִּים אֱלִילִים
וַיהוָה שָׁמַיִם עָשָׂה:

CALL TO ALL PEOPLES TO WORSHIP

IT is not enough if Israel acknowledges God. His Sovereignty must be accepted by all the nations of the world. With the advent of the redemption this song will be sung. All the nations will be called to behold the marvelous works of God. The prophet Isaiah (lxv. 17, lxvi. 22) speaks of 'new heavens and a new earth,' a metaphorical expression for a new world order. This will result in a 'new song' which will be sung by 'all the earth' and by all the nations of the world who will all be the beneficiaries of this 'new world'. In 1 Chron. xvi. 23-33 this Psalm is reproduced almost verbatim, and there it is said to have been composed by David when he brought the Ark of the covenant to Jerusalem.

1-3 PRAISE TO GOD

1. *sing*. See on xcvi. 1.

sing ... song. Same in Isa. xlii. 10.

all the earth. A feminine singular noun, whereas the verb *sing* is masc. plural, signifying that the inhabitants of the world are meant (cf. c. 1).

2. *His name*. His self-revelation in mighty deeds.

proclaim. lit. 'announce the good tidings of' the great deliverance daily, that it be known throughout the earth and induce all peoples to pay Him homage.

3. Cf. ix. 2.

4. *great ... praised*. From xlviii. 2.

above all gods. See on xcv. 3.

5. *things of nought*. Lacking reality; the prophet used the weapon of irony to prove this (Isa. xl. 19ff., xliv. 12ff.).

made the heavens. Upon His creative acts rests His claim to be recognized as God (cf. Job xxxviii. 4ff.).

6 Honour and majesty are before
   Him;
   Strength and beauty are in His
   sanctuary.

7 Ascribe unto the LORD, ye kindreds of the peoples,
   Ascribe unto the LORD glory and
   strength.

8 Ascribe unto the LORD the glory
   due unto His name;
   Bring an offering, and come into
   His courts.

9 O worship the LORD in the beauty
   of holiness;
   Tremble before Him, all the
   earth.

10 Say among the nations: 'The
   LORD reigneth.'

הוֹד־וְהָדָר לְפָנָיו 6
עֹז וְתִפְאֶרֶת ° בְּמִקְדָּשׁוֹ׃
הָבוּ לַיהוָה מִשְׁפְּחוֹת עַמִּים 7
הָבוּ לַיהוָה כָּבוֹד וָעֹז׃
הָבוּ לַיהוָה כְּבוֹד שְׁמוֹ 8
שְׂאוּ־מִנְחָה וּבֹאוּ לְחַצְרוֹתָיו׃
הִשְׁתַּחֲווּ לַיהוָה בְּהַדְרַת־קֹדֶשׁ 9
חִילוּ מִפָּנָיו כָּל־הָאָרֶץ׃
אִמְרוּ בַגּוֹיִם ׀ יְהֹוָה מָלָךְ 10

6. *honour and majesty.* In civ. 1, God is
said to be clothed in these attributes. Hirsch
sees these attributes as those that man can
truly attain only before God's countenance.

strength and beauty. Qualities applied to the
Ark of the covenant (lxxviii. 61). Malbim
defines 'strength' as internal, while 'beauty'
is external, displayed before others.

in His sanctuary. Hirsch declares that it is in
God's sanctuary that man's moral fortitude
and full spiritual development ('strength and
beauty') can unfold.

7-9   ALL PEOPLES INVITED
TO WORSHIP HIM

7. Cf. xxix. 1.

kindreds of the peoples. Cf. xxii. 28.

8. *His courts.* A reference to the various
courtyards of the Temple (Kimchi). Meiri
declares that the purpose of coming into His
courts is to pay homage to Him.

9. *beauty of holiness.* Cf. xxix.2. A reference to the Temple beautified with holiness
(Metsudath David). Sforno sees this as a
description of the worship: worship the LORD
because of the beauty of His holiness and not
out of fear of punishment.

tremble. In contemplation of His awesome
majesty.

10-13   ALL NATURE INVITED
TO ACCLAIM HIM

10. *reigneth.* Better, 'hath become King'
(as in xciii. 1)

The world also is established that
   it cannot be moved; ·
He will judge the peoples with
   equity.

11 Let the heavens be glad, and let
    the earth rejoice;
   Let the sea roar, and the fulness
    thereof;

12 Let the field exult, and all that is
    therein;
   Then shall all the trees of the
    wood sing for joy;

13 Before the Lord, for He is come;
   For He is come to judge the earth;
   He will judge the world with
    righteousness,
   And the peoples in His faithful-
    ness.

אַף־תִּכּוֹן תֵּבֵל בַּל־תִּמּוֹט
יָדִין עַמִּים בְּמֵישָׁרִים:
יִשְׂמְחוּ הַשָּׁמַיִם וְתָגֵל הָאָרֶץ 11
יִרְעַם הַיָּם וּמְלֹאוֹ:
יַעֲלֹז שָׂדַי וְכָל־אֲשֶׁר־בּוֹ 12
אָז יְרַנְּנוּ כָּל־עֲצֵי־יָעַר:
לִפְנֵי יְהוָה | כִּי בָא 13
כִּי בָא לִשְׁפֹּט הָאָרֶץ
יִשְׁפֹּט־תֵּבֵל בְּצֶדֶק
וְעַמִּים בֶּאֱמוּנָתוֹ:

world ... moved. Again from xciii. 1.

He will judge ... equity. From ix. 9. In combining these two quotations, the Psalmist's
aim seem to have been to suggest a parallel
between the physical universe and the social
order. Alike their stability rests upon the will
of God.

11. The establishment of God's righteous
rule will produce the great happiness expressed in these figures of speech (Kimchi).

rejoice. Hebrew 'exult.'

let the sea ... thereof. Repeated in xcviii. 7.
Roar is literally 'make a noise like thunder.'

fulness thereof. All that live in the seas (cf.
the earth is the Lord's, and the fulness

thereof, xxiv. 1).

12. *the field.* i.e. the open country as distinct from the land upon which cities are
built.

then. At the time when God's Kingdom will
be recognized throughout the world.

trees ... sing for joy. Cf. Isa. xliv. 23, lv. 12.

13. The verse is similar to xcviii. 9.

judge. Rule over. When it is God Who is the
Judge, the occasion is one for universal gladness, for His judgment is *in His faithfulness,*
i.e. just and fitting (Metsudath David).

He will judge ... righteousness. Cf. ix. 9.

faithfulness. Cf. xcii. 3. Fidelity to His
promises.

צז

97

1 The Lord reigneth; let the earth
   rejoice;
   Let the multitude of isles be glad.

יְהוָה מָלָךְ תָּגֵל הָאָרֶץ
יִשְׂמְחוּ אִיִּים רַבִּים׃

2 Clouds and darkness are round
   about Him;
   Righteousness and justice are the
   foundation of His throne.

2 עָנָן וַעֲרָפֶל סְבִיבָיו
צֶדֶק וּמִשְׁפָּט מְכוֹן כִּסְאוֹ׃

3 A fire goeth before Him,
   And burneth up His adversaries
   round about.

3 אֵשׁ לְפָנָיו תֵּלֵךְ
וּתְלַהֵט סָבִיב צָרָיו׃

4 His lightnings lighted up the world;
   The earth saw, and trembled.

4 הֵאִירוּ בְרָקָיו תֵּבֵל
רָאֲתָה וַתָּחֵל הָאָרֶץ׃

5 The mountains melted like wax at
   the presence of the Lord,
   At the presence of the Lord of the
   whole earth.

5 הָרִים כַּדּוֹנַג נָמַסּוּ מִלִּפְנֵי יְהוָה
מִלִּפְנֵי אֲדוֹן כָּל־הָאָרֶץ׃

6 The heavens declared His righteousness,
   And all the peoples saw His glory.

6 הִגִּידוּ הַשָּׁמַיִם צִדְקוֹ
וְרָאוּ כָל־הָעַמִּים כְּבוֹדוֹ׃

THE UNIVERSAL KING

This Psalm develops the theme of the concluding verse of the preceding Psalm. It tells of the
effects which result from God's assumption of the Judgeship over the world: the dismay it
creates for the wicked and the light it brings to the righteous. 'Only the downfall of all the
enemies of God's kingdom and of all the powers and forces that men mistakenly worship can
pave the way for a time when the whole world will be truly aware of the existence of God and
of His sovereign power' (Hirsch). Meiri states that this Psalm, too, discusses the advent of the
redemption to strengthen peoples' hearts so that they should not abandon hope of its coming.

1-3 GOD'S MANIFESTATION AS KING

1. *reigneth. Hath become King*, as in
xciii. 1.

let the earth rejoice. From xcvi. 11.

multitude of isles. The numerous islands and
coastlands (cf. lxxii. 10) which will all
benefit by the establishment of God's kingdom, since its happy consequences will be
universal.

2. *clouds and darkness.* The setting in which
God reveals Himself (xviii. 10ff.).

righteousness ... throne. From lxxxix. 15.

3. *a fire goeth before Him.* Cf. l. 3.

burneth up His adversaries. Cf. Mal iii. 19.

4-6 HIS REVELATION

4. From lxxvii. 19, which relates to the
exodus from Egypt.

5. Cf. Micah i. 4. *Mountains* represent the
most solid part of the universe; even they
dissolved in fear at God's appearance.
'*Mountains* refer to the great powers on earth
to which men had hitherto looked up in
admiration' (Hirsch).

6. *the heavens ... righteousness.* From l. 6.
declared. Gave testimony to.

all the peoples saw His glory. Cf. Isa.xxxv.
2, xl. 5.

7 Ashamed be all they that serve
    graven images,
  That boast themselves of things of
    nought;
  Bow down to Him, all ye gods.

8 Zion heard and was glad,
  And the daughters of Judah re-
    joiced;
  Because of Thy judgments, O
    LORD.

9 For Thou, LORD, art most high
    above all the earth;
  Thou art exalted far above all gods.

10 O ye that love the LORD, hate
    evil;
  He preserveth the souls of His
    saints;
  He delivereth them out of the
    hand of the wicked.

11 Light is sown for the righteous,
  And gladness for the upright in
    heart.

12 Be glad in the LORD, ye righteous;
  And give thanks to His holy
    name.

7 יֵבֹשׁוּ ׀ כָּל־עֹבְדֵי פֶסֶל
הַמִּתְהַלְלִים בָּאֱלִילִים
הִשְׁתַּחֲווּ־לוֹ כָּל־אֱלֹהִים׃
8 שָׁמְעָה וַתִּשְׂמַח ׀ צִיּוֹן
וַתָּגֵלְנָה בְּנוֹת יְהוּדָה
לְמַעַן מִשְׁפָּטֶיךָ יְהוָה׃
9 כִּי־אַתָּה יְהוָה עֶלְיוֹן
עַל־כָּל־הָאָרֶץ
מְאֹד נַעֲלֵיתָ עַל־כָּל־אֱלֹהִים׃
10 אֹהֲבֵי יְהוָה שִׂנְאוּ רָע
שֹׁמֵר נַפְשׁוֹת חֲסִידָיו
מִיַּד רְשָׁעִים יַצִּילֵם׃
11 אוֹר זָרֻעַ לַצַּדִּיק
וּלְיִשְׁרֵי־לֵב שִׂמְחָה׃
12 שִׂמְחוּ צַדִּיקִים בַּיהוָה
וְהוֹדוּ לְזֵכֶר קָדְשׁוֹ׃

7-9   EFFECT UPON IDOLATERS AND ISRAEL

7. *ashamed…images.* Cf. Isa. xlv. 16. They
will be filled with shame when they discover
how impotent their deities are to help them.
Such was the experience of the Babylonians
when their might was shattered and Israel
was restored to its homeland.

boast themselves. In the belief that their successes were caused, and will be maintained,
by the idols they serve.

things of nought. So Metsudath David. Cf.
xcvi. 5.

bow … gods. Better, 'all gods have been
prostrated before Him' (cf. Isa. xlvi. 1). He
has proved Himself mighty, whereas their
helplessness was exposed. Cf. 1 Sam. v. 3-4.

8.   From xlviii. 12, with the difference that
in this verse Zion *heard* reports of God's triumph wrought against Israel's enemies, but
in the other passage Zion witnesses it.

9.   *most high … earth.* From lxxxiii. 19.

exalted far above all gods. The heavenly
bodies they worshipped hitherto (Kimchi).

10-12   ISRAEL'S DUTY

10.   *hate evil.* The essential characteristic
of those who acknowledge the rule of God
(cf. *the fear of the LORD is to hate evil,* Prov.
viii. 13).

His saints. They who love God and whom He
loves in return (see on iv. 4.)

11.   *light is sown.* 'It is only in the distant
future that the true good to which he renders
homage will bloom and ripen on earth. But
the seed has been sown by the LORD of time
in the womb of time' (Hirsch). 'It may for the
present be hidden like the seed in the earth,
but it is sure to spring forth. Let the righteous
therefore go on hating evil' (Hertz).

12.   *be glad … righteous.* From xxxii. 11.

and give thanks … name. From xxx. 5.

1 A Psalm.
  O sing unto the LORD a new song;
  For He hath done marvellous things;
  His right hand, and His holy arm,
    hath wrought salvation for Him.

2 The LORD hath made known His
    salvation;
  His righteousness hath He re-
    vealed in the sight of the nations.

3 He hath remembered His mercy
    and His faithfulness toward the
    house of Israel;
  All the ends of the earth have seen
    the salvation of our God.

מִזְמֹ֗ור

שִׁ֤ירוּ לַֽיהוָ֨ה ׀ שִׁ֣יר חָדָ֔שׁ

כִּֽי־נִפְלָא֥ות עָשָׂ֑ה

הֹושִֽׁיעָה־לֹּ֥ו יְ֝מִינֹ֗ו וּזְרֹ֥ועַ קָדְשֹֽׁו׃

²הֹודִ֣יעַ יְ֭הוָה יְשׁוּעָתֹ֑ו

לְעֵינֵ֥י הַ֝גֹּויִ֗ם גִּלָּ֥ה צִדְקָתֹֽו׃

³זָ֘כַ֤ר חַסְדֹּ֨ו ׀ וֶֽאֱֽמוּנָתֹו֮ לְבֵ֪ית יִשְׂרָ֫אֵ֥ל

רָא֥וּ כָל־אַפְסֵי־אָ֑רֶץ

אֵ֝֗ת יְשׁוּעַ֥ת אֱלֹהֵֽינוּ׃

CALL TO NATURE TO WORSHIP

ALL nature is summoned to join in the acclamation of the Supreme King for His redemption of Israel from captivity. This Psalm is largely made up of quotations, and yet retains a refreshing spontaneity.

1-3 PRAISE GOD FOR HIS SALVATION

1. *a Psalm.* Cf. xxx. 1.

a new song. Cf. xcvi. 1.

His right hand and His holy arm. A reminiscence of xliv. 4, where it is emphasized that Israel's victory over the Canaanite peoples was not won by Israel's 'sword and arm' but by *Thy right hand and Thine arm.* Cf. Exod. xv. 6.

His holy arm. Found in Isa. lii. 10. It means power exercised in a holy cause.

wrought salvation. Better, 'His saving right hand and His holy arm (alone) has assisted Him.' God is not dependent on any auxiliary power to effect salvation (Metsudath David, Hirsch).

2. *salvation … righteousness.* The former was the effect of the latter (cf. Kimchi). For the combination, cf. lxxi. 15.

in the sight of the nations. So publicly that all the peoples could discern His intervention.

3. *He hath remembered.* Although the cry of the exiles had been *the LORD hath forgotten me* (Isa. xlix. 14).

mercy … faithfulness. Combined in xcii. 3.

all the ends … our God. Cf. the promise in Isa. lii. 10.

4 Shout unto the LORD, all the earth;
  Break forth and sing for joy, yea,
    sing praises.

5 Sing praises unto the LORD with
    the harp;
  With the harp and the voice of
    melody.

6 With trumpets and sound of the
    horn
  Shout ye before the King, the
    LORD.

7 Let the sea roar, and the fulness
    thereof;
  The world, and they that dwell
    therein;

8 Let the floods clap their hands;
  Let the mountains sing for joy
    together;

9 Before the LORD, for He is come
    to judge the earth;
  He will judge the world with
    righteousness,
  And the peoples with equity.

4 הָרִיעוּ לַיהוָה כָּל־הָאָרֶץ
פִּצְחוּ וְרַנְּנוּ וְזַמֵּרוּ׃

5 זַמְּרוּ לַיהוָה בְּכִנּוֹר
בְּכִנּוֹר וְקוֹל זִמְרָה׃

6 בַּחֲצֹצְרוֹת וְקוֹל שׁוֹפָר
הָרִיעוּ לִפְנֵי ׀ הַמֶּלֶךְ יְהוָה׃

7 יִרְעַם הַיָּם וּמְלֹאוֹ
תֵּבֵל וְיֹשְׁבֵי בָהּ׃

8 נְהָרוֹת יִמְחֲאוּ־כָף
יַחַד הָרִים יְרַנֵּנוּ׃

9 לִפְנֵי־יְהוָה כִּי בָא
לִשְׁפֹּט הָאָרֶץ
יִשְׁפֹּט־תֵּבֵל בְּצֶדֶק
וְעַמִּים בְּמֵישָׁרִים׃

4-6 ACCLAIM HIM WITH MUSIC

4. *shout ... earth*. Again in c. 1. As so often
in the Psalter, God's display of salvation to
Israel is to be heralded by all the nations,
because it is the prelude to a worldwide
recognition of His Sovereignty over the whole
earth, inaugurating the era of universal peace
(Kimchi).

break forth and sing for joy. The same verbs
in Isa. lii. 9.

sing praises. Better, 'make melody,' either
with the voice, or musical instruments, or
both. So also in the next verse.

5. *the voice of melody*. Also in Isa. li. 3.

6. *trumpets*. Made of silver (Num. x. 2).

horn. Hebrew *shofar*, ram's horn.

7-9 LET ALL NATURE JOIN IN PRAISE

7. *let the sea ... thereof*. Also in xcvi. 11.

the world ... therein. Also in xxiv. 1.

8. *floods clap their hands*. Instead of *floods*,
read 'rivers.' The imagery is not the crashing
of the waves on the shore, but meant to evoke
the happy clapping of rejoicers in dance. In
Isa. lv. 12, the mountains are called upon to
sing and the trees of the forest to clap their
hands.

9. Cf. xcvi. 13.

1 The LORD reigneth; let the peoples
 tremble;
 He is enthroned upon the cherubim; let the earth quake.

2 The LORD is great in Zion;
 And He is high above all the
 peoples.

3 Let them praise Thy name as great
 and awful;
 Holy is He.

4 The strength also of the king who
 loveth justice—
 Thou hast established equity,
 Thou hast executed justice and
 righteousness in Jacob.

5 Exalt ye the LORD our God,
 And prostrate yourselves at His
 footstool;
 Holy is He.

יְהֹוָה מָלָךְ יִרְגְּזוּ עַמִּים
יֹשֵׁב כְּרוּבִים תָּנוּט הָאָרֶץ:
2 יְהֹוָה בְּצִיּוֹן גָּדוֹל
וְרָם הוּא עַל־כָּל־הָעַמִּים:
3 יוֹדוּ שִׁמְךָ גָּדוֹל וְנוֹרָא
קָדוֹשׁ הוּא:
4 וְעֹז מֶלֶךְ מִשְׁפָּט אָהֵב
אַתָּה כּוֹנַנְתָּ מֵישָׁרִים
מִשְׁפָּט וּצְדָקָה בְּיַעֲקֹב
אַתָּה עָשִׂיתָ:
5 רוֹמְמוּ יְהֹוָה אֱלֹהֵינוּ
וְהִשְׁתַּחֲווּ לַהֲדֹם רַגְלָיו
קָדוֹשׁ הוּא:

CALL TO WORSHIP RENEWED

THE theme of XCIII and XCVII is repeated.

1-3 GOD IS ENTHRONED

1. *reigneth.* 'Hath become King.'

tremble. Be awestruck.

enthroned upon the cherubim. See on lxxx. 2.

let the earth quake. Cf. lxxvii. 19.

2. *great in Zion.* Cf. xlviii. 2. God's greatness was indeed revealed in Zion, the city of
his Temple. He will now be exalted universally, with all nations acknowledging His
supremacy (see Meiri, Sforno, Hirsch).

3. *Thy name is great and awful.* Cf. cxi. 9.

holy is He. A refrain which recurs in verses 5
and 9. Holiness is God's essential attribute
and the supreme ethical inspiration to all who
acknowledge Him (Lev. xix. 2) (cf. Hirsch).

4-5 GOD'S RULE IS JUST

4. *the strength ... loveth justice.* Unlike
human monarchs who use their power des-
potically, the Divine King allows His might
to be controlled by justice which He loves
(Midrash Shocher Tov).

Thou. Emphatic in the Hebrew to mark the
contrast with the kings of the earth.

equity ... justice ... righteousness. All evi-
denced in the laws of the Torah (Ibn Ezra).

5. *exalt ye.* Cf. xxxiv. 4.

His footstool. That upon which His glory
rests; applied to the earth (Isa. lxvi. 1), the Ark
of the covenant (1 Chron.. xxviii. 2), Zion
(Lam. ii. 1), and the Temple (cxxxii. 7). The
last-mentioned passage is akin to the phrase
in this Psalm.

6 Moses **and** Aaron among His
   priests,
And Samuel among them that call
   upon His name,
Did call upon the LORD, and He
   answered them.

7 He spoke unto them in the pillar
   of cloud;
They kept His testimonies, and
   the statute that He gave them.

8 O LORD our God, Thou didst answer them;
A forgiving God wast Thou unto
   them,
Though Thou tookest vengeance
   of their misdeeds.

9 Exalt ye the LORD our God,
And worship at His holy hill;
For the LORD our God is holy.

6 מֹשֶׁה וְאַהֲרֹן ׀ בְּכֹהֲנָיו
וּשְׁמוּאֵל בְּקֹרְאֵי שְׁמוֹ
קֹרִאים אֶל־יְהֹוָה וְהוּא יַעֲנֵם׃
7 בְּעַמּוּד עָנָן יְדַבֵּר אֲלֵיהֶם
שָׁמְרוּ עֵדֹתָיו וְחֹק נָתַן־לָמוֹ׃
8 יְהֹוָה אֱלֹהֵינוּ אַתָּה עֲנִיתָם
אֵל נֹשֵׂא הָיִיתָ לָהֶם
וְנֹקֵם עַל־עֲלִילוֹתָם׃
9 רוֹמְמוּ יְהֹוָה אֱלֹהֵינוּ
וְהִשְׁתַּחֲווּ לְהַר קָדְשׁוֹ
כִּי־קָדוֹשׁ יְהֹוָה אֱלֹהֵינוּ׃

6-9 HIS RELATION WITH ISRAEL'S LEADERS

The exhortation in the first section of the Psalm is reinforced by recalling God's response to the prayers offered through these names as an indication of the honour due 'His footstool'; for people as great as Moses, Aaron and Samuel had served therein. Cf. Jer. xv.1.

6. Even if Moses had not officiated as a priest during the seven-day consecration of the Tabernacle, he would be deserving of the title 'priest' by its basic meaning of exerting influence through words and deeds (Hirsch). Moses prayed for the people in connection with the sin of the Golden Calf and the spies. Aaron interceded on behalf of the community during the plague which followed Korah's revolt (Num. xvii. 11ff.). For an example of Samuel's intercession, cf. 1 Sam. vii. 8.

7. *in the pillar of cloud.* Cf. Exod. xxxiii. 9.

they kept. God accepted their petitions as a reward of their faithfulness to His laws (Meiri).

8. *forgiving God ... unto them.* Better, 'because of them'. A forgiving God wast Thou unto [Israel] because of them [Moses, Aaron and Samuel] (Rashi).

Thou tookest vengeance. Though He pardoned the people in answer to the prayer of the leaders, He exacted justice from their leaders for their own deeds.

9. *His holy hill.* Mount Zion (ii. 6).

Exalt ye ... the LORD our God is holy. Alshich interprets this verse as a summary of the entire Psalm. Exalt Him and exclaim that though He is sublime over the heavens, he does not absent Himself from earth. Therefore, worship not only at the Temple, His footstool, but also at His holy hill (a reference to the times when there is no Temple) for the LORD our God is holy.

100

ק

1 A Psalm of thanksgiving.
  Shout unto the LORD, all the earth.

2 Serve the LORD with gladness;
  Come before His presence with
  singing.

3 Know ye that the LORD He is God;
  It is He that hath made us, and we
  are His,
  His people, and the flock of His
  pasture.

מִזְמוֹר לְתוֹדָה
הָרִיעוּ לַיהֹוָה כָּל־הָאָרֶץ׃
2 עִבְדוּ אֶת־יְהֹוָה בְּשִׂמְחָה
בֹּאוּ לְפָנָיו בִּרְנָנָה׃
3 דְּעוּ כִּי־יְהֹוָה הוּא אֱלֹהִים
הוּא עָשָׂנוּ וְלֹא אֲנַחְנוּ
עַמּוֹ וְצֹאן מַרְעִיתוֹ׃

v. 3. ולו ק'

CALL TO GOD'S SERVICE

THIS brief Psalm is a worthy climax to the 'accession' group which commenced with XCIII.
Its few verses summarize the teachings contained therein. All the peoples of the earth are
invited to join with Israel in the worship of God, to serve Him in gladness, and thereby form
a united band to do His will. Then will His loving-kindness and faithfulness be universally
enjoyed (cf. Hirsch).

1. *thanksgiving.* The Targum renders 'for
the thank-offering,' and the Psalm was originally intended to accompany the bringing of
that sacrifice. It has therefore been prescribed
in the Jewish liturgy for days other than the
Sabbath and Festivals, when that offering
was brought (*P.B.*, p. 20).

shout ... earth. As in xcviii. 4.

2. *serve the* LORD *with gladness.* A human
being approaches his king with trepidation;
he should approach God with a joyful heart.
His service is not irksome but *rejoicing the
heart* (xix. 9) (Kimchi).

3. *know ye that the* LORD *He is God.* The
cardinal doctrine upon which the service of
Israel's God rests (1 Kings xviii. 39). You
should now know that *the* LORD *He is God* and

He is the Almighty over the entire universe
(Kimchi). Sforno interprets 'He is judge';
that is, 'Know ye that the LORD He is judge
over all.' In your service to God, your beliefs
and your prayers, know that the LORD [only]
He is God. Do not think, as do the heretics,
that He Who created good cannot create evil,
and that, therefore, there are two gods. Know
that the LORD of compassion is the very same
LORD of justice (Hazeh Zion).

hath made us. Israel, to be the instrument
of His purpose to mankind (xcv. 6; Deut.
xxxii. 6).

and we are His. This is the rendering of the
kerë; the *kethib* means: 'and not we (have
made) ourselves.'

the flock of His pasture. Cf. xcv. 7.

4 Enter into His gates with thanks-
    giving,
  And into His courts with praise;
  Give thanks unto Him, and bless
    His name.

5 For the Lord is good; His mercy
    endureth for ever;
  And His faithfulness unto all
    generations.

בָּאוּ שְׁעָרָיו ן בְּתוֹדָה 4
חֲצֵרֹתָיו בִּתְהִלָּה
הוֹדוּ לוֹ בָּרְכוּ שְׁמוֹ:
כִּי־טוֹב יְהוָה לְעוֹלָם חַסְדּוֹ 5
וְעַד־דֹּר וָדֹר אֱמוּנָתוֹ:

4. *gates.* Of the Temple.

thanksgiving. Probably the sacrifice of
thanksgiving (cf. xcvi. 8), itself a symbol of
gratitude. The Rabbis affirmed that while all
other offerings would cease, not so the thank-
offering (Midrash Shocher Tov). By this they
intended that the need for sin-offerings, etc.
might conceivably be no more, but the call on
man's sentiment of gratitude to God must
always exist (cf. Redak, Hirsch).

praise. Of His goodness.

give thanks ... name. Cf. xcvii. 12, and xcvi.
2. The verse throws light on the spirit with
which the Israelites were to rebuild the Temple
as the centre of religious worship. Its Service
was more than the offering of sacrifices upon
the altar; this was but the means to a higher
purpose, as the verse indicates. Giving thanks
to God and blessing His name define the
loftier levels of prayer (see Maimonides,
Guide for the Perplexed 3: xxxii; cf. Hirsch).

5. *good.* The Psalmist urges the people to
'spread the message that the Lord is the sole
absolute good' after which man should strive
(Hirsch).

good ... for ever. This is the thanks, praise
and blessing that will be recited by the Israelites (Ibn Ezra).

His mercy endureth for ever. Cf. the similar
refrain in cxxxvi., 'the Great Hallel.'

for ever. God's goodness and His mercy are
not rare and extraordinary occurrences, but
are with us daily and for ever (Hirsch).

101

קֵא

לְדָוִד מִזְמֹר
חֶסֶד־וּמִשְׁפָּט אָשִׁירָה
לְךָ יְהוָה אֲזַמֵּרָה:
2 אַשְׂכִּילָה ׀ בְּדֶרֶךְ תָּמִים
מָתַי תָּבוֹא אֵלָי
אֶתְהַלֵּךְ בְּתָם־לְבָבִי
בְּקֶרֶב בֵּיתִי:
3 לֹא־אָשִׁית ׀ לְנֶגֶד עֵינַי
דְּבַר־בְּלִיָּעַל

1 A Psalm of David.
I will sing of mercy and justice;
Unto Thee, O LORD, will I sing
praises.

2 I will give heed unto the way of
integrity;
Oh when wilt Thou come unto
me?
I will walk within my house in the
integrity of my heart.

3 I will set no base thing before
mine eyes;

AN IDEAL KINGSHIP

MANY commentators agree that in this Psalm we have the utterance of a king who formulates the principles which will guide him in his reign. As such it sets forth an ideal of the throne which is on the highest plane (cf. Meiri, Kimchi, Sforno). The poignant question at the opening, *Oh when wilt Thou come unto me?* receives its most pointed explanation on a hypothesis that the Psalm was composed by David at the beginning of his reign. His ardent wish was to instal the Ark of the covenant, captured from the Philistines, in Jerusalem. The untoward incident, the death of Uzzah, which frustrated his first attempt to realize that hope, filled him with fear and caused him to exclaim, *How shall the ark of the LORD come unto me?* (2 Sam. vi. 9). His question implied that before Jerusalem could have the privilege of housing the Ark, the city must be made fit for its reception by a thorough eradication of evil. His purpose in making this reformation is voiced in this Psalm. This interpretation also explains why it was included immediately after the 'accession' Psalms. Zion could only become a fitting resting-place of the Ark after the city had been cleansed of all unrighteousness, as the earth could only become the Kingdom of God when wickedness had been eliminated.

1-2 THE KING'S LONGING FOR GOD

1. *I will sing.* I will extol the virtues of.

mercy and justice. Cf. *Righteousness and justice are the foundation of Thy throne; mercy and truth go before Thee* (lxxxix. 15). These qualities of Divine rule are lauded by the Psalmist and will be made the guiding principles of his reign.

will I sing praises. Not merely in words, but in imitating the Divine attributes in his own kingship.

2. *I will give heed.* He will deliberately choose *the way of integrity* to walk in as the ruler of his people.

when wilt Thou come. This is the goal that inspired his resolution, for the attainment of which he specifies the steps he will take.

within my house. Here the beginning is to be made. His private life will not be tarnished by the corruption and self-indulgence which were usual with an Eastern monarch (cf. Rashi, Hirsch).

3-4 HE WILL SHUN EVERYTHING BASE

3. *base thing.* lit. 'matter of Belial' (cf. xviii. 5, xli. 9). He will avoid every unworthy aim and ambition.

I hate the doing of things crooked;
It shall not cleave unto me.

4 A perverse heart shall depart from
    me;
  I will know no evil thing.

5 Whoso slandereth his neighbour
    in secret, him will I destroy;
  Whoso is haughty of eye and proud
    of heart, him will I not suffer.

6 Mine eyes are upon the faithful
    of the land, that they may dwell
    with me;
  He that walketh in a way of integ-
    rity, he shall minister unto me.

7 He that worketh deceit shall not
    dwell within my house;
  He that speaketh falsehood shall
    not be established before mine
    eyes.

8 Morning by morning will I destroy
    all the wicked of the land;
  To cut off all the workers of in-
    iquity from the city of the LORD.

עֲשֹׂה־סֵטִים שָׂנֵאתִי
לֹא יִדְבַּק בִּי:
4 לֵבָב עִקֵּשׁ יָסוּר מִמֶּנִּי
רָע לֹא אֵדָע:
5 מְלוֹשְׁנִי בַסֵּתֶר רֵעֵהוּ
אוֹתוֹ אַצְמִית
גְּבַהּ־עֵינַיִם וּרְחַב לֵבָב
אֹתוֹ לֹא אוּכָל:
6 עֵינַי בְּנֶאֶמְנֵי־אֶרֶץ
לָשֶׁבֶת עִמָּדִי
הֹלֵךְ בְּדֶרֶךְ תָּמִים
הוּא יְשָׁרְתֵנִי:
7 לֹא־יֵשֵׁב בְּקֶרֶב בֵּיתִי
עֹשֵׂה רְמִיָּה
דֹבֵר שְׁקָרִים לֹא־יִכּוֹן לְנֶגֶד עֵינָי:
8 לַבְּקָרִים אַצְמִית כָּל־רִשְׁעֵי־אֶרֶץ
לְהַכְרִית מֵעִיר־יְהוָה
כָּל־פֹּעֲלֵי אָוֶן:

---

things crooked. lit. '(deeds which) swerve
(from that which is right).'

shall not cleave. Should an evil deed come to
his hand, he will at once free himself of it.

4. *a perverse heart.* lit. 'crooked heart' (cf.
Prov. xi. 20). Only what is straightforward
will remain in his heart.

I will know. i.e. be intimate with.

5-6   HIS MINISTERS MUST BE RIGHTEOUS

5. *slandereth.* A common vice in a king's
court (cf. Hirsch).

haughty ... proud. Such men are likely to
imperil the peace of the state.

6. *dwell with me.* Be my associates (cf.
Ibn Ezra).

walketh in a way of integrity. Each of his
ministers must be like himself (verse 2).

7-8   HE WILL PURGE JERUSALEM
      OF THE WICKED

7. *shall not dwell.* As in xv. 1, with a different verb. A deceitful man will not have entry
to the palace.

shall not be established. He will be dismissed
when his character is discovered.

8. *morning by morning.* Each morning the
king will sit to administer justice (cf. Jer. xxi.
12). The capital, as well as the court, must be
morally clean (cf. Rashi, Kimchi, Ibn Ezra,
Metsudath David).

city of the LORD. Jerusalem (Meiri).

102

1 A Prayer of the afflicted, when he
  fainteth, and poureth out his
  complaint before the LORD.

2 O LORD, hear my prayer,
  And let my cry come unto Thee.

3 Hide not Thy face from me in the
  day of my distress;
  Incline Thine ear unto me;
  In the day when I call answer me
  speedily.

4 For my days are consumed like
  smoke,
  And my bones are burned as a
  hearth.

5 My heart is smitten like grass, and
  withered;
  For I forget to eat my bread.

קב

‫תְּפִלָּה לְעָנִי כִי־יַעֲטֹף‬
‫וְלִפְנֵי יְהוָה יִשְׁפֹּךְ שִׂיחוֹ׃‬
‫יְהוָה שִׁמְעָה תְפִלָּתִי 2‬
‫וְשַׁוְעָתִי אֵלֶיךָ תָבוֹא׃‬
‫אַל־תַּסְתֵּר פָּנֶיךָ ׀ מִמֶּנִּי 3‬
‫בְּיוֹם צַר לִי‬
‫הַטֵּה־אֵלַי אָזְנֶךָ‬
‫בְּיוֹם אֶקְרָא מַהֵר עֲנֵנִי׃‬
‫כִּי־כָלוּ בְעָשָׁן יָמָי 4‬
‫וְעַצְמוֹתַי כְּמוֹקֵד נִחָרוּ׃‬
‫הוּכָּה־כָעֵשֶׂב וַיִּבַשׁ לִבִּי 5‬
‫כִּי־שָׁכַחְתִּי מֵאֲכֹל לַחְמִי׃‬

AN EXILE'S PLAINT

RASHI identifies the speaker of the Psalm with Israel, the afflicted. Most all of the commentators agree that the Psalm describes the dreadful state of Israel, suffering the agonies of exile. One gleam of hope pierces the enveloping darkness, and that is God's eternity which kindles faith in Zion's restoration. He will not discard His people for ever. The day will come for the fulfilment of the promise that Jerusalem shall be the centre to which all nations will rally in His service.

1. The superscription has allusion to the Psalm's liturgical use. It is appropriate for recital by any sufferer whose overcharged heart seeks relief in prayer.

2-3 INTRODUCTORY INVOCATION

Although the opening appeal is couched in conventional language, it vibrates with earnestness and urgency.

2. *O LORD ... prayer.* As in xxxix. 13.

let my cry ... Thee. As in xviii. 7.

3. *hide not ... from me.* As in xxvii. 9.

in the day of my distress. As in lix. 17.

incline ... unto me. As in xxxi. 3.

in the day when I call. As in lvi. 10.

answer me speedily. As in lxix. 18.

4-12 HIS DESPERATE STATE

4. *like smoke.* The Hebrew is 'in smoke' which gives the true meaning. To be consumed *like* smoke is a simile for extinction. The Psalmist likens Israel to a sick man inflamed by fever.

bones. The bodily frame (cf. vi. 3).

hearth. A place of burning, or a mass of burning material.

5. *heart.* Source of vitality and strength (Kimchi).

grass. Better, 'herbage.' Scorched by the sun's heat, it shrivels. Similarly his blood is dried up by his travails.

6 By reason of the voice of my
 sighing
 My bones cleave to my flesh.

7 I am like a pelican of the wilderness;
 I am become as an owl of the
 waste places.

8 I watch, and am become
 Like a sparrow that is alone upon
 the housetop.

9 Mine enemies taunt me all the day;
 They that are mad against me do
 curse by me.

10 For I have eaten ashes like bread,
 And mingled my drink with
 weeping.

11 Because of Thine indignation and
 Thy wrath;
 For Thou hast taken me up, and
 cast me away.

12 My days are like a lengthening
 shadow;
 And I am withered like grass.

מִקּוֹל אַנְחָתִי 6
דָּבְקָה עַצְמִי לִבְשָׂרִי׃
דָּמִיתִי לִקְאַת מִדְבָּר 7
הָיִיתִי כְּכוֹס חֳרָבוֹת׃
שָׁקַדְתִּי וָאֶהְיֶה 8
כְּצִפּוֹר בּוֹדֵד עַל־גָּג׃
כָּל־הַיּוֹם חֵרְפוּנִי אוֹיְבָי 9
מְהוֹלָלַי בִּי נִשְׁבָּעוּ׃
כִּי־אֵפֶר כַּלֶּחֶם אָכָלְתִּי 10
וְשִׁקֻּוַי בִּבְכִי מָסָכְתִּי׃
מִפְּנֵי־זַעַמְךָ וְקִצְפֶּךָ 11
כִּי נְשָׂאתַנִי וַתַּשְׁלִיכֵנִי׃
יָמַי כְּצֵל נָטוּי 12
וַאֲנִי כָּעֵשֶׂב אִיבָשׁ׃

to eat. Troubles destroy his appetite.

6. *my bones … my flesh*. His body is wasted by lack of food and by worry (cf. Job xix. 20).

7. *pelican*. 'The pelican, which subsists on fish, must go daily from its desert habitat to the rivers to find its sustenance. So, says the Psalmist, am I in exile; dwelling in deserts, separated from the populace, stealthily approaching the populated areas for my sustenance' (Malbim).

owl. Called by the Arabs 'mother of ruins,' because it makes its home in desolate places and derelict buildings.

8. *I watch*. Better, 'I have been startled into restless wakefulness' (Hirsch).

a sparrow … alone. Having been separated from my mate (Meiri). Kimchi sees this description as an allusion to the prolonged and dispersed exile. The scattered nation laments: 'Wherever I go in exile, I find myself alone in a foreign nation, just as the sparrow, separated from its mate, is alone on the housetops.'

9. *taunt*. Mock his forlorn condition and ask why his God does not come to his aid (cf. xlii. 11).

cursed by me. Use his name when execrating a person, saying, 'May you become as wretched as he (the Psalmist).'

10. *eaten … bread*. Not literally. Ashes were sprinkled upon the head in mourning (Joshua vii. 6); Israel resorted to them as a man naturally partakes of food (Metsudath David). See also Lam. iii. 16.

mingled my drink with weeping. And not with spices as ordinarily happened. Or, the phrase may be figurative as in xlii. 4, lxxx. 6.

11. *indignation*. As usual in the Bible, calamity is recognized as evidence of God's wrath.

taken … me away. As a gale lifts a man off his feet and hurls him some distance away.

12. *a … shadow*. Towards evening, when the sun is about to set, the shadow is extended (Rashi). Israel feels swallowed up by the darkness of exile (Kimchi).

grass. Herbage, as in verse 5.

13 But Thou, O Lord, sittest enthroned for ever;
  And Thy name is unto all generations.

14 Thou wilt arise, and have compassion upon Zion;
  For it is time to be gracious unto
  her, for the appointed time is
  come.

15 For Thy servants take pleasure
  in her stones,
  And love her dust.

16 So the nations will fear the name
  of the Lord,
  And all the kings of the earth Thy
  glory;

17 When the Lord hath built up
  Zion,
  When He hath appeared in His
  glory;

18 When He hath regarded the
  prayer of the destitute,
  And hath not despised their
  prayer.

וְאַתָּה יְהוָה לְעוֹלָם תֵּשֵׁב 13
וְזִכְרְךָ לְדֹר וָדֹר׃

אַתָּה תָקוּם תְּרַחֵם צִיּוֹן 14
כִּי־עֵת לְחֶנְנָהּ
כִּי־בָא מוֹעֵד׃

כִּי־רָצוּ עֲבָדֶיךָ אֶת־אֲבָנֶיהָ 15
וְאֶת־עֲפָרָהּ יְחֹנֵנוּ׃

וְיִירְאוּ גוֹיִם אֶת־שֵׁם יְהוָה 16
וְכָל־מַלְכֵי הָאָרֶץ אֶת־כְּבוֹדֶךָ׃

כִּי־בָנָה יְהוָה צִיּוֹן 17
נִרְאָה בִּכְבוֹדוֹ׃

פָּנָה אֶל־תְּפִלַּת הָעַרְעָר 18
וְלֹא־בָזָה אֶת־תְּפִלָּתָם׃

13-23 ZION WILL BE RESTORED

Israel is convinced of Zion's glorious future.
Each generation carries the conviction and
hope that it will yet merit the final redemption, for 'Thou, O Lord, sittest enthroned
forever' (Kimchi).

13. An almost identical verse appears in
Lam. v. 19., with the substitution of *Thy throne*
for *Thy name*.

but Thou. Emphasized in the Hebrew text, to
stress the basis for Israel's unshaken confidence. 'Thou sittest … forever; you swore to
us in Your Name. Therefore, Thou wilt arise
… ' (Rashi).

name. lit. 'memorial' (cf. Exod. iii. 15). The
aspect in which God is remembered from
generation to generation is His kingship.

14. *have compassion upon Zion.* In her
desolate condition, bereft of her children (cf.
Kimchi).

appointed time. For restoration to her former
glory. In the national disaster, the prophets
reassured the people with God's message
that the captivity was the expiation for sin
and would terminate when He deemed the
penalty to have been exacted (cf. Isa. xl. 2;
Jer. xxix. 10).

15. *take pleasure in her stones.* An additional plea for God's compassion. Far from
having forgotten Zion, the exiles constantly
think with affection even of her rubble heaps
(cf. Rashi, Ibn Ezra, Kimchi).

16. Still another reason for God to restore
Israel to its former glory: the effect it will
produce throughout the world. This thought
is met with in Isaiah (e.g. lix. 19, lx. 3).

17. *appeared in His glory.* Revealed Himself in a manner which redounds to His glory.

18. *the destitute.* The exiled nation.

19 This shall be written for the
   generation to come;
   And a people which shall be
   created shall praise the LORD.

20 For He hath looked down from
   the height of His sanctuary;
   From heaven did the LORD behold the earth;

21 To hear the groaning of the
   prisoner;
   To loose those that are appointed
   to death;

22 That men may tell of the name of
   the LORD in Zion,
   And His praise in Jerusalem;

23 When the peoples are gathered
   together,
   And the kingdoms, to serve the
   LORD.

24 He weakened my strength in the
   way;
   He shortened my days.

19 תִּכָּתֶב זֹאת לְדוֹר אַחֲרוֹן
וְעַם נִבְרָא יְהַלֶּל־יָהּ:

20 כִּי־הִשְׁקִיף מִמְּרוֹם קָדְשׁוֹ
יְהוָה מִשָּׁמַיִם ׀ אֶל־אֶרֶץ הִבִּיט:

21 לִשְׁמֹעַ אֶנְקַת אָסִיר
לְפַתֵּחַ בְּנֵי תְמוּתָה:

22 לְסַפֵּר בְּצִיּוֹן שֵׁם יְהוָה
וּתְהִלָּתוֹ בִּירוּשָׁלָ͏ִם:

23 בְּהִקָּבֵץ עַמִּים יַחְדָּו
וּמַמְלָכוֹת לַעֲבֹד אֶת־יְהוָה:

24 עִנָּה בַדֶּרֶךְ כֹּחוֹ
קִצַּר יָמָי:

כחי ק׳   v. 24.

---

19. *shall be written.* Zion's restoration will be recorded and read by future generations (Rashi, Metsudath David).

a people which shall be created. Israel revived and entering upon a new epoch in its history will have cause to praise God for His abundant mercies (Rashi, Meiri).

the LORD. Hebrew *Jah*, the designation frequently used in the Psalter for God as Israel's Saviour.

20. *hath looked down.* The prophetic perfect; or, the conjunction *for* may be rendered 'when.' For the language, cf. xiv. 2, xxxiii. 13.

from the height of His sanctuary. From heaven, His holy abode above.

21. Similar to lxxix. 11.

22. *that men may tell.* lit. 'to tell'; the subject may be the reprieved exiles of the preceding verse, or *the peoples* mentioned in verse 23. Possibly both are intended.

23. The return to Zion will be the prelude to the universal acknowledgment of God, in fulfilment of the prophecy of Isa. ii. 2ff and lvi. 7. 'God has caused them to go through all varied experiences of suffering and redemption so that they might become His messengers in Zion and Jerusalem to teach the nations of the world to recognize God and His mighty acts, when at long last those nations will have gathered together as one, to enter into the service of the LORD forever' (Hirsch).

24-25 THE PSALMIST RENEWS HIS PLAINT

24. Before concluding his composition, the Psalmist returns to the subject of his condition, with which he began.

He weakened my strength. This is the reading of the *kerë*; the rendering of the *kethib* is 'His strength hath afflicted (me).'

in the way. In my journey through exile.

25 I say: 'O my God, take me not
    away in the midst of my days,
    Thou whose years endure
    throughout all generations.

26 Of old Thou didst lay the foun-
    dation of the earth;
    And the heavens are the work of
    Thy hands.

27 They shall perish, but Thou shalt
    endure;
    Yea, all of them shall wax old like
    a garment;
    As a vesture shalt Thou change
    them, and they shall pass away;

28 But Thou art the selfsame,
    And Thy years shall have no end.

29 The children of Thy servants
    shall dwell securely,
    And their seed shall be estab-
    lished before Thee.'

25 אֹמַר אֵלִי אַל־תַּעֲלֵנִי בַּחֲצִי יָמָי

בְּדוֹר דּוֹרִים שְׁנוֹתֶיךָ׃

26 לְפָנִים הָאָרֶץ יָסַדְתָּ

וּמַעֲשֵׂה יָדֶיךָ שָׁמָיִם׃

27 הֵמָּה ׀ יֹאבֵדוּ וְאַתָּה תַעֲמֹד

וְכֻלָּם כַּבֶּגֶד יִבְלוּ

כַּלְּבוּשׁ תַּחֲלִיפֵם וְיַחֲלֹפוּ׃

28 וְאַתָּה־הוּא

וּשְׁנוֹתֶיךָ לֹא יִתָּמּוּ׃

29 בְּנֵי־עֲבָדֶיךָ יִשְׁכּוֹנוּ

וְזַרְעָם לְפָנֶיךָ יִכּוֹן׃

He shortened my days. The Psalmist laments
the thought of his death being near at hand
which circumstance would deprive him of
the happiness of seeing Zion rebuilt (Kimchi).

25. *I say*. His meditation forces the prayer
from his lips.

in the midst of my days. lit. 'in the half of my
days' (cf. lv. 24).

years endure. As in verses 12f. he sets his
fleeting days beside God's permanence, and
dwells on the theme in conclusion.

26-29   GOD ETERNAL AND UNCHANGING

26. *of old*. God, being the Creator of the
universe, must necessarily have been without beginning in time (Metsudath David).

work of Thy hands. What has been made by
God can be destroyed by Him; it is not eternal
like the Maker.

27. *they shall perish*. Man thinks of heaven
and earth, the physical world, as symbols of
permanence, but even after they come into

being as the work of Thy hands, they are for
ever dependent on Thee. But Thou art not
dependent on anything. Even if they shall
perish, if Thou changest them, Thou wilt
remain unchanged for ever.

wax old like a garment. For the language, cf.
Deut. viii. 4.

change them … pass away. Both verbs are
derived from the same root, and although the
former may mean 'change,' there is no thought
here of a new world replacing the old. The
preferable rendering is: 'shalt Thou make to
pass away and they shall pass away.'

28. *Thou are the selfsame*. lit. 'Thou art He'
—an emphatic assertion of the personality of
God, which is in its very nature unchanging
(cf. Rashi, Malbim).

29. *shall dwell securely*. Hebrew 'shall
dwell,' viz. in the rebuilt homeland (cf. lxix.
36) (Kimchi, Sforno).

before Thee. Maintaining God's favour (cf.
Malbim).

1 [A Psalm] of David.
Bless the LORD, O my soul;
And all that is within me, bless
His holy name.

2 Bless the LORD, O my soul,
And forget not all His benefits;

3 Who forgiveth all thine iniquity;
Who healeth all thy diseases;

4 Who redeemeth thy life from the
pit;
Who encompasseth thee with lovingkindness and tender mercies;

5 Who satisfieth thine old age with
good things;
So that thy youth is renewed like
the eagle.

לְדָוִד ׀
בָּרֲכִי נַפְשִׁי אֶת־יְהוָֹה
וְכָל־קְרָבַי אֶת־שֵׁם קָדְשׁוֹ:
2 בָּרֲכִי נַפְשִׁי אֶת־יְהוָֹה
וְאַל־תִּשְׁכְּחִי כָּל־גְּמוּלָיו:
3 הַסֹּלֵחַ לְכָל־עֲוֺנֵכִי
הָרֹפֵא לְכָל־תַּחֲלוּאָיְכִי:
4 הַגּוֹאֵל מִשַּׁחַת חַיָּיְכִי
הַמְעַטְּרֵכִי חֶסֶד וְרַחֲמִים:
5 הַמַּשְׂבִּיעַ בַּטּוֹב עֶדְיֵךְ
תִּתְחַדֵּשׁ כַּנֶּשֶׁר נְעוּרָיְכִי:

HYMN OF PRAISE

WE have in this Psalm one of the most joyful compositions in the Psalter. Only in happy
circumstances could such an outburst have been possible. Sforno suggested that the Psalmist
summons himself and others to make public the favours that God does for mankind. Thus the
love for God will find inroads into all hearts, and mankind, universally, will serve Him out
of love. The composition also presents the Psalmist's personal declaration of the significance
of God in his own life, both physical and spiritual (Hirsch).

1-5 CALL TO PRAISE GOD

1. *Bless … my soul.* A call to that part of
man which has a relationship with God, from
Whom it emanates, and is, therefore, immortal (Hirsch).

all … within me. The body (Ibn Ezra). Man is
called to praise God with body and soul.

2. *benefits.* lit. 'awards,' the proofs of His
mercy and love which are specified in the
following verses.

3. *thine iniquity.* God had healed his moral
ills by His pardon as well as his ailments.
Kimchi asserts that 'diseases' refer to spiritual ailments; that is, sins as in xli. 5.

4. *pit.* Grave. He did not perish, but was

granted life because of God's mercy and
compassion (Ibn Ezra).

5. *thine old age.* So the Targum. The ordinary meaning is 'ornament,' which Targum
sees as a reference to old age. Kimchi and Ibn
Ezra translate *edyaich* 'your mouth' as in
xxxii. 9. God, with His compassion, satisfies
your mouth (which in illness loathed food)
with good things, via good health. Ibn Ezra
sees the *ornaments* as a reference to the soul.
Only by satisfying your soul with good things
can your youthfulness be renewed.

thy youth. In exile the nation was like a de-
crepit person, but now, with the advent of
redemption, it displayed the freshness of
youth again (cf. Sforno).

6 The LORD executeth righteousness,
And acts of justice for all that are
oppressed.

7 He made known His ways unto
Moses,
His doings unto the children of
Israel.

8 The LORD is full of compassion
and gracious,
Slow to anger, and plenteous in
mercy.

9 He will not always contend;
Neither will He keep His anger for
ever.

10 He hath not dealt with us after
our sins,
Nor requited us according to our
iniquities.

11 For as the heaven is high above
the earth,
So great is His mercy toward
them that fear Him.

12 As far as the east is from the west,
So far hath He removed our
transgressions from us.

6 עֹשֵׂה צְדָקוֹת יְהוָֹה
וּמִשְׁפָּטִים לְכָל־עֲשׁוּקִים:
7 יוֹדִיעַ דְּרָכָיו לְמֹשֶׁה
לִבְנֵי יִשְׂרָאֵל עֲלִילוֹתָיו:
8 רַחוּם וְחַנּוּן יְהוָֹה
אֶרֶךְ אַפַּיִם וְרַב־חָסֶד:
9 לֹא־לָנֶצַח יָרִיב
וְלֹא לְעוֹלָם יִטּוֹר:
10 לֹא כַחֲטָאֵינוּ עָשָׂה לָנוּ
וְלֹא כַעֲוֹנֹתֵינוּ גָּמַל עָלֵינוּ:
11 כִּי כִגְבֹהַּ שָׁמַיִם עַל־הָאָרֶץ
גָּבַר חַסְדּוֹ עַל־יְרֵאָיו:
12 כִּרְחֹק מִזְרָח מִמַּעֲרָב
הִרְחִיק מִמֶּנּוּ אֶת־פְּשָׁעֵינוּ:

like the eagle. The eagle grows new feathers in the place of old, and it lives to a great age and yet retains its vitality. Cf. Isa. xl. 31 (Rashi, Meiri).

6-18 DIVINE GRACIOUSNESS

6. *righteousness.* Better, 'righteous acts,' the noun being plural, more particularly 'acts of salvation' which are the effect of His righteousness. The deliverance from Babylon is in his mind.

acts of justice. lit. 'judgments,' with which oppressors are penalized (cf. Malbim).

7. *His ways.* In answer to Moses' prayer *snow me now Thy ways* (Exod. xxxiii. 13), the attributes which dispose His dealings towards men (Kimchi).

8. Based upon Exod. xxxiv. 6.

9. Cf. Isa. lvii. 16.

contend. A technical term for bringing a suit before a judge. As a righteous God, He cannot overlook sin; but in His mercy, He is sparing in punishment.

11. *heaven ... earth.* An immeasurable distance.

great. Beyond measure and description.

them that fear Him. In a general sense, and here especially of the faithful in Israel for whose sake God had revealed His mercy to the nation as a whole.

12. *transgressions.* Acts of rebellion against His Sovereignty.

13 Like as a father hath compassion
   upon his children,
   So hath the LORD compassion
   upon them that fear Him.

14 For He knoweth our frame;
   He remembereth that we are dust.

15 As for man, his days are as grass;
   As a flower of the field, so he
   flourisheth.

16 For the wind passeth over it, and
   it is gone;
   And the place thereof knoweth it
   no more.

17 But the mercy of the LORD is from
   everlasting to everlasting upon
   them that fear Him,
   And His righteousness unto children's children;

18 To such as keep His covenant,
   And to those that remember His
   precepts to do them.

19 The LORD hath established His
   throne in the heavens;
   And His kingdom ruleth over all.

כְּרַחֵם אָב עַל־בָּנִים 13
רִחַם יְהֹוָה עַל־יְרֵאָיו׃
כִּי־הוּא יָדַע יִצְרֵנוּ 14
זָכוּר כִּי־עָפָר אֲנָחְנוּ׃
אֱנוֹשׁ כֶּחָצִיר יָמָיו 15
כְּצִיץ הַשָּׂדֶה כֵּן יָצִיץ׃
כִּי רוּחַ עָבְרָה־בּוֹ וְאֵינֶנּוּ 16
וְלֹא־יַכִּירֶנּוּ עוֹד מְקוֹמוֹ׃
וְחֶסֶד יְהֹוָה מֵעוֹלָם וְעַד־עוֹלָם 17
עַל־יְרֵאָיו
וְצִדְקָתוֹ לִבְנֵי בָנִים׃
לְשֹׁמְרֵי בְרִיתוֹ 18
וּלְזֹכְרֵי פִקֻּדָיו לַעֲשׂוֹתָם׃
יְהֹוָה בַּשָּׁמַיִם הֵכִין כִּסְאוֹ 19
וּמַלְכוּתוֹ בַּכֹּל מָשָׁלָה׃

13. *compassion*. He demonstrated one of His attributes (verse 8).

14. *our frame*. The noun is connected with the verb in Gen. ii. 7, *the LORD God* formed, *man of the dust of the ground*; hence the meaning is: He knows how man was formed, that he is a mortal creature destined to return to dust. Such knowledge arouses His pity and He acts mercifully with him (cf. Metsudath David).

15. *man*. Hebrew *enosh* (see on viii. 5).

grass. Cf. xc. 5. The 'hatzir' dries earlier than other types of grass (Malbim).

flower. Cf. Isa. xl. 6f.

16. *and the place … more*. Repeated in Job. vii. 10.

17. *from everlasting to everlasting*. See on xc. 2. In his frail and erring nature man has

nothing else to depend upon than God's eternal mercy (cf. Kimchi).

18. *to such as keep His covenant*. According to the assurance of the Decalogue (Exod. xx. 6).

keep … to do. Kimchi observes that 'the LORD's mercy … everlasting … unto children's children' depends upon the children's purpose in studying the imperatives of the covenant to be their practice. Academic knowledge unaccompanied by concrete practice is not sufficient.

19-22 GOD THE UNIVERSAL KING

As often in the Psalter, the experience of Israel is recounted as teaching a lesson for all mankind. If the whole human race acknowledged His rule, His benefits would be enjoyed by all men.

20 Bless the Lord, ye angels of His,
   Ye mighty in strength, that fulfil
     His word,
   Hearkening unto the voice of His
     word.

21 Bless the Lord, all ye His hosts;
   Ye ministers of His, that do His
     pleasure.

22 Bless the Lord, all ye His
     works,
   In all places of His dominion;
   Bless the Lord, O my soul.

20 בָּרֲכוּ יְהוָֹה מַלְאָכָיו
גִּבֹּרֵי כֹחַ עֹשֵׂי דְבָרוֹ
לִשְׁמֹעַ בְּקוֹל דְּבָרוֹ:
21 בָּרֲכוּ יְהוָֹה כָּל־צְבָאָיו
מְשָׁרְתָיו עֹשֵׂי רְצוֹנוֹ:
22 בָּרֲכוּ יְהוָֹה כָּל־מַעֲשָׂיו
בְּכָל־מְקֹמוֹת מֶמְשַׁלְתּוֹ
בָּרֲכִי נַפְשִׁי אֶת־יְהוָֹה:

19. *established … heavens.* Unlike earthly dynasties which are liable to change, the Divine throne is firmly in heaven, everlasting and unchanging.

His kingdom ruleth over all. Not only over Israel; would that the other peoples recognized this truth!

20. *angels.* The celestial beings are invoked to praise the name of God (xxix. 1 cxlviii. 3) as His attendants, thus setting an example to the dwellers upon earth.

ye mighty in strength. lit. 'mighty ones (or, warriors) of strength,' i.e. mighty warriors. The angels are again so described in Joel iv. 11 where they are summoned to fight in aid of Israel (Kimchi, op. cit.).

word. Command.

21. *hosts.* The heavenly bodies and the forces of nature which serve His purposes (civ. 4, cxlviii. 3). 'His hosts' denotes the extraterrestrial world with its myriads of stars and the forces of the elements which all stand under the direct command of God, and which are His ministers (Hirsch).

22. *all ye His works.* In the terrestrial world (Kimchi).

in all places of His dominion. Both in heaven and earth.

bless the Lord, O my soul. He ends on the note with which he began. As one of God's creatures, he feels the urge to join in the chorus of praise due to Him. There is no anti-climax when the Psalm passes from praise to God uttered by *angels* and *hosts* to that which issues from the *soul* of a humble individual. It rather points to the dignity of the human being who has the privilege of sharing this duty with the heavenly creatures. According to Rabbinic teaching the purpose of man's creation was to afford him an opportunity of glorifying his Maker, and praise from him was most acceptable to God. 'From the beginning of the world's formation, praise ascended to the Holy One, blessed be He, only from the waters (cf. xciii. 4); and God declared, "If these, which possess neither mouth nor speech, offer Me such praise, how much more will I be extolled when I create man!"' (Midrash Rabbah, Gen. 5a, b).

104

קד

1 Bless the Lord, O my soul.
O Lord my God, Thou art **very**
great;
Thou art clothed with glory and
majesty.

2 Who coverest Thyself with light as
with a garment,
Who stretchest out the heavens
like a curtain;

3 Who layest the beams of Thine
upper chambers in the waters,
Who makest the clouds Thy
chariot,
Who walkest upon the wings of
the wind;

בָּרְכִי נַפְשִׁי אֶת־יְהֹוָה
יְהֹוָה אֱלֹהַי גָּדַלְתָּ מְּאֹד
הוֹד וְהָדָר לָבָשְׁתָּ:
2 עֹטֶה־אוֹר כַּשַּׂלְמָה
נוֹטֶה שָׁמַיִם כַּיְרִיעָה:
3 הַמְקָרֶה בַמַּיִם עֲלִיּוֹתָיו
הַשָּׂם־עָבִים רְכוּבוֹ
הַמְהַלֵּךְ עַל־כַּנְפֵי־רוּחַ:

GOD THE CREATOR

THIS outstanding song of praise describes the mighty acts of God as they are revealed in nature.
The Psalmist portrays the wonders of the six days of creation and sketches the eternal salvation
of those who exult in His glory and the destruction of those who reject Him. He outlines the
interdependence of every component created by God and then depicts the formation of man,
the crown of creation. This Psalm is included in the liturgy to be recited on the beginning of
every month (Rosh Hodesh).

1-4 GOD'S MAJESTY IN HIS CREATION

1. *Thou art very great.* His quintessential
greatness is incomprehensible to man. Only
in the revealed wonders of the universe He
created, did God's immeasurable greatness
become apparent to man (cf. Meiri, Malbim).

Thou art clothed. Render, 'Thou hast clothed
Thyself,' by the act of creation.

glory and majesty. See on viii. 6.

2. The Psalmist follows the account in Gen.
i. The first creative acts of God had been light
and the heavenly firmament.

coverest Thyself. All had been darkness until
God said, *Let there be light,* and on its appearance the light enwrapped Him like a robe

(Ibn Ezra). The verbs in these three verses are
present participles. The original act of creation continues into the present as a daily
renewal of the universe. This concept finds
expression in the daily liturgy of the Jews: 'In
Thy goodness Thou renewest the creation
every day continually' (P.B., p. 37 and Etz
Yosef, op.).

3. *who layest the beams.* The Psalmist, with
poetic license, pictures God's heavenly abode
as floating upon the waters above (cf. Amos
ix. 6). For the stores of water above the
firmament, cf. Gen. i. 7.

the clouds Thy chariot. Cf. Isa. xix. 1. God
reveals Himself in rain-storms.

the wings of the wind. He also reveals Himself in the whirlwind.

4 Who makest winds Thy messen-
    gers,
  The flaming fire Thy ministers.

5 Who didst establish the earth
    upon its foundations,
  That it should not be moved for
    ever and ever;

6 Thou didst cover it with the deep
    as with a vesture;
  The waters stood above the moun-
    tains.

7 At Thy rebuke they fled,
  At the voice of Thy thunder they
    hasted away—

8 The mountains rose, the valleys
    sank down—
  Unto the place which Thou hadst
    founded for them;

9 Thou didst set a bound which they
    should not pass over,
  That they might not return to
    cover the earth.

10 Who sendest forth springs into
    the valleys;
  They run between the mountains;

עֹשֶׂה מַלְאָכָיו רוּחוֹת 4
מְשָׁרְתָיו אֵשׁ לֹהֵט:
יָסַד־אֶרֶץ עַל־מְכוֹנֶיהָ 5
בַּל־תִּמּוֹט עוֹלָם וָעֶד:
תְּהוֹם כַּלְּבוּשׁ כִּסִּיתוֹ 6
עַל־הָרִים יַעַמְדוּ־מָיִם:
מִן־גַּעֲרָתְךָ יְנוּסוּן 7
מִן־קוֹל רַעַמְךָ יֵחָפֵזוּן:
יַעֲלוּ הָרִים יֵרְדוּ בְקָעוֹת 8
אֶל־מְקוֹם זֶה וְיָסַדְתָּ לָהֶם:
גְּבוּל־שַׂמְתָּ בַּל־יַעֲבֹרוּן 9
בַּל־יְשׁוּבוּן לְכַסּוֹת הָאָרֶץ:
הַמְשַׁלֵּחַ מַעְיָנִים בַּנְּחָלִים 10
בֵּין הָרִים יְהַלֵּכוּן:

---

4. *winds Thy messengers.* Cf. cxlviii. 8.

flaming fire. Flashes of lightning.

5-9   CREATION OF EARTH

5. *foundations.* Kimchi asserts that the 'foundations' which prevents the earth from 'moving' is a reference to the principle of gravity.

6. The verse describes the earth before the division was made between sea and dry land (Gen. i. 9f.).

7. *Thy rebuke.* When God said *Let the waters under the heaven be gathered together into one place* (Gen. i. 9). From the *voice* of that declaration all the waters *hasted away* from where they were and gathered together

unto the place that Thou hadst founded for them (Rashi).

fled … hasted away. Better, 'flee … haste away.' The writer pictures the scene as taking place.

8. *rose … sank.* Render, 'rise … sink.'
for them. The waters.

10-13   CREATION OF SPRINGS AND RAIN

10. A meaningful description of how God engineered the waters for the benefit of the entire creation; the salty oceans and the fresh spring waters; water for humans and animals, for crops, for cooling the air and moisture for the body; waters that flow through the mountains into the wilderness and even in the deserts (see Kimchi).

11 They give drink to every beast of
the field,
The wild asses quench their thirst.

12 Beside them dwell the fowl of the
heaven,
From among the branches they
sing.

13 Who waterest the mountains from
Thine upper chambers;
The earth is full of the fruit of
Thy works.

14 Who causest the grass to spring
up for the cattle,
And herb for the service of man;
To bring forth bread out of the
earth,

15 And wine that maketh glad the
heart of man,
Making the face brighter than
oil,
And bread that stayeth man's
heart.

11 יַשְׁקוּ כָּל־חַיְתוֹ שָׂדָי
יִשְׁבְּרוּ פְרָאִים צְמָאָם׃
12 עֲלֵיהֶם עוֹף־הַשָּׁמַיִם יִשְׁכּוֹן
מִבֵּין עֳפָאיִם יִתְּנוּ־קוֹל׃
13 מַשְׁקֶה הָרִים מֵעֲלִיּוֹתָיו
מִפְּרִי מַעֲשֶׂיךָ תִּשְׂבַּע הָאָרֶץ׃
14 מַצְמִיחַ חָצִיר ׀ לַבְּהֵמָה
וְעֵשֶׂב לַעֲבֹדַת הָאָדָם
לְהוֹצִיא לֶחֶם מִן־הָאָרֶץ׃
15 וְיַיִן ׀ יְשַׂמַּח לְבַב־אֱנוֹשׁ
לְהַצְהִיל פָּנִים מִשָּׁמֶן
וְלֶחֶם לְבַב־אֱנוֹשׁ יִסְעָד׃

11. *beast of the field.* Wild animals whose
needs are not supplied by man, as distinct
from domestic animals.

wild asses. For a graphic description of the
animal, cf. Job xxxix. 5ff., and for its sufferings in a time of drought, Jer. xiv. 6. Owing
to its avoidance of inhabited places, it, in
particular, depends upon water supplied by
God (Kimchi).

12. *beside them.* viz. the springs, grow the
trees which provide habitation for the birds
(Metsudath David).

branches. Or, foliage (see Dan. iv. 9).

13. *mountains.* The fields on the mountain
slopes (see on lxxii. 16).

upper chambers. See on verse 3.

Thy works. The effect of rain is an ample
supply of vegetation for food, as the next
section details (cf. Kimchi).

14-18 CREATION OF FOOD

14. *herb.* The word used in Gen. i. 11f., a

general term for the vegetable kingdom.

for the service of man. Both the Hebrew and
English translation can mean either 'for the
use of man' (cf. Hirsch) or 'for man's labour,'
i.e. by toil man obtains his food (Kimchi).

to bring forth ... earth. That he (man) may
make the earth yield bread for himself. The
words are the source of the Jewish Grace
before meals (*P.B.*, p. 278).

15. *that maketh glad.* Cf. Judges ix. 13,
wine which cheereth God and man, and
Eccles. x. 19, *wine maketh glad the life* (see
Tal. Pes. 109a). Judaism does not regard the
drinking of wine as a vice because its abuse
leads to degrading intoxication. Moderation,
not abstinence, is advocated; and before
drinking wine, a benediction is to be pronounced, 'Blessed art Thou ... Who createst
the fruit of the vine' (*P.B.*, p. 287).

making the face brighter than oil. Better, 'that
he may make the face to shine with oil.'

stayeth. lit. 'supporteth,' sustains.

16 The trees of the LORD have their
fill,
The cedars of Lebanon, which
He hath planted:

17 Wherein the birds make their
nests;
As for the stork, the fir-trees are
her house.

18 The high mountains are for the
wild goats;
The rocks are a refuge for the
conies.

19 Who appointedst the moon for
seasons;
The sun knoweth his going down.

20 Thou makest darkness, and it is
night,
Wherein all the beasts of the
forest do creep forth.

21 The young lions roar after their
prey,
And seek their food from God.

22 The sun ariseth, they slink away,
And couch in their dens.

16 יִשְׂבְּעוּ עֲצֵי יְהֹוָה
אַרְזֵי לְבָנוֹן אֲשֶׁר נָטָע:
17 אֲשֶׁר־שָׁם צִפֳּרִים יְקַנֵּנוּ
חֲסִידָה בְּרוֹשִׁים בֵּיתָהּ:
18 הָרִים הַגְּבֹהִים לַיְּעֵלִים
סְלָעִים מַחְסֶה לַשְׁפַנִּים:
19 עָשָׂה יָרֵחַ לְמוֹעֲדִים
שֶׁמֶשׁ יָדַע מְבוֹאוֹ:
20 תָּשֶׁת־חֹשֶׁךְ וִיהִי לָיְלָה
בּוֹ־תִרְמֹשׂ כָּל־חַיְתוֹ־יָעַר:
21 הַכְּפִירִים שֹׁאֲגִים לַטָּרֶף
וּלְבַקֵּשׁ מֵאֵל אָכְלָם:
22 תִּזְרַח הַשֶּׁמֶשׁ יֵאָסֵפוּן
וְאֶל־מְעוֹנֹתָם יִרְבָּצוּן:

16. *trees of the LORD.* i.e. trees planted by
God—as against those planted and watered
by man—of which the cedar is specified as
the most notable example (Kimchi).

their fill. Of rain.

17. *birds.* The Hebrew denotes the species
of birds that nest in high cedars (Malbim).

the stork. Hebrew *chasidah*, from *chesed*
'lovingkindness.' It is said it is so named
because of its great affection for its young.

fir-trees. The stork selects tall, protective
trees for its nest, and for this purpose the fir
tree, whose wide leaves serve as a protection
from rain, is very convenient.

18. *wild goats.* lit. 'climbers.'

conies. They are afraid of man and run to
hide in the rocks. God provided care and
protection for each of His creations (cf.

Meiri, Malbim).

19-23 CREATION OF MOON AND SUN

19. *the moon.* Mentioned before the sun,
because Scripture reckons the day as beginning at nightfall (Gen. i. 5ff.).

for seasons. The Jewish calendar is based
upon a lunar year.

20. *Thou makest darkness.* Night and
darkness are not merely the lack of light but
are positive aspects of creation. Some animals are nocturnal, hunting only at night;
man needs night for rest and the process of
growth takes place during the night (Kimchi).

21. *roar.* Interpreted by the poet as a petition to God to send them food (Kimchi).

22. *couch in their dens.* lit. 'to their dens
they couch,' i.e. retire to their lairs and lie
down in them.

23 Man goeth forth unto his work
   And to his labour until the
   evening.

24 How manifold are Thy works, O
   LORD!
   In wisdom hast Thou made them
   all;
   The earth is full of Thy creatures.

25 Yonder sea, great and wide,
   Therein are creeping things innumerable,
   Living creatures, both small and
   great.

26 There go the ships;
   There is leviathan, whom Thou
   hast formed to sport therein.

27 All of them wait for Thee,
   That Thou mayest give them
   their food in due season.

יָצֵא אָדָם לְפָעֳלוֹ 23
וְלַעֲבֹדָתוֹ עֲדֵי־עָרֶב:
מָה־רַבּוּ מַעֲשֶׂיךָ ׀ יְהֹוָה 24
כֻּלָּם בְּחָכְמָה עָשִׂיתָ
מָלְאָה הָאָרֶץ קִנְיָנֶךָ:
זֶה ׀ הַיָּם גָּדוֹל וּרְחַב יָדָיִם 25
שָׁם־רֶמֶשׂ וְאֵין מִסְפָּר
חַיּוֹת קְטַנּוֹת עִם־גְּדֹלוֹת:
שָׁם אֳנִיּוֹת יְהַלֵּכוּן 26
לִוְיָתָן זֶה־יָצַרְתָּ לְשַׂחֶק־בּוֹ:
כֻּלָּם אֵלֶיךָ יְשַׂבֵּרוּן 27
לָתֵת אָכְלָם בְּעִתּוֹ:

---

23. *until the evening*. Sunset marks also a *season* for man, the end of the day's toil.

24-30 REFLECTION UPON GOD'S WORKS

24. *manifold*. Many in number and variety.

in wisdom. All are the product of God's incomprehensible wisdom, whether man can appreciate their place in the Divine plan or not (cf. Prov. iii. 19, viii. 22ff.).

Thy creatures. This special meaning of the root *kanah* 'acquire' occurs in the designation of God as *Maker* (*koneh*) *of heaven and earth* (Gen. xiv. 22).

25. *wide*. lit. 'broad on both hands.' Having detailed the marvels of creation regarding man and animal on land, the Psalmist now turns to the vastness of the oceans and the countless inhabitants of the deep, an area in life on this earth which is mostly hidden from the eyes of man (Kimchi).

26. *ships*. The Psalmist stood amazed at the myriad forms of life which find habitation *in* the sea; now he marvels at the sight presented by its surface. The ships sailing by excite his wonder.

leviathan. The huge sea-monsters. See Job xl. 25.

to sport therein. In the sea. So Kimchi, pointing out that all the creatures of the sea are sport for the leviathan who rules over them and feeds on any he wishes.

27. *all of them*. All living beings depend upon God for sustenance (cf. cxlv. 15 and cxxxvi. 25) (Kimchi).

28 Thou givest it unto them, they
   gather it;
   Thou openest Thy hand, they
   are satisfied with good.

29 Thou hidest Thy face, they
   vanish;
   Thou withdrawest their breath,
   they perish,
   And return to their dust.

30 Thou sendest forth Thy spirit,
   they are created;
   And Thou renewest the face of
   the earth.

31 May the glory of the Lord endure for ever;
   Let the Lord rejoice in His works!

32 Who looketh on the earth, and it
   trembleth;
   He toucheth the mountains, and
   they smoke.

33 I will sing unto the Lord as long
   as I live;

28 תִּתֵּן לָהֶם יִלְקֹטוּן
תִּפְתַּח יָדְךָ יִשְׂבְּעוּן טוֹב׃
29 תַּסְתִּיר פָּנֶיךָ יִבָּהֵלוּן
תֹּסֵף רוּחָם יִגְוָעוּן
וְאֶל־עֲפָרָם יְשׁוּבוּן׃
30 תְּשַׁלַּח רוּחֲךָ יִבָּרֵאוּן
וּתְחַדֵּשׁ פְּנֵי אֲדָמָה׃
31 יְהִי כְבוֹד יְהוָה לְעוֹלָם
יִשְׂמַח יְהוָה בְּמַעֲשָׂיו׃
32 הַמַּבִּיט לָאָרֶץ וַתִּרְעָד
יִגַּע בֶּהָרִים וְיֶעֱשָׁנוּ׃
33 אָשִׁירָה לַיהוָה בְּחַיָּי

28. *Thou openest … good.* Cf. cxlv. 16.

29. *Thou hidest Thy face.* To withhold the essential provision (Kimchi).

withdrawest their breath. The same word as in (God) *breathed into his nostrils the breath of life* (Gen. ii. 7) and *the spirit returneth unto God who gave it* (Eccles. xii. 7). Death is the withdrawal of the God-given breath.

return to their dust. As in Gen. iii. 19.

30. *Thou renewest … the earth.* With living creatures the dead are succeeded by their offspring; each generation brings new faces to the world. Cf. Ecc. i. 4 (Kimchi).

31-35 CONCLUDING PRAYER AND VOW

31. *rejoice in His works.* As when, on their completion, *God saw everything that He had made, and, behold, it was very good* (Gen. i. 31); because should He ever be dissatisfied with the universe, He has the power to reduce it to chaos (Kimchi).

32. *looketh … it trembleth.* Hirsch sees this verse as a continuation of the previous one where in God is described as delighting in his creatures for their voluntary obedience. In this verse the point is made that God could easily force obedience, for He need only to cause the earth to tremble.

33. Almost identical with cxlvi. 2.

as long as I live. Because throughout the remainder of his life his mind will be impressed by the consciousness of God's marvellous

I will sing praise to my God while
I have any being.

34 Let my musing be sweet unto
Him;
As for me, I will rejoice in the
LORD.

35 Let sinners cease out of the earth,
And let the wicked be no more.
Bless the LORD, O my soul.
Hallelujah.

אֹמְרָה לֵאלֹהַי בְּעוֹדִי:
34 יֶעֱרַב עָלָיו שִׂיחִי
אָנֹכִי אֶשְׂמַח בַּיהוָה:
35 יִתַּמּוּ חַטָּאִים ׀ מִן־הָאָרֶץ
וּרְשָׁעִים ׀ עוֹד אֵינָם
בָּרְכִי נַפְשִׁי אֶת־יְהוָה
הַלְלוּיָהּ:

works, and also, perhaps, because he is aware
that *the dead praise not the* LORD (cxv. 17).

34. *let my musing be sweet unto Him.* The
same hope as in xix. 15. The verb *be sweet* is
used of a sacrifice which is acceptable to God
(Jer. vi. 20; Hosea ix. 4). His hope is, accordingly, that his meditation would find favour
with Him.

I will rejoice in the LORD. As God rejoices in
His works (verse 31), the Psalmist will re-
joice in God, finding in contemplation of
Him an unfailing source of joy (Ibn Ezra).

35. *let sinners cease.* A prayer (Ibn Ezra) or
an expectation: 'and sinners will cease.' In
contrast, Eccl. (vii. 20) reads that there can be
no man who 'sinneth not,' but there it refers
to one who occasionally errs, whilst our
verse focuses on those who sin on purpose.
The Psalmist awaits the day that men will
eventually heed their innate inclination to
God, and deliberate disobedience of God's
law will vanish from the earth (Hirsch). The

Tal. (Ber. 10a) relates that Rabbi Meir, when
vexed by the conduct of some lawless men,
prayed that they should perish. His wife,
overhearing the remark, quoted this verse,
with a slight change of vowels, as meaning,
'Let sins be consumed out of the earth and
then the wicked will be no more,' because
they will have repented. A daily prayer in the
Jewish liturgy similarly petitions that 'Thou
wilt turn unto Thyself all the wicked of the
earth,' as the fulfilment of the hope that
'Thou wilt remove the abominations from
the earth' (*P.B.*, pp. 76f.).

let the wicked be no more Their disappear-
ance is prayed for because they strike a dis-
cordant note in God's world.

bless the LORD, *O my soul.* The same ending
as in the previous Psalm.

Hallelujah. 'Praise ye the LORD (jah).' This is
the first occurrence of this term, limited to the
Psalter, which has passed into the language
of prayer.

105

קה

1 O give thanks unto the Lord, call
upon His name;
Make known His doings among
the peoples.

2 Sing unto Him, sing praises unto
Him;
Speak ye of all His marvellous
works.

3 Glory ye in His holy name;
Let the heart of them rejoice that
seek the Lord.

4 Seek ye the Lord and His strength;
Seek His face continually.

5 Remember His marvellous works
that He hath done,
His wonders, and the judgments of
His mouth;

הוֹדוּ לַיהוָה קִרְאוּ בִשְׁמוֹ
הוֹדִיעוּ בָעַמִּים עֲלִילוֹתָיו:
2 שִׁירוּ־לוֹ זַמְּרוּ־לוֹ
שִׂיחוּ בְּכָל־נִפְלְאוֹתָיו:
3 הִתְהַלְלוּ בְּשֵׁם קָדְשׁוֹ
יִשְׂמַח לֵב ׀ מְבַקְשֵׁי יְהוָה:
4 דִּרְשׁוּ יְהוָה וְעֻזּוֹ
בַּקְּשׁוּ פָנָיו תָּמִיד:
5 זִכְרוּ נִפְלְאוֹתָיו אֲשֶׁר־עָשָׂה
מֹפְתָיו וּמִשְׁפְּטֵי־פִיו:

THANKSGIVING TO GOD FOR HIS PAST ACTS

Like LXXVIII the Psalm gives a retrospect of God's dealings with Abraham and his
descendants to the time of their taking possession of the promised land. If He had then
enlarged a small family into a great people, He was capable of developing Israel into a mighty
nation. The Psalm was composed by David when he brought the Ark from the house of Obed
Edom the Gittite to the City of David. It was recited in front of the Ark daily until Solomon
placed the Ark in its permanent sanctuary in the Temple. Verses 1-15 have been incorporated
in 1 Chron. xvi. 8-22.

1-6 EXHORTATION TO PRAISE GOD

1. The verse forms part of Isa. xii. 4.

call upon His name. His dealings with Israel
are a matter of universal concern, and Israel's
duty is to spread a knowledge of them to the
end that all mankind may swear allegiance to
Him.

2. *sing praises.* Or, 'make melody.'

marvellous works. Acts of deliverance.

3. *His holy name.* See on xxxiii. 21.

rejoice. From the confidence that they do not
seek Him in vain (Malbim).

4. *seek ye.* A different verb from *seek His
face;* it means 'to inquire to obtain a knowledge of' (see Ezek. xxxiv. 6) (cf. Malbim).

His strength. As a power to save.

seek His face. This verb is the same as in
verse 3. *Face* signifies 'presence.' Man should
constantly strive to have the consciousness
that he is under Divine scrutiny so that he can
say, *I have set the Lord always before me*
(xvi. 8).

5. *remember.* An exhortation to Israel often repeated by Moses (cf. especially Deut.
xxxii. 7). From the recollection of past history inspiration for the present is derived.

works ... wonders. The terms include all the
miracles God performed in Egypt, the desert
and the Holy Land (Kimchi).

judgments of His mouth. The plagues executed upon Egypt (cf. Exod. vi. 6, vii. 4)
(Kimchi).

6 O ye seed of Abraham His servant,
Ye children of Jacob, His chosen
ones.

7 He is the LORD our God;
His judgments are in all the earth.

8 He hath remembered His covenant for ever,
The word which He commanded
to a thousand generations;

9 [The covenant] which He made
with Abraham,
And His oath unto Isaac;

10 And He established it unto Jacob
for a statute,
To Israel for an everlasting covenant;

11 Saying: 'Unto thee will I give
the land of Canaan,
The lot of your inheritance.'

12 When they were but a few men in
number,
Yea, very few, and sojourners in
it,

זֶרַע אַבְרָהָם עַבְדּוֹ 6
בְּנֵי יַעֲקֹב בְּחִירָיו:
הוּא יְהוָה אֱלֹהֵינוּ 7
בְּכָל־הָאָרֶץ מִשְׁפָּטָיו:
זָכַר לְעוֹלָם בְּרִיתוֹ 8
דָּבָר צִוָּה לְאֶלֶף דּוֹר:
אֲשֶׁר כָּרַת אֶת־אַבְרָהָם 9
וּשְׁבוּעָתוֹ לְיִשְׂחָק:
וַיַּעֲמִידֶהָ לְיַעֲקֹב לְחֹק 10
לְיִשְׂרָאֵל בְּרִית עוֹלָם:
לֵאמֹר לְךָ אֶתֵּן אֶת־אֶרֶץ כְּנָעַן 11
חֶבֶל נַחֲלַתְכֶם:
בִּהְיוֹתָם מְתֵי מִסְפָּר 12
כִּמְעַט וְגָרִים בָּהּ:

6. *Abraham His servant*. Again in verse
42. 1 Chron. has *Israel*.

chosen ones. Again in verse 43. The sense in
which Israel was *chosen* is defined in the
following verses.

7-11 COVENANT WITH THE PATRIARCHS

7. *He is ... our God*. The God of the patriarchs is now our God. Neither time nor place
have been able to effect the slightest change
in the nature of our relationship to God, nor
will they be able to do so in the future (Hirsch).

8. *He hath remembered*. Better, 'He
remembereth.' His memory has no limitations (cf. cxi. 9 where 'God is mindful of His
covenant for ever') (Hirsch).

word. The Word, the Law and promise of the
covenant (Hirsch).

commanded. Render 'the word which He
commanded endures for a thousand generations' (Malbim).

a thousand generations. Cf. Deut. vii. 9.

Thousand stands for a large number and is
not to be interpreted literally.

9. *with Abraham*. Gen. xvii. 2ff.

unto Isaac. Gen. xxvi. 3. The covenant was
renewed with Isaac to indicate that the other
sons of Abraham were excluded from the
promise (see Gen. xxv. 5, 6).

10. *unto Jacob*. Gen. xxviii. 13ff., to the
exclusion of Esau.

a statute. A fixed decree.

11. *unto thee*. Referring to each of the patriarchs (Kimchi).

your inheritance. Alluding to the people of
Israel (Kimchi).

12-15 PROTECTION OF THE PATRIARCHS

12. *they*. The patriarchs and their families
(Kimchi).

but a few men in number. So Jacob described
himself and his children (Gen. xxxiv. 30).

sojourners in it. They resided in a land which

13 And when they went about from
    nation to nation,
    From one kingdom to another
    people,

14 He suffered no man to do them
    wrong,
    Yea, for their sake He reproved
    kings:

15 'Touch not Mine anointed ones,
    And do My prophets no harm.'

16 And He called a famine upon the
    land;
    He broke the whole staff of bread.

17 He sent a man before them;
    Joseph was sold for a servant;

18 His feet they hurt with fetters,
    His person was laid in iron;

13 וַיִּתְהַלְּכוּ מִגּוֹי אֶל־גּוֹי
מִמַּמְלָכָה אֶל־עַם אַחֵר:

14 לֹא־הִנִּיחַ אָדָם לְעָשְׁקָם
וַיּוֹכַח עֲלֵיהֶם מְלָכִים:

15 אַל־תִּגְּעוּ בִמְשִׁיחָי
וְלִנְבִיאַי אַל־תָּרֵעוּ:

16 וַיִּקְרָא רָעָב עַל־הָאָרֶץ
כָּל־מַטֵּה־לֶחֶם שָׁבָר:

17 שָׁלַח לִפְנֵיהֶם אִישׁ
לְעֶבֶד נִמְכַּר יוֹסֵף:

18 עִנּוּ בַכֶּבֶל רַגְלָיו
בַּרְזֶל בָּאָה נַפְשׁוֹ:

v. 18. רגלו ק׳

was not theirs and were dependent upon the good will of the inhabitants. Their position was consequently precarious.

13. All the patriarchs were compelled to migrate from Canaan (Gen. xii. 10, xxvi. 1, xxviii. 10) (Rashi).

14. *reproved kings.* Cf. Gen. xii. 17, xx. 3 (Rashi).

15. *touch not.* Cf. Gen. xxvi. 11, xx. 6.

Mine anointed ones. The term is used in a wide sense in connection with the patriarchs as men designated by God to become the progenitors of *a kingdom of priests*. Rabbi Judah (Tal. Sab. 119b) beautifully applied the words to schoolchildren whose education must be regarded as a primary duty.

My prophets. Men to whom God had communicated His will. Abraham is so designated (Gen. xx. 7). The Talmud (ibid.) sees in these words a reference to the sages.

16-22   HIS CARE OF JOSEPH

16. *He called a famine.* A common Hebrew idiom. To be noted is the Psalmist's interpretation of the famine in Egypt as ordained by God for the fulfilment of His purpose with Israel (cf. Rashi, Kimchi).

broke … bread. Reminiscent of Lev. xxvi. 26. Bread is the *staff of life* (cf. civ. 15) upon which man leans for his sustenance. This was snapped by God in the famine.

17. *a man before them.* Joseph preceded his brethren in Egypt to make their immigration possible. He said of himself, *God did send me before you to preserve life* (Gen. xlv.5).

18. *with fetters.* A poetical elaboration of *Joseph was bound* (Gen. xl. 3).

his person was laid in iron. lit. 'his soul (i.e. he) entered into iron (chains). Both the LXX and Targum render: 'the iron entered his soul,' which denotes the humiliation and mental suffering resulting from imprisonment (Kimchi).

<table>
<tr><td valign="top">

19 Until the time that his word came
    to pass,
    The word of the LORD tested him.

20 The king sent and loosed him;
    Even the ruler of peoples, and
    set him free.

21 He made him lord of his house,
    And ruler of all his possessions;

22 To bind his princes at his
    pleasure,
    And teach his elders wisdom.

23 Israel also came into Egypt;
    And Jacob sojourned in the land
    of Ham.

24 And He increased His people
    greatly,
    And made them too mighty for
    their adversaries.

25 He turned their heart to hate His
    people,
    To deal craftily with His servants.

</td><td valign="top" dir="rtl">

19 עַד־עֵת בֹּא־דְבָרוֹ
אִמְרַת יְהוָה צְרָפָתְהוּ:
20 שָׁלַח מֶלֶךְ וַיַּתִּירֵהוּ
מֹשֵׁל עַמִּים וַיְפַתְּחֵהוּ:
21 שָׂמוֹ אָדוֹן לְבֵיתוֹ
וּמֹשֵׁל בְּכָל־קִנְיָנוֹ:
22 לֶאְסֹר שָׂרָיו בְּנַפְשׁוֹ
וּזְקֵנָיו יְחַכֵּם:
23 וַיָּבֹא יִשְׂרָאֵל מִצְרָיִם
וְיַעֲקֹב גָּר בְּאֶרֶץ־חָם:
24 וַיֶּפֶר אֶת־עַמּוֹ מְאֹד
וַיַּעֲצִמֵהוּ מִצָּרָיו:
25 הָפַךְ לִבָּם לִשְׂנֹא עַמּוֹ
לְהִתְנַכֵּל בַּעֲבָדָיו:

</td></tr>
</table>

19. *his word came to pass*. i.e. Joseph's interpretation of Pharaoh's dreams (Metsudath David) foreshadowing his future eminence (cf. *but his father kept the saying* (lit. *word*) *in mind*, Gen. xxxvii. 11).

the word of the LORD *tested him*. Better, 'cleansed him.' The Hebrew for *word* has a different meaning from the Hebrew *davar* which precedes it. It signifies the decree of God which came to test Joseph by way of slavery and imprisonment. These trials served to refine his faith and character (Rashi).

20. Gen. xli. 14.

21. Gen. xli. 40ff.

lord of his house. Cf. Gen. xlv. 8.

22. *bind*. He had the power to imprison others as Potiphar had done to him (Gen. xxxix. 20); so Ibn Ezra.

his princes. The Hebrew for *prince* occurs in the phrases 'chief of the butlers, *chief* of the bakers'; it means the higher rank of officials.

at his pleasure. At his own discretion, with-

out direction from Pharaoh (Kimchi).

elders. The king's councillors.

23-28   HIS CARE OF ISRAEL IN EGYPT

23. *Israel*. The family which became the nation (Hirsch).

the land of Ham. Again in verse 27 (see on lxxviii. 51).

24. The verbs recall those of Exod. i. 7, *and the children of Israel were* fruitful ... *and* waxed *exceeding* mighty. Render here: 'and He made His people greatly fruitful, and caused them to be mightier than their adversaries.'

25. *He turned their heart*. viz. of the adversaries, the Egyptians. Their oppression of the Israelites is ascribed to God as part of His scheme for their deliverance. The Targum has 'their heart turned,' probably as a result of Israel's unnatural growth referred to in the previous verse (cf. Hirsch).

to deal craftily. Cf. *come, let us deal wisely with them* (Exod. i. 10).

26 He sent Moses His servant,
And Aaron whom He had chosen.

27 They wrought among them His
manifold signs,
And wonders in the land of Ham.

28 He sent darkness, and it was
dark;
And they rebelled not against His
word.

29 He turned their waters into blood,
And slew their fish.

30 Their land swarmed with frogs,
In the chambers of their kings.

31 He spoke, and there came swarms
of flies,
And gnats in all their borders.

32 He gave them hail for rain,
And flaming fire in their land.

33 He smote their vines also and
their fig-trees;
And broke the trees of their
borders.

26 שָׁלַח מֹשֶׁה עַבְדּוֹ
אַהֲרֹן אֲשֶׁר בָּחַר־בּוֹ:

27 שָׂמוּ־בָם דִּבְרֵי אֹתוֹתָיו
וּמֹפְתִים בְּאֶרֶץ חָם:

28 שָׁלַח חֹשֶׁךְ וַיַּחְשִׁךְ
וְלֹא־מָרוּ אֶת־דְּבָרָיו:

29 הָפַךְ אֶת־מֵימֵיהֶם לְדָם
וַיָּמֶת אֶת־דְּגָתָם:

30 שָׁרַץ אַרְצָם צְפַרְדְּעִים
בְּחַדְרֵי מַלְכֵיהֶם:

31 אָמַר וַיָּבֹא עָרֹב
כִּנִּים בְּכָל־גְּבוּלָם:

32 נָתַן גִּשְׁמֵיהֶם בָּרָד
אֵשׁ לֶהָבוֹת בְּאַרְצָם:

33 וַיַּךְ גַּפְנָם וּתְאֵנָתָם
וַיְשַׁבֵּר עֵץ גְּבוּלָם:

v. 28. דברו ק׳

---

26. *Moses His servant.* As in Exod. xiv. 31
and elsewhere.

Aaron. Cf. Exod. iv. 14ff., 27.

27. *they wrought.* Moses and Aaron acting
on behalf of God (Metsudath David).

His manifold signs. lit. 'the words (matters)
of His signs'; the intention being 'the instructive content' of His signs (Hirsch).

28. *darkness.* The Psalmist does not follow
the Exodus account of the plagues. He begins
with the ninth, omits the fifth and sixth, and
inverts the order of the third and fourth. Why
he began with the ninth is uncertain. Ibn Ezra
thinks it was because this plague forced Pharaoh to consider releasing the Israelites (Exod.
x. 21ff.). It has been suggested that the
Psalmist classified the plagues: the first two
attacked elements, the next three involved

animal life, and the two that followed attacked crops.

they rebelled not against His word. The
plagues took effect precisely as commanded
(Rashi, Kimchi). Ibn Ezra adds that the subject may be Moses and Aaron; they were
faithful to their mission although it involved
them in danger.

29. The first plague, Exod. vii. 14ff.

30. The second plague, Exod. vii. 26ff.

their kings. Pharaoh's household.

31. The fourth and third plagues, Exod.
viii. 16, 12.

32. *hail.* The seventh plague, Exod. ix.
18ff.

flaming fire. Lightning (Exod. ix. 23f.).

33. An elaboration of Exod. ix. 25.

34 He spoke, and the locust came,
And the canker-worm without
number,

35 And did eat up every herb in their
land,
And did eat up the fruit of their
ground.

36 He smote also all the first-born
in their land,
The first-fruits of all their
strength.

37 And He brought them forth with
silver and gold;
And there was none that stumbled
among His tribes.

38 Egypt was glad when they departed;
For the fear of them had fallen
upon them.

39 He spread a cloud for a screen;
And fire to give light in the night.

40 They asked, and He brought
quails,
And gave them in plenty the
bread of heaven.

41 He opened the rock, and waters
gushed out;
They ran, a river in the dry places.

34 אָמַר וַיָּבֹא אַרְבֶּה
וְיֶלֶק וְאֵין מִסְפָּר:
35 וַיֹּאכַל כָּל־עֵשֶׂב בְּאַרְצָם
וַיֹּאכַל פְּרִי אַדְמָתָם:
36 וַיַּךְ כָּל־בְּכוֹר בְּאַרְצָם
רֵאשִׁית לְכָל־אוֹנָם:
37 וַיּוֹצִיאֵם בְּכֶסֶף וְזָהָב
וְאֵין בִּשְׁבָטָיו כּוֹשֵׁל:
38 שָׂמַח מִצְרַיִם בְּצֵאתָם
כִּי־נָפַל פַּחְדָּם עֲלֵיהֶם:
39 פָּרַשׂ עָנָן לְמָסָךְ
וְאֵשׁ לְהָאִיר לָיְלָה:
40 שָׁאַל וַיָּבֵא שְׂלָו
וְלֶחֶם שָׁמַיִם יַשְׂבִּיעֵם:
41 פָּתַח צוּר וַיָּזוּבוּ מָיִם
הָלְכוּ בַּצִּיּוֹת נָהָר:

שליו ק׳   v. 40.

---

34. *locust.* The eighth plague, Exod. x. 4ff.

canker-worm. There are several Hebrew words for 'locusts,' and a different word occurs in lxxviii. 46.

36. The tenth plague, Exod. xi. 1ff.

first-fruits and all their strength. A term for the firstborn (Gen. xlix. 3; Deut. xxi. 17).

37. *with silver and gold.* Cf. Exod. xii. 35f. These *spoils* were in lieu of the wages for their labour which had been withheld.

none that stumbled. Cf. Isa. v. 27. None of the Israelites at the exodus suffered from poverty (Ibn Ezra, Kimchi).

His tribes. Like *the tribes of the* LORD (cxxii. 4).

38. *Egypt was glad.* Cf. Exod. xii. 33.

fear ... upon them. The dread of Israel upon the Egyptians (Exod. xv.16).

39-41   GOD'S CARE OF ISRAEL
IN THE DESERT

39. Cf. Exod. xiii. 21.

40. *they asked.* Hebrew 'he (the people) asked.'

quails. Exod. xvi. 13.

the bread of heaven. Exod. xvi. 4, manna.

41. *opened the rock.* Exod. xvii. 6; cf. lxxviii. 20.

42 For He remembered His holy
   word
   Unto Abraham His servant;

43 And He brought forth His people
   with joy,
   His chosen ones with singing.

44 And He gave them the lands of
   the nations,
   And they took the labour of the
   peoples in possession;

45 That they might keep His
   statutes,
   And observe His laws.
   Hallelujah.

42 כִּי־זָכַר אֶת־דְּבַר קָדְשׁוֹ
אֶת־אַבְרָהָם עַבְדּוֹ:

43 וַיּוֹצִא עַמּוֹ בְשָׂשׂוֹן
בְּרִנָּה אֶת־בְּחִירָיו:

44 וַיִּתֵּן לָהֶם אַרְצוֹת גּוֹיִם
וַעֲמַל לְאֻמִּים יִירָשׁוּ:

45 בַּעֲבוּר ׀ יִשְׁמְרוּ חֻקָּיו
וְתוֹרֹתָיו יִנְצֹרוּ
הַלְלוּיָהּ:

42-45   GOD'S WORD REALIZED

42. After his historical survey, the Psalmist reverts to his earlier theme of verses 8ff., to show how the promise had been fulfilled.

His holy word. The promise guaranteed by God's holiness.

43. *singing.* The song at the Red Sea (Exod. xv.). The Psalmist is perhaps drawing a parallel between the remote past and the great event of his own time, the return of the Ark from captivity, another occasion of going forth *with singing* (cf. *and the ransomed of the LORD shall return, and come with singing unto Zion,* Isa. li. 11).

44. *He gave them.* Cf. the promise in Deut. vi. 10f.

the labour. i.e. the fruits of their labour. viz., the houses they had built, plantations, etc.

45. *that they might keep.* God's fulfillment of His side of the covenant was to be the inducement for the Israelites to be true to their undertaking. The land was given to them so that they would be able to dedicate their lives to the fulfillment of God's laws and to the cultivation of His teachings, while enjoying a peaceful and unmolested existence. The retention of this rich gift was conditional upon loyalty to the covenant (Deut. iv. 40, xxxi. 20) (Kimchi).

106   קו

1 Hallelujah.
O give thanks unto the Lord;
  for He is good;
For His mercy endureth for ever.

2 Who can express the mighty acts
  of the Lord,
Or make all His praise to be heard?

3 Happy are they that keep justice,
That do righteousness at all times.

4 Remember me, O Lord, when
  Thou favourest Thy people;
O think of me at Thy salvation;

5 That I may behold the prosperity
  of Thy chosen,
That I may rejoice in the gladness
  of Thy nation,
That I may glory with Thine inheritance.

הַלְלוּיָהּ ׀

הוֹדוּ לַיהוָה כִּי־טוֹב

כִּי לְעוֹלָם חַסְדּוֹ׃

2 מִי יְמַלֵּל גְּבוּרוֹת יְהוָה

יַשְׁמִיעַ כָּל־תְּהִלָּתוֹ׃

3 אַשְׁרֵי שֹׁמְרֵי מִשְׁפָּט

עֹשֵׂה צְדָקָה בְכָל־עֵת׃

4 זָכְרֵנִי יְהוָה בִּרְצוֹן עַמֶּךָ

פָּקְדֵנִי בִּישׁוּעָתֶךָ׃

5 לִרְאוֹת ׀ בְּטוֹבַת בְּחִירֶיךָ

לִשְׂמֹחַ בְּשִׂמְחַת גּוֹיֶךָ

לְהִתְהַלֵּל עִם־נַחֲלָתֶךָ׃

NATIONAL INFIDELITY

After reviewing the early history of Israel to demonstrate God's faithfulness to His covenant, the Psalmist makes another retrospect for the purpose of bringing into prominence how constant had been Israel's disloyalty and the dire consequences which ensued. Israel is unique in confessing to sin in its own hymns. For the returned exiles it was a salutary theme, because it emphasized the thought that the welfare of the people would be determined by their obedience or disobedience to God's will. Verses i, 47 and 48 are quoted in 1 Chron. xvi. 34-6.

1-5   INTRODUCTORY PRAISE AND PRAYER

1.   A similar liturgical invocation is found at the beginning of cvii., cxviii., cxxxvi.

good. Gracious and lenient.

His mercy. Without which Israel's sinfulness would long ago have brought an end to its national existence.

2.   *who can express.* Human language is inadequate for so tremendous a theme (cf. *If I would declare and speak of them* (God's wondrous works), *they are more than can be told,* xl. 6) (Kimchi).

3.   *justice ... righteousness.* The essential principles of conduct which win God's ap-

proval and bring man true happiness.

at all times. Even when it is to a man's material disadvantage; e.g. *he sweareth to his own hurt, and changeth not* (xv. 4).

4.   The two verses are a personal petition inserted into a congregational liturgy. The individual prays to have the privilege of himself sharing in the better times which are in store for the nation (Metsudath David).

when Thou favourest Thy people. lit. 'in favour of Thy people,' i.e. in the favour which Thou wilt display unto Thy people.

5.   *Thy chosen.* Cf. cv. 6, 43.

Thine inheritance. Israel (xxxiii. 12).

6 We have sinned with our fathers,
We have done iniquitously, we
have dealt wickedly.

7 Our fathers in Egypt gave no heed
unto Thy wonders;
They remembered not the multitude of Thy mercies;
But were rebellious at the sea, even
at the Red Sea.

8 Nevertheless He saved them for
His name's sake,
That He might make His mighty
power to be known.

9 And He rebuked the Red Sea, and
it was dried up;
And He led them through the
depths, as through a wilderness.

10 And He saved them from the
hand of him that hated them,
And redeemed them from the
hand of the enemy.

6 חָטָאנוּ עִם־אֲבוֹתֵינוּ
הֶעֱוִינוּ הִרְשָׁעְנוּ׃
7 אֲבוֹתֵינוּ בְמִצְרַיִם ׀ לֹא־הִשְׂכִּילוּ
נִפְלְאוֹתֶיךָ
לֹא זָכְרוּ אֶת־רֹב חֲסָדֶיךָ
וַיַּמְרוּ עַל־יָם בְּיַם־סוּף׃
8 וַיּוֹשִׁיעֵם לְמַעַן שְׁמוֹ
לְהוֹדִיעַ אֶת־גְּבוּרָתוֹ׃
9 וַיִּגְעַר בְּיַם־סוּף וַיֶּחֱרָב
וַיּוֹלִיכֵם בַּתְּהֹמוֹת כַּמִּדְבָּר׃
10 וַיּוֹשִׁיעֵם מִיַּד שׂוֹנֵא
וַיִּגְאָלֵם מִיַּד אוֹיֵב׃

6-12 ISRAEL AT THE RED SEA

6. The Psalmist now enters upon the subject of his composition, the persistent backsliding of the nation, of which seven illustrations are cited.

we have sinned with our fathers. More than
the idea that the present generation has been
as culpable as the generations of the past is
intended in the verse. *We have done iniquitously ... wickedly* stresses that our sinning
has been deliberate and planned, while that
of our forefathers was solely a result of succumbing to temptations (Malbim). The three
verbs for the act of sinning occur together in
1 Kings viii. 47.

7. *gave no heed unto*. The national mentality should have been left with an indelible
impression by the miraculous happenings in
Egypt. It failed in this because of lack of
understanding. (Cf. Moses' denunciation in
Deut. xxxii. 28ff.).

rebellious at the sea. Before the crossing they
had cried, *It were better for us to serve the
Egyptians, than that we should die in the
wilderness* (Exod. xiv. 12), in spite of what
God had done for them in Egypt.

8. *for His name's sake*. God overlooked the
people's want of faith in Him and wrought
salvation for them although they did not
deserve it. In doing so, He had two motives:
first, as the prophet declared, *I wrought for
My name's sake, that it should not be profaned in the sight of the nations, among
whom they were, in whose sight I made
Myself known unto them* (Ezek. xx. 9)
(Malbim); and second, which follows from
the first, to establish the truth for all men and
nations that there was a Power protecting the
weak against the ruthless strong.

9. *rebuked*. See on civ. 7.

a wilderness. The sea bed dried up so thoroughly that it became arid like a desert
(Malbim).

11 And the waters covered their
   adversaries;
   There was not one of them left.

12 Then believed they His words;
   They sang His praise.

13 They soon forgot His works;
   They waited not for His counsel;

14 But lusted exceedingly in the
   wilderness,
   And tried God in the desert.

15 And He gave them their request;
   But sent leanness into their soul.

16 They were jealous also of Moses
   in the camp,
   And of Aaron the holy one of the
   LORD.

17 The earth opened and swallowed
   up Dathan,
   And covered the company of
   Abiram.

18 And a fire was kindled in their
   company;
   The flame burned up the wicked.

11 וַיְכַסּוּ־מַ֫יִם צָרֵיהֶ֑ם
אֶחָ֥ד מֵהֶ֗ם לֹ֣א נוֹתָֽר׃
12 וַיַּאֲמִ֥ינוּ בִדְבָרָ֑יו
יָ֝שִׁ֗ירוּ תְּהִלָּתֽוֹ׃
13 מִֽ֭הֲרוּ שָׁכְח֣וּ מַעֲשָׂ֑יו
לֹֽא־חִ֝כּ֗וּ לַעֲצָתֽוֹ׃
14 וַיִּתְאַוּ֣וּ תַ֭אֲוָה בַּמִּדְבָּ֑ר
וַיְנַסּוּ־אֵ֗ל בִּישִׁימֽוֹן׃
15 וַיִּתֵּ֣ן לָ֭הֶם שֶׁאֱלָתָ֑ם
וַיְשַׁלַּ֖ח רָז֣וֹן בְּנַפְשָֽׁם׃
16 וַיְקַנְא֣וּ לְ֭מֹשֶׁה בַּֽמַּחֲנֶ֑ה
לְ֝אַהֲרֹ֗ן קְד֣וֹשׁ יְהֹוָֽה׃
17 תִּפְתַּח־אֶ֭רֶץ וַתִּבְלַ֣ע דָּתָ֑ן
וַ֝תְּכַ֗ס עַל־עֲדַ֥ת אֲבִירָֽם׃
18 וַתִּבְעַר־אֵ֥שׁ בַּעֲדָתָ֑ם
לֶ֝הָבָ֗ה תְּלַהֵ֥ט רְשָׁעִֽים׃

11. Recalling Exod. xiv. 28.

12. *then believed they.* Exod. xiv. 31.

they sang His praise. Exod. xv. 1.

13-15 ISRAEL LUSTED FOR MEAT

13. *they soon forgot.* lit. 'they hurried and forgot.' Only three days after the crossing they began to murmur for water (Exod. xv. 22), and six weeks later for food (Exod. xvi. 3).

waited not for His counsel. They did not allow God the opportunity of revealing His plan to provide for them.

14. *lusted exceedingly.* From Num. xi. 4.

tried. lit. 'put to the test,' by their demand for the immediate satisfaction of their needs and refusal to trust Him.

15. The eating of meat did not improve their physical condition. On the contrary, in place of life and vigour, they were stricken with sickness and death. The 'graves of lust' marked the scene of their sin and its punishment (Metsudath David).

16-18 ISRAEL'S REVOLT

16. *jealous also of Moses.* Num. xvi.

the holy one of the LORD. Aaron had been designated by God for the holy office of priesthood; but Korah and his followers advanced the plea *all the congregation were holy*, to which Moses retorted, *the LORD will show ... who is holy.*

17. *Dathan ... Abiram.* As in Deut. xi. 6. Rashi remarks that the Psalmist omitted the name of Korah in connection with the revolt from consideration of the Korahites who ministered in the Temple.

18. Num. xvi. 35.

the wicked. The rebels, Num. xvi. 26.

19 They made a calf in Horeb,
And worshipped a molten image.

20 Thus they exchanged their glory
For the likeness of an ox that
eateth grass.

21 They forgot God their saviour,
Who had done great things in
Egypt;

22 Wondrous works in the land of
Ham,
Terrible things by the Red Sea.

23 Therefore He said that He would
destroy them,
Had not Moses His chosen stood
before Him in the breach,
To turn back His wrath, lest He
should destroy them.

24 Moreover, they scorned the
desirable land,
They believed not His word;

25 And they murmured in their tents,
They hearkened not unto the
voice of the Lord.

26 Therefore He swore concerning
them,
That He would overthrow them
in the wilderness;

19‏ יַעֲשׂוּ־עֵגֶל בְּחֹרֵב

וַיִּשְׁתַּחֲווּ לְמַסֵּכָה׃

20‏ וַיָּמִירוּ אֶת־כְּבוֹדָם

בְּתַבְנִית שׁוֹר אֹכֵל עֵשֶׂב׃

21‏ שָׁכְחוּ אֵל מוֹשִׁיעָם

עֹשֶׂה גְדֹלוֹת בְּמִצְרָיִם׃

22‏ נִפְלָאוֹת בְּאֶרֶץ חָם

נוֹרָאוֹת עַל־יַם־סוּף׃

23‏ וַיֹּאמֶר לְהַשְׁמִידָם

לוּלֵי מֹשֶׁה בְחִירוֹ

עָמַד בַּפֶּרֶץ לְפָנָיו

לְהָשִׁיב חֲמָתוֹ מֵהַשְׁחִית׃

24‏ וַיִּמְאֲסוּ בְּאֶרֶץ חֶמְדָּה

לֹא־הֶאֱמִינוּ לִדְבָרוֹ׃

25‏ וַיֵּרָגְנוּ בְאָהֳלֵיהֶם

לֹא שָׁמְעוּ בְּקוֹל יְהֹוָה׃

26‏ וַיִּשָּׂא יָדוֹ לָהֶם

לְהַפִּיל אוֹתָם בַּמִּדְבָּר׃

19-23   SIN OF THE GOLDEN CALF

19.   *a calf.* Exod. xxxii.

in Horeb. Deut. ix. 8ff. Horeb is identical to Sinai, where the Golden Calf was made.

20.   *their glory.* God Who had revealed Himself in His glorious attributes. According to tradition the text should read 'His glory' (Targum 'the glory of their Lord'), but was toned down from a sense of reverence.

22.   *land of Ham.* See on lxxviii. 51.

23.   *destroy them.* Cf. Deut. ix. 25.

stood ... breach. Like a soldier who, in peril of his life, takes his stand where the enemy has made an opening in the city's defences, so Moses stood between the sinful people and God in His anger (cf. Metsudath David).

24-27   INCIDENT OF THE SPIES

24.   *scorned.* Or 'rejected' (Num. xiv. 31).

the desirable land. Canaan is again so described in Jer. iii. 19; Zech. vii. 14.

they believed not His word. And urged the sending of spies to report on the land and its inhabitants (Deut. i. 22).

25.   *they murmured in their tents.* From Deut. i. 27.

26.   *He swore.* lit. 'He raised His hand.' A man, when taking an oath, lifts his hand heavenwards, invoking God as his Witness. The same phrase is used of God in the act of swearing (cf. Exod. vi. 8; Deut. xxxii. 40).

27 And that He would cast out **their**
   seed among the nations,
   And scatter them in the lands.

28 They joined themselves also **unto**
   Baal of Peor,
   And ate the sacrifices of the dead.

29 Thus they provoked Him with
   their doings,
   And the plague broke in upon
   them.

30 Then stood up Phinehas, and
   wrought judgment,
   And so the plague was stayed.

31 And that was counted unto him
   for righteousness,
   Unto all generations **for ever.**

32 They angered Him also at **the**
   waters of Meribah,
   And it went ill with Moses because of them;

33 For they embittered his spirit,
   And he spoke rashly with his lips.

כז וַלְהַפִּיל זַרְעָם בַּגּוֹיִם
וּלְזָרוֹתָם בָּאֲרָצוֹת:
כח וַיִּצָּמְדוּ לְבַעַל פְּעוֹר
וַיֹּאכְלוּ זִבְחֵי מֵתִים:
כט וַיַּכְעִיסוּ בְּמַעַלְלֵיהֶם
וַתִּפְרָץ־בָּם מַגֵּפָה:
ל וַיַּעֲמֹד פִּינְחָס וַיְפַלֵּל
וַתֵּעָצַר הַמַּגֵּפָה:
לא וַתֵּחָשֶׁב לוֹ לִצְדָקָה
לְדֹר וָדֹר עַד־עוֹלָם:
לב וַיַּקְצִיפוּ עַל־מֵי מְרִיבָה
וַיֵּרַע לְמֹשֶׁה בַּעֲבוּרָם:
לג כִּי־הִמְרוּ אֶת־רוּחוֹ
וַיְבַטֵּא בִּשְׂפָתָיו:

---

27. Almost verbatim from Ezek. xx. 23.

    28-31 SIN AT PEOR

28. *joined themselves.* Num. xxv. 3.

Baal of Peor. The heathen deity worshipped
in Peor (Num. xxiii. 28, xxiv. 3; cf. Rashi).

ate the sacrifices of the dead. An elaboration
of *and the people did eat* (Num. xxv. 2). The
allusion is to the meal eaten in common as a
religious rite, contemptuously described as
the flesh of offerings to *dead* gods, lifeless
idols.

29. *plague.* Num. xxv. 8f.

30. *wrought judgment.* So Ibn Ezra; another rendering is: 'and he prayed' (Targum).

31. *counted unto him for righteousness.*
The same commendation as Abraham earned
(Gen. xv. 6).

unto all generations. His reward was *the*

covenant of an everlasting priesthood (Num.
xxv. 13).

   32-33 MURMURING AT MERIBAH

32. *Meribah.* Cf. xcv. 8; Num. xx. 13.

it went ill with Moses. He then committed the
act which had as its consequence his exclusion from Canaan (Num. xx. 12).

33. *they embittered his spirit.* A.J., following Kimchi, takes *they* as the people and
his to allude to Moses, whom the people
caused to lose self-control and utter rash
words (Num. xx.10). According to Rashi and
Ibn Ezra, *they* are Moses and Aaron, and *his
spirit* is God's (cf. Isa. lxiii.10). Moses and
Aaron were both involved in striking the rock
rather than speaking to it, causing God's
wrath to be roused and His forbidding their
entry into the promised land.

34 They did not destroy the peoples,
As the Lord commanded them;

35 But mingled themselves with the
nations,
And learned their works;

36 And they served their idols,
Which became a snare unto them;

37 Yea, they sacrificed their sons
and their daughters unto
demons,

38 And shed innocent blood, even
the blood of their sons and of
their daughters,
Whom they sacrificed unto the
idols of Canaan;
And the land was polluted with
blood.

39 Thus were they defiled with their
works,
And went astray in their doings.

40 Therefore was the wrath of the
Lord kindled against His
people,
And He abhorred His inheritance.

41 And He gave them into the hand
of the nations;
And they that hated them ruled
over them.

42 Their enemies also oppressed
them,
And they were subdued under
their hand.

לֹא־הִשְׁמִידוּ אֶת־הָעַמִּים 34
אֲשֶׁר אָמַר יְהוָה לָהֶם:
וַיִּתְעָרְבוּ בַגּוֹיִם 35
וַיִּלְמְדוּ מַעֲשֵׂיהֶם:
וַיַּעַבְדוּ אֶת־עֲצַבֵּיהֶם 36
וַיִּהְיוּ לָהֶם לְמוֹקֵשׁ:
וַיִּזְבְּחוּ אֶת־בְּנֵיהֶם 37
וְאֶת־בְּנוֹתֵיהֶם לַשֵּׁדִים:
וַיִּשְׁפְּכוּ דָם נָקִי 38
דַּם־בְּנֵיהֶם וּבְנוֹתֵיהֶם
אֲשֶׁר זִבְּחוּ לַעֲצַבֵּי כְנָעַן
וַתֶּחֱנַף הָאָרֶץ בַּדָּמִים:
וַיִּטְמְאוּ בְמַעֲשֵׂיהֶם 39
וַיִּזְנוּ בְּמַעַלְלֵיהֶם:
וַיִּחַר־אַף יְהוָה בְּעַמּוֹ 40
וַיְתָעֵב אֶת־נַחֲלָתוֹ:
וַיִּתְּנֵם בְּיַד־גּוֹיִם 41
וַיִּמְשְׁלוּ בָהֶם שֹׂנְאֵיהֶם:
וַיִּלְחָצוּם אוֹיְבֵיהֶם 42
וַיִּכָּנְעוּ תַּחַת יָדָם:

34-39   DISOBEDIENCE AFTER
ENTERING CANAAN

34. The command of Deut. vii. 2ff. was not
obeyed (Judges i. 21, 27ff.).

35. *mingled themselves*. By intermarriage.

36. *which became*. Render, 'and they (the
inhabitants of Canaan) became.'

a snare. As foretold in Exod. xxiii. 33.

37. *demons*. Hebrew *shedim* (cf. Deut.
xxxii.17). A reference to the idols worshipped by the nations (Meiri). Hirsch explains 'shedim' as invisible forces injurious
to growth and prosperity.

38. That Israelites at times assimilated this
rite is attested by Ezek. xvi. 20f.

land was polluted. Cf Num. xxxv. 33.

39. *went astray*. The Hebrew denotes immorality, and is used of disloyalty to God
because the covenant relationship is likened
to the marriage vow.

40-43   RESULTANT PUNISHMENT

40. *wrath ... people*. A recurrent phrase in
the Book of Judges.

His inheritance. Israel.

41. *the nations*. Heathen peoples.

43 Many times did He deliver them;
But they were rebellious in their
counsel,
And sank low through their
iniquity.

44 Nevertheless He looked upon
their distress,
When He heard their cry;

45 And He remembered for them
His covenant,
And repented according to the
multitude of His mercies.

46 He made them also to be pitied
Of all those that carried them
captive.

47 Save us, O Lord our God,
And gather us from among the
nations,
That we may give thanks unto
Thy holy name,
That we may triumph in Thy
praise.

48 Blessed be the Lord, the God of
Israel,
From everlasting even to ever-
lasting.
And let all the people say:
'Amen.'
Hallelujah.

43 פְּעָמִים רַבּוֹת יַצִּילֵם
וְהֵמָּה יַמְרוּ בַעֲצָתָם
וַיָּמֹכּוּ בַּעֲוֺנָם׃
44 וַיַּרְא בַּצַּר לָהֶם
בְּשָׁמְעוֹ אֶת־רִנָּתָם׃
45 וַיִּזְכֹּר לָהֶם בְּרִיתוֹ
וַיִּנָּחֵם כְּרֹב חֲסָדָו׃
46 וַיִּתֵּן אוֹתָם לְרַחֲמִים
לִפְנֵי כָּל־שׁוֹבֵיהֶם׃
47 הוֹשִׁיעֵנוּ ׀ יְהוָה אֱלֹהֵינוּ
וְקַבְּצֵנוּ מִן־הַגּוֹיִם
לְהֹדוֹת לְשֵׁם קָדְשֶׁךָ
לְהִשְׁתַּבֵּחַ בִּתְהִלָּתֶךָ׃
48 בָּרוּךְ יְהוָה ׀ אֱלֹהֵי יִשְׂרָאֵל
מִן־הָעוֹלָם ׀ וְעַד הָעוֹלָם
וְאָמַר כָּל־הָעָם אָמֵן
הַלְלוּיָהּ׃

חסדיו ק׳ v. 45.

42. *were subdued*. Better, 'brought into subjection.'

43. *many times*. Through judges like Gideon, Jephthah and Samson.

rebellious in their counsel. Refusing to take to heart the lesson of past experience and persisting in their evil ways.

44-46 GOD REMEMBERED HIS COVENANT

45. *repented*. See on xc. 13.

46. *made them also to be pitied*. Made them the objects of pity (cf. 1 Kings viii. 50).

47 CONCLUDING PRAYER

The last two verses of the Psalm take the form of a direct plea to God. We must hope and pray that in view of the loving kindness He has shown us in the past, the Lord may also bring about our ultimate deliverance so that we may render homage to His name by devoting our lives to Him and thus glory in His greatness which will be clearly displayed to all (Hirsch).

1 'O give thanks unto the LORD,
    for He is good,
  For His mercy endureth for ever.'

2 So let the redeemed of the LORD
    say,
  Whom He hath redeemed from
    the hand of the adversary;

3 And gathered them out of the
    lands,
  From the east and from the west,
  From the north and from the sea.

דּוּ לַיהוָה כִּי־טֽוֹב
כִּי לְעוֹלָם חַסְדּֽוֹ:
יֹאמְרוּ גְּאוּלֵי יְהוָה   2
אֲשֶׁר גְּאָלָם מִיַּד־צָֽר:
וּֽמֵאֲרָצוֹת קִבְּצָם   3
מִמִּזְרָח וּמִֽמַּעֲרָב
מִצָּפוֹן וּמִיָּֽם:

DIVINE PROVIDENCE

ALTHOUGH a new Book begins with this Psalm, it is closely linked with the preceding and may
be regarded as a continuation of the series. Four word-pictures are drawn by the poet as
circumstances of distress in which man is dependent upon God's mercy, and they are all
applicable to the bitter experience of Israel in exile. That the people survived the hardships
and trials provides occasion for heartfelt praise to be offered to Him. At verse 33 the subject
matter assumes a different form, and the Psalmist meditates upon the changes in fortune which
befall countries generally and sees in them also the working of God's purpose. There is a
difference of opinion concerning the historical setting of the composition. Alshich opines that
the Psalm is a form of thanksgiving for the redemption from Egyptian bondage and the
subsequent passage through sea and desert. Sforno sees it as a future song for those who will
survive the present exile, while Ibn Yahiya connects it again with David's own troubled times
when the holy Ark was captured, and later safely returned to its sanctuary.

1-3 SUMMONS TO PRAISE GOD
FROM THE REDEEMED SLAVES

1. See on cvi.1.

2. *the redeemed of the LORD*. Cf. Isa. lxii.
12, *and they shall call them* (the returned
captives) *the holy people, the redeemed of
the LORD*.

adversary. Perhaps to be translated 'adversity.' It is the same word as *trouble* in verse 6.

3. *gathered them out of the lands*. God had
answered the prayer of cvi. 47, *gather us from*

among the nations. The mention of *lands* (in
the plural) signifies that the Israelites will be
scattered the world over before final redemption (Midrash Shocher Tov).

from the sea. This term usually means the
west, but here the south is required. The
Targum renders 'the sea of the south,' which
may indicate the Red Sea or the part of the
Mediterranean that borders on Egypt. The
words bring to mind those of Isa. xlix.12,
although 'sea' there means west.

4 They wandered in the wilderness
    in a desert way;
  They found no city of habitation.

5 Hungry and thirsty,
  Their soul fainted in them.

6 Then they cried unto the Lord
    in their trouble,
  And He delivered them out of
    their distresses.

7 And He led them by a straight way,
  That they might go to a city of
    habitation.

8 Let them give thanks unto the
    Lord for His mercy,
  And for His wonderful works to
    the children of men!

9 For He hath satisfied the longing
    soul,
  And the hungry soul He hath filled
    with good.

10 Such as sat in darkness and in the
    shadow of death,
  Being bound in affliction and
    iron—

11 Because they rebelled against the
    words of God,
  And contemned the counsel of
    the Most High.

4 תָּעוּ בַמִּדְבָּר בִּישִׁימוֹן דָּרֶךְ
עִיר מוֹשָׁב לֹא מָצָאוּ:

5 רְעֵבִים גַּם־צְמֵאִים
נַפְשָׁם בָּהֶם תִּתְעַטָּף:

6 וַיִּצְעֲקוּ אֶל־יְהוָה בַּצַּר לָהֶם
מִמְּצוּקוֹתֵיהֶם יַצִּילֵם:

7 וַיַּדְרִיכֵם בְּדֶרֶךְ יְשָׁרָה
לָלֶכֶת אֶל־עִיר מוֹשָׁב:

8 יוֹדוּ לַיהוָה חַסְדּוֹ
וְנִפְלְאוֹתָיו לִבְנֵי אָדָם:

9 כִּי־הִשְׂבִּיעַ נֶפֶשׁ שֹׁקֵקָה
וְנֶפֶשׁ רְעֵבָה מִלֵּא־טוֹב:

10 יֹשְׁבֵי חֹשֶׁךְ וְצַלְמָוֶת
אֲסִירֵי עֳנִי וּבַרְזֶל:

11 כִּי־הִמְרוּ אִמְרֵי־אֵל
וַעֲצַת עֶלְיוֹן נָאָצוּ:

4-9   FIRST ILLUSTRATION:
GOD'S CARE OF LOST TRAVELLERS

4. *they wandered.* The verb denotes aimless wandering and in the Hebrew idiom the subject is not specified, being understood from the context. In English the paraphrase would be, 'travellers went astray.'

in a desert way. Or, 'a path of desolation' where no marked paths are to be found as a guide of direction, and is, therefore, difficult to follow (Hirsch).

city of habitation. A place of lodging and food; again in verses 7, 36.

5. *their soul fainted in them.* They were in an exhausted condition.

6. The verse occurs, with variation of verb, as a refrain in the four illustrations, verses 13, 19, 28.

7. *by a straight way.* By the quickest and easiest route.

8. *let them give thanks.* The travellers who had experienced God's mercy. The verse is repeated in verses 15, 21, 31.

9. Cf. Jer. xxxi. 25.

10-16   SECOND ILLUSTRATION:
GOD'S CARE OF CAPTIVES

10. *sat in darkness.* Used in Isa. xlii. 7 of exiles. It may be understood literally of prisoners whose dungeons were without light.

shadow of death. See on xxiii. 4.

being bound in affliction and iron. Cf. cv. 18; Job xxxvi. 8.

11. Their sufferings were the penalty of transgressing God's will; so again in verses 17, 34.

12 Therefore He humbled their
    heart with travail,
    They stumbled, and there was
    none to help—

13 They cried unto the LORD in their
    trouble,
    And He saved them out of their
    distresses.

14 He brought them out of darkness
    and the shadow of death,
    And broke their bands in sunder.

15 Let them give thanks unto the
    LORD for His mercy,
    And for His wonderful works to
    the children of men!

16 For He hath broken the gates of
    brass,
    And cut the bars of iron in
    sunder.

17 Crazed because of the way of
    their transgression,
    And afflicted because of their
    iniquities—

18 Their soul abhorred all manner
    of food,
    And they drew near unto the
    gates of death—

19 They cried unto the LORD in their
    trouble,
    And He saved them out of their
    distresses;

12 וַיַּכְנַע בֶּעָמָל לִבָּם

כָּשְׁלוּ וְאֵין עֹזֵר:

13 וַיִּזְעֲקוּ אֶל־יְהוָה בַּצַּר לָהֶם

מִמְּצֻקוֹתֵיהֶם יוֹשִׁיעֵם:

14 יוֹצִיאֵם מֵחֹשֶׁךְ וְצַלְמָוֶת

וּמוֹסְרוֹתֵיהֶם יְנַתֵּק:

15 יוֹדוּ לַיהוָה חַסְדּוֹ

וְנִפְלְאוֹתָיו לִבְנֵי אָדָם:

16 כִּי־שִׁבַּר דַּלְתוֹת נְחֹשֶׁת

וּבְרִיחֵי בַרְזֶל גִּדֵּעַ:

17 אֱוִלִים מִדֶּרֶךְ פִּשְׁעָם

וּמֵעֲוֹנֹתֵיהֶם יִתְעַנּוּ:

18 כָּל־אֹכֶל תְּתַעֵב נַפְשָׁם

וַיַּגִּיעוּ עַד־שַׁעֲרֵי־מָוֶת:

19 וַיִּזְעֲקוּ אֶל־יְהוָה בַּצַּר לָהֶם

מִמְּצֻקוֹתֵיהֶם יוֹשִׁיעֵם:

12. *He humbled.* Better, 'He brought into subjection,' as in cvi. 42.

14. *bands.* The fetters in which they were bound.

16. Though the dungeons be guarded with heavy iron gates, reinforced with bolts, God will break through them to redeem its prisoners (Kimchi).

    17-22 THIRD ILLUSTRATION:
    GOD HEALS THOSE SMITTEN WITH
    SICKNESS FOR THEIR SINS

17. In this section the words are similar to those in Job xxxiii.19-26.

crazed. lit. 'fools.' *The foolish despise wisdom and discipline* (Prov. i. 7), preferring the path of sin which leads to afflictions.

afflicted. The form of the verb may signify 'afflicted themselves,' i.e. brought sufferings upon themselves (cf. Hirsch).

18. *abhorred all manner of food.* A common symptom in very sick people.

the gates of death. See on ix. 14.

20 He sent His word, and healed
   them,
   And delivered them from their
   graves.

21 Let them give thanks unto the
   LORD for His mercy,
   And for His wonderful works to
   the children of men!

22 And let them offer the sacrifices
   of thanksgiving,
   And declare His works with
   singing.

23 They that go down to the sea in
   ships,
   That do business in great waters—

24 These saw the works of the LORD,
   And His wonders in the deep;

25 For He commanded, and raised
   the stormy wind,
   Which lifted up the waves thereof;

26 They mounted up to the heaven,
   they went down to the deeps;
   Their soul melted away because
   · of trouble;

27 They reeled to and fro, and stag-
   gered like a drunken man,
   And all their wisdom was swallowed up—

20 יִשְׁלַח דְּבָרוֹ וְיִרְפָּאֵם
   וִימַלֵּט מִשְּׁחִיתוֹתָם:
21 יוֹדוּ לַיהוָה חַסְדּוֹ
   וְנִפְלְאוֹתָיו לִבְנֵי אָדָם:
22 וְיִזְבְּחוּ זִבְחֵי תוֹדָה
   וִיסַפְּרוּ מַעֲשָׂיו בְּרִנָּה:
23 יוֹרְדֵי הַיָּם בָּאֳנִיּוֹת
   עֹשֵׂי מְלָאכָה בְּמַיִם רַבִּים:
24 הֵמָּה רָאוּ מַעֲשֵׂי יְהוָה
   וְנִפְלְאוֹתָיו בִּמְצוּלָה:
25 וַיֹּאמֶר וַיַּעֲמֵד רוּחַ סְעָרָה
   וַתְּרוֹמֵם גַּלָּיו:
26 יַעֲלוּ שָׁמַיִם יֵרְדוּ תְהוֹמוֹת
   נַפְשָׁם בְּרָעָה תִתְמוֹגָג:
27 יָחוֹגּוּ וְיָנוּעוּ כַּשִּׁכּוֹר
   וְכָל־חָכְמָתָם תִּתְבַּלָּע:

20. *sent His word*. As in cxlvii. 15, 18, God's *word* is personified as His messenger fulfilling His command.

graves. lit. 'pits' (cf. ciii. 4), to which their bodies would have been consigned after death.

22. *sacrifices of thanksgiving*. As in cxvi. 17.

23-32 FOURTH ILLUSTRATION:
GOD'S CARE OF SEA-VOYAGERS

23. *that do business*. Whose trade requires them to make journeys in ships.

24. *works ... wonders*. God's acts of de-

liverance from the perils of the sea.

25. The portrayal is of a seafarer during a storm, who is entirely at the mercy of God. The waves are called 'His' because they are at His command and execute His will with regard to ships that sail on them (Hirsch).

26. *they mounted up*. The subject is the passengers (Kimchi) or the waves (Ibn Ezra).

their soul melted away. In terror (cf. Exod. xv. 15).

27. *all their wisdom*. In the art of naviga-tion (Ibn Ezra). A.V. and R.V. paraphrase, *and are at their wits' end*.

28 They cried unto the LORD in their
    trouble,
    And He brought them out of
    their distresses.

29 He made the storm a calm,
    So that the waves thereof were
    still.

30 Then were they glad because
    they were quiet,
    And He led them unto their de-
    sired haven.

31 Let them give thanks unto the
    LORD for His mercy,
    And for His wonderful works to
    the children of men!

32 Let them exalt Him also in the
    assembly of the people,
    And praise Him in the seat of the
    elders.

33 He turneth rivers into a wilder-
    ness,
    And watersprings into a thirsty
    ground;

34 A fruitful land into a salt waste,
    For the wickedness of them that
    dwell therein.

35 He turneth a wilderness into a
    pool of water,
    And a dry land into watersprings.

28 וַיִּצְעֲקוּ אֶל־יְהוָה בַּצַּר לָהֶם
וּמִמְּצוּקֹתֵיהֶם יוֹצִיאֵם׃
29 יָקֵם סְעָרָה לִדְמָמָה
וַיֶּחֱשׁוּ גַּלֵּיהֶם׃
30 וַיִּשְׂמְחוּ כִי־יִשְׁתֹּקוּ
וַיַּנְחֵם אֶל־מְחוֹז חֶפְצָם׃
31 יוֹדוּ לַיהוָה חַסְדּוֹ
וְנִפְלְאוֹתָיו לִבְנֵי אָדָם׃
32 וִירוֹמְמוּהוּ בִּקְהַל־עָם
וּבְמוֹשַׁב זְקֵנִים יְהַלְלוּהוּ׃
33 יָשֵׂם נְהָרוֹת לְמִדְבָּר
וּמֹצָאֵי מַיִם לְצִמָּאוֹן׃
34 אֶרֶץ פְּרִי לִמְלֵחָה
מֵרָעַת יוֹשְׁבֵי בָהּ׃
35 יָשֵׂם מִדְבָּר לַאֲגַם־מַיִם
וְאֶרֶץ צִיָּה לְמֹצָאֵי מָיִם׃

---

29. *He made the storm a calm.* lit. 'He
maketh a storm to rise to silence,' meaning:
after raising a storm He reduces it to silence.

30. *they were quiet.* i.e., the waves.

haven. In Assyrian and in the Talmud the
word has the meaning of 'city,' especially a
market-town.

32. *in the assembly of the people.* Whenever an opportunity of public acknowledgment occurs.

33-38   GOD'S CONTROL
       OF MAN'S HABITATION

33. *rivers into a wilderness.* Cf. Isa. l. 2. By
rivers is meant land which is abundantly
watered by streams.

watersprings ... ground. Cf. Isa. xxxv. 7.

34. *a salt waste.* Descriptive of barren soil,
to which Sodom [and Gomorrah] were reduced (Deut. xxix. 22) (Targum).

35. Cf. Isa. xli. 18.

36 And there He maketh the hungry
  to dwell,
 And they establish a city of
  habitation;

37 And sow fields, and plant vine-
  yards,
 Which yield fruits of increase.

38 He blesseth them also, so that
  they are multiplied greatly,
 And suffereth not their cattle to
  decrease.

39 Again, they are minished and
  dwindle away
 Through oppression of evil and
  sorrow.

40 He poureth contempt upon
  princes,
 And causeth them to wander in
  the waste, where there is no
  way.

41 Yet setteth He the needy on high
  from affliction,
 And maketh his families like a
  flock.

42 The upright see it, and are glad;
 And all iniquity stoppeth her
  mouth.

43 Whoso is wise, let him observe
  these things,
 And let them consider the mercies
  of the LORD.

וַיּוֹשֶׁב שָׁם רְעֵבִים 36
וַיְכוֹנְנוּ עִיר מוֹשָׁב:
וַיִּזְרְעוּ שָׂדוֹת וַיִּטְּעוּ כְרָמִים 37
וַיַּעֲשׂוּ פְּרִי תְבוּאָה:
וַיְבָרֲכֵם וַיִּרְבּוּ מְאֹד 38
וּבְהֶמְתָּם לֹא יַמְעִיט:
וַיִּמְעֲטוּ וַיָּשֹׁחוּ 39
מֵעֹצֶר רָעָה וְיָגוֹן:
שֹׁפֵךְ בּוּז עַל־נְדִיבִים 40
וַיַּתְעֵם בְּתֹהוּ לֹא־דָרֶךְ:
וַיְשַׂגֵּב אֶבְיוֹן מֵעוֹנִי 41
וַיָּשֶׂם כַּצֹּאן מִשְׁפָּחוֹת:
יִרְאוּ יְשָׁרִים וְיִשְׂמָחוּ 42
וְכָל־עַוְלָה קָפְצָה פִּיהָ:
מִי־חָכָם וְיִשְׁמָר־אֵלֶּה 43
וְיִתְבּוֹנְנוּ חַסְדֵי יְהוָה:

36. *maketh the hungry to dwell.* Because the former wilderness has now become fertile.

38. *blesseth them.* Who had previously been *hungry* (verse 36). (Ibn Ezra).

39-42 HE DEFENDS HIS PEOPLE AGAINST ATTACKERS

39. Translate: 'And when they are reduced in numbers and brought low by oppressive empires and [physical] harm and [financial] woe.' Their prosperity will lead them to sin and the neighbouring countries will attack them, bringing upon them misery and suffering (cf. Kimchi, Malbim).

40. Also in Job. xii. 21, 24. The *princes* are the rulers of the invading nations whom God overthrows and scatters.

41. *on high.* Above the reach of affliction which is compared to rising waters.

like a flock. Many in number.

42. *the upright ... glad.* Cf. Job xxii. 19.

all iniquity ... mouth. Cf. Job v. 16. Evil-doers will cease their taunts when they take note of the downfall of the unscrupulous, as a result of God's judgment.

43 MORAL FOR THE WISE

From the facts detailed above, those who are understanding of heart will learn to see the hand of God at work in the affairs of man (cf. Hosea xiv.10).

108   קח

1 A Song, a Psalm of David.

2 My heart is stedfast, O God;
I will sing, yea, I will sing praises,
even with my glory.

3 Awake, psaltery and harp;
I will awake the dawn.

4 I will give thanks unto Thee, O
LORD, among the peoples;
And I will sing praises unto Thee
among the nations.

5 For Thy mercy is great above the
heavens,
And Thy truth reacheth unto the
skies.

6 Be Thou exalted, O God, above
the heavens;
And Thy glory be above all the
earth.

שִׁיר מִזְמוֹר לְדָוִד׃

2 נָכוֹן לִבִּי אֱלֹהִים
אָשִׁירָה וַאֲזַמְּרָה אַף־כְּבוֹדִי׃

3 עוּרָה הַנֵּבֶל וְכִנּוֹר
אָעִירָה שָּׁחַר׃

4 אוֹדְךָ בָעַמִּים יְהוָה
וַאֲזַמֶּרְךָ בַּלְאֻמִּים׃

5 כִּי־גָדֹל מֵעַל־שָׁמַיִם חַסְדֶּךָ
וְעַד־שְׁחָקִים אֲמִתֶּךָ׃

6 רוּמָה עַל־שָׁמַיִם אֱלֹהִים
וְעַל כָּל־הָאָרֶץ כְּבוֹדֶךָ׃

THANKSGIVING AND PRAYER

Two extracts from earlier Psalms are the constituents of this Psalm. Verses 2-6 correspond with lvii. 8-12, and verses 7-14 with lx. 7-14. It seems that the selection and combination here bring a new meaning to the future when the Messiah will deliver Israel from exile and lead them in the conquest over their enemies (Kimchi). In the Commentary the points of variation are noted and the reader is referred to the original Psalms for the exposition.

1. Since the two Psalms which are the source are ascribed to David, his name is attached to the composition in its present form.

2-6 THANKSGIVING FOR GOD'S MERCIES

2. *my heart is stedfast.* In lvii. 8, the phrase is repeated after *O God* .

even with my glory. Omitted in lvii., but *my glory* appears in a clause *awake, my glory* added at the beginning of verse 9.

3. *awake, psaltery and harp.* According to the Talmud (Ber. 3b) David's harp hung over his bed and at midnight the north wind caused it to play by itself. At that point David would arise to sing hymns and songs of praise to God. This is what is meant by this verse (cf. Rashi).

4. *O LORD.* For the Tetragrammaton here lvii. 10 has *Adonai*.

and I will sing. The conjunction is omitted in lvii.

5. *above the heavens.* In lvii. 11, *unto the heavens*. The Talmud explains the variation thus: The Divine mercy is great *above* the heavens to those who perform God's commands for their own sake, but *unto* the heavens to those who are obedient from an ulterior motive.

6. *the heavens.* The Hebrew here omits the definite article.

and Thy glory. The conjunction is omitted in lvii. 12.

7 That Thy beloved may be delivered,
  Save with Thy right hand, and
  answer me.

8 God spoke in His holiness, that I
  would exult;
  That I would divide Shechem,
  and mete out the valley of
  Succoth.

9 Gilead is mine, Manasseh is mine;
  Ephraim also is the defence of my
  head;
  Judah is my sceptre.

10 Moab is my washpot;
  Upon Edom do I cast my shoe;
  Over Philistia do I cry aloud.

11 Who will bring me into the
  fortified city?
  Who will lead me unto Edom?

12 Hast not Thou cast us off, O
  God?
  And Thou goest not forth, O
  God, with our hosts.

13 Give us help against the adversary;
  For vain is the help of man.

14 Through God we shall do
  valiantly;
  For He it is that will tread down
  our adversaries.

7 לְמַעַן יֵחָלְצוּן יְדִידֶיךָ
הוֹשִׁיעָה יְמִינְךָ וַעֲנֵנוּ׃

8 אֱלֹהִים ׀ דִּבֶּר בְּקָדְשׁוֹ
אֶעְלֹזָה אֲחַלְּקָה שְׁכֶם
וְעֵמֶק סֻכּוֹת אֲמַדֵּד׃

9 לִי גִלְעָד ׀ וְלִי מְנַשֶּׁה
וְאֶפְרַיִם מָעוֹז רֹאשִׁי
יְהוּדָה מְחֹקְקִי׃

10 מוֹאָב ׀ סִיר רַחְצִי
עַל־אֱדוֹם אַשְׁלִיךְ נַעֲלִי
עָלַי־פְּלֶשֶׁת אֶתְרוֹעָע׃

11 מִי יֹבִלֵנִי עִיר מִבְצָר
מִי נָחַנִי עַד־אֱדוֹם׃

12 הֲלֹא־אֱלֹהִים זְנַחְתָּנוּ
וְלֹא־תֵצֵא אֱלֹהִים בְּצִבְאֹתֵינוּ׃

13 הָבָה־לָּנוּ עֶזְרָת מִצָּר
וְשָׁוְא תְּשׁוּעַת אָדָם׃

14 בֵּאלֹהִים נַעֲשֶׂה־חָיִל
וְהוּא יָבוּס צָרֵינוּ׃

v. 7. רוֹנְנִי ק׳

7-14 PRAYER IN DANGER

9. *Manasseh.* In lx. 9 *and* precedes.

10. *over Philistia do I cry aloud.* lx. 10 reads
Philistia, cry aloud because of me. There the
idea is 'let Philistia dare shout because of
me,' since the enemy will no longer have

occasion to exult over Israel (cf. Hirsch).

11. *the fortified city.* In lx. 11, a different
word is employed for *fortified.*

12. *Thou cast us off.* In lx. 12, the subject
is emphasized by the addition of the pronoun
attah.

109

קט

לַמְנַצֵּחַ לְדָוִד מִזְמוֹר
אֱלֹהֵי תְהִלָּתִי אַל־תֶּחֱרַשׁ:
2 כִּי פִי רָשָׁע וּפִי־מִרְמָה עָלַי פָּתָחוּ
דִּבְּרוּ אִתִּי לְשׁוֹן שָׁקֶר:
3 וְדִבְרֵי שִׂנְאָה סְבָבוּנִי
וַיִּלָּחֲמוּנִי חִנָּם:

1 For the Leader. A Psalm of
  David.
  O God of my praise, keep not
  silence;

2 For the mouth of the wicked and
  the mouth of deceit have they
  opened against me;
  They have spoken unto me with
  a lying tongue.

3 They compassed me about also
  with words of hatred,
  And fought against me without a
  cause.

A CRY FOR HELP

THE Psalm tells of suffering under relentless persecution, and is to be compared to earlier Psalms of the same type, especially XXV and LXIX. Though there is no clue to the author's identity or the circumstances, it is presumed that David composed the Psalm while being pursued by Saul after having been the victim of treacherous slander. In verses 6-19 David lashes out at his enemies with a string of the most vehement curses. The singular form is used as he is primarily referring to his arch-enemy Doeg, the Edomite (Kimchi). Malbim and Hirsch, following a different line of thought, maintain that the maledictions are not spoken by the author against his persecutors, but express the evil wishes of the latter against the man they were hounding to death. This might account for the fact that the adversaries are in the plural, whereas the curses are directed against a subject in the singular. Moreover, in verse 28 the Psalmist explicitly prays, 'Let them curse, but bless Thou,' and it is natural to understand his words as referring to the imprecations in the Psalm.

1-5 PLEA FOR HELP

1. *God of my praise.* The God Whom I praised in the past for mercies granted to me. Relying upon that experience, the Psalmist again turns to Him in his distress (cf. Sforno).

keep not silence. By withholding a response to the prayer.

2. *mouth of the wicked.* lit. 'mouth of a wicked man,' which may mean that his ill-wishers had put forward an unscrupulous person to bring false charges against him, as Jezebel did against Naboth.

spoken unto me. Hebrew 'with me.' Whenever I chanced to be with them, they would make friendly overtures towards me, but inwardly they hated and despised me (Kimchi).

3. *words of hatred.* Their false allegations, inspired by animosity, caused Saul to turn against me, even to the point that he battles against me (Kimchi).

without a cause. Their attack upon him is without justification.

4 In return for my love they are my
    adversaries;
  But I am all prayer.

5 And they have laid upon me evil
    for good,
  And hatred for my love:

6 'Set Thou a wicked man over him;
  And let an adversary stand at his
    right hand.

7 When he is judged, let him go
    forth condemned;
  And let his prayer be turned into
    sin.

8 Let his days be few;
  Let another take his charge.

9 Let his children be fatherless,
  And his wife a widow.

4 תַּחַת־אַהֲבָתִי יִשְׂטְנוּנִי
וַאֲנִי תְפִלָּה׃
5 וַיָּשִׂימוּ עָלַי רָעָה תַּחַת טוֹבָה
וְשִׂנְאָה תַּחַת אַהֲבָתִי׃
6 הַפְקֵד עָלָיו רָשָׁע
וְשָׂטָן יַעֲמֹד עַל־יְמִינוֹ׃
7 בְּהִשָּׁפְטוֹ יֵצֵא רָשָׁע
וּתְפִלָּתוֹ תִּהְיֶה לַחֲטָאָה׃
8 יִהְיוּ־יָמָיו מְעַטִּים
פְּקֻדָּתוֹ יִקַּח אַחֵר׃
9 יִהְיוּ־בָנָיו יְתוֹמִים
וְאִשְׁתּוֹ אַלְמָנָה׃

4. *my love.* Acts of friendship which he had performed for them.

they are my adversaries. Rather, 'they accuse (or, prosecute) me'; the verb recurs in verse 20, 29, and the noun is used in verse 6.

but... prayer. Hebrew 'but I am prayer'; cf. *I am peace* (cxx. 7). He means that he had devoted himself to prayer on their behalf when they had been in trouble (cf. xxxv. 13) (Kimchi).

5. Cf. xxxv. 12, xxxviii. 21.

6-20 IMPRECATIONS

In the interpretation of this section adopted by Malbim and Hirsch (see Introduction), we must understand a word like 'saying' before verse 6. A.J. accordingly prints quotation marks at the beginning and end. They who hold that the Psalmist curses his persecutors explain the singular in a collective or distributive (each one of them) sense or as referring to Doeg (see Introduction).

6. *set Thou.* Equals 'may there be set.'

a wicked man. An unscrupulous judge.

adversary. Hebrew *satan,* 'accuser, perse-cutor' (see on verse 4).

at his right hand. The prosecutor stood at the right of the accused (Zech. iii. 1).

7. *when ... judged.* The first part of the imprecation deals with a trial before a judge, and in the Psalm's opening verses the writer complained that *he* was the defendant on a false charge. This harmonizes with the view that the Psalmist is the object of the curses.

and let his prayer be turned into sin. Better, 'so that his prayer will be for sin.' The accused prays to God to vindicate him; his condemnation, despite his prayer, will be accepted as proof that he was really guilty.

8. *his charge.* i.e. his office of honour and responsibility which seems to be alluded to in verses 16ff. (cf. Rashi). Possibly the word means *his possessions* as in Isa. xv. 7, *and that which they have laid up shall they carry away* (cf. Kimchi).

9. The malevolence of his enemies extended to his dependants. Orphans and widows, lacking a protector, were often the victims of exploitation.

10 Let his children be vagabonds,
    and beg;
  And let them seek their bread
    out of their desolate places.

11 Let the creditor distrain all that
    he hath;
  And let strangers make spoil of
    his labour.

12 Let there be none to extend kind-
    ness unto him;
  Neither let there be any to be
    gracious unto his fatherless
    children.

13 Let his posterity be cut off;
  In the generation following let
    their name be blotted out.

14 Let the iniquity of his fathers be
    brought to remembrance unto
    the Lord;
  And let not the sin of his mother
    be blotted out.

15 Let them be before the Lord
    continually,
  That He may cut off the memory
    of them from the earth.

16 Because that he remembered not
    to do kindness,
  But persecuted the poor and
    needy man,
  And the broken in heart he was
    ready to slay.

10 וְנ֤וֹעַ יָנ֣וּעוּ בָנָ֣יו וְשִׁאֵ֑לוּ
וְֽדָרְשׁ֗וּ מֵחָרְבֽוֹתֵיהֶֽם׃

11 יְנַקֵּ֣שׁ נ֭וֹשֶׁה לְכָל־אֲשֶׁר־ל֑וֹ
וְיָבֹ֖זּוּ זָרִ֣ים יְגִיעֽוֹ׃

12 אַל־יְהִי־ל֭וֹ מֹשֵׁ֣ךְ חָ֑סֶד
וְֽאַל־יְהִ֥י ח֝וֹנֵ֗ן לִיתוֹמָֽיו׃

13 יְהִֽי־אַחֲרִית֥וֹ לְהַכְרִ֑ית
בְּד֥וֹר אַחֵ֗ר יִמַּ֥ח שְׁמָֽם׃

14 יִזָּכֵ֤ר ׀ עֲוֺ֣ן אֲ֭בֹתָיו אֶל־יְהֹוָ֑ה
וְחַטַּ֥את אִ֝מּ֗וֹ אַל־תִּמָּֽח׃

15 יִהְי֣וּ נֶֽגֶד־יְהֹוָ֣ה תָּמִ֑יד
וְיַכְרֵ֖ת מֵאֶ֣רֶץ זִכְרָֽם׃

16 יַ֗עַן אֲשֶׁ֤ר ׀ לֹ֥א זָכַר֮ עֲשׂ֢וֹת חָ֥סֶד
וַיִּרְדֹּ֡ף אִישׁ־עָנִ֣י וְ֭אֶבְיוֹן
וְנִכְאֵ֨ה לֵבָ֬ב לְמוֹתֵֽת׃

10. *their bread.* Not in the Hebrew but to be understood from the context.

desolate places. Their ruined home.

11. *distrain.* lit. 'ensnare,' take by trickery more than was due to him.

his labour. The fruits of his toil.

12. *unto him.* In the remainder of his life.

gracious unto. Have pity on.

13. *his posterity.* His children.

14. *iniquity of his fathers.* May the penalties incurred by them be visited upon him, in accordance with the declaration of Exod. xx. 5 (Metsudath David).

be blotted out. From the records preserved by God (see on li. 3).

15. *let them be.* viz. the iniquity of his fathers and the sin of his mother.

the memory of them. Of his forefathers and all their descendants.

16. This and the following verses contain the substance of the allegations made by his enemies against him in justification of their hostility.

and the broken ... slay. This rendering follows the traditional punctuation; but the verse is better translated: 'persecuted the poor and needy man, also the crushed of heart, unto (their) death.'

17 Yea, he loved cursing, and it
   came unto him;
   And he delighted not in blessing,
   and it is far from him.

18 He clothed himself also with
   cursing as with his raiment,
   And it is come into his inward
   parts like water,
   And like oil into his bones.

19 Let it be unto him as the garment
   which he putteth on,
   And for the girdle wherewith he
   is girded continually.'

20 This would mine adversaries
   effect from the LORD,
   And they that speak evil against
   my soul.

21 But Thou, O God the LORD, deal
   with me for Thy name's sake;
   Because Thy mercy is good,
   deliver Thou me.

22 For I am poor and needy,
   And my heart is wounded within
   me.

23 I am gone like the shadow when
   it lengtheneth;
   I am shaken off as the locust.

17 וַיֶּאֱהַב קְלָלָה וַתְּבוֹאֵהוּ
וְלֹא־חָפֵץ בִּבְרָכָה וַתִּרְחַק מִמֶּנּוּ:
18 וַיִּלְבַּשׁ קְלָלָה כְּמַדּוֹ
וַתָּבֹא כַמַּיִם בְּקִרְבּוֹ
וְכַשֶּׁמֶן בְּעַצְמוֹתָיו:
19 תְּהִי־לוֹ כְּבֶגֶד יַעְטֶה
וּלְמֵזַח תָּמִיד יַחְגְּרֶהָ:
20 זֹאת פְּעֻלַּת שֹׂטְנַי מֵאֵת יְהוָה
וְהַדֹּבְרִים רָע עַל־נַפְשִׁי:
21 וְאַתָּה יְהוִה אֲדֹנָי
עֲשֵׂה־אִתִּי לְמַעַן שְׁמֶךָ
כִּי־טוֹב חַסְדְּךָ הַצִּילֵנִי:
22 כִּי־עָנִי וְאֶבְיוֹן אָנֹכִי
וְלִבִּי חָלַל בְּקִרְבִּי:
23 כְּצֵל כִּנְטוֹתוֹ נֶהֱלָכְתִּי
נִנְעַרְתִּי כָּאַרְבֶּה:

17. 'He has rebelled against the Divine
decree; he had deliberately and intentionally
striven after things that he knew could bring
nothing but ruin' (Hirsch).

18. *clothed … raiment*. He cursed the weak
as habitually as he put on his garments, so
that it became a constant feature of his
behaviour.

like water … oil. A normal person drinks water and massages himself with oil for refreshment, but he is alleged to have found his
refreshment in curses.

19. *as the garment*. May the maledictions
which comes from his lips envelop him and
cling as closely as does the girdle to the body
(Malbim).

20-25 HE APPEALS FOR GOD'S MERCY

20. On the interpretation that the curses are

uttered by the Psalmist, the verse is rendered;
'This is the reward of mine adversaries'
(R.V.); such is the treatment by God that they
deserve. For the other interpretation, the
translation is: 'This is my accusers' request
(lit. what they wish to be done) of the LORD';
this is what they ask Him to do unto me.

21. *deal with me*. He calls upon God to
judge between him and them, confident that
the verdict will be in his favour, and that He
will act in accordance with His attribute of
holiness and justice.

because Thy mercy is good. Cf. lxix. 17.

22. *poor*. Afflicted.

wounded. Because of my many enemies
(Kimchi).

23. *I am gone*. Traversed the term of life.

shadow when it lengtheneth. See on cii. 12.

24 My knees totter through fasting;
   And my flesh is lean, and hath no
      fatness.

25 I am become also a taunt unto
      them;
   When they see me, they shake
      their head.

26 Help me, O LORD my God;
   O save me according to Thy
      mercy;

27 That they may know that this is
      Thy hand;
   That Thou, LORD, hast done it.

28 Let them curse, but bless Thou;
   When they arise, they shall be
      put to shame, but Thy servant
      shall rejoice.

29 Mine adversaries shall be clothed
      with confusion,
   And shall put on their own shame
      as a robe.

30 I will give great thanks unto the
      LORD with my mouth;
   Yea, I will praise Him among the
      multitude;

31 Because He standeth at the right
      hand of the needy,
   To save him from them that
      judge his soul.

24 בִּרְכַּי כָּשְׁלוּ מִצּוֹם
וּבְשָׂרִי כָּחַשׁ מִשָּׁמֶן:

25 וַאֲנִי הָיִיתִי חֶרְפָּה לָהֶם
יִרְאוּנִי יְנִיעוּן רֹאשָׁם:

26 עָזְרֵנִי יְהֹוָה אֱלֹהָי
הוֹשִׁיעֵנִי כְחַסְדֶּךָ:

27 וְיֵדְעוּ כִּי־יָדְךָ זֹּאת
אַתָּה יְהֹוָה עֲשִׂיתָהּ:

28 יְקַלְלוּ־הֵמָּה וְאַתָּה תְבָרֵךְ
קָמוּ וַיֵּבֹשׁוּ וְעַבְדְּךָ יִשְׂמָח:

29 יִלְבְּשׁוּ שׂוֹטְנַי כְּלִמָּה
וְיַעֲטוּ כַמְעִיל בָּשְׁתָּם:

30 אוֹדֶה יְהֹוָה מְאֹד בְּפִי
וּבְתוֹךְ רַבִּים אֲהַלְלֶנּוּ:

31 כִּי־יַעֲמֹד לִימִין אֶבְיוֹן
לְהוֹשִׁיעַ מִשֹּׁפְטֵי נַפְשׁוֹ:

shaken off as the locust. I am cast about from place to place like a locust that is constantly being shaken off from its place of rest (Malbim).

24. *through fasting.* In his anguish he lost his appetite for food (cii. 5).

and hath no fatness. As a result of incessant fasting, my body has become weak and lean.

25. *a taunt.* An object of reproach.

shake their head. In contempt.

    26-31 HIS CERTAINTY OF DIVINE AID

26. *according to Thy mercy.* So often evinced in the past and not exhausted.

27. *this is Thy hand.* The deliverance which has come to me is the effect of Thy will.

28. *arise.* To put their schemes against me into operation.

29. *adversaries.* Or, 'accusers.'

clothed with confusion. Cf. xxxv. 26, lxxi. 13.

robe. The outer garment which is not hidden from view; so will their shame be visible to all (Malbim).

30. *with my mouth.* Aloud and publicly.

31. *at the right hand.* Not as prosecutor (verse 6) but as Protector.

judge his soul. i.e. have as their aim his condemnation to death (Kimchi).

110

קִי

1 A Psalm of David.
The LORD saith unto my lord:
'Sit thou at My right hand,
Until I make thine enemies thy
footstool.'

2 The rod of thy strength the LORD
will send out of Zion:
'Rule thou in the midst of thine
enemies.'

לְדָוִד מִזְמוֹר
נְאֻם יְהֹוָה ׀ לַאדֹנִי
שֵׁב לִימִינִי
עַד־אָשִׁית אֹיְבֶיךָ הֲדֹם לְרַגְלֶיךָ׃
2 מַטֵּה עֻזְּךָ יִשְׁלַח יְהֹוָה מִצִּיּוֹן
רְדֵה בְּקֶרֶב אֹיְבֶיךָ׃

A KING'S VICTORY

FROM the allusion to Melchizedek, the Rabbis (Tal. Ned. 32b) expounded this Psalm as relating to Abraham and his victory over Amraphel (Gen. xiv). Rashi, in his commentary, follows this theme, but Ibn Ezra (cf. Kimchi) named David as the king, maintaining that the superscription signifies 'a Psalm for (concerning) David' and is connected to the events of the battle with Ammon. David was foresworn from going to battle as his men felt it more productive for him to attend to affairs of state at home. Joab was sent in his stead (Malbim). Kimchi, quoting Ibn Ezra, presents this Psalm as having been composed in the early stages of David's reign. The Philistines, hearing of the new king's appointment, launched an attack on Judah, but retreated in the wake of the battle of Emek Rephaim (see on verse 6).

1-3 GOD'S ASSURANCE OF TRIUMPH

1. *the* LORD *saith.* The Hebrew phrase, common in the prophetical literature, occurs only here in the Psalter. It is literally 'the oracle of the LORD' and expresses a solemn declaration made upon the authority of God.

my lord. Hebrew *adoni*, a title of respect when addressing a superior, such as a king (Gen. xxiii. 6; 1 Kings i. 2, 17).

sit thou at My right hand. To be given a seat at the right hand was a mark of distinction (1 Kings ii. 19). Such an honour God figuratively confers upon David at a critical moment when neighbouring nations were showing themselves hostile towards him. By this invitation the thought is conveyed that while God is the supreme King, David, as the chosen ruler of the people, shared His authority. In this sense David declared, *He hath chosen Solomon my son to sit upon the throne of the kingdom of the* LORD *over Israel* (1 Chron. xxviii. 5); and it is recorded, *Then*

Solomon sat on the throne of the LORD *as king instead of David his father* (1 Chron. xxix. 23) (cf. Malbim).

until. God's special measure of help will be at his disposal and will not fail him so long as the crisis lasts .

make...footstool. A metaphor for the decisive defeat of enemies, originating in the custom of the victor placing his foot upon the neck of the conquered general or king (Joshua x. 24).

2. *the rod of thy strength.* A Hebrew idiom for 'thy powerful sceptre,' the symbol of regal authority. That authority, invested with Divinely ordained power (1 Sam. ii. 10), will be directed by God Himself out of His abode in Zion on the field of battle.

rule ... enemies. Printed in inverted commas to denote our interpretation that they exclusively are words spoken by God in this verse. The command to *rule* was intended to inspire the king with the certainty that the victory would be his.

3 Thy people offer themselves wil-
    lingly in the day of thy warfare;
  In adornments of holiness, from
    the womb of the dawn,
  Thine is the dew of thy youth.

4 The Lord hath sworn, and will
    not repent:
  'Thou art a priest for ever
  After the manner of Melchizedek.'

5 The Lord at thy right hand
  Doth crush kings in the day of His
    wrath.

עַמְּךָ נְדָבֹת בְּיוֹם חֵילֶךָ 3
בְּהַדְרֵי־קֹדֶשׁ מֵרֶחֶם מִשְׁחָר
לְךָ טַל יַלְדֻתֶךָ:
נִשְׁבַּע יְהֹוָה וְלֹא יִנָּחֵם 4
אַתָּה־כֹהֵן לְעוֹלָם
עַל־דִּבְרָתִי מַלְכִּי־צֶדֶק:
אֲדֹנָי עַל־יְמִינְךָ 5
מָחַץ בְּיוֹם־אַפּוֹ מְלָכִים:

3. *offer themselves willingly.* lit. 'are willingnesses,' the same root as in Judges v. 2, *The people offer themselves freely.* Animated by a sense of loyalty to the king, they eagerly rally to his standard.

thy warfare. lit. 'thy army'; when the forces mobilise.

in adornments of holiness. A similar phrase in xxix. 2, xcvi. 9, to describe the vestments of the priests. Here it is better rendered '(because you are) adorned with the holiness etc,' the reference being David, was from youth righteous and God-fearing (Rashi) and was anointed at a young age with sanctified oil to lead his people (Malbim). Others see this as a reference to Jerusalem and translate 'majesty of the sanctuary' (Kimchi, Hirsch).

from the womb … youth. The dew falls at dawn, poetically called its mother. It is a metaphor of freshness and is applied to David who, from a young age showed promise as the future anointed leader of his people (cf. Kimchi).

4 THE KING'S PRIESTHOOD

The status of David is defined here. He was not just a king like those in heathen nations. In addition to his regal dignity he was a *priest*, not of the same standing as Aaron and his male descendants, but in the sense that Melchizedek had been a *priest* of God (cf. Malbim).

the Lord hath sworn. i.e. He has made an unalterable decree.

repent. Revoke what He has ordained.

priest for ever. The distinctive kingship of David would be continued in his successors. The word *priest* (Heb. *cohen*) is used in reference to David and his sons, of the latter in *And David's sons were chief ministers* (Hebrew 'priests') (2 Sam. viii. 18); and of the former, who wore the sacerdotal ephod (2 Sam. vi. 14), in *and David offered burnt-offerings and peace-offerings before the Lord* (2 Sam. vi. 17).

after the manner of Melchizedek. In Gen. xiv. 18, he is described as *king of Salem priest of God Most High.* He, as David, was not consecrated to the priesthood, but he ruled his people in the light of God's will and as such was a priest-king. That was the ideal set to the Davidic dynasty (Malbim).

5-7 THE SCENE OF BATTLE

5. *at thy right hand.* To assist in the fight and guarantee victory (Malbim).

doth crush. Rather, 'shall shatter'; the prophetic perfect (Meiri).

kings. Of neighbouring peoples who rise against His appointed ruler.

day of His wrath. The day of battle when He will decide the issue.

6 He will judge among the nations;
He filleth it with dead bodies,
He crusheth the head over a wide
land.
7 He will drink of the brook in the
way;
Therefore will he lift up the head.

6 יָדִין בַּגּוֹיִם מָלֵא גְוִיּוֹת
מָחַץ רֹאשׁ עַל־אֶרֶץ רַבָּה:
7 מִנַּחַל בַּדֶּרֶךְ יִשְׁתֶּה
עַל־כֵּן יָרִים רֹאשׁ:

6. *judge.* He will mete out judgment among the nations till the battlefield will be filled with dead bodies (Kimchi).

He filleth it. Better, 'He will fill (the arena)'; prophetic perfect.

dead bodies. The Hebrew word denotes both living (cf. Gen. xlvii. 18) and dead bodies. Ibn Ezra understands it here in the former sense: 'the nations which are full of bodies,' i.e. numerically strong. Other commentators agree that it alludes to the corpses of the slain amongst the defeated nations. Hirsch explains the verse to mean 'He will judge the nations whose wealth is built up through the murder of others,' i.e. the 'dead bodies' not of the wicked but of their victims.

He crusheth the head. Render: 'He will shatter heads.' The noun, singular in the Hebrew, may be employed in a collective sense (Kimchi) or it may signify the leader of the opposing army or the head of the fighting men (cf. Rashi). The occurrence of the phrase in lxviii. 22 supports the latter interpretation.

over a wide land. Better, 'of a great land.' A victory will be won over a mighty empire and will bring the king much territory. Kimchi and Malbim render 'the land of Rabbah,' identifying the occasion of the Psalm to be the outset of David's war with Ammon, when he captured Rabbah, the capital (2 Sam. xii. 26ff.)

7. *he will drink.* A metaphor. Surrounded by a multitude of corpses, he will be drunk with the success of victory. His thirst for revenge shall have been quenched (cf. Metsudath David).

therefore. Victory will be achieved solely as a consequence of God's intervention and, with that thought in mind, he may proudly lift his head over the vanquished (Metsudath David).

lift up the head. In final triumph (see xxvii. 6).

111

קיא

הַלְלוּיָהּ׀
אוֹדֶה יְהֹוָה בְּכָל־לֵבָב
בְּסוֹד יְשָׁרִים וְעֵדָה׃
2 גְּדֹלִים מַעֲשֵׂי יְהֹוָה
דְּרוּשִׁים לְכָל־חֶפְצֵיהֶם׃
3 הוֹד־וְהָדָר פָּעֳלוֹ
וְצִדְקָתוֹ עֹמֶדֶת לָעַד׃
4 זֵכֶר עָשָׂה לְנִפְלְאוֹתָיו
חַנּוּן וְרַחוּם יְהֹוָה׃
5 טֶרֶף נָתַן לִירֵאָיו

1 Hallelujah.
I will give thanks unto the LORD
with my whole heart,
In the council of the upright, and
in the congregation.

2 The works of the LORD are great,
Sought out of all them that have
delight therein.

3 His work is glory and majesty;
And His righteousness endureth
for ever.

4 He hath made a memorial for His
wonderful works;
The LORD is gracious and full of
compassion.

5 He hath given food unto them that
fear Him;

GOD'S SAVING ACTS

THE Psalm is constructed on the lines of an acrostic, each half verse beginning with a letter of the alphabet. The theme is the glorification of God for His acts of mercy to Israel.

1. *Hallelujah.* See on civ. 35; the call of the precentor to the Levite singers to join in the recital of the Psalm (Kimchi).

with my whole heart. Hebrew 'with a whole heart,' with a heart completely absorbed in the duty to offer Him praise.

council of the upright. Select scholars who have attained insight into God and His ways, and who form an intimate group amongst His people (Sforno).

and in the congregation. He has the obligation to proclaim thanks to the LORD, not only in the presence of individuals but also before the entire congregation, the laymen who make up the House of Israel; they, too, yearn to learn God's wonders (cf. Malbim).

2. *works.* In providing for the needs of His devotees (verse 5) and in His special acts on behalf of Israel (verses 6, 9).

sought out. Those *works* are the subject of inquiry and meditation by men whose *delight* is to gain a full understanding of them.

3. *work.* A different Hebrew word from that in verse 2 meaning 'His Providence.'

is glory and majesty. The attributes in which God is *clothed* (civ. 1). His dealings with mankind reveal these qualities.

His righteousness. The eternal characteristic of His *work.*

4. *His wonderful works.* The miracles He wrought for Israel in redeeming them from Egypt were perpetuated in the memory of the people by the institutions of the Sabbath and the Holydays which are called 'a remembrance of the departure from Egypt' in the Hebrew liturgy (*P.B.*, p. 124; cf. Exod. xiii. 8, Lev. xxiii. 43, Deut. v. 15, xvi. 3, 12).

gracious and full of compassion. Cf. ciii. 8; Exod. xxxiv. 6.

5. *food.* Usually, the word means a wild beast's prey. It was chosen here not only for the acrostic, but it signifies food for human

He will ever be mindful of His covenant.

6 He hath declared to His people the power of His works,
In giving them the heritage of the nations.

7 The works of His hands are truth and justice;
All His precepts are sure.

8 They are established for ever and ever,
They are done in truth and uprightness.

9 He hath sent redemption unto His people;
He hath commanded His covenant for ever;
Holy and awful is His name.

10 The fear of the LORD is the beginning of wisdom;
A good understanding have all they that do thereafter;
His praise endureth for ever.

יִזְכֹּר לְעוֹלָם בְּרִיתוֹ׃

6 כֹּחַ מַעֲשָׂיו הִגִּיד לְעַמּוֹ
לָתֵת לָהֶם נַחֲלַת גּוֹיִם׃

7 מַעֲשֵׂי יָדָיו אֱמֶת וּמִשְׁפָּט
נֶאֱמָנִים כָּל־פִּקּוּדָיו׃

8 סְמוּכִים לָעַד לְעוֹלָם
עֲשׂוּיִם בֶּאֱמֶת וְיָשָׁר׃

9 פְּדוּת שָׁלַח לְעַמּוֹ
צִוָּה לְעוֹלָם בְּרִיתוֹ
קָדוֹשׁ וְנוֹרָא שְׁמוֹ׃

10 רֵאשִׁית חָכְמָה יִרְאַת יְהוָה
שֵׂכֶל טוֹב לְכָל־עֹשֵׂיהֶם
תְּהִלָּתוֹ עֹמֶדֶת לָעַד׃

consumption also in Prov. xxxi. 15.

covenant. With the patriarchs (cf. cv. 8ff.).

6. *heritage of the nations*. Of the inhabitants of Canaan who were dispossessed by Israel; an overwhelming demonstration of God's might (Metsudath David).

7. *truth and justice*. God does not exercise His power in an arbitrary spirit, but is actuated by righteous principles.

all His precepts are sure. Whatever He ordains man to do is reliable as guidance (see on xix. 8), and also, like *the works of His hands*, grounded in *truth*. The words for *sure* and *truth* are derived from the same root.

8. *established*. God's *precepts*, unlike man's enactments, are everlastingly valid, because they have been instituted by Him in accord with the immutable dictates of right.

9. *redemption*. The redemption from Egyptian bondage was primarily for the purpose of giving the Torah, the foundation rock of the eternal *covenant* between God and His people (Exod. xxxiv.27) (Sforno, Metsudath David).

holy and awful is His name. Better, 'awesome.' *Awful* is used in the sense of 'awe-inspiring.' His acts of deliverance from Egypt revealed that He was a God Whose purposes are holy and Whose power is such as to arouse man's awe.

10. *fear of the LORD*. Cf. Prov. i. 7, ix. 10. By 'fear' is to be understood total commitment to God and His commandments (cf. Deut. xiii. 5) (Kimchi); the starting point of life on a plane higher than an animal existence, a thought developed in the next Psalm.

a good understanding. Man's ideal is to find *grace and good favour* (the same phrase in the Hebrew) *in the sight of God and man* (Prov. iii. 4), and *good understanding giveth grace* (Prov. xiii. 15). It has been defined as an understanding of what is good for ourselves and the world we live in. It comes to those who make the fear of God the content of their everyday living (Hirsch).

His praise. Others render 'his praise,' the praise of one who fears the LORD and possesses *good understanding* (as above) (cf. Ibn Ezra, Metsudath David).

1 Hallelujah.
Happy is the man that feareth the
LORD,
That delighteth greatly in His
commandments.

2 His seed shall be mighty upon
earth;
The generation of the upright
shall be blessed.

3 Wealth and riches are in his house;
And his merit endureth for ever.

4 Unto the upright He shineth as a
light in the darkness,
Gracious, and full of compassion,
and righteous.

5 Well is it with the man that dealeth
graciously and lendeth,
That ordereth his affairs rightfully.

קיב

הַלְלוּיָהּ ׀

אַשְׁרֵי־אִישׁ יָרֵא אֶת־יְהֹוָה
בְּמִצְוֹתָיו חָפֵץ מְאֹד:

2 גִּבּוֹר בָּאָרֶץ יִהְיֶה זַרְעוֹ
דּוֹר יְשָׁרִים יְבֹרָךְ:

3 הוֹן־וָעֹשֶׁר בְּבֵיתוֹ
וְצִדְקָתוֹ עֹמֶדֶת לָעַד:

4 זָרַח בַּחֹשֶׁךְ אוֹר לַיְשָׁרִים
חַנּוּן וְרַחוּם וְצַדִּיק:

5 טוֹב־אִישׁ חוֹנֵן וּמַלְוֶה
יְכַלְכֵּל דְּבָרָיו בְּמִשְׁפָּט:

THE RIGHTEOUS MAN

THIS Psalm is a companion to the preceding and has similar acrostic construction. It develops the theme of the closing verses of CXI and describes the life of the man inspired by the ideal of 'the imitation of God.'

1. *that feareth the* LORD. Who has adopted the doctrine that *the fear of the* LORD *is the beginning of wisdom* (cxi. 10).

delighteth. As in cxi. 2 (see on i. 2).

2. *his seed*. The merit of the God-fearing man will also be enjoyed by his descendants (cf. xxv. 13).

mighty. *Gibbor* normally means physically strong or heroic in battle. Here it denotes honourable and secure, and the word was chosen to fit into the acrostic.

generation. Parallel to seed and with the same meaning (Rashi). It may refer to a chain of generations that will be blessed (Hirsch).

3. *wealth and riches*. Cf. the assertion in xxxvii. 25f.

merit. lit. 'righteousness.' As it was stated in cxi. 3, that God's righteousness *endureth for ever*, a similar claim is made for the good man. With such a guarantee in his support, he will certainly reap the reward of his virtue.

4. Since the Psalm consists of a description of the God-fearing, some prefer the translation: 'light shines in the darkness for the upright (for him who is) gracious, full of compassion, and righteous' (cf. xcvii. 11). The righteous man shares the Divine attributes (Exod. xxxiv. 6).

5. *dealeth graciously and lendeth*. He is ready to extend a helping hand to the needy by making them a loan, and in such a way as not to hurt their feelings (Kimchi).

ordereth his affairs rightfully. He is scrupulous and considerate in the conduct of his business (Kimchi).

6 **For** he shall never be moved;
The righteous shall be had in everlasting remembrance.

7 He shall not be afraid of evil
tidings;
His heart is stedfast, trusting in
the LORD.

8 His heart is established, he shall
not be afraid,
Until he gaze upon his adversaries.

9 He hath scattered abroad, he hath
given to the needy;
His righteousness endureth for
ever;
His horn shall be exalted in
honour.

10 The wicked shall see, and be
vexed;
He shall gnash with his teeth,
and melt away;
The desire of the wicked shall
perish.

כִּי־לְעוֹלָם לֹא־יִמּוֹט 6
לְזֵכֶר עוֹלָם יִהְיֶה צַדִּיק׃
מִשְּׁמוּעָה רָעָה לֹא יִירָא 7
נָכוֹן לִבּוֹ בָּטֻחַ בַּיהֹוָה׃
סָמוּךְ לִבּוֹ לֹא יִירָא 8
עַד אֲשֶׁר־יִרְאֶה בְצָרָיו׃
פִּזַּר נָתַן לָאֶבְיוֹנִים 9
צִדְקָתוֹ עֹמֶדֶת לָעַד
קַרְנוֹ תָּרוּם בְּכָבוֹד׃
רָשָׁע יִרְאֶה וְכָעָס 10
שִׁנָּיו יַחֲרֹק וְנָמָס
תַּאֲוַת רְשָׁעִים תֹּאבֵד׃

6. *never be moved.* His prosperity will be lasting.

in everlasting remembrance. Suggested by cxi. 4, where it is declared that God's works are a *memorial* to Him. Likewise the good deeds of the righteous man will be an endur-ing *remembrance* (the same Hebrew word) of his life. 'There is no need to set up monuments to the righteous; their acts are their memorial' (Talmud).

7. *not be afraid of evil tidings.* He will not be exempt from setbacks in his lifetime; but when he hears of them, they will not disturb him unduly. His trust in God enables him to face them with fortitude (see on i. 3; cf. Prov. x. 24f.).

8. *established.* The same word as in cxi. 8, and selected because of the acrostic. It is literally 'supported' by his reliance upon God.

gaze upon. See on xcii. 12.

9. *scattered abroad.* Spent his money freely in worthy causes.

his righteousness ... ever. Repeated from verse 3.

horn. See on lxxv. 6.

10. *wicked shall see.* The triumph of the righteous. The verb is the same as gaze in verse 8 and a contrast may be intended be-tween the destiny of the righteous and the wicked. The former sees the downfall of the evil-doer; the latter sees the vindication of the upright.

melt away. Through envy or the rage of vexa-tion (Kimchi).

desire ... perish. What he wishes to attain by evil means shall never be realised (Kimchi, Hirsch).

1 Hallelujah.
  Praise, O ye servants of the LORD,
  Praise the name of the LORD.

2 Blessed be the name of the LORD
  From this time forth and for ever.

3 From the rising of the sun unto the
    going down thereof
  The LORD's name is to be praised.

4 The LORD is high above all nations,
  His glory is above the heavens.

5 Who is like unto the LORD our
    God,
  That is enthroned on high,

הַלְלוּיָהּ |
הַלְלוּ עַבְדֵי יְהֹוָה
הַלְלוּ אֶת־שֵׁם יְהֹוָה׃
2 יְהִי שֵׁם יְהֹוָה מְבֹרָךְ
מֵעַתָּה וְעַד־עוֹלָם׃
3 מִמִּזְרַח־שֶׁמֶשׁ עַד־מְבוֹאוֹ
מְהֻלָּל שֵׁם יְהֹוָה׃
4 רָם עַל־כָּל־גּוֹיִם | יְהֹוָה
עַל הַשָּׁמַיִם כְּבוֹדוֹ׃
5 מִי כַּיהֹוָה אֱלֹהֵינוּ
הַמַּגְבִּיהִי לָשָׁבֶת׃

PRAISE GOD

PSALMS CXIII-CXVIII are named in the Talmud 'the Hallel (praise) of Egypt' because of the mention of the exodus at the opening of CXIV, in contradistinction to 'the Great Hallel,' defined as CXX-CXXIV ('The Songs of Ascents') or more commonly CXXXVI. They are included in the Jewish liturgy on the New Moon, the Pilgrim Festivals and the Feast of Dedication (cf. the rubric in *P.B.*, p. 219).

1-3 SUMMONS TO PRAISE GOD

1. *ye servants of the LORD*. This phrase refers to the loyal among Israel. In verse 3 the call is made to all, Israelites and Gentiles, who acknowledge God.

the name of the LORD. It is God as He revealed Himself (*the name*) that men are exhorted to praise (Daath Sofrim).

2. *from this time forth*. From the time of the writing of these words. It is an event of eternal significance, and so His praise must continue for all time.

3. *from the rising ... thereof*. It is also an event of universal import, so that all men, east to west, throughout the world, may discern His might and supremacy, and offer Him praise (Kimchi, Metsudath David).

4-6 GOD'S EMINENCE

4. *the LORD ... nations*. See on xcix. 2.

His glory is above the heavens. The heavens declare the glory of God (xix. 2), but they can only convey a partial impression of it. His glory transcends what they reveal.

5. *that is enthroned on high*. lit. 'Who exalteth to dwell.' He designated His dwelling-place high above the universe, and as such He is a transcendent God.

6 That looketh down low
Upon heaven and upon the
earth?

7 Who raiseth up the poor out of the
dust,
And lifteth up the needy out of the
dunghill;

8 That He may set him with princes,
Even with the princes of His
people.

9 Who maketh the barren woman to
dwell in her house
As a joyful mother of children.
Hallelujah.

6 הַמַּשְׁפִּילִי לִרְאוֹת
בַּשָּׁמַיִם וּבָאָרֶץ׃

7 מְקִימִי מֵעָפָר דָּל
מֵאַשְׁפֹּת יָרִים אֶבְיוֹן׃

8 לְהוֹשִׁיבִי עִם־נְדִיבִים
עִם נְדִיבֵי עַמּוֹ׃

9 מוֹשִׁיבִי ׀ עֲקֶרֶת הַבַּיִת
אֵם־הַבָּנִים שְׂמֵחָה
הַלְלוּיָהּ׃

6. *that looketh down low.* lit. 'Who cometh down low to look.' God was always recognized as being 'on high.' The conviction that He is also 'near'; that He looks into the heavens and down unto earth, that He is concerned about the welfare of even the lowliest of creatures, is that which distinguishes the Jewish concept of God from that held by other nations (Hirsch).

upon heaven and upon the earth. i.e. upon the universe in its entirety, as the combination of the two nouns indicates in Gen. i. 1.

7-9 HIS CARE FOR THE LOWLY

7. This verse and the first half of the next are quoted from 1 Sam. ii. 8.

poor. Hebrew *dal* as in xli. 2, a person 'brought low' by illness or misfortune.

out of the dust. Cf. *Come down, and sit in the dust* (Isa. xlvii. 1), alluding to the practice of sitting on the ground in a time of mourning.

dunghill. The home of those who live in extreme poverty. Even those who have abandoned all hope can be elevated to positions of honour and influence (cf. Daath Sofrim).

8. *set him with princes.* Elevate his social status (cf. Job xxxvi. 7).

the princes of His people. More honourable than the *princes* of heathen nations (Ibn Ezra). The phrase is omitted in 1 Sam. ii. 8 and is added here for the purpose of the parallelism.

9. *the barren woman.* The Psalmist, no doubt, had the instance of Hannah in mind, having quoted her song (1 Sam. ii. 1-10); but he may also have been influenced by the imagery of Isa. liv. 1 and lxvi. 8, where Zion in her desolation is compared to a barren woman, and in her restoration, to a mother with her children happily gathered about her (Rashi). The Targum paraphrases: 'maketh the community of Israel, which was like a barren woman who sat pale (with longing) for the menfolk of her house, to dwell full of crowds like a mother rejoicing over her children.'

114

קיד

1 When Israel came forth out of
   Egypt,
   The house of Jacob from a people
   of strange language;

2 Judah became His sanctuary,
   Israel His dominion.

3 The sea saw it, and fled;
   The Jordan turned backward.

4 The mountains skipped like rams,
   The hills like young sheep.

בְּצֵאת יִשְׂרָאֵל מִמִּצְרָיִם
בֵּית יַעֲקֹב מֵעַם לֹעֵז:
2 הָיְתָה יְהוּדָה לְקָדְשׁוֹ
יִשְׂרָאֵל מַמְשְׁלוֹתָיו:
3 הַיָּם רָאָה וַיָּנֹס
הַיַּרְדֵּן יִסֹּב לְאָחוֹר:
4 הֶהָרִים רָקְדוּ כְאֵילִים
גְּבָעוֹת כִּבְנֵי־צֹאן:

THE EXODUS

FROM the point of view of poetry, this Psalm is a lyric of surpassing beauty. In construction
and language it is among the finest in the Psalter. It may be regarded as a comment on the
closing verses of the previous Psalm and supplies the supreme historical illustration of the
claim there made. In a few short verses the Psalmist describes the effects of the exodus on
Israel and on the rest of the world. So glorious were the wonders that God wrought for Israel,
the splitting of the Red Sea and the giving of the Torah at Sinai, that even the inanimate
creations of God are affected and make up the subjects of the Psalm. The mountains and seas
are disturbed from their natural courses so as to assist in the spiritual birth of the Israelite
nation. It is not man but nature itself which is pictured as witnessing God's miraculous deeds
for the sake of His people.

1-2 ISRAEL'S CHOICE BY GOD

1. *a people of strange language*. Despite
two hundred and ten years in Egypt, the
Israelites (especially the Levites) mostly
remained in Goshen and refused to mingle
with the Egyptians. Among themselves they
spoke only their own language, hence the
Egyptian language was *strange*.

2. *Judah ... Israel*. At an early stage in the
nation's history, the tribe of Judah showed
remarkable leadership qualities. They were
the first to enter the Red Sea, and this sancti-
fying of God's name proved them worthy
candidates for royalty (Rashi, Kimchi).

3-4 NATURE'S CONSTERNATION
AT GOD'S MIGHT

3. *fled ... turned backward*. In terror, to
present no obstacle to Israel's advance towards Canaan.

4. *mountains skipped*. They shook when
the thunders at Sinai heralded the Revelation
(cf. lxviii. 9, and, for the imagery, xxix.6).

5 What aileth thee O thou sea,
    that thou fleest?
  Thou Jordan, that thou turnest
    backward?

6 Ye mountains, that ye skip like
    rams;
  Ye hills, like young sheep?

7 Tremble, thou earth, at the pres-
    ence of the Lord,
  At the presence of the God of
    Jacob;

8 Who turned the rock into a pool of
    water,
  The flint into a fountain of waters.

מַה־לְּךָ הַיָּם כִּי תָנוּס 5
הַיַּרְדֵּן תִּסֹּב לְאָחוֹר:
הֶהָרִים תִּרְקְדוּ כְאֵילִים 6
גְּבָעוֹת כִּבְנֵי־צֹאן:
מִלִּפְנֵי אָדוֹן חוּלִי אָרֶץ 7
מִלִּפְנֵי אֱלוֹהַּ יַעֲקֹב:
הַהֹפְכִי הַצּוּר אֲגַם־מָיִם 8
חַלָּמִישׁ לְמַעְיְנוֹ־מָיִם:

5-6   NATURE QUESTIONED
ABOUT THE EFFECTS

5. *what aileth thee.* lit. 'what to thee?' i.e. what has happened to produce such extraordinary phenomena? The answer is not specified, but implied in what follows. They had been awestruck by *the presence of the LORD* at the events which are recalled by the Psalmist. He continues with the moral that these are not isolated happenings in which the Divine Presence was concerned: God is present everywhere on earth at all times.

7-8   EARTH BIDDEN TO TREMBLE
AT GOD'S PRESENCE

7. *tremble.* Cf. xcvii. 4. Not only the *mountains* and *hills*, but the whole of the universe, should shake before the Divine Presence.

the LORD. Hebrew *adon*, the 'Ruler' of the universe, Who is identified with *the God of Jacob.*

8. The incidents at Rephidim and Kadesh (lxxviii. 15f., 20; Exod. xvii. 6; Num. xx. 11) are quoted as evidence that He is indeed the Ruler of the universe, and Nature must yield to his will (Kimchi). Ibn Ezra sees the verses as allusions to the splitting of the Red Sea and the river Jordan mentioned earlier in the Psalm.

115

קטו

1 Not unto us, O Lord, not unto us,
But unto Thy name give glory,
For Thy mercy, and for Thy
truth's sake.

2 Wherefore should the nations say:
'Where is now their God?'

3 But our God is in the heavens;
Whatsoever pleased Him He hath
done.

4 Their idols are silver and gold,
The work of men's hands.

5 They have mouths, but they speak
not;
Eyes have they, but they see not;

לֹא לָנוּ יְהוָה לֹא־לָנוּ

כִּי־לְשִׁמְךָ תֵּן כָּבוֹד

עַל־חַסְדְּךָ עַל־אֲמִתֶּךָ:

2 לָמָּה יֹאמְרוּ הַגּוֹיִם

אַיֵּה־נָא אֱלֹהֵיהֶם:

3 וֵאלֹהֵינוּ בַשָּׁמָיִם

כֹּל אֲשֶׁר־חָפֵץ עָשָׂה:

4 עֲצַבֵּיהֶם כֶּסֶף וְזָהָב

מַעֲשֵׂה יְדֵי אָדָם:

5 פֶּה־לָהֶם וְלֹא יְדַבֵּרוּ

עֵינַיִם לָהֶם וְלֹא יִרְאוּ:

NATIONAL TRUST IN GOD

A PRAYER by the people for God's help and an exhortation to retain confidence in Him are the subject of the Psalm. The honour of God must be defended against the scorn of the mockers who question His divinity. The form of the Psalm suggests that verses 1-8 and 16-18 were sung by the Levite choir, and each verse from 9-15 was rendered by the precentor with a response from the choir. This antiphonal method is mentioned in Ezra iii. 11, *and they* (the priests and Levites) *sang one to another in praising.*

1-3 APPEAL TO GOD FOR AID

1. *not unto us.* Governed by *give glory.* In appealing for His help, they were not solely motivated by the desire to secure their welfare. Their thought was also for His recognition by all peoples as the supreme Ruler of the universe Who upheld the righteous when assailed by the wicked. His *name* was compromised in the esteem of the heathen nations when Israel appeared to be abandoned by Him.

mercy ... truth. Show Your compassion to us by Your mercy, if we have sinned , and by Your truth, for we are Your nation (Meiri).

2. See on lxxix.10. *Now* may mean 'at this time'; or it is a particle enforcing the question: 'Where, pray, is their God?' (Daath Sofrim).

3. *is in the heavens.* Answers the question 'where?' but adds that whereas the gods of the heathens are material objects and visible, God is invisible and incorporeal. The idols are inert images, but He has the power of doing His will (Kimchi). If therefore, God permitted Israel to suffer national humiliation, it was the consequence of His decree and not of His inability to avert it.

4-8 IMPOTENCE OF IDOLS

Substantially reproduced in cxxxv. 15-18.

4. *silver and gold.* Wood plated with precious metal (Hab. ii. 19).

5. *they speak not.* Their will to man.

they see not. The plight of those who worship them to come to their help.

6 They have ears, but they hear not;
  Noses have they, but they smell
    not;

7 They have hands, but they handle
    not;
  Feet have they, but they walk not;
  Neither speak they with their
    throat.

8 They that make them shall be like
    unto them;
  Yea, every one that trusteth in
    them.

9 O Israel, trust thou in the LORD!
  He is their help and their shield!

10 O house of Aaron, trust ye in the
    LORD!
  He is their help and their shield!

11 Ye that fear the LORD, trust in
    the LORD!
  He is their help and their shield.

6 אָזְנַיִם לָהֶם וְלֹא יִשְׁמָעוּ
אַף לָהֶם וְלֹא יְרִיחוּן:

7 יְדֵיהֶם וְלֹא יְמִישׁוּן
רַגְלֵיהֶם וְלֹא יְהַלֵּכוּ
לֹא־יֶהְגּוּ בִּגְרוֹנָם:

8 כְּמוֹהֶם יִהְיוּ עֹשֵׂיהֶם
כֹּל אֲשֶׁר־בֹּטֵחַ בָּהֶם:

9 יִשְׂרָאֵל בְּטַח בַּיהֹוָה
עֶזְרָם וּמָגִנָּם הוּא:

10 בֵּית אַהֲרֹן בִּטְחוּ בַיהֹוָה
עֶזְרָם וּמָגִנָּם הוּא:

11 יִרְאֵי יְהֹוָה בִּטְחוּ בַיהֹוָה
עֶזְרָם וּמָגִנָּם הוּא:

6. *they hear not*. Prayers offered to them.

they smell not. Incense and sacrifices burnt in their honour.

7. *they have hands*. The grammatical form is changed and the more literal rendering is: 'as for their hands, they (the idols) cannot touch; as for their feet, they (the idols) cannot walk.'

handle. Better, 'touch.' Lacking the power of touch, the hands of the idols are merely ornamental and mean nothing.

neither speak they. Not the same verb as in verse 5. It signifies making an inarticulate sound. Even this they are incapable of doing, because they are completely dumb (Kimchi).

8. *shall be*. Ibn Ezra construes this as a prayer: 'may they that make them be like unto them.'

like unto them. Bereft of their faculties. 'Since they put their trust in the figments of folly, they forfeit their significance as human beings and, lost and helpless, they perish' (Hirsch).

9-11 TRUST IN GOD

9. *O Israel*. The three categories are also mentioned in cxviii. 2-4 and cxxxv. 19f. In the latter passage *house of Israel* occurs and *house of Levi* is added.

He is their help. The choral response to the precentor's invocation in the first half of the verse. Hence the third person *their*. The combination of *help* and *shield* is found in xxxiii. 20.

11. *ye that fear the LORD*. Rashi takes this as a reference to proselytes, while, according to Kimchi, it means those totally devoted to Torah study.

12 The Lord hath been mindful of
 us, He will bless—
 He will bless the house of Israel;
 He will bless the house of Aaron.

13 He will bless them that fear the
 Lord,
 Both small and great.

14 The Lord increase you more and
 more,
 You and your children.

15 Blessed be ye of the Lord,
 Who made heaven and earth.

16 The heavens are the heavens of
 the Lord;
 But the earth hath He given to the
 children of men.

17 The dead praise not the Lord,
 Neither any that go down into
 silence;

18 But we will bless the Lord
 From this time forth and for ever.
 Hallelujah.

12 יְהֹוָה זְכָרָנוּ יְבָרֵךְ
יְבָרֵךְ אֶת־בֵּית יִשְׂרָאֵל
יְבָרֵךְ אֶת־בֵּית אַהֲרֹן:

13 יְבָרֵךְ יִרְאֵי יְהֹוָה
הַקְּטַנִּים עִם־הַגְּדֹלִים:

14 יֹסֵף יְהֹוָה עֲלֵיכֶם
עֲלֵיכֶם וְעַל־בְּנֵיכֶם:

15 בְּרוּכִים אַתֶּם לַיהֹוָה
עֹשֵׂה שָׁמַיִם וָאָרֶץ:

16 הַשָּׁמַיִם שָׁמַיִם לַיהֹוָה
וְהָאָרֶץ נָתַן לִבְנֵי־אָדָם:

17 לֹא הַמֵּתִים יְהַלְלוּ־יָהּ
וְלֹא כָּל־יֹרְדֵי דוּמָה:

18 וַאֲנַחְנוּ נְבָרֵךְ יָהּ
מֵעַתָּה וְעַד־עוֹלָם
הַלְלוּיָהּ:

12-15 God's Blessing Assured

12. *the Lord ... bless.* Rather, 'the Lord Who hath been mindful of us will bless.' Israel acknowledges that God has always watched over them even if, at times, it did not appear obvious (Daath Sofrim).

13. *both small and great.* An idiom for total inclusiveness. Hirsch perceptively explains that the young thereby retain an eternal link with the old.

14. *increase you.* A prophecy (Kimchi). The Psalmist gives an assurance that though they will suffer population decline during exile, they will dramatically proliferate in the era preceding the Messiah (Abarbanel).

15. *Who made heaven and earth.* And therefore endowed with power to confer blessings, unlike the inert idols of the heathens.

16-18 The Earth and Heaven

16. The statement of the preceding verse is taken up and a practical moral drawn from it. Heaven is God's dwelling place from which He directs the destinies of His creatures; earth is assigned to man as the stage on which he plays his part during his term of existence.

17. *the dead praise not the Lord.* 'Man should occupy himself with Torah and benevolent acts before he dies; for on his death he cannot any longer do this and the Holy One, blessed be He, finds nought to praise in him' (Talmud; see on vi. 6).

go down into silence. Descend to Sheol (cf. xciv. 17).

18. *but we.* Emphasized in the Hebrew: we who are living.

and for ever. For the remainder of our life, as in lxxxvi. 12.

116

1 I love that the LORD should hear
My voice and my supplications.

2 Because He hath inclined His ear
  unto me,
Therefore will I call upon Him
  all my days.

3 The cords of death compassed me,
And the straits of the nether-world
  got hold upon me;
I found trouble and sorrow.

4 But I called upon the name of the
  LORD:
'I beseech Thee, O LORD, deliver
  my soul.'

5 Gracious is the LORD, and righteous;
Yea, our God is compassionate.

6 The LORD preserveth the simple;
I was brought low, and He saved
  me.

קטז

אָהַבְתִּי כִּי־יִשְׁמַע ׀ יְהוָה,
אֶת־קוֹלִי תַּחֲנוּנָי:
כִּי־הִטָּה אָזְנוֹ לִי 2
וּבְיָמַי אֶקְרָא:
אֲפָפוּנִי ׀ חֶבְלֵי־מָוֶת 3
וּמְצָרֵי שְׁאוֹל מְצָאוּנִי
צָרָה וְיָגוֹן אֶמְצָא:
וּבְשֵׁם־יְהוָה אֶקְרָא 4
אָנָּה יְהוָה מַלְּטָה נַפְשִׁי:
חַנּוּן יְהוָה וְצַדִּיק 5
וֵאלֹהֵינוּ מְרַחֵם:
שֹׁמֵר פְּתָאיִם יְהוָה 6
דַּלֹּתִי וְלִי יְהוֹשִׁיעַ:

PERSONAL THANKSGIVING TO GOD

IN contrast to CXV which concerns the nation as a whole, this Psalm is strongly individualistic throughout. As the people had cause to praise God for deliverance from the sufferings in captivity, the Psalmist records his personal experience as testimony to His saving power. Who he was is unknown. Some think of king Hezekiah after his illness (Malbim), but there are indications that David composed it after Saul's death upon being proclaimed king (Rashi).

1-2 GOD ANSWERS PRAYER

1. *I love … hear*. So most commentators. Another possible rendering is: 'I love (Him), because the LORD heareth' (Metsudath David).

my voice and my supplications. The Hebrew has no *and*, so the phrase must be translated either 'my voice (even) my supplications,' or better 'the voice of my supplications.'

2. *because*. Rather 'for He hath inclined … and in (all) my days will I call (upon Him).' Having proved by experience that God does hearken to his prayer, he will turn to Him whenever help is needed. What that experience was he now proceeds to relate.

3-6 THE PSALMIST TELLS OF HIS PERIL

With this section, cf. xviii. 6-7.

3. *the cords of death compassed me*. Verbatim from xviii. 5.

straits. The confined space of Sheol in which he felt himself entrapped; opposite of a broad place in which he is able to move about freely (cf. cxviii. 5).

4. *I called*. More lit. 'I kept calling.'

the name of the LORD. i.e. the LORD in His revealed attributes which are enumerated in the next verse.

5. Cf. cxi. 4.

6. *the simple*. See on xix. 8.

7 Return, O my soul, unto thy rest;
    For the LORD hath dealt bounti-
      fully with thee.

8 For Thou hast delivered my soul
      from death,
    Mine eyes from tears,
    And my feet from stumbling.

9 I shall walk before the LORD
    In the lands of the living.

10 I trusted even when I spoke:
     'I am greatly afflicted.'

11 I said in my haste:
     'All men are liars.'

12 How can I repay unto the LORD
     All His bountiful dealings toward
      me?

13 I will lift up the cup of salvation,
    And call upon the name of the
      LORD.

7 שׁוּבִי נַפְשִׁי לִמְנוּחָיְכִי

כִּי־יְהֹוָה גָּמַל עָלָיְכִי:

8 כִּי חִלַּצְתָּ נַפְשִׁי מִמָּוֶת

אֶת־עֵינִי מִן־דִּמְעָה

אֶת־רַגְלִי מִדֶּחִי:

9 אֶתְהַלֵּךְ לִפְנֵי יְהֹוָה

בְּאַרְצוֹת הַחַיִּים:

10 הֶאֱמַנְתִּי כִּי אֲדַבֵּר

אֲנִי עָנִיתִי מְאֹד:

11 אֲנִי אָמַרְתִּי בְחָפְזִי

כָּל־הָאָדָם כֹּזֵב:

12 מָה־אָשִׁיב לַיהֹוָה

כָּל־תַּגְמוּלוֹהִי עָלָי:

13 כּוֹס־יְשׁוּעוֹת אֶשָּׂא

וּבְשֵׁם יְהֹוָה אֶקְרָא:

7-11   HIS CONFIDENCE IN GOD

7. *return ... rest.* Cease to be anxious and regain tranquillity of spirit (Daath Sofrim). *Rest* is plural in Hebrew, the plural of intensity, signifying perfect rest (cf. Hirsch).

hath dealt bountifully. Cf. xiii. 6.

8. Very similar to lvi. 14.

9. *I shall walk before the LORD.* Cf. the exhortation to Abraham (Gen. xvii. 1).

in the lands of the living. As opposed to *the straits of the nether-world* (verse 3) (Kimchi).

10. Render: 'I trusted (God) even when I was saying, "I am greatly afflicted."' His faith held firm during the time his distress was acute.

11. *I said in my haste.* Same as in xxxi. 23. For *haste* substitute 'alarm' or 'panic.'

Whereas in the earlier Psalm the writer felt during the crisis that he was cut off from before God's eyes and was utterly forlorn, this Psalm expresses strengthened reliance upon God, the thought possessing the author being the futility of human aid.

all men are liars. Rather, 'all of mankind is deceptive,' his power to assist is unreliable (cf. *vain is the help of man,* lx. 13). The noun from this root occurs in lxii. 10, *men of low degree are vanity, and men of high degree are a lie.*

12-14   VOWS OF GRATITUDE

13. *the cup of salvation.* Alluding to the drink-offering which he will bring to the Temple in recognition of his release from danger (Rashi).

call upon. Openly proclaim God as his Rescuer.

14 My vows will I pay unto the
   LORD,
   Yea, in the presence of all His
   people.
15 Precious in the sight of the LORD
   Is the death of His saints.
16 I beseech Thee, O LORD, for I
   am Thy servant;
   I am Thy servant, the son of Thy
   handmaid;
   Thou hast loosed my bands.
17 I will offer to Thee the sacrifice
   of thanksgiving,
   And will call upon the name of
   the LORD.
18 I will pay my vows unto the LORD,
   Yea, in the presence of all His
   people;
19 In the courts of the LORD's house,
   In the midst of thee, O Jerusalem.
   Hallelujah.

14 נְדָרַי לַיהֹוָה אֲשַׁלֵּם
   נֶגְדָה־נָּא לְכָל־עַמּוֹ:
15 יָקָר בְּעֵינֵי יְהֹוָה
   הַמָּוְתָה לַחֲסִידָיו:
16 אָנָּה יְהֹוָה כִּי־אֲנִי עַבְדֶּךָ
   אֲנִי עַבְדְּךָ בֶּן־אֲמָתֶךָ
   פִּתַּחְתָּ לְמוֹסֵרָי:
17 לְךָ־אֶזְבַּח זֶבַח תּוֹדָה
   וּבְשֵׁם יְהֹוָה אֶקְרָא:
18 נְדָרַי לַיהֹוָה אֲשַׁלֵּם
   נֶגְדָה־נָּא לְכָל־עַמּוֹ:
19 בְּחַצְרוֹת ׀ בֵּית יְהֹוָה
   בְּתוֹכֵכִי־יְרוּשָׁלָ͏ִם
   הַלְלוּיָהּ:

14. Repeated in verse 18. What he had promised to do in his time of peril, if God sent him relief, he will publicly discharge, thereby testifying that he owes his life to Divine mercy (Metsudath David).

15-19 HE WILL OFFER HIS THANKSGIVING SACRIFICE

15. *precious.* God does not regard their death lightly and therefore hastens to protect them (cf. lxxii. 14) (Kimchi, Metsudath David).

His saints. Hebrew *chasid* (see on iv. 4). The Psalmist includes himself in that category (Kimchi).

16. *I beseech Thee.* This Hebrew particle is normally followed by a petition, as in cxviii. 25. Accordingly, *Thou hast loosed* is understood by Malbim as 'the precative perfect,' i.e. it equals 'mayest Thou loosen'; but the context speaks of the deliverance as already accomplished. Most commentators render 'I thank thee for Thou hast loosened my bands.' The word *anah* indicates acknowledgement of a debt of gratitude (cf. Exod. xxxii. 31) (Hirsch).

Thy servant ... handmaid. See on lxxxvi. 16. The humble self-description expresses the speaker's feeling of dependence for the future as well as in the past.

loosed my bands. No longer hemmed in by danger and suffering (cf. cvii. 14).

17. *sacrifice of thanksgiving.* Described in Lev. vii. 11ff.

and will call. Repeated from verse 13.

19. *in the courts.* Where the Israelites assembled; only the priests entered the holy precincts of the Temple.

קיז

הַלְלוּ אֶת־יְהֹוָה כָּל־גּוֹיִם
שַׁבְּחוּהוּ כָּל־הָאֻמִּים:
2 כִּי גָבַר עָלֵינוּ ׀ חַסְדּוֹ
וֶאֱמֶת־יְהֹוָה לְעוֹלָם
הַלְלוּיָהּ:

117

1 O praise the LORD, all ye nations;
  Laud Him, all ye peoples.

2 For His mercy is great toward us;
  And the truth of the LORD en-
    dureth for ever.
  Hallelujah.

SUMMONS TO ALL NATIONS TO PRAISE GOD

THIS, the shortest of the Psalms, alludes to the Messianic era when the world will be formed of two groups praising the LORD: the nation of Israel, who will continue to serve God by fulfilling His Torah, and the Gentiles of the world, who will acknowledge God by fulfilling the Noahide laws (Kimchi). Its insertion in the Psalter is a witness to the universal aspiration of Judaism. The mission of Israel remains unfulfilled until the hope voiced in this Psalm becomes a reality. On the day it does, Israel will address the rest of mankind, summoning them to render homage to the Almighty, and to proclaim His greatness (Hirsch). The two verses are in truth *multum in parvo*. Some Hebrew MSS do not treat it as a separate Psalm, but attach it either to the end of CXVI or the beginning of CXVIII. Its message, however, is distinct from both of them, and LXX conforms to the arrangement of M.T., which regards it as a separate Psalm.

1. *laud.* lit. 'to improve.' Those of the nations who had never done so previously, will praise the LORD. Those who had acknowledged and praised him heretofore, will now improve upon this by lauding Him (Malbim).

2. *mercy.* Hebrew *chesed*, 'love.'

great toward us. The Hebrew is literally 'has been mighty upon us.' The meaning is that Divine love prevailed over Divine justice, and in spite of the nation's sins an event has happened which was a marvellous demonstation of God's clemency.

truth of the LORD. This and *His mercy* are God's two main attributes in His dealings with men (cxv. 1), and the recognition of them compels praise of Him.

Hallelujah. A song of praise to God for the fulfillment of His promises (Metsudath David).

118

1 'O give thanks unto the LORD,
    for He is good,
  For His mercy endureth for ever'.

2 So let Israel now say,
  For His mercy endureth for ever.

3 So let the house of Aaron now say,
  For His mercy endureth for ever.

4 So let them now that fear the
    LORD say,
  For His mercy endureth for ever.

5 Out of my straits I called upon
    the LORD;
  He answered me with great en-
    largement.

6 The LORD is for me; I will not
    fear;
  What can man do unto me?

קיח

הוֹדוּ לַיהוָה כִּי־טוֹב

כִּי לְעוֹלָם חַסְדּוֹ:

2 יֹאמַר־נָא יִשְׂרָאֵל

כִּי לְעוֹלָם חַסְדּוֹ:

3 יֹאמְרוּ־נָא בֵית־אַהֲרֹן

כִּי לְעוֹלָם חַסְדּוֹ:

4 יֹאמְרוּ־נָא יִרְאֵי יְהוָה

כִּי לְעוֹלָם חַסְדּוֹ:

5 מִן־הַמֵּצַר קָרָאתִי יָּהּ

עָנָנִי בַמֶּרְחָב יָהּ:

6 יְהוָה לִי לֹא אִירָא

מַה־יַּעֲשֶׂה לִי אָדָם:

NATIONAL THANKSGIVING

A JOYFUL proclamation of the people in the Temple on the occasion of the final redemption is the scene of this Psalm, and the feelings of gratitude which animated their hearts are expressed in glowing language. According to a second Rabbinic view, the Psalm was composed by David upon the death of Saul. It expresses his relief from the relentless pressure to which he had been subjected during Saul's reign (Kimchi).

1-4 INVOCATION TO PRAISE GOD

1. See on cvi. 1.

2ff. For the three categories, *Israel, house of Aaron,* and *that fear the LORD,* see on cxv. 9, 11.

5-9 THE DIVINE ALLY

5. *straits ... enlargement.* See on cxvi. 3. Here 'straits' refers to the difficulties David encountered while being pursued by Saul.

Alternatively, Israel in exile, called upon God until He relieved them from their oppressive circumstances (Kimchi).

the LORD. Hebrew *Jah,* the Redeemer of their ancestors from Egypt (Exod. xv. 2), Who had extended His protection to them also (cf. Abarbanel).

6. Cf. lvi. 10 (end), 12.

7. *as my helper.* lit. 'among my helpers'; but the implication is not that the Jews had

7 The LORD is for me as my helper;
  And I shall gaze upon them that
    hate me.

8 It is better to take refuge in the
    LORD
  Than to trust in man.

9 It is better to take refuge in the
    LORD
  Than to trust in princes.

10 All nations compass me about;
   Verily, in the name of the LORD I
     will cut them off.

11 They compass me about, yea,
     they compass me about;
   Verily, in the name of the LORD
     I will cut them off.

12 They compass me about like
     bees;
   They are quenched as the fire of
     thorns;
   Verily, in the name of the LORD
     I will cut them off.

13 Thou didst thrust sore at me that
     I might fall;
   But the LORD helped me.

7 יְהוָה לִי בְּעֹזְרָי
וַאֲנִי אֶרְאֶה בְשֹׂנְאָי׃

8 טוֹב לַחֲסוֹת בַּיהוָה
מִבְּטֹחַ בָּאָדָם׃

9 טוֹב לַחֲסוֹת בַּיהוָה
מִבְּטֹחַ בִּנְדִיבִים׃

10 כָּל־גּוֹיִם סְבָבוּנִי
בְּשֵׁם יְהוָה כִּי אֲמִילַם׃

11 סַבּוּנִי גַם־סְבָבוּנִי
בְּשֵׁם יְהוָה כִּי אֲמִילַם׃

12 סַבּוּנִי כִדְבֹרִים
דֹּעֲכוּ כְּאֵשׁ קוֹצִים
בְּשֵׁם יְהוָה כִּי אֲמִילַם׃

13 דַּחֹה דְחִיתַנִי לִנְפֹּל
וַיהוָה עֲזָרָנִי׃

additional assistance besides God. It simply
means that 'those who helped me were messengers of God sent to execute His plans' (cf.
Ibn Ezra, Hirsch).

gaze upon. See on xcii.12.

8f. It is better to look with confidence
toward the help of God, though it be far off,
than to trust in the aid of men, though it be
present now — even if those men are of noble
character who show kindness and compassion (Hirsch).

10-14 TRIUMPH OVER ENEMIES

10. *all nations.* David was surrounded by
enemies when he sought refuge with King
Achish in Philistia. Alternatively, Israel has
been surrounded by hostile nations during its
exile (Kimchi).

in the name of the LORD. Relying upon His
help (cf. David's challenge to Goliath, *I come*

to thee in the name of the LORD of hosts, 1 Sam.
xvii. 45).

I will cut them off. That is the thought of the
Jews when the contest is forced upon them.
At the time of the redemption it will be an
accomplished fact.

11. *yea, they compass me about.* Repeated
to fill in the metrical line.

12. *like bees.* Cf. Deut. i. 44.

quenched ... thorns. Their malice blazed like
thorns on fire which shoot out flames but
soon are consumed and leave nought but
ashes. It, too, lasted only a brief while and
quickly ceased to do harm (Ibn Ezra).

13. *thou didst thrust sore at me.* The community, personified as an individual, addresses itself to the enemy nations similarly
personified.

14 The LORD is my strength and
  song;
  And He is become my salvation.

15 The voice of rejoicing and salvation is in the tents of the
  righteous;
  The right hand of the LORD doeth
  valiantly.

16 The right hand of the LORD is
  exalted;
  The right hand of the LORD
  doeth valiantly.

17 I shall not die, but live,
  And declare the works of the
  LORD.

18 The LORD hath chastened me
  sore;
  But He hath not given me over
  unto death.

19 Open to me the gates of righteousness;
  I will enter into them, I will give
  thanks unto the LORD.

עָזִּי וְזִמְרָת יָהּ 14
וַיְהִי־לִי לִישׁוּעָה:
קוֹל ׀ רִנָּה וִישׁוּעָה בְּאָהֳלֵי צַדִּיקִים 15
יְמִין יְהוָֹה עֹשָׂה חָיִל:
יְמִין יְהוָֹה רוֹמֵמָה 16
יְמִין יְהוָֹה עֹשָׂה חָיִל:
לֹא־אָמוּת כִּי־אֶחְיֶה 17
וַאֲסַפֵּר מַעֲשֵׂי יָהּ:
יַסֹּר יִסְּרַנִּי יָּהּ 18
וְלַמָּוֶת לֹא נְתָנָנִי:
פִּתְחוּ־לִי שַׁעֲרֵי־צֶדֶק 19
אָבֹא־בָם אוֹדֶה יָהּ:

14.   Quoted from the song at the Red Sea (Exod. xv. 2).

15-18   JOY OF THE DELIVERED NATION

15.   *tents*. Poetical term for dwelling-places, as in xci. 10.

righteous. Israel vindicated by God in the defeat of the heathen.

right hand. See on xvii. 7.

16.   *is exalted*. Or, 'exalteth (me).'

17.   *I shall not die*. Israel speaks as a nation that escaped from the annihilation which had threatened.

declare the works of the LORD. The perpetuation of the national life would be eloquent and convincing witness to the truth that God decides the destinies of peoples (cf. Hirsch).

18.   *chastened me sore*. During the long exile, so that sins should be forgiven and, as a result, He did not put me to death (Rashi) (see Tal. Ber. 5a,b).

19-25   THE PROCESSION
ENTERS THE TEMPLE

19.   *open to me*. The gates are closed, and the king with his entourage claim admission (Malbim).

gates of righteousness. Leading to the Temple where the Presence of the righteous God abides and from which He sent forth His help to the distressed (Metsudath David).

the LORD. Hebrew *Jah*, the Victor over the forces of evil.

20 This is the gate of the LORD;
   The righteous shall enter into it.

21 I will give thanks unto Thee, for
   Thou hast answered me,
   And art become my salvation.

22 The stone which the builders rejected
   Is become the chief corner-stone.

23 This is the LORD's doing;
   It is marvellous in our eyes.

24 This is the day which the LORD
   hath made;
   We will rejoice and be glad in it.

25 We beseech Thee, O LORD, save
   now !
   We beseech Thee, O LORD, make
   us now to prosper!

20 זֶה־הַשַּׁעַר לַיהֹוָה
צַדִּיקִים יָבֹאוּ בוֹ׃
21 אוֹדְךָ כִּי עֲנִיתָנִי
וַתְּהִי־לִי לִישׁוּעָה׃
22 אֶבֶן מָאֲסוּ הַבּוֹנִים
הָיְתָה לְרֹאשׁ פִּנָּה׃
23 מֵאֵת יְהֹוָה הָיְתָה זֹּאת
הִיא נִפְלָאת בְּעֵינֵינוּ׃
24 זֶה־הַיּוֹם עָשָׂה יְהֹוָה
נָגִילָה וְנִשְׂמְחָה בוֹ׃
25 אָנָּא יְהֹוָה הוֹשִׁיעָה נָּא
אָנָּא יְהֹוָה הַצְלִיחָה נָּא׃

20. The response of the Levites who act as gate-keepers.

the righteous. 'It does not say, "The priests, the Levites and Israel shall enter," but *the righteous shall enter*—the righteous Gentile also' (Sifra on Lev. xviii. 5; cf. Isa. xxvi. 2, where the Rabbis interpret *righteous nation* as 'a pious non-Israelite').

21. Now the procession has passed through the outer gates and the purpose of the assembly is stated (Malbim).

and art ... my salvation. Based on Exod. xv. 2.

22. *chief corner-stone.* Either the top stone which completes the edifice (Zech. iv. 7), or the large stone at the foundation which binds two layers at right angles (Isa. xxviii. 16; Jer. li. 26). On either explanation, it is a stone which holds an important place in the structure. Similarly, Israel, despised by neighbouring peoples, has been appointed by God for an essential function to discharge in the construction of His kingdom upon earth (cf. Hirsch). That was the interpretation placed upon their survival by those who gathered in the Temple to thank and praise Him.

23. *this is the LORD's doing.* lit. 'from the LORD has this come to pass' (cf. Nehem. vi. 16).

marvellous. A miraculous happening due to Divine agency.

24. *the day.* Of redemption which led to national rejoicing and thanksgiving.

in it. On this great occasion, or in the event which is being celebrated. It may also mean *in Him* (cf. xxxii. 11) (Daath Sofrim).

25. *save now.* Hebrew *hoshiah-na*; in its contracted form *hosha-na*, it appears in the name given to the seventh day of Tabernacles, Hoshana Rabbah. *Now* may equal 'we pray Thee' (see on cxv. 2).

make us now to prosper. The phrase occurs in Nehem. i. 11. The prayer is for continued support in the future.

26 Blessed be he that cometh in the
    name of the LORD;
    We bless you out of the house of
    the LORD.

27 The LORD is God, and hath given
    us light;
    Order the festival procession with
    boughs, even unto the horns of
    the altar.

28 Thou art my God, and I will give
    thanks unto Thee;
    Thou art my God, I will exalt
    Thee.

29 O give thanks unto the LORD, for
    He is good,
    For His mercy endureth for ever.

26 בָּרוּךְ הַבָּא בְּשֵׁם יְהֹוָה
בֵּרַכְנוּכֶם מִבֵּית יְהֹוָה:
27 אֵל יְהֹוָה וַיָּאֶר לָנוּ
אִסְרוּ־חַג בַּעֲבֹתִים
עַד־קַרְנוֹת הַמִּזְבֵּחַ:
28 אֵלִי אַתָּה וְאוֹדֶךָּ
אֱלֹהַי אֲרוֹמְמֶךָּ:
29 הוֹדוּ לַיהֹוָה כִּי־טוֹב
כִּי לְעוֹלָם חַסְדּוֹ:

26-29   THE SERVICE IN THE TEMPLE

26. *blessed be he*. Spoken by the priests to each member of the procession (Kimchi).

in the name of the LORD. Better, 'with,' to be attached to *blessed be he*, not to *cometh* (cf. cxxix. 8; Deut. xxi.5) (Hirsch).

27. *is God*. Hebrew *el*, the Mighty One Who has demonstrated His infinite power by dispelling the darkness of captivity.

hath given us light. Symbol of deliverance (Esther viii. 16). The darkness of national anxiety and tribulation has given place to the light of freedom (Kimchi).

order the festival procession with boughs. Render as A.V. and R.V., *bind the sacrifice with cords* (so Rashi and Ibn Ezra) referring to the offerings which were brought. For the verb *asar* in the sense of *order*, vf. 1 Kings xx. 14, where it means marshalling troops for battle.

horns of the altar. Upward projections at the sides of the altar upon which the priests poured blood of sacrificial animals (Lev. iv. 7). Unapproachable by non-priests, they marked the limit to which they would proceed.

28. This (similar to Exod. xv. 2) and the next verse are sung by the procession. *My God* is said by each pilgrim (Ibn Ezra) or the national body, in acknowledging God's delivering him from exile (Kimchi).

29. Ending the Psalm as it began. According to Ibn Ezra, the verse is the response of the priests and Levites to the declaration in the preceding verse.

ALEPH

1 Happy are they that are upright
  in the way,
   Who walk in the law of the LORD.
2 Happy are they that keep His
   testimonies,
   That seek Him with the whole
   heart;
3 Yea, they do no unrighteousness;
   They walk in His ways.
4 Thou hast ordained Thy precepts,
   That we should observe them
   diligently.
5 Oh that my ways were directed
   To observe Thy statutes!

אַשְׁרֵי תְמִימֵי־דָרֶךְ
הַהֹלְכִים בְּתוֹרַת יְהֹוָה:
2 אַשְׁרֵי נֹצְרֵי עֵדֹתָיו
בְּכָל־לֵב יִדְרְשׁוּהוּ:
3 אַף לֹא־פָעֲלוּ עַוְלָה
בִּדְרָכָיו הָלָכוּ:
4 אַתָּה צִוִּיתָה פִקֻּדֶיךָ
לִשְׁמֹר מְאֹד:
5 אַחֲלַי יִכֹּנוּ דְרָכָי
לִשְׁמֹר חֻקֶּיךָ:

TORAH THE WAY OF LIFE

AN extraordinary declaration of the joy and help which Torah brings to those who conduct their life under its direction fills the longest of the Psalms. It consists of twenty-two stanzas corresponding with the number of letters in the Hebrew alphabet. All eight verses of each stanza begin with the letter of the alphabet following the one in the previous stanza, until the alphabet is completed. The author also adopts the key-words used in xix. 8-10, and taking them and others as his motif, weaves them into a verbal fugue. As spokesman of many co-religionists who endorse his tribute, he draws lavishly upon his resources of language to convey his love of Torah and the force it is in his life. Many commentators identify David as the composer of the Psalm (but see Ibn Ezra).

1-8 ALEPH

1. *upright*. The same Hebrew word as in Gen. xvii. 1, *walk before Me and be thou whole-hearted*. Those to whom the epithet applies are undivided in their allegiance and completely guided by the Torah.

the way. The path of life delineated for man in the Divine Revelation.

the law. Hebrew *Torah*, the first and most comprehensive of the key-words. 'Law,' denotes a legal system. The true meaning is 'teaching, direction,' and it connotes the whole will of God imparted to man for his guidance (cf. Daath Sofrim).

2. *testimonies*. The second key-word: rules of conduct which attest to the Divine will (Hirsch).

that seek Him. Cf. verse 10 and Deut. iv. 29. They earnestly set out on the quest to discover how God desires man to live (Hirsch).

with the whole heart. With the fullest concentration of the mental faculty upon the task of learning.

3. *do no unrighteousness*. Because the fundamental purpose of Torah is to withhold man from the path of evil.

His ways. Ways of righteousness.

4. *precepts*. The third key-word, denoting particularized rules which are man's duty to obey.

5. *my ways*. Daily conduct.

6 Then should I not be ashamed,
   When I have regard unto all Thy
   commandments.

7 I will give thanks unto Thee with
   uprightness of heart,
   When I learn Thy righteous ordinances.

8 I will observe Thy statutes;
   O forsake me not utterly.

9 Wherewithal shall a young man
   keep his way pure?
   By taking heed thereto according
   to Thy word.

10 With my whole heart have I
    sought Thee;
    O let me not err from Thy com-
    mandments.

11 Thy word have I laid up in my
    heart,
    That I might not sin against Thee.

אָז לֹא־אֵבוֹשׁ 6
בְּהַבִּיטִי אֶל־כָּל־מִצְוֹתֶיךָ׃
אוֹדְךָ בְּיֹשֶׁר לֵבָב 7
בְּלָמְדִי מִשְׁפְּטֵי צִדְקֶךָ׃
אֶת־חֻקֶּיךָ אֶשְׁמֹר 8
אַל־תַּעַזְבֵנִי עַד־מְאֹד׃

BETH

בַּמֶּה יְזַכֶּה־נַּעַר אֶת־אָרְחוֹ 9
לִשְׁמֹר כִּדְבָרֶךָ׃
בְּכָל־לִבִּי דְרַשְׁתִּיךָ 10
אַל־תַּשְׁגֵּנִי מִמִּצְוֹתֶיךָ׃
בְּלִבִּי צָפַנְתִּי אִמְרָתֶךָ 11
לְמַעַן לֹא אֶחֱטָא־לָךְ׃

statutes. The fourth key-word, which does not occur in xix. Its literal meaning is 'that which is engraved' on stone, the common form the laws of a community were published. It signifies laws which control our physical drives (Hirsch) as well as those which regulate the life of an individual as a member of society. Many of these laws have no obvious rationale and are kept purely out of faith in God.

6. *not be ashamed*. The reasons for most commandments are discernable, thus there will be no embarrassment (Ibn Ezra).

commandments. The fifth key-word: a general term for a law of God in the sphere of the religious life.

7. *when I learn*. An in-depth study of God's ordinances is necessary in order to become fully acquainted with them. Even while pursuing this aim, the learners will acquire 'uprightness of heart' (cf. Hirsch).

ordinances. The sixth key-word: lit. 'judgments' which regulate man's relationship with his neighbour, and are characterized by righteousness.

8. *O forsake me not utterly*. Mindful of Israel's fate when guilty of transgression, he prayed to be spared that penalty because his endeavour will be to adhere faithfully to what God commands.

9-16   BETH

9. *a young man*. Beset by temptations.

word. Hebrew *dabar*, the seventh key-word: a general term for the expressed will of God.

10. *with ... heart ... Thee*. Cf. verse 2.

let me not err. Not intentionally, but inadvertently through defective knowledge (cf. Hirsch).

11. *word*. Hebrew *imrah*, the eighth and last key-word: a poetical variant of *dabar* (verse 9; cf. the parallelism in *they have rejected the law* (Torah) *of the LORD of hosts, and contemned the word* (imrah) *of the Holy One of Israel*, Isa. v. 24).

have I laid up. The verb is commonly used of safeguarding a precious object (Daath Sofrim). So has the Psalmist treated God's word.

12 Blessed art Thou, O Lord;
   Teach me Thy statutes.

13 With my lips have I told
   All the ordinances of Thy mouth.

14 I have rejoiced in the way of Thy
     testimonies,
   As much as in all riches.

15 I will meditate in Thy precepts,
   And have respect unto Thy ways.

16 I will delight myself in Thy
     statutes;
   I will not forget Thy word.

GIMEL

17 Deal bountifully with Thy ser-
     vant, that I may live,
   And I will observe Thy word.

18 Open Thou mine eyes, that I may
     behold
   Wondrous things out of Thy law.

19 I am a sojourner in the earth;
   Hide not Thy commandments
     from me.

בָּרוּךְ אַתָּה יְהֹוָה 12
לַמְּדֵנִי חֻקֶּיךָ׃

בִּשְׂפָתַי סִפַּרְתִּי 13
כֹּל מִשְׁפְּטֵי־פִיךָ׃

בְּדֶרֶךְ עֵדְוֺתֶיךָ שַׂשְׂתִּי 14
כְּעַל כָּל־הוֹן׃

בְּפִקּוּדֶיךָ אָשִׂיחָה 15
וְאַבִּיטָה אֹרְחֹתֶיךָ׃

בְּחֻקֹּתֶיךָ אֶשְׁתַּעֲשָׁע 16
לֹא אֶשְׁכַּח דְּבָרֶךָ׃

גְּמֹל עַל־עַבְדְּךָ אֶחְיֶה 17
וְאֶשְׁמְרָה דְבָרֶךָ׃

גַּל־עֵינַי וְאַבִּיטָה 18
נִפְלָאוֹת מִתּוֹרָתֶךָ׃

גֵּר אָנֹכִי בָאָרֶץ 19
אַל־תַּסְתֵּר מִמֶּנִּי מִצְוֺתֶיךָ׃

12. *blessed art Thou.* 'In the relation of man to God, "to bless" means to prosper His cause by our consecration of heart, soul, and might to the advancement of His kingdom' (Hertz).

13. *with my lips have I told.* In addition to laying them up in his heart (verse 11), he took every opportunity to speak of them for the instruction of others.

14. *in all riches.* He found joyful satisfaction in the Torah such as others derive from the acquisition of wealth.

15. *meditate.* The precepts will be the subject which occupy his thoughts.

16. *delight myself.* Others look for their pleasures in things material, but he delights in meditation upon God's will.

17-24 GIMEL

17. The translation of A.J. wrongly conveys the impression that the Psalmist un-

dertakes to keep God's word in return for His bounty. A better rendering is: 'Grant to Thy servant that I may live, so that I may keep Thy word' (cf. Kimchi).

18. *open.* Rather, 'unveil,' lit. 'roll away' whatever obscures discernment.

wondrous things. The Hebrew word is only used of works of God; therefore the signification here is the Divine teachings contained in the Torah.

19. *a sojourner.* Hebrew *ger.* In xxxix. 13 the Psalmist called himself *a stranger* (ger) *with Thee,* where he alluded to his temporary stay in the world. Here the meaning is different: as an alien needs to learn the roads and paths of the new country in which he resides lest he get lost, so the Psalmist begs to be taught the commandments enacted by God for the dwellers upon His earth (Ibn Ezra).

20 My soul breaketh for the longing
   That it hath unto Thine ordin-
     ances at all times.
21 Thou hast rebuked the proud
   that are cursed,
   That do err from Thy command-
     ments.
22 Take away from me reproach and
   contempt;
   For I have kept Thy testimonies.
23 Even though princes sit and talk
   against me,
   Thy servant doth meditate in
     Thy statutes.
24 Yea, Thy testimonies are my
   delight,
   They are my counsellors.

DALETH

25 My soul cleaveth unto the dust;
   Quicken Thou me according to
     Thy word.
26 I told of my ways, and Thou
   didst answer me;
   Teach me Thy statutes.

20 גָּרְסָה נַפְשִׁי לְתַאֲבָה
אֶל־מִשְׁפָּטֶיךָ בְכָל־עֵת׃
21 גָּעַרְתָּ זֵדִים אֲרוּרִים
הַשֹּׁגִים מִמִּצְוֺתֶיךָ׃
22 גַּל מֵעָלַי חֶרְפָּה וָבוּז
כִּי עֵדֹתֶיךָ נָצָרְתִּי׃
23 גַּם יָשְׁבוּ שָׂרִים כִּי נִדְבָּרוּ
עַבְדְּךָ יָשִׂיחַ בְּחֻקֶּיךָ׃
24 גַּם־עֵדֹתֶיךָ שַׁעֲשֻׁעָי
אַנְשֵׁי עֲצָתִי׃

25 דָּבְקָה לֶעָפָר נַפְשִׁי
חַיֵּנִי כִּדְבָרֶךָ׃
26 דְּרָכַי סִפַּרְתִּי וַתַּעֲנֵנִי
לַמְּדֵנִי חֻקֶּיךָ׃

20. A continuation of the thought of the last verse giving the mood which prompted the request.

my soul breaketh. Equals 'I am crushed, overwhelmed, with longing for Thine ordinances at all times.'

21. As a consequence of their defections, they have arrived at fallacious interpretations of God's pronouncements. They attempt to justify their theories by persuading their contemporaries that their own understanding of God's law is more 'correct.' It is fervently wished that their endeavours meet with little success (Hirsch).

22. *take away.* The same verb as in verse 18, *open.* Again the meaning is 'to unveil,' *reproach* and *contempt* being thought of as a covering garment (cf. cix. 29). The fate of the *proud* (verse 21) will be to be covered in this manner; but he prays to be spared from the ridicule and scorn that the sinners heap upon him as a result of his unbending faith (Kimchi).

23. *princes.* Again in verse 161 he speaks of his persecutors as *princes.* They were the influential rulers of the community who sat in conclave and conspired to ruin him.

24. *my delight.* When he is harassed by these oppressors and his life is made bitter by them, he turns to God's testimonies for solace (cf. Hirsch).

my counsellors. To foil their schemes.

25-32 DALETH

25. *my soul … dust.* I am sunk to the ground under the weight of trouble and grief.

quicken. Revive, renew my vitality and give me fresh strength.

according to Thy word. He has in mind an utterance such as that in Deut. xxx. 19f.

26. *I told of my ways.* The Psalmist affirms that he had laid bare before God all his vicissitudes, and the petitions addressed to Him had been answered. Accordingly he is emboldened to offer another prayer, viz. that

27 Make me to understand the way
   of Thy precepts,
   That I may talk of Thy wondrous
   works.

28 My soul melteth away for heaviness;
   Sustain me according unto Thy
   word.

29 Remove from me the way of
   falsehood;
   And grant me Thy law graciously.

30 I have chosen the way of faithfulness;
   Thine ordinances have I set
   [before me].

31 I cleave unto Thy testimonies;
   O Lord, put me not to shame.

32 I will run the way of Thy commandments,
   For Thou dost enlarge my heart.

HE

33 Teach me, O Lord, the way of
   Thy statutes;
   And I will keep it at every step.

כז הֶרֶךְ־פִּקּוּדֶיךָ הֲבִינֵנִי
וְאָשִׂיחָה בְּנִפְלְאוֹתֶיךָ׃

כח דָּלְפָה נַפְשִׁי מִתּוּגָה
קַיְּמֵנִי כִּדְבָרֶךָ׃

כט דֶּרֶךְ־שֶׁקֶר הָסֵר מִמֶּנִּי
וְתוֹרָתְךָ חָנֵּנִי׃

ל דֶּרֶךְ־אֱמוּנָה בָחָרְתִּי
מִשְׁפָּטֶיךָ שִׁוִּיתִי׃

לא דָּבַקְתִּי בְעֵדְוֺתֶיךָ
יְהוָה אַל־תְּבִישֵׁנִי׃

לב דֶּרֶךְ־מִצְוֺתֶיךָ אָרוּץ
כִּי תַרְחִיב לִבִּי׃

לג הוֹרֵנִי יְהוָה דֶּרֶךְ חֻקֶּיךָ
וְאֶצְּרֶנָּה עֵקֶב׃

God would enable him to gain a full knowledge of His statutes (Kimchi, Hirsch).

27. *talk of.* Or, 'reflect upon.'

Thy wondrous works. The same word as in
verse 18 with the same meaning: the wonderful doctrines of the Torah.

28. *my soul melteth away.* I dissolve in tears.

heaviness. The Hebrew denotes grief and
anxiety.

29. *the way of falsehood.* Which leads
away from, instead of to God.

grant … graciously. lit. 'favour me with Thy
law'; be gracious and instruct me in its teachings, that I may perceive the way of truth and
walk therein.

30. *the way of faithfulness.* In contrast to
the way of falsehood (Kimchi).

have I set. The same verb as in *I have set the
Lord always before me* (xvi. 8).

31. *put me not to shame.* By failing to show

me Thy favour, in consequence of which I am
taunted in a time of distress by evil-doers on
the futility of obeying the commandments
(cf. Malbim).

32. *run.* An indication of pleasurable eagerness to discharge religious duties (cf. 'Run
to do even a slight precept' and 'Be as fleet as
a hart to do the will of Thy Father Who is in
Heaven'—Aboth).

enlarge my heart. Free it of distressing worries so that all energies are concentrated upon
loyal obedience (cf. Hirsch).

33-40 HE

33. *teach.* The Hebrew verb from which
the noun *Torah* is derived.

at every step. Rashi renders: in all the paths of
the Torah; but Ibn Ezra gives the word the
same meaning it has in xix. 12, viz. *a great
reward.* Keeping the laws of the Torah will
lead to *great reward.*

34 Give me understanding, that I
keep Thy law
And observe it with my whole
heart.

35 Make me to tread in the path of
Thy commandments;
For therein do I delight.

36 Incline my heart unto Thy testimonies,
And not to covetousness.

37 Turn away mine eyes from beholding vanity,
And quicken me in Thy ways.

38 Confirm Thy word unto Thy
servant,
Which pertaineth unto the fear of
Thee.

39 Turn away my reproach which I
dread;
For Thine ordinances are good.

40 Behold, I have longed after Thy
precepts;
Quicken me in Thy righteousness.

צ34 הֲבִינֵנִי וְאֶצְּרָה תוֹרָתֶךָ
וְאֶשְׁמְרֶנָּה בְכָל־לֵב:

35 הַדְרִיכֵנִי בִּנְתִיב מִצְוֹתֶיךָ
כִּי־בוֹ חָפָצְתִּי:

36 הַט־לִבִּי אֶל־עֵדְוֹתֶיךָ
וְאַל אֶל־בָּצַע:

37 הַעֲבֵר עֵינַי מֵרְאוֹת שָׁוְא
בִּדְרָכֶךָ חַיֵּנִי:

38 הָקֵם לְעַבְדְּךָ אִמְרָתֶךָ
אֲשֶׁר לְיִרְאָתֶךָ:

39 הַעֲבֵר חֶרְפָּתִי אֲשֶׁר יָגֹרְתִּי
כִּי מִשְׁפָּטֶיךָ טוֹבִים:

40 הִנֵּה תָּאַבְתִּי לְפִקֻּדֶיךָ
בְּצִדְקָתְךָ חַיֵּנִי:

34. *with my whole heart.* If he possesses an adequate understanding of the Torah, it will result in absorbing his whole thought with the aim of observing the Divine precepts (cf. Hirsch).

35. *delight.* The pleasure which accompanied the performance of God's commands is a theme upon which the Rabbis expatiated.

36. *covetousness.* lit. (love of) gain,' the acquisition of material wealth especially by dishonest methods (cf. Isa. xxxiii. 15).

37. *from beholding vanity.* i.e. from desiring things of unreal worth as compared with the true and abiding value of the merits which accrue from loyalty to God's will.

quicken me in Thy ways. Strengthen me to be stedfast in the ways of righteousness and to overcome the temptation to go astray.

38. *Thy word.* The Divine promise.

which pertaineth ... Thee. Better, 'which is to those who revere Thee.'

39. *my reproach.* The shame that he was subjected to as a result of his sins. He asks that he be forgiven so that his enemies no longer have reason to taunt him (Rashi).

are good. And should yield happiness to him who submits to them.

40. *in Thy righteousness.* Since God is righteous, He will support His loyal servants. Another possible rendering is: 'by Thy righteousness,' which is embodied in the *precepts*. From this source he prays to be refreshed to meet the troubles of life.

VAU

41 Let Thy mercies also come unto
    me, O LORD,
  Even Thy salvation, according to
    Thy word;

42 That I may have an answer for
    him that taunteth me;
  For I trust in Thy word.

43 And take not the word of truth
    utterly out of my mouth;
  For I hope in Thine ordinances;

44 So shall I observe Thy law con-
    tinually
  For ever and ever;

45 And I will walk at ease,
  For I have sought Thy precepts;

46 I will also speak of Thy testi-
    monies before kings,
  And will not be ashamed.

47 And I will delight myself in Thy
    commandments,
  Which I have loved.

48 I will lift up my hands also unto
    Thy commandments, which I
    have loved;
  And I will meditate in Thy
    statutes.

וִיבֹאֻנִי חֲסָדֶךָ יְהֹוָה 41
תְּשׁוּעָתְךָ כְּאִמְרָתֶךָ:
וְאֶעֱנֶה חֹרְפִי דָבָר 42
כִּי־בָטַחְתִּי בִּדְבָרֶךָ:
וְאַל־תַּצֵּל מִפִּי דְבַר־אֱמֶת עַד־מְאֹד 43
כִּי לְמִשְׁפָּטֶךָ יִחָלְתִּי:
וְאֶשְׁמְרָה תוֹרָתְךָ תָמִיד 44
לְעוֹלָם וָעֶד:
וְאֶתְהַלְּכָה בָרְחָבָה 45
כִּי פִקֻּדֶיךָ דָרָשְׁתִּי:
וַאֲדַבְּרָה בְעֵדֹתֶיךָ נֶגֶד מְלָכִים 46
וְלֹא אֵבוֹשׁ:
וְאֶשְׁתַּעֲשַׁע בְּמִצְוֹתֶיךָ 47
אֲשֶׁר אָהָבְתִּי:
וְאֶשָּׂא כַפַּי אֶל־מִצְוֹתֶיךָ 48
אֲשֶׁר אָהָבְתִּי
וְאָשִׂיחָה בְחֻקֶּיךָ:

41-48   VAV

41. *Thy mercies.* Demonstrated in *Thy salvation.*

word. Hebrew *imrah*, promise.

42. *an answer.* In its most convincing form for a loyal subject of God when taunted by the godless, viz. Divine salvation.

word. Hebrew *dabar* (see on verse 9).

43. *take not ... mouth.* In the absence of the manifestation of God's favour for which he prayed, he would be derived of the power of testifying to the rightness of his chosen way of life when challenged by the mockers (cf. Hirsch).

44. *so shall I observe.* His prayer, on the other hand, having been granted, he would be in a position to fulfil his wish to be observant of the Torah until his dying day (*for ever and ever*).

45. *at ease.* Freed from anxiety (see on verse 32).

sought. See on verse 2.

46. *before kings.* Without being overawed by their majesty, he will witness to the excellence of God's commandments and not feel abashed (Malbim).

47. *delight myself.* See on verse 16.

I have loved. Rather, 'I love'; so again in the next verse.

48. *lift up my hands.* The phrase usually denotes the attitude of prayer; here it is devotion or longing.

ZAIN

49 Remember the word unto Thy
    servant,
    Because Thou hast made me to
    hope.

50 This is my comfort in my
    affliction,
    That Thy word hath quickened
    me.

51 The proud have had me greatly
    in derision;
    Yet have I not turned aside from
    Thy law.

52 I have remembered Thine ordi-
    nances which are of old, O
    LORD,
    And have comforted myself.

53 Burning indignation hath taken
    hold upon me, because of the
    wicked
    That forsake Thy law.

54 Thy statutes have been my songs
    In the house of my pilgrimage.

55 I have remembered Thy name,
    O LORD, in the night,
    And have observed Thy law.

56 This I have had,
    That I have kept Thy precepts.

49 זְכֹר־דָּבָר לְעַבְדֶּךָ

עַל אֲשֶׁר יִחַלְתָּנִי:

50 זֹאת נֶחָמָתִי בְעָנְיִי

כִּי אִמְרָתְךָ חִיָּתְנִי:

51 זֵדִים הֱלִיצֻנִי עַד־מְאֹד

מִתּוֹרָתְךָ לֹא נָטִיתִי:

52 זָכַרְתִּי מִשְׁפָּטֶיךָ מֵעוֹלָם ׀ יְהֹוָה

וָאֶתְנֶחָם:

53 זַלְעָפָה אֲחָזַתְנִי מֵרְשָׁעִים

עֹזְבֵי תּוֹרָתֶךָ:

54 זְמִרוֹת הָיוּ־לִי חֻקֶּיךָ

בְּבֵית מְגוּרָי:

55 זָכַרְתִּי בַלַּיְלָה שִׁמְךָ יְהֹוָה

וָאֶשְׁמְרָה תּוֹרָתֶךָ:

56 זֹאת הָיְתָה־לִּי

כִּי פִקֻּדֶיךָ נָצָרְתִּי:

49-56 ZAIN

49. *the word.* Hebrew *dabar*, but meaning 'promise.' God's promise had inspired him with hope; may God therefore be mindful of it to save him from disappointment (cf. Hirsch).

50. *hath quickened me.* In past crises and will have the same effect in similar circumstances.

51. *proud.* Corresponds to *scornful* in i. 1.

52. *comforted myself.* In the lesson taught by past experience that the *proud* are ultimately humbled (Ibn Ezra).

53. *burning indignation.* In verse 136 these apostates are said to have caused the Psalmist to shed tears on their behalf.

54. *my songs.* The themes of songs.

house of my pilgrimage. In verse 19 he declared himself to be a *sojourner* (the same root as *pilgrimage*) *in the earth* wishing to possess a knowledge of God's laws which govern it and which become such a source of gladness to him that he is inspired to sing with joy while learning them (Malbim).

55. *I have remembered.* Better, 'I am mindful of.' God is constantly in His thoughts, even during the night (cf. i. 2) (Daath Sofrim).

56. *this I have had.* lit. 'this has been to me,' spiritual comfort and joy.

HETH

57 My portion is the LORD,
　　I have said that I would observe
　　　Thy words.

58 I have entreated Thy favour with
　　my whole heart;
　　Be gracious unto me according to
　　　Thy word.

59 I considered my ways,
　　And turned my feet unto Thy
　　　testimonies.

60 I made haste, and delayed not,
　　To observe Thy commandments.

61 The bands of the wicked have
　　enclosed me;
　　But I have not forgotten Thy law.

62 At midnight I will rise to give
　　thanks unto Thee
　　Because of Thy righteous ordi-
　　　nances.

63 I am a companion of all them
　　that fear Thee,
　　And of them that observe Thy
　　　precepts.

64 The earth, O LORD, is full of Thy
　　mercy;
　　Teach me Thy statutes.

חֵֽלְקִי יְהֹוָה 57
אָמַרְתִּי לִשְׁמֹר דְּבָרֶֽיךָ:
חִלִּֽיתִי פָנֶֽיךָ בְכָל־לֵב 58
חָנֵּֽנִי כְּאִמְרָתֶֽךָ:
חִשַּׁבְתִּי דְרָכָי 59
וָאָשִֽׁיבָה רַגְלַי אֶל־עֵדֹתֶֽיךָ:
חַֽשְׁתִּי וְלֹא הִתְמַהְמָהְתִּי 60
לִשְׁמֹר מִצְוֹתֶֽיךָ:
חֶבְלֵי רְשָׁעִים עִוְּדֻֽנִי 61
תּֽוֹרָתְךָ לֹא שָׁכָֽחְתִּי:
חֲצוֹת־לַֽיְלָה אָקוּם לְהוֹדוֹת לָךְ 62
עַל מִשְׁפְּטֵי צִדְקֶֽךָ:
חָבֵר אָֽנִי לְכָל־אֲשֶׁר יְרֵאֽוּךָ 63
וּלְשֹׁמְרֵי פִּקּוּדֶֽיךָ:
חַסְדְּךָ יְהֹוָה מָלְאָה הָאָֽרֶץ 64
חֻקֶּֽיךָ לַמְּדֵֽנִי:

57-64 HETH

57. *my portion is the LORD.* An alternative
rendering is: 'My portion, O LORD, I have
(inwardly) said, is to keep Thy words'
(Hirsch).

58. *Thy favour.* lit. 'Thy face,' Presence.

59. *considered my ways.* He examined his
conduct and, finding it defective, repented
and returned to the path God commanded.

60. *I made haste.* To abandon the evil
course.

61. *bands … enclosed me.* When he was

caught in their machinations like an animal
trapped by the snarer (cf. verse 110).

62. *I will rise.* Rather, 'I rise.' He is so
mindful of God that he shortens his sleep to
rise and thank Him (cf. verse 55) (Kimchi).

63. *a companion.* He chooses his associates only from those who are like-minded to
himself.

64. *the earth … mercy.* Cf. xxxiii. 5. Because God has been so gracious to the universe of His creation, his wish is to have a full
knowledge of His will (cf. Kimchi).

TETH

65 Thou hast dealt well with Thy servant,
    O Lord, according unto Thy word.

66 Teach me good discernment and knowledge;
    For I have believed in Thy commandments.

67 Before I was afflicted, I did err;
    But now I observe Thy word.

68 Thou art good, and doest good;
    Teach me Thy statutes.

69 The proud have forged a lie against me;
    But I with my whole heart will keep Thy precepts.

70 Their heart is gross like fat;
    But I delight in Thy law.

71 It is good for me that I have been afflicted,
    In order that I might learn Thy statutes.

72 The law of Thy mouth is better unto me
    Than thousands of gold and silver.

טוֹב עָשִׂיתָ עִם־עַבְדְּךָ 65
יְהוָה כִּדְבָרֶךָ׃
טוּב טַעַם וָדַעַת לַמְּדֵנִי 66
כִּי בְמִצְוֹתֶיךָ הֶאֱמָנְתִּי׃
טֶרֶם אֶעֱנֶה אֲנִי שֹׁגֵג 67
וְעַתָּה אִמְרָתְךָ שָׁמָרְתִּי׃
טוֹב־אַתָּה וּמֵטִיב 68
לַמְּדֵנִי חֻקֶּיךָ׃
טָפְלוּ עָלַי שֶׁקֶר זֵדִים 69
אֲנִי בְּכָל־לֵב אֶצֹּר פִּקּוּדֶיךָ׃
טָפַשׁ כַּחֵלֶב לִבָּם 70
אֲנִי תּוֹרָתְךָ שִׁעֲשָׁעְתִּי׃
טוֹב־לִי כִי־עֻנֵּיתִי 71
לְמַעַן אֶלְמַד חֻקֶּיךָ׃
טוֹב־לִי תוֹרַת־פִּיךָ 72
מֵאַלְפֵי זָהָב וָכָסֶף׃

65-72 TETH

65. *dealt well.* Acted graciously, showed kindness.

66. *good discernment.* lit. 'goodness of taste,' ethical insight to appreciate the moral worth of God's commandments. He has *believed* in them, knowing that since they emanate from a Divine source they must be right; but he also desires to possess both understanding and knowledge of them (Kimchi, Hirsch).

67. *before I was afflicted.* His erring from the right path had its sequel in affliction (Targum), and his suffering was the means whereby he came to submit to God's rule (cf. the striking utterance in verse 71) (Hirsch).

68. *good, and doest good.* Being a benefi-cent God, He reveals graciousness towards His creatures. Realizing this truth, the Psalmist is eager to be instructed in His precepts (Daath Sofrim).

69. *forged a lie against me.* Better, 'have besmeared me with falsehood.' By their slan-derous allegations they gave him a hypocriti-cal character utterly different from what was his; nevertheless he remained firm in his adherence to the Torah, because to God the truth is known (Kimchi, Metsudath David).

70. *heart is gross.* They are impervious to spiritual ideals (see on xvii. 10) (Hirsch, cf.).

71. See on verse 67.

72. *thousands.* i.e. thousands of pieces. For the thought, cf. verse 14.

IOD

73 Thy hands have made me and
  fashioned me;
  Give me understanding, that I
  may learn Thy commandments.

74 They that fear Thee shall see me
  and be glad,
  Because I have hope in Thy word.

75 I know, O Lord, that Thy judgments are righteous,
  And that in faithfulness Thou
  hast afflicted me.

76 Let, I pray Thee, Thy lovingkindness be ready to comfort
  me,
  According to Thy promise unto
  Thy servant.

77 Let Thy tender mercies come
  unto me, that I may live;
  For Thy law is my delight.

78 Let the proud be put to shame,
  for they have distorted my
  cause with falsehood;
  But I will meditate in Thy precepts.

79 Let those that fear Thee return
  unto me,
  And they that know Thy testimonies.

80 Let my heart be undivided in
  Thy statutes,
  In order that I may not be put
  to shame.

73 יָדֶיךָ עָשׂוּנִי וַיְכוֹנְנוּנִי
הֲבִינֵנִי וְאֶלְמְדָה מִצְוֹתֶיךָ׃

74 יְרֵאֶיךָ יִרְאוּנִי וְיִשְׂמָחוּ
כִּי לִדְבָרְךָ יִחָלְתִּי׃

75 יָדַעְתִּי יְהוָה כִּי־צֶדֶק מִשְׁפָּטֶיךָ
וֶאֱמוּנָה עִנִּיתָנִי׃

76 יְהִי־נָא חַסְדְּךָ לְנַחֲמֵנִי
כְּאִמְרָתְךָ לְעַבְדֶּךָ׃

77 יְבֹאוּנִי רַחֲמֶיךָ וְאֶחְיֶה
כִּי־תוֹרָתְךָ שַׁעֲשֻׁעָי׃

78 יֵבֹשׁוּ זֵדִים כִּי־שֶׁקֶר עִוְּתוּנִי
אֲנִי אָשִׂיחַ בְּפִקּוּדֶיךָ׃

79 יָשׁוּבוּ לִי יְרֵאֶיךָ
וְיֹדְעֵי עֵדֹתֶיךָ׃

80 יְהִי־לִבִּי תָמִים בְּחֻקֶּיךָ
לְמַעַן לֹא אֵבוֹשׁ׃

v. 79 וידעי ק׳

73-80 YOD

73. *Thy hands have made me*. As a creature of God, it is his duty to understand the purpose for which he had been created.

74. *they that fear*. Or, 'may they that fear Thee see me.' May Thy favour, bestowed upon me as a loyal adherent of the Torah, be an encouragement to others (cf. Metsudath David, Malbim).

75. *righteous*. lit. 'righteousness,' founded upon right; so that if He brings sufferings, He acts in *faithfulness* with the decree that evil is punished.

76. *be … comfort me*. Omit *ready* to which nothing corresponds in Hebrew. In time of affliction may he find consolation in God's love. He will then be sure that his distress is sent to discipline him, not to crush him.

77. *that I may live*. Better, 'that I may be revived.' He asks that he may be instilled with renewed energy essential to the study of Torah (cf. Hirsch).

78. *distorted my cause*. lit. 'twisted me'; the same verb as in *to subvert a man in his cause, the Lord approveth not* (Lam. iii. 36).

79. *return unto me*. Those who had wavered in their faith and left my company while under the influence of the sinners may now return, now that the sinners have been put to shame (Metsudath David).

and they that know. Better, 'even they that know.' This is the translation of the *kerë* to which the LXX and Targum conform; the *kethib* means 'and they shall know.'

CAPH

81 My soul pineth for Thy salvation;
   In Thy word do I hope.
82 Mine eyes fail for Thy word,
   Saying: 'When wilt Thou com-
      fort me?'
83 For I am become like a wine-
      skin in the smoke;
   Yet do I not forget Thy statutes.
84 How many are the days of Thy
      servant?
   When wilt Thou execute judg-
      ment on them that persecute
      me?
85 The proud have digged pits for
      me,
   Which is not according to Thy
      law.
86 All Thy commandments are
      faithful;
   They persecute me for nought;
      help Thou me.
87 They had almost consumed me
      upon earth;
   But as for me, I forsook not Thy
      precepts.
88 Quicken me after Thy loving-
      kindness,
   And I will observe the testimony
      of Thy mouth.

81 כָּלְתָה לִתְשׁוּעָתְךָ נַפְשִׁי
   לִדְבָרְךָ יִחָלְתִּי:
82 כָּלוּ עֵינַי לְאִמְרָתֶךָ
   לֵאמֹר מָתַי תְּנַחֲמֵנִי:
83 כִּי־הָיִיתִי כְּנֹאד בְּקִיטוֹר
   חֻקֶּיךָ לֹא שָׁכָחְתִּי:
84 כַּמָּה יְמֵי־עַבְדֶּךָ
   מָתַי תַּעֲשֶׂה בְרֹדְפַי מִשְׁפָּט:
85 כָּרוּ־לִי זֵדִים שִׁיחוֹת
   אֲשֶׁר לֹא כְתוֹרָתֶךָ:
86 כָּל־מִצְוֺתֶיךָ אֱמוּנָה
   שֶׁקֶר רְדָפוּנִי עָזְרֵנִי:
87 כִּמְעַט כִּלּוּנִי בָאָרֶץ
   וַאֲנִי לֹא־עָזַבְתִּי פִקֻּדֶיךָ:
88 כְּחַסְדְּךָ חַיֵּנִי
   וְאֶשְׁמְרָה עֵדוּת פִּיךָ:

81-88   CAPH

81. *my soul pineth.* The verb is used of the
eyes in the next verse and verse 123; lit. 'is
consumed' and corresponds with the English
idiom 'I am dying for.'

82. *fail.* His sight is strained by looking out
for relief which is delayed in coming.

83. *like a wine-skin.* In the East bottles are
made of skin and, when not in use, are hung
up in the room which has no chimney for the
escape of smoke; they become shrivelled in
consequence. The Psalmist declares himself
to be so affected by his trials that he is
similarly shrivelled (Daath Sofrim).

84. *how many.* The implied answer is that
they are very few; therefore let his judgment
come quickly or it may be too late (Metsudath
David).

85. *dug pits.* Cf. lvii. 7.

which… according to Thy law. Since the deed
of *the proud* violates the teaching of the Torah,
the Psalmist expects God to take action against
them. Another possible rendering is: 'who fail
(to act) according to Thy law.'

86. *faithful.* lit. 'faithfulness.' That is the
distinguishing feature of God's ordinances
which are deliberately set aside by *the proud*,
because 'with falsehood they pursue me' (so
translate). As a victim of men's unrighteousness, he claims the help of God Who has
given commandments based on the principle
of faithfulness (cf. Hirsch).

87. *consumed.* lit. 'made an end'; *almost*,
but not completely, because he was under
God's protection.

88. *and I will observe.* Better, 'that I may
observe.' For that purpose he longs to continue in life and escape the destruction planned
by his persecutors.

LAMED

89 For ever, O Lord,
    Thy word standeth fast in heaven.

90 Thy faithfulness is unto all
    generations;
    Thou hast established the earth,
    and it standeth.

91 They stand this day according to
    Thine ordinances;
    For all things are Thy servants.

92 Unless Thy law had been my
    delight,
    I should then have perished in
    mine affliction.

93 I will never forget Thy precepts;
    For with them Thou hast quick-
    ened me.

94 I am Thine, save me;
    For I have sought Thy precepts.

95 The wicked have waited for me
    to destroy me;
    But I will consider Thy testi-
    monies.

96 I have seen an end to every
    purpose;
    But Thy commandment is ex-
    ceeding broad.

89 לְעוֹלָם יְהוָֹה
דְּבָרְךָ נִצָּב בַּשָּׁמָיִם:
90 לְדֹר וָדֹר אֱמוּנָתֶךָ
כּוֹנַנְתָּ אֶרֶץ וַתַּעֲמֹד:
91 לְמִשְׁפָּטֶיךָ עָמְדוּ הַיּוֹם
כִּי הַכֹּל עֲבָדֶיךָ:
92 לוּלֵי תוֹרָתְךָ שַׁעֲשֻׁעָי
אָז אָבַדְתִּי בְעָנְיִי:
93 לְעוֹלָם לֹא־אֶשְׁכַּח פִּקּוּדֶיךָ
כִּי בָם חִיִּיתָנִי:
94 לְךָ־אֲנִי הוֹשִׁיעֵנִי
כִּי פִקּוּדֶיךָ דָרָשְׁתִּי:
95 לִי קִוּוּ רְשָׁעִים לְאַבְּדֵנִי
עֵדֹתֶיךָ אֶתְבּוֹנָן:
96 לְכָל־תִּכְלָה רָאִיתִי קֵץ
רְחָבָה מִצְוָתְךָ מְאֹד:

89-96   LAMED

89. God's revelation is for all time and immutable, as are all things which belong to the realm of heaven. Continuity of nature depends on His word and He proclaims the ultimate destiny of mankind (Malbim, Hirsch).

90. As God's work in the creation of the universe is constant, it testifies to the permanence of His attribute of faithfulness which governs His relationship with man.

91. *they stand.* The subject is 'heaven and earth' (Ibn Ezra).

according to. As decreed by God. But a better translation is: 'for Thine ordinances,' i.e. ready to obey the commands given to them.

Everything in the universe is subservient to the Divine will (Kimchi).

92. *perished.* Because he would have been without any force to encourage him to persist.

93. *never forget.* He feels he may need them in future perils which may befall him.

94. *I am Thine.* A devoted follower of Thy Revelation.

95. *consider.* Give heed to, as the means of enlisting God's help in foiling the plans of my enemies who are bent on destroying me (Malbim).

96. *to every purpose.* Better, 'to every limit.' All things upon earth are limited in scope or size; only God's commandments are without such limitation (Kimchi).

MEM

<table>
<tr><td>

97 Oh how love I Thy law!
It is my meditation all the day.

98 Thy commandments make me
wiser than mine enemies;
For they are ever with me.

99 I have more understanding than
all my teachers;
For Thy testimonies are my
meditation.

100 I understand more than mine
elders,
Because I have kept Thy pre-
cepts.

101 I have refrained my feet from
every evil way,
In order that I might observe
Thy word.

102 I have not turned aside from
Thine ordinances;
For Thou hast instructed me.

103 How sweet are Thy words unto
my palate!
Yea, sweeter than honey to my
mouth!

104 From Thy precepts I get under-
standing;
Therefore I hate every false
way.

</td><td>

97 מָה־אָהַבְתִּי תוֹרָתֶךָ
כָּל־הַיּוֹם הִיא שִׂיחָתִי:
98 מֵאֹיְבַי תְּחַכְּמֵנִי מִצְוֹתֶךָ
כִּי לְעוֹלָם הִיא־לִי:
99 מִכָּל־מְלַמְּדַי הִשְׂכַּלְתִּי
כִּי עֵדְוֹתֶיךָ שִׂיחָה לִי:
100 מִזְּקֵנִים אֶתְבּוֹנָן
כִּי פִקּוּדֶיךָ נָצָרְתִּי:
101 מִכָּל־אֹרַח רָע כָּלִאתִי רַגְלָי
לְמַעַן אֶשְׁמֹר דְּבָרֶךָ:
102 מִמִּשְׁפָּטֶיךָ לֹא־סָרְתִּי
כִּי־אַתָּה הוֹרֵתָנִי:
103 מַה־נִּמְלְצוּ לְחִכִּי אִמְרָתֶךָ
מִדְּבַשׁ לְפִי:
104 מִפִּקּוּדֶיךָ אֶתְבּוֹנָן
עַל־כֵּן שָׂנֵאתִי ׀ כָּל־אֹרַח שָׁקֶר:

</td></tr>
</table>

<table>
<tr><td>

97–104 MEM

98. *make me wiser.* Cf. Deut. iv. 6.

they are ever with me. Rather, 'they are ever mine,' my eternal possession. It is to be noted that although *commandments* is plural, the verb *make me wiser* is singular, as is also the pronoun in the second clause which is liter-ally, 'it is ever mine.' Although the Torah consists of numerous precepts, it is essen-tially a unity (Hirsch).

99. *I have more understanding.* No conceit is implied in the claim. He had received instruction from many teachers; but he main-tains that by constant meditation upon God's testimonies, he has obtained the truest dis-cernment of Torah as the best guide of living (Ibn Ezra). In Pirke Aboth (4:1) the clause is quoted with the meaning, 'From all my

</td><td>

teachers have I derived understanding.'

100. *elders.* Whose knowledge is obtained from long experience. The source of his understanding of life is superior to theirs, viz. obedience of God's precepts (Metsudath David, Malbim).

101. *in order that I might observe.* His love of God and longing to conform to His will deterred him from evil.

102. *Thou.* Emphatic in the Hebrew: Thou and no human teacher. Following such an Instructor, he could not go astray.

103. *sweet.* lit. 'smooth,' i.e. agreeable. The Psalmist may have had xix. 11 in mind, though a different word is employed there.

104. *understanding.* To distinguish be-tween right and wrong and give preference to the former.

</td></tr>
</table>

NUN

105 Thy word is a lamp unto my
    feet,
    And a light unto my path.

106 I have sworn, and have con-
    firmed it,
    To observe Thy righteous ordi-
    nances.

107 I am afflicted very much;
    Quicken me, O LORD, according
    unto Thy word.

108 Accept, I beseech Thee, the
    freewill-offerings of my
    mouth, O LORD,
    And teach me Thine ordinances.

109 My soul is continually in my
    hand;
    Yet have I not forgotten Thy
    law.

110 The wicked have laid a snare for
    me;
    Yet went I not astray from Thy
    precepts.

111 Thy testimonies have I taken as
    a heritage for ever;
    For they are the rejoicing of my
    heart.

112 I have inclined my heart to per-
    form Thy statutes,
    For ever, at every step.

נֵר־לְרַגְלִי דְבָרֶךָ 105
וְאוֹר לִנְתִיבָתִי:
נִשְׁבַּעְתִּי וָאֲקַיֵּמָה 106
לִשְׁמֹר מִשְׁפְּטֵי צִדְקֶךָ:
נַעֲנֵיתִי עַד־מְאֹד 107
יְהוָה חַיֵּנִי כִדְבָרֶךָ:
נִדְבוֹת פִּי רְצֵה־נָא יְהוָה 108
וּמִשְׁפָּטֶיךָ לַמְּדֵנִי:
נַפְשִׁי בְכַפִּי תָמִיד 109
וְתוֹרָתְךָ לֹא שָׁכָחְתִּי:
נָתְנוּ רְשָׁעִים פַּח לִי 110
וּמִפִּקּוּדֶיךָ לֹא תָעִיתִי:
נָחַלְתִּי עֵדְוֹתֶיךָ לְעוֹלָם 111
כִּי־שְׂשׂוֹן לִבִּי הֵמָּה:
נָטִיתִי לִבִּי לַעֲשׂוֹת חֻקֶּיךָ 112
לְעוֹלָם עֵקֶב:

105-112 NUN

105. *a lamp unto my feet.* Lighting up the true way of life so that he does not err (cf. Prov. vi. 23) (Kimchi, Hirsch).

106. *confirmed.* Or, 'fulfilled'; he kept his oath.

107. Cf. verse 25.

108. *freewill-offerings of my mouth.* Prayer and praise (Hirsch).

109. *my soul ... hand.* I have often been in danger of death; like *I put my life in my hand* (Judges xii. 3; cf. 1 Sam. xix. 5) (Hirsch).

110. *have laid a snare.* If the verse is the sequel to the preceding, it explains how the Psalmist's life was menaced (cf. Hirsch).

111. *have I taken as a heritage.* The ordinances which testify to God's divinity and omnipotence have become the property of man, and living by them brings great joy to the heart (cf. Daath Sofrim).

112. *at every step.* Better, 'to the utmost' (Hirsch).

SAMECH

113 I hate them that are of a double
     mind;
     But Thy law do I love.
114 Thou art my covert and **my**
     shield;
     In Thy word do I hope.
115 Depart from me, ye evil-doers;
     That I may keep the command-
     ments of my God.
116 Uphold me according unto Thy
     word, that I may live;
     And put me not to shame in my
     hope.
117 Support Thou me, and I shall
     be saved;
     And I will occupy myself with
     Thy statutes continually.
118 Thou hast made light of all them
     that err from Thy statutes;
     For their deceit is vain.
119 Thou puttest away all the
     wicked of the earth like dross;
     Therefore I love Thy testi-
     monies.
120 My flesh shuddereth for fear of
     Thee;
     And I am afraid of Thy judg-
     ments.

סְעֲפִים שָׂנֵאתִי 113
וְתוֹרָתְךָ אָהָבְתִּי׃
סִתְרִי וּמָגִנִּי אָתָּה 114
לִדְבָרְךָ יִחָלְתִּי׃
סוּרוּ מִמֶּנִּי מְרֵעִים 115
וְאֶצְּרָה מִצְוֺת אֱלֹהָי׃
סָמְכֵנִי כְאִמְרָתְךָ וְאֶחְיֶה 116
וְאַל־תְּבִישֵׁנִי מִשִּׂבְרִי׃
סְעָדֵנִי וְאִוָּשֵׁעָה 117
וְאֶשְׁעָה בְחֻקֶּיךָ תָמִיד׃
סָלִיתָ כָּל־שׁוֹגִים מֵחֻקֶּיךָ 118
כִּי־שֶׁקֶר תַּרְמִיתָם׃
סִגִים הִשְׁבַּתָּ כָל־רִשְׁעֵי־אָרֶץ 119
לָכֵן אָהַבְתִּי עֵדֹתֶיךָ׃
סָמַר מִפַּחְדְּךָ בְשָׂרִי 120
וּמִמִּשְׁפָּטֶיךָ יָרֵאתִי׃

113-120   SAMECH

113. *them ... of a double mind.* The same
root occurs in the phrase, *How long halt ye
between two opinions?* (1 Kings xviii. 21).
Who exactly is intended is uncertain; but
whoever they were, these were irresolute
people who would follow the right path one
moment and the wrong path the next (Hirsch).

114. *my covert.* Refuge in days of storm;
the same word as in *Thou art my* hiding-place
(xxxii. 7).

my shield. Cf. iii. 4, vii. 11, xviii. 3.

115. *depart from me.* Cf. vi. 9.

that I may keep. Their persecution was a hin-
drance to his observing the commandments
(Kimchi).

116. *put me not to shame in my hope.* Do not
disappoint me in my expectation of deliverance (Kimchi).

117. *occupy myself with.* lit. 'gaze'; regard

with devotion (cf. Daath Sofrim).

118. *made light of.* See Hirsch.
Alternatively, 'trampled' (Kimchi, Malbim).

their deceit is vain. Rather, 'their deceit is
falsehood.' Their spurious teachings have
led them to wander from the Torah and to lure
others astray in their wake. Their views and
interpretations have proven to be nothing but
false justifications for their actions (Hirsch).

119. *Thou puttest away.* lit. 'causest to
cease.' As a refiner separates dross from pure
metal, God cuts off the wicked; and to escape
sharing their doom, the Psalmist declares his
love of the Torah.

120. *my flesh shuddereth.* On contemplating the fate of those who are disobedient.

Thy judgments. Either acts of judgment, punishments inflicted upon the wicked (Rashi),
or the laws and commandments which, if
neglected, are followed by retribution (Daath
Sofrim).

AIN

121 I have done justice and righteousness;
Leave me not to mine oppressors.

122 Be surety for Thy servant for
good;
Let not the proud oppress me.

123 Mine eyes fail for Thy salvation,
And for Thy righteous word.

124 Deal with Thy servant according unto Thy mercy,
And teach me Thy statutes.

125 I am Thy servant, give me
understanding;
That I may know Thy testimonies.

126 It is time for the LORD to work;
They have made void Thy law.

127 Therefore I love Thy commandments
Above gold, yea, above fine gold.

128 Therefore I esteem all [Thy]
precepts concerning all things
to be right;
Every false way I hate.

עָשִׂיתִי מִשְׁפָּט וָצֶדֶק121
בַּל־תַּנִּיחֵנִי לְעֹשְׁקָי:
עֲרֹב עַבְדְּךָ לְטוֹב122
אַל־יַעַשְׁקֻנִי זֵדִים:
עֵינַי כָּלוּ לִישׁוּעָתֶךָ123
וּלְאִמְרַת צִדְקֶךָ:
עֲשֵׂה עִם־עַבְדְּךָ כְחַסְדֶּךָ124
וְחֻקֶּיךָ לַמְּדֵנִי:
עַבְדְּךָ־אָנִי הֲבִינֵנִי125
וְאֵדְעָה עֵדֹתֶיךָ:
עֵת לַעֲשׂוֹת לַיהוָֹה126
הֵפֵרוּ תּוֹרָתֶךָ:
עַל־כֵּן אָהַבְתִּי מִצְוֹתֶיךָ127
מִזָּהָב וּמִפָּז:
עַל־כֵּן ׀ כָּל־פִּקּוּדֵי כֹל יִשָּׁרְתִּי128
כָּל־אֹרַח שֶׁקֶר שָׂנֵאתִי:

121-128   AIN

121. *justice and righteousness.* The qualities which God loves (xxxiii. 5) and which
form the foundation of His throne (lxxxix.
15). These have been his principles of conduct. In recognition of his integrity he pleads
that God may exercise those attributes and
release him from his distress.

122. *be surety.* Stand guarantee for my
welfare (Rashi).

123. *mine eyes fail.* See on verse 82.

Thy righteous word. God's promise guaranteed by His righteousness.

124. *according unto Thy mercy.* If he be
lacking in merits, he appeals to God's mercy
and asks to be instructed in His statutes
(Metsudath David) and their hidden meanings (Malbim).

125. *I am Thy servant.* Desirous of proving
dutiful, and to that end fuller knowledge is
necessary (Kimchi).

126. *to work.* To deal with wicked and
punish them; the verb is so used in Jer. xviii.
23; Ezek. xxxi. 11. A special application was
given to this verse by the Rabbis who read
into the words the meaning, 'At a time of
working for the LORD, they violated Thy
Torah,' to justify the temporary abrogation
of a commandment in an emergency when
the purpose is to maintain the Torah's general integrity (Tal. Ber. 63a).

127. *therefore I love.* Because others *have
made void Thy law* (Kimchi).

above gold. From xix. 11.

128. An alternative rendering is: 'Therefore I declare all (Thy) precepts, concerning
all things, to be fair and just' (cf. Hirsch).

PE

129 Thy testimonies are wonderful;
   Therefore doth my soul keep
   them.

130 The opening of Thy words
   giveth light;
   It giveth understanding unto
   the simple.

131 I opened wide my mouth, and
   panted;
   For I longed for Thy commandments.

132 Turn Thee towards me, and be
   gracious unto me,
   As is Thy wont to do unto those
   that love Thy name.

133 Order my footsteps by Thy word;
   And let not any iniquity have
   dominion over me.

134 Redeem me from the oppression
   of man,
   And I will observe Thy precepts.

135 Make Thy face to shine upon
   Thy servant;
   And teach me Thy statutes.

136 Mine eyes run down with rivers
   of water,
   Because they observe not Thy
   law.

פְּלָאוֹת עֵדְוֹתֶיךָ 129
עַל־כֵּן נְצָרָתַם נַפְשִׁי׃
פֵּתַח דְּבָרֶיךָ יָאִיר 130
מֵבִין פְּתָיִים׃
פִּי־פָעַרְתִּי וָאֶשְׁאָפָה 131
כִּי לְמִצְוֺתֶיךָ יָאָבְתִּי׃
פְּנֵה־אֵלַי וְחָנֵּנִי 132
כְּמִשְׁפָּט לְאֹהֲבֵי שְׁמֶךָ׃
פְּעָמַי הָכֵן בְּאִמְרָתֶךָ 133
וְאַל־תַּשְׁלֶט־בִּי כָל־אָוֶן׃
פְּדֵנִי מֵעֹשֶׁק אָדָם 134
וְאֶשְׁמְרָה פִּקּוּדֶיךָ׃
פָּנֶיךָ הָאֵר בְּעַבְדֶּךָ 135
וְלַמְּדֵנִי אֶת־חֻקֶּיךָ׃
פַּלְגֵי־מַיִם יָרְדוּ עֵינָי 136
עַל לֹא־שָׁמְרוּ תוֹרָתֶךָ׃

129-136 PE

129. *wonderful.* Of Divine origin; the same
root as the word in verse 18.

130. *opening.* lit. 'doorway.' Thy words
are so comprehensible and enlightening that
even the simplest man will desire wisdom
and ethics by studying the narratives of the
Torah (Malbim).

simple. See on xix. 8.

131. *opened wide.* To take in the spiritual
food offered in the Torah.

panted. In eager longing.

132. *turn Thee ... unto me.* Repeated from
xxv. 16, lxxxvi. 16.

as is Thy wont to do. Even if I be undeserving,
have mercy and treat me as You would those
who accept Your judgments wholeheartedly
(Malbim).

133. *order.* Guide.

iniquity. Infraction of the moral law. May the
study of Torah save him from succumbing to
his evil inclination and being guilty of this
(Midrash Shocher Tov).

134. *oppression.* Which might stand in the
way of his carrying out his obligations (cf.
verse 121f.) (Kimchi).

135. *make Thy face to shine.* Dispelling the
darkness of oppression (cf. lxxx. 4).

136. *mine eyes ... water.* Cf. Lam. iii. 48.
He is overcome with sorrow at the lawlessness of the wicked.

119. 137

137 Righteous art Thou, O Lord,
And upright are Thy judgments.

138 Thou hast commanded Thy
testimonies in righteousness
And exceeding faithfulness.

139 My zeal hath undone me,
Because mine adversaries have
forgotten Thy words.

140 Thy word is tried to the uttermost,
And Thy servant loveth it.

141 I am small and despised;
Yet have I not forgotten Thy
precepts.

142 Thy righteousness is an everlasting righteousness,
And Thy law is truth.

143 Trouble and anguish have overtaken me;
Yet Thy commandments are my
delight.

144 Thy testimonies are righteous
for ever;
Give me understanding, and I
shall live.

145 I have called with my whole
heart; answer me, O Lord;
I will keep Thy statutes.

146 I have called Thee, save me,
And I will observe Thy testimonies.

TZADE

137 צַדִּיק אַתָּה יְהֹוָה
וְיָשָׁר מִשְׁפָּטֶיךָ:

138 צִוִּיתָ צֶדֶק עֵדֹתֶיךָ
וֶאֱמוּנָה מְאֹד:

139 צִמְּתַתְנִי קִנְאָתִי
כִּי־שָׁכְחוּ דְבָרֶיךָ צָרָי:

140 צְרוּפָה אִמְרָתְךָ מְאֹד
וְעַבְדְּךָ אֲהֵבָהּ:

141 צָעִיר אָנֹכִי וְנִבְזֶה
פִּקֻּדֶיךָ לֹא שָׁכָחְתִּי:

142 צִדְקָתְךָ צֶדֶק לְעוֹלָם
וְתוֹרָתְךָ אֱמֶת:

143 צַר־וּמָצוֹק מְצָאוּנִי
מִצְוֹתֶיךָ שַׁעֲשֻׁעָי:

144 צֶדֶק עֵדְוֹתֶיךָ לְעוֹלָם
הֲבִינֵנִי וְאֶחְיֶה:

KOPH

145 קָרָאתִי בְכָל־לֵב עֲנֵנִי יְהֹוָה
חֻקֶּיךָ אֶצֹּרָה:

146 קְרָאתִיךָ הוֹשִׁיעֵנִי
וְאֶשְׁמְרָה עֵדֹתֶיךָ:

137-144 TZADE

137. *upright.* The adjective is singular,
signifying each one of Thy judgments (Ibn
Ezra).

138. Cf. verses 86, 144.

139. *my ... hath undone me.* See lxix. 10.

140. *tried.* 'Refined' completely free of
dross (xii. 7).

141. *small.* Insignificant in the esteem of
his fellows. Their contempt cannot influence

him to be false to His loyalty.

142. *everlasting.* Eternal like God.

is truth. Cf. xix. 10, and below verses 151,
160.

144. *righteous for ever.* Like the eternal
righteousness of God (verse 142).

live. In conformity with Torah precepts.

145-152 KOPH

146. *and I will observe.* Better, 'that I may
observe.'

147 I rose early at dawn, and cried;
　　I hoped in Thy word.

148 Mine eyes forestalled the night-
　　watches,
　　That I might meditate in Thy
　　word.

149 Hear my voice according unto
　　Thy lovingkindness;
　　Quicken me, O LORD, as Thou
　　art wont.

150 They draw nigh that follow after
　　wickedness;
　　They are far from Thy law.

151 Thou art nigh, O LORD;
　　And all Thy commandments are
　　truth.

152 Of old have I known from Thy
　　testimonies
　　That Thou hast founded them
　　for ever.

RESH

153 O see mine affliction, and rescue
　　me;
　　For I do not forget Thy law.

154 Plead Thou my cause, and re-
　　deem me;
　　Quicken me according to Thy
　　word.

155 Salvation is far from the wicked;
　　For they seek not Thy statutes.

156 Great are Thy compassions, O
　　LORD;
　　Quicken me as Thou art wont.

קִדַּ֤מְתִּי בַנֶּ֣שֶׁף וָאֲשַׁוֵּ֑עָה 147
לִדְבָרְךָ֥ יִחָֽלְתִּי׃

קִדְּמ֣וּ עֵ֭ינַי אַשְׁמֻר֑וֹת 148
לָ֝שִׂ֗יחַ בְּאִמְרָתֶֽךָ׃

ק֭וֹלִי שִׁמְעָ֣ה כְחַסְדֶּ֑ךָ 149
יְ֝הֹוָ֗ה כְּֽמִשְׁפָּטֶ֥ךָ חַיֵּֽנִי׃

קָ֭רְבוּ רֹדְפֵ֣י זִמָּ֑ה 150
מִתּוֹרָתְךָ֥ רָחָֽקוּ׃

קָר֣וֹב אַתָּ֣ה יְהֹוָ֑ה 151
וְֽכׇל־מִצְוֺתֶ֥יךָ אֱמֶֽת׃

קֶ֣דֶם יָ֭דַעְתִּי מֵעֵדֹתֶ֑יךָ 152
כִּ֖י לְעוֹלָ֣ם יְסַדְתָּֽם׃

רְאֵ֣ה עׇנְיִ֣י וְחַלְּצֵ֑נִי 153
כִּי־ת֝וֹרָתְךָ֗ לֹ֣א שָׁכָֽחְתִּי׃

רִיבָ֣ה רִ֭יבִי וּגְאָלֵ֑נִי 154
לְאִמְרָתְךָ֥ חַיֵּֽנִי׃

רָח֣וֹק מֵרְשָׁעִ֣ים יְשׁוּעָ֑ה 155
כִּֽי־חֻ֝קֶּ֗יךָ לֹ֣א דָרָֽשׁוּ׃

רַחֲמֶ֖יךָ רַבִּ֥ים ׀ יְהֹוָ֑ה 156
כְּֽמִשְׁפָּטֶ֥יךָ חַיֵּֽנִי׃

v. 147. לדברך ק׳

147. *I rose early.* More exactly, 'I fore-stalled' (the same verb as in the next verse); arose before dawn to pray for help.

word. The *kethib* is plural.

148. *night-watches.* See on lxiii. 7. He reduced his sleep for Torah study (Rashi).

149. *as Thou art wont.* See on verse 132; the noun here is plural.

150. *draw nigh.* And stick to their evil ways (Kimchi).

151. *Thou art nigh.* Nevertheless, to all those who call on You (Kimchi).

152. *of old.* From long reflection upon God's testimonies he has become convinced that they are eternally valid, and so he trusts in them at all times.

153-160 RESH

153. *see mine affliction.* From ix. 14; again Lam. i. 9.

154. *plead Thou my cause.* The issue between him and his persecutors (cf. xxxv. 1, xliii. 1) (Malbim).

156. *as Thou art wont.* See on verse 149.

157 Many are my persecutors and
    mine adversaries;
    Yet have I not turned aside from
    Thy testimonies.

158 I beheld them that were faith-
    less, and strove with them;
    Because they observed not Thy
    word.

159 O see how I love Thy precepts;
    Quicken me, O LORD, according
    to Thy lovingkindness.

160 The beginning of Thy word is
    truth;
    And all Thy righteous ordinance
    endureth for ever.

SHIN

161 Princes have persecuted me
    without a cause;
    But my heart standeth in awe of
    Thy words.

162 I rejoice at Thy word,
    As one that findeth great spoil.

163 I hate and abhor falsehood;
    Thy law do I love.

164 Seven times a day do I praise
    Thee,
    Because of Thy righteous ordi-
    nances.

157 רַבִּים רֹדְפַי וְצָרָי

מֵעֵדְוֹתֶיךָ לֹא נָטִיתִי:

158 רָאִיתִי בֹגְדִים וָאֶתְקוֹטָטָה

אֲשֶׁר אִמְרָתְךָ לֹא שָׁמָרוּ:

159 רְאֵה כִּי־פִקּוּדֶיךָ אָהָבְתִּי

יְהֹוָה כְּחַסְדְּךָ חַיֵּנִי:

160 רֹאשׁ־דְּבָרְךָ אֱמֶת

וּלְעוֹלָם כָּל־מִשְׁפַּט צִדְקֶךָ:

SHIN

161 שָׂרִים רְדָפוּנִי חִנָּם

וּמִדְּבָרְךָ פָּחַד לִבִּי:

162 שָׂשׂ אָנֹכִי עַל־אִמְרָתֶךָ

כְּמוֹצֵא שָׁלָל רָב:

163 שֶׁקֶר שָׂנֵאתִי וָאֲתַעֵבָה

תּוֹרָתְךָ אָהָבְתִּי:

164 שֶׁבַע בַּיּוֹם הִלַּלְתִּיךָ

עַל מִשְׁפְּטֵי צִדְקֶךָ:

v. 161 וּמדברך ק׳

---

158. *faithless.* To God's teachings.

strove with them. Cf. *supra* verse 95. Ibn Ezra
renders 'felt disgust.' The same root occurs
in xcv. 10, where the subject is God (cf. Job
x. 11).

160. *beginning.* lit. 'head.' Its meaning here
is 'totality'; the whole of it is truth (Hirsch,
cf. Rashi).

161–168 SHIN

161. *princes.* See on verse 23.

standeth in awe. In spite of his trials, he remained firm in his submission to the disci-

pline of Torah (Kimchi).

words. So the *kethib*; the *kerë* is to be translated as singular.

162. *rejoice.* His obedience is induced by
joy as well as awe.

great spoil. The warrior's prize on the battlefield is rich booty; his own prize in living
under the Torah is the happiness it brings to
him (cf. Hirsch).

163. *falsehood.* Opposite of the truth embodied in Thy law (Kimchi).

164. *seven times.* Frequently (Kimchi).

165 Great peace have they that love
Thy law;
And there is no stumbling for
them.

166 I have hoped for Thy salvation,
O Lord,
And have done Thy command-
ments.

167 My soul hath observed Thy
testimonies;
And I love them exceedingly.

168 I have observed Thy precepts
and Thy testimonies;
For all my ways are before Thee.

TAU

169 Let my cry come near before
Thee, O Lord;
Give me understanding accord-
ing to Thy word.

170 Let my supplication come before Thee;
Deliver me according to Thy
word.

171 Let my lips utter praise:
Because Thou teachest me Thy
statutes.

172 Let my tongue sing of Thy
word;
For all Thy commandments are
righteousness.

שָׁלוֹם רָב לְאֹהֲבֵי תוֹרָתֶךָ 165
וְאֵין־לָמוֹ מִכְשׁוֹל:
שִׂבַּרְתִּי לִישׁוּעָתְךָ יְהוָה 166
וּמִצְוֹתֶיךָ עָשִׂיתִי:
שָׁמְרָה נַפְשִׁי עֵדֹתֶיךָ 167
וָאֹהֲבֵם מְאֹד:
שָׁמַרְתִּי פִקּוּדֶיךָ וְעֵדֹתֶיךָ 168
כִּי כָל־דְּרָכַי נֶגְדֶּךָ:

תִּקְרַב רִנָּתִי לְפָנֶיךָ יְהוָה 169
כִּדְבָרְךָ הֲבִינֵנִי:
תָּבוֹא תְּחִנָּתִי לְפָנֶיךָ 170
כְּאִמְרָתְךָ הַצִּילֵנִי:
תַּבַּעְנָה שְׂפָתַי תְּהִלָּה 171
כִּי תְלַמְּדֵנִי חֻקֶּיךָ:
תַּעַן לְשׁוֹנִי אִמְרָתֶךָ 172
כִּי כָל־מִצְוֹתֶיךָ צֶּדֶק:

---

165. *great peace.* Two interpretations are possible. The Psalmist may mean that even when assailed by malicious opponents, the lovers of Torah derive an inner feeling of *peace*, a sense of confidence, from medita-tion upon its doctrines, and that 'nothing which life may bring can cause [them] to fall (Hirsch). Alternatively, *peace* has a material connotation, the common love they have for Torah brings them to form bonds of friend-ship that endure despite periods of setbacks. For them there is no stumbling in the way to this goal of harmony; temporary obstacles are overcome (Daath Sofrim).

166. *I have hoped ... O Lord.* Quotation from Gen. xlix. 18, with a different word for *hoped* as required by the acrostic.

167. *my soul.* As commonly, equals 'I.'

168. *my ways.* Daily conduct, as in verse 5. His life is an open book which he confidently presents for God's inspection, inasmuch as he had been observant of the precepts (cf. Kimchi).

169-176 TAV

169. *cry.* See on xvii. 1. Here it is a cry of anguish and entreaty (Kimchi).

170. *supplication.* lit. '(prayer for) grace, favour.'

171. *utter.* Rather, 'pour forth.' The word for 'fountain' comes from the same root (Kimchi).

172. The note of joy in the commandments, because of their moral perfection, is a distinct Torah perspective.

173 Let Thy hand be ready to help
    me;
    For I have chosen Thy precepts.

174 I have longed for Thy salvation,
    O Lord;
    And Thy law is my delight.

175 Let my soul live, and it shall
    praise Thee;
    And let Thine ordinances help
    me.

176 I have gone astray like a lost
    sheep; seek Thy servant;
    For I have not forgotten Thy
    commandments.

173 תְּהִי־יָדְךָ לְעָזְרֵנִי

כִּי פִקּוּדֶיךָ בָחָרְתִּי:

174 תָּאַבְתִּי לִישׁוּעָתְךָ יְהוָה

וְתוֹרָתְךָ שַׁעֲשֻׁעָי:

175 תְּחִי־נַפְשִׁי וּתְהַלְלֶךָּ

וּמִשְׁפָּטֶךָ יַעֲזְרֻנִי:

176 תָּעִיתִי כְּשֶׂה אֹבֵד בַּקֵּשׁ עַבְדֶּךָ

כִּי מִצְוֺתֶיךָ לֹא שָׁכָחְתִּי:

173. He pleads three reasons for an answer to his prayers: he has deliberately resolved to obey God's precepts (cf. verse 30); he has long been waiting eagerly for deliverance from the hindrances to obedience which surround him (cf. verses 40, 166), he yearns to devote himself entirely to Torah, which will become his constant delight (verse 174).

174. *I have longed for Thy salvation.* A variant of verse 166.

175. *and it shall praise.* Rather, 'that it may praise.' The purpose of living is to praise God (cf. cxv. 17f., cxlvi. 2), and with that aim in view he craves to live.

help me. As principles regulating the life which is in fact praise of God.

176. *I have gone astray.* The Hebrew accentuation supports the rendering: 'If I have gone astray like a lost sheep, seek Thy servant.' The Psalmist may be alluding to the frailty which is part of human nature, and prays that, should he ever succumb to his weakness and err, God will speedily restore him to the fold, because His commandments are always in his mind and he longs to be obedient to them (Hirsch). He may, on the other hand, be using the image of a lost sheep as the symbol of forlorn helplessness. If he is in such a condition and at the mercy of the wicked, may God be to him like a watchful shepherd (cf. Kimchi, Metsudath David, Malbim).

I have ... Thy commandments. Even under circumstances extremely difficult for keeping all the Torah's commandments, its fundamentals were not forgotten and he strove for maximum observance (Daath Sofrim).

PSALMS CXX-CXXXIV

ṢONGS OF ASCENTS

A GROUP of fifteen Psalms now occurs, each bearing the title *Shir ha-ma'aloth* (CXXI *la-ma'aloth*). There is disagreement on the meaning of *ma'aloth, ascending stages,* and the use for which these Psalms were composed. In the Mishnaic description of the Temple it is stated: 'Fifteen steps led up from within it (the Court of the Women) to the Court of the Israelites, corresponding to the fifteen Songs of Ascent in the Psalms, and upon them the Levites would sing' (Middoth ii. 5). At the ceremony of Rejoicing at the place of Water-drawing on the Festival of Tabernacles, the Levites were stationed 'upon the fifteen steps leading from the Court of the Israelites to the Court of the Women, corresponding to the fifteen Songs of Ascents in the Psalms. It was upon these that the Levites stood with their musical instruments and sang their songs' (Sukkah v. 4).

From these references it was deduced that the fifteen Psalms received their title from these steps (Rashi, Ibn Ezra, Kimchi).

Another theory is that the title was given after an episode which occurred during the building of the Temple. According to the Talmud (ibid. 53a, b), after the foundations were dug, the water level rose and threatened to inundate the entire area. David inscribed the [Ineffable] Name upon a shard, cast it into the Deep which then subsided sixteen thousand cubits into the earth. Exclaiming, "the nearer it is to the earth, the better the earth can be kept watered" he uttered the fifteen Songs of Ascent and the Deep reascended fifteen thousand cubits remaining but one thousand cubits [below the surface].

Still another theory put forward is that of Rabbi Saadia Gaon (cf. Meiri, Ibn Ezra). He suggests that the songs were part of a musical arrangement that was begun in a low voice which progressively grew louder. He further comments that their composer is not named, and they might have been of a Divine source, their intention being to offer solace to those in exile who could only pray to God for deliverance.

Yet another explanation is suggested by Kimchi. The ascents relate to the redemption of the Jews from exile and their return to the land of Israel, which will take place in three stages (*ma-aloth*). Others see it as referring to the release from the Babylonian exile and the eventual return to Judea (cf. Psalm CXXVI).

120

קכ

1 A Song of Ascents.
   In my distress I called unto the
   LORD,
   And He answered me.

2 O LORD, deliver my soul from
   lying lips,
   From a deceitful tongue.

3 What shall be given unto thee, and
   what shall be done more unto
   thee,
   Thou deceitful tongue?

4 Sharp arrows of the mighty,
   With coals of broom.

שִׁיר הַמַּעֲלוֹת
אֶל־יְהוָה בַּצָּרָתָה לִּי
קָרָאתִי וַיַּעֲנֵנִי׃
2 יְהוָה הַצִּילָה נַפְשִׁי מִשְּׂפַת־שֶׁקֶר
מִלָּשׁוֹן רְמִיָּה׃
3 מַה־יִּתֵּן לְךָ וּמַה־יֹּסִיף לָךְ
לָשׁוֹן רְמִיָּה׃
4 חִצֵּי גִבּוֹר שְׁנוּנִים
עִם גַּחֲלֵי רְתָמִים׃

THE SLANDEROUS TONGUE

OPINIONS are divided whether an individual prays for deliverance from a campaign of slander, or it is the nation which is suffering from this cause. Perhaps it was originally a personal cry, and was afterwards applied to a national emergency, such as the lying allegations of the Samaritans to hinder the rebuilding of the Temple (Ezra iv. 1ff.), or the intrigues of Sanballat and Tobiah to stop the construction of the wall around Jerusalem (Neh. iv. 1ff.).

1-2 PRAYER FOR DELIVERANCE

1. *unto the* LORD. In the Hebrew these words are placed at the beginning of the sentence to add to their emphasis: 'Unto the LORD in my distress I called.' (cf. Ibn Ezra). In his present straits he brings to mind past vicissitudes when prayer to God resulted in relief, and employs the same means to escape his enemy (cf. Hirsch).

2. Cf. lii. 3ff., where a similar situation is graphically described.

lips. Hebrew is sing. in a collective sense.

deceitful tongue. lit. 'tongue (which is, i.e. full of) deceit.'

3-4 GOD PUNISHES SLANDERERS

3. *shall be given … shall be done more.* What

other protective measures can be taken against the tongue which has already been placed behind two protective gates (Rashi) (see Tal. Arachin 15b).

4. *sharp arrows of the mighty.* Rather, 'sharpened arrows of a warrior.' God's punishment will correspond to the crime. The guilty person who had shot verbal arrows at him to ruin his character (Jer. ix. 7) will be struck down by the arrows of an archer appointed by God.

coals of broom. The roots of the *rothem* are still used as fuel and throw out much heat (cf. Tal. B.B. 74b). The persecutor who had kindled strife and contention will be consumed in the fiercely burning fire of Gehinnom (Tal. Arachin 15b).

5 Woe is me, that I sojourn with
    Meshech,
  That I dwell beside the tents of
    Kedar!
6 My soul hath full long had her
    dwelling
  With him that hateth peace.
7 I am all peace;
  But when I speak, they are for war.

אֽוֹיָה־לִי כִּי־גַרְתִּי מֶשֶׁךְ 5
שָׁכַנְתִּי עִם־אָהֳלֵי קֵדָר:
רַבַּת שָׁכְנָה־לָּהּ נַפְשִׁי 6
עִם שׂוֹנֵא שָׁלוֹם:
אֲנִי־שָׁלוֹם 7
וְכִי אֲדַבֵּר הֵמָּה לַמִּלְחָמָה:

5-7 LAMENT OF AN EXILE

5. *Meshech ... Kedar.* The first is named
among the sons of Japheth (Gen. x. 2) and
designates people such as Persians and Greeks
(Rashi). The other bears the name of the
second son of Ishmael (Gen. xxv. 13) and
stands for the Bedouin Arabs (cf. Kimchi,
Ibn Ezra). Alike they are typical of barbarian
races; the Psalmist does not actually dwell
amongst them. Forced into flight by persecution, his residence is with those whose way of
life is as rude as that among the peoples
named. (cf. Daath Sofrim).

tents. Some commentators see in this word
an allusion to the nomadic life of those tribes
(Hirsch). It may, however, be nothing more
than a poetical term for dwelling-places (cf.
cxviii. 15, cxxxii. 3).

6. *my soul.* Possibly the equivalent of 'I' as

often in the Psalter; or it may express his
spiritual nature which is distressingly affected by the ways of the people with whom
circumstances have forced him to dwell
(Hirsch).

full long ... hateth peace. Malbim renders 'All
the worse (is my predicament) that my soul
dwells with those (from my own people) who
hate peace.' Targum and the Midrash see this
as a reference to the peace-despising Edomites.

7. *I am all peace.* lit. 'I am peace,' like *I am
all prayer* (cix. 4); all my thoughts are for
peace.

when I speak. i.e. of peace, make peaceful
overtures to them. They, however, prefer
war. Even if they agree to live in peace, they
continue to hate me because of the truth that
I represent, and they seek every opportunity
to resume hostilities (Hirsch, Malbim).

121

קכא

שִׁיר לַמַּעֲלוֹת

אֶשָּׂא עֵינַי אֶל־הֶהָרִים

מֵאַיִן יָבֹא עֶזְרִי:

2 עֶזְרִי מֵעִם יְהוָה

עֹשֵׂה שָׁמַיִם וָאָרֶץ:

3 אַל־יִתֵּן לַמּוֹט רַגְלֶךָ

אַל־יָנוּם שֹׁמְרֶךָ:

4 הִנֵּה לֹא־יָנוּם וְלֹא יִישָׁן

שׁוֹמֵר יִשְׂרָאֵל:

5 יְהוָה שֹׁמְרֶךָ

יְהוָה צִלְּךָ עַל־יַד יְמִינֶךָ:

1 A Song of Ascents.
  I will lift up mine eyes unto the
    mountains:
  From whence shall my help come?

2 My help cometh from the LORD,
  Who made heaven and earth.

3 He will not suffer thy foot to be
    moved;
  He that keepeth thee will not
    slumber.

4 Behold, He that keepeth Israel
  Doth neither slumber nor sleep.

5 The LORD is thy keeper;
  The LORD is thy shade upon thy
    right hand.

GOD THE HELPER

ONE of the most popular hymns in the Psalter, a perfect expression of trust in God, this Psalm
has been on the lips of countless men and women throughout the generations whenever they
felt the need of help beyond that which mortals could offer. It differs from the other songs in
this group, in that the second word is *lama-aloth*, 'to the ascents,' rather than 'hamaaloth,' of
the ascents. It is addressed to the One who grants the righteous the merit of ascending to the
afterworld (Yalkut).

1-2 HELP COMES FROM GOD

1. *the mountains.* He looks up to the mountains hoping that assistance will come from
that direction (Ibn Ezra).

from whence. The question is only asked to
elicit the answer which follows.

2. *Who made … earth.* The existence of the
universe, the work of His hands, is witness to
His power to aid (see cxv. 15).

3-4 THE SLEEPLESS GUARDIAN

3. Although the Hebrew negative is *al* and
not *lo*, there is no need to render with R.V.

margin, 'may He not suffer … may He that
keepeth.' Its use here is 'the subjective negative' with the meaning: 'He will not, nay,
cannot possibly.'

4. *sleep.* Contrast the mocking words of
Elijah about Baal (1 Kings xviii. 27). Even in
the dark days of exile, He constantly watches
over us and thwarts the enemy's attempts to
destroy us (Kimchi).

5-6 DIVINE PROTECTION

5. *shade.* Cf. xci. 1.

upon thy right hand. The position taken by
one's champion (see on cix. 31).

6 The sun shall not smite thee by
     day,
  Nor the moon by night.

7 The LORD shall keep thee from all
     evil;
  He shall keep thy soul.

8 The LORD shall guard thy going
     out and thy coming in,
  From this time forth and for ever.

6 יוֹמָם הַשֶּׁמֶשׁ לֹא־יַכֶּ֑כָּה
  וְיָרֵחַ בַּלָּֽיְלָה׃

7 יְהוָה יִשְׁמָרְךָ מִכָּל־רָע
  יִשְׁמֹר אֶת־נַפְשֶֽׁךָ׃

8 יְהוָה יִשְׁמָר־צֵאתְךָ וּבוֹאֶ֑ךָ
  מֵעַתָּה וְעַד־עוֹלָֽם׃

6. The metaphor of *shade* is elaborated (cf. Isa. xlix. 10). The heat during the day and the cold at night are controlled by God so that their effects should not be harmful (Kimchi). Alternatively, the sun allegorically refers to the glitter of good fortune that can dazzle and cause arrogance. God will shade you from these consequences. The latter half of the verse is rendered 'and there will be a moon at night.' Even during periods of misfortune He will dispel the gloom of sorrow as the moon brightens the darkness of night (Hirsch).

7-8   GOD'S CARE ASSURED

7. *evil.* Calamity. The addition of *all* points to the comprehensiveness of the Divine protective power. Life exposes man to a great variety of mishaps, but none are beyond God's sheltering care.

keep thy soul. Guard thy life.

going out and thy coming in. All thine affairs and undertakings (cf. Deut. xxviii. 6, xxxi. 2) (Daath Sofrim). Alternatively, *going out* refers to man's departure from the House of Study to attend to his daily business and return to it (Targum). In the Psalm there may also be an implied allusion to the departure of the people of Israel from their countries of exile and the return to their homeland (Kimchi).

from this time ... ever. See on cxv. 18.

122

קכב

1 A Song of Ascents; of David.
  I rejoiced when they said unto me:
  'Let us go unto the house of the
  LORD.'
2 Our feet are standing
  Within thy gates, O Jerusalem;
3 Jerusalem, that art builded
  As a city that is compact together:
4 Whither the tribes went up, even
  the tribes of the LORD,
  As a testimony unto Israel,
  To give thanks unto the name of
  the LORD.

שִׁיר הַמַּעֲלוֹת לְדָוִד
שָׂמַחְתִּי בְּאֹמְרִים לִי
בֵּית יְהֹוָה נֵלֵךְ:
2 עֹמְדוֹת הָיוּ רַגְלֵינוּ
בִּשְׁעָרַיִךְ יְרוּשָׁלָ͏ִם:
3 יְרוּשָׁלַ͏ִם הַבְּנוּיָה
כְּעִיר שֶׁחֻבְּרָה־לָּהּ יַחְדָּו:
4 שֶׁשָּׁם עָלוּ שְׁבָטִים
שִׁבְטֵי־יָהּ עֵדוּת לְיִשְׂרָאֵל
לְהֹדוֹת לְשֵׁם יְהֹוָה:

THE PILGRIM'S JOY

ONE interpretation makes the Psalm a pilgrim's happy meditation after he had returned home from his visit to Jerusalem. According to other expositors, it describes the pilgrim's sensations while he is standing within the Temple precinct.

1. INVITATION TO JOIN THE PILGRIMAGE

of David. Not all the Psalms in this group have this title, and they were possibly composed by various poets (Kimchi). Ibn Ezra quotes two opinions. The first maintains that the song was composed by David to be sung by the choir after the Temple's completion. The second believes that David did not compose it but his name is mentioned as it was through his efforts that the Temple was constructed.

let us go. Better, 'we will go.'

2-5 REFLECTIONS IN JERUSALEM

2. *are standing.* The verbal form is called the 'perfect of experience.' It suggests that when the pilgrims came to Jerusalem, their feet stood still within the gates of the city as if transfixed by the view of its magnificence which spread out before their eyes (Hirsch).

3. *as a city that is compact together.* Or, 'as a city in which companionship together was fostered. Peoples from all walks of life and from various countries would meet in Jerusalem on the occasion of the festival and the effect would be to unite them into one homogeneous group (Kimchi). The Talmud (Taan. 5a) applies deeper meaning to the verse. David intended that the earthly city of Jerusalem would correspond to the heavenly Jerusalem, and would become a city totally dedicated to the ideals of God. Hence he built it with the hope that it would be united with its sister-city on high.

4. *whither the tribes went up.* The city recalled the glories of the past, when the tribes came in crowds on the three Pilgrim Festivals, in obedience of the ancient *testimony* in Exod. xxiii. 17, Deut. xvi. 16.

the tribes of the LORD. Not 'the tribes of Israel,' but a more honourable title that associates them with God, since their sole objective in the pilgrimage to Jerusalem was acknowledgement of Him and a demonstration of their allegiance to His Torah (Kimchi).

5 For there were set thrones for
  judgment,
  The thrones of the house of David.

6 Pray for the peace of Jerusalem;
  May they prosper that love thee.

7 Peace be within thy walls,
  And prosperity within thy palaces.

8 For my brethren and companions'
  sakes,
  I will now say: 'Peace be within
  thee.'

9 For the sake of the house of the
  LORD our God
  I will seek thy good.

5 כִּי שָׁמָּה ׀ יָשְׁבוּ כִסְאוֹת לְמִשְׁפָּט
כִּסְאוֹת לְבֵית דָּוִד:
6 שַׁאֲלוּ שְׁלוֹם יְרוּשָׁלָ͏ִם
יִשְׁלָיוּ אֹהֲבָיִךְ:
7 יְהִי־שָׁלוֹם בְּחֵילֵךְ
שַׁלְוָה בְּאַרְמְנוֹתָיִךְ:
8 לְמַעַן אַחַי וְרֵעָי
אֲדַבְּרָה־נָּא שָׁלוֹם בָּךְ:
9 לְמַעַן בֵּית־יְהֹוָה אֱלֹהֵינוּ
אֲבַקְשָׁה טוֹב לָךְ:

5. *thrones for judgment.* Cf. ix. 5, 8 where the reference is to God's seat of judgment. Here the plural denotes not only God's seat of judgment, but also that of the Davidic dynasty which exercised its authority in the city (Kimchi).

6-9 PRAYER FOR JERUSALEM'S WELFARE

From dwelling upon the happy past, the pilgrim's thoughts naturally turn to the present and future, and he prays for its prosperity, inviting others to join in the prayer.

6. There is a word play in the Hebrew which cannot be reproduced in translation.

peace. Hebrew *shalom*, lit. condition of 'wholeness' in which nothing desirable is lacking.

Jerusalem. Hebrew *Yerushalayim*, the latter half being connected with *shalom*.

may they prosper. Hebrew *yishlayu*. He invokes a blessing upon Zion's well-wishers, just as in cxxix. 5 the Psalmist hopes that her haters may be *ashamed and turned backward.*

7. *walls ... palaces.* The same words as in xlviii. 14.

8. *my brethren and companions' sakes.* He prays not only for his own sake but also on behalf of all the children of Israel, especially for those in exile, that they shall return to Jerusalem (Rashi, Kimchi).

I will now say ... thee. Or, 'let me now speak peace concerning thee,' i.e. pray for the city's welfare.

9. *the house.* His final thought is for the Temple which will give Jerusalem its distinctive and sacred character (cf. Alshich).

I will seek. In prayer (Hirsch).

קכג

שִׁיר הַמַּעֲלוֹת
אֵלֶיךָ נָשָׂאתִי אֶת־עֵינַי
הַיֹּשְׁבִי בַּשָּׁמָיִם:
2 הִנֵּה כְעֵינֵי עֲבָדִים
אֶל־יַד אֲדוֹנֵיהֶם
כְּעֵינֵי שִׁפְחָה אֶל־יַד גְּבִרְתָּהּ
כֵּן עֵינֵינוּ אֶל־יְהוָה אֱלֹהֵינוּ
עַד שֶׁיְּחָנֵּנוּ:
3 חָנֵּנוּ יְהוָה חָנֵּנוּ
כִּי־רַב שָׂבַעְנוּ בוּז:
4 רַבַּת שָׂבְעָה־לָּהּ נַפְשֵׁנוּ
הַלַּעַג הַשַּׁאֲנַנִּים
הַבּוּז לִגְאֵיוֹנִים:

‏v. 4. ‏לִגְאֵי־יוֹנִים ק׳

123

1 A Song of Ascents.
Unto Thee I lift up mine eyes,
O Thou that art enthroned in the
heavens.

2 Behold, as the eyes of servants
unto the hand of their master,
As the eyes of a maiden unto the
hand of her mistress;
So our eyes look unto the LORD
our God,
Until He be gracious unto us.

3 Be gracious unto us, O LORD, be
gracious unto us;
For we are full sated with contempt.

4 Our soul is full sated
With the scorning of those that are
at ease,
And with the contempt of the
proud oppressors.

HYMN OF FAITH

AN individual speaks for his people. He begins with the singular pronoun, but from verse 2 uses the plural. The Psalm was composed in a time of trouble, and the faithful look yearningly to God for relief. Quite probably the historical background is the malicious hostility of their new neighbours during their exile.

1-2 HOPE IN GOD

1. *I lift up mine eyes.* Cf. cxxi. 1.

enthroned in the heavens. As King and Judge (ii. 4).

2. *the hand.* Which supplies their needs.

3-4 PRAYER FOR HIS FAVOUR

3. *full sated with contempt.* Humiliation had been their constant experience at the hands of their neighbours.

4. *scorning.* The verb from this root is found in *they laughed us to scorn* and *they mocked the Jews* (Nehem. ii. 19, iii. 33).

are at ease. The Jews, toiling to reconstruct their life in exile, contrast their despised condition with the boastful and secure lot of their opponents.

proud oppressors. The *kethib* means 'the proud'; the *kerë* reads as two words: 'valley of doves,' i.e. Jerusalem. The phrase thus means, 'Jerusalem was the object of their contempt' (Rashi).

שִׁיר הַמַּעֲלוֹת לְדָוִד

לוּלֵי יְהוָה שֶׁהָיָה לָנוּ

יֹאמַר־נָא יִשְׂרָאֵל:

2 לוּלֵא יְהוָה שֶׁהָיָה לָנוּ

בְּקוּם עָלֵינוּ אָדָם:

3 אֲזַי חַיִּים בְּלָעוּנוּ

בַּחֲרוֹת אַפָּם בָּנוּ:

4 אֲזַי הַמַּיִם שְׁטָפוּנוּ

נַחְלָה עָבַר עַל־נַפְשֵׁנוּ:

5 אֲזַי עָבַר עַל־נַפְשֵׁנוּ

הַמַּיִם הַזֵּידוֹנִים:

6 בָּרוּךְ יְהוָה

שֶׁלֹּא נְתָנָנוּ טֶרֶף לְשִׁנֵּיהֶם:

7 נַפְשֵׁנוּ כְּצִפּוֹר נִמְלְטָה

מִפַּח יוֹקְשִׁים

הַפַּח נִשְׁבָּר וַאֲנַחְנוּ נִמְלָטְנוּ:

8 עֶזְרֵנוּ בְּשֵׁם יְהוָה

עֹשֵׂה שָׁמַיִם וָאָרֶץ:

1 A Song of Ascents; of David.
'If it had not been the LORD who
    was for us',
Let Israel now say;

2 'If it had not been the LORD who
    was for us,
When men rose up against us,

3 Then they had swallowed us up
    alive,
When their wrath was kindled
    against us;

4 Then the waters had overwhelmed
    us,
The stream had gone over our
    soul;

5 Then the proud waters
Had gone over our soul.'

6 Blessed be the LORD,
Who hath not given us as a prey to
    their teeth.

7 Our soul is escaped as a bird out of
    the snare of the fowlers;
The snare is broken, and we are
    escaped.

8 Our help is in the name of the
    LORD,
Who made heaven and earth.

SONG OF DELIVERANCE

THE Psalm was clearly occasioned by the passing of a recent danger; and like so many in this group, it could possibly refer to any of the enemies who arose against the people of Israel in exile (cf. Kimchi).

1-5 THE PERIL

1. *of David.* As in cxxii. 1, and here the Targum renders that it was recited by others regarding David.

if it had not been ... us. Their survival through centuries of suffering depended on God alone (Hirsch).

now. In times of exile (Kimchi) (cf. cxviii. 2).

2. *men.* Hebrew *adam* (see on viii. 5). The Talmud (Meg. 11a) identifies this 'man' as Haman.

3. *their wrath.* They were over-eager to destroy us like a starving man, who, in his haste, will devour even raw ('alive') meat (Kimchi).

4. *stream.* A mountain torrent swollen by heavy rains.

5. *the proud waters.* The Hebrew adjective connotes wilful wickedness. The waters in their swollen state thus typify the enemy (Kimchi).

6-8 THANKSGIVING TO GOD

6. *blessed.* Has the force of 'praised.'

8. *in the name of the LORD.* In God's attribute of Protector of the weak.

שִׁיר הַמַּעֲלוֹת
הַבֹּטְחִים בַּיהוָֹה
כְּהַר־צִיּוֹן לֹא־יִמּוֹט
לְעוֹלָם יֵשֵׁב:

1 A Song of Ascents.
They that trust in the LORD
Are as mount Zion, which cannot
  be moved, but abideth for ever.

2 יְרוּשָׁלַם הָרִים סָבִיב לָהּ
וַיהוָֹה סָבִיב לְעַמּוֹ
מֵעַתָּה וְעַד־עוֹלָם:

2 As the mountains are round about
  Jerusalem,
So the LORD is round about His
  people,
From this time forth and for ever.

3 כִּי לֹא יָנוּחַ שֵׁבֶט הָרֶשַׁע
עַל גּוֹרַל הַצַּדִּיקִים
לְמַעַן לֹא־יִשְׁלְחוּ הַצַּדִּיקִים
בְּעַוְלָתָה יְדֵיהֶם:

3 For the rod of wickedness shall not
  rest upon the lot of the righteous;
That the righteous put not forth
  their hands unto iniquity.

4 הֵיטִיבָה יְהוָֹה לַטּוֹבִים
וְלִישָׁרִים בְּלִבּוֹתָם:

4 Do good, O LORD, unto the good,
And to them that are upright in
  their hearts.

5 וְהַמַּטִּים עֲקַלְקַלּוֹתָם
יוֹלִיכֵם יְהוָֹה אֶת־פֹּעֲלֵי הָאָוֶן
שָׁלוֹם עַל־יִשְׂרָאֵל:

5 But as for such as turn aside unto
  their crooked ways,
The LORD will lead them away
  with the workers of iniquity.
Peace be upon Israel.

SECURITY IN GOD

THE conviction that to rely upon God in a time of trouble is the surest source of endurance breathes through this Psalm. The righteous were being harried by evil-doers, and the composition may relate to the future resettlement of the Jewish people in their homeland after the ingathering of the exiles—they will enjoy Divine protection and thus live in total security (Sforno).

1. *as mount Zion.* To the residents of Jerusalem the holy mount would represent the symbol of permanence (cf. Kimchi).

2. *as the mountains.* Hills typify the encircling protection of God.

from this time ... ever. For all eternity; not, as in cxv. 18, cxxi. 8, during our lifetime.

3. *rod of wickedness.* Rather, 'sceptre of wickedness,' foreign domination characterized by tyranny.

the lot of the righteous. Israel's land (Ibn Ezra).

put not forth their hands. Long-continued rule by heathen governors might induce some Israelites to lose faith, and in despair throw in their lot with the oppressors, abandoning their ancestral religion (Kimchi).

4. *the good ... upright.* The good in their deeds and the upright in their hearts (Kimchi).

5. *turn aside ... ways.* Hirsch renders 'those who turn their crooked ways even further from the straight path.'

the LORD will lead. Or, 'may the LORD lead,' to share like condemnation.

peace ... Israel. Cf. cxxii. 6ff. Peace in Israel is possible only when the nation rids itself of its renegades. Their presence among the people brings disharmony as they attempt to lead others away from God (Daath Sofrim).

126

קכו

שִׁיר הַמַּעֲלוֹת
בְּשׁוּב יְהוָה אֶת־שִׁיבַת צִיּוֹן
הָיִינוּ כְּחֹלְמִים:
2 אָז יִמָּלֵא שְׂחוֹק פִּינוּ
וּלְשׁוֹנֵנוּ רִנָּה
אָז יֹאמְרוּ בַגּוֹיִם
הִגְדִּיל יְהוָה לַעֲשׂוֹת עִם־אֵלֶּה:
3 הִגְדִּיל יְהוָה לַעֲשׂוֹת עִמָּנוּ
הָיִינוּ שְׂמֵחִים:
4 שׁוּבָה יְהוָה אֶת־שְׁבוּתֵנוּ
כַּאֲפִיקִים בַּנֶּגֶב:
5 הַזֹּרְעִים בְּדִמְעָה
בְּרִנָּה יִקְצֹרוּ:
6 הָלוֹךְ יֵלֵךְ וּבָכֹה נֹשֵׂא מֶשֶׁךְ־הַזָּרַע
בֹּא־יָבֹא בְרִנָּה נֹשֵׂא אֲלֻמֹּתָיו:

שביתנו ק׳ v. 4.

1 A Song of Ascents.
When the LORD brought back
those that returned to Zion,
We were like unto them that
dream.

2 Then was our mouth filled with
laughter,
And our tongue with singing;
Then said they among the nations:
'The LORD hath done great things
with these.'

3 The LORD hath done great things
with us;
We are rejoiced.

4 Turn our captivity, O LORD,
As the streams in the dry land.

5 They that sow in tears
Shall reap in joy.

6 Though he goeth on his way weeping that beareth the measure of
seed,
He shall come home with joy
bearing his sheaves.

THE ASCENT FROM EXILE

THE Psalm prophesies the feelings and thoughts of the people during the final redemption. The hopes are high and happiness abounds. Contrast with CXXXVII which describes the nation's descent into exile. The Psalm is chanted prior to the recitation of the grace after meals on the Sabbath and Holy days.

1. *When … back.* Better: 'will bring back.' Rashi interprets the verse as speaking of the returning captives from exile, while Kimchi suggests it to be a reference to repentance and renders 'when the LORD will bring back the penitents of Zion (to His faith).'

We … that dream. Better, 'we will have been like those who dream.' Past events will seem as if they never happened (Kimchi).

2. *Then was our mouth.* Render, 'then will our mouth be filled.' Cf. Job. viii. 21.

singing. Praises to God for salvation.

then said they. Render 'then they will say.' The remarkable series of events will impress the surrounding nations (Hirsch, Malbim).

3. *the LORD hath done.* If the heathens acknowledge this, how much more so the people who benefited from God's act! (Cf. Metsudath David).

4. *turn our captivity.* i.e., restore our fortunes.

the dry land. Better, 'in the South,' the sandy tract in the south of the land of Israel (Hirsch).

5. The metaphor changes to life on the land. The peasant sows his seed with tears of anxiety; but when the time of reaping comes, tears give place to joyful singing.

in joy. Rather, 'with cries of joy.'

127

קכז

1 A Song of Ascents; of Solomon.
Except the LORD build the house,
They labour in vain that build it;
Except the LORD keep the city,
The watchman waketh but in vain.

2 It is vain for you that ye rise early,
   and sit up late,
Ye that eat the bread of toil;
So He giveth unto His beloved
   in sleep.

שִׁיר הַמַּעֲלוֹת לִשְׁלֹמֹה
אִם־יְהֹוָה ׀ לֹא־יִבְנֶה בַיִת
שָׁוְא ׀ עָמְלוּ בוֹנָיו בּוֹ
אִם־יְהֹוָה לֹא־יִשְׁמָר־עִיר
שָׁוְא ׀ שָׁקַד שׁוֹמֵר׃
2 שָׁוְא לָכֶם ׀ מַשְׁכִּימֵי קוּם
מְאַחֲרֵי־שֶׁבֶת
אֹכְלֵי לֶחֶם הָעֲצָבִים
כֵּן יִתֵּן לִידִידוֹ שֵׁנָא׃

GOD'S HELP ESSENTIAL

Two lines of thought run through this Psalm. One teaching is general and concerns the problems of building a successful and lasting home. Human planning and effort need to be supplemented by God's blessing if it is to endure (Hirsch, Malbim). In addition, the Psalm takes David's experience as a vivid example of human reliance on Divine favour. Though he invested time and effort in gathering materials for the building of the Temple, it was God's wish that only David's son Solomon would be honoured with the task of constructing it (Kimchi).

1-2 MAN'S WORK FUTILE WITHOUT GOD

1. *of Solomon.* The commentators do not understand this as indicating his authorship of the Psalm. They takes it to mean 'concerning Solomon' as the builder of the Temple.

the house. Rather, 'a house'; no definite article appears in the Hebrew.

labour. The Hebrew verb means to toil until one is weary.

the city. Rather, 'a city,' there being no definite article.

waketh. Render, 'keepeth watch.'

2. *rise early, and sit up late.* Even the most industrious, who begin their day's toil early in the morning and continue it into the late evening, labour in vain without His aid (Rashi). It may be referring specifically to David's son Absalom who was the first to rebel against his father and to Adoniyahu who rebelled later (Kimchi).

the bread of toil. Better, 'of troubles.' Food gained by hard work despite setbacks (Cf. Hirsch, Malbim).

so He giveth. Possibly *ken* does not signify *so* but 'what is right, suitable,' and the translation is: 'what is due He giveth.' The teaching is that God provides for those who gain His favour even when they are not engaged in their work, as during the time of sleep; not that they may be idle, but freed from anxiety they will not lack the necessities of life (cf. Hirsch).

3 Lo, children are a heritage of the
    LORD;
  The fruit of the womb is a reward.

4 As arrows in the hand of a mighty
    man,
  So are the children of one's youth.

5 Happy is the man that hath his
    quiver full of them;
  They shall not be put to shame,
  When they speak with their en-
    emies in the gate.

3 הִנֵּה נַחֲלַת יְהוָה בָּנִים
שָׂכָר פְּרִי הַבָּטֶן:
4 כְּחִצִּים בְּיַד־גִּבּוֹר
כֵּן בְּנֵי הַנְּעוּרִים:
5 אַשְׁרֵי הַגֶּבֶר אֲשֶׁר מִלֵּא
אֶת־אַשְׁפָּתוֹ מֵהֶם
לֹא־יֵבֹשׁוּ
כִּי־יְדַבְּרוּ אֶת־אוֹיְבִים בַּשָּׁעַר:

3-5 THE BLESSING OF CHILDREN

3.   That children are a gift bestowed by the
grace of God is a characteristic teaching of
the Bible. Hence the statement, *And God
healed Abimelech, and his wife, and his maid-
servants; and they bore children. For the
LORD had fast closed up all the wombs of the
house of Abimelech* (Gen. xx. 17f.), and the
retort of Jacob, *Am I in God's stead, Who
hath withheld from thee the fruit of the womb?*
to Rachel's complaint, *Give me children, or
else I die* (Gen. xxx. 1f.). The Rabbis declared that a child has three parents: God in
addition to father and mother.

children. The Hebrew term can denote 'sons'
or *children* generally. In view of the comparison with *arrows* in the next verse, the
intention is doubtless sons who alone could
defend their father; but the parallelism *fruit
of the womb* indicates that daughters are not
excluded, since the phrase must mean 'offspring' (cf. Daath Sofrim).

reward. Cf. cxxviii. 4.

4.   *as arrows.* A great aid, as are arrows
against attackers (Kimchi).

a mighty man. A warrior.

children of one's youth. Born while the father
was still young, so that when grown to manhood they are able to safeguard his interests
in his old age (cf. Kimchi).

5.   *his quiver.* Continuing the metaphor of
children as arrows.

they shall not. viz. the fathers who have many
adult sons. The plural may also indicate the
father surrounded by his sons.

speak with their enemies. Defend their cause
in a matter under dispute. When justice was
not impartially administered, the presence of
these stalwart sons by the side of their father
to uphold his interests would impress the
judges (cf. Kimchi).

in the gate. See on lxix. 13. Lawsuits were
heard there (cf. Deut. xxi. 19). Rashi sees this
verse as reference to scholars who 'battle'
with their 'enemies' in the understanding of
Torah law.

128

קכח

שִׁיר הַמַּעֲלוֹת
אַשְׁרֵי כָּל־יְרֵא יְהוָה
הַהֹלֵךְ בִּדְרָכָיו:

2 יְגִיעַ כַּפֶּיךָ כִּי תֹאכֵל
אַשְׁרֶיךָ וְטוֹב לָךְ:

3 אֶשְׁתְּךָ ׀ כְּגֶפֶן פֹּרִיָּה
בְּיַרְכְּתֵי בֵיתֶךָ
בָּנֶיךָ כִּשְׁתִלֵי זֵיתִים
סָבִיב לְשֻׁלְחָנֶךָ:

4 הִנֵּה כִי־כֵן יְבֹרַךְ גָּבֶר
יְרֵא יְהוָה:

5 יְבָרֶכְךָ יְהוָה מִצִּיּוֹן
וּרְאֵה בְּטוּב יְרוּשָׁלָ͏ִם
כֹּל יְמֵי חַיֶּיךָ:

6 וּרְאֵה־בָנִים לְבָנֶיךָ
שָׁלוֹם עַל־יִשְׂרָאֵל:

1 A Song of Ascents.
  Happy is every one that feareth
    the LORD,
  That walketh in His ways.

2 When thou eatest the labour of thy
    hands,
  Happy shalt thou be, and it shall
    be well with thee.

3 Thy wife shall be as a fruitful vine,
    in the innermost parts of thy
    house;
  Thy children like olive plants,
    round about thy table.

4 Behold, surely thus shall the man
    be blessed
  That feareth the LORD.

5 The LORD bless thee out of Zion;
  And see thou the good of Jeru-
    salem all the days of thy life;

6 And see thy children's children.
  Peace be upon Israel!

HAPPINESS OF THE GOD-FEARING

A COMPANION Psalm to the preceding, the link being the mention of a prolific family as a blessing from God. It contains a beautiful cameo picture of an ideal homelife. Happiness is brought about by a combination of 'the fear of God' and 'labour,' and is composed of a successful marriage that brings blessing to the home (Hirsch).

1. *feareth.* Shows reverence of God by conformity to His precepts.

2. *when thou eatest.* i.e., when you are able to enjoy the fruits of your toil and do not depend on charity (Kimchi).

happy ... with thee. A favourite text of the Rabbis when teaching the dignity of honest work.

3. *thy wife.* This idealistic picture of the home presupposes a state of monogamy, as does Prov. xxxi. 10ff.

fruitful vine. Bearing numerous grape-clus-ters; so the God-fearing man's wife will bring him many children.

innermost parts of thy house. The modest woman keeps to the privacy of her home, reserving her beauty for her husband alone (Midrash Tanchuma, Gen. Vayishlach).

5. *the good of Jerusalem.* The welfare of the Israelite is bound up with the city.

6. *see thy children's children.* Thus attaining a good old age.

peace be upon Israel. See on cxxv. 5.

129

קכט

שִׁיר הַמַּעֲלוֹת
רַבַּת צְרָרוּנִי מִנְּעוּרַי
יֹאמַר־נָא יִשְׂרָאֵל:
2 רַבַּת צְרָרוּנִי מִנְּעוּרָי
גַּם לֹא־יָכְלוּ לִי:
3 עַל־גַּבִּי חָרְשׁוּ חֹרְשִׁים
הֶאֱרִיכוּ לְמַעֲנוֹתָם:
4 יְהֹוָה צַדִּיק
קִצֵּץ עֲבוֹת רְשָׁעִים:
5 יֵבֹשׁוּ וְיִסֹּגוּ אָחוֹר
כֹּל שֹׂנְאֵי צִיּוֹן:

v. 3. למעניתם ק׳

1 A Song of Ascents.
  'Much have they afflicted me from
    my youth up,'
  Let Israel now say;

2 'Much have they afflicted me from
    my youth up;
  But they have not prevailed against
    me.

3 The plowers plowed upon my
    back;
  They made long their furrows.

4 The LORD is righteous;
  He hath cut asunder the cords of
    the wicked.'

5 Let them be ashamed and turned
    backward,
  All they that hate Zion.

A SUFFERER'S PLEA

The commentators describe the Psalm as Israel's yearning, while in exile, for Zion. The commentators contrast it with the fleeting pleasures, devoid of all blessing and permanence, of those who hate Zion and regard it as their life's mission to fight against the teaching that comes forth from Zion and its people (Hirsch).

1-4 ISRAEL'S OPPRESSION AND DELIVERANCE

1. The construction of this and the next verses has the same form as cxxiv. 1f.

my youth. From the earliest days of history (Hirsch).

3. *the plowers ... back.* As land is gashed by the plough, so the backs of the Israelites were exposed to the torture of their oppressors (Malbim).

they made long their furrows. There was no letup from the torment and suffering inflicted on Israel by her enemies.

4. *cords.* The word is employed in Job xxxix. 10, for the rope which harnesses the ox to the plough. The Israelites, under the subjection of heathen rulers, are likened to the ox yoked for work in the field. By God's aid the cords were broken and freedom was regained.

5-8 NATIONAL ENEMIES IMPRECATED

5. *ashamed.* Disappointed by failure of their schemes to harm Israel (Kimchi).

Zion. A symbol of the nation.

6 Let them be as the grass upon the
    housetops,
    Which withereth afore it springeth
    up;

7 Wherewith the reaper filleth not
    his hand,
    Nor he that bindeth sheaves his
    bosom;

8 Neither do they that go by say:
    'The blessing of the Lord be upon
    you;
    We bless you in the name of the
    Lord.'

6 יִהְיוּ כַּחֲצִיר גַּגּוֹת
שֶׁקַּדְמַת שָׁלַף יָבֵשׁ:
7 שֶׁלֹּא מִלֵּא כַפּוֹ קוֹצֵר
וְחִצְנוֹ מְעַמֵּר:
8 וְלֹא אָמְרוּ ׀ הָעֹבְרִים
בִּרְכַּת־יְהוָֹה אֲלֵיכֶם
בֵּרַכְנוּ אֶתְכֶם בְּשֵׁם יְהוָֹה:

6. *grass upon the housetops.* Cf. Isa. xxxvii. 27. The wind carries seed from the field which sometimes falls upon a roof. It may begin to grow, but with no depth of soil, it quickly shrivels under the sun's heat (Kimchi).

springeth up. lit. 'is unsheathed,' commonly used of the sword, here of the blade of grass. So may Israel's foes perish before their plans fructify.

7. Even when the grass grows, it will wither before it can be reaped. The reaper will not be able 'to fill his hand' with what is left. Similarly, the ill-wishers of Zion will meet with little success. What they hold in their grip will be shrivelled and worthless only to be thrown aside. They will gain nothing from their schemes (cf. Hirsch). Alternatively, just as the remaining corn is spread around in various areas, so will the wicked be dispersed and disunited and their evil ideas doomed to certain failure (Malbim).

his bosom. Also governed by the verb *filleth.*

8. *neither do they that go by say.* It was customary for a passer-by to address a blessing to the reapers, such as *the Lord be with you* (Ruth ii. 4). No blessing of God can be invoked upon men engaged upon work of so malicious a character (Kimchi, Ibn Ezra, Metsudath David).

we bless you in the name of the Lord. In ordinary circumstances the prayer would imply, 'May God prosper your work'; but who could utter such a hope in this connection!

130

קל

שִׁיר הַמַּעֲלוֹת
מִמַּעֲמַקִּים קְרָאתִיךָ יְהֹוָה:
2 אֲדֹנָי שִׁמְעָה בְקוֹלִי
תִּהְיֶינָה אָזְנֶיךָ קַשֻּׁבוֹת
לְקוֹל תַּחֲנוּנָי:
3 אִם־עֲוֹנוֹת תִּשְׁמָר־יָהּ
אֲדֹנָי מִי יַעֲמֹד:
4 כִּי־עִמְּךָ הַסְּלִיחָה
לְמַעַן תִּוָּרֵא:
5 קִוִּיתִי יְהֹוָה קִוְּתָה נַפְשִׁי
וְלִדְבָרוֹ הוֹחָלְתִּי:

1 A Song of Ascents.
  Out of the depths have I called
  Thee, O LORD.

2 Lord, hearken unto my voice;
  Let Thine ears be attentive
  To the voice of my supplications.

3 If Thou, LORD, shouldest mark
  iniquities,
  O Lord, who could stand?

4 For with Thee there is forgiveness,
  That Thou mayest be feared.

5 I wait for the LORD, my soul doth
  wait,
  And in His word do I hope.

A SINNER'S CRY

THE Psalm is best understood as an expression of remorse for sin and a plea for forgiveness on the part of an individual Israelite. Although it is a personal confession and prayer, he is the spokesman of his people, and the hardships he is undergoing are due to national distress. He concludes with a call for repentance which will surely cause God to bring about redemption.

1-2 THE PENITENT'S CRY

1. *depths.* Of waters; a common metaphor for troubles (cf. cxxiv. 4f.) (cf. Kimchi).

have I called. In Hebrew the perfect of experience, to be rendered 'do I call.'

2. *let Thine ears be attentive.* The phrase in the singular occurs in Nehemiah's prayer (Nehem. i. 6).

3-4 GOD IS FORGIVING

3. *mark.* Take account of; pardon can only ensue from God's clemency.

LORD. Different words are employed. The first is *Jah*, the designation of God as the Saviour of Israel (Exod. xv. 2); the second means 'my Master,' expressing dependence upon His kindness.

stand. Before the Divine tribunal and endure the ordeal of judgment.

4. *for.* Better, 'but,' answering the point raised in verse 3. Conscious of sin, he yet pleads with God because He is forgiving and does not *mark iniquities.*

with Thee. With Thee alone and not with any intermediaries, such as ministering angels (Kimchi, Metsudath David).

mayest be feared. God pardons and removes the penalty of sin from the penitent in order to turn men's hearts away from sin and towards Him in reverence (cf. Ibn Ezra).

5-6 HE AWAITS GOD'S DELIVERANCE

5. *I wait.* lit. 'waited,' perfect of experience; similarly *do I hope.*

my soul. The change from 'I' to *my soul* denotes the intentness and complete concentration of the act of waiting (Metsudath David).

6 My soul waiteth for the Lord,
  More than watchmen for the
    morning;
  Yea, more than watchmen for the
    morning.

7 O Israel, hope in the LORD;
  For with the LORD there is mercy,
  And with Him is plenteous re-
    demption.

8 And He will redeem Israel
  From all his iniquities.

נַפְשִׁי לַאדֹנָי 6
מִשֹּׁמְרִים לַבֹּקֶר
שֹׁמְרִים לַבֹּקֶר׃
יַחֵל יִשְׂרָאֵל אֶל־יְהֹוָה 7
כִּי־עִם־יְהֹוָה הַחֶסֶד
וְהַרְבֵּה עִמּוֹ פְדוּת׃
וְהוּא יִפְדֶּה אֶת־יִשְׂרָאֵל 8
מִכֹּל עֲוֹנֹתָיו׃

His word. Promise to forgive sins and deliver from hardship.

6. *my soul waiteth.* The verb has to be supplied, the Hebrew being lit. 'my soul (is turned) to the LORD' (Kimchi, Ibn Ezra). Another possibility is not to insert the verb 'waiteth' but to translate 'my soul is one from among those who pray and hope to the LORD for the light of redemption'; i.e., the Psalmist is one of those who aspires to God during the darkness of exile (Meiri, Metsudath David).

watchmen. According to the Targum, the allusion is to the Levites in the Temple eagerly looking for the appearance of dawn to offer the morning sacrifice. It may refer to the sentinels upon the city walls impatiently awaiting the passing of the night to be relieved of their duties (cf. Ibn Ezra).

yea, more than watchmen. The repetition produces the effect of urgency.

7-8 EXHORTATION TO THE PEOPLE

7. The Psalmist addresses his co-religionists and exhorts them to share his convictions.

mercy. Hebrew *chesed*, 'love.' The definite article is prefixed to the noun, perhaps indicating *the* love which is the assurance of *the forgiveness* (so lit.) of which he had spoken in verse 4 (cf. Daath Sofrim).

plenteous redemption. Unlimited power to deliver. God has demonstrated in the past His readiness to redeem His nation from troubles (Kimchi).

8. *and He.* Emphasized in the Hebrew implying that redemption is assured because of the attribute of mercy ascribed to Him.

will redeem Israel. From his iniquities and the national distress which followed thereon (cf. the petition in xxv. 22, *Redeem Israel, O God, out of all his troubles*).

131

שִׁיר הַמַּעֲלוֹת לְדָוִד
יְהוָה ׀ לֹא־גָּבַהּ לִבִּי
וְלֹא־רָמוּ עֵינַי
וְלֹא־הִלַּכְתִּי ׀ בִּגְדֹלוֹת
וּבְנִפְלָאוֹת מִמֶּנִּי ׃
2 אִם־לֹא שִׁוִּיתִי ׀ וְדוֹמַמְתִּי נַפְשִׁי
כְּגָמֻל עֲלֵי אִמּוֹ
כַּגָּמֻל עָלַי נַפְשִׁי ׃
3 יַחֵל יִשְׂרָאֵל אֶל־יְהוָה
מֵעַתָּה וְעַד־עוֹלָם ׃

קלא

1 A Song of Ascents; of David.
Lord, my heart is not haughty,
  nor mine eyes lofty;
Neither do I exercise myself in
  things too great, or in things too
  wonderful for me.

2 Surely I have stilled and quieted
  my soul;
Like a weaned child with his
  mother,
My soul is with me like a weaned
  child.

3 O Israel, hope in the Lord
From this time forth and for ever.

THE HUMBLE SPIRIT

The Psalm is a literary gem of exquisite beauty and surpassing spirituality. David speaks of himself but has the nation in mind, for the time when they will languish in exile. If the people will emulate his behaviour and act with humility and modesty, God will consequently show mercy and redeem them (Kimchi).

1. *mine eyes lofty.* Cf. *the haughty eyes* (xviii. 28 and cf. ci. 5).

neither ... for me. He is content to follow a humble course of life, not aspiring to high office in the community. *Exercise myself* is literally 'walk about,' i.e. strive for things which were too great and too remote for me to reach (Hirsch).

2. *like a weaned child.* A remarkable piece of imagery. An infant in its mother's arms instinctively yearns for her milk; but after being weaned, it still finds happy security when held by her although the earlier longing had passed. Such is the Psalmist's condition after weaning himself from the desire for prominence (Kimchi).

3. May his people follow his example, not longing for imperial eminence and power, but waiting continually and submissively for God to guide their destiny (Daath Sofrim).

O Israel, hope in the Lord. Repeated from cxxx. 7.

from this time ... ever. See on cxxv. 2.

132

קלב

1 A Song of Ascents.
  LORD, remember unto David
  All his affliction;

2 How he swore unto the LORD,
  And vowed unto the Mighty One
    of Jacob:

3 'Surely I will not come into the
    tent of my house,
  Nor go up into the bed that is
    spread for me;

4 I will not give sleep to mine eyes,
  Nor slumber to mine eyelids;

5 Until I find out a place for the
    LORD,
  A dwelling-place for the Mighty
    One of Jacob.'

שִׁיר הַמַּעֲלוֹת
זְכוֹר־יְהוָה לְדָוִד
אֵת כָּל־עֻנּוֹתוֹ׃
אֲשֶׁר נִשְׁבַּע לַיהוָה 2
נָדַר לַאֲבִיר יַעֲקֹב׃
אִם־אָבֹא בְּאֹהֶל בֵּיתִי 3
אִם־אֶעֱלֶה עַל־עֶרֶשׂ יְצוּעָי׃
אִם־אֶתֵּן שְׁנַת לְעֵינָי 4
לְעַפְעַפַּי תְּנוּמָה׃
עַד־אֶמְצָא מָקוֹם לַיהוָה 5
מִשְׁכָּנוֹת לַאֲבִיר יַעֲקֹב׃

GOD'S PROMISE WILL BE FULFILLED

THIS Psalm is different from all the other Songs of Ascents in length and style. Verses 8-10 reappear substantially in 2 Chron. vi. 41f. at the end of Solomon's Prayer of Dedication and verses 7-14 point to its celebration of the solemn moment when the ark of the Law was brought into the Temple built by Solomon. Through this act, the Temple was dedicated to the presence of God in Israel's midst (Hirsch). Ibn Ezra and Kimchi connect this Psalm with events that occurred in the latter days of David's reign (2 Sam. xxiv. 18-25, 1 Chron. xxi. 18-30): A plague which had overrun Israel, killing thousands, then threatened Jerusalem. David was told to build an altar for sacrifices on the future Temple site to stem the destruction, but the identity of the site was unknown (verse 6). The Psalm also recollects David's pain upon learning that he was not to be the builder of the Temple and the zeal he nevertheless showed in his preparations for it.

1-5 DAVID'S VOW TO BUILD A TEMPLE

1. *unto David.* In David's favour.

all his affliction. It was no easy task for David to arrange for the construction of the Temple, as the following verses relate. In 1 Chron. xxii. 14, David cries, *Now, behold, in my straits* (lit. affliction) *I have prepared for the house of the LORD.*

2. *how he swore.* Implied in his strong wish to erect a Temple (2 Sam. vii.).

the Mighty One of Jacob. Again verse 5, originally in Gen. xlix. 24. God raised Jacob from the lowly state of fugitive to a position which enabled him to overcome even such powerful adversaries as Esau and Laban. He was also elevated from shepherd to leader of his people (cf. Hirsch).

3. David is uncomfortable with staying in his palace while the Presence of God, as represented by the Holy Ark, is without a fixed abode (Kimchi).

the tent of my house. i.e. the tent which is my house. *Tent* is employed poetically.

5. *a place for the LORD.* Explained by *he*

6 Lo, we heard of it as being in
   Ephrath;
  We found it in the field of the
   wood.

7 Let us go into His dwelling-place;
  Let us worship at His footstool.

8 Arise, O LORD, unto Thy resting-
   place;
  Thou, and the ark of Thy strength

9 Let Thy priests be clothed with
   righteousness;
  And let Thy saints shout for joy.

10 For Thy servant David's sake
   Turn not away the face of Thine
   anointed.

6 הִנֵּה שְׁמַעֲנוּהָ בְאֶפְרָתָה
מְצָאנוּהָ בִּשְׂדֵי־יָעַר:

7 נָבוֹאָה לְמִשְׁכְּנוֹתָיו
נִשְׁתַּחֲוֶה לַהֲדֹם רַגְלָיו:

8 קוּמָה יְהוָה לִמְנוּחָתֶךָ
אַתָּה וַאֲרוֹן עֻזֶּךָ:

9 כֹּהֲנֶיךָ יִלְבְּשׁוּ־צֶדֶק
וַחֲסִידֶיךָ יְרַנֵּנוּ:

10 בַּעֲבוּר דָּוִד עַבְדֶּךָ
אַל־תָּשֵׁב פְּנֵי מְשִׁיחֶךָ:

prepared a place for the ark of God (1 Chron. xv. 1).

a dwelling-place. The Hebrew is plural, as in verse 7 (see on xliii. 3).

6-7 TRANSPORTATION OF THE ARK

The poet expresses the joy of the people when the ark is conveyed to Jerusalem.

6. *we heard of it.* viz. the ark, specifically mentioned in verse 8.

Ephrath. Usually a name for Bethlehem (Gen. xxxv. 19). Kimchi renders 'we heard (from the sages) in Ephrath (that the identity of the permanent site for the Temple is soon to be revealed).' Ibn Ezra explains 'we heard (from the prophets) that the chosen place for the Temple is near Ephrath (but not precisely where).'

field of the wood. The Temple was built on the site of the granary of Aravnah the Jebusite, which was densely forested (Kimchi).

7. Eventually the ark was brought to Jerusalem and housed in a permanent Sanctuary. The verse conveys the eagerness of the people at that time to visit it.

dwelling-place. The Hebrew is plural, as in verse 5.

His footstool. See on xcix. 5.

8-10 PRAYERS IN CONNECTION WITH THE SANCTUARY

8. *arise, O, LORD.* Cf. Num. x. 35.

Thy resting-place. The abode of the *Shechinah*, Divine Presence.

the ark of Thy strength. Cf. lxxviii. 61. God's power was gloriously manifested when the ark entered the Holy of Holies. A cloud accompanied the ark on its passage and *the priests could not stand to minister by reason of the cloud; for the glory of the LORD filled the house of God* (2 Chron. v. 13-14).

Thy saints. The Levites whose joyous songs accompanied the service (Ibn Ezra).

10. Though Solomon was given the task of erecting the Temple, David is not to be forgotten for his tireless efforts in arranging its construction (cf. Hirsch). On this account, may God be ever favourably inclined towards him and his dynasty.

11 The LORD swore unto David in
   truth;
   He will not turn back from it:
   'Of the fruit of thy body will I
   set upon thy throne.

12 If thy children keep My covenant
   And My testimony that I shall
   teach them,
   Their children also for ever shall
   sit upon thy throne.'

13 For the LORD hath chosen Zion;
   He hath desired it for His habitation:

14 'This is My resting-place for ever;
   Here will I dwell; for I have
   desired it.

15 I will abundantly bless her provision;
   I will give her needy bread in
   plenty.

16 Her priests also will I clothe with
   salvation;
   And her saints shall shout aloud
   for joy.

17 There will I make a horn to shoot
   up unto David,
   There have I ordered a lamp for
   Mine anointed.

18 His enemies will I clothe with
   shame;
   But upon himself shall his crown
   shine.'

נִשְׁבַּע־יְהֹוָה ׀ לְדָוִד 11
אֱמֶת לֹא־יָשׁוּב מִמֶּנָּה
מִפְּרִי בִטְנְךָ
אָשִׁית לְכִסֵּא־לָךְ:
אִם־יִשְׁמְרוּ בָנֶיךָ ׀ בְּרִיתִי 12
וְעֵדֹתִי זוֹ אֲלַמְּדֵם
גַּם־בְּנֵיהֶם עֲדֵי־עַד
יֵשְׁבוּ לְכִסֵּא־לָךְ:
כִּי־בָחַר יְהוָה בְּצִיּוֹן 13
אִוָּהּ לְמוֹשָׁב לוֹ:
זֹאת־מְנוּחָתִי עֲדֵי־עַד 14
פֹּה אֵשֵׁב כִּי אִוִּתִיהָ:
צֵידָהּ בָּרֵךְ אֲבָרֵךְ 15
אֶבְיוֹנֶיהָ אַשְׂבִּיעַ לָחֶם:
וְכֹהֲנֶיהָ אַלְבִּישׁ יֶשַׁע 16
וַחֲסִידֶיהָ רַנֵּן יְרַנֵּנוּ:
שָׁם ׀ אַצְמִיחַ קֶרֶן לְדָוִד 17
עָרַכְתִּי נֵר לִמְשִׁיחִי:
אוֹיְבָיו אַלְבִּישׁ בֹּשֶׁת 18
וְעָלָיו יָצִיץ נִזְרוֹ:

11-18 GOD'S RESPONSE TO THE PRAYER

11. *the* LORD *swore.* Cf. lxxxix. 4.

in truth. Or, 'what is true,' what is certain to
be accomplished.

12. *children.* Better, 'sons,' since the succession to the throne is in mind.

13. *chosen Zion.* The selection of Zion as
the Divine abode preceded the choice of
David as the founder of the royal house (cf.
Deut. xii. 11ff., lxxviii. 68ff., cf. Hirsch).

14. From this point to the end of the Psalm
we have God's utterance.

15. The Presence of God in Zion will bring

material blessings upon the people.

16. Response to the prayer of verse 9.

17. *there.* In Zion (Metsudath David).

make a horn to shoot up. He will be strong
and victorious.

ordered a lamp. To burn perpetually, symbolizing the dynasty's preservation.

18. *clothe with shame.* Not with *righteousness* (verse 9) or *salvation* (verse 16).

upon himself. David (Metsudath David), and
also each of his descendants upon the throne
(Hirsch).

133

1 A Song of Ascents; of David.

    Behold, how good and how pleas-
       ant it is
    For brethren to dwell together in
       unity!

2 It is like the precious oil upon the
       head,
    Coming down upon the beard;
    Even Aaron's beard,
    That cometh down upon the
       collar of his garments;

3 Like the dew of Hermon,
    That cometh down upon the
       mountains of Zion;
    For there the Lord commanded
       the blessing,
    Even life for ever

קלג

שִׁיר הַמַּעֲלוֹת לְדָוִד
הִנֵּה מַה־טּוֹב וּמַה־נָּעִים
שֶׁבֶת אַחִים גַּם־יָחַד:
2 כַּשֶּׁמֶן הַטּוֹב ׀ עַל־הָרֹאשׁ
יֹרֵד עַל־הַזָּקָן זְקַן־אַהֲרֹן
שֶׁיֹּרֵד עַל־פִּי מִדּוֹתָיו:
3 כְּטַל־חֶרְמוֹן שֶׁיֹּרֵד עַל־הַרְרֵי צִיּוֹן
כִּי שָׁם ׀ צִוָּה יְהוָה אֶת־הַבְּרָכָה
חַיִּים עַד־הָעוֹלָם:

BLESSING OF UNIFICATION

THIS beautiful short poem on the theme of brotherly relationship is regarded by Rashi as alluding to the effect that the presence of the Holy Spirit in its permanent abode produced on the inhabitants of Zion. Ibn Ezra suggests that the Psalm refers to the priests who performed their holy work in unity. Hence, the mention of Aaron, the first High Priest. Kimchi maintains that the 'brothers' of the Psalm are the King and the High Priest who shall together rule the nation in total harmony, both carrying out their appointed tasks without overstepping their limits and infringing on each other's authority. Metsudath David takes it as a request for unity in precognition of Israel's splintering into two kingdoms in the days of Rehoboam. The commentary will follow this interpretation.

1. *of David.* Omitted in the Targum.

good. Fine and beneficial, making for social happiness and national vitality.

dwell together in unity. lit. 'the dwelling of brethren also together.' What is advocated is not concord but co-habitation. The nation should not be split into two kingdoms, as in Solomon's son's days (Metsudath David).

2. *the... oil.* Anointing oil was poured on the head of High Priest at his consecration (Exod. xxix. 7) and would flow down on to his beard. Similarly, the effect of living together would spread through the nation (Metsudath David).

even Aaron's beard. Aaron was the first Jewish leader to be anointed with oil (Kimchi). His beard was so long that it covered the upper hem of his vestment (Malbim).

3. *like ... Hermon.* Mount Hermon is noted for the abundance of dew that forms on its slopes (Daath Sofrim). This dew gives fertility to the soil and, similarly, the influence created by a single king shall invigorate the whole nation towards unity (Metsudath David).

upon ... Zion. The poet cannot intend that the dew of Hermon actually flows as far as the hills upon which Jerusalem is situated, about 200 miles distant. The intention is that if a heavy dew, such as that which falls on Mount Hermon, falls on the mountains of Zion, it will be a blessing for the land (Ibn Ezra).

life. To the nation of Israel.

for ever. To be connected with *commanded*. In Zion is His eternal dwelling-place, and from that centre His blessing will always radiate (Hirsch).

134

1 A Song of Ascents.
  Behold, bless ye the LORD, all ye
    servants of the LORD,
  That stand in the house of the
    LORD in the night seasons.

2 Lift up your hands to the sanc-
    tuary,
  And bless ye the LORD.

3 The LORD bless thee out of Zion;
  Even He that made heaven and
    earth.

קלד

שִׁיר הַמַּעֲלוֹת

הִנֵּה ׀ בָּרְכוּ אֶת־יְהוָה

כָּל־עַבְדֵי יְהוָה

הָעֹמְדִים בְּבֵית־יְהוָה בַּלֵּילוֹת׃

2 שְׂאוּ־יְדֵכֶם קֹדֶשׁ

וּבָרְכוּ אֶת־יְהוָה׃

3 יְבָרֶכְךָ יְהוָה מִצִּיּוֹן

עֹשֵׂה שָׁמַיִם וָאָרֶץ׃

BLESSING THE LORD

THE Songs of Ascents, associated with the Temple service, have an appropriate conclusion in this Psalm which contains the instruction for the priests to reciprocate God's blessings (*supra*) with blessings to Him (Ibn Ezra, Kimchi). Others suggest that the song is not connected with the Temple service at all, but is a general call to all servants of God who continue to pray and study into the night (Tal. Men. 110a). A promise is made that if they continue to bless God, they too shall be blessed (Kimchi).

1. *servants of the* LORD. The priests in the Temple (Ibn Ezra).

stand. Who remain at their posts (Malbim).

in the night seasons. Or, 'at night.' The genuine servant of God shows his faith not only in times of freedom, of success and comfort; even in the dark nights of exile he remains a staunch supporter of the LORD and turns his home into a miniature sanctuary where he can continue to serve his Creator (cf. Hirsch).

2. *lift up your hands*. In prayer (xxviii. 2, cxli. 2).

to the sanctuary. In the direction of the Holy of Holies (Hirsch).

3. Either the same poet continuing with the promise that God will reciprocate with another blessing or the response of the officiants (Kimchi). Cf. cxxviii. 5.

bless thee. Each one of you.

made heaven and earth. See on cxv. 15.

135

קלה

1 Hallelujah.
  Praise ye the name of the Lord;
  Give praise, O ye servants of the
  Lord,

2 Ye that stand in the house of the
  Lord,
  In the courts of the house of our
  God.

3 Praise ye the Lord, for the Lord
  is good;
  Sing praises unto His name, for it
  is pleasant.

4 For the Lord hath chosen Jacob
  unto Himself,
  And Israel for His own treasure.

5 For I know that the Lord is great,
  And that our Lord is above all
  gods.

6 Whatsoever the Lord pleased,
  that hath He done,
  In heaven and in earth, in the seas
  and in all deeps;

הַלְלוּיָהּ ׀
הַלְלוּ אֶת־שֵׁם יְהוָה
הַלְלוּ עַבְדֵי יְהוָה:
שֶׁעֹמְדִים בְּבֵית יְהוָה 2
בְּחַצְרוֹת בֵּית אֱלֹהֵינוּ:
הַלְלוּיָהּ כִּי־טוֹב יְהוָה 3
זַמְּרוּ לִשְׁמוֹ כִּי נָעִים:
כִּי־יַעֲקֹב בָּחַר לוֹ יָהּ 4
יִשְׂרָאֵל לִסְגֻלָּתוֹ:
כִּי אֲנִי יָדַעְתִּי כִּי־גָדוֹל יְהוָה 5
וַאֲדֹנֵינוּ מִכָּל־אֱלֹהִים:
כֹּל אֲשֶׁר־חָפֵץ יְהוָה עָשָׂה 6
בַּשָּׁמַיִם וּבָאָרֶץ
בַּיַּמִּים וְכָל־תְּהֹמוֹת:

GOD IN NATURE AND HISTORY

A HYMN composed for use in the Temple, mainly built up from Scriptural citations, it traces
the hand of God at work in the physical universe and the early history of Israel. It speaks of
a time when the Israelites, having forfeited its independence and having suffered the abuse
of the nations, will await the judgment of the Lord and the coming of the Messiah to change
its bitter lot (Hirsch). In contrast, the nations of the world rely on false gods and idols whose
worthlessness makes them an object of scorn for the Psalmist.

1-4 CALL TO PRAISE GOD

1. Identical with cxiii. 1, but with the order
of the clauses reversed.

2. *stand.* The priests who serve in the House
of God and the Israelites who pray in the
Temple courtyard (Kimchi).

3. *for it is pleasant.* Either God's name is
pleasant, like *Give thanks unto Thy name, O
Lord, for it is good* (liv. 8) (Kimchi, Ibn Ezra);
or, 'let your singing express how pleasant are
the thoughts which are derived from a knowledge of His name' (Hirsch).

4. *the Lord.* Hebrew *Jah,* Israel's Saviour.

The verse is derived from Deut. vii. 6.

5-7 GOD'S MIGHT IN NATURE

5. *I know.* The subject is emphatic in the
Hebrew. Whatever the heathens may believe, I, as an Israelite, have definite knowledge of God's unique supremacy.

above all gods. Better, forces of nature (cf.
Kimchi). It is impossible to imagine that the
Psalmist accepted the reality of other gods in
view of what he says in verse 15ff.

6. *whatsoever ... done.* Quoted from cxv. 3.

deeps. The waters beneath the earth (see on
xxiv. 2).

7 Who causeth the vapours to
   ascend from the ends of the
   earth;
   He maketh lightnings for the rain;
   He bringeth forth the wind out of
   His treasuries.

8 Who smote the first-born of
   Egypt,
   Both of man and beast.

9 He sent signs and wonders into the
   midst of thee, O Egypt,
   Upon Pharaoh, and upon all his
   servants.

10 Who smote many nations,
   And slew mighty kings:

11 Sihon king of the Amorites,
   And Og king of Bashan,
   And all the kingdoms of Canaan;

12 And gave their land for a heritage,
   A heritage unto Israel His people.

13 O LORD, Thy name endureth for
   ever;
   Thy memorial, O LORD, throughout all generations.

7 מַעֲלֶה נְשִׂאִים מִקְצֵה הָאָרֶץ
בְּרָקִים לַמָּטָר עָשָׂה
מוֹצֵא רוּחַ מֵאוֹצְרוֹתָיו׃

8 שֶׁהִכָּה בְּכוֹרֵי מִצְרָיִם
מֵאָדָם עַד־בְּהֵמָה׃

9 שָׁלַח ׀ אוֹתֹת וּמֹפְתִים
בְּתוֹכֵכִי מִצְרָיִם
בְּפַרְעֹה וּבְכָל־עֲבָדָיו׃

10 שֶׁהִכָּה גּוֹיִם רַבִּים
וְהָרַג מְלָכִים עֲצוּמִים׃

11 לְסִיחוֹן ׀ מֶלֶךְ הָאֱמֹרִי
וּלְעוֹג מֶלֶךְ הַבָּשָׁן
וּלְכֹל מַמְלְכוֹת כְּנָעַן׃

12 וְנָתַן אַרְצָם נַחֲלָה
נַחֲלָה לְיִשְׂרָאֵל עַמּוֹ׃

13 יְהוָה שִׁמְךָ לְעוֹלָם
יְהוָה זִכְרְךָ לְדֹר־וָדֹר׃

7. Cf. Jer. x. 13, li. 16.

vapours. Rain clouds.

from the ends of the earth. From the sea which
engirdles the world (Kimchi).

lightnings for the rain. Lightnings which accompanied the rainstorm. One of the wonders of nature is here described. The lightning, a form of fire, seems to come from the
sky together with the rainwater, yet it is not
extinguished (Kimchi).

His treasuries. God's storehouse where [po-
etically] the winds were kept in stock. Similar figures of speech describe *treasuries* for
the waters (xxxiii. 7), and snow and hail (Job
xxxviii. 22).

8-12   GOD'S MIGHT IN ISRAEL'S HISTORY

8. *both of man and beast.* Exod. xii. 29,
xiii. 15.

9. *signs and wonders.* Exod. vii. 3.

10. *many nations.* Cf. Deut. vii. 1.

11. *Sihon ... Og.* Num. xxi. 21ff., 33ff.

12. Bashan was inhabited by half the tribe
of Manasseh and the land of the Amorites,
including part of Moab conquered by them,
by the tribe of Reuben.

13-18   GOD'S ETERNITY AND
THE IDOLS' IMPOTENCE

13. *name ... memorial.* Cf. Exod. iii. 15,
and see on cii. 13.

14 For the LORD will judge His
   people,
   And repent Himself for His
   servants.

15 The idols of the nations are
   silver and gold,
   The work of men's hands.

16 They have mouths, but they
   speak not;
   Eyes have they, but they see not;

17 They have ears, but they hear
   not;
   Neither is there any breath in
   their mouths.

18 They that make them shall be
   like unto them;
   Yea, every one that trusteth in
   them.

19 O house of Israel, bless ye the
   LORD;
   O house of Aaron, bless ye the
   LORD;

20 O house of Levi, bless ye the
   LORD;
   Ye that fear the LORD, bless ye
   the LORD.

21 Blessed be the LORD out of Zion,
   Who dwelleth at Jerusalem.
   Hallelujah.

14 כִּי־יָדִין יְהֹוָה עַמּוֹ
וְעַל־עֲבָדָיו יִתְנֶחָם:
15 עֲצַבֵּי הַגּוֹיִם כֶּסֶף וְזָהָב
מַעֲשֵׂה יְדֵי אָדָם:
16 פֶּה־לָהֶם וְלֹא יְדַבֵּרוּ
עֵינַיִם לָהֶם וְלֹא יִרְאוּ:
17 אָזְנַיִם לָהֶם וְלֹא יַאֲזִינוּ
אַף אֵין־יֶשׁ־רוּחַ בְּפִיהֶם:
18 כְּמוֹהֶם יִהְיוּ עֹשֵׂיהֶם
כֹּל אֲשֶׁר־בֹּטֵחַ בָּהֶם:
19 בֵּית יִשְׂרָאֵל בָּרְכוּ אֶת־יְהֹוָה
בֵּית אַהֲרֹן בָּרְכוּ אֶת־יְהֹוָה:
20 בֵּית הַלֵּוִי בָּרְכוּ אֶת־יְהֹוָה
יִרְאֵי יְהֹוָה בָּרְכוּ אֶת־יְהֹוָה:
21 בָּרוּךְ יְהֹוָה מִצִּיּוֹן
שֹׁכֵן יְרוּשָׁלִָם
הַלְלוּיָהּ:

14. Quoted from Deut. xxxii. 36. 'The very
extremity of Israel's need will move Him to
vindicate Israel against foes and detractors'
(Hertz).

repent Himself. Rescind His hard decrees
against Israel when they suffer the penalty of
disobedience, and not abandon the people to
destruction.

15-18. Repeated with slight variation from
cxv. 4-8.

19-21   SUMMONS TO PRAISE GOD

19. For the invocation, cf. cxv. 9-11,
cxviii. 2-4.

20. *O house of Levi, bless ye the* LORD. An
addition to this Psalm as compared with the
others mentioned.

21. *blessed ... out of Zion.* Here *blessed*
means the same as 'praised' (cf. cxxiv. 6). As
God sends His blessings from Zion (cxxxiv.
3), so from the centre of His worship should
the praise of Him echo far and wide.

136

1 O give thanks unto the LORD, for
   He is good,
   For His mercy endureth for ever.

2 O give thanks unto the God of
   gods,
   For His mercy endureth for ever.

3 O give thanks unto the Lord of
   lords,
   For His mercy endureth for ever.

4 To Him who alone doeth great
   wonders,
   For His mercy endureth for ever.

5 To Him that by understanding
   made the heavens,
   For His mercy endureth for ever.

6 To Him that spread forth the earth
   above the waters,
   For His mercy endureth for ever.

7 To Him that made great lights,
   For His mercy endureth for ever;

8 The sun to rule by day,
   For His mercy endureth for ever;

9 The moon and stars to rule by
   night,
   For His mercy endureth for ever.

קלו

הוֹדוּ לַיהוָה כִּי־טוֹב
כִּי לְעוֹלָם חַסְדּוֹ:
2 הוֹדוּ לֵאלֹהֵי הָאֱלֹהִים
כִּי לְעוֹלָם חַסְדּוֹ:
3 הוֹדוּ לַאֲדֹנֵי הָאֲדֹנִים
כִּי לְעוֹלָם חַסְדּוֹ:
4 לְעֹשֵׂה נִפְלָאוֹת גְּדֹלוֹת לְבַדּוֹ
כִּי לְעוֹלָם חַסְדּוֹ:
5 לְעֹשֵׂה הַשָּׁמַיִם בִּתְבוּנָה
כִּי לְעוֹלָם חַסְדּוֹ:
6 לְרֹקַע הָאָרֶץ עַל־הַמָּיִם
כִּי לְעוֹלָם חַסְדּוֹ:
7 לְעֹשֵׂה אוֹרִים גְּדֹלִים
כִּי לְעוֹלָם חַסְדּוֹ:
8 אֶת־הַשֶּׁמֶשׁ לְמֶמְשֶׁלֶת בַּיּוֹם
כִּי לְעוֹלָם חַסְדּוֹ:
9 אֶת־הַיָּרֵחַ וְכוֹכָבִים לְמֶמְשְׁלוֹת
בַּלָּיְלָה
כִּי לְעוֹלָם חַסְדּוֹ:

HYMN OF PRAISE

THE Psalm is often called 'The Great Hallel' (see Introduction to CXIII). Like the previous Psalm it is a compilation for liturgical use, lauding God as the controlling Power of Nature and Israel's history. It is possible that the refrain was sung by the choir of the Levites or the congregation.

1-3 INVOCATION TO THANKSGIVING

1. Identical with the opening of cvi, cvii, cxviii.

2f. The phrases *God of gods* and LORD *of lords* are taken from Deut. x. 17. They mean nothing more than the supreme God and LORD, like *heaven of heavens*, for 'the highest heavens.'

4-9 GOD THE CREATOR

4. *who alone ... wonders.* From lxxii. 18 (cf. lxxxvi. 10).

5. *by understanding made the heavens.* Cf. Jer. x. 12; Prov. iii. 19.

6. Based on xxiv. 2; Isa. xlii. 5, xliv. 24.

7-9. Recalling Gen. i. 14-16.

10 To Him that smote Egypt in their
   first-born,
   For His mercy endureth for ever;

11 And brought out Israel from
   among them,
   For His mercy endureth for ever;

12 With a strong hand, and with an
   outstretched arm,
   For His mercy endureth for ever.

13 To Him who divided the Red
   Sea in sunder,
   For His mercy endureth for ever;

14 And made Israel to pass through
   the midst of it,
   For His mercy endureth for ever;

15 But overthrew Pharaoh and his
   host in the Red Sea,
   For His mercy endureth for ever.

16 To Him that led His people
   through the wilderness.
   For His mercy endureth for ever.

17 To Him that smote great kings;
   For His mercy endureth for ever;

18 And slew mighty kings,
   For His mercy endureth for ever;

19 Sihon king of the Amorites,
   For His mercy endureth for ever;

20 And Og king of Bashan,
   For His mercy endureth for ever;

21 And gave their land for a heritage,
   For His mercy endureth for ever;

22 Even a heritage unto Israel His
   servant,
   For His mercy endureth for ever.

10 לְמַכֵּה מִצְרַיִם בִּבְכוֹרֵיהֶם

כִּי לְעוֹלָם חַסְדּוֹ:

11 וַיּוֹצֵא יִשְׂרָאֵל מִתּוֹכָם

כִּי לְעוֹלָם חַסְדּוֹ:

12 בְּיָד חֲזָקָה וּבִזְרוֹעַ נְטוּיָה

כִּי לְעוֹלָם חַסְדּוֹ:

13 לְגֹזֵר יַם־סוּף לִגְזָרִים

כִּי לְעוֹלָם חַסְדּוֹ:

14 וְהֶעֱבִיר יִשְׂרָאֵל בְּתוֹכוֹ

כִּי לְעוֹלָם חַסְדּוֹ:

15 וְנִעֵר פַּרְעֹה וְחֵילוֹ בְיַם־סוּף

כִּי לְעוֹלָם חַסְדּוֹ:

16 לְמוֹלִיךְ עַמּוֹ בַּמִּדְבָּר

כִּי לְעוֹלָם חַסְדּוֹ:

17 לְמַכֵּה מְלָכִים גְּדֹלִים

כִּי לְעוֹלָם חַסְדּוֹ:

18 וַיַּהֲרֹג מְלָכִים אַדִּירִים

כִּי לְעוֹלָם חַסְדּוֹ:

19 לְסִיחוֹן מֶלֶךְ הָאֱמֹרִי

כִּי לְעוֹלָם חַסְדּוֹ:

20 וּלְעוֹג מֶלֶךְ הַבָּשָׁן

כִּי לְעוֹלָם חַסְדּוֹ:

21 וְנָתַן אַרְצָם לְנַחֲלָה

כִּי לְעוֹלָם חַסְדּוֹ:

22 נַחֲלָה לְיִשְׂרָאֵל עַבְדּוֹ

כִּי לְעוֹלָם חַסְדּוֹ:

10-15   GOD THE DELIVERER FROM EGYPT

This section is analogous to cxxxv. 8f.

12.   *strong ... arm.* From Deut. iv. 34.

15.   *overthrew.* The same unusual word as
in Exod. xiv. 27, lit. 'shook off.'

16-22   IN THE WILDERNESS

Analogous to cxxxv. 10-12.

23 Who remembered us in our low
   estate,
   For His mercy endureth for ever;

24 And hath delivered us from our
   adversaries,
   For His mercy endureth for ever.

25 Who giveth food to all flesh,
   For His mercy endureth for ever.

26 O give thanks unto the God of
   heaven,
   For His mercy endureth for ever.

כג שֶׁבְּשִׁפְלֵנוּ זָכַר לָנוּ
כִּי לְעוֹלָם חַסְדּוֹ:
כד וַיִּפְרְקֵנוּ מִצָּרֵינוּ
כִּי לְעוֹלָם חַסְדּוֹ:
כה נֹתֵן לֶחֶם לְכָל־בָּשָׂר
כִּי לְעוֹלָם חַסְדּוֹ:
כו הוֹדוּ לְאֵל הַשָּׁמָיִם
כִּי לְעוֹלָם חַסְדּוֹ:

23-26   GOD—ISRAEL'S HELPER AND UNIVERSAL PROVIDER

23. *in our low estate*. Whenever Israel was brought low by enemies. Rashi sees in the phrase a reference to Egyptian bondage, and Ibn Ezra to the Babylonian exile. According to Hirsch, the Psalmist has in mind the whole course of Israel's history with it numerous periods of vicissitude.

24. *delivered*. The verb is commonly used in the sense of breaking a yoke from off the neck, and naturally refers to the release from captivity.

25. *all flesh*. 'Flesh' designates animate creatures as a whole, and the thought agrees with civ. 27f., cxlv. 16. The Psalmist enumerated God's favours to His people and now applies the theme universally by stressing that His kindness is extended to all creatures (Kimchi). This is a common feature of the Psalter. In explaining the proximity to verses 13ff., Rabbi Elazar ben Azariah remarked: 'A man's sustenance is as difficult [to provide] as the dividing of the Red Sea.' i.e., the fact that everyone is provided for is considered miraculous. (Tal. Pes. 118a).

26. *the God of heaven*. This title of God is found in Jonah i. 9, and then frequently in the later Books of the Bible, Ezra, Nehemiah, Daniel and Chronicles.

137

1 By the rivers of Babylon,
There we sat down, yea, we wept,
When we remembered Zion.

2 Upon the willows in the midst
thereof
We hanged up our harps.

3 For there they that led us captive
asked of us words of song,
And our tormentors asked of us
mirth:
'Sing us one of the songs of Zion.'

4 How shall we sing the Lord's
song
In a foreign land?

קלז

עַל נַהֲרוֹת ׀ בָּבֶל
שָׁם יָשַׁבְנוּ גַּם־בָּכִינוּ
בְּזָכְרֵנוּ אֶת־צִיּוֹן:
עַל־עֲרָבִים בְּתוֹכָהּ ‏2
תָּלִינוּ כִּנֹּרוֹתֵינוּ:
כִּי שָׁם ׀ שְׁאֵלוּנוּ שׁוֹבֵינוּ דִּבְרֵי־שִׁיר ‏3
וְתוֹלָלֵינוּ שִׂמְחָה
שִׁירוּ לָנוּ מִשִּׁיר צִיּוֹן:
אֵיךְ נָשִׁיר אֶת־שִׁיר־יְהֹוָה ‏4
עַל אַדְמַת נֵכָר:

AMONG THE RUINS OF JERUSALEM

THE feelings which moved the writer of this Psalm will best be understood if we think of him as an exile recently back from Babylon, viewing with horror the havoc wrought in the city he dearly loved (Kimchi). Refugees from Europe, when they returned and saw how their native cities had been turned into masses of rubble by the Germans, surely shared this mood. The Talmud (Git. 57b) maintains that David was the author and was provided with a prophetic vision in which the destruction of the first Temple (verse 1) and the second Temple (verse 7) were foreseen.

1-3 THE EXILES' SINGING SILENCED

1. *rivers.* Babylon was invoked as *thou that dwellest upon many waters* (Jer. li. 13), her many streams and canals being a feature of the country.

there we sat down. Amidst the shade and solitude to mourn the nation's calamity (Kimchi). *Sat down* may denote settling down in their new land (Malbim).

Zion. The Holy City with its sacred associations.

2. *willows.* Possibly the poplar is intended which was common in Babylon.

hanged up our harps. The harps were used to accompany the songs of the Levites in the Temple. When led away in captivity, the Levites hid their harps among the willows, away from enemy view (Metsudath David).

3. *words of songs.* Idiomatic for 'some songs.'

our tormentors. An obscure word; perhaps 'they who were mocking us.' (Metsudath Zion)

mirth. lit. 'gladness,' a lively song out of accord with their mood. There was obviously malice in such a request, and a desire to make the captives conscious of their humiliation.

one of the songs of Zion. lit. 'from the songs of Zion,' some of the chants used in the Temple. The meaning may be 'accept Babylon as your new homeland, and sing her praises as you would of Zion' (Malbim).

4-6 THEIR REFUSAL TO SING

4. *the Lord's song.* Cf. *and when the burnt-offering began, the song of the Lord began also* (2 Chron. xxix. 27). These hymns were reserved for use in the Temple-worship and contained praises of God; accordingly they would have been both out of time and place in an environment of idol worshippers (Sforno).

5 If I forget thee, O Jerusalem,
　Let my right hand forget her
　　cunning.

6 Let my tongue cleave to the roof
　　of my mouth,
　If I remember thee not;
　If I set not Jerusalem
　Above my chiefest joy.

7 Remember, O LORD, against the
　　children of Edom
　The day of Jerusalem;
　Who said: 'Rase it, rase it,
　Even to the foundation thereof.'

8 O daughter of Babylon, that art to
　　be destroyed;
　Happy shall he be, that repayeth
　　thee
　As thou hast served us.

9 Happy shall he be, that taketh and
　　dasheth thy little ones
　Against the rock.

5 אִם־אֶשְׁכָּחֵךְ יְרוּשָׁלָםִ
　תִּשְׁכַּח יְמִינִי׃
6 תִּדְבַּק־לְשׁוֹנִי ׀ לְחִכִּי
　אִם־לֹא אֶזְכְּרֵכִי
　אִם־לֹא אַעֲלֶה אֶת־יְרוּשָׁלַםִ
　עַל רֹאשׁ שִׂמְחָתִי׃
7 זְכֹר יְהוָֹה ׀ לִבְנֵי אֱדוֹם
　אֵת יוֹם יְרוּשָׁלָםִ
　הָאֹמְרִים עָרוּ ׀ עָרוּ
　עַד הַיְסוֹד בָּהּ׃
8 בַּת־בָּבֶל הַשְּׁדוּדָה
　אַשְׁרֵי שֶׁיְשַׁלֶּם־לָךְ
　אֶת־גְּמוּלֵךְ שֶׁגָּמַלְתְּ לָנוּ׃
9 אַשְׁרֵי ׀ שֶׁיֹּאחֵז וְנִפֵּץ אֶת־עֹלָלַיִךְ
　אֶל־הַסָּלַע׃

5. *if I forget thee.* Not only in the sense of abandoning memories of the city, but also becoming unmindful of what was due from them in respect of it. To have acceded to the request would be contempt of what they must hold sacred.

her cunning. Not in the Hebrew, but forcefully added in translation.

6. *let my tongue cleave.* May I lose all power to speak or sing.

remember thee not. In love and reverence.

set ... joy. Give Jerusalem first place in the experiences which afford me happiness.

7-9 IMPRECATION UPON
EDOM AND BABYLON

7. *remember.* With a view to their due punishment.

children of Edom. Despite the kinship of the Edomites, descended from Esau, they had proved themselves inveterate enemies of Israel, and the prophets often condemn them (Isa. xxiv; Jer. xlix. 7ff.; Amos i. 11, etc.). In particular Obad. 10ff. denounces in scathing terms the heartless conduct of the Edomites when *thou wast as one of them*, i.e. abetting the Babylonians in the destruction of Judea.

the day of Jerusalem. viz. of its fall and destruction.

rase it. 'lay (it) bare,' of houses and inhabitants.

8. *daughter of Babylon.* City of Babylon.

that art to be destroyed. lit. 'that art destroyed,' the participle used like the prophetic perfect.

9. This barbarity was often perpetrated against Israel (2 Kings viii. 12; Hosea x. 14), and the Babylonians were guilty of it (cf. Jer. li. 24 with Isa. xiii. 16). The tables will be turned and Babylon will suffer a taste of its own medicine (Malbim).

138

קלח

1 [A Psalm] of David.
  I will give Thee thanks with my
    whole heart,
  In the presence of the mighty will
    I sing praises unto Thee.

2 I will bow down toward Thy holy
    temple,
  And give thanks unto Thy name
    for Thy mercy and for Thy
    truth;
  For Thou hast magnified Thy
    word above all Thy name.

3 In the day that I called, Thou
    didst answer me;
  Thou didst encourage me in my
    soul with strength.

לְדָוִד ׀
אוֹדְךָ בְכָל־לִבִּי
נֶגֶד אֱלֹהִים אֲזַמְּרֶךָּ:
2 אֶשְׁתַּחֲוֶה אֶל־הֵיכַל קָדְשְׁךָ
וְאוֹדֶה אֶת־שְׁמֶךָ
עַל־חַסְדְּךָ וְעַל־אֲמִתֶּךָ
כִּי־הִגְדַּלְתָּ עַל־כָּל־שִׁמְךָ אִמְרָתֶךָ:
3 בְּיוֹם קָרָאתִי וַתַּעֲנֵנִי
תַּרְהִבֵנִי בְנַפְשִׁי עֹז:

THANKSGIVING TO GOD

THE key-word of the Psalm is 'thanks.' As the interpreter of the people's sense of gratitude, the Psalmist acknowledges indebtedness to God for His saving acts. These will so impress *the kings of the earth* that they too will come to thank Him. Though the composition has the title *of David*, the speaker might just as likely be the nation of Israel who, by virtue of its history, has paved the way for the eventual universal worship of God on earth (Hirsch).

1-3 GOD THANKED FOR HIS MERCIES

1. *I will give ... heart.* Based on ix. 2.

in the presence of the mighty. Hebrew *elohim.* The Targum renders by 'judges' (as in lxxxii. 1), which is followed by Ibn Ezra; the LXX has 'angels' which is favoured by Rashi. Hirsch, in view of the context, particularly verse 4, retains the literal meaning of 'gods.' The other nations of the earth have various deities to whom they pay homage, and the Psalmist challenges them by extolling his God to their faces, thus testifying to His might in contrast with their helplessness.

2. *I will bow ... temple.* From v. 8.

mercy ... truth. The combination of these Divine attributes is common in the Psalter

(xxv. 10, lvii. 4, lxi. 8, etc.).

Thou hast magnified ... name. Word must mean 'promise,' and the sense is: God's *name*, His revealed nature as the perfection of truth and other such qualities, gave us confidence that He would honour His plighted word to us; but what He has actually done for us exceeds what we anticipated (cf. Rashi).

3. *I called ... answer me.* Cf. xvii. 6.

didst encourage me. lit. 'didst make me proud.' Through God's response to his prayer, he became conscious of a power within him of which he had been before unaware, and this power inspired him with a proud certainty that he must eventually triumph (cf. Kimchi, Hirsch).

4 All the kings of the earth shall give
   Thee thanks, O Lord,
For they have heard the words of
   Thy mouth.

5 Yea, they shall sing of the ways of
   the Lord;
For great is the glory of the Lord.

6 For though the Lord be high, yet
   regardeth He the lowly,
And the haughty He knoweth
   from afar.

7 Though I walk in the midst of
   trouble, Thou quickenest me;
Thou stretchest forth Thy hand
   against the wrath of mine
   enemies,
And Thy right hand doth save me.

8 The Lord will accomplish that
   which concerneth me;
Thy mercy, O Lord, endureth for
   ever;
Forsake not the work of Thine
   own hands.

4 יוֹדוּךָ יְהוָה כָּל־מַלְכֵי־אָרֶץ
כִּי שָׁמְעוּ אִמְרֵי־פִיךָ׃

5 וְיָשִׁירוּ בְּדַרְכֵי יְהוָה
כִּי גָדוֹל כְּבוֹד יְהוָה׃

6 כִּי־רָם יְהוָה וְשָׁפָל יִרְאֶה
וְגָבֹהַּ מִמֶּרְחָק יְיֵדָע׃

7 אִם־אֵלֵךְ ׀ בְּקֶרֶב צָרָה תְּחַיֵּנִי
עַל־אַף אֹיְבַי תִּשְׁלַח יָדֶךָ
וְתוֹשִׁיעֵנִי יְמִינֶךָ׃

8 יְהוָה יִגְמֹר בַּעֲדִי
יְהוָה חַסְדְּךָ לְעוֹלָם
מַעֲשֵׂי יָדֶיךָ אַל־תֶּרֶף׃

4-6   GOD WILL BE WORSHIPPED
BY ALL KINGS

4. With the thought of this verse cf. cii.
16ff.

for. Or, 'when.'

the words of Thy mouth. Promises made to
his people and how they have been accomplished.

5. *ways.* His dealings with men (ciii. 7).

the glory of the Lord. The manifestation of
His redemptive might on behalf of Israel;
used of the termination of the captivity in Isa.
xl. 5, lx. 1.

6. *the Lord be high … lowly.* The thought
is forcibly expounded in cxiii. 5ff.

He knoweth from afar. God's dwelling in
heaven does not give immunity to the haughty
by reason of the distance from Him of their
sphere of malevolent activity (Kimchi, Hirsch).

7-8   GOD WILL FULFILL HIS PURPOSES

7. *trouble.* lit. 'narrowness,' hemmed in by
dangers and trials.

Thou quickenest me. Thou keepest me alive;
any plot to bring about my destruction will
fail.

stretchest forth Thy hand. To turn aside the
weapons used in their wrath against me by
my enemies.

Thy right hand. See on xvii. 7.

8. *accomplish.* As in lvii. 3, the implied
object being His purposes. The literal meaning of the verb is 'to complete,' i.e. carry out
to the full (cf. Kimchi).

Thy mercy, O Lord, endureth for ever. Upon
this truth he bases his assurance for the future.

forsake not. Withdraw not Thine activity until
the tasks ordained by Thee as affecting Israel
are finally completed.

PSALM CXXXIX

139

1 For the Leader. A Psalm of
David.
  O Lord, Thou hast searched me,
and known me.

2 Thou knowest my downsitting
and mine uprising,
  Thou understandest my thought
afar off.

3 Thou measurest my going about
and my lying down,
  And art acquainted with all my
ways.

4 For there is not a word in my
tongue,
  But, lo, O Lord, Thou knowest it
altogether.

קלט

לַמְנַצֵּחַ לְדָוִד מִזְמוֹר
יְהֹוָה חֲקַרְתַּנִי וַתֵּדָע:

2 אַתָּה יָדַעְתָּ שִׁבְתִּי וְקוּמִי
בַּנְתָּה לְרֵעִי מֵרָחוֹק:

3 אָרְחִי וְרִבְעִי זֵרִיתָ
וְכָל־דְּרָכַי הִסְכַּנְתָּה:

4 כִּי אֵין מִלָּה בִּלְשׁוֹנִי
הֵן יְהֹוָה יָדַעְתָּ כֻלָּהּ:

GOD OMNISCIENT AND OMNIPRESENT

Like Psalms XL and CIX before it, which have similar headings, this Psalm is written on a personal note (Daath Sofrim). It tells of man's recognition of God's omniscience and omnipresence; of man's realization that He attends to his every word and thought. Ibn Ezra remarked, 'This Psalm is most glorious on the theme of the ways of God and is unequalled in the five Books of the Psalter.' David's realization of God is most intimate and personal, the effect of religious experience rather than of rational meditation alone. Midrash Shocher Tov remarks that the thoughts in the Psalm were those of Adam and were later adapted by David into the written word.

1-6 GOD'S OMNISCIENCE

1. *Thou hast searched me.* i.e. my heart (cf. verse 23; Jer. xvii. 10) (Kimchi).

and known me. The object *me* is not in the Hebrew, and is probably to be understood as 'all that is in my heart, my thoughts and feelings' (cf. Hirsch).

2. *Thou knowest.* The subject *Thou* is emphasized in the Hebrew. Thou only, being omniscient, canst have such intimate knowledge of me.

downsitting ... uprising. Only again in verse 17. It is an Aramaic word meaning 'inclination, wish.'

afar off. See on cxxxviii. 6.

3. *measurest ... my going about.* Better, 'encompasseth,' the verb being obtained from the word 'zer,' a crown or border (Exod. xxv.

11) (Rashi, Ibn Ezra). Hirsch connects the word with the verb 'to winnow' (cf. Isa. xxx. 24) or 'to scatter' (cf. Ezek. xii. 15) and renders 'Thou hast set apart my going about and my lying down.' The two aspects of man's nature—his moral qualities and his physical, animal aspects—do not conflict with each other. Thus, regardless of the sensual aspects of his personality which he holds in common with the beast, he can discharge his task as a moral human being on a spiritual plane.

ways. Dealing with one's fellows. Used of God in cxxxviii. 5.

4. The meaning is that God is aware of the thought to be expressed before it is even put into words (Ibn Ezra). It can also be understood as 'He knows the intention of every word even if it does not as yet express a thought' (Hirsch).

5 Thou hast hemmed me in behind
    and before,
    And laid Thy hand upon me.

6 Such knowledge is too wonderful
    for me;
    Too high, I cannot attain unto it.

7 Whither shall I go from Thy
    spirit?
    Or whither shall I flee from Thy
    presence ?

8 If I ascend up into heaven, Thou
    art there;
    If I make my bed in the nether-
    world, behold, Thou art there.

9 If I take the wings of the morning,
    And dwell in the uttermost parts
    of the sea;

10 Even there would Thy hand lead
    me,
    And Thy right hand would hold
    me.

5 אָח֣וֹר וָקֶ֣דֶם צַרְתָּ֑נִי
וַתָּ֖שֶׁת עָלַ֣י כַּפֶּֽכָה׃

6 פְּלִיאָ֣ה דַ֣עַת מִמֶּ֑נִּי
נִ֝שְׂגְּבָ֗ה לֹא־א֥וּכַל לָֽהּ׃

7 אָ֭נָה אֵלֵ֣ךְ מֵרוּחֶ֑ךָ
וְ֝אָ֗נָה מִפָּנֶ֥יךָ אֶבְרָֽח׃

8 אִם־אֶסַּ֣ק שָׁ֭מַיִם שָׁ֣ם אָ֑תָּה
וְאַצִּ֖יעָה שְּׁא֣וֹל הִנֶּֽךָּ׃

9 אֶשָּׂ֥א כַנְפֵי־שָׁ֑חַר
אֶ֝שְׁכְּנָ֗ה בְּאַחֲרִ֥ית יָֽם׃

10 גַּם־שָׁ֭ם יָדְךָ֣ תַנְחֵ֑נִי
וְֽתֹאחֲזֵ֥נִי יְמִינֶֽךָ׃

v. 6. פליאה ק׳

---

5. *hemmed me in.* It is the verb to describe laying siege to a city. God has, as it were, besieged him so that there is no escape (Malbim).

laid Thy hand upon me. Grasped me and I cannot get away (cf. verse 10).

6. *such knowledge.* Which God possesses of him as of every individual.

too wonderful. Beyond human comprehension.

7-12 GOD'S OMNIPRESENCE

7. *whither shall i go.* i.e. where could I go, if I desired to remove myself from the sphere of Thy influence?

Thy spirit. God as active in the world (cf. *the spirit of God hovered over the face of the waters.* Gen. i. 2).

Thy presence. Which fills the universe and manifests His relationship with humans.

8. For the thought and language, cf. Amos ix. 2; Job. xvii. 13.

ascend. The text has the common Aramaic verb for 'going up.'

make my bed in the nether-world. More lit. 'make Sheol my couch.' The language passes from one extreme of space to the other.

9. *wings of the morning.* The image is that of sunrise which instantly spreads its wings of light from one horizon to the other. Similarly, the poet imagines having wings which would carry him instantaneously to the other end of the earth (Rashi, Ibn Ezra).

the sea. Mediterranean; i.e. go as far west as *the wings of the morning,* the utmost limit.

10. *lead me ... hold me.* Wherever he was, he would find himself within the sphere of God's control.

11 And if I say: 'Surely the darkness
    shall envelop me,
    And the light about me shall be
    night';

12 Even the darkness is not too dark
    for Thee,
    But the night shineth as the day;
    The darkness is even as the light.

13 For Thou hast made my reins;
    Thou hast knit me together in my
    mother's womb.

14 I will give thanks unto Thee, for
    I am fearfully and wonderfully
    made;
    Wonderful are Thy works;
    And that my soul knoweth right
    well.

15 My frame was not hidden from
    Thee,
    When I was made in secret,
    And curiously wrought in the
    lowest parts of the earth.

16 Thine eyes did see mine un-
    formed substance,
    And in Thy book they were all
    written—

11 וָאֹמַר אַךְ־חֹשֶׁךְ יְשׁוּפֵנִי
וְלַיְלָה אוֹר בַּעֲדֵנִי:
12 גַּם־חֹשֶׁךְ לֹא־יַחְשִׁיךְ מִמֶּךָ
וְלַיְלָה כַּיּוֹם יָאִיר
כַּחֲשֵׁיכָה כָּאוֹרָה:
13 כִּי־אַתָּה קָנִיתָ כִלְיֹתָי
תְּסֻכֵּנִי בְּבֶטֶן אִמִּי:
14 אוֹדְךָ עַל כִּי נוֹרָאוֹת נִפְלֵיתִי
נִפְלָאִים מַעֲשֶׂיךָ
וְנַפְשִׁי יֹדַעַת מְאֹד:
15 לֹא־נִכְחַד עָצְמִי מִמֶּךָּ
אֲשֶׁר־עֻשֵּׂיתִי בַסֵּתֶר
רֻקַּמְתִּי בְּתַחְתִּיּוֹת אָרֶץ:
16 גָּלְמִי רָאוּ עֵינֶיךָ
וְעַל־סִפְרְךָ כֻּלָּם יִכָּתֵבוּ

11. *surely the darkness shall envelop me.*
Better, 'let the darkness enshroud me and the
night shall hide me even in the day.' It is futile
to attempt to evade God's all-seeing eye by
hiding in the dark (Malbim).

12. *it is not too dark for Thee.* Render,
'does not darken from Thee'; God's glance
penetrates the darkness.

13-18 GOD'S WONDROUS WORK

13. *for Thou.* The subject *Thou* is emphatic
as in verse 2. The force of the conjunction *for*
is: God must know me through and through,
because he controlled my existence and development even as an embryo (cf. Kimchi).

made. For this meaning of the verb, cf. Gen.
xiv. 19; Deut. xxxii. 6.

my reins. The kidneys (see on vii. 10), here
are representative of all the internal organs.

knit me together. Cf. *and Thou hast knot me*

together with bones and sinews (Job. x. 11).

14. *fearfully and wonderfully made.* Reflections upon the marvels of the human
body inspired the Psalmist with awe and
wonder.

my soul. Equals 'I.'

15. *frame.* Skeleton.

in secret. Within the womb (Ibn Ezra).

curiously wrought. lit. 'embroidered,' alluding to the veins and arteries which run through
the body like coloured threads (Kimchi).

in the lowest parts of the earth. Poetical description of the darkness in the womb (Rashi).

16. *mine unformed substance.* The early
embryo (Kimchi).

they were all written. Ibn Ezra took the subject to be all the limbs which would develop
from the embryo. Alternatively, God has a
book in which are recorded all the phenomena

Even the days that were fashioned,
When as yet there was none of
them.

17 How weighty also are Thy
thoughts unto me, O God!
How great is the sum of them!

18 If I would count them, they are
more in number than the sand;
Were I to come to the end of
them, I would still be with
Thee.

19 If Thou but wouldest slay the
wicked, O God—
Depart from me therefore, ye
men of blood;

20 Who utter Thy name with
wicked thought,
They take it for falsehood, even
Thine enemies—

יָמִים יֻצָּרוּ
וְלֹא אֶחָד בָּהֶם:
17 וְלִי מַה־יָּקְרוּ רֵעֶיךָ אֵל
מֶה עָצְמוּ רָאשֵׁיהֶם:
18 אֶסְפְּרֵם מֵחוֹל יִרְבּוּן
הֱקִיצֹתִי וְעוֹדִי עִמָּךְ:
19 אִם־תִּקְטֹל אֱלוֹהַּ ׀ רָשָׁע
וְאַנְשֵׁי דָמִים סוּרוּ מֶנִּי:
20 אֲשֶׁר יֹמְרוּךָ לִמְזִמָּה
נָשׂוּא לַשָּׁוְא עָרֶיךָ:

וְלוֹ ק׳ v. 16.

of the order of creation that will appear as living realities in the world (Hirsch).

when as yet there was none of them. This translation follows the *kethib*; the *kerë* has to be rendered: 'and for it there was one among,' i.e. among the days entered in the book was one for the embryo to come to birth (Hirsch).

17. *weighty.* Beyond the Psalmist's power to comprehend (Kimchi).

is the sum. lit. 'are the sums,' plural of full-ness, 'their vast sum.' Each *thought* of God is itself unfathomable by man and in totality immeasurable (Kimchi).

18. *were I to come to the end of them.* Rashi connects with *kets*, 'end'; but others render 'when I am awake.' Kimchi explains that the task of counting would occupy not only his waking hours but even his dreams; and after he came out of his sleep, he would still be with God, enumerating His thoughts, be-cause they were inexhaustible.

19-24 PRAYER AGAINST THE WICKED

This section should be compared with civ. 35, where, after recounting the wonders of

God in the universe, the Psalmist prays *let sinners cease out of the earth*, because they are out of harmony with his beautiful world. So in this Psalm the writer feels that God, Who has a minute knowledge of each one of His family, should not tolerate those who conduct their lives contrary to His will.

19. *slay the wicked.* Whose evil living pro-fanes the name of their Maker.

depart from me. Cf. vi. 9, cxix. 115. He will have no intercourse with them.

men of blood. Cf. v. 7.

20. *utter Thy name.* lit. 'they speak Thee.' They cloak their evil schemes by making use of God's name (Rashi). Metsudath David and Malbim, however, render 'they exalt Thee for the purpose of wicked scheming'; i.e. they claim that it is beneath God's dignity to bother about their wickedness.

they take it for falsehood. Or, *in vain*, the Hebrew corresponding to the Third Com-mandment (Exod. xx. 7).

Thine enemies. The word employed is an Aramaism.

21 Do not I hate them, O Lord, that
     hate Thee?
     And do not I strive with those
       that rise up against Thee?

22 I hate them with utmost hatred;
     I count them mine enemies.

23 Search me, O God, and know my
     heart,
     Try me, and know my thoughts;

24 And see if there be any way in me
     that is grievous,
     And lead me in the way ever-
     lasting.

21 הֲלוֹא־מְשַׂנְאֶיךָ יְהוָה ׀ אֶשְׂנָא
וּבִתְקוֹמְמֶיךָ אֶתְקוֹטָט׃

22 תַּכְלִית שִׂנְאָה שְׂנֵאתִים
לְאוֹיְבִים הָיוּ לִי׃

23 חָקְרֵנִי אֵל וְדַע לְבָבִי
בְּחָנֵנִי וְדַע שַׂרְעַפָּי׃

24 וּרְאֵה אִם־דֶּרֶךְ־עֹצֶב בִּי
וּנְחֵנִי בְּדֶרֶךְ עוֹלָם׃

21. *strive.* Better, 'feel disgust' (see on xcv. 10 and cxix. 158). he burns with zeal for God and His cause; consequently, all who are at enmity with Him he regards as his personal enemies, and every affront to the purposes which He approves creates within him fierce resentment.

22. 'It is the uprisings and not the evil men themselves that I hate with the utmost hatred. Therefore it is not I who became their foe; it was they who became my enemies '(Hirsch).

23. *search me.* After mentioning the evil thoughts of the wicked he asks to be subject to scrutiny by God and his heart be shown to be completely honest and pure (Kimchi). A similar prayer occurs in xxvi. 2 and there its purpose is specified.

thoughts. The same word as in xciv. 19 translated *cares*, lit. 'dividing (distracting)' thoughts.

24. *any way ... that is grievous.* lit. 'way of pain,' thoughts that cause God distress because they are against His will (Ibn Ezra). The Targum, on the basis of Isa. xlviii. 5, renders 'way of idolatry.'

the way everlasting. he asks to be guided in the way of truth that leads to eternity. Others see a different meaning in the phrase and read it as a threat: 'If there be any way in me which causes grief, then lead me to my death'; i.e. better that I die than live a life of wickedness. The word 'olam' is commonly used in describing the destination of man at the end of his life. Cf. Eccl. xii. 5 (Kimchi, Malbim).

140

1 For the Leader. A Psalm of David.

2 Deliver me, O Lord, from the evil man;
Preserve me from the violent man;

3 Who devise evil things in their heart;
Every day do they stir up wars.

4 They have sharpened their tongue like a serpent;
Vipers' venom is under their lips. Selah

5 Keep me, O Lord, from the hands of the wicked;
Preserve me from the violent man;
Who have purposed to make my steps slip.

6 The proud have hid a snare for me, and cords;
They have spread a net by the wayside;
They have set gins for me. Selah

7 I have said unto the Lord: 'Thou art my God';
Give ear, O Lord, unto the voice of my supplications.

קמ

לַמְנַצֵּחַ מִזְמוֹר לְדָוִד׃

2 חַלְּצֵנִי יְהוָה מֵאָדָם רָע
מֵאִישׁ חֲמָסִים תִּנְצְרֵנִי׃

3 אֲשֶׁר חָשְׁבוּ רָעוֹת בְּלֵב
כָּל־יוֹם יָגוּרוּ מִלְחָמוֹת׃

4 שָׁנְנוּ לְשׁוֹנָם כְּמוֹ־נָחָשׁ
חֲמַת עַכְשׁוּב תַּחַת שְׂפָתֵימוֹ
סֶלָה׃

5 שָׁמְרֵנִי יְהוָה מִידֵי רָשָׁע
מֵאִישׁ חֲמָסִים תִּנְצְרֵנִי
אֲשֶׁר חָשְׁבוּ לִדְחוֹת פְּעָמָי׃

6 טָמְנוּ־גֵאִים פַּח לִי
וַחֲבָלִים פָּרְשׂוּ רֶשֶׁת לְיַד־מַעְגָּל
מֹקְשִׁים שָׁתוּ־לִי סֶלָה׃

7 אָמַרְתִּי לַיהוָה אֵלִי אָתָּה
הַאֲזִינָה יְהוָה קוֹל תַּחֲנוּנָי׃

PRAYER FOR PROTECTION

It is generally agreed that Psalms CXL-CXLIII form a distinctive group, reflecting the same conditions and possessing many literary similarities. Alike they tell of a time when the pious suffered at the hands of the ungodly within the ranks of Israel. This Psalm was recorded during one of the most difficult times in David's life. Though he had been anointed by Samuel as the future leader of his people, Saul sought his blood, and he was forced to live as a fugitive to escape the king and his men. See 1 Sam. xxiii. (Ibn Ezra, Malbim).

2-4 CRY FOR HELP

2. *evil man … violent man.* Both are collective, the verbs in verse 3 being plural.

3. *wars.* Plural of intensity, 'bitter strife.'

4. *sharpened … serpent.* The clause combines two similes: slander likened to swords and a serpent's fang.

under their lips. Like the bag containing poison beneath the viper's tongue.

5-6 HIS ENEMIES' INSIDIOUS PLOTS

5. *make my steps slip.* So that I stumble.

6. *snare.* Used to trap hunted animals.

cords. Translated *noose* in Job. xviii. 10, concealed in the ground to catch the leg.

gins. Traps to catch birds; again in cxli. 9.

7-9 PLEA TO GOD FOR AID

7. *I have said.* Or, 'I say.'

8 O God the Lord, the strength of
   my salvation,
  Who hast screened my head in
   the day of battle,
9 Grant not, O Lord, the desires of
   the wicked;
  Further not his evil device, so that
   they exalt themselves.   Selah
10 As for the head of those that
   compass me about,
  Let the mischief of their own lips
   cover them.
11 Let burning coals fall upon them;
  Let them be cast into the fire,
  Into deep pits, that they rise not
   up again.
12 A slanderer shall not be established in the earth;
  The violent and evil man shall be
   hunted with thrust upon thrust.
13 I know that the Lord will maintain the cause of the poor,
  And the right of the needy.
14 Surely the righteous shall give
   thanks unto Thy name;
  The upright shall dwell in Thy
   presence.

יְהֹוִה אֲדֹנָי עֹז יְשׁוּעָתִי 8
סַכֹּתָה לְרֹאשִׁי בְּיוֹם נָשֶׁק׃
אַל־תִּתֵּן יְהֹוָה מַאֲוַיֵּי רָשָׁע 9
זְמָמוֹ אַל־תָּפֵק יָרוּמוּ סֶלָה׃
רֹאשׁ מְסִבָּי 10
עֲמַל שְׂפָתֵימוֹ יְכַסּוֹמוֹ׃
יִמֹּטוּ עֲלֵיהֶם גֶּחָלִים 11
בָּאֵשׁ יַפִּלֵם
בְּמַהֲמֹרוֹת בַּל־יָקוּמוּ׃
אִישׁ לָשׁוֹן בַּל־יִכּוֹן בָּאָרֶץ 12
אִישׁ־חָמָס רָע יְצוּדֶנּוּ לְמַדְחֵפֹת׃
יָדַעְתָּ כִּי־יַעֲשֶׂה יְהֹוָה דִּין עָנִי 13
מִשְׁפַּט אֶבְיֹנִים׃
אַךְ צַדִּיקִים יוֹדוּ לִשְׁמֶךָ 14
יֵשְׁבוּ יְשָׁרִים אֶת־פָּנֶיךָ׃

v. 10. יכסימו ק׳ v. 11. ימוטו ק׳ v. 13. ידעתי ק׳

8. *Who hast screened.* It may be the perfect of experience, 'who screenest,' as with a helmet to protect the head.

battle. lit. 'armour,' a day when armour is necessary. Here used figuratively as protection against their spears and arrows (Kimchi).

9. *further not his evil device.* lit. 'let not his evil device issue (successfully).'

so that ... themselves. If they succeed in overcoming me, they will consider themselves invincible (Hirsch).

10-12 PRAYER AGAINST HIS FOES

10. May what they schemed against me recoil upon their own heads.

11. *burning coals.* From heaven, representing God's anger. Cf. xviii. 9, 18; xiii. 14, 6.

deep pits. The Hebrew word occurs nowhere else. Hirsch has 'clay pits.'

12. *slanderer.* lit. 'man of tongue.' His fate is to be destroyed by God (ci. 5).

the violent ... thrust. Better, 'as for the evil man of wrongdoing, it catches him with thrust upon thrust' (Kimchi, cf. Hirsch). He will be pursued relentlessly by God's retribution as he had pursued the innocent without mercy.

13-14 CONFIDENCE IN GOD

13. *I know.* The Psalmist is convinced of this truth.

14. *surely.* Expressing the certainty that the righteous will escape the machinations of their persecutors and have cause to thank their Rescuer.

dwell in Thy presence. In a state of serenity (cf. cii. 29).

141　　　　　　　　　　　　　　　　　**קמא**

1 A Psalm of David.
  Lord, I have called Thee; make
    haste unto me;
  Give ear unto my voice, when I
    call unto Thee.

2 Let my prayer be set forth as
    incense before Thee,
  The lifting up of my hands as the
    evening sacrifice.

3 Set a guard, O Lord, to my
    mouth;
  Keep watch at the door of my lips.

4 Incline not my heart to any evil
    thing,
  To be occupied in deeds of
    wickedness
  With men that work iniquity;
  And let me not eat of their
    dainties.

מִזְמוֹר לְדָוִד
יְהוָה קְרָאתִיךָ חוּשָׁה לִּי
הַאֲזִינָה קוֹלִי בְּקָרְאִי־לָךְ׃
2 תִּכּוֹן תְּפִלָּתִי קְטֹרֶת לְפָנֶיךָ
מַשְׂאַת כַּפַּי מִנְחַת־עָרֶב׃
3 שִׁיתָה יְהוָה שָׁמְרָה לְפִי
נִצְּרָה עַל־דַּל שְׂפָתָי׃
4 אַל־תַּט־לִבִּי לְדָבָר רָע
לְהִתְעוֹלֵל עֲלִלוֹת בְּרֶשַׁע
אֶת־אִישִׁים פֹּעֲלֵי־אָוֶן
וּבַל־אֶלְחַם בְּמַנְעַמֵּיהֶם׃

PRAYER AGAINST SINNERS

This Psalm describes David's experiences when, during his flight, Saul fell into his grip and he prayed that he should not be confronted by an urge to kill him (Malbim). It elucidates the feelings of anyone suffering from his fellowmen's offensive actions who needs God's help to resist falling into sin through retaliation.

1-4 SUPPLICATION FOR DIVINE AID

1. *make haste.* To help me in my straits; as in lxx. 6.

my voice. Of appeal.

2. *as incense.* As in lxvi. 15, *the sweet smoke of rams*, the word is employed of the odour of the sacrifice burning on the altar. The Psalmist is evidently precluded from bringing an offering and hopes that his prayer will be an efficacious substitute (cf. Hosea xiv. 3) (Midrash Shocher Tov).

lifting up of my hands. The attitude of prayer (xxviii. 2, lxiii. 5).

the evening sacrifice. Cf. Num. xxviii. 4. The mention of this particular offering led Kimchi to comment that the Psalm was possibly composed during the evening.

3. *set a guard.* His enemies had resorted to language of a blasphemous character; may God withhold him from allowing similar words to pass his lips!

4. *incline not my heart.* Now he prays that he be not tempted to throw in his lot with the wicked and share their nefarious acts. Specifically, he pleads that he not be incited to dispose of Saul who had caused him so much suffering (Malbim).

men. Hebrew *ishim,* which may indicate that they were men of high standing and influence (Meiri).

let me not eat of their dainties. He wishes to have no association at all with his enemies (Rashi). Or, afraid that he might be led to follow their evil ways, expresses the hope that he not be lured from the path of righteousness by worldly pleasures (Kimchi).

5 Let the righteous smite me in
   kindness, and correct me;
  Oil so choice let not my head
   refuse;
  For still is my prayer because of
   their wickedness.

6 Their judges are thrown down by
   the sides of the rock;
  And they shall hear my words,
   that they are sweet.

7 As when one cleaveth and breaketh up the earth,
  Our bones are scattered at the
   grave's mouth.

8 For mine eyes are unto Thee, O
   God the Lord;
  In Thee have I taken refuge, O
   pour not out my soul.

9 Keep me from the snare which
   they have laid for me,
  And from the gins of the workers
   of iniquity.

10 Let the wicked fall into their own
   nets,
  Whilst I withal escape.

5 יֶהֶלְמֵנִי צַדִּיק חֶסֶד וְיוֹכִיחֵנִי
שֶׁמֶן רֹאשׁ אַל־יָנִי רֹאשִׁי
כִּי־עוֹד וּתְפִלָּתִי בְּרָעוֹתֵיהֶם׃

6 נִשְׁמְטוּ בִידֵי־סֶלַע שֹׁפְטֵיהֶם
וְשָׁמְעוּ אֲמָרַי כִּי נָעֵמוּ׃

7 כְּמוֹ פֹלֵחַ וּבֹקֵעַ בָּאָרֶץ
נִפְזְרוּ עֲצָמֵינוּ לְפִי שְׁאוֹל׃

8 כִּי אֵלֶיךָ יְהוִה אֲדֹנָי עֵינָי
בְּכָה חָסִיתִי אַל־תְּעַר נַפְשִׁי׃

9 שָׁמְרֵנִי מִידֵי פַּח יָקְשׁוּ לִי
וּמֹקְשׁוֹת פֹּעֲלֵי אָוֶן׃

10 יִפְּלוּ בְמַכְמֹרָיו רְשָׁעִים
יַחַד אָנֹכִי עַד־אֶעֱבוֹר׃

5-7 MAY HE NOT REJECT SOUND REPROOF

Here David alludes to a specific episode in which he resisted killing Saul when he found him asleep in a cave. See 1 Sam. xxiv (Malbim).

5. A better translation of the verse is 'let the righteous strike me, it shall be kindness, and let Him reprove me; it shall be as oil for my head, so let not my head refuse it; but still let my prayer be against their evil doings' (cf. Rashi, Hirsch). Various explanations have been applied to this verse. According to Malbim, David is troubled by the indignity he caused Saul to suffer by tearing off a piece of the cloak worn by Saul, God's anointed king, though continuing to pray for the failure of the evil schemes the king had plotted against him.

6. *their judges ... thrown.* Render, 'when judges ... the rock, they will hear my words.' Immediately before the evil judges or rulers against whom he has been praying, meet with being hurled to destruction from a high rock (cf. 2 Chron. xxv. 12), they will admit David had been right in rebuking them and regret that they had ignored him (Rashi, Kimchi).

7. David and his men are in grave danger of capture by Saul. They are afraid that they cannot escape and are at the brink of death.

breaketh ... earth. Rather, 'choppeth (wood) on the earth'; so Rashi and Kimchi, the verb meaning that in Job xvi. 13 and Eccles. x. 9. David and his men are terrified at the prospect of their bodies being cut up by the enemy as scattered chips of wood when logs are cut up. They feel themselves as if at the entrance of Sheol. (cf. Kimchi).

8-10 THE PRAYER RENEWED

8. *for.* Better, 'surely.'

mine eyes are unto Thee. Cf. xxv. 15.

pour not out my soul. Drain not my body of life which is identical with the blood in it (Lev. xvii. 11).

9. Cf. cxl. 5f.

10. *into their own nets.* lit. 'into his own nets,' alluding to each one of *the wicked.*

whilst I withal escape. lit. 'together (i.e. at the same time as they fall), I (emphatic in the Hebrew) will pass by (in safety)' (Kimchi).

142   קמב

מַשְׂכִּיל לְדָוִד

בִּהְיוֹתוֹ בַמְּעָרָה תְפִלָּה:

1 Maschil of David, when he was in the cave; a Prayer.

קוֹלִי אֶל־יְהֹוָה אֶזְעָק ²

קוֹלִי אֶל־יְהֹוָה אֶתְחַנָּן:

2 With my voice I cry unto the LORD;
With my voice I make supplication unto the LORD.

אֶשְׁפֹּךְ לְפָנָיו שִׂיחִי ³

צָרָתִי לְפָנָיו אַגִּיד:

3 I pour out my complaint before Him,
I declare before Him my trouble;

בְּהִתְעַטֵּף עָלַי רוּחִי ⁴

וְאַתָּה יָדַעְתָּ נְתִיבָתִי

בְּאֹרַח־זוּ אֲהַלֵּךְ

טָמְנוּ פַח לִי:

4 When my spirit fainteth within me—
Thou knowest my path—
In the way wherein I walk
Have they hidden a snare for me.

הַבֵּיט יָמִין וּרְאֵה ⁵

וְאֵין־לִי מַכִּיר

אָבַד מָנוֹס מִמֶּנִּי

אֵין דּוֹרֵשׁ לְנַפְשִׁי:

5 Look on my right hand, and see,
For there is no man that knoweth me;
I have no way to flee;
No man careth for my soul.

PLEA FOR HELP

THE pathetic tone of the Psalm is most appropriate to the occasion in David's life mentioned in the superscription, and his prayers are in addition to those already voiced in LVII. Noticeably lacking is the mention of revenge although Saul had pursued him relentlessly (Hirsch). Though it is written in the form of a personal cry, the Psalm has often been recited during times of national plight when people find themselves in similar circumstances to those of David (Ibn Yachya). This may explain the title *Maschil*, 'instruction.'

1. *Maschil*. See on xxxii.1.

when he was in the cave. See on lvii. 1. Or it may have been the cave of the preceding Psalm in En-Gedi (1 Sam. xxiv) (Kimchi).

a Prayer. Cf. xvii. 1, lxxxvi. 1.

2-5 HIS COMPLAINT

2. *with my voice.* Equals 'aloud' (Hirsch). His anguish must find relief in the earnest cry of supplication.

3. *pour out my complaint.* Cf. cii. 1.

4. *Thou knowest my path.* Better, 'but Thou knowest' etc. Interrupting his description of spiritual exhaustion, David is impelled to declare that God Himself knows his true intentions, even the path he has chosen, and [David] does not deserve the distress of the enemy's attempts to trap and turn him away from the life he values (Hirsch).

hidden a snare. As in cxl. 6, cxli. 9.

5. *look on my right hand.* Where a champion should be standing to defend me. None of Saul's retine, however, supported my cause (Rashi).

knoweth. lit. 'recognizeth.' Used in Ruth ii. 19 for one who befriends another.

careth for my soul. Concerned to help in saving my life (cf. Jer. xxx. 17).

6 I have cried unto Thee, O LORD;
I have said: 'Thou art my refuge,
My portion in the land of the
living.'

7 Attend unto my cry;
For I am brought very low;
Deliver me from my persecutors;
For they are too strong for me.

8 Bring my soul out of prison,
That I may give thanks unto Thy
name;
The righteous shall crown themselves because of me;
For Thou wilt deal bountifully
with me.

6 זָעַקְתִּי אֵלֶיךָ יְהֹוָה
אָמַרְתִּי אַתָּה מַחְסִי
חֶלְקִי בְּאֶרֶץ הַחַיִּים:
7 הַקְשִׁיבָה ׀ אֶל־רִנָּתִי
כִּי־דַלּוֹתִי מְאֹד
הַצִּילֵנִי מֵרֹדְפַי
כִּי אָמְצוּ מִמֶּנִּי:
8 הוֹצִיאָה מִמַּסְגֵּר ׀ נַפְשִׁי
לְהוֹדוֹת אֶת־שְׁמֶךָ
בִּי יַכְתִּרוּ צַדִּיקִים
כִּי תִגְמֹל עָלָי:

6-8 HIS PETITION

Although the two verses, 6 and 7, as analysis reveals, are made up almost in their entirety from phrases which are found elsewhere in the Psalms, they do not read like an artificial compilation but have an intensity which is unmistakable.

6. *cried ... said*. Better, 'cry ... say.' What he did before in times of crisis he does now.

refuge. The word used in xci. 2.

my portion. Cf. xvi. 5, lxxiii. 26.

in the land of the living. See on xxvii. 13.

7. *attend unto my cry*. Cf. xvii. 1.

for I am brought very low. Cf. lxxix. 8.

deliver ... persecutors. Cf. vii. 2, xxxi. 16.

for they are too strong for me. Cf. xviii. 18.

8. *bring my soul out of prison*. A metaphor for wretchedness and a life hampered by besetting foes. It may also be an allusion to the cave in which he was hiding and from whence he offers a prayer for relief (Kimchi). Cf. Isa. xlii. 7, where it means the land of captivity.

give thanks unto Thy name. In gratitude for deliverance (cf. cxl. 14).

crown themselves because of me. My deliverance will cause the righteous to exult since it implies their vindication also (Ibn Ezra). The phrase may alternatively mean 'because of me shall the righteous crown Thee,' i.e. with praises (Rashi). Kimchi has 'On account of me the righteous will crown themselves with me,' i.e. they will use his example as proof that faith leads to redemption.

deal bountifully with me. Cf. xiii. 6, cxvi. 12.

143

1 A Psalm of David.
  O LORD, hear my prayer, give ear
    to my supplications;
  In Thy faithfulness answer me,
    and in Thy righteousness.

2 And enter not into judgment with
    Thy servant;
  For in Thy sight shall no man liv-
    ing be justified.

3 For the enemy hath persecuted my
    soul;
  He hath crushed my life down to
    the ground;
  He hath made me to dwell in dark
    places, as those that have been
    long dead.

4 And my spirit fainteth within me;
  My heart within me is appalled.

5 I remember the days of old;
  I meditate on all Thy doing;
  I muse on the work of Thy hands.

קמג

מִזְמוֹר לְדָוִד
יְהֹוָה ו שְׁמַע תְּפִלָּתִי
הַאֲזִינָה אֶל־תַּחֲנוּנַי
בֶּאֱמֻנָתְךָ עֲנֵנִי בְּצִדְקָתֶךָ:
2 וְאַל־תָּבוֹא בְמִשְׁפָּט אֶת־עַבְדֶּךָ
כִּי לֹא־יִצְדַּק לְפָנֶיךָ כָל־חָי:
3 כִּי רָדַף אוֹיֵב ו נַפְשִׁי
דִּכָּא לָאָרֶץ חַיָּתִי
הוֹשִׁיבַנִי בְמַחֲשַׁכִּים כְּמֵתֵי עוֹלָם:
4 וַתִּתְעַטֵּף עָלַי רוּחִי
בְּתוֹכִי יִשְׁתּוֹמֵם לִבִּי:
5 זָכַרְתִּי יָמִים ו מִקֶּדֶם
הָגִיתִי בְכָל־פָּעֳלֶךָ
בְּמַעֲשֵׂה יָדֶיךָ אֲשׂוֹחֵחַ:

CALL FOR GOD'S HELP

THIS Psalm resembles the preceding one very closely in tone and circumstance. David, trapped in the cave, finds himself in a desperate situation and invokes the mercy of God, Who has come to his aid on previous occasions (Kimchi, Hirsch). The latter half of the Psalm, in particular, is constructed mainly from quotations.

1-2 PLEA FOR MERCY

1. *in Thy righteousness.* The term cannot be employed here in its usual meaning of strict equity, because in the next verse the Psalmist begs to be spared the ordeal of a trial by God in which neither he nor any other mortal could justify himself. Accordingly the word has to be understood in the sense of God's character as One Who forgives (Metsudath David, Daath Sofrim).

2. *enter not into judgment.* Do not try me in Thy capacity of Judge of mankind.

Thy servant. He acknowledges his insignificance before God's awesome majesty.

be justified. lit. 'be righteous,' in its technical sense of 'acquitted as innocent.'

3-4 HE IS OVERCOME BY PERSECUTION

3. *in dark places.* The confinement in the cave and, in lxxxviii. 7, an allusion to the darkness of the grave, a metaphor for death. (Kimchi).

long dead. And completely forgotten. The last four words of the verse occur in a different order in Lam. iii. 6.

4. *appalled.* Benumbed by pain and worry so that it fails to function normally.

5-6 RECOLLECTION OF GOD'S MERCIES

5. *Thy doing ... the work of Thy hands.* As in xcii. 5f., the manifestations of Divine Providence.

6 I spread forth my hands unto
   Thee;
  My soul [thirsteth] after Thee, as
    a weary land.   Selah

7 Answer me speedily, O LORD,
  My spirit faileth;
  Hide not Thy face from me;
  Lest I become like them that go
   down into the pit.

8 Cause me to hear Thy lovingkind-
    ness in the morning,
  For in Thee do I trust;
  Cause me to know the way where-
    in I should walk,
  For unto Thee have I lifted up my
    soul.

9 Deliver me from mine enemies,
   O LORD;
  With Thee have I hidden myself.

10 Teach me to do Thy will,
   For Thou art my God;
   Let Thy good spirit
   Lead me in an even land.

11 For Thy name's sake, O LORD,
    quicken me;
   In Thy righteousness bring my
    soul out of trouble.

12 And in Thy mercy cut off mine
    enemies,
   And destroy all them that harass
    my soul;
   For I am Thy servant.

6 פֵּרַשְׂתִּי יָדַי אֵלֶיךָ
נַפְשִׁי ׀ כְּאֶרֶץ־עֲיֵפָה לְךָ סֶלָה׃
7 מַהֵר עֲנֵנִי ׀ יְהֹוָה כָּלְתָה רוּחִי
אַל־תַּסְתֵּר פָּנֶיךָ מִמֶּנִּי
וְנִמְשַׁלְתִּי עִם־יֹרְדֵי בוֹר׃
8 הַשְׁמִיעֵנִי בַבֹּקֶר ׀ חַסְדֶּךָ
כִּי־בְךָ בָטָחְתִּי
הוֹדִיעֵנִי דֶּרֶךְ־זוּ אֵלֵךְ
כִּי־אֵלֶיךָ נָשָׂאתִי נַפְשִׁי׃
9 הַצִּילֵנִי מֵאֹיְבַי ׀ יְהֹוָה
אֵלֶיךָ כִסִּתִי׃
10 לַמְּדֵנִי ׀ לַעֲשׂוֹת רְצוֹנֶךָ
כִּי־אַתָּה אֱלוֹהָי
רוּחֲךָ טוֹבָה תַּנְחֵנִי בְּאֶרֶץ מִישׁוֹר׃
11 לְמַעַן־שִׁמְךָ יְהֹוָה תְּחַיֵּנִי
בְּצִדְקָתְךָ ׀ תוֹצִיא מִצָּרָה נַפְשִׁי׃
12 וּבְחַסְדְּךָ תַּצְמִית אֹיְבָי
וְהַאֲבַדְתָּ כָּל־צֹרְרֵי נַפְשִׁי
כִּי אֲנִי עַבְדֶּךָ׃

---

6. *spread forth my hands.* In appeal.

as a weary land. See on lxiii. 2.

    7-8 MAY GOD ANSWER HIS PRAYER

7. *answer me speedily.* From lxix. 18.

my spirit faileth. Cf. lxxxiv. 3.

hide not Thy face from me. From cii. 3.

lest I become … pit. From xxviii. 1.

8. *cause me … morning.* See on xc. 14.

for … my soul. Based on xxv. 1f., 4.

    9-10 PLEA FOR DELIVERANCE

9. *deliver me … LORD.* From lix. 2.

have I hidden myself. lit. 'unto Thee have I
concealed,' the object being unexpressed.
The verb in this form has a reflexive meaning
in Ezek. xxxi. 15, but what the writer seems

to convey is : 'unto Thee only have I revealed
my plight' (Rashi).

10. *Thy good spirit.* The graciousness of
God towards His creatures.

in an even land. The phrase occurs as a
geographical term in Deut. iv. 43 for level
country unobstructed by hills. Here it is
figurative of conditions freed from the
temptation to sin (Kimchi).

    11-12 CONFIDENCE IN GOD'S RESPONSE

12. *for I am Thy servant.* I serve Thee and
am worthy of a fate different from that of
the wicked. An alternative explanation is: I
am devoted to Thy cause, and were I to
succumb to these evil men, that cause would
be compromised in the eyes of my contemporaries.

144

קמד

1 [A Psalm] of David.
Blessed be the LORD my Rock,
Who traineth my hands for war,
And my fingers for battle;

2 My lovingkindness, and my fortress,
My high tower, and my deliverer;
My shield, and He in whom I
take refuge;
Who subdueth my people under
me.

3 LORD, what is man, that Thou
takest knowledge of him?
Or the son of man, that Thou
makest account of him?

לְדָוִד ׀
בָּרוּךְ יְהוָה ׀ צוּרִי
הַמְלַמֵּד יָדַי לַקְרָב
אֶצְבְּעוֹתַי לַמִּלְחָמָה:
2 חַסְדִּי וּמְצוּדָתִי
מִשְׂגַּבִּי וּמְפַלְטִי לִי
מָגִנִּי וּבוֹ חָסִיתִי
הָרוֹדֵד עַמִּי תַחְתָּי:
3 יְהוָה מָה־אָדָם וַתֵּדָעֵהוּ
בֶּן־אֱנוֹשׁ וַתְּחַשְּׁבֵהוּ:

JOY IN GOD'S PROTECTION

THIS joyous Psalm is largely a mosaic of citations from other Psalms. The Targum sees in verse 10 a reference to Goliath's *hurtful sword* and, indeed, the Midrash (Shocher Tov) considers this Psalm to be David's song of joy after his victory over the Philistine giant. David acknowledges that he owes all his victories to God alone. He includes a request that God's miracles should manifest themselves so that the nations will recognize His power and omnipotence and come to fear Him (Malbim). According to some customs in the Jewish liturgy, it prefaces the service for the termination of the Sabbath (P.B., p. 210). The Jew's re-entry into weekday life and the imminent renewal of the weekday struggle is accompanied by this Psalm that invokes God's protective hand and expresses optimism and certainty that God is the support of all human life and endeavour. After the Sabbath calm, the ideas expressed in this Psalm help to reinforce the ability to face the intrusion of the world.

1-2 VICTORY IN GOD

1. *blessed be ... my Rock.* From xviii. 47.

traineth ... for battle. An elaboration of xviii. 35. The word for *war* is an Aramaism. *Fingers* are trained to manipulate the bow and *hands* the sword.

2. *my lovingkindness.* Abbreviated from *God of my lovingkindness* (lix. 11, 18).

my deliverer. lit. 'my deliverer for myself,' agreeing with 2 Sam. xxii. 2, as against Ps. xviii. 3, which omits 'for myself.'

subdueth my people under me. In xviii. 48 and 2 Sam. xxii. 48 the text has *people*, i.e. heathen nations. Here, the speaker is the king who thanks God for help in suppressing rebellious elements within the Israelite ranks (Hirsch).

3-4 MAN'S INSIGNIFICANCE

The nature of God, as disclosed in His Providence, becomes enhanced when set beside man's smallness.

3. A variant of viii. 5.

4 Man is like unto a breath;
  His days are as a shadow that
      passeth away.

5 O LORD, bow Thy heavens, and
      come down;
  Touch the mountains, that they
      may smoke.

6 Cast forth lightning, and scatter
      them;
  Send out Thine arrows, and dis-
      comfit them.

7 Stretch forth Thy hands from on
      high;
  Rescue me, and deliver me out of
      many waters,
  Out of the hand of strangers;

8 Whose mouth speaketh falsehood,
  And their right hand is a right
      hand of lying.

9 O God, I will sing a new song
      unto Thee,
  Upon a psaltery of ten strings
      will I sing praises unto Thee;

10 Who givest salvation unto kings,
   Who rescuest David Thy servant
       from the hurtful sword.

4 אָדָם לַהֶבֶל דָּמָה

יָמָיו כְּצֵל עוֹבֵר:

5 יְהוָה הַט־שָׁמֶיךָ וְתֵרֵד

גַּע בֶּהָרִים וְיֶעֱשָׁנוּ:

6 בְּרוֹק בָּרָק וּתְפִיצֵם

שְׁלַח חִצֶּיךָ וּתְהֻמֵּם:

7 שְׁלַח יָדֶיךָ מִמָּרוֹם

פְּצֵנִי וְהַצִּילֵנִי מִמַּיִם רַבִּים

מִיַּד בְּנֵי נֵכָר:

8 אֲשֶׁר פִּיהֶם דִּבֶּר־שָׁוְא

וִימִינָם יְמִין שָׁקֶר:

9 אֱלֹהִים שִׁיר חָדָשׁ אָשִׁירָה לָּךְ

בְּנֵבֶל עָשׂוֹר אֲזַמְּרָה־לָּךְ:

10 הַנּוֹתֵן תְּשׁוּעָה לַמְּלָכִים

הַפּוֹצֶה אֶת־דָּוִד עַבְדּוֹ

מֵחֶרֶב רָעָה:

4. *a breath.* Cf. xxxix. 6, 7, 12, lxii. 10.

his days ... passeth away. Cf. cii. 12; Job viii. 9. The Rabbis remarked: 'Would that life were like the shadow cast by a wall or a tree; but it is like the shadow of a bird in flight.'

5-8 PRAYER FOR DELIVERANCE

5. *bow ... come down.* From xviii. 10 changing a statement of fact into an entreaty.

touch ... that they may smoke. From civ. 32, with a similar change which continues in the following verses.

6. Derived from xviii. 15. *Them* refers to his enemies of whom he is thinking.

7. From xviii. 17.

rescue. Better, 'release me.' See lxvi. 14 where the verb means 'to utter' (open the mouth) (Kimchi).

strangers. lit. *sons of a stranger*, as in xviii. 45f.

8. *falsehood.* lit. 'vanity' (cf. xii. 3).

right hand. Raised heavenward in taking an oath; they swear falsely (Rashi).

9-11 HIS ASSURANCE OF VICTORY

9. From xxxiii. 2f. The triumph, of which he is certain, will necessitate a fresh song of praise.

10. *givest salvation unto kings.* God controls the destinies of all peoples and determines which side will win in a war.

rescuest David. In particular He protects His chosen king of Israel.

the hurtful sword. See Introduction.

11. Repetition of the prayer of verses 7f. after extolling the might of God.

11 Rescue me, and deliver me out of
the hand of strangers,
Whose mouth speaketh falsehood,
And their right hand is a right
hand of lying.

12 We whose sons are as plants
grown up in their youth;
Whose daughters are as corner-
pillars carved after the fashion
of a palace;

13 Whose garners are full, affording
all manner of store;
Whose sheep increase by thousands and ten thousands in our
fields;

14 Whose oxen are well laden;
With no breach, and no going
forth,
And no outcry in our broad
places;

15 Happy is the people that is in
such a case,
Yea, happy is the people whose
God is the LORD.

11 פְּצֵנִי וְהַצִּילֵנִי מִיַּד בְּנֵי־נֵכָר
אֲשֶׁר פִּיהֶם דִּבֶּר־שָׁוְא
וִימִינָם יְמִין שָׁקֶר׃
12 אֲשֶׁר בָּנֵינוּ ׀ כִּנְטִעִים
מְגֻדָּלִים בִּנְעוּרֵיהֶם
בְּנוֹתֵינוּ כְזָוִיֹּת
מְחֻטָּבוֹת תַּבְנִית הֵיכָל׃
13 מְזָוֵינוּ מְלֵאִים מְפִיקִים מִזַּן אֶל זַן
צֹאונֵנוּ מַאֲלִיפוֹת מְרֻבָּבוֹת
בְּחוּצוֹתֵינוּ׃
14 אַלּוּפֵינוּ מְסֻבָּלִים
אֵין פֶּרֶץ וְאֵין יוֹצֵאת
וְאֵין צְוָחָה בִּרְחֹבֹתֵינוּ׃
15 אַשְׁרֵי הָעָם שֶׁכָּכָה לּוֹ
אַשְׁרֵי הָעָם שֶׁיהוה אֱלֹהָיו׃

12-15 EFFECT UPON ISRAEL
OF GOD'S PROTECTION

Heretofore David repeated freely verses from other Psalms in praising God for rescuing him from enemies. In this section he describes the state of the people after the enemy's fall. The verses present a picture of a happy and prosperous homestead, with numerous and beautiful children and well-filled barns, the lot of the members of a people enjoying the care and blessing of God.

12. *plants*. Rather, 'saplings.' The meaning of the clause is: our sons in their youth are like grown saplings. They are already sending out shoots and give promise of developing into fruitful trees (cf. cxxviii. 3) (cf. Kimchi, Metsudath David).

as corner-pillars. The daughters are as graceful as the elegant carvings which adorn the pillars of a palace (cf. Kimchi, Metsudath David).

13. *all manner of store*. lit. 'from kind to kind,' of every sort.

fields. lit. 'what is outside'; usually *streets* (so A.V.), but 'fields' is more appropriate to the context. They are the open spaces outside the city (cf. Job v. 10) (Hirsch).

14. *well laden*. With the produce of the field which the oxen carry to the garners.

no breach. In the city's wall by an invading army. The land is blessed with peace and security (Ibn Ezra, Kimchi).

no going forth. Of the population as captives of the conqueror (Kimchi).

no outcry. Of alarm and distress on the part of the defeated (Jer. xiv. 2) (Ibn Ezra).

broad places. The open spaces of a city into which the citizens pour in a time of panic.

15. *that is in such a case*. lit. 'to whom it is thus,' whose privilege it is to receive these evidences of Divine favour (Kimchi, Metsudath David).

yea, happy ... LORD. From xxxiii. 12.

145　　　　　　　　　　　　　　קמה

[A Psalm of] praise; of David.
I will extol Thee, my God, O
   King;
And I will bless Thy name for
   ever and ever.

2 Every day will I bless Thee;
And I will praise Thy name for
   ever and ever.

3 Great is the Lord, and highly to
   be praised;
And His greatness is unsearchable.

4 One generation shall laud Thy
   works to another,
And shall declare Thy mighty
   acts.

תְּהִלָּה לְדָוִד
אֲרוֹמִמְךָ אֱלוֹהַי הַמֶּלֶךְ
וַאֲבָרְכָה שִׁמְךָ לְעוֹלָם וָעֶד:
2 בְּכָל־יוֹם אֲבָרְכֶךָּ
וַאֲהַלְלָה שִׁמְךָ לְעוֹלָם וָעֶד:
3 גָּדוֹל יְהוָה וּמְהֻלָּל מְאֹד
וְלִגְדֻלָּתוֹ אֵין חֵקֶר:
4 דּוֹר לְדוֹר יְשַׁבַּח מַעֲשֶׂיךָ
וּגְבוּרֹתֶיךָ יַגִּידוּ:

GLORY TO GOD

This Psalm is a glorious hymn of praise describing the majesty of God and the wonders He
performs for His creations in attending to their every physical need (cf. Kimchi). Many of the
verses were culled from other Psalms and are in the form of an alphabetic acrostic with the
omission of the verse beginning with the letter 'nun.' According to Rabbi Yochanan (Tal. Ber.
4b), the verse was deliberately left out because it would have been one of ill omen, such as
'Fallen (*naphelah*) is the virgin of Israel, she shall no more rise ' (Amos v. 2). The composition
was considered of great significance and led the Rabbis to declare (Tal. ibid.) 'whoever recites
this Psalm thrice daily may be assured that he is a son of the World to Come, because it contains
the verse, *Thou openest Thy hand and satisfiest every living thing with favour,*' i.e. an acknowledgment of man's dependence upon God's grace. In conformity with this teaching the
Psalm occurs three times in the Jewish liturgy for every day (P.B., pp. 29, 71, 94). This Psalm
inaugurates the concluding group which rounds up the Psalter with a series of hymns of praise,
reaching its climax in the superb Hallelujah of cl.

1. *praise.* Only this Psalm bears this heading.

of David. By David.

my God. Contrast *I will extol Thee, O Lord*
(xxx. 2). The use of *elohim* strikes the universal note which is a distinguishing feature
of the Psalm (cf. Kimchi).

O King. Ruler of all the world.

2. *bless.* The same as 'praise' (cf. the vari-

ant in verse 2).

for ever and ever. As long as I live (see on
cxix. 44).

3. *great ... praised.* From xlviii. 2, xcvi. 4.

unsearchable. Beyond human comprehension.

4. *Thy mighty acts.* Bringing salvation to
the weak.

5 The glorious splendour of Thy
   majesty,
And Thy wondrous works, will I
   rehearse.

6 And men shall speak of the might
   of Thy tremendous acts;
And I will tell of Thy greatness.

7 They shall utter the fame of Thy
   great goodness,
And shall sing of Thy righteousness.

8 The LORD is gracious, and full of
   compassion;
Slow to anger, and of great mercy.

9 The LORD is good to all;
And His tender mercies are over
   all His works.

10 All Thy works shall praise Thee,
   O LORD;
And Thy saints shall bless Thee.

11 They shall speak of the glory of
   Thy kingdom,
And talk of Thy might;

12 To make known to the sons of
   men His mighty acts,
And the glory of the majesty of
   His kingdom.

הֲדַר כְּבוֹד הוֹדֶךָ 5
וְדִבְרֵי נִפְלְאֹתֶיךָ אָשִׂיחָה׃
וֶעֱזוּז נוֹרְאֹתֶיךָ יֹאמֵרוּ 6
וּגְדֻלּוֹתֶיךָ אֲסַפְּרֶנָּה׃
זֵכֶר רַב־טוּבְךָ יַבִּיעוּ 7
וְצִדְקָתְךָ יְרַנֵּנוּ׃
חַנּוּן וְרַחוּם יְהוָה 8
אֶרֶךְ אַפַּיִם וּגְדָל־חָסֶד׃
טוֹב־יְהוָה לַכֹּל 9
וְרַחֲמָיו עַל־כָּל־מַעֲשָׂיו׃
יוֹדוּךָ יְהוָה כָּל־מַעֲשֶׂיךָ 10
וַחֲסִידֶיךָ יְבָרְכוּכָה׃
כְּבוֹד מַלְכוּתְךָ יֹאמֵרוּ 11
וּגְבוּרָתְךָ יְדַבֵּרוּ׃
לְהוֹדִיעַ לִבְנֵי הָאָדָם גְּבוּרֹתָיו 12
וּכְבוֹד הֲדַר מַלְכוּתוֹ׃

v. 6. וגדולתך ק׳

5. *glorious splendour.* lit. 'the splendour of
the glory of.' All three terms, *splendour,
glory and majesty*, are attributed to God's
Kingship (verse 12, xxi. 6, xcvi. 6, civ. 1).

Thy wondrous works. lit. 'the word of Thy
wondrous works'; for the idiom, see on cv.
27.

6. *Thy tremendous acts.* lit. 'awe-inspiring
acts' of judgment upon the heathen peoples
which they too will acknowledge (Malbim);
hence *men* (lit. they) *shall speak.*

Thy greatness. So the *kerë*; the *kethib* means
'Thy great deeds.'

7. *utter.* See on cxix. 171.

Thy great goodness. Better, 'Thine abundant
goodness,' as in xxxi. 20. The adjective is not
the same as that translated *great* in verse 8.

Thy righteousness. The nations will bear

witness to God's fidelity to His attributes as
a just and merciful King with exultant song.

9. *good to all.* To every creature, human or
animal, created by Him (Kimchi). No words
can more adequately conveys the thought of
God as the universal Father.

10. *praise.* Better, 'thank.' God's creatures
will acknowledge with gratitude His goodness to them.

Thy saints. See on iv. 4.

11. *they shall speak.* The subject is *Thy
saints*; they will be the medium through
which all mankind comes to know of God's
worldwide Kingship (Malbim).

12. *His mighty acts.* The change to the third
person may be accounted for by regarding
the verse as containing the substance of the
saints' testimony.

13 Thy kingdom is a kingdom for
    all ages,
    And Thy dominion endureth
    throughout all generations.

14 The LORD upholdeth all that fall,
    And raiseth up all those that are
    bowed down.

15 The eyes of all wait for Thee,
    And Thou givest them their food
    in due season.

16 Thou openest Thy hand,
    And satisfiest every living thing
    with favour.

17 The LORD is righteous in all His
    ways,
    And gracious in all His works.

18 The LORD is nigh unto all them
    that call upon Him,
    To all that call upon Him in
    truth.

19 He will fulfil the desire of them
    that fear Him;
    He also will hear their cry, and
    will save them.

20 The LORD preserveth all them
    that love Him;
    But all the wicked will He de-
    stroy.

21 My mouth shall speak the praise
    of the LORD;
    And let all flesh bless His holy
    name for ever and ever.

13 מַלְכוּתְךָ מַלְכוּת כָּל־עֹלָמִים
וּמֶמְשַׁלְתְּךָ בְּכָל־דּוֹר וָדֹר:

14 סוֹמֵךְ יְהֹוָה לְכָל־הַנֹּפְלִים
וְזוֹקֵף לְכָל־הַכְּפוּפִים:

15 עֵינֵי כֹל אֵלֶיךָ יְשַׂבֵּרוּ
וְאַתָּה נוֹתֵן־לָהֶם אֶת־אָכְלָם בְּעִתּוֹ:

16 פּוֹתֵחַ אֶת־יָדֶךָ
וּמַשְׂבִּיעַ לְכָל־חַי רָצוֹן:

17 צַדִּיק יְהֹוָה בְּכָל־דְּרָכָיו
וְחָסִיד בְּכָל־מַעֲשָׂיו:

18 קָרוֹב יְהֹוָה לְכָל־קֹרְאָיו
לְכֹל אֲשֶׁר יִקְרָאֻהוּ בֶאֱמֶת:

19 רְצוֹן־יְרֵאָיו יַעֲשֶׂה
וְאֶת־שַׁוְעָתָם יִשְׁמַע וְיוֹשִׁיעֵם:

20 שׁוֹמֵר יְהֹוָה אֶת־כָּל־אֹהֲבָיו
וְאֵת כָּל־הָרְשָׁעִים יַשְׁמִיד:

21 תְּהִלַּת יְהֹוָה יְדַבֶּר־פִּי
וִיבָרֵךְ כָּל־בָּשָׂר שֵׁם קָדְשׁוֹ
לְעוֹלָם וָעֶד:

13. This verse is quoted in Aramaic translation in Dan. iii. 33, iv. 31.

14. *raiseth up*. Only again in cxlvi. 8, but
common in Aramaic.

15. Derived from civ. 27.

16. *Thou openest Thy hand*. From civ. 28.

with favour. Either (Thy) graciousness
openeth Thy hand (Malbim), or the word
may have the same meaning as in verse 19,
'satisfiest every living thing with (its) desire'
(Hirsch).

17. *ways*. See on ciii. 7.

18. *nigh*. Commenting on Deut. iv. 7, the
Talmud asks, 'Can one imagine God nearer
to us, Who is ready to bring His ear close to

the mouth of every one of His creatures?'
This universalistic touch in the comment is in
the spirit of this verse.

19. *fear*. Whereas one who fears a mortal
king is satisfied not to be harmed by him, God
fulfills the will of one who fears Him (Ibn
Ezra).

20. *love*. 'Greater is he who serves God
from love than he who serves Him from fear'
(Talmud).

all flesh. Corresponding to *every thing that
hath breath* (cl. 6). The Psalmist is not content to proclaim the unique greatness of God;
his aspiration is that all mankind will join the
chorus of adulation as long as the world
endures.

146

קמו

1 Hallelujah.
Praise the LORD, O my soul.

2 I will praise the LORD while I live;
I will sing praises unto my God
while I have my being.

3 Put not your trust in princes,
Nor in the son of man, in whom
there is no help.

4 His breath goeth forth, he returneth to his dust;
In that very day his thoughts
perish.

5 Happy is he whose help is the God
of Jacob,
Whose hope is in the LORD his
God,

6 Who made heaven and earth,
The sea, and all that in them is;
Who keepeth truth for ever;

הַלְלוּיָהּ

הַלְלִי נַפְשִׁי אֶת־יְהוָֹה:

2 אֲהַלְלָה יְהוָה בְּחַיָּי

אֲזַמְּרָה לֵאלֹהַי בְּעוֹדִי:

3 אַל־תִּבְטְחוּ בִנְדִיבִים

בְּבֶן־אָדָם ׀ שֶׁאֵין לוֹ תְשׁוּעָה:

4 תֵּצֵא רוּחוֹ יָשֻׁב לְאַדְמָתוֹ

בַּיּוֹם הַהוּא אָבְדוּ עֶשְׁתֹּנֹתָיו:

5 אַשְׁרֵי שֶׁאֵל יַעֲקֹב בְּעֶזְרוֹ

שִׂבְרוֹ עַל־יְהוָה אֱלֹהָיו:

6 עֹשֶׂה ׀ שָׁמַיִם וָאָרֶץ

אֶת־הַיָּם וְאֶת־כָּל־אֲשֶׁר־בָּם

הַשֹּׁמֵר אֱמֶת לְעוֹלָם:

GOD THE HELPER

SEVERAL affinities may be noted between this Psalm and its predecessor. It is general in character and seemingly unconnected with any special circumstances. The theme is that in God alone is an unfailing source of help is to be discovered.

1-2 THE PSALMIST'S URGE TO PRAISE GOD

1. *praise ... soul.* Comparable to *Bless the LORD, O my soul*, the opening of ciii and civ.

2. Cf. civ. 33, cxlv. 2.

3-4 TRUST NOT IN MORTALS

3. *princes.* Cf. cxviii. 8f. and Jer. xvii. 5, 7. To secure protection trust cannot be placed in men of wealth and influence. The Psalmist indicates a more reliable Protector.

help. lit. 'salvation.' Human aid often proves a broken reed.

4. *breath.* The vitality derived from God (Gen. ii. 7).

goeth forth. From the body.

returneth to his dust. Cf. civ. 29.

thoughts. Only here in the Bible, but com-mon in Aramaic; its meaning is 'purposes.'

5-10 THE POWER OF GOD

5. *the God of Jacob.* See on xx. 2. But He is no tribal deity; He is the Creator and Controller of the universe.

hope. An Aramaism; the verb of the same root occurs in cxlv. 15.

6. In contrast to the powerlessness of mor-tal creatures, the infinite might of God is extolled.

in them. viz. heaven, earth and sea.

keepeth truth for ever. True to the Hebraic spirit, the Psalmist does not rest his confi-dence in God only because of His power; an even more cogent reason is His providential dealings with His creatures in accordance with His revealed attributes.

7 Who executeth justice for the
    oppressed;
  Who giveth bread to the hungry.
  The Lord looseth the prisoners;

8 The Lord openeth the eyes of the
    blind;
  The Lord raiseth up them that are
    bowed down;
  The Lord loveth the righteous;

9 The Lord preserveth the
    strangers;
  He upholdeth the fatherless and
    the widow;
  But the way of the wicked He
    maketh crooked.

10 The Lord will reign for ever,
   Thy God, O Zion, unto all genera-
   tions.
   Hallelujah.

עֹשֶׂה מִשְׁפָּט ׀ לָעֲשׁוּקִים 7
נֹתֵן לֶחֶם לָרְעֵבִים
יְהֹוָה מַתִּיר אֲסוּרִים:
יְהֹוָה ׀ פֹּקֵחַ עִוְרִים 8
יְהֹוָה זֹקֵף כְּפוּפִים
יְהֹוָה אֹהֵב צַדִּיקִים:
יְהֹוָה ׀ שֹׁמֵר אֶת־גֵּרִים 9
יָתוֹם וְאַלְמָנָה יְעוֹדֵד
וְדֶרֶךְ רְשָׁעִים יְעַוֵּת:
יִמְלֹךְ יְהֹוָה ׀ לְעוֹלָם 10
אֱלֹהַיִךְ צִיּוֹן לְדֹר וָדֹר
הַלְלוּיָהּ:

7. *executeth justice for the ... oppressed.*
Derived from ciii. 6. He constantly protects
the innocent's rights and metes out justice to
the wicked on their behalf (Kimchi).

giveth bread to the hungry. Cf. cvii. 9. Upon
God's will, as the Creator of the universe,
depends the fruitfulness of the soil (cf. Daath
Sofrim).

looseth the prisoners. The words may be applied literally to the exiles or figuratively to
those who are in the grip of trouble (Kimchi).

8. *openeth the eyes of the blind.* This may
also be understood as figuratively referring
to intellectual enlightenment (Malbim). (Cf.
the use of *blind* in Lev. xix. 14).

raiseth up ... bowed down. Cf. cxlv. 14.

loveth the righteous. And is consequently their
Ally against their oppressors.

9. *strangers ... fatherless and the widow.*
Mentioned together in xciv. 6 as helpless
persons needing protection. Their rights were
only secure when justice was faithfully administered; therefore God as the supreme
Judge upholds their cause.

maketh crooked. Their goal is unworthy and
the path to it marked by corruption. God
diverts them so that they do not attain their
desire but are led to ruin (Kimchi, Metsudath
David cf. Hirsch).

10. *the Lord will reign for ever.* From Exod.
xv. 18. Unlike the princes of earth who die
(verses 3f.), the reign of God is eternal.

Thy God, O Zion. Jerusalem being the seat of
His Kingship (xcix. 1f.). From His chosen
centre, Zion, (Metsudath David) God will
reign over all peoples who will unite in recognition of His Kingship (Kimchi).

147

קמז

הַלְלוּיָהּ ׀

כִּי־טוֹב זַמְּרָה אֱלֹהֵינוּ

כִּי־נָעִים נָאוָה תְהִלָּה׃

2 בּוֹנֵה יְרוּשָׁלַ͏ִם יְהוָה

נִדְחֵי יִשְׂרָאֵל יְכַנֵּס׃

3 הָרֹפֵא לִשְׁבוּרֵי לֵב

וּמְחַבֵּשׁ לְעַצְּבוֹתָם׃

4 מוֹנֶה מִסְפָּר לַכּוֹכָבִים

לְכֻלָּם שֵׁמוֹת יִקְרָא׃

5 גָּדוֹל אֲדוֹנֵינוּ וְרַב־כֹּחַ

לִתְבוּנָתוֹ אֵין מִסְפָּר׃

1 Hallelujah;
   For it is good to sing praises unto our God;
   For it is pleasant, and praise is comely.

2 The LORD doth build up Jerusalem,
   He gathereth together the dispersed of Israel;

3 Who healeth the broken in heart,
   And bindeth up their wounds.

4 He counteth the number of the stars;
   He giveth them all their names.

5 Great is our Lord, and mighty in power;
   His understanding is infinite.

GOD'S LOVE AND POWER

THE Psalmist adduces four reasons for praising God: His regard for Israel as will be proved by the future Restoration; the bounteous provision He has made for the sustenance of His creatures; His control of the forces of nature; and His revelation to Israel, constituting a declaration of its uniqueness vis-a-vis the other nations. The Psalm 'imparts to Israel ... an awareness of its enduring relationship to God ... and its permanent position as messenger of His word amidst mankind' (Hirsch). A notable feature in this and the succeeding Psalms is the stress laid upon the thought of God as the Creator of the universe and the Director of its forces, and it may be Israel's answer to the pagan ideas which were current in those times.

1-3 PRAISE GOD FOR HIS GOODNESS

1. *for.* Since *Halleluah* is an introductory invocation, it is better to translate 'surely.' The verse is based on cxxxv. 3 and xxxiii. 1.

2. *doth build up Jerusalem.* The present tense is used although the reference is to the future. A better rendering might be, 'The builder of Jerusalem, the LORD,' ... i.e. He is the founder of the city (cf. lxxvi. 2; Hirsch).

He gathereth ... Israel. A reminiscence of Isa. lvi. 8.

3. *broken in heart.* The exiles in a state of extreme dejection as pictured in cxxxvii (cf. also Isa. lxi. 1).

wounds. Of the spirit rather than the flesh (Malbim).

4-11 THE MIGHT OF GOD

4. Cf. Isa. xl. 26.

He counteth the number. An indication of omnipotence, since it is a task beyond human power (Gen. xv. 5) (Kimchi). Perhaps a more correct translation is: 'He determineth a number to the stars' (Hirsch). As the creator of the universe He decided with how many stars the firmament should be studded.

He giveth ... names. He knows each one of them; but more probably the clause means: 'He calls all of them by name' (Hirsch). Each of them has a particular mission to influence a specific part of the universe, however minute. Cf. Tal. Chulin 7a (Kimchi). A similar thought is found in Isa. xl. 26, where the stars are likened to an army of soldiers.

5. *mighty in power.* lit. 'abundant of power' (cf. Isa. xl. 26).

6 The LORD upholdeth the humble;
He bringeth the wicked down to
the ground.

7 Sing unto the LORD with thanksgiving,
Sing praises upon the harp unto
our God;

8 Who covereth the heaven with
clouds,
Who prepareth rain for the earth,
Who maketh the mountains to
spring with grass.

9 He giveth to the beast his food,
And to the young ravens which
cry.

10 He delighteth not in the strength
of the horse;
He taketh no pleasure in the legs
of a man.

11 The LORD taketh pleasure in
them that fear Him,
In those that wait for His mercy.

12 Glorify the LORD, O Jerusalem;
Praise thy God, O Zion.

6 מְעוֹדֵד עֲנָוִים יְהֹוָה

מַשְׁפִּיל רְשָׁעִים עֲדֵי־אָרֶץ:

7 עֱנוּ לַיהֹוָה בְּתוֹדָה

זַמְּרוּ לֵאלֹהֵינוּ בְכִנּוֹר:

8 הַמְכַסֶּה שָׁמַיִם ׀ בְּעָבִים

הַמֵּכִין לָאָרֶץ מָטָר

הַמַּצְמִיחַ הָרִים חָצִיר:

9 נוֹתֵן לִבְהֵמָה לַחְמָהּ

לִבְנֵי עֹרֵב אֲשֶׁר יִקְרָאוּ:

10 לֹא בִגְבוּרַת הַסּוּס יֶחְפָּץ

לֹא־בְשׁוֹקֵי הָאִישׁ יִרְצֶה:

11 רוֹצֶה יְהֹוָה אֶת־יְרֵאָיו

אֶת־הַמְיַחֲלִים לְחַסְדּוֹ:

12 שַׁבְּחִי יְרוּשָׁלַ͏ִם אֶת־יְהֹוָה

הַלְלִי אֱלֹהַיִךְ צִיּוֹן:

His understanding is infinite. lit.'numberless,'
incalculable, a variant of *His discernment*
(the same word as *understanding*) *is past
searching out* (Isa. xl. 28)

6. *upholdeth the humble.* As in cxlvi. 7ff.
the thought is stressed that the might of God
is exercised in His dealings with man as well
as in the physical world. He controls the stars
but also men's fortunes.

7. The renewed call to praise introduces a
fuller account of Divine creative power.

sing praises upon the harp. From xcviii. 5.

8. The verse illustrates the distinctive Hebraic conception, that the whole of nature's
functioning is ascribed to one God instead of
a multiplicity of departmental deities.

the mountains. Specifically mentioned because they are not cultivated by man (Kimchi).

9. *the beast.* God's considerateness for
animal welfare is an aspect of His love
featured by the Psalter (civ. 11ff., cxlv. 15f.).

the young ravens. The raven's young are
cited as manifesting the goodness and care
God provides His lower creatures. Abandoned by their mother at a tender age and left
to cry for their at best scanty food, they must
seek nourishment over a wide expanse of
country. God comes to their aid and supplies
them with insects (cf. Rashi, Kimchi).

10. *the horse.* Used in battle (xxxiii. 17).

the legs of a man. Of a soldier, firm and
nimble on his feet to counter assault and, if
necessary, make a swift retreat. God is not
interested in those who rely upon their own
power for success. Cf. Amos ii. 14ff (Kimchi).

11. God's 'warriors,' in whom He delights,
are not the strong in limb, but the firm in faith
and reverence.

12-14 GOD'S GRACIOUSNESS
TO JERUSALEM

The thought of the previous verses is continued. It is through Zion and Jerusalem that the

147. 13

13 For He hath made strong the bars
   of thy gates;
   He hath blessed thy children
   within thee.

14 He maketh thy borders peace;
   He giveth thee in plenty the fat
   of wheat.

15 He sendeth out His commandment upon earth;
   His word runneth very swiftly.

16 He giveth snow like wool;
   He scattereth the hoar-frost like
   ashes.

17 He casteth forth His ice like
   crumbs;
   Who can stand before His cold?

18 He sendeth forth His word, and
   melteth them;
   He causeth His wind to blow,
   and the waters flow.

19 He declareth His word unto
   Jacob,
   His statutes and His ordinances
   unto Israel.

20 He hath not dealt so with any
   nation;
   And as for His ordinances, they
   have not known them.
   Hallelujah.

13 כִּי־חִזַּק בְּרִיחֵי שְׁעָרָיִךְ
בֵּרַךְ בָּנַיִךְ בְּקִרְבֵּךְ׃
14 הַשָּׂם־גְּבוּלֵךְ שָׁלוֹם
חֵלֶב חִטִּים יַשְׂבִּיעֵךְ׃
15 הַשֹּׁלֵחַ אִמְרָתוֹ אָרֶץ
עַד־מְהֵרָה יָרוּץ דְּבָרוֹ׃
16 הַנֹּתֵן שֶׁלֶג כַּצָּמֶר
כְּפוֹר כָּאֵפֶר יְפַזֵּר׃
17 מַשְׁלִיךְ קַרְחוֹ כְפִתִּים
לִפְנֵי קָרָתוֹ מִי יַעֲמֹד׃
18 יִשְׁלַח דְּבָרוֹ וְיַמְסֵם
יַשֵּׁב רוּחוֹ יִזְּלוּ־מָיִם׃
19 מַגִּיד דְּבָרוֹ לְיַעֲקֹב
חֻקָּיו וּמִשְׁפָּטָיו לְיִשְׂרָאֵל׃
20 לֹא עָשָׂה כֵן ׀ לְכָל־גּוֹי
וּמִשְׁפָּטִים בַּל־יְדָעוּם
הַלְלוּיָהּ׃

v. 19. דבריו ק׳

wonders of God and the frailty of man shall
be demonstrated (Hirsch).

the bars of thy gates. To strengthen the en-
trances to the city against attack (Metsudath
David).

children. He will cause the population to
multiply (Metsudath David.).

14. *maketh thy borders peace.* lit.
'appointeth thy boundary (to be in a state of)
peace.'

15. *His commandment.* To the elements,
such as rain which produces the rich corn (cf.
Kimchi).

16. Snow is rare in urban Israel and falls
mainly in the hilly areas where it adds consid-
erably to the water supply (Daath Sofrim).

17. *ice.* Hail which scatters over the ground
like bread-crumbs.

who can stand. Its occurrence must be very
trying to the population.

18. *His word.* He countermands His order
which gripped the land in snow.

His wind. Bringing a rise of temperature.

19-20 HIS REVELATION TO ISRAEL

The last ground for praise of God is that He
had committed His laws into the keeping of
Israel.

19. *word.* So the *kethib*, but the *kerë* denotes
'words,' a general term for Revelation.

20. The other nations lack knowledge,
not only of statutes which confine the
physical aspects of the individual personality within the bounds of moral purity, but
also the ordinances built upon absolute values which govern the life of a stable society
(Hirsch).

148

קמח

הַלְלוּיָהּ ׀

הַלְלוּ אֶת־יְהֹוָה מִן־הַשָּׁמַיִם
הַלְלוּהוּ בַּמְּרוֹמִים:

2 הַלְלוּהוּ כָל־מַלְאָכָיו
הַלְלוּהוּ כָּל־צְבָאָו:

3 הַלְלוּהוּ שֶׁמֶשׁ וְיָרֵחַ
הַלְלוּהוּ כָּל־כּוֹכְבֵי אוֹר:

4 הַלְלוּהוּ שְׁמֵי הַשָּׁמָיִם
וְהַמַּיִם אֲשֶׁר ׀ מֵעַל הַשָּׁמָיִם:

5 יְהַלְלוּ אֶת־שֵׁם יְהֹוָה
כִּי הוּא צִוָּה וְנִבְרָאוּ:

6 וַיַּעֲמִידֵם לָעַד לְעוֹלָם
חָק־נָתַן וְלֹא יַעֲבוֹר:

7 הַלְלוּ אֶת־יְהֹוָה מִן־הָאָרֶץ
תַּנִּינִים וְכָל־תְּהֹמוֹת:

צבאיו ק׳ v. 2.

1 Hallelujah.
Praise ye the Lord from the heavens;
Praise Him in the heights.

2 Praise ye Him, all His angels;
Praise ye Him, all His hosts.

3 Praise ye Him, sun and moon;
Praise Him, all ye stars of light.

4 Praise Him, ye heavens of heavens,
And ye waters that are above the heavens.

5 Let them praise the name of the Lord;
For He commanded, and they were created.

6 He hath also established them for ever and ever;
He hath made a decree which shall not be transgressed.

7 Praise the Lord from the earth,
Ye sea-monsters, and all deeps;

ALL CREATION PRAISE GOD

EVERY THING in heaven and earth is invited to join in a universal chorus of laudation. The occasion for this signal outburst of praise is indicated in the closing verse of the Psalm which is an allusion to Israel's eventual return after the exile. It will be an event of significance for the whole world, the triumph of the Divine purpose which has meaning for the entire universe.

1-6 PRAISE FROM HEAVEN

1. *from the heavens.* Cf. *from the earth* in verse 7. The thanksgiving was to begin with the angels and then re-echo through the earth.

2. *His angels.* Cf. ciii. 20.

His hosts. See on ciii. 21. The *kethib* is singular, but the *kerë* is plural.

4. *heavens of heavens.* The far away heavens (Metsudath David).

waters ... heavens. Cf. civ. 3; Gen. i. 7.

5. *He commanded.* The subject is emphasized: He and none other.

6. *established.* lit. 'caused to stand.' The thought is that in addition to creating the heavenly bodies, God maintains them.

He hath made ... transgressed. Render: 'He hath given (each of them) a statute which it cannot transgress.' God instituted the laws to which they have to conform (Metsudath David). The 'laws of Nature' of the scientist are actually the ordinances of God.

7-13 PRAISE FROM EARTH

7. *sea-monsters.* Gen. i. 21.

deeps. Of the seas where they live.

8 Fire and hail, snow and vapour,
  Stormy wind, fulfilling His word;

9 Mountains and all hills,
  Fruitful trees and all cedars;

10 Beasts and all cattle,
   Creeping things and winged
     fowl;

11 Kings of the earth and all peoples,
   Princes and all judges of the
     earth;

12 Both young men and maidens,
   Old men and children;

13 Let them praise the name of the
     LORD,
   For His name alone is exalted;
   His glory is above the earth and
     heaven.

14 And He hath lifted up a horn for
     His people,
   A praise for all His saints,
   Even for the children of Israel, a
     people near unto Him.
   Hallelujah.

8 אֵשׁ וּבָרָד שֶׁלֶג וְקִיטוֹר
רוּחַ סְעָרָה עֹשָׂה דְבָרוֹ׃

9 הֶהָרִים וְכָל־גְּבָעוֹת
עֵץ פְּרִי וְכָל־אֲרָזִים׃

10 הַחַיָּה וְכָל־בְּהֵמָה
רֶמֶשׂ וְצִפּוֹר כָּנָף׃

11 מַלְכֵי־אֶרֶץ וְכָל־לְאֻמִּים
שָׂרִים וְכָל־שֹׁפְטֵי אָרֶץ׃

12 בַּחוּרִים וְגַם־בְּתוּלוֹת
זְקֵנִים עִם־נְעָרִים׃

13 יְהַלְלוּ אֶת־שֵׁם יְהוָה
כִּי־נִשְׂגָּב שְׁמוֹ לְבַדּוֹ
הוֹדוֹ עַל־אֶרֶץ וְשָׁמָיִם׃

14 וַיָּרֶם קֶרֶן לְעַמּוֹ
תְּהִלָּה לְכָל־חֲסִידָיו
לִבְנֵי יִשְׂרָאֵל עַם קְרֹבוֹ
הַלְלוּיָהּ׃

---

8. *fire and hail.* Cf. xviii. 13. Hailstorms are usually accompanied by flashes of lightning.

vapour. Warm mists that arise from the earth.

9. *fruitful trees.* lit. 'fruit-tree' (collective), as in Gen. i. 11; fruit-bearing trees.

cedars. Typical of trees which do not produce fruit.

10. *beasts.* Wild animals.

cattle. Domestic animals.

11. The Psalmist follows the sequence of Gen. i and places man last as the culminating point of God's creation (Kimchi).

kings, etc. The higher the rank the greater the duty to join in the praise.

12. *and maidens.* Better, 'and also maidens.' The young men will not praise together with the maidens, as will the old men and children. The mingling of two groups is unbecoming, especially in view of the spiritual atmosphere of the occasion (Daath Sofrim).

13. *His name alone is exalted.* From Isa. xii. 4. What He does for Israel has the effect of magnifying Him before all peoples and making it evident that His majesty (not *glory*) transcends the universe.

14. OCCASION FOR THE PRAISE

lifted up a horn. See on lxxxix. 18. God will have restored Israel's honour after the humiliation of the exile (Kimchi).

a praise for all His saints. This redemptive act is a theme for Israel to whom God has manifested His love (Kimchi).

a people near unto Him. God has proved Himself near to Israel (Deut. iv. 7) in coming to their rescue, and thereby acknowledged the people's nearness to Him as *a kingdom of priests and a holy nation* (Exod. xix. 6). For this recognition, *the children of Israel,* in particular, had the obligation of praising Him.

149

קמט

הַלְלוּיָהּ
שִׁירוּ לַיהוָֹה שִׁיר חָדָשׁ
תְּהִלָּתוֹ בִּקְהַל חֲסִידִים:
2 יִשְׂמַח יִשְׂרָאֵל בְּעֹשָׂיו
בְּנֵי־צִיּוֹן יָגִילוּ בְמַלְכָּם:
3 יְהַלְלוּ שְׁמוֹ בְמָחוֹל
בְּתֹף וְכִנּוֹר יְזַמְּרוּ־לוֹ:
4 כִּי־רוֹצֶה יְהוָֹה בְּעַמּוֹ
יְפָאֵר עֲנָוִים בִּישׁוּעָה:
5 יַעְלְזוּ חֲסִידִים בְּכָבוֹד
יְרַנְּנוּ עַל־מִשְׁכְּבוֹתָם:

1 Hallelujah.
  Sing unto the Lord a new song,
  And His praise in the assembly of
     the saints.

2 Let Israel rejoice in his Maker;
  Let the children of Zion be joyful
     in their King.

3 Let them praise His name in the
     dance;
  Let them sing praises unto Him
     with the timbrel and harp.

4 For the Lord taketh pleasure in
     His people;
  He adorneth the humble with
     salvation.

5 Let the saints exult in glory;
  Let them sing for joy upon their
     beds.

HYMN OF TRIUMPH

This Psalm was composed to celebrate the final redemption when the nation of Israel will triumph over their enemies and regain their former splendour.

1-4 ISRAEL'S PRAISE DUE TO GOD

1. *sing ... song.* See on xcvi. 1.

in the assembly of the saints. It will be a time for national rejoicing and thanksgiving. The *saints* are identical with Israel (verse 2), as in cxlviii. 14 (Kimchi).

2. *his Maker.* See on xcv. 6.

their King. The seat of Whose Kingdom is in Zion. There may be an allusion to the Messiah who will be crowned king (Sforno).

3. *in the dance.* Religious fervour expresses itself in dancing (cf. Exod. xv. 20; Judges xi. 34; 2 Sam. vi. 14).

timbrel. Cf. lxviii. 26.

4. *the Lord taketh pleasure.* Cf. cxlvii. 11. The evidence of His renewed favour will be the end of exile and the return to Zion.

the humble. They who have been oppressed and degraded by their conquerors. Now they will be, so to speak, beautified by Divine salvation.

5-9 THEIR ENEMIES TO BE DESTROYED

5. *in glory.* In the restored honour of the nation.

upon their beds. Where they can retire to sleep in safety, their foes having been vanquished (Hirsch).

6 Let the high praises of God be in
   their mouth,
   And a two-edged sword in their
     hand;

7 To execute vengeance upon the
   nations,
   And chastisements upon the
     peoples;

8 To bind their kings with chains,
   And their nobles with fetters of
     iron;

9 To execute upon them the judg-
   ment written;
   He is the glory of all His saints.
   Hallelujah.

6 רוֹמְמוֹת אֵל בִּגְרוֹנָם
וְחֶרֶב פִּיפִיּוֹת בְּיָדָם:
7 לַעֲשׂוֹת נְקָמָה בַּגּוֹיִם
תּוֹכֵחוֹת בַּלְאֻמִּים:
8 לֶאְסֹר מַלְכֵיהֶם בְּזִקִּים
וְנִכְבְּדֵיהֶם בְּכַבְלֵי בַרְזֶל:
9 לַעֲשׂוֹת בָּהֶם׀ מִשְׁפָּט כָּתוּב
הָדָר הוּא לְכָל־חֲסִידָיו
הַלְלוּיָהּ:

6. *high praises*. Praises extolling God.

mouth. lit. 'throat.'

two-edged sword. lit. 'a sword of the mouths.' The two-edged sword alludes to the power of prayer and the dual purpose that it must serve. 'On the one hand it will serve to protect them against attack from their fellows who will persist in opposing their way of life, and on the other hand it will guard them from any adverse involvement in the Divine judgment described in the following verses' (Hirsch, cf. Kimchi).

7. *vengeance*. Revenge against one's fellow man is denounced in the Torah (Lev. xix. 18). Here, however, the reference is to retribution for the crimes committed by the nations against the Jewish people, whom they were bent on destroying. Their acts of genocide are inexcusable (cf. Daath Sofrim).

chastisements. The penalties for the sins of which they were guilty. The kings and rulers utilized their positions of power for unlawful purposes (Hirsch).

8. *to bind their kings*. The language recalls the Messianic prophecies of Isa. xlv. 14, xlix. 7, 23.

nobles. More lit. 'honoured men,' whose example and influence had led the common people astray (Daath Sofrim).

9. *upon them*. i.e. all who were specified in the preceding verse, the peoples as well as their leaders.

the judgment written. The sentence passed upon them by the heavenly Judge and recorded by Him (Isa. lxv. 6 and Ezek. xxv. 14) (cf. Rashi).

He is the glory. Or, 'It shall be glory for all His saints,' the final overcoming of these enemies is an obligation upon God's people which will redound to their glory (Metsudath David).

150

קנ

1 Hallelujah.
  Praise God in His sanctuary;
  Praise Him in the firmament **of**
    His power.

2 Praise Him for His mighty acts;
  Praise Him according to His
    abundant greatness.

3 Praise Him with the blast of the
    horn;
  Praise Him with the psaltery and
    harp.

הַלְלוּיָהּ ׀
הַלְלוּ־אֵל בְּקָדְשׁוֹ
הַלְלוּהוּ בִּרְקִיעַ עֻזּוֹ׃
הַלְלוּהוּ בִגְבוּרֹתָיו 2
הַלְלוּהוּ כְּרֹב גֻּדְלוֹ׃
הַלְלוּהוּ בְּתֵקַע שׁוֹפָר 3
הַלְלוּהוּ בְּנֵבֶל וְכִנּוֹר׃

HALLELUJAH

THE group of praise-Psalms and the whole Psalter reach their culmination in this unequalled hymn of extolment in which can be noted thirteen expressions of praise, corresponding to the thirteen attributes with which God governs the world (Kimchi). No close more fitting to this section of sacred Hebrew literature could be conceived than the outburst of ecstatic exultation which rings through this song. With its concluding call to *everything that hath breath* the Psalmist sums up the aspiration and aim of Israel's mission and the purpose of its existence as God's appointed messenger to mankind.

1. *God.* Hebrew *el*, the Power directing the universe and all it contains.

in His sanctuary. Not the Temple in Zion, but His holy temple in *heaven* (xi. 4, cii. 20) as the parallelism shows (Kimchi). From His abode there He rules the earth, and all hearts should be directed upwards in praise of Him. Alshich sees in this verse an invocation to the angels to proclaim the sanctity of God, an act which is repeated daily.

the firmament of His power. Firmament is a synonym of heaven (Gen. i). Its appearance was one of the first phases in the creation of the world, and is therefore a witness of His infinite power (cf. Hirsch).

2. *mighty acts.* In the government of man-kind, which are beyond human telling (cvi. 2).

abundant greatness. Which is *unsearchable* by man (cxlv. 3).

3. *horn,* etc. Nine types of instruments are enumerated altogether. Each of them pro-duces a sound which expresses a particular feeling of human nature such as happiness, sadness, awe and solemnity (cf. Hirsch). The ram's horn, associated with the praise of God (xlvii. 6f., xcviii 6) was sounded by the priests in the Temple and was often accom-panied by the sounding of the trumpets. The Psalmist has these in mind, too (Kimchi).

psaltery and harp. These, together with *cymbals,* were played by the Levites (1 Chron. xxv. 1).

4 Praise Him with the timbrel and
    dance;
  Praise Him with stringed instru-
    ments and the pipe.

5 Praise Him with the loud-sound-
    ing cymbals;
  Praise Him with the clanging
    cymbals.

6 Let every thing that hath breath
    praise the LORD.
  Hallelujah.

4 הַלְלוּהוּ בְתֹף וּמָחוֹל
  הַלְלוּהוּ בְּמִנִּים וְעֻגָב:

5 הַלְלוּהוּ בְצִלְצְלֵי־שָׁמַע
  הַלְלוּהוּ בְּצִלְצְלֵי תְרוּעָה:

6 כֹּל הַנְּשָׁמָה תְּהַלֵּל יָהּ
  הַלְלוּיָהּ:

4. *timbrel and dance.* See on cxlix. 3. The *timbrel* was a woman's instrument.

stringed instruments. Mentioned for secular use in xlv. 9.

pipe. An ancient wind instrument (Gen. iv. 21), used on occasions of rejoicing (Job xxi. 12). If the stringed instruments and pipe were played by laymen, the call is made to all sections of the community: priests, Levites, laymen and women.

5. *loud-sounding cymbals.* lit. 'cymbals of hearing' (cf. *cymbals of brass to sound aloud*, 1 Chron. xv. 19, xvi. 5) used for the ac-companiment of the Levite singers.

clanging cymbals. lit. 'cymbals with a shrill sound.' These were smaller than the loud-sounding cymbals.

6. *every thing that hath breath.* lit. 'all the breath.' In Deut. xx. 16, Joshua x. 40 the phrase denotes human beings, and it is only said of man that God *breathed into his nostrils the breath of life* (Gen. ii. 7). According to Hirsch the Psalmist intended to include animals as creatures of God (as in cxlviii. 10). It may also refer to the intellectual 'soul' of the person that appreciates the goodness of God more than anything else (Kimchi).

AUTHORITIES QUOTED

Abarbanel, Don Isaac (1437–1509), Bible commentator.

Daath Sofrim (1983)—Rabinowitz, Chaim Dov, contemporary Bible commentator and historian.

Hertz, J. H. (Chief Rabbi), Commentaries on the Pentateuch and Hebrew Prayer Book.

Hirsch, Samson Raphael (nineteenth century leader of German Orthodoxy), Commentary on Psalms.

Ibn Ezra, Abraham (1092–1167), Bible commentator, Commentary on Psalms.

Ibn Yachya, Yosef (1494–1534), Bible commentator.

Kimchi, David (Redak, 1160–1235), Bible commentator, Commentary on Psalms.

Maimonides, Moshe (Rambam, 1135–1204), Leading medieval authority on Jewish law, philosophy and medicine, *Guide to the Perplexed.*

Malbim, Meir Leibush (1809–1879), Bible commentator, Commentary on Psalms, *Yair Ohr.*

Maharal, Yehudah Loewe (c. 1512–1609), Chief Rabbi of Prague, Jewish philosopher and commentator.

Meiri, Menachem (thirteenth century), Talmudist and Bible commentator, Commentary on Psalms.

Metzudath David (Tower of David), Commentary on Psalms by David Altschul (seventeenth century).

Metzudath Zion (Tower of Zion), Definitions of words of the Bible by David Altschul (seventeenth century).

Midrash—Rabbinic homilies on the Pentateuch, etc.

Midrash Shocher Tov, or Midrash Tehillim—Homiletic explanation on Book of Psalms. Authorship not definitely established.

Pesikta—Midrashic compilation

Pirkei Aboth (*The Sayings of the Fathers*)—Mishnah tractate.

Ramban (Nachmanides, Rabbi Moshe ben Nachman, 1194–c.1270), Talmudist, Kabbalist, Biblical exegete, Commentary on Psalms.

Rashi (Rabbi Shlomo ben Isaac, 1040–1105), Bible commentator, Commentary on Psalms.

Saadia (Rabbi Saadia Gaon, 892–942), Head of the Academy in Sura, Babylon; Bible commentator and philosopher, central figure and sage of Gaonic period.

Septuagint—Greek Translation of the Bible, begun in third century B.C.E.

Sifra—Ancient Rabbinical commentary on Leviticus.

Sforno, Obadiah (1475–1550), Bible commentator.

Talmud—Corpus of Jewish law and thought, compiled at the end of the fifth century C.E.

Tanchuma—Midrashic commentary on the Pentateuch (original version fourth century C.E.).

Targum—Aramaic translation of the Bible (first and second centuries C.E.).

Tosefta—Tannaitic compilation elaborating on the Mishnah.

Tristram, H. B. (Natural Scientist), *The Natural History of the Bible.*

Yaavetz (Rabbi Yitzchak ben Tzvi), Bible commentator (sixteenth century).

Yalkut—Midrash compilation (thirteenth century).

PSALMS CLASSIFIED FOR READING AND MEDITATION

THE GODLY LIFE, i, xv, xxiv, xxxiv, ci, cxi, cxii, cxxxi.

GOD'S REVELATION. xix, cxix.

MEDITATION ON HUMAN LIFE. xlix, xc, cxxxix.

PENITENTIAL. vi. xxv, xxxii, xxxviii, li, cii, cxxx, cxliii.

PROBLEM OF GOOD AND EVIL. xxxvii, lxxiii.

THE RIGHTEOUS AND WICKED. ix-xiv, xxviii, xxxvi, xliv, lii, liii, lviii, lix, lxiv, xciv, cix.

GOD AND NATURE. viii, xix, xxix, lxv, civ.

GOD IN HISTORY. lxviii, lxxviii, lxxxi, cv, cvi, cxiv, cxxxvi.

KINGSHIP OF GOD. xlvii, xciii, xcv-c.

YEARNING FOR GOD. xlii, xliii, lxiii, lxxxiv.

GOD'S JUDGMENT. l, lviii, lxxv, lxxxii, lxxxiii.

GOD A SURE REFUGE. vii, xvii, xviii, xxvii, xxxi, lxii, lxxxi, xci, cxxi, cxlii.

GOD THE DELIVERER. xlvi, liv-lvii, lxxiv, lxxvii, lxxix, lxxx, lxxxv, cvii, cxvi, cxl, cxli, cxliv.

SUBMISSION TO GOD. ii, vii, xx, xxvi, xxx, xxxii, xlii, lii, lxiii, lxvii, lxxvii, lxxxiv, cxxviii, cxli, cxlii.

CONFIDENCE IN GOD. iii, iv, ix, xi, xiii, xiv, xvi, xxi, xxiii, xxvii, xxxiv, xxxvi, xxxvii, xl, xli, xliv, xlvi, liii, lvi, lxii, lxv, lxxiii, xci, xciv, cviii, cxxi, cxxiii, cxxiv, cxxv, cxxvii.

PRAYER IN TROUBLE. v, vi, x, xii, xiii, xvii, xxi, xxv, xxviii, xxxi, xxxv, xxxviii, xxxix, xliii, li, liv, lv, lvii, lix, lxiv, lxix, lxx, lxxi, lxxiv, lxxxvi, lxxxviii, cii, cxxx, cxl, cxliii.

PRAISE OF GOD. viii, xviii, xxiv, xxix, xxxiii, xxxiv, xlvii, xlviii, lxvi, lxviii, lxxxix, xcii, xciii, xcv-c, ciii, civ, cvii, cxi, cxiii-cxviii, cxxxv, cxxxvi, cxxxviii, cxlv-cl.

TERMS AND ABBREVIATIONS

A.J.   American-Jewish Translation of the Scriptures.

B.C.E.   Before the Common Era.

c.   About.

C.E.   Common Era.

c.f.   Compare, Refer to.

e.g.   For example.

etc.   And so forth.

f.   Following verse or chapter (plural, ff.).

ibid.   The same reference.

i.e.   That is.

kerë.   The Hebrew text as it is to be read.

kethib.   The Hebrew text as it is written.

lit.   Literally.

loc. cit.   In the place cited.

LXX.   Septuagint (see Authorities Quoted)

MS.   Manuscript (plural MSS).

M.T.   The Masoretic Text.

op. cit.   In the work cited.

P.B.   *Authorised Daily Prayer Book*, (ed. S. Singer).

Prophetic perfect.   Explained in iii. 8.

Ps.   Psalm (plural Pss).

Selah.   Explained on iii. 3.

Sheol.   Explained on vi. 6.

viz.   Namely.

TALMUDIC TRACTATES

B.B.   *Baba Bathra*

Ber.   *Berachoth*

B.K.   *Baba Kama*

B.M.   *Baba Metzia*

Eruv.   *Eruvin*

Git.   *Gittin*

Ket.   *Kethuboth*

M.K.   *Moed Katan*

Meg.   *Megillah*

Ned.   *Nedarim*

Pes.   *Pesachim*

R.H.   *Rosh Hashanah*

Sab.   *Sabbath*

San.   *Sanhedrin*

Sot.   *Sotah*

Suc.   *Succoth*

Taan.   *Taanith*

Yeb.   *Yebamoth*

Zeb.   *Zebachim*

INDEX

INDEX

I. NAMES AND SUBJECTS

282, 287, 289f., 291, 293, 294, 304, 306, 316, 317, 318, 320, 322, 325, 326, 333, 334f., 364, 374, 376, 382, 385, 388, 389, 399, 403, 404, 406, 412, 413, 414, 431, 441, 444, 449, 462, 463, 464, 467f., 469, 472; Creator, 19, 53, 69, 96, 239, 291, 313, 315, 332, 337f., 384, 406, 420, 425, 440, 441, 444, 470, 472; eternity of, 175, 297f., 305, 307, 330, 332, 442, 469, 471; fear of, 5, 11, 36, 54, 73, 100, 208, 228, 245, 335, 376, 383, 384, 389, 399, 404, 430, 433, 443, 469, 473; glory of, 70, 230, 278, 300, 316, 318, 330, 337, 342, 354, 378, 450, 476; healer, 13, 333, 472; helper, 7, 26, 38, 79, 81, 85, 87, 100, 103, 112, 116, 119, 123ff., 159, 171, 174, 175, 179, 191, 194f., 198, 218, 235, 238, 282, 303, 310, 385f., 390, 418, 420f., 424, 425, 428, 450, 457, 470; Holy One of Israel, 226, 254, 292; imitation of, 326; in history, 202, 209ff., 248, 249ff., 264, 269, 344ff., 351ff., 358ff., 442; jealousy of, 257, 261; judge, 2, 10, 16f., 20f., 23, 28, 33, 40, 84, 88, 97, 107, 133, 157, 162, 178. 180, 184, 198, 208, 241f., 244, 270f., 305, 308, 317, 321, 334, 345, 373, 404, 409, 412, 423, 433, 443, 471; king, 10, 26, 57, 66, 84, 136, 147f., 149, 213, 238, 275, 292, 307, 312, 316, 318, 321, 322, 330, 335, 424, 467, 468f., 471, 477; 'Lord of hosts,' 70, 145, 146, 186, 217, 264, 266, 275, 276, 290; love of God for man *see under* God, mercy of; love of man for God, 12, 91, 130, 221, 385, 411, 469; manifestation of, 45, 83, 157, 210f., 239, 243f., 248, 249ff., 317, 321, 331, 375, 380f.; mercy of, 13, 32, 75, 139, 161, 167, 181, 188, 196, 206, 218, 254, 278, 281, 291, 293, 294, 300, 310, 325, 333, 334f., 351, 357, 358, 363, 364, 369, 370, 388, 389, 400, 402, 404, 410, 413, 434, 444f., 450, 463, 468, 473; might of, 41, 84, 135, 145f., 170, 188, 196, 202, 204f., 212, 214, 215, 225, 239, 243f., 248, 249ff., 262, 263, 282, 290f., 307, 316, 320, 344, 352, 362, 437, 467f., 472, 479; name of, 12, 17, 18, 19, 21, 56, 57, 65, 67, 69, 72, 86, 88, 97, 136, 167,

171, 192, 221, 241, 261, 266, 274, 291, 293, 303, 304, 315, 319, 322, 325, 330, 331, 344, 357, 369, 375, 378, 382, 385, 386, 390, 401, 422, 425, 441, 442, 449, 461, 463, 467, 469, 475, 476; nearness of, 235, 241, 413, 469; omnipresence of, 452; omniscience of, 16, 28, 138, 309, 451f.; praise of, 441, 467–480; provider, 100, 202f., 252f., 269, 338f., 341f., 359, 363, 374, 438, 446, 469, 471, 473, 474; rebellion against, 3, 12, 205, 273, 334; refuge, 5, 12, 15, 21, 27, 34, 37, 41, 44, 49, 78f., 88, 91, 100, 102, 109, 144, 180, 188, 192, 195, 200, 223, 224, 235, 301, 302, 311, 390, 409, 426, 459, 461, 464; shepherd, 67, 82, 236, 248, 256, 262, 263, 313, 324; shield, 6, 12, 44, 49, 82, 98, 187, 266, 276, 301, 383, 409; vindicator, 8, 30, 51, 181, 202, 308, 319, 323, 370, 392; 'voice' of, 45, 83f., 145, 215, 269; 'ways' of, 11, 47, 71, 80, 281, 303, 314, 334, 394, 450

God's 'book,' 161, 178, 453

God's 'bottle,' 178

God's footstool,' 322, 437

God's 'gentleman,' 35

God's 'guest,' 35f., 68, 78, 167, 192

Goshen, 251

Grace, before meals, 339

H

Hagrites, 273

Ham, land of, 347, 348, 354; 'tents' of, 256

Heart, seat of thought, 17, 33

Heman, 285

Hermon, dew of, 439; mount, 131, 211f., 291

Hertz, J. H., *quoted*, 72, 102, 105, 298, 300, 308, 319, 396, 443

Hezekiah, 204

Horn, symbol of strength, 44, 241f., 291, 293, 306

Horse, in battle, 57, 97

Humble, the, 72, 435, 473, 477

I

Idols, 382f., 443

Immortality, xiv, 39

Imprecations, 174, 184, 219f., 261, 273f.,

II. HEBREW WORDS

AF412733